Law in Culture and Society

Edited by LAURA NADER

UNIVERSITY OF CALIFORNIA PRESS
Berkeley · Los Angeles · London

University of California Press
Berkeley and Los Angeles, California

University of California Press, Ltd.
London, England

Copyright © 1969 by the Wenner-Gren Foundation
for Anthropological Research, Inc.

First Paperback Printing 1997

Library of Congress Cataloging-in-Publication Data
Law in culture and society / edited by Laura Nader.
     p.   cm.
     Originally published: Chicago, Ill. : Aldine Pub., 1969.
     Includes bibliographical references and index.
     ISBN 0-520-20833-1 (alk. paper)
     1. Law and anthropology. 2. Ethnological jurisprudence. 3. Law,
Primitive. I. Nader, Laura.
K487.A57L385 1997
340'.115—dc20   96-34175
                                             CIP

Printed in the United States of America

This book is a print-on-demand volume. It is manufactured using toner
in place of ink. Type and images may be less sharp than the same
material seen in traditionally printed University of California Press
editions.

The paper used in this publication meets the minimum requirements
of ANSI/NISO Z39.48–1992 (R 1997)
(Permanence of paper.)

Contents

Preface to the Paperback Edition

Since the first publication of *Law in Culture and Society* in 1969, there has been a virtual revolution in thinking about law by practitioners in sister disciplines. The story of what has happened is written about elsewhere in long and protracted form. Here I will merely note that movements made the difference, in the direction of scholarship at least. The Development Movement sought to democratize the third world by exporting Europe-American legal education and legal codes and statutes, an inexpensive kind of development which is currently being renewed by efforts in Eastern Europe. The Law and Society Movement made a niche for law and society scholars who were marginal or who did not fit in law schools, political science, sociology, psychology, criminology, history or anthropology departments—people who saw in law the tools for research and reform related to poverty, racism, and sexism, for example. The Critical Legal Studies Movement is a progressive examination of the assumptions of American law and legal education that revealed a law that was more political than neutral, results that might not surprise the downtrodden. Law and Economics, Chicago style, was a reactionary move that loosely paralleled the Reagan Revolution. For scholars there was excitement, for example, in discoveries of law as a vehicle for cultural transmissions or legal imperialisms. When the same patterns were found on home ground there was a crisis of contradictions. The law was not neutral as supposed.

Finally, there has come a recognition of dead-ends. Law and Society is increasingly encapsulated, and more and more replicating that which many sought to escape—boundary controls. Critical Legal Studies is often caught in disembodied literatures and narrative techniques that focus on more discourse-based positions to the exclusion of other factors involved in the creation of social beings.thus, whether about the everyday or the abstract, the original power of the "new thinking" wanes just as new thinking about law is taking hold in places like Italy or France.

From the perspective of anthropology as a discipline the change was cumulative, not dramatic, because intellectually the anthropology of law gave to the movements perhaps more than we received. "Our" terrain—the non-western other—our approaches and methods such as participant observation, and what we had learned about social and cultural processes through ethnography, filtered into other disciplines. Notions of critique and comparison, culture and local knowledge, and the various ideas about pluralism and perception had now moved horizontally into sister disciplines, albeit in altered forms.

But there were also subtle changes during this period. Anthropologists learned about the power of law and in law, something more obvious to lawyers than anthropologists. The ethnographic study of law in other cultures, a study that had already yielded a small number of classic ethnographies, continued to be small in number while distinguished anthropologists chose to write ethnographies of law in the United States. New work in Africa diminished and a few outstanding monographs began to appear in Mexico, Brazil, Tibet, Indonesia and the Pacific and elsewhere.

In 1969, dispute resolution was a subject matter that engaged empirically-grounded ethnographers concerned with what law does instead of what law is. In 1996, dispute resolution is an industry that has penetrated the neighborhoods, the schools, the prisons, the corporations, the NAFTA and the GATT, and once again, third world countries dealing with conflicts accompanying decolonization. Throughout this period mainstream legal thought has been severely shaken.

In 1969, anthropologists were treated with disdain by fellow social scientists for examining the everyday in law life because for them real social dramas were elsewhere—in the prisons, in the judgeships, in the streets, or in jurisprudential exploration. By 1996, the anthropological domain had been run over by our fellow social scientists with interest in everyday life and the part played by law in communities. Legal pluralism and dispute resolution interested activists and juridical planners, as well as "identity construction." Now, it is more difficult to tell who is an anthropologist and who is not, or indeed to respond to assertions that by the late 1990s "there are more anthropologists of law who are lawyers than anthropologists," but it is clear that there is a continued interest in anthropologically-rooted studies concerned with the less visible face of law and the view from below.

Since 1969, the view from below has expanded upward and outward. Anthropologists had consistently underestimated the role of legal ideologies in the construction or deconstruction of culture writ large. Legal ideologies such as the harmony law model were used as techniques of pacification among colonized peoples, in nation-states and as well in the international arena. Yet, the effort to understand the political economy of legal models as adumbrated in our volume in papers on legal styles, historical changes in the law of nation-states, colonialism and the politics of law, and even the Bohannan-Gluckman controversy over folk and analytic categories was more political in nature than either of them might admit.

Arguments over the notion of autonomous systems were embedded in boundary concerns. Could there be a legal system that operated independent of its environment? In our volume, indigenous systems of law are described ethnographically as part of the indigenous culture and society. Years later we were to realize that the study of colonialisms shifted our entire perspective as to what constituted indigenous culture and society. In 1996, we include legal transplants, missionary justice, AID programs, economic globalization as part of the local ethnographic picture. We were correct to be uneasy about drawing boundaries in 1969; boundaries are continually erased as knowledge and political domains shift.

In my first Preface, I indicated that the conference which produced the volume had been tumultuous. Clearly, the intellectual issues about ethnography and interpretation were all there simmering—whose categories do we use, the Other or the West? What is ethnography? When is ethnography ethnographic? Should we standardize data collection? When do we include colonials and missionaries? Do we recognize Pueblo law as a result of forces of conquest?

The political differences between us were there, but they were unmentionable. Only later are we coming to realize the tightrope that many ethnographers were walking between advocacy and objectivity, between generalization and interpretation. A rereading of these essays from the vantage of the 1990s with an improved understanding of the impact of colonialism, the Cold War, and the competition for world resources, suggests the lasting worth of these detailed studies which span generations, disciplines, nationalities, and four continents.

Laura Nader
Berkeley, California
August 1996

Preface

This volume does not attempt to sum up the anthropologist's study of law in culture and society; rather, it intends to contribute to the continuing definition of various problem areas on which effort has been expended in the past and on which it should be expended in the future. That anthropological studies of law do not form a single systematic body of data and concepts has been illustrated at two Wenner-Gren conferences. The first conference was held at the Center for Advanced Study in the Behavioral Sciences, Stanford, California, April 2–4, 1964. The results of that conference were published as a special issue of the *American Anthropologist* in December 1965. A second, and this time international, Wenner-Gren conference was held at the Burg Wartenstein, Gloggnitz, Austria, August 3–13, 1966; the results are published in this book.

The principal aim of both conferences was to stimulate more and improved research in areas the potential of which has not yet been well mined. The value of both conferences for the participants has been summarized by Professor Isaac Schapera as "the pooling of topics, learning particular problems people are interested in, and then the stimulation of others to pursue problems in their own work." To date the field has been one in which individual scholars have contributed as individuals, with little, if any, of the work's reflecting the cumulative effort of the small group of interested scholars. Both volumes aim at providing new data and analysis that will encourage the building of ideas and the development of intellectual dialogues heretofore virtually absent in this field. In particular this volume seeks to contribute to discourse between nationals —to bring together scholars whose paths might not easily cross, in spite of their overlapping interests.

The focus of the Burg Wartenstein conference was to be the understanding and analysis of legal systems *as they operate in particular cultural and societal contexts.* Neither the live interest in the philosophy of law, which is the traditional study of lawyers and of scholars of jurisprudence, nor the recent interest of a more practical sort in policy formation, contemporary problems of legal pluralism, and restatement projects was to be our central concern. Although such subject matters are of general importance and although they overlap with any substantive research in the ethnography of law, we believed that a better conference would result (1) if we were to include mainly studies based on extensive field work or on knowledge of the cross-cultural materials on law, (2) if the goal of the research were "scientific"—or, more specifically, generalizing in nature—rather than applied or philosophical, and (3) if theory were derived from empirical field research. We were focusing the papers in a way that we believed had been neglected in anthropological conferring.

Search letters were sent to various countries to find scholars prepared to contribute to such a conference. The conference had an international anthropological representation of the following order: Paul Bohannan, Northwestern University; Frank Cancian, Stanford University (now of Cornell University); Max Gluckman, University of Manchester; James Gibbs, University of Minnesota (now of Stanford University); Phillip Gulliver, School of Oriental and African Studies, London; E. Adamson Hoebel, University of Minnesota; André Köbben, University of Amsterdam; Sally Falk Moore, University of Southern California; Laura Nader, University of California, Berkeley; Leopold Pospisil, Yale University; Isaac Schapera, London School of Economics and Political Science; Richard Werbner, University of Manchester. One contributor—Charles Frake, Stanford University—was unable to attend the conference. In addition, two sociologists—Vilhelm Aubert, University of Oslo; and Gresham Sykes, University of Denver—and three legal scholars—Herma Kay, University of California, Berkeley; Geert van den Steenhoven, Catholic University at Nijmegen; and Raymond Verdier, Faculté de Droit et des Sciences Economiques de Paris—also participated. Three students, then graduates at the University of California, Berkeley, acted as rapporteurs: Klaus Koch (presently at Harvard University), John Rothenberger (at Hayward State College), and Carl McCarthy.

All the contributions presented at the conference, with the exception of the film "To Make the Balance," shown by Laura Nader, are included in this volume. Bohannan, Frake, and Nader wrote their papers after the conference.

It would be simple distortion for me to describe those stimulating ten days at the Burg Wartenstein as anything but turbulent. We disagreed on both personal and intellectual levels, but in so doing I believe we arrived at better ideas of how—individually if not collectively, in small groups if not by general consensus—we would undertake to build knowledge in this field. A member of the staff said to me then, "We worry more about the long-range results when all goes ultra-smoothly." If long-range results are guaranteed by a rocky conference, our future is certainly secured. At any rate, as Gresham Sykes said before he left, "It was a memorable conference!" Sitting around that illustrious round table were all this century's anthropological pioneers in this field, in particular Professors Schapera, Hoebel, and Gluckman. This is a very young field, in which the excitement is just beginning.

We are glad and grateful to the Wenner-Gren Foundation for its generous support and gracious hospitality and to Anne Brower, Sylvia Forman, Dorothy Dake, and Gobi Stromberg for their patient, careful aid in editing and preparing the manuscript for publication.

LAURA NADER

Introduction

This essay, introducing the volume, attempts to describe briefly, in the context of past and present anthropological arguments, what I believe has been and what will be the style of future anthropological studies of law. Since World War II there has been in anthropology a proliferation of various subdisciplines—such as the anthropology of religion, political anthropology, the anthropology of law—that will presumably merge into problem areas in the next decade; in the meantime we have developed these narrower fields in order to make some systematic progress in data accumulation and theory building. We can sometimes profit from looking at the parallel patterns of developments in the subfields, and in this essay I will make specific reference to the development of socio-linguistic studies as it relates to developments in the anthropology of law. For similar reasons I will cite extensively from a memorandum written at the request of the conference members by the sociologist Vilhelm Aubert. In order that a variety of views might be expressed, separate introductions to the four sections were written by other participants. These introductions, better than anything I could say, summarize the sometimes convergent positions expressed at the conference.

Over forty years ago Robert Lowie wrote a chapter in Ogburn and Goldenweiser's book, *The Social Sciences*, entitled "Anthropology and Law." It is interesting perhaps to note the flavor and content of that article as a backdrop for the present volume. Lowie was interested in how anthropology might benefit from a neighboring branch of learning. He writes: "The jurisprudence of advanced civilizations, refined by centuries of acute intellects, is marked by a clarification of basic concepts

1

such as the student of anthropology may well envy. There are obvious pitfalls to be avoided. Primitive customary law does not present the rigid formalism of codified law. It would assuredly be the acme of artificiality to pigeonhole the rules of inheritance in a North American aboriginal community according to the standards of English jurisprudence. But the comparative fluidity of primitive conditions is fully recognized at the present time, and little danger threatens from that source." Lowie then briefly summarizes the results of anthropological investigations as they bear on what he sees as four main problems of legal theory: family law, property, associations, and the state.

It is of interest to note a continued interest in the "pigeonhole problem" and the general lack of interest at this conference in substantive law and, for the most part, in questions having to do with political development—questions that were the core of Lowie's summary of anthropology and law forty years ago. In our groping for concepts, problem formation, and method, we moved from anthropology and law to law in culture and society as it is affected by and affects the individuals who make the law both similar and different.

Major Discussions

The major discussions of this conference swung between two different subjects, having as a common denominator a concern with various aspects of method: the position of jurisprudence in social science and the study of dispute settlement in terms of processes relating to society and the individual. Vilhelm Aubert, a scholar trained in both the formal law and behavioral science commented on the first question in a memo sent to me shortly after the Burg Wartenstein conference (n.d.):

> There are several ways in which law and social science may be brought into touch with each other. One may use social science to analyze legal problems. Fact-finding surveys, on attitudes or other social items, may be utilized as a means to substantiate legal propositions. . . . The analytical scheme into which the sociological findings are fed, remains legal or jurisprudential. One may, on the other hand, use sociological or anthropological concepts and theories to interpret legal phenomena. It may be necessary to know something about legal thinking in order to get the empirical basis straight, but the analytical scheme remains sociological.
>
> Although there is considerable interest among lawyers in employing sociological methods for purely legislative or juridical purposes . . . there was little of this represented at the conference. There were some, however, who seemed to come close to maintaining that certain parts of Western jurisprudence might furnish a framework within which legal facts in tribal societies might be interpreted (Gluckman and Hoebel). Their intention was probably not to aid jurisprudence by pointing to new data which might lend

new credence to old legal assumptions. Rather, it seemed these scholars believe that . . . Western legal thought has developed concepts (like the "reasonable man" or Hohfeld's scheme) . . . which may be applied also to furnish order in otherwise meaningless anthropological findings relating to social order and conflict resolution.

This point of view was strongly opposed by Bohannan who finds it necessary to grasp, from the inside, the legal concepts of that society which is being studied. I felt that the discussion on this point to a large extent hinged on questions of empirical observations. For it may well be that a good way of understanding what goes on in the other people's minds is to use the schemes which are available in one's own mind. They may, or may not, fit, but this method seems to be one of those we always have to use. Some do it well, others do it less well. Some read into others what they find in themselves, but some also fail to see parallels which are actually there. The one fallacy is as dangerous as the other one. But I do not think this is a point which can profitably be pursued in abstract debates without simultaneously having a chance to inspect the data. . . .

In one sense I find it difficult to believe that Western legal concepts can be applied to tribal materials . . . that is, if it were to be claimed that the Western legal concepts apply with implications identical to those which they have in Western law. Since legal concepts are defined in relation to a complete legal system it is highly unlikely that they should fit in a very different social system if one wants to be precise and specific. The concept of "the reasonable man" is, of course, on a level so general that its application in a non-Western society has the ring of truth. However, if we were to include its specific implications in a certain Western system, its applications to a non-Western society might fail. In both types of societies, however, one interesting point is that such loose concepts are used in juridical argumentation, and that this provides the decision-maker with a certain amount of freedom vis-à-vis a set of rules by which he is, in principle, bound. This tells us something about the need for elasticity, loopholes, malleability, etc., in a normative system. In order to characterize this aspect of the legal system, and of the enforcement of norms, we would use concepts derived from social science and not from law.

The analytical position of the Hohfeldian scheme is probably slightly different. Hohfeld's concepts do not, as I have understood them, belong to the working tools of the practicing lawyer. They represent some kind of generalization of the terms and concepts actually applied in legal work. Although they have been developed by a lawyer as a means to understand law, they seem, nevertheless, to belong more than halfway in the social sciences. They are applicable to all normative phenomena, to all situations where rights and obligations obtain between actors, whether these are legal in origin or not. This, of course, does not detract from the usefulness of Hohfeld's scheme, which is amply illustrated in Hoebel's "Law of Primitive Man." The usefulness of Hohfeld should not, however, be misinterpreted as a symptom that law and social science are closer to each other than they actually seem to be for the moment.

The application of Hohfeld's scheme makes it possible to discern a number of conflict-resolving situations and to bring out their affinity, but not identity, to court decisions in Western systems. The final conceptualization, however, should not, in my opinion, remain on this level. When comparing conflict-resolving devices and institutions it seems advisable not to classify institutions in term of concepts derived from procedural law, but to apply general sociological concepts. Among these latter belong concepts used in describing group structures (dyad-triad, etc.), the pattern variables (specificity-diffuseness, universalism-particularism, etc.). My impression is that the greatest scientific profit can be extracted also from the writings of Gluckman and Hoebel when their findings are analyzed in these terms.

The question of anthropological use of jurisprudential terminology, basic to an earlier disagreement between Max Gluckman and Paul Bohannan, was discussed and summarized at this conference. Intellectual agreement between Bohannan and Gluckman was arrived at by Professor Hoebel's skillful statement of the question by means of the following diagram, and the group expressed the belief that the argument had now been dissolved and need no longer occupy the attention and energies of scholars interested in law.

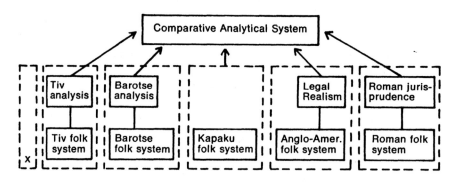

Bohannan's position focused on the importance of the ethnographer's getting at what the Tiv think about their own system; this is the Tiv analytical system. Gluckman has proved that the Barotse also have a folk analytical system. We need further a comparative analytical system competent to deal with all the folk systems. We can draw concepts from any of the lower levels to obtain the concepts for our comparative analytical system (or, Aubert would say and I would agree, from sociological or anthropological concepts). Bohannan suggested that for analytical purposes the folk system should be seen to include Tiv law as well as the Tiv folk analytical system (as is suggested by the dotted lines above). Selected parts of what is in the folk analytical systems can be taken to the comparative analytical box. It was at one time felt that the folk analysis of Western jurisprudence was sufficient in itself for the comparative box. This view is no longer considered valid; Gluckman and Bohannan agreed on this point, at least at that time. The fact that all participants were so anxious to have this as part of the printed record indicated a degree of impatience with what many thought was indeed a nonproblem. As Frank Cancian said in his summation at the conference, he now concluded that there was no Bohannan-Gluckman controversy. He had previously thought that Bohannan wanted to use native categories and that Gluckman wanted "adequate" categories, which could be native or Western, and that Bohannan in turn had found Western categories inadequate. In fact, the disagreement is not on the level of description but on the next step of analysis. The intricacies of this discussion are summarized by Moore's introduction.

Be this as it may—an illustration of dispute settlement among two highly respected anthropologists—we are left with the general proposition that a field does not develop by deciding from where its terminology should be chosen. To find out whether any kind of analytical system should be used, it must be tried out on a problem. This is what Hoebel did in *The Law of Primitive Man* (1954). If it works, the product can be advertised. Jurisprudential scholars have often commented on how useful their language would be to anthropology. Someone at the conference even offered to compile a dictionary of such words for anthropological use. "Show me by doing" is my motto, and in the meantime I remain comfortable with Aubert's position on this subject.

How should this field develop, then? It was the feeling among several of the participants that an exploration of dispute settlement or conflict resolution could lead to some findings in the ethnography of law that are verifiable, and that such an investigation could well be an area of inquiry from which we could take off to other related domains, such as the question of the interrelationship between manifest and latent functions. There was no feeling that this was the central topic for study or that other subjects were not more interesting. It was simply a place to start, as Gulliver indicates in his section introduction. In 1965 I called attention to the lack of mutual interest between those who study something called "conflict resolution" and those who study "legal procedure" and "judicial process." Many of the papers in this volume indicate that there is value in joining forces among those interested in conflict resolution, legal procedure, and dispute settlement—a recognition that we are all interested in the same, or at least in related, materials. Aubert (n.d.) is particularly interested in this direction of study:

> Information of institutions and methods of conflict resolution may be used for several analytical purposes. They may be used as a means to tap important general characteristics of the social system which employs a certain method of conflict resolution. Thus, Gulliver's study throws important light on the social structure of the Ndendeuli, as it is revealed in the course of the moots where the conflicts are discussed and settled. . . .

One may also conduct a different type of comparative study, namely by comparing institutions of conflict resolution as such. The institutions may belong to the same society, for example, in the form of a battery of methods, like courts, boards of arbitration, mediation, etc. . . . Thus, one may discover that typically legal methods are preferred in some situations and shunned under different circumstances. One may, of course, combine the comparison of legal and other conflict-resolving methods with the comparison of societies, thus clarifying the reasons why some social systems rely more upon law than others.

Some felt, in addition, that if we were going to concern ourselves with process we must not neglect studies of the individual's role. Although in the development of political anthropology there apparently has been a steady progression of interests that led from a preoccupation with taxonomy, structure, and function to a concern with political processes (Swartz, Tuden, and Turner 1966), law studies from the start have been interested in process. In this volume the interest in taxonomy is conceived of as a way of getting at process in terms of specified functions. The papers here are not simply static, or structural. As Sykes suggested, the beginnings of a typology could develop out of categories such as: settlement or negotiation, decision-making, appeal, rule formation, rule alteration, and the execution of decisions. Any one of these categories could be taken as a sector for study of process. A discussion of various negotiation models, for example, led Schapera to ask, "Is there a difference between the type of negotiation where there is an anticipation of going to court, of where there is even the possibility of going to court, and where there is not?" Moore then suggested that there is a distinction between societies where there are professional intermediaries and those where there are not, implying that professional intermediaries have a stake in prolonging the process of negotiation. We know little about the influence of the possibility of resort to a third party upon negotiation processes in particular or upon the time problem in general.

The concern with process started with society and ended with the individual. When we began to focus upon the individual, two types of questions were raised. What changes result in legal institutions as a result of specific personality types? What is the effect of type of personalities on the use or application of the legal institution? The discussion that dealt with legal change as it is affected by an authority's legislative act (for example, a judge's decision) or by an individual's criminal act indicated that we needed to know more. Specifically we need to have more case studies taken within a single society in order to establish criteria for describing an innovation as effecting basic changes. Indeed, the question was raised as to the possibility of producing proof for an argument based on the proposition, "Individual variation causes innovation." Hoebel's comment on the permanence of tension within a system

—on the range of variation respective of conformity—led Bohannan to propose viewing a dispute case as an instance of boundary testing of personalities (which is another way of viewing change in law ways and which leads into the problem that Gibbs deals with in his introduction).

A Unifying Theme

As late as 1953, Harry Hoijer, in a review article entitled "The Relation of Language to Culture," found it necessary to examine the proposition that language does not stand separate from culture but is an essential part of it. In the process of examining this assumption and of answering the challenges specifically posed by Voegelin (1949), he returned to a statement by Sapir (1933:11) that language "does not as a matter of fact stand apart from or run parallel to direct experience but completely interpenetrates with it." It is this interpenetration, which is not apparent immediately, that has recently concerned an increasing number of linguists and anthropologists and sociologists (for example, Gumperz and Hymes, in press).

The notion of language *and* culture assumes that language is measurable apart from culture. As a result of the work of the American school of descriptive linguistics—which, especially in the 1930's, concentrated upon physical cues—the notion developed that grammar was built on sounds and that language could be viewed and studied as an independent system. In order to understand the peculiarities of language, linguists then isolated language as an independent system, in much the same way a physiologist isolates certain parts of an organism for analysis. It is probably futile to ask whether language is in reality an independent pattern; we can say that it can be studied independently, with results that are limited, at least to one point in time. We can find out something if we are interested in the logical structure of the human ability to verbalize or if we are curious about the varieties of language structures the human mind has invented.

If, however, we are interested in questions of the relation of language to culture and society and if we are interested in understanding change, then, in the minds of such specialists as Gumperz and Hymes, such a view of language is likely to impede research. By saying that on the one hand there is language and on the other there is society and culture, the researcher cuts himself off from study of causal connections and from posing such questions as "Can certain social practices generate certain language practices and the reverse?" Such a question would probably never arise if we looked at independent linguistic phenomena and independent social phenomena; and indeed, in our field work, we would be collecting data accordingly, without taking into account the social context in which speech takes place, neglecting all those factors relevant to understanding relationships.[1]

In sum, then, it is safe enough to isolate linguistic behavior as an independent system for limited purposes as long as we do not fall prey to the fallacy that because linguistic behavior may be treated independently, it is in reality independent of society and culture. If we are, and if we need to be, interested in the relation of language to society and culture, we cannot view language as independent.

At a recent Law and Society Association meeting the suggestion that that name of the society be changed from "Law *and* Society" to "Law *in* Society" was met with a sharp retort: "It *is* law *and* society, and *not* law *in* society. There is nothing hierarchical about this relationship." This reply exposed with complete spontaneity an attitude that has stood squarely in the way of even posing for research problems of law *in* society. Somehow law is conceived of as in reality being a system independent of society and culture; in the case of legal scholars in particular, their "professionalism" seems to encourage such a position.[2]

The contrast—law *in*, versus law *and* society—has not been much explored in recent social-science and law discussions about the subject. Professor Lon Fuller (n.d.) does note, however:

> The intensified interest in the sociology of law that has developed in recent years has come to assume the proportions of something like an intellectual movement. In the United States this movement has found a kind of sloganized expression in the title, Law and Society. . . .
>
> . . . there are, I believe, some dangers in this new title and in the allocation of intellectual energies it seems to imply. By speaking of law *and* society we may forget that law is itself a part of society, that its basic processes are social processes, that it contains within its own internal workings social dimensions worthy of the best attentions of the sociologist.
>
> My misgivings about the possible implications of a newly coined slogan would hardly be worth communicating to you if there were not powerful streams of thought in both sociology and jurisprudence that tend toward

1. These and similar questions are treated in Gumperz and Hymes, *Directions in Sociolinguistics* (in press). I am grateful to John Gumperz for the various conversations we have had that sought to compare developments in the fields of our respective interests.

2. See Pound's classic "The causes of popular dissatisfaction with the administration of justice" (1906) for an example of the social repercussions of such an attitude. Or see his article "Sociological Jurisprudence: Stage One" (1907), where he concludes: "To this end it is the duty of teachers of law, while they teach scrupulously the law that the courts administer, to teach it in the spirit and from the standpoint of the political, economic, and sociological learning of today. It is their task to create in this country a true sociological jurisprudence, to develop a thorough understanding between the people and the law, to insure that the common law remain what its exponents have always insisted it is—the custom of the people, the expression of their habits of thought and action as to the relations of men with each other" (p. 615).

drawing a sharp line or division between the study of legal institutions and procedures, on the one hand, and the basic study of society itself, on the other.

As with the example of language in society and culture, for purposes of some kinds of analysis one may want to draw sharp lines of division between the study of legal institutions and the study of society, but such an approach would not raise such questions as "What are the social and cultural factors that determine the forms and/or substance of dispute settlement?" Or "What are the social dimensions (to paraphrase Fuller) which mold the adjudicative process and determine adjudicative results?"

In summarizing the situation in anthropology, I (1965b:17, 18) concluded several years ago:

> During the past two decades the major contributions to the ethnography of law have been descriptive, functional analyses of systems both in isolated and in contact situations. The tendency has been to treat the legal system as an institution virtually independent and isolated from other institutions in society, except insofar as "society" is gleaned from the law materials. . . .
>
> In most of the recent monographs, Gulliver (1963) being a major exception, the law has been treated as isolated from other social control systems, and indeed in some monographs it has been left for the reader to place the law in its socio-cultural context.

Although at the Wenner-Gren conference in Austria there was no discussion of whether law was a system independent of society, whether law was a system independent of culture, and whether it should or should not be viewed as such, it was clear that some of the underlying tensions in the discussions could be traced to basic disagreements, often more subconcious than articulate, on the issue of law as "something apart." For example, in discussing the use of jurisprudential terms, Max Gluckman commented, "An analysis of the mechanics of 'dispute settlement' could profitably be made by the use of sociological and anthropological methods, whereas a study of the 'judicial process' would better employ concepts taken from jurisprudence." Vilhelm Aubert, on the other hand, thought that the question of applicability of jurisprudential terms was irrelevant to problem conceptions in the field of the sociology of law. He saw a better chance of communication and integration of sociological and anthropological studies if we concerned ourselves with basic problems in conflict resolution, typological classification, and the like; and he did not include legal studies because he views legal scholars as having quite different aims from those of social scientists (see Aubert 1963).

There were indications at this conference that anthropologists are ready to consider studies of law in culture and society as core interests and that they are contributing to enriching knowledge of what Professor Fuller has called "the social dimensions of the law itself." Some indications of shifting interests in the direction of law studies were the reluctance to draw tight boundaries around the domain of law or to expend effort in the search for a conclusive definition of law and the reluctance to accept jurisprudential terminology, without qualification, as the vocabulary for the anthropological study of law. Another indicator, and a more positive one, was the desire to focus on something intensively enough to make some intellectual headway: the single most dominant theme in the discussions and the papers was dispute settlement. The study of dispute settlement focuses on only one of the many functions of law. As a topic it crosscuts a segment of the law domain by incorporating a particular type of settlement—judicial process—into the broader domain —dispute settlement, which perforce leads us to dwell on problems of law in culture and society. The consideration of judicial process as one point of the continuum of the broader category of public forms of dispute settlement leads us to considerations of an anthropological nature in trying to explain process, use, and function of various dispute-settling mechanisms as they relate to the presence or absence of a judicial process.

PART I

Case Studies of Law in Non-Western Societies

INTRODUCTION BY P. H. GULLIVER

My brief for this introductory essay concerns the anthropological study of law in non-Western societies. I do not intend to review the essays of my colleagues that follow in this section of the book, for they can speak for themselves well enough. I shall keep fairly closely to my brief and attempt a research-oriented operational survey of potentialities and needs in this subject. More sophisticated problems of comparative jurisprudence and of sociological theory are therefore not my concern here.

Anthropologists have been studying the legal systems of non-Western societies ever since their discipline became established on a reasonably firm foundation. There are a number of earlier landmarks that retain their ethnographic and theoretical importance beyond their purely historical significance: for example, Barton's *Ifugao Law* (1919), Malinowski's *Crime and Custom in Savage Society* (1926), Rattray's *Ashanti Law and Constitution* (1929), and Hogbin's *Law and Order in Polynesia* (1934). But undoubtedly a major watershed was passed with the publication in 1941 of *The Cheyenne Way* by Llewellyn and Hoebel. This book marks the beginning of modern studies in the anthropology of law, and particularly in its clear identification and detailed treatment of the case study as the unit of analysis. The number of thoroughgoing studies has slowly grown since that time; but unfortunately they are still rather few, and they compare unfavorably in number with contemporaneous publications in most other main fields of anthropology—kinship, politics, ritual, or economics, for example. There is still a great deal to be done; and the development of general anthropological theory and expertise makes the demand even more pressing.

11

A noteworthy feature emerged from the discussions at the Wenner-Gren Symposium on "The Ethnography of Law," the source of the following papers. This was the marked disinclination—indeed, positive refusal—by scholars from several countries and several disciplines to become involved in attempts to define and delimit the focal term, "law." A number of participants expressed themselves strongly of the opinion that it would be a waste of time and a misdirection of intellectual effort to seek to establish a single, universally applicable connotation for this term, and there was little dissension from this view.

In part this general consensus came from a weariness with past endeavors to achieve acceptable and useful definitions and from weariness with the vast amounts of words that have been spilled out in increasingly fruitless controversy. Such controversy has too often led to dogmatic or doctrinaire approaches, arguments in vacuo, and rarefied hairsplitting, with little genuine advance in anthropological research, analysis, and understanding. The not unreasonable view that "law," a Western term and concept, should be defined by Western criteria, led to difficulties: first, that there are many non-Western societies in which "law," thus defined, is then absent; and second, that alternative institutions and processes in non-Western societies have their comparable counterparts in Western societies, both within and without the legal system. Definitions have been widened—or perhaps, diluted—in attempts to include the varieties of non-Western phenomena, until the term has become so diffuse, including so much, that in fact it has come to mean less and less. It has become increasingly useless as a basis of discourse or a tool of analysis and comparative study, except in the widest and most general sense.

It may perhaps seem singularly odd that some general agreement has not, and apparently cannot, be reached. Yet the rejection—for this is what it amounts to—of the need and value of definition is not out of keeping with the situation in other fields of anthropological study. Operationally, it is by and large agreed to leave the definition of such comparable terms as "political system" or "religion." Not merely is there disillusion as to the possibility of useful agreement—and especially in the face of a still poorly understood cross-cultural diversity—but, more importantly, it is seen that these terms are useful only if they are not rigidly defined but are left as loose labels of general areas of interest. The real problems, and the interesting ones leading to further understanding, are not, and probably never have been, concerned with definitions and classifications.

Thus it should be possible to ignore some of the older, and bitterly contested, controversies: does "law" necessarily entail the possibility of the use of force, or the practice of adjudication, or the existence of a court? For example, do conciliation processes, duels, song contests, and various types of self-help come within its realm? It is more desirable to analyze these kinds of phenomena in their own contexts, in order to understand the social processes and ideas at work and to perceive the comparable factors and the significant variable at both the intra- and the cross-cultural levels.

I believe that I express more than a personal view in asserting that the prime concern in the general field of anthropology of law is the study of processes, and in particular the processes of dispute settlement. This is not exhaustive of our interests, but it seems to be at least the most useful and productive focus. Here the fundamental unit of study is the case, the empirical dispute, and its mode of treatment. The thorough examination of detailed case material is likely to be the most rewarding procedure, as it has already been in the best literature. But, of course, it must be an examination within the full socio-cultural context of the dispute cases.

In saying this, I am saying nothing new. As long ago as 1942, Hoebel rightly declared that anthropologists must reach their "generalizations from particulars which are case, cases, and more cases" (Hoebel 1942: 966). The seminal *The Cheyenne Way* (1941) was a remarkable exposition and demonstration of what could and should be done. Unfortunately, a quarter of a century later, the stock of well-described and adequately analyzed cases in context is still small and insufficient. Still, in the intervening years there has been a rather continued preoccupation with generalized accounts of legal systems and processes—models, in fact—and all too brief citations of some illustrative cases. These models may (but, on the other hand, they may not) have been legitimately constructed from the anthropologists' own notebooks of recorded cases. But this is to give the conclusions without showing the evidence on which they are based —a procedure that is nonjudicial and unscientific. Nor does it allow other students to ask fresh questions of the data in the light of comparative experience and theoretical developments. To be sure, it is no easy matter to record fully a sufficiently large number of adequate cases; there are linguistic problems and many severe practical difficulties. Yet until we do accumulate a rich store of empirical materials, both analytical development and comparative study will be gravely hampered. With such a store, it becomes possible to appreciate what is comparable and what is not. Doubtless it will be unusual, and probably not especially useful, to compare whole systems. Rather, it will be fruitful to compare and gain deeper understanding of particular aspects, particular kinds of processes and variables, particular institutional arrangements, limitations, and opportunities. And this development should lead back to older studies and stimulate new studies of dispute cases, both to examine suggestive hypotheses and to ask new questions.

The problem focus of research and analysis in non-Western societies is then the *process of dispute settlement,* set in the empirical basis of detailed cases. As a synonym or alternative to "dispute settlement," some writers have used the term "conflict resolution." This latter seems, however, to be less satisfactory and less specific. The word "conflict" has been legitimately used in sociology and in psychology with a range of connotations that are not of direct concern here. Although the word "dispute" (or any other, for that matter) cannot be free of alternative meanings, it seems to be less susceptible to confusion; and it is one that most anthropologists have come to use.

By *dispute* I intend to mean something like the following—but without seeking to make a dogmatic definition that might exclude potentially significant marginal phenomena. A dispute arises out of disagreement between persons (individuals or subgroups) in which the alleged rights of one party are claimed to be infringed, interfered with, or denied by the other party. The second party may deny the infringement, or justify it by reference to some alternative or overriding right, or acknowledge the accusation; but he does not meet the claim. The right-claimant may, for whatever reason, accede to this, in which case no dispute arises. If he is unwilling to accede, he then takes steps to attempt to rectify the situation by some regularized procedure in the public arena. The intent is to gain the rights affected, to secure freedom from further infringement, perhaps to obtain compensation or the administration of retribution, and to gain some definition of the relevant rights. Somewhat arbitrarily, perhaps, I suggest that no dispute exists unless and until the right-claimant, or someone on his behalf, actively raises the initial disagreement from the level of dyadic argument into the public arena, with the express intention of doing something about the denied claim. There may, of course, be scarcely any initial disagreement or quarrel, for a plaintiff may directly activate the matter into a dispute without approaching the defendant first.

The word *settlement,* in reference to a dispute, may also appear arbitrary, for I do not necessarily refer to a final resolution of the matter. Final resolution is not always gained; indeed, sometimes it is not even sought if there is considered to be value in keeping the dispute going as a means of expressing or maintaining interrelationships and interaction. But once a disagreement or quarrel is activated—that is, made a dispute—some kind of result must follow. This may be a clear-cut decision, but it need not be, at least not overtly and directly. The plaintiff, the right-claimant, may be unable to bring the matter to any decisive consideration for lack of sufficient evidence and support, inadequacy of institutional means, political interference, direct and indirect social pressure to desist, failure to persist in the face of relative disadvantages (such as costs) that accrue, movement of the other party out of social range, and so forth. But in that event, no decision is, in fact, a decision more or less in favor of the defendant. Beyond that, some sort of a positive result is reached in any dispute as the action proceeds and eventually ends in the settlement. The original quarrel may be solved more or less, or it may continue and be reactivated into a further dispute. The outcome will depend on the nature of the dispute process in the particular society.

I wish, then, to preserve the term "dispute" for the matter in active process of settlement. However, an adequate case history should include more if full understanding is to be gained. Briefly, there are three main stages: the prehistory of the dispute, the dispute itself, and the social consequences that follow settlement.

The prehistory consists of two parts that, though obviously related, need to be kept analytically separate. First, where we are concerned with fairly small-scale societies, dominated by status relations of a multiplex kind, it is necessary to understand as fully as possible the previous development and state of relations between the two parties, both dyadically and in their interconnection with other involved persons. Seemingly simple cases of theft, adultery, or slander may often be shown to be more complex, and more understandable, in the context of the prehistory. Second, account is required of the occurrence of the alleged infringement and the emergence of disagreement or quarrel. Much of this will, of course, reappear during the phase of active dispute settlement (that is, in the evidence provided). But it should not be assumed that all the significant information will appear in evidence, nor that the anthropologist-observer will be able to pick up all the relevant tacit assumptions and elliptical references of the participants in the course of the dispute proper. Claims, counterclaims, rebuttals, emphases of evidence, tactics, and so on, may all change during the process, and it is most important to know of this in order to take it into account.

Undoubtedly the best case documentation is achieved when, by good fortune or painstaking field work, the anthropologist is able to record the genesis of a conflict before it becomes a dispute, and therefore before there begins to be either modification or stereotyping of evidence, inferences, and attitudes. For instance, it is unlikely that I could have understood the Ndendeuli Case No. 4, below, even as well as I did, had I not already obtained fairly full records of the interrelations of the disputants over the preceding two decades. Furthermore, I happened to be present when the initial quarrel erupted at a beer party. This happenstance was largely fortuitous, since it was naturally impossible for me to be present at more than a small proportion of all social occasions in the particular community; but partly it was the fortunate result of assiduously attending and participating in as many as I could. Nevertheless, even in this favorable situation, I was not present at the earlier stage, when the aggrieved cousin was (or maybe was not) invited to that beer party.

Indeed, I never discovered with any certainty whether or not he was invited, or having been invited, if he actually received the message. This matter was probably in some degree crucial to the dispute, even though the two men would most probably have come to dispute on some other issue, as they sought to redefine and express their relationship to one another and to the other members of their community.

A full consideration of the consequences of a dispute settlement is equally important, both for general analysis and in the examination of social processes among a particular cluster of people. The dispute may be settled (in the sense previously outlined), but the form and content of the settlement, and its subsequent enforcement as relevant, must necessarily affect relations between the disputants and others involved in some way or other. Dispute settlement does not occur in a social vacuum, insulated from the continuous stream of interaction that makes up ongoing social life—although too often anthropological analysis seems to give the contrary, and false, impression. Very often, though not invariably, the participants in a dispute are more or less aware of this fact, and the settlement itself is modified by that knowledge. In any case, however, the settlement in effect defines, or redefines, statuses, rights, and obligations, both for the disputants themselves and for other people. Status expectations may be reaffirmed, weakened, strengthened, or altered, and all this has some effect on subsequent relationships and social action. Take the example of a divorce case: the couple may be induced or compelled to remain together, yet the marital relationship is most likely going to be different thereafter—better or worse or something of each, but different. If divorce is obtained, then an important set of relationships is obviously affected. The settlement of a dispute may effectively resolve the disagreement, it may exacerbate it or reduce it or even change its character. Without considering these sorts of consequences, we are leaving our task uncompleted and we miss therefore a most important dimension of the anthropology of law. Indeed I would assert that anthropologists nullify a great deal of their work if they fail to examine fully the consequences of dispute settlement.

It is of much interest that Gluckman, in the second edition of *The Judicial Process among the Barotse*, has reiterated his acknowledgment of failure to accomplish the full task of case study (Gluckman 1967:370–372; also Gluckman 1961). In that outstanding contribution to our subject, he neglected to take account of both the prehistory and the consequences of the dispute cases he described so well in process of settlement. He himself attributes this defect to a blocking of the mind resulting from overconcentration on processes in the Lozi courts. The most significant, not to say distressing, feature of this event, however, is that the many reviewers and critics of Gluckman's well-read book have apparently not raised the matter at all. Presumably they have not perceived any defect or have thought it merely trivial. Awareness of the deficiency by Gluckman himself, and by some other anthropologists, has come mainly from research and hypotheses in other, contiguous fields of social anthropology; that is, from detailed investigation of social processes in the continuous flow of human interaction, and especially in the inter-action among roughly the same clusters of persons (for example, Mitchell 1956, Turner 1957, Middleton 1960, Van Velsen 1964). Although under-standable in some ways, it nevertheless remains unfortunate, even strange, that there should have been so little interest in and concern for the consequences of dispute settlement and legal action. No doubt this circumstance can be traced in part to preoccupation with disputes them-selves and with legal mechanisms and perhaps to an overly legalistic viewpoint among social scientists. But I suggest that it may also come in part from the fruitless concern with what "law" is, instead of con-centrating on what "law" does.

To say all this is not to deny the central importance of the actual processes of dispute settlement. In the study of these we should, I think, as a first step distinguish at least two structurally different modes. One is dispute settlement by *negotiation* between the disputants, each as-sisted by socially relevant supporters, representatives and spokesmen. Each party seeks to exert what strength it can against the other, such strength ranging from forensic argument and skill to the threat of phys-ical force, from moral pressures to offers or denials of other advantages. Here the result, the settlement, is in effect some mutually acceptable, tolerable resolution of the matter in dispute, based on the assessed or demonstrated strengths of the parties. It is useful to distinguish further between straight negotiations between the two parties and negotiations mediated by some third party or one who is a member of both parties, who has no ability to issue any binding decision.

The second mode of dispute settlement is by *adjudication*, where a binding decision is given by a third party with a degree of authority. Such a decision is in some way coercive in that the adjudicator (judge or the like) has not only both the right and obligation to reach and enunciate a decision but also power to enforce it. The ability to enforce may range from the virtually absolute to little more than the effective public expression of accepted norms and standards of expectations in their application to the particular dispute. Authority in whatever de-gree is commonly reinforced to a greater or lesser extent by the addi-tional pressures of diplomatic persuasion, inducement, moral stricture, and appeal to the supernatural.

Essentially the difference is between judgment by an authorized third party, on the one hand, and negotiated agreement without judgment, on the other; that is, the difference between the presence or absence of overriding authority. Adjudicators may, and often do, attempt to obtain the agreement of the parties—or at least their accedence—to the decision and to reconcile the disputants both to the judgment and to each other. They need not attempt this, and they may fail in the attempt; but the judgment stands, nevertheless, as the decision and settlement. The adjudicator may be to some extent unintelligent, ignorant, biased, dishonest, unskillful, or he may be as just and able as is humanly possible; but he gives, and is committed to giving, the decision. The disputants may argue their cases before him, seeking to influence his decision, suggesting compromise, appealing to rational and irrational factors. That is, they seek to affect the judgment in their own interests, but they do not participate in the decision-making. In contrast, in negotiations with or without a mediator the disputants and their parties participate directly in the settlement; and they must be in agreement with it and must accept it as the best that can be obtained in the circumstances. Acceptance is by compulsion, of course; but it is the compulsion exercised by the other party and not by overriding, external authority. More than this, however: such agreement is not the result only of consideration and application of norms and rules and of standard expectations. Indeed, there is no one in this situation to determine which norms apply, and how; there may be no ultimate agreement on that score. There is, however, the additional and critical factor of the relative strengths of the two parties, in terms of physical numbers and force, political power, supernatural power, and various social advantages and disadvantages to be gained or lost, offered or withheld.

From this I would suggest the hypothesis that, on the whole, there is greater reliance on, appeal to, and operation of rules, standards, and norms where adjudication rather than negotiation is the mode of dispute settlement. Apart from downright, idiosyncratic arbitrariness, the adjudicator reaches his decision by reference to acknowledged standards that he interprets to meet the particular case. This is an oversimplified statement, but it touches the core of the distinction and its implications. In negotiated settlement, reference and appeal to acknowledged standards is likely to be insufficient without supporting bargaining strength. Probably those standards are only infrequently almost entirely neglected —though this can occur when one party has a virtual monopoly of strength over the other. More commonly—in fact, almost generally— negotiation involves both argument in terms of norms and standard expectations and also operational assessment of relative bargaining strength. Most commonly each party has some strength it can exert against the other to its own advantage. Thus compromise of some kind is the typical result.

If this hypothesis is viable, it leads to the further hypothesis that standards are both more vaguely defined and more flexible in areas of social life where negotiation procedures occur than in areas where adjudication is the mode. This does not mean, of course, that standards are inevitably clearly defined, nor that they lack a degree of flexibility, under adjudication; but definition and rigidity tend to be greater. A corollary of this is that where adjudication occurs, there tends to be considerably more explicit exposition and justification of argument and decision-making. Unless the adjudicator is merely capricious, he seeks logically to identify relevant standards, to apply them, and to show how and why they apply, for these are the fundamentals of his decision. Standards tend to be less carefully examined and declared—significantly, they are often less precise—in negotiations, when the ultimate determining factor is the relative strength of the parties deriving at least in part from other factors. There is less need for and value in careful exposition; neither is there any single person with the responsibility of making an explicit specification of the standards.

These hypotheses require cross-cultural testing and, doubtless, modification in the light of empirical material. It is doubtful if there is at the moment sufficient adequate evidence on which to reach a proper conclusion, for records of dispute processes are too often overly brief. Too often anthropologists have been content to give the results of dispute settlement without an account of the processes of ratiocination, exposition, and the reaching of agreement or decision. Nevertheless, with the two modes of dispute settlement in mind, such hypotheses should lead to more sophisticated recording and analysis of processes and to an improved appreciation of the significance and operation of standards (laws, and the like). It should be possible to focus more constructively on the procedures of the presentation of cases, cross-examination, evaluation of evidence, specification of relevant standards and their particular application, and the relation of all these factors to the settlement of disputes. It should be possible to examine more realistically the standards and the general principles that underly them.

I would think that almost all anthropologists agree that the compilation of a list of laws, rules, norms—a *corpus juris*—is by itself a somewhat arid undertaking. It is most likely to conceal as much or more than it reveals. No doubt this is true even in a fully literate society, with full formal documentation of laws and rulings; but in largely nonliterate societies, without such cumulative documentation (and especially where highly formalized procedures are unknown), lists of rules, and so on, are most probably idealized versions that hang in a vacuum. We need to know how the rules are used in actual practice, in what ways and under what circumstances they are modified or even ignored. The mode of application and the mode of determining behavior and assessing it in the light of the rules is quite crucial. Nevertheless, it is obviously essential to examine the rules themselves and their formulation, because they define the matter in dispute and because the disputants and others involved inevitably resort to them in seeking to establish their cases. The rules at least inform the starting point of a dispute, even though they may not necessarily provide clear and unambiguous conclusion to it.

Deliberately I do not seek here to tackle the problem of defining and distinguishing the range of standards that can be used in the process of dispute settlements: such standards as ethical principles, basic cultural premises, norms of conduct, customs, laws, rulings and precedents, reasonable expectations and leeways of toleration, and so on. All of this is by no means unimportant, but concentration on it seems to lead too often to sterile logic chopping. It seems to me that the realistic approach should be first through actual dispute cases. Thus we may see what rules (to use a neutral term) are brought forward overtly or by assumption by various participants, how these are manipulated, modified, and used as measures and as justification of behavior and of rights and obligations, and the relative weighting given to different ones in varying contexts. In practice, of course, any anthropologist will obtain stereotyped versions of rules from his informants, both during disputes and at other times; but the reality and significance of them can be perceived only as they are seen actually in operation in dispute processes.

This approach will bring out a further important point that has tended to be neglected by anthropologists. There is always, I believe, some hierarchy of rules that can be discovered and examined in their operation. This hierarchy is of two interrelated kinds—perhaps two sides of the same coin. First, there is a range from the highly specific to the more general and inclusive: here the more specific rules derive from the general, "superior" ones. For example, there is likely to be a range from the prescription of, say, larceny to basic principles concerning the nature of property; or from the definition of certain rights and obligations between specified kinsmen to principles of kinship or of lineage organization. Secondly, there is a hierarchy in which certain rules are superior to (that is, take precedence over) other and therefore less important ones. For example, "thou shalt not kill" can perhaps be overridden by the rule that a person may defend himself by force, even to the extent of homicide, in the face of violent attack and where no other defense is possible. The first rule may also be overridden by "superior," contrary rules appertaining to warfare, capital punishment, or sacrifice, or it may be subject to modification by reference to rank and status. Other suggestive examples can be given. The rules allocating rights between brothers may be overridden by the rules of family unity or paternal authority; and rules defining rights between families may be subject to the "superior" rules of lineage unity. Bridewealth may be specified as a certain number of animals, amount of currency, or the like, but principles of affinal relationships may, in certain situations at least, override this rule. Support of a kinsman may be held superior to the support of a neighbor, and the latter superior to support of some more distant person. An adequate perception of these kinds of hierarchies is one further way to avoid simplistic listings of laws. But it is more important than that, for these hierarchies are intrinsic to the processes of dispute settlement. They provide one way in which rules are interrelated and interdependent and therefore affect the operation of and appeal to rules in dispute cases. In many instances a "superior" rule overarches and subsumes a number of "inferior" rules, bringing them together systematically and giving them, when necessary, additional validity and force. For example, close kinsmen should behave toward one another in certain specified ways in particular contexts, but those prescriptions and expectations are made coherent and are strengthened by reference, say, to the rules of lineage membership and the values of lineage unity. The hierarchies of rules also suggest possible solutions to conflicts or alleged conflicts between rules in the course of reaching a settlement. It seems probable that an important method of procedure, conscious or not, is to discover the overarching rule that applies indisputably to both disputants as the bridge of initial consensus. From this a further narrowing of the differences can be attempted, and some assessment of priorities can be made among these. I think that adjudicators at least sometimes work in that way; and it would be useful to know in what kinds of circumstances and by what kinds of steps they so act. My experience of negotiation processes suggests that mediators—or, alternatively, certain members of each opposing party—often seek to identify the overarching rule as a means of initiating the positive phase leading to some form of agreement. Much more work is required to elucidate this kind of operation, but it may well lead to more sophisticated analysis. In particular it should throw light on the operational significance of rules and values in dispute processes.

To revert to the two principal modes of dispute settlement—negotiation and adjudication. Some societies are characterized by the absence of adjudication, but probably no society is without some forms of negotiation as a means of dealing with disputes. Negotiations may operate within fairly distinct subsystems (such as small clusters of neighbors, kin groups, voluntary associations) where the members are roughly equals who wish to avoid outside interference. Here negotiations may well be the regular method of treating disputes between members, even though access to adjudication remains a possibility. Negotiations may, however, be a preliminary or a possible alternative to adjudication.

Many disputes are subject to treatment by a combination of the two modes operating in different phases. The adjudicator may be content to accept, and perhaps formalize, the agreed results of negotiation; he may be the instigator of those negotiations; he may step in when they falter; or he may set limits within which they take place. Negotiations may serve to clarify the area of dispute in which adjudication is required. The possibility of a resort or appeal to adjudication will be likely to affect the course and results of negotiations. All this requires much more examination by anthropologists. For instance, what determines whether a dispute goes to negotiation or adjudication—the kind of matter in dispute, the nature of relations between the disputants, the desire to avoid or to appeal to authority? It is of some importance to understand the differences in the kinds of settlements reached by the two processes in the same society and the kinds of social consequences entailed by them.

The distinction between these two modes of dispute settlement seems to be not only valid but also analytically useful. This fact need not, however, lead to an insistence upon rigidly exclusive categories of social processes. Such rigidity is always likely to be dangerous. In this instance there is no absolute dividing line between the two modes. Certainly intermediate cases occur where it is difficult, and scarcely worthwhile, to attempt to allocate them firmly to one category or the other. These cases may, instead, teach us a good deal about the similarities, rather than the differences, in these phenomena. For instance, it is obviously hard to say when an adjudicator begins to become more a mediator between the disputants than a decision-maker. Alternatively, a mediator may in certain circumstances arrive at a position where he is able, or allowed, to give a more or less binding decision. In negotiations without a mediator, a spokesman for one party may have sufficient influence and skill to come to a position where he can act in effect almost as an adjudicator; whereas an adjudicator may sometimes find it convenient or politic or more efficient to act as a mediator. These leading roles in the dispute process may be flexible, and the circumstances in which modifications can occur may require examination.

Furthermore, we need to examine not only the differences but also the similarities between the two modes of settlement. Certain aspects of particular processes of negotiation are directly comparable with certain aspects of particular adjudication processes: for example, the verification of evidence, the operation of the notion of reasonable expectations, or the specification of overarching values. It should be clear also that social pressures impinging on a dispute from outside, and thus affecting the settlement, are not confined to negotiations alone. Pressures of one sort or another can be brought to bear on the adjudicator in order to influence, even to control, his decision: bribery, flattery, appeal to prejudices, threat to his own interests, and the like. The differences between the two modes in respect to the social consequences of dispute settlement are by no means clear. Doubtless a good deal depends on the nature of the dispute and the disputants; but there is no a priori justification for making a rigid distinction in this respect.

Despite my insistence on the significant distinctions between the two modes of dispute settlement, I wish to avoid the establishment of precise ideal types or models. The distinction is intended to be primarily heuristic and exploratory, and therefore I have deliberately written in general terms, without seeking to specify the constitution of either mode and without giving ethnographic substance to each. Taken to extremes, the two modes would present overcontrasted, distorted models: on the one hand, the autocratic judge, all wise and all powerful, handing down a decision determined precisely and justly in accordance with clearly enunciated, unambiguous law; and on the other hand, two disputing parties, with little or no regard for acknowledged standards, fighting the matter out purely in terms of their relative strengths derived from any and all available sources. These are caricatures; neither is likely to occur in real life. Authority is invariably limited in some degree; uncertainty of law is inevitable; negotiation through strength is always restricted by some adherence to common, accepted values and standards; settlements are all more or less opportunistic. Clearly, every dispute is affected not only by the rules and standards that are relevantly applicable to the behavior and statuses involved, but also by external factors and forces that in one way or another can be brought to bear on the matter, and on any participant, to influence the settlement.

Nevertheless I believe that there is genuine advantage to be gained from the heuristic identification and contradistinction of processes of negotiation and adjudication. Not least among the advantages, perhaps, may be the stimulation of more careful study of processes of negotiation, for these have been unduly neglected by anthropologists in their predilection for the more obvious mode of adjudication. But irrespective of these distinctions, I suggest that only with the detailed recording of the full processes relating to dispute settlements, including both their prehistories and their social consequences, will anthropological progress be achieved. Whatever particular aspects we may be concerned with, and whether intra- or cross-culturally, more case studies of dispute settlement in their socio-cultural context will provide the essential material for their understanding.

Dispute Settlement Without Courts: The Ndendeuli of Southern Tanzania

In considering law and especially the processes of dispute settlement in simpler societies, anthropologists have most generally dealt with situations in which courts or courtlike institutions operate. By a court I mean some kind of more or less formal assembly presided over by a designated person (or group of persons) who has both the responsibility and the authority to hear the cases of the disputants, their witnesses, and arguments, and to determine and pronounce a decision. In other words, there is *adjudication* by a *judge* who is not, or should not be, committed to either disputing party but who acts as a third party. To some extent the judge acts on behalf of the community and/or the established political authority. He may be virtually a spokesman for public opinion, summing up consensus of views on a matter in dispute; or he may be more truly magisterial, with the responsibility of decision-making firmly in his hands, though with reference to established rules and precedents. Often, though not invariably, the judge has sanctions at his disposal with which to enforce his decisions; but this seems to be a secondary consideration. He may occupy a specialized, formal status in the established political system and enjoy the backing of coercion available in that system to those in positions of political authority; this is typical of those societies with centralized, institutionalized political systems. The best example we have is that of the Lozi of central Africa, described by Gluckman (1955); but there are many other similar, if less well described, systems in Africa and elsewhere. In other societies, certain roles, only partly political and jural in content, carry the obligation and the right to adjudicate or at least arbitrate in disputes and to give considered opinions and decisions with some expectation of their acceptance and enforcement. Examples of such roles are lineage head, ritual leader, age-group leader, band leader, village head, seniormost kinsman, secret-society official, and the like. In yet other societies influential men of varying kinds—neighbors, elderly men, or others neutral to the disputing parties —may be pressed into temporary adoption of the role of arbitrator or even of adjudicator on something of an ad hoc basis—as among the Ifugao of Northern Luzon, for example (Barton 1919).

To repeat: in all these societies someone, or some body of persons, who is not directly implicated in the dispute, acts as judge or arbitrator. He gives, and has to give, a decision. Epstein, a lawyer-anthropologist, has described the simplest form of the situation thus: "Arguments are presented, witnesses are called or supporters heard, until finally the matter is concluded when the *acknowledged spokesmen of the group* give their opinions on the case." [1] Almost all of the best anthropological analyses of the processes of dispute settlement refer to this sort of situation —to "courts" and to "judges"; those of Llewellyn and Hoebel, Bohannan, Gluckman, Hoebel, Hogbin, Pospisil are some that spring immediately to mind.

Much less consideration, to any degree of analytical depth, has been given to societies and social situations where the adjudicator, judge, arbitrator, is absent. The literature has many references to feud as an alternative to adjudication, but there seems to be no really adequate and convincing analysis of feud as a dispute-solving process rather than as a political process. Sooner or later—at least if the two parties belong to the same community network of continuing social relationships and interaction [2]—hostility or the constant threat of it must give way to discussion, negotiation, and an attempt to reach some kind of *rapprochement* and a settlement of the matter in dispute. Precisely how this stage is reached, and how the settlement is reached, and what sort of a settlement, we are seldom told in any detail. The hostilities of groups and the end results of reconciliation and peace seem to have interested anthropologists more than the essential intervening process of reaching a settlement—and that process is far more difficult to record adequately. Barton (1949) on the Kalingas and Colson (1962) on the Plateau Tonga are notable exceptions to this. But in any case, not all peoples who have no adjudicators and arbitrators necessarily practice an institutionalized resort to force and feud in the event of dispute; nor, no doubt, are all disputes treated by feuding even in those societies where that is prac-

---

1. Epstein 1954:2, my italics.
2. Persistent feuds seem often to operate not within the same community, nor with an immediately neighboring one, but with a slightly more distant one with whom peaceful, continuous interaction is not essential—as Peters (1967) has pointed out for Senusi of Cyrenaica.

ticed, for such disruption can scarcely be allowed within fairly small face-to-face local groups. Even in societies with well-organized courts, disputes occurring within local communities are sometimes settled without recourse to the formal court system: Beattie (1957) has briefly described one such instance. Moreover, as shown elsewhere in this volume, a very considerable number of disputes in modern, industrial societies are settled within the group (such as office, club, college) or by some kind of conciliation process (for example, meeting of attorneys) without recourse to the courts. In short, there is a range of communities and social situations in which neither courts nor coercion provide the means of treating and settling disputes.

Previously, for the Arusha of northern Tanzania, I have described the processes of essentially peaceful settlement of disputes (from petty offenses to homicide) where there is no intervention of adjudicators. Put in the simplest way: when a dispute occurs among the Arusha, each disputant recruits a body of supporters, and the two parties meet in peaceful assembly to discuss the matter and to negotiate an agreed settlement. Supporters are recruited on the basis of patrilineal affiliation, coevality, and neighborhood. Each disputant attempts to gain the support particularly of those publicly influential men (lineage counselors, age-group spokesmen, and other notables) who are linked in these ways more nearly to him than to his opponent. But these influential men act as leaders and advocates on a disputant's behalf and are in no way third parties, let alone arbitrators or adjudicators. Although reference and appeal is made by both disputing parties to accepted expectations of behavior and alleged breaches of them, a settlement of the matter is some kind of negotiated compromise between the conflicting claims. Social pressures of any and every kind are brought to bear on the other party as each disputant and his supporters feel able to make use of them. Settlements frequently disregard ideal norms, as indeed they must by the logic of the situation: if an agreement is to be reached at all, each party must be ultimately prepared—and induced—to shift its ground and to accept compromise. The problem of enforcement arises only marginally: since it is an agreed settlement, both sides are prepared to accept it as the best solution available in the circumstances. Preferably it is put into effect immediately, thus avoiding the necessity of further action—for example, the agreed compensation is handed over, the abducted girl is returned to her father, the field boundary is marked out. But ritual means can be used, and they are held to bind both parties to the settlement. This is a very brief summary of a rather complex process (Gulliver 1963: Part IV).

In this paper I examine data from another African society in which there are no courts or courtlike institutions, no judges or arbitrators, but where also the use of coercion by force is abjured as a means of dispute settlement or of obtaining redress for injury.

The Ndendeuli

The Ndendeuli, a Bantu-speaking people, are shifting cultivators living in the eastern part of the Songea area of southern Tanzania. The country is covered with dry woodland. With simple slash-and-burn technique and rather poor soils, fields can be cultivated for no more than three successive seasons under the staple crop of maize. There is the usual high proportion of uncultivatable land typical of so much of central Africa, and consequently no household seems able to remain permanently in one place. Available woodland from which to make new fields becomes exhausted before regeneration of abandoned land is completed. Over-all density of population is about five persons per square mile, but there are extensive areas of uninhabited woodland. The people congregate in local communities of from thirty to fifty households—150 to 250 people—so that purely local densities of population are something like sixty persons per square mile.

A local community is established when a man of initiative assembles a cluster of some of his kinsmen—cognates and affines—and together they pioneer an unoccupied area of woodland. Being all related to the leader, the pioneers (and their households—immediate families plus dependents) are directly or indirectly all related to one another. A newcomer is generally welcome to join the community so long as he is related by cognatic or affinal kinship to an existing resident member, who acts as his sponsor, guarantor, and supporter. Being related to his sponsor, the newcomer is therefore linked directly or indirectly to all of his neighbors, members of the community. As increasing numbers of newcomers join the community (because available land is worked out elsewhere, because of difficulties in the previous community, and the like), the indirectness of kinship linkages between heads of households increases. Men become unable and unconcerned to trace their linkages with many of their neighbors. They recognize and cooperate with a range of acknowledged kin, cognatic and affinal, and they know of and occasionally cooperate with a range of the kin of those kin; but others are merely neighbors. Yet empirically, as a result of the collation of genealogical knowledge by the anthropologist, the members of a local community can all be placed in a single extended genealogy. This is a logical consequence of the mode of recruitment to a community, and it has most important significance in the processes of dispute settlement, as I shall show presently.

An example of one such Ndendeuli local community is given in Figure

1. It can be seen that the community comprises a single kinship network. Ndendeuli kinship is nonunilineal in character: in the nature of relationships, interaction, rights, and obligations, there is little essential difference between cognatic and affinal kin. Kinship ties do not carry highly specific kinds of rights and obligations but involve imprecisely defined, generalized cooperation and interests. Genealogically nearer kin tend to acknowledge stronger obligations to give assistance of many kinds that more distant kin. But a man has similar expectations of, say, his father's brother, mother's brother, and wife's father, or of his first cousins and his wife's brother.

The original leader of the pioneers who founded the local community does not necessarily continue to have an influential role once the community is established. He does not become a kind of headman. Whether he does retain particular influence depends mainly on his personal qualities and abilities, together with the nature of the range of his direct kinsmen among his neighbors. As residents move away for whatever reason and newcomers move in, he may come to have many kin-neighbors or only a few. And he is in no better position than any other well-favored member of the community to exert influence and leadership.

Such a local community consists of a number of hamlets of from one to five autonomous households, scattered over an area of three or four square miles. They are separated from similar communities by stretches of uninhabited, unused woodland. It is an independent unit: communities do not combine into any larger group. A man has many other kinsmen who are scattered in other communities but with whom he has less close association than with his neighbors. There is no regular character to that cluster of kin-neighbors.

In this paper I consider the settlement of disputes within a local community—that is, between neighbors. Disputes do, of course, occur between people of different communities, and the basic principles of their treatment are largely the same. It is, however, easier to describe the processes within a community. But there is an additional important reason for my choice of presentation. From my field data I am able to describe and discuss a chronological series of cases that occurred in a single community during one year and that to a greater or lesser extent affected the same collection of people. These cases were most significantly affected by the developing neighborly and kinship relations among those people. This is quite crucial, and a proper understanding of Ndendeuli dispute processes cannot be obtained from a consideration of isolated single examples. These processes are intimately involved in and affected by the dynamic continuum of community life. The processes and results in one case directly and indirectly affect the relationships that operate in subsequent cases. Furthermore, relations between neighbors that are activated and utilized when disputes arise are also concerned in various

Figure I

LIGOMBA LOCAL COMMUNITY
Skeleton genealogy.

The numbered men are the heads of the autono-mous domestic groups which constitute the local community. The many other kin resident elsewhere and females (unnumbered) are shown only where they provide linkages in the Ligomba kinship net-work. Dependent children are not shown.

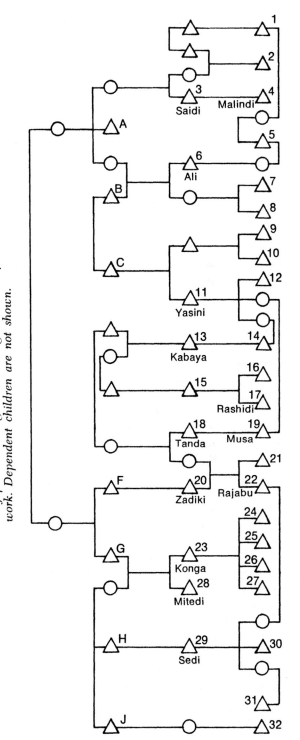

kinds of cooperation and competition in other kinds of activities in community life.[3]

Collective action is required by a member of a local community to pursue or defend his interests in a number of ways that are beyond the means of his own household—for example, in cooperative work parties for various agricultural tasks (clearing virgin woodland and making new fields, hoeing and planting, fencing fields, and so on) and for building, for ritual performances, and at marriages, funerals, and the like. Similarly, and drawing on the same neighbors, collective action is required when a man seeks recompense for injuries to or rejection of his rights and when he seeks to prevent interference with his legitimate interests. To obtain such collective action a man recruits an *action-set* from among his neighbors. Principally he recruits his own kin-neighbors; but as far as he wishes and is able, he recruits his kin-neighbors' kin who are only indirectly related to him—for example, a cousin's cousin, an affine's affine. The extent of recruitment by a man (Ego) broadly speaking depends on a number of factors. One is the importance of the interests involved and thus of the amount of assistance needed. Secondly, the simultaneous recruitment of an action-set by some other neighbor may limit the number of neighbors Ego can recruit—Ego may be in direct conflict with that other neighbor, as in a dispute with him; or both may be engaged in the same activity, as in hoeing their fields. Thirdly, recruitment is affected by the strength of the claims that Ego can exert upon his kin-neighbors and, through them, upon their own kin-neighbors not directly related to him.

Action-sets are purely ephemeral, with no corporate character. Once the interest for which a set was recruited has been achieved, the set dissolves. Subsequent action-sets, in other interests of the same Ego or of some other man, will not have the same composition in all probability because of the changing patterns of the factors involved, mentioned above, which largely determine their composition. In this nonunilineal kinship system no two men, however closely related, have quite the same range of kinship relations upon which to call in the recruitment of action-sets. It is characteristically an Ego-oriented system.

The Ndendeuli say—and so, for brevity and with caution, may the anthropologist—that men expect help from one another and accede to recruitment to an action-set to assist and support Ego because of their kinship relation with him. A more realistic explanation, however, is that men are willing to help Ego, and to become involved in collective ac-

3. All this is no doubt true of similar processes in other societies, but anthropologists have tended to ignore this vital factor. In a different context Turner (1957) has well shown the importance and value of analyzing a chronological succession of social events—what he calls "social drama"—among the same collection of interrelated people. Turner now uses the term, "phase development" rather than "social drama"—see his Introduction to Swartz, Tuden, and Turner 1966.

tion, because of the help they themselves have received and expect in the future to receive from Ego. The principle of reciprocity is crucial. Kinsmen are in practice those who more or less regularly help a person; those who do not are in effect not kinsmen. The kinsman of a kinsman, with whom regular cooperation develops, becomes and is acknowledged as a kinsman, even though the genealogical link may be tenuous. But the kinsman's kinsman who seldom becomes involved remains only indirectly linked and remains only a neighbor. Kinship provides in effect a shorthand way of expressing mutually advantageous interaction, though to a considerable extent genealogical patterns provide the working "rules of the game" and allow a systematization of cooperation and of expectations.

Thus A joins B's action-set to help hoe B's field in the cultivation season, and he expects B to join in hoeing A's field or to join A's action-set when A comes into dispute with some other neighbor. But the organization of collective action is usually rather more complex. A may help B because he wishes to express and strengthen his association with C, who is also helping B; and A may further wish to express his opposition to D, who is in conflict with B. The permutations and complexities of motivation and alignment are considerable. They are, at least at first, best indicated by illustration, as in the following account of dispute cases and the action-sets these precipitated. For the Ndendeuli, however, they are overtly expressed in a kinship idiom.

The Process of Dispute Settlement

Occasionally nonresident individuals are drawn into a dispute between neighbors in order to support their kinsmen who are residents in the community. But even when they do participate, they are seldom prominent in the typical interaction that leads to some kind of settlement of the dispute. This interaction is very largely channeled through the kinship network that links neighbors together. Through the network—that is, through kinship linkages—a man is able to obtain active supporters in his own interests; but at the same time he is liable to limitations and pressures exercised by his opponent and by the latter's supporters because of the linkages that extend between them and his own supporters. Neighbors in dispute are compelled to take into account the whole range of linkages, interests, and operative relationships among the rest of their neighbors and to reach some agreement with that context.

A greatly simplified model will serve as an introduction to the nature of the social processes concerned. In a dispute between neighbors A and E (who are not directly related and who do not regard each other as kin), A expects the support of his kin-neighbor B; and B may well seek the support of his own kin-neighbor C (who is not kin to A) to the side of A. But C might be similarly expected to give his support in the matter to another kin-neighbor D (who is not kin to B) on the side of E who is kin to D. Thus A and E are connected: their fields of social action impinge on each other's and are mutually limiting. C is placed in a structurally intermediate position, where he may be compelled to act as mediator; B and D may seek to influence each other and to prevent their own co-operative relations (via C) from undue disruption. Very roughly, the basic situation is illustrated in the following diagram, where all lines represent actual interpersonal relationship: uninterrupted lines represent direct, acknowledged kinship links; interrupted lines represent indirect linkages.

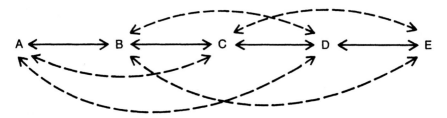

An actual dispute situation would, of course, be far less simple. It is certain that A and E—and, indeed, any other of these men—would be linked in other effective ways through the kinship network; more neighbors would be involved, and the impingement of the fields of action of A and E would therefore be much more complex. As I have already remarked, a dispute is not a self-contained, isolated social event, for it occurs in the context of the continuum of community life. A or E, or both, may have supported C on some recent occasion, and they both probably participate in C's work parties and he in theirs; A and D, B and D, and B and E may also have been giving each other reciprocal assistance. And all will expect to give and obtain assistance in the future. A real dispute situation is commonly affected by the efforts of particular men to demonstrate and perhaps enlarge their influence over their neighbors and by particular friendliness or hostility between individual men as a result of past encounters and structural relationships.

Matters of public interest and concern, including disputes, are discussed whenever men come together in any number. A gathering of neighbors may be primarily for some other purpose—a beer-drink, a feast, the performance of rituals, and the like—or it may be an arranged and rather more formal assembly convened for a specific discussion. Such a purposive assembly will be referred to as a "moot"; Ndendeuli simply call it a "meeting," *mkutano.* A moot can be convened by one of the disputants who wishes to bring the matter to active, public consideration; or it may be convened by a neighbor who is structurally intermediate between the disputants or who, definitely on one side or the other, is influential and active enough to assume initiative and leadership. Moots are usually held on neutral ground—very often at the house of an intermediary—though if the dispute is not too serious, it may be held at the house of the defendant.

Each disputant recruits his own action-set, although a younger man (who is nevertheless head of his own autonomous household) may sometimes leave this to his father or other senior kin-neighbor. The members of the action-set advise their principal, sit with him in the moot, speak on his behalf, cross-examine speakers from the other side, and assist him to negotiate his case. Though it is an arranged arena of dispute, a moot is fairly informal, as men sit on the verandah or under the eaves of the house and on the ground in front of it. There is generally a certain amount of moving about, and the two action-sets are often not clearly distinguishable by eye. Those participants who are structurally intermediate tend to sit in the middle of the gathering, demonstrating their lack of definite allegiance to one side or the other. Neutral neighbors, if any, usually sit at the edge of the group. There are few rules of procedure and no formal head who can act as chairman. The matter is normally described first by the plaintiff, and the defendant then replies with his own account; but not infrequently the defendant starts off, rebutting what is already a well-known complaint and perhaps making a counterclaim. Thereafter discussion is free, open to anyone present, even occasionally to neutrals, though on the whole discussion tends to be dominated by the principals, one or two of their more influential supporters, and influential intermediaries. Often two or more men speak at once, especially when discussion becomes heated, but for the most part each man is allowed his uninterrupted say, as ideally he should be. A speaker remains sitting where he is, and he may be interrupted or questioned while he is speaking. The men know one another well, of course, for they are neighbors who meet frequently in all sorts of circumstances. There is an assumption of equality among them and, even when emotions run high, a willingness to let each man have his say and to listen to him with tolerance and respect. Discussion is often disorganized and rambling, but only the grossest irrelevancies are summarily checked by the impatience of the audience. Men are not obliged to speak, although unless they are clearly neutral, they should indicate their support of their own principal and of the final decision, if any, that is reached.

In the following account and analysis of actual dispute cases a number of special terms are used to refer to the roles of participants. *Plaintiff* and *defendant*, referred to in common as the *principals* in the dispute, are the men who respectively bring and rebut the complaint or claim. Usually they are the actual men who allegedly have suffered and caused the injury or offense that is the subject of the dispute, or the heads of the households of which the injured and offender are members. Sometimes, however, their role as principal is taken by a "father"—that is, a kin-neighbor of senior generation.

A neighbor who is more or less equally related in the kinship network to both principals is referred to as an *intermediary* (for example, C in the preceding diagram). This is a purely structural placement, resulting from the relative position of the two principals in the particular case. The actual role of an intermediary varies: he may be actively partial to one of the principals, though he seldom entirely opposes the other; or he may avoid embarrassing participation by deliberately absenting himself from the community temporarily and thus remaining inactively neutral; or he may become a *mediator*. A mediator attempts to act as broker between the principals, but he may be active in suggesting and pressing positive means of reaching an agreed settlement. He is at most, however, a con-ciliator. He does not act as an arbitrator, for he cannot give a decision and a settlement, nor is he expected to. Not every dispute and moot brings forth a mediator, though most do.

In a local community a few men are acknowledged to have particular ability in the processes of dispute settlement and have marked influence over their neighbors in general, to the point of becoming informal lead-ers. Such a man is called simply a "big man" (*mundu mukurungwa*) and is referred to in this account as a *notable*. In Ndendeuli usage this is a rather vague term, applicable to anyone who takes an informal lead in some situation or whose reputation, personality, and seniority afford him a certain respect and influence. Most men of the senior generation in the community can be, and sometimes are, described in this way, and it would be insulting openly to suggest that such an older household head is not a "big man." However, invariably two or three men are consistently acknowledged publicly to be notables: they exercise accepted influence and tend to take the lead on most occasions of public dispute, discussion, and action. It is to these men that the term "notable" is given without qualification in this account. Their role is not at all well defined. Cer-tainly it does not afford authority in the sense that their lead must more or less be followed, and they have no active sanctions at their disposal to support their leadership. They do not adjudicate, and they can be ignored. A notable who attempts to extend his accepted influence to authoritarianism raises resentment and opposition among his neighbors. He may well lose his influence by such an attempt, for he loses the good will and trust that is so necessary for the continuation of a notable's success.

The role of the notable in a dispute case depends on his position in the kinship network vis-à-vis the two principals and their kin-neighbors. If, on the one hand, he is so clearly linked with one of the principals that he is included in the latter's action-set recruited for the case, then he usually shares the leadership of it with the principal, and he may even become the chief exponent of the promotion or defense of the interests at stake. If, on the other hand, he is an intermediary—and even, sometimes, a neutral—he may act as a mediator. According to the situation, notables may become leaders of either side in the moot, or one may be leading an action-set while another acts as mediator. Rivalry between notables can be important in the process of dispute settlement as well as in community affairs in general, as will be illustrated in the cases that follow.

Some Disputes in Ligomba Community

At the time of field research, in 1953, this local community comprised thirty-two households, the heads of which are shown in a single linking genealogy, as given in Figure 1. Each household head had many other acknowledged kinsmen who were at that time resident in other communities elsewhere in the country; and one or two heads were linked through these other kinsmen. However, the chief interconnections, and the ones emphasized by the men themselves, are those given in that genealogy.

I present an account of five successive disputes that arose in Ligomba during 1953 and that I recorded and discussed in the field. They illustrate how disputes are treated in the context of the kinship network of a Ndendeuli local community and how the events and results of one dispute have some effect on the events and results of the following ones. I should note that I am still engaged in the analysis of my field material on the Ndendeuli; these case studies are but a part of that material, though an integral part.

Case 1. A Claim for Additional Bridewealth (June). In June 1953 Rajabu (22 in Fig. 2) returned to Ligomba after more than a year away as a labor migrant. The day after his return he visited his wife's parents (29 and wife) and presented them with a blanket and a length of cheap cloth. He apologized that he offered them no more, saying that he had managed to bring little home with him. Sedi (29) appeared to be satisfied—at least he commended Rajabu on the gifts. A few days later, however, Sedi made a demand for money from Rajabu as an additional contribution to bridewealth. Rajabu claimed that he had completed all bridewealth obligations before he had left home at the end of 1951; and he claimed that Sedi had at that time been satisfied with the transaction. In support of this statement he said that Sedi had not at that time made further demands for future payments and that his daughter (Rajabu's wife) had continued to live in her house in the hamlet of her father-in-law, Zadiki (20), while Rajabu had been away; that is, her father-in-law had assumed responsibility for her. Sedi

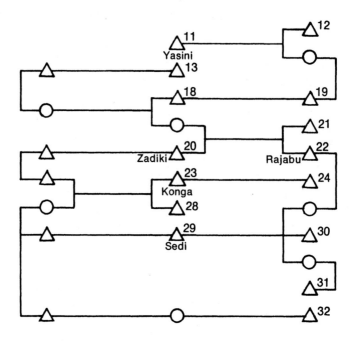

Figure 2

denied that this fact was any proof of completed bridewealth; it was merely a demonstration of good and proper affinal relations. He repudiated any idea that he had ever expressed final satisfaction with the bridewealth. A stalemate followed as Rajabu was fully supported by his father, Zadiki. After these private discussions Sedi consulted with his kin-neighbors and then asked for a moot to consider his persisting claim. His request was negotiated by Konga (23, his father's sister's son), who was first cousin of Zadiki (20), and the moot was eventually held at Konga's house.

The action-sets at the moot were composed as follows. Sedi recruited and led his own set. Rajabu was a young man, about twenty-four years old, who had been absent from Ligomba a great deal in labor migration since becoming an adult; his father therefore acted as principal in the case and recruited the action-set; Rajabu himself, though present, took very little part. Also present were Konga (23) with his eldest son (24); they were equally closely related to both principals, therefore equally obligated formally and in an obvious position to act as mediators. But 28, no less intermediary, preferred to opt out of what he judged to be too difficult a situation; he left Ligomba on a temporary visit. Konga took the lead as mediator, as he was a notable. It was a small moot and, as it turned out, the only one required to settle the dispute. Because of the fairly close and interconnected kinship linkages the action-sets were limited, and there was in the event no need for either principal to appeal to more distantly linked neighbors. The only other men present were 7 and 14, who joined the moot after it had begun, ap-

Action-set of Zadiki (20) °

21, 22 (S)
   18 (WB)
   19 (WBS)
   13 (18's MBS)
   12 (19's WB)
   11 (19's WF)
   (8 men)

Action-set of Sedi (29)

30 (S)
31 (DH)
32 (FBDS)

MBS, nonresident
(5 men)

° Conventional signs denoting kinship relations are used throughout as follows: F-father, M-mother, S-son, D-daughter, B-brother, Z-sister, H-husband, W-wife. Thus, for example, MBS denotes "mother's brother's son."

parently attracted from their fields nearby where they were working, and 15, who arrived toward the end of the proceedings. None of these three men took any part in the moot.

Zadiki argued, in opening the moot, that the request for more bridewealth was really a demand for a larger share of the savings that Rajabu had brought home after his period of labor migration. At the intervention of 18, the gifts to himself and his wife were admitted by Sedi; but he claimed that these represented the obligation of any young son-in-law on his return from abroad. Sedi insisted that he had a right to more bridewealth, and that Rajabu was in a position to give it. Rajabu called out that he had brought home very little, but Sedi refused to listen to this. The amounts of cash previously given in bridewealth were described by Zadiki and admitted by Sedi after some minor argument. But Sedi refused to admit to Zadiki's assertion that the completion of payment had even been acknowledged. He restated his current claim but set it at no specific figure. After further discussion Zadiki was forced to admit that his son had brought some money savings home, but he said that they were small and were needed for other purposes by his sons and himself. Zadiki was supported in this by 18, who also raised the point that Sedi and his wife had been given generous gifts when Rajabu had returned home from his previous spell of labor migration. Sedi conceded this, and also the implication, pointed out by Zadiki and the notable, 13, that Rajabu had shown himself to be a good son-in-law. Then 13 stated baldly that Sedi had no claim at all against Rajabu and Zadiki and suggested that he was showing himself to be a poor father-in-law by attempting to make a claim. The notable continued to review the discussion so far and the evidence produced in order to show the absence of a basis for Sedi's claim. He was followed by Yasini (11), who mainly reiterated the substance of the arguments of 18 and 13.

This intervention by Yasini brought a crisis to the discussion, for 30 inquired aloud what interest he had in the matter. Yasini said that he was supporting his "brother"; and 18 elaborated on this by explaining, "Is he not the father of my son's wife? my brother, then? He goes with [supports] me because I am brother of Zadiki. It is right that we are here, and I and Zadiki invited him." And 13 called out that Yasini was his brother too. "We go with our brothers, yes," retorted Sedi, "but is it not true that Yasini has not yet received all the bridewealth for his daughter? Where is the rest to come from? Who gives Musa [Yasini's son-in-law, 19] the money for bridewealth, for he has not been to the Coast [that is, has not been a labor migrant] for a long time? Is Musa getting money from Rajabu so that he can give bridewealth to Yasini?"

After further discussion it appeared that Sedi's suggestion was correct, although it was not explicitly admitted by Zadiki and his supporters. I am uncertain how much of this was previously known by Sedi and how far he was probing on the basis of suspicion, for nothing of this aspect of the dispute had been raised beforehand. The explanation—not fully detailed in the moot—was that two years previously, on returning from labor migration, 19 had lent money to Rajabu, his father's sister's son, to use for bridewealth payments to Sedi. Now on Rajabu's return from employment abroad he was expected to repay the loan so that 19 could himself complete his own bridewealth payments to Yasini (11) (see genealogy, Figure 1).

Until this stage Konga (23) had taken no part in the proceedings of the moot, but now, with the details of the case fairly well established and at least tacitly admitted by both sides, he began to take the initiative in negotiating an acceptable settlement. It became clear that he was not an entirely neutral mediator, for, though cautiously, he leaned to the side of Sedi. It was he who finally stated that Sedi's allegations were substantially correct—Zadiki's side remained silent, thus accepting the statement—and he added that Sedi had a right, as father-in-law, to a larger gift than he had so far received since Rajabu returned home. He commended Rajabu on his desire to repay his debt to his cousin, 19; but he declared—cutting across remonstrations by Zadiki to the same opinion—that it was equally commendable to be generous to a father-in-law who had given his daughter. There was a good deal of general discussion by speakers from both sides on the relative strengths of the conflicting claims of father-in-law and creditor cousin of Rajabu; but in the end—mainly, I think, owing to Konga's insistent advocacy quietly backed by 24—it was agreed that Rajabu should give Sedi another twenty-five shillings and that 19 should receive 50. Konga asked Yasini (11) directly to agree; and this he did, implying that he was prepared to accept for the moment a bridewealth installment of 50 shillings from 19—a smaller amount than he had been expecting. With Yasini's agreement, Zadiki could now scarcely withstand Konga's request for his agreement also. But Zadiki demanded that Sedi should state there in the moot that no further bridewealth obligation lay against Rajabu. After some attempt by Sedi to avoid so committing himself, he eventually agreed to this. Rajabu went off to his house, less than a mile away, and returned to hand over the 25 shillings to Sedi. The moot ended at this point in the joint drinking of some beer provided by Konga.

The significance of the role of Konga (23) in this moot and settlement was emphasized to me afterward in conversations with Yasini (11) and my field assistant, and with the notable (6) who had not attended the moot. These informants explained that Konga—and 24—could have thrown their weight on the side of Zadiki by arguing that Sedi had already received an adequate bridewealth,[4] where as Rajabu owed a genuine debt to 19, who had a need for the money for his own bridewealth payment. But Zadiki and Konga, though first cousins, had long been antagonistic to one another;[5] they still continued to participate in each other's work parties and were sometimes co-members of the same action-sets in other matters, but their relations were largely formal and without warmth. In contrast, Konga was concerned to maintain close cooperation with Sedi and his kin-neighbors. Strictly logically Konga should, or at least could, have given equal support to both principals. As far as I understood the issues in the dispute, and in the opinions of my informants, there was no clear-cut solution. Had Sedi not already received an average-sized bridewealth, for instance, there would have been a better case for his claim at this time. Of course other factors affected the settlement also. Had Yasini (11) been more insistent in his undisputed claim for bridewealth from 19, or had 18 been a more influential person or a better speaker, or had Zadiki been more stubborn rather than being prepared in the end to placate his son's father-in-law, the actual settlement could have been rather different. Fathers-in-law commonly attempt to obtain generous gifts from the savings of returned labor migrants, but they do not invariably succeed, especially where other valid debts are proved. In this instance Sedi did succeed, and without endangering his daughter's marriage; though he did nothing to improve his affinal relations and put his son-in-law in a somewhat difficult position between himself and Zadiki. The role of Konga nevertheless seems to have been crucial, and his generally accepted influence and his persuasive skill in discussion gave him an advantage. Yet he had no wish to alienate his cousin, Zadiki, entirely. There was useful cooperation between them and between each man and the other's kin-neighbors in the community—a break with Zadiki might well have meant a break also with 18, for example. Konga's support of Sedi had to be tempered by these considerations, and consequently he made much show of backing Zadiki's demand that Sedi should declare the end of bridewealth claims against Rajabu. Fairly skillfully Konga managed to bring off something of a personal success in the event, enhancing his reputation for ability and influence in Ligomba.

I should note also that a moderately successful settlement of the actual dispute was achieved in that the various claims of the men concerned were mutually adjusted and community life was able to continue. However, as will be seen in Case 4, relations between Zadiki and Konga were not made any easier as a result of this case and its settlement; and rela-

---

4. It was agreed in the moot that Sedi had received 185 shillings in cash previously from Rajabu. This is roughly an average sum for Ndendeuli bridewealth and therefore in itself gave no particular support to a claim or rejection of further bridewealth.
5. See Case 4, below.

tions between Zadiki and Sedi were less cordial than previously—a situation that became important in Case 3.

Case 2. A Claim for Compensation for Injuries in a Fight (August). During the early dry season, Yasini (11 in Figure 3) convened a work party to cut and clear a piece of woodland and make a new field. Including himself, thirteen men participated in the day's work—a fairly large party. At the beer-drink that followed in the midafternoon these men were gradually augmented by other neighbors, until the large majority of Ligomba men were present. There was plenty of beer and it was a highly convivial affair, as these parties are at that time of year. A number of men grew intoxicated, among them Malindi (4) and Rashidi (17), who began to quarrel. Fighting broke out between them, but this was stopped by some of the others, and

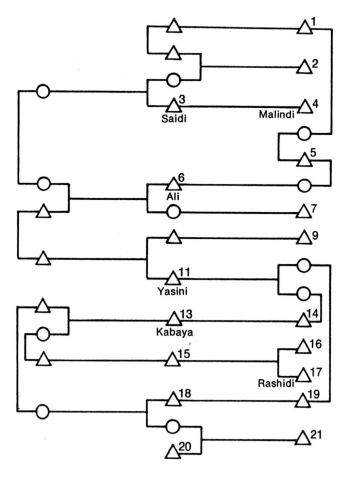

Figure 3

Malindi moved away as if to leave the party. As he left, he shouted abuse at Rashidi, who ran after him and started the fight again. The two men were finally separated, but Malindi was now in a bad state—his clothes were torn and his face and arm were bloody—and his father and his cousin (2) took him off home. There it was found that, in addition to cuts, bruises, and torn clothing, he had received a broken arm.

Next day his father, Saidi (3), sent a younger adult son as messenger to Rashidi to demand compensation. The latter denied responsibility for the fight, saying that Malindi had begun it by grossly insulting him. The messenger, Malindi's younger brother, after some altercation, threatened to take up the fight again and had to leave hurriedly to avoid assault by Rashidi and his brothers.

The father, Saidi (3), consulted with his cousin, Ali (6), as apparently he usually did at times of trouble. Ali advised that renewed direct negotiation with Rashidi was not feasible, and with Saidi's agreement he went to see Kabaya (13), a Ligomba notable and first cousin of Rashidi's father. The two men agreed to try to arrange a moot, and Kabaya persuaded Rashidi to concur. The moot was held the second day following at the house of Konga (23)—that is, on neutral ground. I was unable to attend and obtained conflicting accounts of what occurred. Certainly the moot broke up fairly quickly as threats of renewed violence were made. Saidi (3) continued to insist that his son should receive compensation and that therefore another moot should be held.

The people of Ligomba expressed much disquiet about this dispute and the way it had gone, for threats of violence had been flung around rather indiscriminately. The two notables, Ali (6) and Kabaya (13), who were already rivals for influence in the community, had quarrelled over the failure of the moot, each blaming the other's side. Neutral opinion condemned Malindi's younger brother as a foolish youth stirring up trouble; and his father was blamed also, first for using him as a messenger and then for allowing him to be present at the moot, in which, as an unmarried man, he scarcely had the right to participate. But Rashidi and his elder brother (16) were also thought to be at fault in the continued threats of violence, whatever the truth about Rashidi's behavior at the time of the fight at the beer-drink. Saidi's demand for a second moot was therefore generally welcomed. After another three days—during which time work parties for 8 and 19 were postponed because of the affair—a moot assembled at the house of Yasini (11). The two notables (Ali and Kabaya) were unable to cooperate in convening this moot, and the initiative was taken by Yasini and his elder nephew (9). By this time Konga had left Ligomba to attend the funeral of an affine elsewhere, so that his house was no longer available as a neutral place for another moot. But in any case, Yasini told me, the fight had occurred at his beer-drink at his house and Rashidi had been a member of his work party earlier that day. On further discussion it was clear that Yasini saw himself put into the role of mediator in the dispute because of his structurally intermediate position between the disputants in the kinship network (see genealogy).

The action-sets at the second moot were composed as follows. Rashidi

(17) was principally responsible for his own set, though the notable Kabaya (13) shared the lead with him. Since Malindi was still incapacitated, the opposing action-set was recruited by his father, Saidi (3), although the lead was largely taken by the notable Ali (6).

Action-set of Saidi (3)	*Action-set of Rashidi (17)*
4 (S)	15 (F)
6 (MZS)	16 (B)
7 (6's ZS)	13, 14, (15's FZS & son)
2 (ZS)	18, 19, (13's MZS & son)
1 (2's FBS)	20, 21, (18's ZH & ZS)
FBS ⎫	
⎬ nonresident	
MSB ⎭	
(8 men)	(9 men)

On this occasion 8—6's other sister's son—did not attend, though he had attended the first moot; he was away visiting. The younger, unmarried brothers of Malindi and Rashidi did not attend either; they were among those who previously had threatened further violence. Also present were Yasini (11) and his nephews, 9 and 10, the intermediaries in this context. In addition, 28, 29, and 31 attended although they were in no way involved and appeared only as spectators. Of the other heads of households then at home in Ligomba, only 27, 30, and 32 were absent from this moot.[6] It was the most comprehensively attended moot that I witnessed, partly because of the relative distance between the principals in the kinship network (compare, for example, the limited action-sets in Case 1) and partly because of the general concern and interest aroused by the dispute as it had developed.

Here I give only a summary version of the proceedings in the moot. In the field and in the records I made at the time I was not especially concerned with the quasi-judicial aspects of the moot but rather with the interaction of these neighbors in the kinship network. Moreover, the moot itself was most informal; often more than one man spoke at the same time, and verbal interchanges between the two sides were too rapid or oblique to be recorded properly. I discussed the whole moot afterward with my assistant and several of the participants in an attempt to verify my understanding of it; their and my afterthoughts may have affected my perception of the case.

In effect the proceedings of the moot fell into two parts, though with a good deal of overlapping and, as far as I am aware, no explicit recognition or attempt by the participants themselves to distinguish and separate the parts. First there was elucidation of the facts, and second there was negotiation of the settlement. The moot began with Saidi's (3) describing his son's injuries and attributing them to Rashidi's drunken ferocity. He asserted that the whole blame for the fight lay with Rashidi, and he noted what was patently true, that Rashidi had suffered little or no damage in the fighting. He ended by demanding compensation of sixty shillings be-

6. 8, 12, 21, 23, 24, 25, and 26 were all absent from Ligomba on what seemed to be legitimate grounds (that is, they were not deliberately opting out of the dispute).

cause his son's injuries prevented him from working at a time when men were engaged in preparing their fields for the following year's cultivation. The only immediate response to this demand was an expletive from Rashidi signifying rejection. Instead, Rashidi, his father, and Kabaya (13) in turn put the responsibility for the fight on Malindi. It was by now well known that Malindi had insulted Rashidi by calling him impotent, and this event was not seriously questioned in the moot, for many men had overheard Malindi's words; Saidi remained silent when the notable Kabaya finally stated as much, and the notable Ali (6) argued only that nevertheless this circumstance did not absolve Rashidi from responsibility for the injuries he had caused. Rashidi claimed that his blows had not in fact broken Malindi's arm, but that the latter had tripped over a tree root and had broken his arm in falling. He admitted, on Ali's insistence, to causing the other, minor injuries and tearing Malindi's clothes, but he excused himself on the basis of the provocation of Malindi's insults. Kabaya spoke in support of this defense.

Ali then made a long speech in support of Saidi, showing that Malindi and Rashidi had quarreled on previous occasions, with Rashidi invariably at fault. He said that Rashidi was well known as a troublemaker, especially at beer-drinks; and he gave examples of such behavior that brought some calls of agreement from his own side of the moot. Rashidi's denial of this reputation was, unfortunately for him, spoiled by Ali's direct appeal to a member of Rashidi's own action-set. Ali was able to extract the grudging agreement from 21 that Rashidi had quarreled with him at a beer-party some weeks previously. Perhaps emboldened by his success, Ali reiterated what he considered to be Rashidi's poor reputation and then went on to suggest, indirectly but fairly obviously, that Rashidi used witchcraft and was a bad neighbor in Ligomba. Amid murmurs of disapproval of Ali's innuendo, Yasini (11) now intervened for the first time. He deprecated the introduction of suggestions of witchcraft, and he appealed to "all my kinsmen" (that is, of both sets) for amity and a speedy settlement. The father of Rashidi (15) indignantly denied any suggestion of witchcraft, saying that if there were witches in Ligomba, they were not among his kinsmen. He admitted that his son had previously quarreled with Malindi and with 21, but he explained this circumstance away as "merely the affairs of young men and beer" and not serious matters relevant to the present dispute. In response, 2 (ZS of Saidi) declared outright that he knew nothing about witchcraft in Ligomba, but Saidi's claim was fair. Another member of Saidi's action-set, 1, remarked that though he was a newcomer to the community, he did not think that his neighbors practiced witchcraft or else he would not have moved to live here. Then 16 began hotly to deny the imputation that his brother used witchcraft, but he was interrupted by Yasini (11), who declared that no one believed this and that it was quite wrong to talk about it at all among kinsmen and neighbors. This fetched general commendation from all sides, while Ali remained silent.

Yasini continued to speak and everyone listened, with no attempt to interrupt. He suggested that although Rashidi was to some extent guilty because he had twice attacked Malindi, yet he was badly abused by Malindi without justification. Rashidi's wife had a child—Rashidi's child, he said—and a man could not be expected to take such an insult quietly at any time. Here there was some inconclusive discussion, begun by Yasini of a recent case of slander alleging impotence in a nearby local community. Kabaya (13) broke in to demand that this discussion should cease as it was irrelevant, for Rashidi was not impotent. Yasini accepted this statement on behalf of the moot, and no one attempted to contradict him.

After a brief pause Saidi revived his demand for compensation of sixty shillings for the admitted injuries sustained by his son. Rashidi again rejected the demand contemptuously. Yasini turned to 28 and 29 and said that he thought that 60 shillings was too much. These two men, both neutrals in the dispute, signified agreement but said nothing. Kabaya said that no payment at all was necessary, nor would it be right. However, 2 and 5 said that some compensation was justified but suggested no figure. Saidi then asked what Rashidi would be prepared to give. After some confused cross-talk Zadiki (20) gained the moot's attention by saying that, although he agreed with Kabaya that no compensation should be given, yet because of neighborliness a small "friendship payment" might be made because of Malindi's broken arm. Another member, 18, brother-in-law and close friend of Zadiki supported this suggestion, saying that some small payment would demonstrate the generosity of 15 and Rashidi. Kabaya agreed but said that the payment must be a small one. Saidi rejected this suggestion, but Yasini asked Rashidi what he would be prepared to give. Rashidi remained silent, but 20 suggested twenty shillings. Kabaya said this was too much and suggested five shillings, the cost of the fare on the truck to Songea (the township of the District), where Malindi had gone to be treated by the European medical officer. Ali said that this was too little, as did Saidi and 5. Yasini urged toleration on both sides; it was important to settle the matter, he said. "We are all kinsmen here, and neighbors. Let us cut the case and carry on in peace. Look! Have not 8 and 19 put off their work parties because of this dispute? We all want to go out and cut woodland and drink beer together. But truly, Malindi went to Songea on that lorry to be treated by the European doctor, and so should we not pay his fare?" He asked Saidi to agree to five shillings, but Saidi refused; 5 asked for a little more. After more discussion, it was agreed that a sum of twelve shillings should be paid. Several members of Rashidi's set, including Kabaya, expressed their approval, as did Yasini, who urged Rashidi to make some payment immediately. At last Rashidi produced two shillings, to which was added one shilling by Kabaya, and fifty cents each by 16 and 19. On Yasini's personal persuasion, 15 produced twenty cents, which, he said, was all he had. This money was handed over to Saidi by Yasini with the comment that the rest would certainly be paid very soon after. Yasini's wife then brought out some beer, and the moot ended in overt amiability over the drink.

As far as I know, only another two shillings were in fact handed over to Saidi—at a beer-drink some days later. Most probably ńo more would ever be paid, in the opinion of several of the men whom I questioned.

There are a number of points to be made about this case. The action-sets of the two principals were fairly clearly defined as the men sat on or near the verandah of Yasini's house, for they clustered more or less on opposite sides of the doorway. The support of members of a set was also made clear—perhaps deliberately—by their early remarks at the commencement of the moot. Of course men were well aware of the relevant alignments in any case, but loyalties were expressed and emphasized in this way. The two kinsmen of Saidi who were not residents of Ligomba took little part in the proceedings beyond occasional brief comments in support of remarks made by Saidi himself.

The first stage of the moot—the elucidation of the facts of the dispute, and of their relevance—was monopolized by the principals and their more influential kin-neighbors: Saidi and Ali on the one side and Rashidi, his father, and Kabaya on the other. The second stage—negotiation of compensation—was initiated by Yasini (11), supported by the less involved members of the action-sets: 2 and 5 on the one side and 20 and 18 on the other—while the principals remained silent or made a show of intransigence but finally acceded to their supporters' compromise.

One of the original disputants, Malindi (4), scarcely contributed to the proceedings at all. He left the initiative to his father, as he had already done in the matter of recruiting the action-set prior to the second moot. He had been away from Ligomba at the time of the first moot, visiting the hospital at Songea. The other disputant, Rashidi, took a leading part, however. The explanation of this difference seems to lie in the character of the two men and in their relations with their fathers. Rashidi was a rather aggressive person, while Malindi was a quieter man of little forcefulness. That both men were still young is not in itself especially significant, for even older men of mild disposition will allow an influential kinsman to take the lead in dispute proceedings. In this instance neither of the fathers was a particularly prominent man in the community, and both were prepared to share the lead with a notable in their action-sets—Ali (6) and Kabaya (13) respectively. It so happened that each of the latter was first cousin to a disputant's father (that is, clearly a kin-neighbor), but that is less important than that each was an acknowledged man of influence in the community, each had both the ability and the ambition to assume leadership, and each sought the opportunity to demonstrate and enhance his influence. These two men were to some extent rivals for influence, and this fact stimulated them to take the lead of the opposed action-sets that developed out of the dispute. In the event, though Kabaya's achievement was not particularly marked, the reputation of Ali was diminished by his unwise and undiplomatic reference to witchcraft. Ali not only reduced his stature as a notable, but he was a definite liability to the interests of Saidi, which was one reason for the repudiation of the witchcraft suggestion by other members of Saidi's set.

The structural position of intermediary imposed on Yasini (11) was quite clear. Yasini himself recognized this and took the role of active mediator once the moot showed the extent of the difference between the principals. He could not remain a passive neutral, although he was not directly related by kinship to either principal. On the one hand, through the marriages of his daughters he was closely linked with members of Rashidi's set, and he and Rashidi and his father generally participated in each other's work parties during the dry season; he was closely associated also with the notable, Kabaya (13). On the other hand, he was equally closely linked with the notable, Ali (6), his first cousin; and he had reciprocal work-party arrangements with some other members of Saidi's set. However, Yashini was not a man of forceful character and seemed to have little ambition for gaining influence in the community at large. Because of this, I think, he made an effective mediator in the circumstances, since he sought no marked advantage of his own. It seemed to me, and to my informants, that Yasini was not altogether impartial; rather, he leaned toward Rashidi's side. The injuries to Malindi were moderately serious, since he could not work in the fields at that busy time of the year; and he might perhaps have obtained a larger compensation, despite his demonstrated fault in provoking the fighting. Yasini was at least partly responsible for the particular settlement that was in fact achieved.

The way in which Yasini played his role of mediator is typical of Ndendeuli processes of dispute settlement. He remained quiet until the stage of real negotiation began, and then, apart from appeals to good will and for concord in the community, he acted in effect as spokesman, stating what he conceived to be the feeling of the moot and opening the way to the next phase of discussion. Thus, after discussion had run on in each instance, he stated that the suggestions of witchcraft were both wrong and irrelevant, that the imputation of impotence was false, and that sixty shillings was too high a compensation, though some payment was justifiable. He finally urged Rashidi not only to agree to the sum of twelve shillings but also to make a part payment straight away. These were critical steps in the movement toward an agreed settlement, although Yasini was supported by other members of the moot in each and was in general only emphasizing their suggestions.

I should also note Yasini's attempt to involve the manifest neutrals, 28 and 29, in support of compromise and agreement. This was not, as it turned out, either important or necessary; but it might have been, had the disputants proved more intransigent. Sedi (29) told me afterward that he did not regard the dispute as any affair of his or of his kinsmen, and therefore he wished to remain passive. But he had been interested enough to attend the moot, and he might possibly have been pushed into the role of assisting the mediator had the dispute continued. Sedi commented to me that, had Konga (23) not been absent from Ligomba, then that notable would probably have attempted to take an active part, even though he was not at all involved. "Konga likes to have power and to show that he is a big man, a man to whom people listen," he said. Thus, in the opinion of Sedi at least, Konga might well have been led by his ambitions to ignore his prescribed status as neutral in this dispute. Unlike Yasini, he would not have been more or less forced into the role of mediator but might have chosen to adopt it. It is unsatisfactory in analysis to resort to supposition of this kind, but the significance of Sedi's opinion is not unimportant to an understanding of the social processes involved.

There was virtually a complete failure to pursue the allegation of impotence made against Rashidi—an acknowledged cause of the fighting. As we have seen, Yasini blocked this line of discussion after both Rashidi and his father had said little beyond blank denials. As a result of later inquiries, I became almost certain that Rashidi was impotent and that his wife's child had been fathered by his elder brother. Ligomba informants were unwilling to discuss the matter, and my inquiries were obviously unwelcome; but my field assistant reported that most men believed the allegation to be true. If this is so, it explains why a more spirited defense was not made, and perhaps it helped persuade Rashidi and his father to accede more readily to compensation demands in order to prevent further discussion. They—and Kabaya, the notable, also—did not want the matter publicly discussed for fear of ridicule and shame. However, whether or not it was a true allegation, it still remained provocation for the violence, and there the fault lay with Malindi.

This matter was related to the way the witchcraft issue was treated. Here the notable Ali (6) overreached himself and weakened his side's cause. There seemed to be no justification of the suggestion—even as obliquely as Ali put it—in the history of Rashidi and his kinsmen. Such accusations are made against people alleged to have committed other offenses, and often against a person who is repeatedly a troublemaker. But such accusation is a grave matter and puts a dispute on a more serious and more intractable level. It is likely to be efficacious only where a dispute is prolonged and where the balance of opinion runs against one principal; often it occurs where a dispute is part of a series of closely interconnected disputes between the same people. It is difficult for Ndendeuli to achieve acceptable agreement and reasonable reconciliation after such an accusation is publicly made; commonly one or other of the parties sooner or later withdraws from the community. This seems to be empirically true; but in any case Ndendeuli think and say that an accused witch and his accuser cannot continue to be neighbors and that a dispute between them is likely to go unsettled. Thus witchcraft accusations raise the possibility, by implication, of a breakdown of intracommunity relations and of a failure to settle a dispute. Ndendeuli certainly believe in and fear witchcraft as such; but they implicitly associate it with the failure of normal social control.

Consequently, Ali's indirect accusation was felt by most men on both sides to be both irrelevant and dangerous, tantamount to suggesting that the dispute could not be settled and that the principals could not remain neighbors. Ali should have perceived this—indeed, I am sure that at other times he did, for I discussed witchcraft with him on other occasions—and it may be surmised that he was too preoccupied with his efforts to demonstrate his influence and leadership and to score against his rival, Kabaya (13). His mistake was unfortunate, too, in another way, for it offered the opportunity to Rashidi and his supporters to make heated, lengthy and self-righteous remonstration and denial, allowing the impotence allegation to be more easily ignored. Fellow members of Saidi's action-set (that is, 2 and 1) were virtually compelled to repudiate Ali's imputation, while Saidi did much the same by remaining silent. Thus, unintentionally no doubt, Ali weakened the case he was promoting and damaged his own personal reputation. In his competition with Kabaya he not only defeated his own ends, but he also endangered his relations with Yasini who, equally closely linked to both men, was here put on the side of Kabaya. As I shall show later, competition between Ali and Kabaya over and through Yasini was persistently significant in the community and its affairs.

Finally, I note that although compensation of twelve shillings was agreed to, only six shillings and twenty cents were actually handed over. People did not expect the rest to be paid. It seemed unlikely that Saidi would reopen the case by making a public issue of the outstanding amount; he probably had little wish for this once Malindi's injuries had healed satisfactorily, and his supporters had little to gain by encouraging it. Yasini told me that the matter was now ended; it should not be raised again, or the whole dispute might be renewed, he explained. He, too, had no wish to see the matter discussed, since it might adversely affect his own neighborly relations. No one had anything to gain, therefore, by insisting on a full payment of the agreed sum, and general opinion was against anything that might threaten good working relationships among neighbors. It was suggested to me by Sedi (29) that possibly the unpaid debt would be raised in the future if Malindi and Rashidi, or their near kin, became involved in some other dispute. His surmise may have been correct; and the chance of another dispute was not fanciful, for although the moot had successfully ended in agreement and settlement, yet the insult of impotence, the suggestion of witchcraft, and the bitterness of the quarrel and of earlier quarrels, all lingered. They were potentially fertile ground for further trouble. On the other hand, however, as community life went on and fresh disputes and conflicts brought rather different alignments of support and opposition, this particular conflict became less and less likely to have the makings of a dominant cleavage in Ligomba such as would produce factions. Too many other people in addition to Yasini bridged the gap between the two sides with their own neighborly relations to allow cleavage of this kind to develop. In this kind of network system persisting factions are both empirically and logically unlikely, as each successive dispute tends to produce its own particular set of ephemeral alignments.

    Case 3. A Creditor's Claim (September). About three weeks after the end of the previous case, a small moot was held at Konga's house to discuss a clash of arrangements for the work parties of 19 and Sedi (29), which, it had been belatedly discovered, had been set for the same day. Thus some men (such as 20 and 22) had obligations to join both parties on the same day. There is nothing unusual about such a clash, since, there being no central organization of work-party schedules, some conflicts of dates are to be expected; and they can be ironed out in a friendly moot attended by interested persons. This moot was attended by the notable, Kabaya (13 in Figure 4), though he was only peripherally involved. In the course of sub-

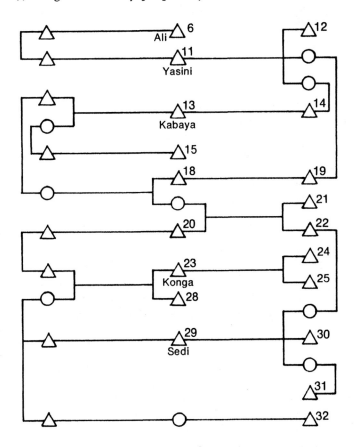

Figure 4

sequent casual gossip over beer, he learned that a young, unmarried son of Sedi had just returned from employment abroad, and therefore he took the opportunity to request that Sedi repay the loan of a goat that Kabaya had provided over a year before for the bridewealth of 30, another of Sedi's sons. Kabaya was unusual in this part of the country in maintaining a small flock of goats, from which he made a modest profit by occasionally lending or selling an animal. Sedi and his son had wished to impress the wife's father and to avoid suitor service and had therefore obtained a goat on promise of payment in cash in the near but unspecified future. Now Kabaya expected to be paid, since he assumed that Sedi's younger son had brought back some money after working as a labor migrant. At first Sedi attempted to deny that his son had brought back any money, and he declared that he himself had had no opportunity to earn money. Kabaya grew indignant, saying that the son must have brought back enough to repay the debt. He grumbled that Sedi had made no attempt at all to try to pay what he owed, and he recalled that this was the second time he had asked for his rightful claim to be met after more than a year. Sedi showed no sign of regret or apology, but on being pressed, he offered five shillings to Kabaya in part payment. He also remarked that the goat had been an old and poor animal, that it had since died, and that the father-in-law was much displeased in consequence. At this point Kabaya lost his temper; he dismissed the denigration of his goat, rejected the part-payment offer, and left the house shouting that he would not let the matter drop and that Sedi was a thief.

Negotiations for a moot were conducted between Kabaya and the notable, Konga (23), and it was agreed to hold it at Konga's house. The action-sets, each recruited by the principal, were as follows:

Action-set of Kabaya (13)	Action-set of Sedi (29)
11 (SWF)	23, 28 (FZS)
12 (SWB)	24, 25 (FZSS)
15 (MBS)	30 (S)
18 (FZS)	31 (DH)
19 (FZSS)	32 (FBDS)
20 (18's ZH)	
(7 men)	(8 men)

It might perhaps have been expected that logically Zadiki (20), as structural intermediary in the context and not directly related to either principal, would have acted as mediator instead of appearing as a member of one of the action-sets. There were, however, good reasons for his choice. Zadiki had long been a close friend and constant associate of his wife's brother (18), and thus he tended to go with him in alignment; and this inclination was strengthened because of his poorly suppressed antagonism toward his cousin Konga, which made him more dependent on 18 and the neighborly links to be gained through him with, for example, 13 and 15. Zadiki felt no need to support either Konga or Sedi. Although Case 1 had been settled and accepted by both Zadiki and Sedi, clearly they were not entirely reconciled to one another; at least Zadiki was not prepared to act as mediator in Sedi's dispute, nor did he choose the course of opting out altogether, as he could easily have done, presumably because he wished to mark his support of 18 and Kabaya. On the other hand, Zadiki's sons, Rajabu (22, son-in-law of Sedi) and 21, were put into a dilemma (especially Rajabu) by their father's action and by the context of the dispute itself. Both chose to opt out and absented themselves from Ligomba for a few days. In consequence there was no intermediary participating in the moot. This circumstance seems to have offered an opening to the notable Ali (6), for he attended the moot and sat, at first, with Kabaya's set; and it was he who came to take on the role of mediator. He had not been invited by Kabaya, nor presumably, in view of their rivalry, did Kabaya wish to have him there. In the moot itself, Ali did not disguise his partiality for Kabaya's claim as legitimate creditor, although he was not so committed as to prevent his acting fairly successfully as mediator. In this role he also made use of his personal and long-standing friendship with Konga (23, his second cousin) in order to gain a workable compromise and reconciliation between the two principals. As a result of his careful intervention, Ali also succeeded in preventing any eruption of hostility between Zadiki and Konga and Sedi.

The moot was not protracted, and with the successful insulation of Zadiki there was no particular complication to prevent agreement being negotiated. The facts of the case were too obvious to everyone to produce any real difference of opinion, and the proceedings were largely devoted to the determination of some payment by Sedi to Kabaya. Eventually Sedi paid twenty shillings before the assembled men—he had the money already in his pocket and had evidently come to the moot prepared to pay something. He promised to pay another four shillings later, though no time limit was fixed for this. It was admitted by Sedi that he knew little about goats or the particular goat in question. He had, he said by way of apology, merely repeated the complaints about its poor quality that had been made by his son's father-in-law. All the men in the moot agreed euphorically that fathers-in-law invariably complain about the bridewealth they obtain (though, of course, several were fathers-in-law themselves); and this was the mood in which they drank the beer together that Sedi supplied.

As the moot ended, the question remained, at least for me as observer, why Ali should have participated uninvited and assumed the role of mediator. My Ligomba informants were not puzzled, however, as I discovered in later conversation with Yasini (11), Konga (23), and 18. According to them, Ali wished to participate in any public issue in the community, for "he is a big man." Although this is not altogether true (Ali had not attended the moot in Case 1, for example), it is most relevant. Notables gain and retain their acknowledged influence by their successful participation in moots. It was further suggested to me that Ali wished to try to recover some of the reputation he had undoubtedly lost as a result of his ill-judged tactics in Case 2. That he was successful is clear. Konga actually complimented him in the moot—though that was as an old friend, speaking and meaning to be helpful. More significantly

Kabaya was obliged, at Yasini's tactful prompting, to express gratitude for Ali's intervention and assistance. As a disputant and principal in the moot, Kabaya was, of course, in no easy position to take a lead in the negotiations toward a settlement, and he had necessarily to accept and to be glad of Ali's help. He could not, in fact, have found a better mediator in the event, and I believe that he was relieved that tensions between Zadiki and Sedi were prevented from interfering in the settlement of his own affairs. Nevertheless, Kabaya disliked admitting an obligation of gratitude to Ali, and probably he had no wish to be the means by which Ali was able to restore something of his reputation in Ligomba.

There was more to Ali's action, however. He was a rival of Kabaya, not only for public influence, but also for the allegiance of their mutual kinsman, Yasini (11). Ali understood that in this case, as doubtless on previous occasions, Yasini was unreservedly obliged to support Kabaya. But this tended to draw Yasini away from Ali himself, and therefore he seems to have chosen to join with Yasini in assisting Kabaya, rather than allowing a separation between them. He said to me afterward: "Is not Yasini my brother? Therefore I must help him and go with [support] him. I cannot leave him on his own when he goes to help another neighbor. We are one, brothers together, and we are nearer together than he and Kabaya.[7] I went with him when he helped Kabaya in order to show how near we are and to show that we are brothers and neighbors." There is no reason to suppose that on this occasion Kabaya had deliberately attempted to emphasize his association with Yasini or to weaken the ties between the latter and Ali. He had every right to expect Yasini's support in the dispute with Sedi. Yet in effect he seemed to threaten Ali's position. In the event, then, Ali was able to emphasize both his tie with Yasini and his capacity for leadership—and both to some extent at the expense of his rival notable, Kabaya; but he accomplished his ends without overly antagonizing Kabaya.

Case 4. A·Quarrel Between Cousins (November). Toward the end of the dry season, 24 and his father, Konga (23), were visited by the father of 24's wife. A small beer-drink was arranged by Konga which was attended, in addition to the visitor, by Konga's sons and by Saidi (3), Ali (6), Mitedi (28), Sedi (29), and 30 (see Figure 1). The following day, while the visitor was still in Ligomba, Zadiki (20) came in great indignation to complain to Konga because, he said, he had not been invited to the beer-drink. He alleged that Konga had ignored him—an unfriendly act—and had made

7. There is no firm Ndendeuli dogma, in fact, which makes a first cousin "nearer," genealogically or in terms of rights and obligations, than a son's wife's father. But in any case Yasini scarcely wished to distinguish the strength of his valuable ties with either of his "brothers." In what was a test case the following wet season, when the work parties of Ali and Kabaya clashed in their timing, Yasini chose to participate in Ali's party, and his son went to work in Kabaya's party.

him appear unimportant to the visitor. Konga claimed that he had sent one of his grandsons to Zadiki's house with news of the beer-drink and that he had assumed that Zadiki had chosen not to attend for some reason. Zadiki insisted that he had had no knowledge of the event (or he would certainly have attended) and asked why Konga had not made sure that the message had been conveyed. He declared that a young grandson was neither a reliable nor a proper messenger. Konga tried to dismiss the matter as an unfortunate accident, but his complacency seemed to irritate Zadiki further. He began to rail against Konga, his first cousin, enumerating past occasions when Konga had failed to extend invitations to him or to help him in other ways. He referred to Case 1, saying that Konga should have supported him then. Zadiki eventually left, after a good deal of recrimination, which ended in a shouting match in which 24 joined (annoyed, he said, because his father-in-law was still there).

Two days later Zadiki returned to Konga's house, again in an angry mood. He had two complaints. First, he alleged that some of Konga's young granddaughters (daughters of 24 and 25) had insulted his wife at the water point, upset a pot of water, and cracked the pot. This incident had happened the day after his earlier visit. Second, he had heard through the women that after he had left on the previous occasion, 27 (youngest married son of Konga) had amused the others by likening him to a strutting cock and had caricatured his walk and gestures. Zadiki now demanded apologies for both incidents, plus the replacement of the damaged water pot. Konga attempted to pass the whole thing off as the playfulness of young girls and a poor attempt at humor by his son (who had the reputation of being a clown). He ignored the claim for a new pot. Another angry scene occurred, and when Zadiki left the house, he shouted out that he would not leave the matter there. Nor did he, for he obtained the support of a number of kin-neighbors in demanding a moot to consider the dispute.

This quarrel and dispute had been imminent for some time, I think; and it was not the first of its kind. Before describing the course of the moot, therefore, the context must be given in the light of the history of relations between the men.

When Ligomba was originally founded, Zadiki had not accompanied his father (F, see Figure 1) as a pioneer there, for at that time he was living in the local community of the father and brother of his first wife, where he had performed suitor service and then married a second time. He came to Ligomba only when his father's serious and prolonged illness left his mother and unmarried sister without male support. His father died soon after. Not long after that, probably in 1938, he came into dispute with his cousin and neighbor Konga (23), alleging that the latter's eldest son (24, then a young unmarried man) had attempted to seduce his junior wife. In the subsequent moot he found himself isolated; his only clear supporter was his mother's sister's son,[8] but Konga was well supported by A, J, Ali (6), Mitedi (28), Sedi (29), and some others now no longer resident in Ligomba. Zadiki's allegation was rejected and, so I was told fifteen years later, Konga's sup-

8. This man has since moved away from Ligomba. At the time of that dispute 13, 15, and 18 had not yet come to live in the community. See the genealogy in Figure 1.

porters were united in condemning Zadiki's junior wife as sexually licentious
—it was on her word, apparently, that her husband's charge mainly depended.
But the moot was a failure because Zadiki adamantly refused to withdraw
the charge against 24. A second moot was agreed to, but the wife in question deserted Zadiki the evening before, declaring that she wanted a divorce
and was going to live with another man. The men, ignorant of this, assembled at Zadiki's house the next morning as prearranged. At the instigation
of A and Ali, Zadiki now agreed to withdraw the allegation against 24; but
this he did with bad grace, complaining that his kinsmen were against him
and did not help him in his difficulties. He accused A and Ali, who were
as closely related to him as to Konga, of favoring Konga instead of being
friendly mediators, and angry exchanges followed. However, J and Zadiki's
mother's sister's son (who were, be it noted, linked independently through
J's wife) combined to act as mediators, persuaded Zadiki to drop all allegations and offered him assistance in the matter of his runaway wife.

Later these two men and Mitedi (28) accompanied Zadiki to the moot
in the local community of that wife's father. A divorce was settled, and some
return of bridewealth was obtained. But apparently Zadiki was not reconciled to his circumstances nor to his cousin, Konga, for at a subsequent
beer-drink he quarreled with him and with Ali because they too had not
gone with him to the divorce moot. There seems to have been no immediate
consequences to this quarrel, but it appears to have set the tone for relations
between these men thereafter.

Soon after this, Zadiki sponsored the brother of his first wife, Tanda (18),
as a newcomer to Ligomba, and later Tanda sponsored Kabaya (13), who
came accompanied by 15. As Ali explained this to me years afterward, either
Zadiki had to obtain new neighbors who would reliably support him or he
must leave Ligomba. The choice may not have been quite as clear-cut as
that, but it was to Zadiki's evident advantage to gain these neighbors, for
then he had less need to depend on Konga, Ali, and others, who doubtless
seemed to him to be unreliable and even hostile. As it turned out, Kabaya
became a serious rival of Ali and Konga for influence and leadership in
Ligomba, and in a number of incidents Zadiki was on the side of Kabaya.
Relations between Zadiki and Konga remained poor. Yet it continued logically in the interests of both of these cousins that at least a minimum of
cooperation and neighborliness should continue; moreover, it was in the
interests of their respective kin-neighbors also to maintain working cooperative relations through the linkages provided by them. Those concerned
were the sons of Zadiki and Konga, as well as Tanda (18), 19, Mitedi (28),
and Sedi (29) (see the genealogy in Figure 1). Some of these men had
been members of each other's work parties and action-sets for years, including the period of field preparation in the current dry season, 1953. And
they wished for such cooperation to continue in the following wet season,
to be expected soon.

On the other hand, relations between Zadiki and Konga were far from
cordial. Only a short time previously (Case 1) Konga as structural intermediary between Zadiki and Sedi (29) had shown himself, in the opinion
of several men including Zadiki himself, to favor Sedi when acting as media-

tor. Later, in Case 3, Zadiki and Konga were members of opposed action-sets; this was partly a function of their own conflict, for in other circumstances two such cousins would most probably have taken the opportunity to join together as mediators in the dispute. These two failed to achieve this or, as far as I could ascertain, even to attempt it.

The present dispute arose out of this history of relations (only briefly told here) between the two men and of their current positions in the kinship network in Ligomba. Konga was probably to blame for initiating the latest phase, for he did not make sure that his cousin was properly invited to the beer-drink—and he may perhaps have not wanted him there. The affair of the water pot was a petty matter, which no doubt could have been settled privately; but Zadiki was angered by it and seemed to have seized the opportunity to use it against Konga. The latter showed little sign of wishing to accommodate his cousin in the matter. In addition, according to one informant (3), Kabaya (13) had encouraged Zadiki to insist on a public apology and reparation. To judge from this evidence, Kabaya sought the chance to embarrass his rival, and Zadiki seemed only too glad to take his advice.

At the moot action-sets were composed as follows:

Action-set of Zadiki (20)	Action-set of Konga (23)
21 (S)	24, 25 (S)
18 (WB)	28 (B)
19 (18's S)	29 (MBS)
13, 14 (18's MBS and son)	32 (MBDS)
15 (13's MBS)	6 (FMBDS)
	3 (FMBDS)
(7 men)	(8 men)

In this context, Yasini (11) was not linked at all closely with either principal; but he was forced into the position of structural intermediary as a result of invitations by Tanda (18) and Kabaya (13), on the one hand, and Ali (6), on the other, to joining their respective sets. He left Ligomba the day before the moot to visit a kinsman, and men at the moot assumed, no doubt rightly, that he had chosen to opt out of a difficult situation that promised no advantage and potential disadvantage to him. Nevertheless, a more ambitious man might well have taken up the role of mediator in this context. Rajabu (22) also was put into an ambivalent position; he clearly should have supported his father, Zadiki (20), but he had no wish to act in a set opposed to one in which his father-in-law, Sedi (29), was acting. As in Case 3, Rajabu decided to opt out, despite the displeasure of his father; but because of his relative juniority and unfamiliarity with his neighbors, he was not (unlike Yasini) a potential mediator.

My account of this moot depends on information from my field assistant and informants in Ligomba, as I was unable to attend. Zadiki began the moot by lengthily repeating his complaints that Konga had allowed him to be insulted in the ways already described; and he went on to refer to previous occasions when Konga had failed to meet expectations. Zadiki spoke with growing indignation; and Konga replied in a similar tone, ignoring Zadiki's complaints and raising complaints of his own against Zadiki's past behavior toward him. The notable Kabaya spoke in support of Zadiki, and the notable Ali followed in support of Konga; 15 also supported Zadiki's allegations and directly attacked Ali.[9] Emotions began to run high as tempers rose, but gradually an alliance of Tanda (18) and 19 on the one side and Mitedi (28) and 24 on the other led to a settlement and to overt reconciliation. As these men continued to insist on a conciliatory solution of the dispute, they were joined and supported by Sedi (29) and 32, and then by Ali. Eventually Kabaya counseled Zadiki to agree to accept an apology from Konga and his son, 27 (who had caricatured him). As 27 was not present at the moot on his brother's advice, his apology was expressed on his behalf by that brother, 24. Zadiki also agreed to drop his complaints against Konga.

On the face of it the moot was inconclusive, in that neither the immediate nor the deeper long-term issues were tackled. Probably it was impossible, or at least not desirable, that they should have been, however, for a real settlement of these and the establishment of friendly "brotherly" and neighborly relations was out of the question because of the personal antagonism between the two men and their structural pulls in opposite directions. Much would depend on future circumstances, of course, but some basis seems to have been laid for the continuance of some kind of working relationship between the two men. The de facto mediators in the moot were concerned to head off continued discussion of the immediate dispute because of the danger that might arise. Sedi (29) told me later that he and the others wished to stop the quarreling, not continue it. The issue of the water pot was not taken up at all by the moot, though Zadiki had made it a complaint in his opening statement.

The moot did achieve the major result—at least for the time being—of preventing the crystallization of hostility, not only between Zadiki and Konga, but also between their respective supporters. There was no breakdown, even temporarily, of neighborly cooperation in Ligomba—this was especially important, as the wet season was expected soon, with all the needs for agricultural cooperation of that season of the Ndendeuli year. Men such as Tanda (18) and 19 on the one hand and 24, Mitedi (28), and Sedi (29) on the other wished to continue reciprocal assistance and to avoid the· threat to this that might have come from some overt schism between Zadiki and Konga. On the occasion of this moot Tanda, for example, was specifically on the side of his brother-in-law, Zadiki; but he had well-established conventions of reciprocal assistance with Konga,

9. Both Saidi (3) and my field assistant believed that 15's attack was the result of Ali's earlier accusation of witchcraft against 15's son (in Case 2). This may have been true, since 15 was not normally an outspoken participant in moots, and on this occasion his obligation to support Zadiki was not very strong; 15 may also have wished to show his association with the notable Kabaya (13).

Mitedi, and others, which were most valuable to him. Sedi had an additional reason for urging a settlement, for he could scarcely afford to allow a worsening of relations with Zadiki, his daughter's husband's father, unless it was impossible to avoid making a choice between Konga and Zadili. In brief, too much was at stake for a number of men for them to want anything other than the opportunity to continue working relations. These considerations were far less important for such men as Ali (6), Kabaya (13), and 15, since their own working relations in the community were not threatened in this way.

All three Ligomba notables were involved in this particular dispute; Konga's role in the case was, of course, limited to that of defendant rather than of leader or mediator. Kabaya sought to lead on 20's side—perhaps in personal opposition to Konga and to Ali—but his influence in the circumstances was limited in effect by the self-interested determination of those others more intimately involved to prevent a thorough-going showdown and to preserve cooperative neighborly relations. Ali supported Konga; but more perceptively, perhaps, than his rival, Kabaya, he fairly quickly joined with the conciliators. Unlike Kabaya, he did not show that he needed to be persuaded and convinced of the satisfactoriness of their advocacy. Kabaya's reputation was not helped in the event, while that of Ali was, if anything, strengthened.

Case 5. An Errant Son-in-Law (December). Yasini (11) had left his house repairs until late in the dry season, and as a matter of urgency (for the rains were soon expected) called on his local "sons" (own son, nephews, and sons-in-law), a few days after the previous moot, to haul and put in place two new wall posts for his house. These had been already cut and prepared about four miles away. One of his sons-in-law, Musa (19), did not turn up the next day, and the work was done by 14, 10, and 12 under Yasini's supervision. But Yasini grumbled about Musa's absence, and the following day he refused to accept Musa's excuse that he had had to go and visit his mother's brother in another community in order to obtain medicines for his sick mother. Yasini then raised the matter of Musa's bridewealth payment. In Case 1, Yasini's willingness to accept a smaller installment of bridewealth than he had at first been promised had been important to the settlement of that dispute between 20 and 29. At that earlier moot he had agreed to receive only fifty shillings instead of the sum of seventy-five shillings; but in fact he had still only received a part payment of forty shillings and had agreed to wait for the remainder. Now he firmly claimed the outstanding ten shillings. Musa said that he no longer had any money, and, for the moment, he could not obtain any. This Yasini refused to accept. He declared that he would no longer be lenient to his son-in-law; he also complained of the latter's failure to help him as he should and alleged that Musa had ill-treated his daughter (Musa's wife).

Consulting with his cousin Ali (6), the notable, Yasini was encouraged to persist with his claim and complaints. Ali set about convening a moot on Yasini's behalf. The moot was easily arranged and was held at the house of Konga (23), where the action-sets were composed as follows (see genealogy in Figure 1):

Action-set of Yasini (11)	Action-set of Musa (19)
12 (S)	18 (F)
6 (FBS)	20 (FZH)
3 (6's MZS)	21, 22 (FZS)
9 (BS)	23, 28 (20's FBS)
14 (DH)	24, 27 (23's S)
	29 (23's MBS/22's WF)
	15, 16 (MBS and son of FMBS, 13)
(6 men)	(12 men)

In this context Kabaya (13) was structurally intermediary and, especially as he was a notable, might have acted as mediator. He chose to opt out, however, by absenting himself from Ligomba; while his son, 14, joined the set of Yasini (wife's father). As far as I could determine, Kabaya did not wish to act as mediator between two sets that would be—and, in fact, were—led by the notables Ali (6) and Konga (23) respectively. He might have gained prestige by negotiating between these notables, but probably he foresaw what was likely to happen. Ali and Konga were, as noted earlier, life-long friends as well as kinsmen; they often supported each other and had contrived to avoid the rivalry and hostility that commonly exists between notables in the same local community. In this moot they cooperated together in effect as mediators after starting off as leading advocates for their own principals. Had Kabaya been present, he would have been squeezed out and made to look superfluous; and so he opted out altogether—probably wisely, from his point of view.

The moot itself was neither difficult nor prolonged. It amounted less to a demand for the acknowledged bridewealth debt to be paid than to a general complaint by a father-in-law against his son-in-law's behavior. Musa was clearly in the wrong, for Yasini had been abundantly tolerant and helpful in Case 1 and since that time, as well, although as a father-in-law he was in a position of some superiority to Musa, who should scarcely have expected favors while still owing bridewealth. After Yasini's opening statement to this effect, Musa made a fairly brief defensive reply, in which he concentrated on his inability to pay anything yet to his father-in-law. He made some play with his imminent obligation to cultivate his fields when the new rains began in order to provide food for his wife (Yasini's daughter) and child (Yasini's grandson). His father-in-law, he protested, could not expect him to go off and find work to earn money when he had to work for his wife, as a husband must. He denied any ill-treatment of his wife. The notable Konga spoke on his behalf, but (it seemed to me) without marked conviction. The notable Ali followed with a summary of Yasini's complaints and then went on to suggest a public apology by Musa to his father-in-law and at least some token payment of bridewealth. Musa remained silent, but Konga expressed willingness to accept the suggestion, though he made the point that no one really thought that Musa mistreated his wife. He then turned to Musa and asked him to agree on condition (though it was more tactfully expressed) that Yasini withdraw his allegation of ill-treatment to the wife. Yasini murmured agreement; and Ali added that as soon as he could, Musa should find temporary work in order to earn money for bridewealth. After a little more discussion all this was affirmed, and Musa gave fifty cents to Yasini. Ali and Konga ended the moot by praising the good sense of Yasini and Musa and the good relations between them. The whole moot lasted little more than half an hour.

Why, then, was Musa's action-set so relatively large, and why did it comprise so many indirectly linked neighbors? The dispute was not a difficult one to settle, and Musa showed little sign of unwillingness to come to terms with his father-in-law. Informants were clear about this: following the previous case by only a week, these men who at that time had been on opposed sides and had managed, as I have described, to produce a working settlement, now wished to emphasize their association together. They were (as 29 told me) less concerned with Musa's case than with their own interrelations; and they took this accidental opportunity to demonstrate their ability and willingness to engage in successful common action. Even Zadiki (20) and Konga (23) sat together in the same set in the moot, though Zadiki himself took little part in the proceedings. Perhaps Yasini and Musa were fortunate that among and between their respective supporters there was no extra antagonism to complicate their own straightforward dispute.

Discussion and Conclusion

In this paper it has been possible to present only five cases of dispute, their treatment and settlement. They were empirical events in the arbitrary period of my field research. First, I have considered it preferable to describe them in some detail and to draw some general principles from them, rather than to concentrate on such principles and to give merely "apt illustrations." These cases were specifically successive ones in a single local community. They do not necessarily demonstrate all the general principles involved in Ndendeuli dispute processes; and their presentation here may permit generalizations other than those I have drawn or the questioning of those I have drawn.

Secondly, I have been more concerned with what Gluckman has described as "the social processes which largely determine the outcome of a dispute," rather than with "analysis of the processes of ratiocination by which negotiations proceed." [10]

Thirdly, it must be emphasized (albeit unfortunately) that a full under-

10. Max Gluckman, personal communication, 1965.

standing of those social processes is not possible without further data on other vital aspects of social life in a Ndendeuli local community: neighborly interaction of many kinds, other occasions and needs of a different kind when action-sets are recruited, alignments made public, and loyalties and antagonisms expressed. Interaction of this sort inevitably affects alignments, action, readiness to mediate or to compromise on the part of the men involved. Dispute processes are but part of a larger continuum. There are necessarily some actions referred to in the present account that do not wholly make sense because of the absence of such related data. This account is, in fact, part of a fuller analysis of Ndendeuli social organization, with special reference to the nonunilineal kinship network system.

A number of features can be highlighted as a result of the case material presented, leading to some conclusions on the nature of dispute settlement in this society.

SIGNIFICANCE OF PAST EVENTS

I re-emphasize what should be clear from my deliberate account of successive disputes among the same group of people: an understanding of one case cannot be adequately gained if the case is treated in isolation from its precedents. It seems at least doubtful if such interpretation is entirely justifiable even in fully juridical systems of courts, judges, laws, established formal procedures, ideal impartiality, and the like. But Ndendeuli disputes are worked out in the full context of the continuum of community life, so that previous disputes and their settlements, and developing relationships of all kinds, impinge on any current case. Extended analysis would have to deal more fully with this most important consideration; but here I merely draw attention to one or two examples. The development of relations between the cousins Zadiki (20) and Konga (23) is essential to an understanding of Case 1; that case clearly affected alignments in Case 3, and then in Cases 4 and 5. The relative failure of the notable Ali (6) in Case 2, and his competition with the notable Kabaya (13), over and through Yasini (11), affected Case 3. The results of Case 4 markedly affected the action-set alignment in Case 5. The significance of past events and immediately preceding dispute cases varies according to the context of following cases; but each contributes to the development pattern of relationships that forms the cumulative network within which subsequent action occurs.

MEDIATORS

In all five cases someone adopted the role of mediator almost of necessity. Principals may negotiate and bargain for a settlement (and before that in clearing up issues that might obstruct negotiation), but they find it easier to do this through, or at least with the assistance of, an interconnected person. In seventeen dispute cases for which really satisfactory records were made in the field, only two were completed without a mediator and by the direct exchange between the principals and committed supporters. Yet the Ndendeuli not only have no word translatable as "mediator," but also do not explicitly recognize such a role and scarcely refer to it indirectly. I find it an indispensable concept for analytical purposes and had little difficulty in identifying the mediators: in Case 1, Konga (23), supported by 24; in Case 2, Yasini (11), supported by 9 and 10; in Case 3, Ali (6); in Case 4 they are less clear, but 18, 24, and 28 allied together as mediators; in Case 5, Ali (6) and Konga (23). Even where a mediator is already fairly obvious (for example, Yasini in Case 2), he does not emerge in action until the principals and their leading supporters have explored the situation and are ready to negotiate. The mediator then acts as broker between them, though he may also offer his own suggestions or modifications. Certainly he does not act as adjudicator; and although sometimes he may announce the agreed settlement or some part of it, this is in his capacity as spokesman and not as judge. A principal often signifies agreement with or acceptance of a suggestion of his opponent by remaining silent (that is, absence of disagreement), but a good mediator makes the point explicitly where doubt might produce later discussion. As we have seen, the mediator is largely precipitated as a structural intermediary in the particular context of the dispute and disputants. The example of Yasini (11) in Case 2 illustrates this most clearly; he did not choose the role but acceded to its necessity, and that even reluctantly. He could have rejected it, however, as too difficult or dangerous to his own interests—as indeed he did in Case 4, and as 28 did in Case 1, and Kabaya (13) in Case 5. Where no intermediary exists, or where (to avoid involvement) he opts out by preference, then one or more members of the opposed action-sets usually adopt the role gradually. Such mediators are either seeking influence and prestige (as did Ali in Case 3), or they are concerned to protect their own interests (as were 18 and 28 in Case 4). In any event, the mediator hopes to assist in the establishment of a settlement and to prevent untoward repercussions within the community. A strongly committed supporter of either principal, like the principals themselves, is unable—at least at first—to make the necessary show of sympathy for both sides and for the community at large; though he, and the principals themselves, often appear relieved when a mediator suggests a way out of an impasse. Ndendeuli declare that they are not prepared to be dictated to by anyone, including their opponents; but they admit that they are willing, even ready, to be persuaded and to follow a lead.

NEUTRALS AND NONRESIDENTS

Practically every intracommunity dispute leaves some residents uncommitted, even indirectly, to either principal (for example, men 1 to 6 in Case 1). They may, but often do not, attend as interested spectators, but no more than that. They seem not to become mediators, for they do not have the kind of interjacent commitment required for the role. Nonresidents are often not involved at all (in only two of the five cases described) and when they are, they seldom take an important part. They are not positively unwelcome, but their weighty intervention would, I think, be resented. They attend, of course, as close kinsmen of one principal, and sometimes they give private counsel before or during the moot. Ndendeuli wish to keep community affairs within the community, if only because any settlement is bound to have repercussions among that group of cooperating neighbors. The only case I witnessed of a nonresident acting as mediator was during a serious and prolonged dispute between brothers (not in Ligomba) where no successful mediator emerged from inside the community. The disputants' father's sister's husband (a notable from another community) and his son were allowed to act in the dangerous impasse that had developed. But members of the community accepted this intervention *faute de mieux*.

NOTABLES

My references to these leaders, men of influence, are unfortunately too abbreviated for full consideration here. These men do not occupy roles of authority; rather, they are men of ability and ambition who are acknowledged to be leaders in context. In Ligomba it was by no means entirely accidental who the notables were; on the whole they tend to assume, and to be allowed to assume, the lead in affairs (and not only disputes) touching members of roughly identifiable clusters of neighbors and they are therefore structurally separated from each other. A glance at Figure 1 indicates as much. But caution is needed in this analysis, for these Ligomba notables (and similarly, notables in other communities) are not faction leaders. Of course there is a tendency for the same clusters of neighbors of a high degree of kinship interrelatedness in the network to combine in collective action (in action-sets), yet membership of action-sets does vary significantly, depending on the structural context of each particular dispute. For example, the action-sets of both Yasini (11) and Musa (19) in Case 5 cut right across the alignment of sets in Case 4. That is to say, the tendency for notables to take the lead over somewhat the same clusters of neighbors can be, and often is, overridden by the necessity of some different and cross-cutting combination. Men are, in their own interests, unable to commit themselves to more or less unreserved allegiance to a specific set of neighbors because each fresh occasion for combination poses, as it were, a fresh problem. Take the example of Yasini (11): in Case 1 he was in the same set as Kabaya (13), although his prime consideration was that he stood to gain directly if Zadiki (20) won the case; in Case 2 he was not committed to Kabaya's lead,[11] but his operation as mediator was somewhat biased to that side; in Case 3 he was firmly on Kabaya's side; in Case 4 the conflict of loyalties was too great and his advantages too small, and he opted out; in Case 5 he needed the support of Ali (6) and others, while Kabaya was too involved with his opponent's side to be of use to him (indeed, Kabaya opted out). Similarly, other individuals shift their allegiances according to circumstances and the relative advantages as these are perceived by them at the time.

In this sort of network situation a man cannot afford to commit himself to one alignment because that would mean ignoring or even breaking valuable relationships with some other kin-neighbors. These other relations may become, or they have been in the past, quite vital when the man becomes a disputant, and also in other collective activities, such as cooperative work parties in agriculture. A man may be obliged to take sides in a dispute, but he does not wish this circumstance to prejudice his opportunities for the future.

I should note also that recruitment to an action-set is largely controlled by the principals in the disputes. Allegiance and support are being given to a neighbor in need, rather than to a notable who shared or took over leadership. Ndendeuli are somewhat skeptical about their notables; they say that a notable is a member of an action-set, not only to assist a principal, but also to further his own interests. Now of course most men participate in an action-set with their own interests in mind, too: if I help X now, he will help me later; or if I follow Y in support of Z, then Y is likely to help me later or is less likely to help a future opponent. But a notable has additional interests to cultivate—his desire to gain influence, prestige, leadership (all somewhat suspect values by Ndendeuli standards).

Notables are, however, conceded to be useful to a disputant who needs advice and encouragement and who himself may not be particularly competent in advocacy and negotiation. Notables have achieved their role primarily because of their abilities, and men are willing to benefit from them. Nevertheless, their rivalry and even hostility toward each other often exacerbate rather than ease dispute (for example, the action of Kabaya, 13, in Case 4) as notables take the opportunity to score off one another or to oppose for the sake of opposing. However, their diplomatic skill can sometimes be decisive in a difficult case.

11. He did not, in fact, attend the first moot in this case, although Kabaya (13) then was a leader in the action-set of Zadiki (20).

ACTION-SETS

Ndendeuli have no word for this concept, although they speak of "my people," "my kinsmen," "those who go with me," and so on, and mean essentially the same thing. Action-sets are the means by which a man recruits the collective support of his associates in his own interests. These associates are primarily kinsmen, and a Ndendeuli would say that they all are. A man gains the support of those he can but (in a dispute case especially) with due recognition of the simultaneous recruitment of kin by his opponent. Thus a man may join the set of his second cousin in one situation but feel compelled to join that of a closer (and potentially more helpful) kin-neighbor in another situation against that cousin. Action-sets are inherently, characteristically ephemeral, as I noted above in reference to the typical absence of persistent factions in a community. It is not enough merely to say that a man calls on his kinsmen (or his kinsmen's kinsmen) when he needs assistance—as Ndendeuli are content to put it, and as some anthropologists have too vaguely described such a situation among peoples wtih nonunilineal kinship networks. It is quite essential to analyze precisely who can be, and actually is, called, and in what situation, and how the range of recruitment varies with the context of action. An action-set is commonly not "all of a man's kin," nor even "all of his kin-neighbors," as I have shown. The precise identification of the action-set is a requisite to any understanding of the social processes by which Ndendeuli deal with disputes and arrange other kinds of valuable cooperation. I regard this concept as essential to the analysis of social networks, but it would be out of place to develop this theme further here.

PERSONAL CONSIDERATIONS

Several examples in the cases illustrate the fact that the processes of dispute settlement, and the way in which the kinship network is used and manipulated to that end, are much affected by interpersonal relations between men. Here I am not particularly concerned for a recognition of the individual personalities and experiences of men that tend to motivate them and to affect their roles and relationships. That needs no emphasis in general, nor is it especially a sociological matter within my competence. Rather, I have something else in mind: the sociological fact that kinship and neighborly relations among Ndendeuli are very little regulated by the authority and necessary requirements of corporate groups, or by political, economic, and ritual leadership and unavoidable obligation. Roles and relationships, and concomitant expectations, are characteristically vaguely defined by these people. In general, nearer kin should give greater assistance than more distant kin; kin of parental generation stand in potentially superior status, those of the sons' generation stand in potentially inferior status, and those of one's own generation are equals. But precise rights and obligations are seldom ascribed; nor is there much real difference between various kinds of, say, more closely related "brothers" (own brother, first cousins, wife's brother). Actual, operative relationships are much dependent on the establishment and maintenance of cooperation and reciprocity between the individuals; and this is open to considerable variation and influence by such interpersonal factors as friendliness and demonstrated reliability, or hostility and unreliability. On the whole, a man is more or less limited to dependence on and liability to his kinsmen among his neighbors. Although subject to the logical necessities of inter- and cross-linkages in the network, a man still retains a good deal of individual inclination and choice. All this affects alignments at times of disputes and in moots, and it affects individuals' behavior in the social processes concerned.

Thus the antagonism between the first cousins Zadiki (20) and Konga (23) or between the rival notables Ali (6) and Kabaya (13) have been noted in context. Similarly the particular friendliness between the brothers-in-law Tanda (18) and Zadiki (20), the notables and second cousins Ali (6) and Konga (23), and the first cousins Konga (23) and Sedi (29) have been shown to be important. The tendency of Saidi (3) to be dependent on his forceful cousin Ali (6) is a further case in point. There were many other similarly influential interpersonal relationships in Ligomba—and in other local communities—that were not wholly governed by straightforward structural considerations and that even cut across such logical requirements.

Doubtlessly judges, court officials, police, specialized lawyers, and the rest are also in some degree affected by personal considerations and relationships (even if, ideally, they should not be), but they do not play their roles and exercise their responsibilities specifically because of these considerations and relationships, but rather in spite of them if and when they are at all relevant. In a Ndendeuli dispute case, however, the roles of each of the participants is a direct function of his personal involvement and his web of linkages with the principals and fellow participants. And therefore the participants are much influenced by the particular character of the pattern of relations and their own place in it.

INDETERMINACY OF NORMS AND EXPECTATIONS

Ndendeuli have few well-defined rules and norms of social behavior against which men's conduct can be easily assessed. To take a single example: all Ndendeuli would agree that a legitimate marriage is possible only by the transfer of bridewealth or the performance of suitor service for the woman's father or some combination of both. But the amount of bridewealth and installment arrangements and the duration and obligations of suitor service are largely undefined, as also is the way of recognizing completion of obligations. "It is all a matter of what you can get from your son-in-law," one man explained to me, "and the strength with which the son-in-law can resist." It is very commonly a matter of genuine (as well, of course, as assumed) difficulty to distinguish between bridewealth/suitor service and the general obligations that any son-in-law owes to his wife's father. Consequently there is ample opportunity for both valid and contrived dispute as to what a man's rights and obligations are at any time.

Similarly, as already noted, there is considerable scope for differences of opinion as to the reciprocal rights between, say, brothers or cousins. A cousin "should" support a man in some situation (a dispute, or in his work party), but he may decide not to do so because of conflicting obligations to that man's opponent or to the one who is forming a work party at the same time. The "rules" by which to gauge expectations and another man's conduct are so imprecise that the range of interpretation is wide. It is, I believe, no accident that this marked indeterminacy of norms operates in a situation where adjudicators do not exist and where negotiation and bargaining is vital to the process of settling disputes. The two features are not merely compatible: they are logically complementary.

Now in Ndendeuli dispute cases it is necessary to look for "reasonable expectations" as these emerge in what men say and do, even though the people themselves poorly articulate the use of this concept as a conscious process. Reference to reasonable expectations and to reasonable, and unreasonable, performance of particular roles—with the notion of tolerable leeways from ideal norms—must be universal in human society, though varying in the degree of application. Obviously in a moot Ndendeuli do attempt to enunciate these expectations, and they seek to measure a man's conduct against them. On the other hand, not only are the expectations rather indeterminate, as I have indicated, but there is also no third party, no adjudicator, and no technique to determine specifically the acceptable, operative, reasonable expectations in the event of a particular dispute. And while men seek their own advantages and attempt to avoid what is disadvantageous, the process of settlement must depend also on other considerations not directly related to the merits of the matter in dispute: the strength with which a defendant can resist his claim, the degree to which a plaintiff can be persuaded to reduce his claim, the degree and kind of support each can obtain from other involved persons.[12]

12. In a rather different ethnographic and sociological context (among the Arusha of northern Tanzania) I have earlier developed this same line of argument and analysis (Gulliver 1963:232 ff. and 296 ff.). In retrospect, however, I would give more emphatic recognition to the significance and operation of "reasonable expectations" than I did in that work.

Thus, in respect to Case 1, no Ndendeuli whom I asked would say whether the claim for more bridewealth was or was not "reasonable," justifiable, or right. Intelligent informants explained that it all depends on the nature of the case. By this they meant two things: the history of the bridewealth transaction up to the time of the dispute, and the nature of relations between the affines and among them and other men concerned. But it was always the latter feature to which most importance (and most interest) was given. Even in the full context of the actual dispute, Ligomba men could give no definite answer. In reply to my questioning, they said that I did not understand Ndendeuli ways or I would not have put the question. To them it was not only a matter of whether the father-in-law was in the right or not, or to what degree, but also how far he could exert pressure on his son-in-law and the latter's father and obtain more bridewealth. In these circumstances not only the bridewealth question had to be taken into account, but also the current state of and future effects on the surrounding relationships of kin and neighbors. In that particular case the father-in-law largely gained his claim, though he had to give way to some extent. Yet it was only in these particular circumstances (probably unique in detail) at that particular time that the settlement was made. The same claim on a different occasion would surely have worked out differently. Similarly, Case 4, between the two cousins, was largely settled in terms of the needs of their supporters for neighborly cooperation, for a break between those two men could not be allowed by their neighbors. In a comparable case, recorded in another community, the breakdown of relations between first cousins held little threat to their respective supporters, who could get along with minimal cooperation from each other, and a quite different settlement was achieved.

In conclusion, the settlement of an intracommunity dispute among the Ndendeuli has these characteristics:

1. It is typically some kind of negotiated compromise between conflicting claims. Even where a principal's claim is very strong and the balance of bargaining power lies with him, he commonly makes some effort to show tolerance and good will by giving way to his opponent in at least some small degree. Where the balance of bargaining power is less one-sided, compromise is a matter of necessity if settlement is to be made.

2. It is dependent not only on ideas of norms, rights, and expectations and on the respective bargaining strengths of both principals and their supporters, but also on considerations of its effects on other men's interests and the continuance of neighborly cooperation and concord.

3. It is, and must be, an agreed settlement, accepted by both principals as the best that can be obtained in the circumstances. Ultimately a principal cannot be compelled to accept an imposed settlement, for

there is no means of enforcing it. Strong pressures from his opponent's side, from mediators, and if necessary even from his own side are brought to persuade him to acceptance and agreement. Only by his agreement can the settlement be put into effect and made good.

4. It is put into effect immediately if at all possible. The compensation or debt is paid, the apology made, the claim renounced, all in the moot. Although not invariably so, a settlement that is not acted upon straight away may be no settlement at all, for the whole dispute may have to be renegotiated at a later date, when the claim is actively exerted again. An agreement, say, to pay compensation later on may be an ephermal success for one principal but perhaps a more practical success for his opponent; that is, the settlement is really an avoidance of settlement, or an agreement to differ. But it may even be one that in effect is in favor of the defendant. Further, by the immediate completion of a settlement it is hoped to remove the dispute altogether and thus allow for the re-establishment of continued working neighborly relations.

With the exception, at least sometimes, of 4, these characteristics are probably common to all processes of dispute settlement by negotiation without courts in all societies, including the many kinds in Western industrial societies. These negotiation processes have not been adequately studied from an empirical base and in a sufficient variety of cultural context for the purposes of comparative analysis. Among the Ndendeuli, relationships—and therefore processes—are largely defined and expressed in a kinship idiom; but obviously this is but one structural and ideological form in which this sociological phenomenon occurs.

Styles of Court Procedure:
To Make the Balance

Judicial Process is the name given to the intellectual procedure by which judges decide cases. It comprehends all the ways of mind, deliberate and subconscious, all the elements in personality, profession and environment which impel toward judgment. Our knowledge of it is limited and colored by the available materials, which are principally "opinions" in which appellate courts explain their decisions.

WALTON H. HAMILTON

In order to describe the main features of style in a Mexican Zapotec court of law, I have used case materials taken from the film *To Make the Balance*. Running through the five cases in the film there is a constant that for present purposes may be briefly described as the value placed on achieving balance between principals in a case. It is compromise arrived at by adjudication or, in some cases, adjudication based on compromise. The particular settlement to a given dispute may fine, jail, ridicule, or acquit the principals in a case, but the aim is to rectify the situation by achieving or reinstating a balance between the parties involved in a dispute, a word that is synonymous with imbalance among the Zapotec. Whatever factors enter into the decision-making process, the restoration of equilibrium determines the final settlement and is the goal of this system of dispute settlement. The profile of the style of procedure that aims at balance may be compared with other societies or with other aspects within the same society.

The main body of the paper is divided into three sections: the sociocultural setting, the case materials, and a discussion and comparison. First I describe the court organization within the broader social organizational features of the town of Ralu'a and comment on the theme of balance in Zapotec culture. The case materials—recorded with the help of a camera, a tape recorder, and pen and paper—provide the data that make up the second segment of this discussion. Only the pen-and-paper version is presented here. I was inspired to film a Zapotec court in action partly because I thought that film was a better medium than the written word for communicating the form and manner of what went on in a court where nonverbal behavior is of primary importance. Here I am faced with describing in words what was so vividly recorded by camera, and I will attempt the job through the use of written case material, much of which is verbatim transcript. In the last part of the paper I will note the elements of dispute settlement that determine the style of settlement processes. This section concentrates on and analyzes the procedures of settlement that remain constant throughout the five cases. The substantive aspects of procedure, which vary from case to case, are determined principally by the type of case and type of participants. The continuous features that permeate court activities and constitute the form and manner of the court give the proceedings their style (Kroeber 1957).

In a final section I comment on the possibilities to the comparative anthropological study of law of an approach specifying the determinants that generate forms or styles of dispute settlement. Comparisons of style may be more likely to stimulate research on law in society—in the context of societal values—than would a comparison of legal families (for example, civil law with common law) or a comparison of institutional arrangements (as court societies with courtless societies) or of techniques for considering a dispute (such as negotiation with adjudication). Any one society may have different styles associated with a range of institutions. The works of Cohn (1959) and Aubert (n.d.) are pioneering contributions directed toward outlining features of the process of dispute settlement. This paper seeks to build on their lead.

Setting

The area known as the Rincon lies approximately 200 kilometers northeast of Oaxaca City and is surrounded by mountains that are part of the Sierra Madre del Sur. The Rincon is peopled by Zapotec pueblos. Ralu'a, a town deep in the Sierra Madre, has the largest population of any of the towns scattered in the area—about 2,000 people, mostly bilingual Zapotec-Spanish speakers. The land produces a livelihoood for the inhabitants in the form of the staples (corn, beans, and sugar cane) and of the cash crop, coffee—a fairly recent introduction. Ralu'a is also a market town, and every Monday morning people from neighboring areas come to Ralu'a and settle down in the market place for a day of trading, talking, and drinking. (Monday is also the day when the greatest number of disputes are brought to the attention of the municipal court.) Trade is the main communication within the Rincon and between the pueblos of the Rincon and other peoples. The impassable mountains that had previously "cornered" the Rinconeros were opened in 1959 by completion of a road that now connects Ralu'a with the Valley of Oaxaca.

Ralu'a was founded in 1525 by Spanish friars in the service of Cortez. The town, unlike the surrounding indigenous pueblos, has a heterogeneous population. At the turn of the century a mine located at a distance of a thirty minutes' walk closed down. The mining families, originally from about fifteen different villages in the area, moved to Ralu'a and took up farming and trading (commerce). Ralu'a still draws new members from nearby towns and is considered by all outsiders as the town most open to change in the area. An earlier study (Nader 1964a) of the social organization of this town describes the many ties that link citizens: ties of kinship, locale, common work interests, and shared obligations and values. Various organizations such as the family, cooperative loan and savings associations, church organization, and the organization of musicians formalize ties between members of the town, as do noncorporate, informal groups that result from the division of labor in agricultural and home and town activities. In this earlier work I pointed out that some ties link a number of people together in a group or as individuals, whereas other ties divide these same persons by linking some of them with different groups. In Ralu'a the groupings, by not coinciding, by countering each other, develop a complexity of relations that serve to integrate or unify the village as a whole.

And unity—or the absence of conflict—is the image these people give to outsiders. Ralu'ans generally deny that disputes occur in their town. A visitor is often told that Ralu'a is a peaceful town, where strife and conflict never or rarely occur, and early in my fieldwork it was difficult to collect dispute cases at all. In the end, however, I had a solid body of data on disputes and their settlement. These were elicited in and out of the court, so that in addition to court materials I gathered further information on disputes that were resolved outside the court system. This preliminary, haphazard elicitation of dispute cases made me realize that the court was only one institution used to settle disputes and that any contextual analysis of dispute settlement in the court could not ignore alternatives that people in this society have (see Van Velsen 1967). Three kinds of agents are found to be used when a dispute develops to a point where a remedy is sought: the court, the family, and supernatural—court officials, family heads, ritual kinsmen, the priest, witches, and even such supernaturals as the saints and the gods. It is obvious that no case (or only the very rare one) begins and ends in the courtroom. For present purposes, however, I will segment the dispute into pre-court, court, and post-court settlement action, and concentrate in this paper on understanding something about the components that best characterize the behavior of the court.

The *municipio* or town hall of Ralu'a is a spacious, rectangular building with two rooms and two small jails; it is the symbol of village government as it is outlined in the Oaxacan state code. Within this town hall there are many officials: the *presidente*, the *sindico*, the *alcalde*, the *policia*, the *regidores*, the *secretario*, the *tesorero*, and the like. In addition to this village officialdom, there are frequent town meetings.

Within this building three officials constitute the town court of justice: the *presidente*, the *alcalde*, and the *sindico*. These three men, nominated by draft and elected by the town citizens (all adult males either married or over the age of twenty-one), are recruited for their experience and skills and serve for one year without pay. They are men deemed capable of *erj goonz*, "making the balance." All three are accountable for their behavior directly to the district court in Villa Alta and to the town citizens of Ralu'a. The greatest variety of disputes appears in the courts.

The *presidente* and the *sindico*, who share one room, have administrative and judicial duties. The duties of the *alcalde* are only judicial, and he and his aides share a room apart. Although the state code of Oaxaca formally defines the duties of these officials, town citizens have their own folk definition of the functions of each. The *presidente* deals with disputes that are easily resolved, such as conflicts between man and wife, between creditor and debtor, between drunken individuals. The *presidente* also handles cases of rebellious behavior, such as the refusal to comply with the obligations of a citizen; those cases of family conflict, debt, and drunken assault and battery that remain unresolved by the *presidente* are passed on to the *alcalde*. If the *alcalde* cannot settle them, they are usually referred to the district court in Villa Alta. The kinds of conflicts handled by the *presidente* and the *alcalde* overlap; it is the seriousness rather than the class of the complaint that determines whether it is passed on to the *alcalde*. Either the *presidente* may decide that the case is too serious for him to handle or the litigants may ask for referral if the decision reached by the *presidente* is not to their liking. The *sindico*, in contrast, is primarily responsible for processing specific kinds of complaints, those classed as crimes (*delitos*). It is the duty of the *sindico* to investigate all cases of crime, such as murder and theft, and to render impartial judgment in the settlement of property disputes. If he is unable to resolve property disputes and theft cases, he is supposed to refer them to the *alcalde*. All cases suggesting the possibility of murder go directly to Villa Alta.

Generally cases enter the court system through the *presidente*'s office, and a powerful and wise *presidente* may succeed in settling cases that one less competent would pass on to the *sindico* or *alcalde*. Disputes that cannot be resolved within these courts—disputes involving decisions that would jeopardize the town and capital crimes—are passed on to the district court at Villa Alta. For a number of reasons Ralu'ans prefer to settle their cases at home. The Villa Alta court officials, being appointees from Oaxaca, might not even admit as proper legal cases many of those brought before the Ralu'an municipal court. More practically, as one Ralu'an has said, "Better that our treasury should flourish than that of Villa Alta."

All three officials have the right to prosecute, judge, and enforce the verdict with the aid of the *policia*—a force of about fifteen men. Although this is the division of labor as described by the court officials themselves, and as understood by the citizens of the town, it is not, in fact, strictly adhered to. The administrative and personal family responsibilities of a *presidente* may make it impossible for him at times to be present to deal with grievances, and in such situations the *sindico* may substitute for him. Or both the *presidente* and the *alcalde* may be averse to making a decision, and in such circumstances the plaintiff must, unless the *alcalde* refers the case to the district court, either withdraw his case or seek aid external to the village court system.

The ideals of office require that these three officials be impartial judges of disputes. They are supposed to listen to a dispute and render a decision that will bind the conflict. Specifically, the duty of these men is *hacer el balance*—to make the balance between the *demandante* and the *demandado* (plaintiff and defendant). Balance is an ideal of many systems of law, but the definition of balance differs among cultures. The Zapotec ideal is not "an eye for an eye," but rather what restores personal relations to equilibrium.

In thinking about the Zapotec idea of balance, I find Foster's work on Tzintzuntzan relevant: "Traditional behavior in Tzintzuntzan is pointed toward maintaining an equilibrium, a state of balance or a status quo in which people must at least feel they are neither threats to, nor threatened by, others" (Foster 1967:12), and "A direct confrontation in which two candidates are in direct opposition—and hence one must lose— . . . is disturbing to all, since an equilibrium is destroyed, and every effort is made to avoid such situations" (Foster 1967:172).[1]

This concern for equilibrium is evident throughout Ralu'a. Upon my making inquiries as to motives for witchcraft in Ralu'a, an informant reported the following as causes: "because one works too much or not enough; because one is too pretty or too ugly or too rich; for being an only child; for being rich and refusing to lend money; for being antisocial—for example, for refusing to greet people." These are all situations that somehow upset the balance as Ralu'ans see it. It is no wonder that the zero-sum game (win or lose) as we know it in some American courts would be a frightening prospect to a plaintiff, even though all "right" might be on his side. The plaintiff need not worry, however, for, as we shall see the *presidente* is equally reluctant to make such a clear-cut

1. Not all peasant or subsistence societies have these values. My materials on a Shia Moslem village indicate that such an emphasis on equilibrium is unlikely to be found or sought in dual organization villages. Rather, the model for the Shias is a dynamic conflict model.

zero-sum-game decision for a variety of reasons—among them that witchcraft is an all too possible tool of retaliation for such behavior. If a plaintiff wanted to play the zero-sum game he would go to a witch and not to the courts, where behavior is far too public.

In many of these cases it is imperative to know something about the prehistory of a dispute in order to understand what the motives for dispute may be. I was once present at a fiesta in Ralu'a, listening to the orchestra play some *pasodobles* and drinking with the people present. The trumpet player was a very talented musician. I praised his performance and asked if I could record his solo. Not long after, a drunken fellow came up and hit the trumpet player, breaking his front tooth—a serious loss to a trumpet player. The case went to court the following day. In one sense the balance had been made when the player was hit and lost his front tooth—his excelling at the trumpet had itself created an imbalance. But the court was now concerned with another, though related, kind of balance. Although the settlement was in favor of the plaintiff, the damages paid were less than minimal: twenty pesos, for which the tooth most certainly could not be replaced. Yet the plaintiff did not ask for more in damages, and he indicated to me that his score would have to be settled by less public means, where retaliation would not be so likely. The case was more complex than I have indicated here. It had many of the same characteristics of the *policia* case recorded in the next section—sides were chosen by Ralu'ans, involving many persons, and many more would have been implicated if the dispute had not been, at least formally, sealed by a court settlement.

The Five Cases [2]

1. *Case of the Damaged Chiles.* On February 24, 1964, in the town of Ralu'a, District of Villa Alta, State of Oaxaca, there arrived at nine thirty before this municipal authority a Mr. Ignacio Andrés Zoalage, merchant, fifty-five years of age. He explained the following: "I am coming to make a complaint about the chauffeur of the cream-colored truck that is on the platform, in the middle of which is a bruised basket of chiles weighing forty-seven and a half kilograms." The chauffeur of the cream-colored truck was called; he arrived fifteen minutes later and said that his name was Mario Valdéz Herrero, chauffeur of the truck. The Court President asked him whether it was true that he had bruised the basket of chiles, and he answered: "Actually, I bruised it, but this happened because I don't have anyone to advise me. It is also the truck owner's fault because he ought to let me have a helper. Also, I could not see because the driver's compartment is high. Besides, it is the señor's fault—they put the things they have for sale on the ground, knowing that there is truck traffic."

2. Cases are presented as recorded by the secretary.

The Municipal Court President asked Mr. Ignacio Andrés: "Why did you put your merchandise down, knowing that the truck would go by?" Mr. Andrés answered that there was room for the truck to pass. The chauffeur then said that this was not true, as the space there was at an angle. Mr. Andrés said: "Look, Mr. President, the truck came this way, then this way and that way." The Municipal Court President said that it would be most convenient in this case if the chauffeur paid for the damage he had caused, and that the basket of chiles should be brought in, so that an estimate could be made of how much of it had been spoiled.

The plaintiff left and the Municipal Court President ordered the magistrate to have the merchandise brought in. The magistrate returned with the owner, carrying a basket of chiles. They emptied it on the floor. The court magistrate observed the chiles on the floor and put aside the damaged chiles; he then told the President that the quantity ruined was about one and a half kilograms. The Municipal Court President asked the owner of the basket how much he wanted to be paid for the damage. Mr. Andrés answered that it was not much—three pesos. The President told the chauffeur that he had to pay three pesos for the damage. Upon this the chauffeur said: "All right, I will go right now for the three pesos." Meanwhile the Municipal Court President reminded the plaintiff to be more careful on the next occasion and to watch where he put his booth—not to put it just anywhere and especially not in front of a truck. Thus this case was closed and the owner walked out with his load of chile, leaving the damaged merchandise with the municipal authority.

2. *Case of the Little Boy with Susto.* In the town of Ralu'a, District of Villa Alta, State of Oaxaca, at twelve noon on February 24, 1964, Mrs. Juan, who was living on a ranch in the adjacent hills between Juquila and Talea, made the following complaint against young Teodoro Garcia. "The son of Teodora assaulted my little son. We were cutting coffee in the field of said Mrs. Quiroz, grandmother of Teodoro, and I asked him why he had hit him. He told me to complain wherever I wished, because he went to the school, and he can defend himself. My little boy got frightened and yells during the night and now has diarrhea because of the fright. Therefore I am asking the President to help me make my little son well again. I asked Teodoro's grandmother why he had been attacking my little boy. He is older, and he started the fight with my little boy, who is only six years old. She answered, 'Fight, fight, and continue to fight; there is enough room in this field.' I am making this claim because Teodoro does not have any right to beat my son, and he hit him."

When the Municipal President was informed of this complaint by Mrs. Juan, young Teodoro was cited to respond to the incidents of which he was accused. When he arrived before this Municipal Presidency, he was informed of what Mrs. Juan had just reported and he said that it was not true, that her boy was stupid and always bothered him, and that his mother defended him and did not say anything to her son. "It is not true, Mr. President," Teodoro said, "He is a mischief-maker and he takes advantage of us because we are working. I will not tolerate his calling me miserable names; he said very ugly things."

The Municipal Court President now said to the señora: "If you know how the young man acts, why don't you leave the work there or don't go there any more for work?" "It is his grandmother who is always asking me to work for her in the field," said Mrs. Juan, "but that Teodoro treated us that way." Teodoro said, "I did not ask you to come to work," and the señora replied, "Your grandmother is the one who did, not you." "You have to work, that's why you came." "I want the President to know that I always have worked, but nobody treats me badly." The President, in order to finish this matter, asked how much Mrs. Juan wanted Teodoro to pay for a treatment. She answered that she wanted thirty pesos for her little son to be cured. Teodoro said that the boy did not have anything wrong with him, but she told him to take the boy home, and then he would see how he yelled at night. Teodoro said he would not do it even if the boy were his son. "Look, Mr. President," he said, "I am not willing to pay thirty pesos, but I would pay twenty." Then the President asked the señora whether she agreed to accept the twenty pesos that he had offered to pay. She accepted, and the accused paid cash, which was given to the señora in his presence. The present session was finished at four o'clock in the afternoon of the same day.

3. *Case of the Bossy Wife.* In Ralu'a, District of Villa Alta, State of Oaxaca, at ten o'clock on February 17, 1964, there appeared before the Municipal President a Mr. Jaime Ruiz, native and inhabitant of this town, married, 45 years of age, to present a complaint against his wife, Carmen Ibarra, native and inhabitant of the same town. He said: "I come to present my complaint about my wife because she cut the coffee without my consent." The Municipal President, after hearing what had been said by the plaintiff, answered: "All right, let's arrange this matter, but we have to call Mrs. Carmen Ibarra so that she can explain what she did and why she did it." It was ordered that Mrs. Carmen Ibarra be called and she appeared at eleven thirty o'clock of the same day.

All parties concerned being present, the Municipal President spoke. He said to the defendant: "I had you called so that you could clarify the matter of the claim made by your husband, who is here, present. Why did you have the coffee cut without his permission?" Here the plaintiff interrupted, saying: "Mr. President, I am here to complain with the help of your authority that this woman, who is my wife, had my coffee cut from a piece of land that belongs to me. I know that the helper of my wife did the cutting on her order, but without my consent or permission, and this is why I am here to claim that this coffee should be delivered to me." Mrs. Carmen Ibarra, wife of the plaintiff, said excitedly: "Mr. President, this man really does not think at all. Why shouldn't I cut the coffee as it belongs to both of us, and besides we have children to support and feed. I am a woman. I do everything to look after our children, and he has left us, left the house, with nobody saying anything to him. He left because he wanted to and he went to the house of his sister so that he could pick up some tales [gossip]—he always had this habit." "I am in the right, Mr. President," explained the plaintiff. "I can't stay with her [the defendant] in the house because she says she is the valuable one, she does nothing but work, and I am the weak one and that is thanks to my mother and father who left me the house and some money."

"He just does it that way; he goes to his [our] house where we are hiding a few things of value, he takes the key or he hides it and at the time when we need something, there we are looking for it everywhere, but he has to have this habit of taking the key. Now he is complaining about the coffee —it is true, I ordered the coffee to be cut. What do I do—me, I have to [take] care of his children, so I think I have my rights, after all we are legally married, and nobody hindered him in carrying out his own wish to get out. The mayor of last year knows this, because I informed him first of it, so that no one could say that I left my husband. Now all I have and what we both have is neither for me nor for him, it is for our children, it is their lives, and we shouldn't be quarreling any more, but this man does not think, no, he does not think of our sons. Look Mr. President, my little girl is at this moment in Mexico [City] for a treatment because she is sick and he does not even think that his daughter needs some money for treatment. He hasn't even asked. He knows very well how sick she is." "I don't agree with that either," said the plaintiff, "because she [the daughter] left without my permission and did not come to tell me, and I didn't even know that she went." "That's how he does things, Mr. President," interrupted Carmen. "Why should his daughter go to him and tell him that she is leaving if he doesn't even help her with the things he could do for her? Now he says that I didn't say anything about her going—if she were dying, would you want me first to ask you permission so that she could die? When there is urgency for a treatment, one has to look for a way. That you should have thought about before leaving us, having a sick daughter." "Mr. President, you heard now how it is, I fully had thought I would not return to her any more for many reasons. First, we have come here to the *municipio* already several times, and always she promises she will behave well and it won't be the same, but after a while she returns to the same thing. Now, for instance, she has a little liquor store; and I don't know anything about it, how it goes, whether there are any money entries, or how she manages it. Clearly she makes out of me a nobody. Now, too, she goes out on her errands and comes back late and I ask where she has gone and she answers angrily, 'Why do you want to know? I had to do my errands because you don't know any-thing.' But I say," continued the plaintiff, " 'It is my right to know where you are going and what kind of business you are attending'—and there are more things she has been doing, but now I don't want this case to drag on longer—I only want her to return the coffee to me." Whereupon Mrs. Carmen Ibarra said: "Yes, I will deliver the coffee, which you said I took, but you have to pay in front of the President the bills of the treatment that our daughter had to have—poor little girl—who wants so much to be cured as she says in her postcard, 'Mama, do sell some interests of my part for the treatment.' And I am doing everything to get hold of some money so that she can take the treatment—and this man, for a little bit of coffee which I went and cut off, he is making such a terrible fuss." "Look, Mr. President," explained the plaintiff, "I planted the coffee seeds for my wife and she has sufficient, and now she tries to take mine and wants to have more, but the only thing I want is for her not to cut [my coffee] without my per-mission."

The Municipal President now having heard what the parties in the lawsuit had to say, pronounced the following: "You should now think like mature people about what you are doing, and the only thing you should do is to get together again, forget the troubles [matters] of the past, think of your sick child and don't think about yourselves. You should both be home worrying about how your daughter can be cured." And directing himself to Mr. Jaime Ruiz: "Nobody has thrown you out [of your house], but you walked out without any motive, therefore return to your home and think about how to resolve the problems of the home. The man as the boss of the house is responsible for the expenditures and necessities of the house, and the chores that have to be done should be the duties of the wife, with the wife letting him know what is being done. Well, the husband should give the orders with regard to what should be done as long as there is the advantage and benefit of the house involved, but in the event the husband abuses his authority in the home, then the wife has every right to protest and has a reason to do so. As to the woman, the obligation of the wife is to be there where the husband orders, as long as it is in agreement and to the benefit of the home; and the woman is also the only one responsible for the food and alike necessities, that is, for the kitchen."

Having listened to what the President had to say and after a long silence and reflection, the couple became reasonable and said that they would unite again and that they would follow the advice of the Municipal President. But Mr. Jaime Ruiz finally added: "I am willing to go [home] if in all ways my wife behaves to me as she should and we are in agreement in everything, as you said. But [only] if you allow me to go home when my daughter returns from her treatment in Mexico [City]. Then I would go back to my house, but as long as she is not here, I will not go." His wife was asked if she would agree to what her husband, Mr. Jaime Ruiz, had just finished saying, whereupon she answered, "Yes, whatever he wishes. He could return now or when our daughter arrives." The Municipal President then said to the plaintiff: "All right, when your daughter returns, then your case will be finished and you may go to your house." And turning to the defendant, "And you may then advise this municipal authority when your daughter arrives in order to settle the case." With these words he finished the proceedings, leaving the case open until further notice from the señora.

4. *Case of the Delinquent Son.* In the town of Ralu'a, District of Villa Alta, State of Oaxaca, at ten o'clock on February 10, 1968, before the undersigned Municipal President there appeared Mr. Benjamin Mendoza Cruz, native of this town, to make a complaint against his son Clemente Mendoza, unmarried, twenty-five years of age, native and inhabitant of the same town. The complaint concerned a violation the son committed on the property of which he [the plaintiff] is the owner and for which he, as the father, demands recompense for loss he has sustained. Taking note of all this, the Municipal President ordered the accused to be cited. Having already been cited earlier, he was present and was now informed of the context of the complaint.

The accused, being allowed to speak, said the following: "Without a witness I can declare that I went to his field in order to cut some coffee. I admit I was at fault, and now he can say how to punish me. A year ago my boss [my father] allowed me to cut some coffee on his property called Suyagtuluc. But now I wish my father would forgive me for the fault I committed. He is in the right and he has his rights, but he might consider how to decide [to view] this matter. I was confident that he would give the coffee to me. I ask for forgiveness and would like to call Professor Raymundo Vasquez to be my legal adviser."

Immediately it was ordered to call the professor, who arrived at ten fifteen of the same day. The professor asked why he had been called and the Municipal President explained that young Clemente, present in the courtroom, had asked that he should be called in order to represent him. The nature of the case was explained to him, and he advised young Clemente, in the presence of the Municipal President, that if he admits his fault and if he has been harvesting the coffee in question, being the son, he should ask forgiveness and pardon from his father. "Apologize to him, because what you did was an abuse," he said. After this he asked permission to leave, as that was all he had to say.

Now Mr. Benjamin Mendoza said the following: "I am, as his father, very sad that my son Clemente should have done this wickedness to me. I did not believe that it was he who had done it until the Juquilena—with whom we have adjacent terrains—informed me. She was the one who told me that it was my son who had cut the coffee, and it hurt me that my son should have done this because on earlier occasions I had noted that coffee was disappearing. I came here to inform his Municipal Presidency and to let it be precisely known to the authorities of the villages of San Juan Juquila that there is a path that is always used, and if there is someone on the ranches that pertain to this municipality who had done this crime, that he be punished so that he would not go on doing it. However, I now know the truth, and I know who has been doing this crime, and now my son even admits his wrongdoing, so I leave it to the criterion [judgment] of this authority to decide what is suitable, because for my part I can tell my son to do this or that when I know he has made a mistake. As his father I have to help him and look after him, but he should not act this way, disposing of the fruit of my harvest, without my consent."

The Municipal President intervened here, saying to Clemente: "Now you heard what your father said, and I will tell you that your father does not have an obligation to give you, his son, anything; nor is he obliged to give you what is his. If a father loves his son very much, he may give him something, but nobody can force him to do so. Now, you have abused him and as you have admitted there is no reason why your father should help you because you committed this wrong."

Young Clemente Mendoza said again: "I am not asking anything of my papa. He is the one free to decide. I admit having taken the coffee without his consent, and you will have to say how you like this matter to be arranged. I don't want this to go on any longer, but I repeat I am guilty." The Municipal President, having taken note of all the father and son had declared, and wanting this case to be solved administratively, asked both parties if they would agree to come to an agreement. They accepted.

The Municipal President now dictated the following: the lost coffee should be restored to the plaintiff; and he should calculate the approximate quantity in kilograms that was lost.

Mr. Benjamin Mendoza said, after making an approximate calculation, that there were approximately twenty-five pounds of dry coffee. "I don't want to say more, because it would not be correct. Many people would do this and sometimes say even much more, but I, for my part, say what I think is suitable; and what I think should be replaced and delivered to me are twenty-five pounds of dried coffee. With regard to the fine, you are authorized to set it in accordance with the form by which you judge the case." The Municipal President said to young Clemente the following: "Without delay you have to deliver the coffee, and the deadline is Friday the twenty-first of this month, and for the wrong you have committed I impose on you a two-hundred-peso fine, which you have to pay today." When defendant Clemente Mendoza heard of the fine and of the coffee that he had to deliver to his father, he accepted in agreement and paid the fine. After that he said: "In case I cannot keep my promise regarding the coffee, my father has the right to claim it from me again."

As both parties had been informed about the agreement and of the imposed fine by this Presidential Municipality, the present document of agreement between both father and son was formalized. On the intervention of the authority it was shown to them, and especially to young Clemente Mendoza, in order that he would realize that once both parties were bound in agreement, he should not inflict reprisals on his father or stepmother and to realize that the plaintiff had the right, as a father, to correct any of his faults and that he, as a son, should ask his father for full permission to harvest some coffee, or to dispose of some of his [father's] interests, to avoid being offensive [making abuse] to his father and stepmother in his father's house, and to behave as a good son is supposed to behave.

With regard to the part relating to the father, he [the Municipal President] said the following: Whenever he wanted to he could dispose of something and give it to his son, help him in mutual agreement, guide him in all work he might undertake, but *de facto* the father does not have any obligation to give his son anything; and on the other hand, the son cannot demand from his father to be given any interests. It is entirely in the hands of the father whether he wants to give or not.

After this disposition was repeated by the Municipal President and both parties again agreed, the present act of investigation and consent was cleared, it then being eleven thirty-five of the same day when the participants signed. We certify.

5. *Case of the* POLICIA. In the town of Talea de Castro, District of Villa Alta, State of Oaxaca, nine o'clock on February 24, 1964, the police of this city hall before the subscribed Municipal President were assembled to testify before the public about a quarrel in the bar "La Frontera." One of them had been bitten in the arm by Vitoriano Bautista Luz, and another said that Efren had hit him a great blow. He [Victoriano] had come with Horacio Dominguez. The Municipal President asked why he had hit him and bitten him. All [the police] said that the night before they had taken his brother

Miguel from the bar because he insulted the police. "When we went with Miguel Bautista because of the disorder he had started, we met Benigno Leon, who said that he would vouch for him and started to impose himself on us; we saw it was useless and that he [Benigno] wanted to free him [Miguel] by force, so we took him, too, into prison and he did not care what was happening to him, and he [now] started an argument." But a few minutes later the Chief of the Section came and declared as follows: "Last night I went to the bar in order to see that they close it, as it was already very late; there came out Miguel Bautista completely drunk; you all go to hell, go away—all of you—and your President [he said], and he tried to kick me but did not touch me; then I called my companions with the help of a whistle in order to get help, and once the other policemen came, we took Miguel Bautista and near the house of Martin Elias we met Benigno who said he would be responsible for this friend and why were we taking him away? He was stupid. After a while Miguel's friends came and his brother, and they raised hell so that we should be forced to let them [Miguel and Benigno] go, and they were vouching for him [Miguel]. He [Victoriano] did not talk like decent people do, he started to insult us, and he bit my companion and delivered a blow in the face to another. All the policemen said the same thing; if they [Victoriano and Miguel's friends?] would have come with good words, as had Horacio Dominguez and Miguel's papa, it would have been different because we [the police] are also decent people, but the way they did it, they hit and insulted us—and we would not accept this. Then there came Pepe, and he said that he had enough money to put down as a guarantee so that we should let Miguel go, but we did not let him go free and they were disgusted and told us they would make a note of this and would take revenge. Also here was the younger brother of Miguel, with the name of Antonio." The Municipal President now had been informed of the complaint the policemen had against Mr. Miguel Bautista Gregorio, who had been arrested and in prison since the night before, together with Mr. Benigno Leon.

Presented now before the City Hall, at the time of ten thirty of the same day.

The Municipal President asked him [Miguel Gregorio] why there was that scandal at night and why they [he and his friends] had insulted the police-men and the authority, as the policemen had testified was their behavior. Mr. Miguel Gregorio, whose turn it was to talk, said: "We did not insult them, all were drunk, and I want the policemen to come here and say it." Then the policemen entered and the Chief of Police said that Mr. Celedonio had said to him to go to the bar to see that the bar was closed when Miguel Bautista G. came out and insulted and kicked him. Miguel Bautista G. then said: "It is not true. The bar was already closed, and as soon as the police-man arrived, he started to whistle." And a policeman said: "He [Miguel] was talking with us." Miguel said that as soon as the police arrived they whistled, and a policeman said that the bar was not closed. The Chief of Police said: "Look Mr. President, what these men did last night, and see how they bit the arm of this policeman" (the policeman showed his arm which had a big mark—it was the left arm). Miguel: "Look, Mr. President, last night when they brought me here they stole from me fifty pesos that I had in my pocket. I don't know which one of them took it out of my pocket." The Municipal President said: "Listen, Miguel, last night after the meeting I passed by the house of Luis Huachic, and I, myself, heard how you insulted me and my secretary. I don't want to oppose you because it is not correct, but I, personally, heard it and you cannot deny it." The Municipal President asked the policemen how they wanted the case arranged, and they said it was in his hands to resolve it, then he continued to say [to Miguel]: "You admit your mistake, so I authorize you to pay fifty pesos—so that you will be careful next time." Mr. Miguel asked to pay only twenty. The Munipical President did not accept this and repeatedly said that the policemen said that "your father came and talked sense." Miguel: "The policemen are to blame, too, they were drunk." President: "It is not possible that they were drunk because at the meeting all were all right, not one of them was drunk." Then Benigno started to talk and said repeatedly that Maurilio should come and testify. Maurilio, the policeman, arrived and said that Benigno had said he vouched for his companion, and he found out enough—he [Benigno] was also drunk. Maurilio continued [to Benigno]: "You started with threats, had you been reasonable nobody would have said anything to you, Benigno." "Because they hit me," [said Benigno?]. Miguel said: "They tore my shirt and the policeman hit me with a stick." Municipal President [to Benigno]: "Listen, son, for the mistake you made I fine you fifteen pesos." Benigno said: "I won't pay anything because they first did damage to me." Municipal President to Benigno: "Why did you get mixed up with this? It was none of your business. When one is doing a favor like this, it always comes out against us [him?]." Benigno replied: "Yes, that is true, but I could not leave my companion." Municipal President: "With reason, yes, but not with menace. Horacio came and spoke decently and then intervened, speaking reasonably as friends do." Benigno: "They grabbed me and hit me, tell me why? So that it hinders me at work because the hand hurts me. I am delicate, and it is quite painful. It is not swollen, but the hand hurts." Municipal President: "In any case, you will have to pay the fine of fifteen pesos." Miguel interrupted and he asked that this matter be arranged and he would give forty pesos—and said that they should not bother his companion. Benigno: "I won't pay for anything because they already have seized me and beat me." President: "It is the sanction which I impose on you so that at another time when there is a dispute among drunks, you should [know] not to take part and get involved or so engaged." Benigno: "Now I know for the next time. But the policemen already have beaten me and put me into jail, they already have made justice twice." Municipal President: "To arrange this matter I will give you another fine, ten pesos, so that you don't insist [argue] any more; Miguel must pay forty pesos, and you must pay ten pesos." They accepted in agreement and said they would come back and pay. The President said that was impossible, but they said, "Yes, we will come back and pay, we will do that and not go somewhere else with the forty pesos." They begged and said they would bring the money the next day. The President gave them permission to pay the next day, and they left. Then the policemen came again, and they said that Victoriano should be called because it was he who had bit one policeman's arm and struck another. They threatened: "If you don't arrange this matter, we all could leave off being policemen." The Municipal President, being advised of this new complaint, cited Mr. Victoriano Bautista in order for him to respond to the charges of the policemen, and he ordered that Victoriano be called, and he answered that he would appear in the afternoon because he was selling meat [he is a butcher] and there was nobody could replace him. When the defendant Victoriano appeared, having received the previous citation by this Municipal Authority, he said the following: "It is true. I came Sunday night to see what had happened, and not knowing that it was my brother who was arrested. I came with Horacio and when I arrived one of the policemen said, 'Now comes the other one.' I thought I would complain to you, for all were drunk. They did an amount of bad things to me and hit me with the stick. I have the marks on my shoulder where Marcelon had hit me and one of Zoloaga's. Zoloaga was very drunk. I had my provocation, but I didn't bite, besides I know I cannot bite. I was not doing anything. I did not get angry. Etziquio was the worst, he used his stick, and no matter how troubled one can become, one has to be able to realize what one is doing. I know I have not beaten anyone. When somebody does a certain thing, naturally one has to admit it. They [police] were pleased when we arrived, but they did not expect us to speak up." Marcelino, the policeman, said: "When you hit me I was not drunk." Victoriano said [to the President]: "If you want to continue the investigation, we can go on, but it is not likely for them to tell the truth. I repeat and say that when I arrived with Horacio I was fine. I repeat, I won't compromise [myself] for anything. If you want that this should be arranged [settled] here, we will arrange it. If we cannot, continue until later; I can go on until they realize this and don't come back later with the same things. Moreover, all the police have done the same, they never wait until one explains to them." Horacio said effectively: "I arrived with Victoriano. The policemen had whistled, but we didn't know whom they were going to bring out [of the bar], and later we knew it was his brother Miguel, and I spoke to them with reason and wanted them in turn to be reasonable, but they did not want to be. I even promised to vouch for him [Miguel] in case they would agree not to present the case." The Municipal President then said in order to settle this now and not to argue further that "If you, Victoriano, recognize your fault [culpability], we can settle this matter here." "All right," said Victoriano B., "so be it. Tomorrow I shall come and pay." "It can't be," said the President. "You have to sign a promissory note first, and then you can come to pay when I so order." After signing a promissory note in favor of the Authority, permission to leave was given to Mr. Victoriano Bautista and to Mr. Horacio Dominguez, and this matter hereby has been closed at eight o'clock, February 24, 1964.

(Please note: In this record of the court stenographer no mention is made of the sum of the fine Victoriano is to pay. Victoriano signs a promissory note, but the amount he thereby promises to pay is not stated.)

Discussion

Professor P. C. Hahm (in press) once commented that "to tell the truth and nothing but the truth" is meaningless for Koreans because they believe no man can tell objective truth. He added that Koreans use no rigid rule of evidence because the individual is viewed in total context —that is, as a son, as a nephew, or the like—that there is no *stare decisis* because Koreans emphasize the particular—no two cases are alike. Koreans, said Professor Hahm, prefer "peace to justice, harmony to truth, and mediation to adjudication." His statements essentially summarize the Zapotec point of view, although the implications of this common view are quite different in both cultures.[3]

In Ralu'a the *presidente* decides cases without using written law and in a court with few formalities. The court, upon being presented with a complaint, attempts to settle it immediately, although not hurriedly. There is time for different points of view to take shape. Many of these cases are linked to previous conflicts known to the *presidente*. In each case the *presidente* offers the litigants advice about avoiding recurrences —to watch where the truck passes through the market place; to reconcile family differences and respect the traditional family· roles of husband and wife, father and son; to consider working at a different place if one does not get along; to be cautious about helping drunken friends when they get themselves in trouble.

The judge is a warden of order and fair play among peers. He resolves conflict by minimizing the sense of injustice and outrage felt by the parties to a case. His investigation of the truth is nondirective and flexible much of the time. His patient stance functions to encourage litigants to decide what relevant issues should be discussed, to present both real and abstract evidence to support their claims. In family cases he is more directive and paternalistic and seeks to remind kinsmen of their responsibilities. He is expected to make use of what he knows of town affairs and is selected for just such knowledge. He is expected to render a verbal and written agreement for each case—an agreement that consensus would label equitable.

The judgment that the *presidente* gives on a matter is always a compromise in that the decision is the "result or embodiment of concession or adjustment." Furthermore, there is always a mutual promise, usually signed, to abide by a decision; the parties to a case have the right to

3. Stanley Lubman's insightful article on "Mao and Mediation: Politics and Dispute Resolution in Communist China" (1967) describes a traditional style of dispute settlement similar to Korea. Lubman's article is particularly fascinating because he begins to document the process of one style of dispute settlement's becoming something new and different. The traditional Confucian mode of mediating disputes is forced into a new Communist pattern.

appeal to the *alcalde*'s office and then to the Villa Alta district court if they are not willing to agree to the decision. Although the judgment has to be agreed upon by both parties, the "compromise" is not always a result of mutual concession because it is the judge (rather than the litigants) who, in listening to the case, decides where the middle ground is. And the decision is the *presidente*'s understanding of what is best for "making the balance"—which as often as not means the restoration of relations to a former condition of equilibrium, a condition when conflict was absent. In addition—or as part of this task—the *presidente*'s judgment may be punitive.

The best way to "make the balance" in the *policia* case was to fine rather than ask for damages, which the defendants would have interpreted as adding insult to injury. The punitive fines go to the third party —the *presidente*'s office. In this same case the *presidente* sought to re-establish a relative condition of peace between the litigants and at the same time to prevent escalation of the conflict to feud proportions. In the chile case and the case of the little boy with fright, damages were the best way to restore the earlier conditions of peace, and advice was given to prevent conflict from breaking out again. In both cases where damages were asked, the litigants did not share a common residence in Ralu'a. In the case of the bossy wife, the *presidente* thought that neither damages nor punitive fines would aid restoration of peace—but that conflict over the division of property would be eliminated if both returned to a normal marital state. In the father-son case there was no hope of "compromise" by virtue of the relationship, but the *presidente* strongly advised the son to fulfill the ideals of the son role, thus eliminating any problem of father-son conflict. In this case the judge succeeded, at least in making the balance, but the son was considered to be greatly out of line. The immediate dispute that gave rise to the theft was the unwillingness of the father to pay the brideprice for his son. The *presidente* could not handle such a dispute because, as he himself said, "This was not a legal question." Had the father not already given the son the equivalent of brideprice several times over, he would certainly have enjoined the father as to his moral obligations, as he did in the husband-wife case.

Settlement and prevention are the tasks of the court, and even punishment is meted out with this in mind. The principle of vengeance cannot dominate even when, as in the *policia* case, the *presidente* personally feels very strongly disinclined toward the defendants' arguments. The *presidente*'s role is that of mediator, adjudicator, group therapist. His principal function seems to be to listen—often asking questions to clear up contradictions. He does not cross-examine, but rather allows the litigants to vent their spleen, and in this way he brings out the nature of the basis of the conflict. The contenders talk about anything they consider relevant, without the *presidente*'s attempting to confine the discussion to the original charge(s). Points of fact are not definitely settled; matters of fault are not ultimately pursued. Implicitly at least these people realize that what is important to settling disputes is not what is "objectively so" but rather the parties' perception of what is so. We therefore find fault-finding and fact-finding in general played down considerably. (This lack of stress on fact-finding is not true, however, in property cases, where boundaries are often visited as part of the settlement procedures.) Given the pattern described above, it is understandable that there is no fiction of judicial ignorance. One has the feeling that what is going on in this court is more expressive, than game-like.

Comparisons of Style

To this point I have been describing certain features of court procedure in a Zapotec town. I would like to concern myself now with the problem of how similarities and differences are made explicit in terms of typology. There have been some attempts at typology in the anthropological study of law, though nowhere near so many as in political anthropology. Maine (1861) distinguished societies in which law is based on status from those in which law is based on contract, in order to illustrate the connection between forms of social groupings and forms of law. Durkheim (2nd ed., 1960) contrasted legal systems on the basis of prevailing sanctions—repressive/restitutive—in order to illustrate the interconnection of types of division of labor with law forms. Hoebel's (1954) whole book is an illustration of types of law forms of varying complexity. Others, such as Bohannan (1965) and Gulliver (in this volume), have thought to distinguish systems of dispute settlement on the basis of type of outcome or mode of settlement—that is, compromise versus decision, negotiation versus adjudication. And generally throughout the literature we find at least an implicit type contrast between court and courtless societies. Rather than depending on a single binary set, the works of Cohn (1959) and Aubert (n.d.) illustrate that a more specific separation for observation of the various features or clusters of features that make up the process of dispute settlement would aid possibilities for comparison within and between societies.[4]

Cohn (1959), on the one hand, addresses the task of factoring out the value conflicts between two systems of procedure: the indigenous Indian and the British system in India. To summarize briefly here, he contrasts British and Indian courts on four points: (1) equality in the eyes of the law; (2) status and contract; (3) importance of the decision; (4) settle-

4. Professor Lon Fuller's paper on "The Forms and Limits of Adjudication" (n.d.) has some useful suggestions as to crucial features of various forms of adjudication.

ment of the case and only the case. In that order, he points out that, whereas Indians consider that men have widely differing inherent worth, the British assume the equality of the individual before the law, and the adversary system functions to equalize persons in court. Whereas, for the Indian, status ties cannot be treated simply as contractual relations, because of the recognition of multiplex relations that cannot be cut by a decision of a court, the British base the court decision on ideas of contract, which do not fit the Indian value system. Whereas the Indian courts postpone clear-cut decisions because the goal is to compromise differences, the British court situation is defined in terms of win or lose. Whereas the Indians discuss a string of disputes to mediate the basis of the dispute, the British deal with the specific case presented by the contending parties.

Aubert (n.d.), on the other hand, has been interested in the features that characterize Norwegian courts and Norwegian administrative agencies. He came up with two models: the court model and the bargain model. Their respective featurs are listed below:

Court Model	*Bargain Model*
a. triad	a. dyad
b. coercive power	b. no coercive power
c. application of highly valued norms	c. pursuit of interests (values)
d. establishment of past facts (guilt)	d. not necessary to establish past facts
e. retroactively oriented reasoning	e. prospectively oriented reasoning
f. legal experts participate (that is, judge)	f. no legal experts participate
g. conclusion is a verdict	g. conclusion is an agreement
h. purely distributive decision	h. distributive/generative decision
i. either/or decision	i. a compromise
j. reaffirmation	j. no necessary implication concerning validity
k. affinity to legal scholarship	k. affinity to science or utilitarian thinking

In observing one Ralu'an court over a period of nine years, I have noted a change in types of cases—a change in the direction of proportionately more family cases, more assault-and-battery cases, fewer property cases. Cases during any one week vary in mode of settlement from adjudication to mediation, depending on the needs of the case; the outcomes vary as to whether the settlement is punitive or restrictive, compromise or decision, but the features noted below do not vary:

1. The procedure is seen as a way of finding out what the trouble is. Instead of the assumption that the cause of the dispute is already known and that the proceedings function to settle, a variety of disputes may be discussed to mediate the basis of the dispute.

2. The goal is to have parties compromise their differences; the minimax principle (give a little, get a little) rather than the zero-sum game (win or lose) prevails.

3. The decisions of the court emanate from the characteristics of a multiplex society. Regardless of who the litigants are, it is the wider network of relations that influence a decision. The greater social relevance is considered in solving a particular dispute. Utilitarian thinking is valued.

4. Norms and interests are recognized.

5. There is a legal expert.

6. It is not necessary to establish past facts or to establish guilt.

7. Conclusion is an agreement.

8. Compromise prevails even if the conclusion is either/or.

9. Agreement is backed by coercive force.

10. Reasoning is prospectively oriented.

11. The principals may exchange positions as ruling may be made on other than the original claim.[5]

It is worth noting that the features of the Zapotec style share something in common with all four models presented by Cohn and Aubert; these features of settlement process define a style that seems to be independent of the shape or organization of the court institution. I have been impressed in comparing the Zapotec data with the work of others—such as that of Yngvesson on the small claims court (n.d.), Hahm on Korea (in press), Cohn on village India (1959), Aubert on the administrative agency (1967), and Gulliver on the Ndendeuli (this volume)—with the general similarities in settlement style, in spite of the great organizational differences between courts described by Cohn (1959), Hahm (in press), Nader (1964a, b, 1966), and Yngvesson (n.d.), and Aubert's agency and Gulliver's settlement by negotiation (in this volume), and *in spite of* the great differences in levels of economic and political development. I was particularly struck by the conclusions in Gulliver's paper—all of which could equally well apply to the Zapotec court.

The similarity is principally in the value placed on the minimax principle, rather than on the zero-sum game. From this principle follows a de-emphasis on establishing past fact; a prospectively oriented reasoning; and the use of proceedings as a technique for expression and for finding out what the trouble really is before reaching a settlement, even though this may be, for Cohn's indigenes, an agreement to avoid a decision.

The style of dispute settlement, it seems, may be viewed independently of its formal expression as court or agency. What factors influence the development of such a style? Yngvesson compared the small-claims courts of Berkeley-Albany and Oakland, California. Both the Berkeley-Albany and Oakland small-claims courts are organized under the same statute;

5. The terms "plaintiff" and "defendant" are not accurate characterizations, since defendant may counterclaim as part of the original case.

yet, she observes, the styles of the courts differ markedly: "Differences existing in the role assumed by the judge in each court are related to the manifest social function of the courts, and correspond roughly to Pound's distinction between the judge who applies rules and the one who applies standards" (n.d.: 2). Yngvesson's paper suggests that there is something above and beyond the strictly "legal" or beyond the shape of the court that molds the proceedings. Upon investigating the social context in which each court is found, she points to several factors that influence the proceedings: types of plaintiffs, types of claims at each court, the role of the judge and the burden of each court.

The fact that 70% of the claims brought to the Oakland court in the sample period were for breach of contract, a claim in which there is rarely any question of who is "right" (and, in fact, it is rare in these cases that the defendant appear at all), suggests that the need in the Oakland court for individualized application of the law is much less than in the Berkeley court, where there is a far greater variety of cases.

An Oakland judge deals predominantly with business group claimants over breach of contract matters, and does not vary his procedure when exceptions to this rule arise. At the Berkeley court, in contrast, there is a much greater variety of cases, many of which require consideration of "special circumstances," and judging procedure is thus of a much more individualistic type.

There is a noticeable difference in the role assumed by the judge in the Oakland and Berkeley courts: In the former, the average judge listens carefully but hurriedly, to what he considers the essential facts of a case. He is pressed by a tight schedule, and has no time to let the litigants talk freely about the issue. As soon as he obtains enough facts to fit the case to a particular rule of law, the hearing is terminated, whether or not the litigants wish to say more on the matter. His role is, generally, that of one who impartially listens to the facts and then fits them into a suitable pigeon-hole. The Berkeley judge, on the other hand, allows the litigants to talk freely, often uncovering issues which, within certain defined bounds, may affect his judgment of the case. He does not appear to be bound by a tight schedule, and will frequently take the time to add a word of advice to the litigants before he dismisses them. . . . His concept of his role would seem to be that of one who comes to a just decision, to the extent that this is possible, given the particular situation, and of one who perhaps remedies grievances as much by listening to them as by merely satisfying one party of the dispute. In contrast, the average Oakland judge would apply a law to the case on the "black and white" evidence, irrespective of personal factors involved.

The Oakland-Piedmont court is in a large metropolitan center, and consequently many of those using it are representatives of business firms or companies in that area. Because its jurisdiction includes a large city, with all the law-breaking and delinquency problems associated with this, its schedule is a busy one, small claims taking up only a few minutes each day in a crowded agenda. The Berkeley-Albany court, on the other hand, is responsible for a more suburban area, where there are far fewer business firms, companies, etc., and where there is generally less litigation going on. [n.d.:11,10,12]

It is important for students of law in society to discover the social and cultural factors that determine the style of dispute proceedings. In the Zapotec situation, three interrelated factors influence the style of the court: (1) the aesthetic and emotional value placed on balance and equality, which is reflected in their ideas related to witchcraft, illness, and economics; (2) the facts of a multiplex, face-to-face society, which recognize that litigants have to be able to continue to live together; (3) the types of cases brought to the *presidente*'s court—that is, those that deal with human conduct. Both Yngvesson's work on the small claims courts and my own work on the Zapotec present special explanations of particular situations. A more general explanation may be sought in the hypothesis suggested in Pound's observations, which should be tested cross-culturally. It may indeed be the types of claims that directly affect the development of a style. Here we get into participation and into patterns of using the courts as they relate to molding courtroom behavior.

> Philosophically the apportionment of the field between rule and discretion which is suggested by the use of rules and of standards respectively in modern law has its basis in the respective fields of intelligence and intuition. Bergson tells us that the former is more adapted to the inorganic, the latter more to life. Likewise rules, where we proceed mechanically, are more adapted to property and to business transactions, and standards, where we proceed upon intuitions, are more adapted to human conduct and to the conduct of enterprises.
>
> In law, some situations call for the product of hands, not of machines, for they involve, not repetitions, where the general elements are significant, but unique events in which the special circumstances are significant. [Pound 1959:70]

My interest in this paper has been primarily descriptive, with comparison an end in mind. I argue that a comparison of styles of dispute settlement may lead us to discover similarities that cross-cut institutional differences (courts, moots, administrative agencies, negotiation proceedings), structurally different modes of dispute settlement (negotiation, adjudication, or mediation, arbitration, adjudication), and types of sanctions imposed (restitutive, repressive). If we begin to work out a typology of dispute settlement along the lines suggested, we will have a delineation by series of features whence we can begin to ask comparative questions, such as what determines or what are the principles underlying the style of dispute settlement. Such determinants may be a mixture of variables: statutes, the types of claims, values and attitudes about dispute, the social groupings in a society, and the personality of the judge. If we look carefully at styles of dispute settlement, we are bound to start viewing as a domain for study the gamut of dispute-settling agencies, rather than the strictly legal agencies—where the features rather than the type agencies (that is, court, noncourt) become of central concern in generating comparative questions.

Both Leach (1961) and Barth (1966) have commented that the purpose of comparison in social anthropology cannot merely be to name and classify, in a tradition of butterfly collection. Yet we have to do some naming and classifying at this stage of the game, for naming and classifying serve to order a wide array of data and to improve description—both necessary prerequisites to wide-scale comparison. Comparison need not await full developments in classification, but the future of any hypothesis testing and the search for determinants or principles in the anthropology of law will be enhanced by some general descriptions of components. If, in the process of developing a classification of styles of dispute settlement, the quality of description is improved, then the classification will have been worth the effort. If, in addition, we find the similarities in style crucial for understanding and specifying the determinants that generate forms or styles of dispute settlement, then all the better. At any rate, because we are in an early stage of development, a variety of methods ought to be explored.[6]

6. This paper has stimulated many an interesting conversation for me. Although I could not incorporate all the helpful suggestions in this version of the work, I am especially grateful for the comments received from Stanley Lubman, Richard Canter, Sylvia Forman, Claire Rosenfield, Harry Todd, and my associates in the Berkeley Department of Anthropology. A version of this paper was presented at a Social Relations Colloquium at Harvard University in April 1968.

Keresan Pueblo Law

Ruth Benedict's *Patterns of Culture* (1934) gave wide currency to an ideal version of the Pueblo cultures of New Mexico, in which an intense degree of social integration is maintained by personal internalization of norms of social cooperation. Pueblo society, as reported by Benedict, operates with a system of social control that is absolutely devoid of coercive physical sanctions. It has, in her terms, no law. This circumstance, if true, would be most significant, for with Pueblo cultures we are dealing with no rudimentary social systems, such as characterize primitive hunters and gatherers. The ceremonial and religious systems of the Pueblos have long evoked admiration for their colorful complexity. The intricacy of Pueblo kinship and the mystery of numerous secret organizations are such as to have denied full understanding to a succession of social anthropologists for nearly a century. Could it really be that such societies had found the secret of harmonious existence without law?

When, in 1943, Karl N. Llewellyn, then Betts Professor of Jurisprudence at Columbia University, and I were invited by the Honorable William Brophy, United States Commissioner of Indian Affairs, to undertake a study of the law of the Pueblos of New Mexico, the opportunity was not to be denied. Field work was carried out for seven successive summers, from 1944 through 1950. Professors S. Mentschikoff and Emma Corstvet also participated for two or more summers each. Most of our field data come from the Keres-speaking Pueblos of Sia and Santa Ana. Less intensive work was done in Santo Domingo, Laguna, and Jemez. Publication has been delayed in order to meet the injunction of our Pueblo friends "not to write anything that would hurt the Pueblo." It also seemed advisable to wait upon the publication of Leslie White's general ethnography of Sia (1962) to provide a fuller cultural background against which the following materials may be set.

The publication of a full-scale monograph, *Zuni Law: A Field of Values* by Watson Smith and John R. Roberts (1954), has already demonstrated in empirical detail the unreality and distortion of the Benedict formulation of Pueblo socialization so far as Zuni is concerned. The results of our Keresan researches parallel those arrived at by Smith and Roberts—the utilization of extreme forms of physical sanction applied by designated officials is a commonplace feature of societal maintenance in the Pueblo cultures of New Mexico.

Pueblo-Government Relations

Under the federal law of the United States, "The Indian tribes still posses their inherent sovereignty and power of self-government excepting only where it has been specifically taken away from them either by treaty or Congressional act" (Jamieson 1957:660). In the instance of the Pueblo Indians of New Mexico and Arizona, it had been held from the time of the acquisition of their territories from Mexico in 1846 until 1912 that they were not "Indians" within the usual meaning of the laws of the United States, but that as pueblos (villages) they were corporations acting under the laws of the Territory of New Mexico (Cohen 1942:385–388). No treaty was ever made between the United States and any Pueblo. Pueblo rights and grants derivative from the King of Spain were transferred unimpaired under the Treaty of Guadelupe Hidalgo (1848), which terminated the Mexican-United States War. With the admission of New Mexico and Arizona to statehood in 1912, control of Southwestern Indian affairs shifted from Santa Fe to Washington, and Pueblos were then administratively and legally defined as Indians—a position sustained by the United States Supreme Court in 1913 (United States 1913:28). This meant that all general laws of the United States government relating to Indians were henceforth applicable to them and at the same time that the jurisdiction of the states in which the Pueblos happened to be located did not extend to the Pueblos. Rather, the federal judiciary in the United States has steadfastly held, since the famous decision of Justice John Marshall in 1832 (*Worcester v. Georgia*), that Indian communities enjoy a limited right of self-government to administer justice among themselves according to their own principles, except for offenses that have been explicitly brought under the jurisdiction of the federal courts by act of congress.[1]

1. They are: assault with a deadly weapon, assault with intent to kill, first and second degree homicide, robbery, burglary, arson, rape, and incest.

As against the internal legal autonomy of the Pueblos, "It is a fact that state governments and administrative officials have frequently trespassed against the realm of tribal autonomy, presuming to govern the Indian tribes through state law or departmental regulation or administrative fiat, but these trespasses have not impaired the vested legal powers of self-government which have been recognized again and agaiı when these trespasses have been challenged by an Indian tribe" (Cohen 1942:125).

Three hundred years of Spanish rule, followed by one hundred years of American, have not been without impact on Pueblo culture. The very presence of state and federal courts, overly zealous administrators, and proselyting missionaries has been an influence that could not be ignored. These factors have definitely had an inhibiting effect upon the free exercise of authority and sanctions in the indigenous system. Since the time of the Spanish conquest, Pueblo officers have never been free from fear that they might be arrested or harassed for the punishments they impose in the exercise of their legal powers. At Zuni in 1897, for example, the five priests of the Bow Society were arrested and imprisoned for beating an old woman into a witchcraft confession. Three troops of cavalry were sent to the pueblo to forestall a possible outbreak in consequence (Pueblo Agency 1897:320).[2] In 1889 the Indian Agent at Albuquerque requested authority "to remove the present officials and replace them with other and better men," because "Pupils who have recently returned from Carlisle school, boys and girls, who refused to take off their [American] dress, have been forcibly stripped of their clothing, tied to a stake and whipped. Parents who refused to make their children put on Indian dress have been tied by their thumbs, hung to posts and flogged. Those who wanted to send their children to school have been subjected to a like indignity" (Pueblo Agency 1889b:46). This particular report brought a special investigator from Washington, who had the governor summarily arrested and jailed (Pueblo Agency 1889a:113).

A decade earlier, Agent Thomas had ordered the Pueblo of Isleta to stop burial of its dead in the churchyard in violation of the health laws of New Mexico Territory, threatening the pueblo governor: "If you do not obey the command I will have you and half of the men of the pueblo before the court for violation of the law and will see that you all suffer the full penalty of the law" (Pueblo Agency 1877:23). In 1879 he threatened the governor of Cochiti with court action if his pueblo did not cease punishment by "hanging and whipping, stocks etc." (Pueblo Agency 1879:101). The governor of San Felipe was ordered to rescind a penalty of confiscation of land that he had imposed upon a former governor for sending his children to school. "Such injustice will not be permitted for a moment" (Pueblo Agency 1882:302).

Arbitrary administrative trespasses against the legal autonomy of the

2. This case is also reported in Smith and Roberts (1954:46–47).

pueblo officers were common in the first decade following establishment of the Pueblo Agency in 1872. In the decade between 1910 and 1920, Courts of Indian Offenses were established in some pueblos by the Bureau of Indian Affairs and staffed by "progressives" chosen by the agents to act as judges. Indian police were also appointed, responsible to the agent. These legal authorities were intended to supersede the indigenous legal administrations, and the law they attempted to apply was not Pueblo law. Charles H. Burke, Commissioner of Indian Affairs, in 1921 quite erroneously informed Santo Domingo, Cochiti, Sandia, and Isleta delegates to Washington that "The powers of the Governor of the Pueblo are limited; it is necessary for him to follow the laws of the states as well as the laws of the Federal Government. The laws of the pueblo are necessarily subservient to the laws of the states and the laws of the Federal Government" (Pueblo Agency 1927).

In 1942 the Keresan Puebloans of the Rio Grande were still very much aware of the kangaroo courts [3] held in the 1920's by the United States District Judge at Albuquerque when the governor and council of Jemez pueblo resisted the construction of a day school in their pueblo. Judge Neblett had bluffed the governor into submission by threatening to send him and all his officials to prison (Pueblo Agency 1931).

In addition to the tendency of government administrators to limit the autonomy of the Pueblos, the repressive nature of pueblo government induces some Pueblo Indians to seek intervention by the Agency administration or by the state or federal courts. Finally, occasional Pueblo governors have themselves sought the easy way out of their problems of internal control by abdicating their judicial responsibility in favor of Spanish or American justices of the peace and of county courts, with their convenient jails.

Against this background in inhibiting experience, encouraged by a "new" (in 1934) Indian Office policy of greater tribal self-determination, officers of even the most conservative Keresan Pueblos were cautiously willing, when approached by us, to explore their legal domain to test its viable boundaries in the hope that their own powers might be made more secure.

Pueblo Social Structure

To understand the responsibilities, prerogatives, and functions of pueblo officers within the life of the Pueblos, it is necessary to review the major features of pueblo social structure and orientation.

3. "*Colloquial*—an unauthorized or irregular court conducted with either a disregard for or a perversion of legal procedure. As a mock court held by prisoners in a jail, or an irregularly conducted court in a frontier district" (Barnhart 1948:666).

The economic base of the Keresan system is that of intensive irrigation agriculture, supplemented by a small amount of rabbit and deer hunting, plus—and this is usually slighted in discussions of the pueblos —very heavy reliance on pastoralism (sheep, cattle, and horses). The mixed horticultural-hunting economy is nearly 2,000 years old. Pastoralism has been added since Spanish contact. A very elaborate and dramatic ritual and ceremonial system focused on fertility, rain-making, and curing is the Pueblos' response to their high-altitude desert environment.

The settlement pattern is that of tightly compacted masonry or adobe multiple-family house units, built around one or more central dance plazas. Most house units are components of a massive "apartment" structure; only a few are isolated, with open space about them. (The "Old Pueblo" at Santa Ana and Acoma is now used only for ceremonial purposes; people live in separated houses in new villages more accessible to a good water supply.)

If judgment were to be passed on the adaptive efficiency of Pueblo technology and social structure, they would rate very high on any scale. The record of archaeological continuity behind contemporary Pueblo culture extends to A.D. 300 (Basketmaker Culture); the Pueblo settlement pattern and basic social structure were elaborated between A.D. 700 and 1050. Then came the Great Period of cultural climax, which endured until an extreme and prolonged drought brought it to a close around 1300. When Coronado first arrived in the Southwest in 1542, there were still a number of heavily populated and flourishing pueblos, but the Pueblo domain was greatly shrunken when compared to its climax of 300 years earlier. The surviving Pueblos of today are but tenacious remnants of a great and exciting cultural efflorescence in a harsh but beautiful environment.

I have suggested a high adaptive rating for Pueblo cultures because of the developmental success of Pueblo cultures over their first millenium and because of their readaptation through successive centuries of devastating drought, intertribal wars, and repressive Spanish religious and political assault, followed by American immigration and administrative meddling. Their present legal practices are in large measure an expression of this adaptive history and success.

Contemporary Pueblo societies are miniscule populations. Sia, which had a population of several thousand in the sixteenth century, at the turn of this century had only 100. In 1960 it had risen to 300 (White 1962:34–36). Acoma's population of 2,000 was reduced to 200 in a massacre by Oñate in 1599. In 1702 Domingo was reduced to a population of 204 (Parsons 1939:11, 892). The story of other surviving pueblos is similar; but more pueblos have died than have survived.

The superstructure of ceremonial organization and priestly personnel, of governmental officials and centralized coercive power, that are carried to this day in the cultures of such minute societies is amazing, except as one keeps in mind the past and the present circumstances of the Pueblos. The structure was originally designed to organize and be managed by much larger populations than now struggle to carry it on. It is clear that for centuries the Pueblos welcomed innovation and change in a dynamic process of growth. Then, in 1300, came stabilization and a dogged conservatism in resistance to change and threatened extinction. Pueblo world view was well formulated and in it man is viewed as existing in precarious balance with his total environment. The ideological phrasing of this balanced relationship among men and their environment is remarkably uniform among all the Pueblos. Laura Thompson (1961: 189) has put it succinctly for the Hopi in the following terms:

> The cosmos is formulated as a living whole in which the subtly balanced relationships of the various parts to one another and to the multidimensional totality are similar to those which characterize living organisms. The parts and the whole are believed to transact for the good of all, according to a single, harmonious, immanent law. Man is a psychophysiological whole, differentiated from the rest of nature by his power of volition, which is an integral part of the scheme and is to be used for the commonweal. He cooperates with other men and with his nonhuman partners in fulfilling the law, through kinship and ceremonial groups. And to the main mechanism through which he expresses symbolically the cosmic process are ritual and art, reinforced by concentrated will-prayer.

Expressed more simply, a Sia Indian replied to my inquiry, "Yes, it's like the Hopi. If I would refuse the request to drum in the Fiesta, it would delay the answers to the people's prayers. There would be no rain. Or else too much rain would come and flood everything. It wouldn't come just right. It is a hard world that requires correct treatment."

The "organic" view described by Thompson and given wide popularity by Ruth Benedict (1934) is sound when perceived as a facet of a larger entity—that is, a culture that is a total lifeway and not just a world view divorced from a system of societal maintenance. It is unbalanced as an analytical approach to an understanding of Pueblo life when it is limited to a picture of Pueblo environmental adjustment as "a kind of glorious fulfillment of a unique world view, a master plan" (Bennett 1946:368).

The total cultural matrix within which a Pueblo system of social control operates, and in accordance with which this analysis of legal forms and processes is done, is found in the more comprehensive summary formulated by Edward Dozier, himself born and reared a Puebloan:

> The dominant integrating factor of Grande Pueblo culture is the view of the universe as an orderly phenomenon. People or things are not merely "good" or "bad." "Evil" is a disturbance in the equilibrium that exists be-

tween man and the universe, while "good" is a positive frame of mind or action that maintains harmonious balance.

To keep man and the universe in harmonious balance, all must work together and with "good" thoughts. Unanimous effort of body and mind is not only a key value, *but it is also enforced.* [italics added] . . . The cacique and the War Captains exert strict control over the activities of village members and see that all physically able members participate in a rigid calendric series of ceremonies. Among the members of a village there is serious concern over a neighbor's behavior and a perpetual watch is maintained over his or her activities. Any action, whether physical or verbal, which is construed by Pueblo authorities to be contrary to group concerns and unanimous will of the village is promptly and severely punished.

Rio Grande Pueblo culture thus makes rigorous demands on the individual and fills him with deep anxiety and suspicion toward his fellow men. Not only is his personal behavior and social interaction strictly circumscribed, but his thoughts as well are rigidly harnessed. He is constantly plagued by an apprehension that he or his fellow man may break the harmonious balance of the universe and bring illness, famine, or some other form of dreaded disaster. [Dozier 1961:122]

Contrary to the theses of Benedict, Thompson, and others, Pueblo thought control and behavioral conformity are not achieved by positive enculturation alone (see especially Bennett 1946, Barnouw 1963:40–48, Hoebel 1960). It is also managed by means of an insistent mechanism of public law, which in the Keresan pueblos is administered by a theocratic bureaucracy.

The quantitative mass of the Pueblo bureaucracy, which is huge relative to the size of the society, is a product of institutional survival from the period of cultural efflorescence plus response to the challenges for survival posed in the historic period. The utilization of this bureaucracy in social control has enabled the Pueblos to persist in the face of pressures that have disintegrated the cultures of most other American Indian tribes.

Keresan Bureaucracy

The units from which the permanent functionaries of Keresan Pueblo bureaucracy are drawn are: (1) households, (2) extended families, (3) clans, (4) medicine—or curing—societies, (5) hunting and warrior societies, (6) kiva-linked "clown" societies, (7) the Catholic Church. In addition, there are two sets of annually chosen officers who hold "at-large" positions; that is, their organizational affiliations are intrinsically irrelevant to their appointment, although in a given year structural affiliation may influence the choice of these officers. The annual at-large officers are: (1) the governor (*dapop*), lieutenant governor (*dapop teniente*), four governor's assistants (*capitani*); (2) the War Captain (*Masewi*) and his twin, *Oyoyewi* (they are named after and symbolically associated with the twin mythological culture-heroes who destroyed the monsters that once inhabited the Pueblo world), plus four or six War Captain's assistants (*gowatcanyi*); and (3) the *fiscale mayor,* the sexton who is responsible for the church and the Catholic aspects of public ceremonies, plus his lieutenant (*fiscale teniente*). The governor and his staff, together with the War Captain and his staff, are the day-to-day executive administrators of Keresan Pueblo law. In the exercise of administrative discretion the governor has a fairly wide range of personal power. The ultimate power, however, resides in a Sacerdotal Council, consisting of the heads of the several medicine societies and the cacique, or Town Priest-Chief, called *tiyamunyi;* he symbolizes the collective entity of the Pueblo and is the ultimate nexus of all activity—sacred and secular. "In the Kachina and medicine cults, and in the selection of officers, his position is preeminent. He is the center of the ceremonial configuration of the pueblo, the custodian of their most sacred customs and traditions, the fountainhead of the power by which the village lives" (White 1932:14).

In some Keresan pueblos the cacique is selected because he is the head of a specific medicine society. In Sia the office "should" be rotated among four clans in a specific sequence. In any event, it is bestowed for life— except that up to the twentieth century the cacique could be impeached for malfeasance by the War Priest. "A degraded cacique seldom, if ever, lives long. There is too much danger in suffering him who is in possession of the most precious arts and knowledge to live while under a cloud. . . . It is the War Captain who, officially at least, attends to such executions. But nobody except a few initiated ones ever know more than that the person had 'died' " (Bandelier 1890:284).

The cacique is freed from physical labor and is supported by the produce of certain fields that are communally cultivated on his behalf under the orders of *Masewi* (the First War Captain). Communal deer and rabbit hunts, directed either by Masewi or the head of the Hunt Society, if one is still active, provide him with meat. He holds surpluses for ceremonial feasts and for dispersal to the needy. He controls the ceremonial cycle and invests the "annual officers," who in the modern situation are his executive officers. He is thus not ordinarily directly involved in the administration of legal affairs.

Within the Keresan Pueblos there is a fluctuating tension over jurisdictional powers between the governor, on the one hand, and the First War Captain, on the other. A hundred years ago it appears that there was a War Priest who exceeded even the cacique in power and authority.

Subsequently, the War Captains gradually replaced the War Priest.[4] If witchcraft accusations are still carried out, they are made and tried by the War Captain. Offenses directly related to society and kiva duties are also dealt with under his direction if they become public affairs. He and his assistants have constituted the watch and ward of Keresan Pueblos from time immemorial. "The war captains," wrote White, in 1932, "keep a watchful eye on all persons to keep them in line and to forestall or punish any breach of ceremonial etiquette or violation of loyalty to the pueblo" (White 1932:15).

In 1942 White had discerned a new trend, however, which our trouble cases clearly document:

> The present writer believes that the office of governor has been increasing in importance during the past few decades and that it is destined to continue to increase in importance in the future. A few generations ago, the cacique, war priests, and medicine men were the important figures in the pueblo. Now the office of cacique is on the wane. The power of the priests and medicine men is doomed to decline as the old life gives way under the impact of American civilization. Contacts with the outside world . . . are made principally through the governor and tend to enhance his importance. Finally, there is the tendency within the pueblo . . . to secularize pueblo government and administration, to take it out of the hands of the priests and medicine men, and concentrate it in the hands of the governor. [White 1942:107–108]

Keresan Justice

The most distinctive feature of Pueblo law, among tribal systems, is that there is no private law.[5] No man or family or clan has the privilege-right of legally exacting a penalty against another. All legal power is centralized in the official bureaucracy, and all procedure must move through it. This does not mean that all cases of grievance and discord come before the War Captain or governor for action. On the contrary, a governor does not intrude in intrafamilial or interpersonal quarrels unless a complaint is brought to him by one of the parties or unless a dis-

4. Much confusion has been generated by the fact that the two War Captains were originally subordinate to a War Priest-Chief who was a lifetime officer outranking even the Town (peace) Chief, or *cacique*. The office of War Priest-Chief has been defunct for some time. When we speak of the War Captain, we refer to Masewi. Ellis (1951) has done much to clarify the confusion.

5. By law we mean: "A social norm is legal if its neglect or infraction is regularly met, in threat or in fact, by the application of physical force by an individual or group possessing the socially recognized right of so acting" (Hoebel 1954:28). Public law is that law in which the privilege-right of enforcement is vested in a public officer rather than in an aggrieved private individual or group.

ruptive public disturbance ensues. Whatever War Priests and Captains may have done in the past, household affairs remain household affairs, to be settled on the household level.

Thus a former governor of Santa Ana explained: "When I was made governor I told them all frankly right then. I said, 'What you do in your house, that is yours, that is not for me. But what you do in the plazas or in the alleys or outside on the Reservation, or what you do in another pueblo, that is for me. That is under my authority, and there you must obey me. I shall not work for myself or for my family. I am governor for the whole pueblo and for the good of the whole pueblo.'"

Most roles in Pueblo culture are rigidly status-defined. To indulge in behavior that goes with a status into which one has not been ritually inducted is exceedingly dangerous; it opens one to the charge of witchcraft. Those who possess ritual knowledge by privilege-right are priests and officers. People who have no such knowledge are *hano sicti*, laymen.

Just as in the Tewa Pueblo of San Ildefonso "Both men and women fear the possession of unauthorized knowledge" (Whitman 1947:117), to say of a person, "He knows something," means he knows something he has no right to know—hence, he is a witch.

In the Keresan judicial process (and policy-making) a sharp distinction is drawn between *tʃikiumi*, authoritative official statements, and *tʃamanu*, personal opinion. *Tʃi* means sacred, or inside, as in *tʃikya*, kiva, and *tʃi'kami*, medicine society. *Tʃa* means outside. Outside talk is dangerous and to be avoided. Thus the very best of informants who would discuss their actions in cases in great detail for the periods when they were governors would profess to know nothing about what happened after they had turned the office over to their successors. Or they would simply say, "You'll have to ask X about that. He was governor that year."

Although it is true that the governor's office was established by the Spanish, it was legitimatized immediately, in Sia at least, by the question's being referred to Utset—the Mother Creator, who authorized the *tʃiamunyi* to install the governor and his staff as established officers of the pueblo.

All Pueblo officers have short batons as insignia of office—staffs that "are sprinkled with meal or with 'holy water' and have a distinctly fetishistic character" (Parsons 1933:620).[6] This was apparently perceived by the Spaniards, who provided the governor of each pueblo with a silver-headed cane as warrant of authority from the King of Spain. In 1863 the United States government provided similar canes in the name of President Lincoln. Possession of the canes is an absolute essential to performance of the governor's role; refusal to give up the canes has been

6. Parsons surmised that Pueblo staffs were but one of many basic Mexican traits that had diffused northward in prehistoric times.

the focal act of several factional fights in non-Keresan pueblos (French 1948; Fenton 1957).

Anything the governor does under the aegis of the canes is *tʃikiumi*, authoritative. Authority as vested in a person is called *stutsuitchatni* (*stutsu*, right + *tʃa*, have + *ini*, I). At the Sia Corn Dance (Fiesta) of 1946 a disturbed returned veteran, who had been contaminated by contact with the Japanese enemy, challenged the authority of the lieutenant governor to confiscate the whiskey he was publicly drinking. The lieutenant hauled him into the dance plaza before the governor. When the angry young man talked back, the governor removed his canes from their place on the wall of the bower that houses the saint and, shaking them in the face of the miscreant, "gave him the word." The veteran stamped off over the desert without his liquor.

At Santa Ana in 1940 the governor was called in the deep of night to subdue two rowdy young drunks (one, the acting cacique's son). They resisted and challenged his authority.

> I had the cacique roused from bed at 3 A.M. "What does the cacique say?" I demanded. "Does the governor have authority? If the governor has no authority, he is going to turn in his canes right now. When I received the canes, did anyone object? Am I the governor?" The cacique avowed that I was indeed the governor and ordered the boys to kneel before me and to apologize. "Now," I said, "if it happens again, there will be no question and no forgiveness."

In this case, no further punishment was imposed—or needed.

The authority of the governor is symbolized not only by the sacred canes, but also by his cat-o'-nine-tails. This is transferred to him along with the canes at the time of his ritual installation on New Year's Eve. At Sia, on the opening fall term of the United States Indian Service day school in the late 1940's the governor addressed the pupils in the presence of the two female teachers, whip in hand, admonishing the children, "My authority goes with these teachers right into this schoolroom. You must obey them. If you do not, they can come to me, and this whip will back them up."

There is also an exorcistic quality to whipping. A governor of Santa Ana developed a case of chronic headache from worrying over "something." The cacique told him he had failed in his duty to keep the church jail in condition. "He made me kneel before him and he whipped me. Then I was all right."

The actual use of the whip as a legal penalty is now done most circumspectly, for fear of punishment of the officers by nonpueblo agencies. In the early phases of our fieldwork it was flatly denied that there is any whipping. Subsequently it was readily acknowledged, and the pueblo of Santa Ana readily accepted a written procedural code in 1949 that carefully spelled out the limited application of the whip as a legal penalty; other Keresan pueblos, in considering written codes, took the sections on whipping as a matter of satisfaction. Traditionally a severe public beating of adulterers, male and female, was regular practice in all Keresan pueblos. In the 1920's and 1930's it still was in one of the Keresan pueblos in which we did not do fieldwork. In January 1922 the Field Matron at Cochiti reported:

> Ventura U. is causing much talk and disturbance of late. Her husband has taken his possessions and gone to the home of his mother. Ventura is continually with another man, Santiago C. Last week they went away together with wagon and team, were gone the entire week returning last night. . . . I am told that Indians last night [one day later] held court, hung and whipped the above offenders, and the home is again restored, husband and wife having gone back together. [Pueblo Agency 1922]

In 1933 a private grudge brought forth charges leading to a fornication and support-of-child trial, with whipping, hanging, damages, and maintenance-of-the-child penalties. The following is a partial transcript of the hearing of a complaint brought to the Agency Superintendent by the penalized defendant, Juan B. G. The testimony is by J. B. G. but recorded in the third person as it was spoken by the interpreter:

Q: What was he charged with?
A: He was charged with getting in trouble with one of the girls up there.
Q: How did they punish him at that time?
A: They gave him a trial and he didn't admit the guilt the first time, so they forced him to admit it by hanging him up, tying his wrists, and while he was hanging there he was given four lashes with a whip.
Q: How long did they leave him hanging there?
A: He hung there somewhere near two hours—a long time anyway.
Q: Were his feet clear off of the floor?
A: His feet were off the floor about so far [indicating about a foot and a half].
Q: Were they hanging him up at that time in order to force him to admit his guilt?
A: Yes, they forced him to.
Q: What does he mean, that they wouldn't let him down until he did admit it?
A: They wouldn't let him down until he said "yes."
Q: What happened then?
A: They gave him this whipping and let him down and they fined him.
Q: How much?
A: He gave one of those black things the ladies wear, a black skirt. He paid one of those, and paid one of those belts, a shawl, a buckskin, a piece of land and——
Q: Was that all the land he had?

A: No, he has a little bit more. And then he gave them one horse, and one sack of flour. That was his fine. They took all those articles from him, including his land.

Q: What happened next?

A: They took the land away from him and then they let him cultivate the land, sow wheat, raise corn or something on it every year but everything that grows from that land has to go to the baby.

Q: What happened after that?

A: That was first, then they dismissed it. Then less than a week ago, sometime after the Fiesta up there, of course he was walking around the village and talking to a lot of boys and all the boys asked him what happened at his trial and of course he told them. The other boys spread it around among the Councilmen and just for that reason they called him in again last week. You know who did it all, that big fellow.

Q: What was he charged with at the second trial?

A: For telling the other young men what happened before.

Q: What did they do to him the second time?

A: They just hung him up again.

Q: Was he entirely off the floor again?

A: Yes, in the same way.

Q: How long did they keep him that way?

A: Until the early hours of the morning.

Q: From what time to what time?

A: He estimates around three hours, but they didn't whip him any more.

Q: That was merely punishment for his telling?

A: Yes.

Q: Was anything said when they let him down this time?

A: When they let him down they warned him if he told some more stuff on them they will catch him again and hang him again.

The witness then testified that he told the governor that he was going to report him. To which the governor replied to go ahead.

Q: He has mentioned some one fellow as being responsible for his being called up both times. Who is he?

A: His name is J. M., not the old man but the other one.

Q: Is he a member of the Council?

A: Yes, he is the main guy.

Q: Does he hold any office?

A: He doesn't hold any kind of office, but is a member of the Council.

Q: Has this man and J. B. G. ever had any trouble before to cause him to want to punish this man?

A: The reason why J. M. is doing this is because it is his relative that got the baby.

Q: What relation is this girl to J. M.?

A: Sister-in-law. J. M. is married to this girl's sister.

Q: How old is this girl?

A: She must be around 27.

Q: Was she present at the first trial? Did she make the statement that he was responsible for getting her into this trouble?

A: Yes, she blamed him, because they already instructed her before they came to the meeting what to say.

Q: Was there any other evidence at the first trial other than this girl's statement?

A: No, there wasn't any other evidence. They forced him to admit it, but he says that it is not his baby, absolutely not. "I say yes just because I was hanging there and I was tired. I had to say something," he says. He told me often that if they would let him down he would give them anything that they wanted.

Q: Has he ever had any relations with this girl?

A: He says he has never touched her once.

Q: Why does he think they picked on him as being responsible if he never had anything to do with her?

A: The only reason they accuse him of this is because he had trouble with J. M. last summer. He fought with him in the field somewhere. J. M. was irrigating that day and when he got through irrigating he shut the water off. Then he went away a short distance and pretty soon he came and wanted to take the water back again. Then he wouldn't let him and he struck him and then the fight started. He says he tore his shirt up, J. M.'s, and ever since he has been trying to get even with him. That is the only thing.

Q: They haven't actually taken his land away from him, but they are going to have him cultivate it and give all the proceeds to this baby, is that right?

A: Yes.

Q: Is that just for this year, or henceforth?

A: As long as the baby lives.

Q: If the baby should die, the land and crops go back to him?

A: They didn't decide that.

Q: All of these other things that he gave as fine, were they given to this girl or to J. M.?

A: To J. M. for the girl. She stays under the same roof.

Q: What does this boy want done?

A: He says he wants your opinion, what do you think about it. He has been hung two times now just for absolutely nothing. He has been trying to work but he thinks he has been hurt in his chest. He is having trouble with his chest and lungs and his hands are crippled up so he can't do any hard work. [Pueblo Agency, 1933]

No further records of this case were found, and we do not have the governor's side of the story. However, the account fits the context of the broader body of data. Although the best of Pueblo officers are devoted to the proposition that a man must set aside his family and personal interests as governor, there is ample evidence that personal grudges and antipathy are frequently the reasons for which a governor seizes the opportunity to prosecute a case. In this instance a private fight over water rights built up into a complaint for damages and maintenance as the means of getting even—presumably J. M. did not have a case in the matter of the ditch fight. We can feel quite sure, however, that the governor and Council went along with J. M.'s demands, not just because J. M. was a "big man on the Council" (which means he was a principal or ex-officer), but also because the Council wanted to put severe pressure on the defendant for other reasons. The fact that he was not dancing in the Fiesta, blabbered to the boys, and went outside the pueblo to complain to the Agency Superintendent indicates that he was a "progressive" recalcitrant who was halfway to being tried as a witch. Thus the extreme physical punishment was for the presumptive criminal aspect of his misbehavior. The punitive damages awarded the mother and child are nominally what we in our law would call compensation for tort, with overtones of a criminal fine.

In 1935, Pablo Sanchez [fictitious name] left his pueblo to marry and live with a Mexican girl living in a nearby Keresan pueblo. He was then a young man with no living relatives; hence no kin ties in his home pueblo.

The governor of his own pueblo for the year ordered him back. A person may not leave his pueblo without permission of the governor because of community work duties. When Pablo refused, the governor had the Agency cut him off the Emergency Conservation Works, a depression program of the U.S. Government rolls. Pablo returned to his home pueblo and was reinstated on the work rolls without the governor's help.

"When I came back here with my wife, I wanted to find a piece of land in the Pueblo up on the mesa to build a house. I couldn't find none nowhere, it seems." His Mexican wife would not be permitted to live in the pueblo. . . .

His next step was to by-pass the governor, who usually allots new land from the public domain, which is then confirmed by the cacique. Instead, "I asked the cacique for some land down here [just below the village]. He said, "Ok." I staked it out. Then *he* called a council meeting, that old man. Right there he said to everyone, "I am giving that piece of land to my son. If anyone has any objection, I want them to speak it out right now. I don't want anyone to say *anything* to him after I am gone." No one said a word.

"Then I started to build this house right here. One day when I was well started, that old man came by from those fields over there. 'Grandson,' he said, 'you are sure building a nice house.'

" 'Thank you, grandfather,' I said. Then he went right up the hill over those rocks there [toward the pueblo]. Halfway up, he turned and waved, just like he was saying goodbye. The very next day he was dead.

"Three days later, a certain fellow (the former governor) rode down here. 'What do you think you are doing here?' he said to me. He started to object to my building there. 'You heard what the old man said,' I told him. 'He didn't want anyone to raise any objections after he was gone. If you want to raise a fuss, take it up with the Council.' He went away and I never heard anything more about it."

Subsequently, as the father of six children, in order to assure deferred status in the draft, Pablo temporarily moved to California for a job in war industry. He wrote the 1944 governor affirming his desire to continue doing his duty in the pueblo as he had always done, but asking to be excused from community work in favor of paying "a fine" instead.

The 1944 governor informed me that he talked it over with his first lieutenant but did not take it up with the Council, because someone, namely the ex-governor might insist that Pablo be ordered back to do his work. The 1944 governor, with an eye to the precedent-setting implications of his decision, decided to deny the request for a substitute payment, "because ——— is a poor Pueblo and such a practice would become a burden on the people." However, he had additional reasons involving the Herrera case (see pp. 112–114 below) for not wanting the idea of cash payments in lieu of community work to get established. Instead, he informed Pablo that his work would be deferred and he would be given special jobs in equivalence when he returned after the war. This was done. A sound and equitable principle was thus established by the 1944 governor and continued by his 1945 successor.

When Pablo returned from California in 1946, however, his old enemy was once again governor; ditch work for that year had already been done. "I decided to put in some corn for my children's sake. It was too late for wheat. That governor cut me off from water without warning. He was just mad at me for ten years ago. He treated me just like then." So Pablo moved to the nearby Spanish-American town where he could live with his wife's relatives.

Two days before the Fiesta in August 1946, Pablo was visited by his Pueblo's War Captain and "twin." Pablo was second ranking officer of the *Koshare* [the so-called clown society] and had himself once served as War Captain. He was informed by his visitors that he was need to dance *Koshare*. Either that, or he would be extruded from the Pueblo forever.

" 'What is the trouble?' they asked me. I told them. 'You are right. The governor has no right to treat you like that. After the Fiesta we are going to take this thing before the council. We will back you up.' "

Pablo returned to his home in the pueblo. He danced *Koshare*. The War Captain convened the Council and took a stand against the governor, who had to back down. The next year [1947] Pablo was appointed Lieutenant Governor. The following year he bought the most famous drum in Cochiti so that his oldest boy could grow up to become a drummer in his own Pueblo. In 1950, he had let his hair grow long and was again Lieutenant Governor—and bursting with pride in his work! [Informants: P.S. and J.M., 1944 Governor]

It will have been noticed that in Pablo's case none of the governors invoked "the Council" to sit as a judicial body; but the War Captain did. A peculiarity of Keresan Pueblo law is the wide leeway in discretionary administrative practice allowed the governor and War Captain. Equally flexible is the constituted personnel that may make up any particular "council."

Two basic rules seem to be at work: (1) no more people should be involved in judging or settling a case than is minimally necessary—cere-

monial duties and field work are so demanding that diversion of manpower should be avoided; (2) quarrels poison the mind and interfere
with the "good thoughts" that are necessary for effective ceremonials
—and Keresans easily get emotionally violent. So it is that people with
small complaints go first to one of the governor's assistants rather than
to the governor with cases that include such matters as petty theft, damages done by wandering animals, and minor car accidents.[7] If the lieutenant and one of the governor's assistants can get the defendant to
pay acceptable damages, the case goes no further. If they fail, and the
plaintiff is insistent, the matter will be taken to the governor. The governor, in turn, makes his own inquiries and issues a judgment.

In the instance of alleged delicts for which the damages or penalty
can normally be expected to be heavy, the careful governor calls in
from two to four *principales* to sit with him as a "council." It is, in fact,
an investigatory commission, which makes its own inquiry and renders
its own decision. In cases in which the convicted defendant fails to pay
the imposed damages or fine, the governor may, after consultation with
the society heads and other officers, decide to convene the full Council.
He thus has prior assurance that he has the backing of the important
men of the pueblo. Adultery and illegitimacy cases, in particular, are
apt to receive the treatment of the full Council—as are criminal cases
involving failure to perform communal duties. Minor delicts are identified as *lepma*, something bad or evil, + *tsowit'tsa'ni*, have done I.
Major delicts are *metsi*, big, *lepma tsowit'tsa'ni*. The emphasis is clearly
on individual culpability.

Incorporation of nonnative members of any pueblo as citizen-residents
requires petition to the full Council by the migrant, after initial approval
and presentation by the governor. Keresan Pueblos are in their official
ideals strongly endogamous (see Lange 1959:18–19, 411–412). To bring
in a spouse from outside the pueblo requires Council approval upon a
request submitted by the head of the family into which the newcomer
is marrying. Acceptance by the Council is followed by ritual incorporation by the cacique. A person marrying in from another pueblo is normally
granted full citizenship immediately. A Mexican, such as Pablo's wife
in the case given above, will not be permitted to live in the pueblo for
a number of years. An Anglo (American white) is ordinarily allowed to
live in the pueblo with the spouse so long as no hostility to the Pueblo
way of life is sensed. Nonetheless, the outsider is barred from all non-
public ceremonies until thoroughly proven.

7. "Last year, I was driving my wagon down from Sam Ysidra. Three boys from
this pueblo were a little drunk. They hit my car and their wagon went in the ditch.
When I got back in the pueblo I went right to the governor and told him what happened and that I wanted damages. He said, 'You want me to settle this thing?' We
agreed. If either of us wanted, it could have gone to the whole Council, but little
things should be taken care of by the governor or his lieutenant."

The Council convened by a War Captain ordinarily consists of the heads of Medicine Societies and the cacique. This is the Council that tries witches and those who refuse to dance in the ceremonies. Whatever the composition of the Council for a given situation (be it judicial or policy making), it is called *hotsenji* (*ho*, highly sacred or mystic, + *tsenji*, ?). The hearing, or trial, is called *hosti*. We were able to be present at two trials before Council; additional data are from *principales*. The setting is usually in the governor's or the War Captain's house; or if the case is of extreme seriousness, in the official residence of the cacique (there is traditionally no other "public" assembly hall). The demeanor of all concerned is most serious. Passions can run very high as the case proceeds, and red-hot anger can lead to vehement speeches and, literally, breast beating. But only one person speaks at a time. The presiding officer (governor or War Captain) opens the proceedings with a statement of the case, including the position he and his staff have taken if it is a criminal case. *In these instances, he or the War Captain are definitely public prosecutors and magistrates, seeking judicial review and acceptance of their findings and judgment.* The Council members sit around the walls of the room in the area farthest from the entrance. Litigants and witnesses face them. Litigants may be advised and assisted by kinsmen or members of their own Medicine Society, who are (at Sia, at least) always invited as a matter of courtesy. There is no swearing in, no conditional curse or oath-taking. Confession and admission of guilt on the part of the defendant are pressed for—and with great pressure. In a desertion case observed at Laguna Pueblo in August 1944, the defendant was harangued for six hours, until he broke down and agreed to reconciliation with the complainant, his wife. "We would have stayed there all night until he gave in. We would have kept it up three days and nights without stopping. If necessary, for a week." This occurred in the most progressive and modernized pueblo. Where traditional methods have been used, hanging from the rafters and beating gets quicker results. Up to the twentieth century incarceration in stocks in a jailroom in the mission church was also used. According to a pueblo *principale:* "And they would fasten a man with his neck in a log, his hands bound together so he could not move. Sometimes eight days without food or drink, until nothing was left but skin and bones. Nobody took care of him. He had to piss and shit right where he lay. Then they would bring him before the Council to promise to do what the Council said. We learned this from Old Mexico. They advised us. When the Americans came, they advised us differently." In "offenses against the public good," wherein action has been initiated by the governor or War Captain, the mere hailing before the Council is in itself evidence of guilt. The prosecuting official has held intensive preliminary consultations with enough of the important members to be assured of their concurrence. The object of the trial is to achieve an official confession and recantation called *tsaitsi tsawia* (*tsaitsi,* totally, all, + *tsa* + *via,* I blame).

Whether these techniques of the Spanish Inquisition and totalitarian police states were pre-Spanish is irrelevant; they fit the ethos and purposes of the Pueblo theocracy. It is possible, however, that a traditional ritual pattern in witchcraft trials among the Keresan Pueblos was more indigenous. The culprit was made to stand within a three-foot cornmeal circle while being unceasingly interrogated. If he fainted or stepped outside the circle, he is said (by my informants) to have been forthwith shot by one of the War Captains, who stood by with drawn bow and arrow throughout the entire trial. When he confessed, he was subsequently executed. To be charged with witchcraft was to be sentenced to death.[8]

Suppression of deviationism and heresy are primary legal concerns for all Pueblos (Hoebel 1960), but enforcement of the duty to perform community work is the focal concern of contemporary Keresan Pueblo law. Apart from participation in the dances, which is also a universal obligation, all able-bodied Pueblo men are required: (1) to cultivate the cacique's field; (2) to join in the deer and rabbit hunts to fill the cacique's larder; (3) to help replaster the Catholic church; (4) to sweep the village plaza for ceremonies; and above all, (5) to join in cleaning and repairing the irrigation ditches each spring, or at any additional times determined by the governor (as at Sia) or the ditch boss (as at Santa Ana). Women share in the last three duties.

On the basis of the evidence, the Wittfogels' and Dozier's assessments of the importance of the irrigation technology for the Rio Grande Pueblos are valid. Dozier's summary is appropriate:

> The Rio Grande Pueblos are located along the Rio Grande and its tributaries and depend upon diverting the waters of these streams into their fields for farming activities. The climate is arid; the annual average rainfall is frequently less than ten inches. Moreover, the limited quantity of rain may not always fall when needed, or may fall in such torrents that crops are uprooted and destroyed. It has been necessary, therefore, in the past and at present to employ irrigation of some sort in order to insure a successful harvest. Unlike the Hopi and Zuni and the several prehistoric regions whence

8. See Hoebel 1952:586–589 for details on Keresan witchcraft. "In his entry of June 21, 1886, Bandelier recorded that the death penalty for practicing witchcraft was certain. He noted that the sentence was carried out secretly and that afterward the information of it was communicated secretly to 'all the other tribes.' He was told that some five or six years before, two witches were killed at Zia 'in a quiet way.' 'They did not use poison but clubbed them to death'" (Lange 1959:254). (I was personally told in Sia that "everyone who helped Mrs. Stevenson somehow died within three years.") The news of these deaths was deliberately spread as far as Taos in 1881 (Miller 1898:92).

the ancestors of the Rio Grande Pueblos might have come, the Rio Grande region provides a permanent water supply. Hopi and Zuni depend more directly on rainfall for flood irrigation, or on springs. The tasks of clearing, terracing, braking, damming, and ditching thus require greater communal effort among the Rio Grande Pueblos. Among the Hopi and Zuni, and probably among the prehistoric Indians, irrigation for crops may have been done by small families or kin groups, perhaps lineage and clan members. In the Rio Grande area, the task of bringing the water to fields, located sometimes at considerable distance from the main streams, requires a large number of individuals, particularly since the technological achievements were simple. Women were required in most pueblos, until recently, to help in maintaining and constructing irrigation ditches.

Large-scale co-operation on irrigation projects has important implications for the nature of Rio Grande Pueblo socio-political and ceremonial organization. These implications have been recently elaborated by K. A. Wittfogel for oriental society and for ancient America (Wittfogel 1957). Wittfogel and Goldfrank (1943) have also presented a provocative article in which the importance of irrigation is discussed with respect to the nature of Pueblo societies. Cautioning that no proof is yet available in the Southwest that the introduction of large scale waterworks had made revolutionary changes in Pueblo societies, the authors report: "If the Pueblos represent a waterwork society in miniature, then we should look for certain authoritative forms of civil and magic leadership, for institutionalized discipline, and a specific social and ceremonial organization." [Dozier 1961:20]

We have already seen how the issue of deferment from ditch work became critical in the case of Pablo Sanchez. In 1924 one Joseph Melchor, a Cochiti Progressive, suffered the penalty of being stripped of his Pueblo land holdings (the governor's staff also tore up all his fences) for refusal to work on a ditch from which he personally drew no water. He professed willingness to work on the ditch that supplied his fields, but not on others. His position rested on the self-centered proposition that community service is an obligation limited by the direct *individual* benefits received. In opposition to this, the fundamental legal postulate of Pueblo law is: *all persons are obligated to the maintenance of the whole as such.* Melchor also refused to dance in the solsticial ceremonies at Christmas time. Intervention on his behalf by the Pueblo Agent in Albuquerque led to a compromise settlement according to which Melchor was reinvested with his land and excused from work on the ditch from which he drew no water; but he was not excused from dancing, sweeping the plaza, and other communal duties (Pueblo Agency 1923). Melchor, who was able to overpower the Cochiti governor and the Superintendent, too, went on to collect $500 damages from the United States Office of Indian Affairs.

In 1909 several Jemez men were whipped for failure to do their ditch work (Pueblo Agency 1909). In fact, there is no Pueblo that is free of "ditch trouble" cases. Interestingly enough, however, except for the J. M. case, we have no evidence of quarrels over water rights between individuals. The distribution of water seems to be so effectively controlled by the central bureaucracy as to keep this potential difficulty to mimimal levels.

Shutting a person off from water is, as already shown in the Sanchez case, an immediate and powerful weapon of control in the hands of a governor or Council seeking to avoid the hazards of engaging in whipping or prosecution for witchcraft in the modern setting.

The case of the Sia "Holy Rollers" is worth discussion as a concluding instance. Various aspects of this case have been previously published by Hawley (1948) and White (1962:67–77); its details need not be spelled out here, except where the legal implications of the matter call for them or where we have additional relevant information not given by the two previous investigators.

In 1928 a Pentacostal woman preacher from California came to the attention of a Sia silversmith, George Herrera, who was frequenting Albuquerque. Herrera had lost his wife in childbirth, and he was drawn to the preaching of Mrs. Crawford in a small Albuquerque congregation, which was mostly Negro. He was, according to his own written account (Herrera n.d.), impressed by her power to cure illness. After instruction by a male member of the congregation, George Herrera returned to Sia. "Then three days after that I received the Holy Ghost in my mother['s] house. . . . I was shaking and I felt the restling wind blowing and hear the sound of the wind blowing and the Holy Ghost spoke to me." After repetition of the experience on the next night, "I couldn't stand it, couldn't hear the words to keep them to myself without telling my people."

He went to L. M., that year's War Captain, asking him to convene the Sacerdotal Council, "the head of all the Indian doctors or priests for me to tell them the message I got and for them what they could think of it." Instead, L. M. called in the governor to hear the story. The governor did not pass the message on to the people, so Herrera gave them the word when they were assembled for Sunday mass. He also had his "teacher" come into the pueblo to preach a number of times.

George Herrera continued to dance in the ceremonies and to do his community work until August 12, 1933, when he stayed away from the practice in the kiva for the forthcoming Corn Dance (Fiesta). The *Koshare* came to get him, but he refused to accompany them. The *Koshare* reported his resistance to the War Captain, and the day after Fiesta was over, the War Captain *and* the governor called a full Council at which George Herrera and his classificatory brother, Viviano Herrera (now also a convert), were asked to recant and to resume participation in the Pueblo religion. They stood fast in their refusal. The Council then ruled that they were never again to enter the mission church, nor could they be given a Pueblo burial (burial involves the services of the Flint Medicine Society). The Pueblo churchyard was to be closed to them for burial. Furthermore, they were ordered not to plant crops on their land, which would henceforth revert to the Pueblo. They were shut off from irrigation water and were told that they must remove their horses and cattle from the Sia range. The judgment was one of total extrusion and denial of a livelihood in the pueblo. "And the people were told in front of us that we are condam [sic] throwing out of Sia like throwing out on the ash pile and even ladies were let known" (Herrera n.d.).

The Herreras stood pat. In spite of their disabilities, they stayed in the Pueblo and went on with their proselyting in utter defiance of the Council. In 1934 another hearing before the War Captain, governor, and staffs (but no full Council) was held, and again recantation was sought and rebuffed. This was apparently the occasion concerning which Hawley reports George Herrara as telling her. "There was even some talk around of the old punishment. This punishment was formerly meted out by the cacique, aided by the war captains, to any villagers who gave information on secret matters. A woman's woven belt was tied around the culprit's waist and the men pulled the belt until he was crushed to death—'or until he was cut in two.' Then his head was cut off and tossed on top of a house. [To Hawley's protest that this could not happen to Herrera] . . . he agreed, although it had been done in his father's time, but suggested that it would not be difficult for the village authorities to arrange" (Hawley 1948:275).

The Herreras' ties to the outside world were too conspicuous for such action to be risked, however, and they were physically safe. In the face of the Herreras' determination to ignore the official sanctions there was seemingly nothing the Pueblo could do. In April 1936 the Pentacostals, now numbering twenty-one, were all called before the Lieutenant Governor's Council and again asked to recant. For the third time they refused; the banishment was renewed—and ignored. The Lieutenant Governor was L. M., the onetime War Captain who was first involved in the case and who as governor was giving Pablo Sanchez such a bad time. L. M. is a strong officer.

In 1939 L. M. was made governor, and William Brophy, then Special Attorney for the Pueblos, was drawn into the case to assist the Pueblo officers toward a final resolution. Mr. Brophy first tried to persuade George Herrera to remove his following from the Pueblo. Herrera understood Brophy to mean that they could relocate on Pueblo lands outside the village. He agreed to this. But when he learned from the governor that the Pueblo intent meant outside of the Sia grant entirely, he reneged.

Finally, on March 1, 1939, a fourth hearing was convened by the governor with full Council. Legal guidance was provided the Council by the Special Attorney for the Pueblos. The Pentacostals came, but they refused to testify. Like martyrs, they sabotaged the proceedings by singing and by crying "Jesus" and "Hallelujah." In spite of the disturbance, a trial record was carefully laid to define the required community work as *citizens' obligations performed in lieu of taxes.* For failure to "pay taxes" over a decade the Pentecostals were ruled by the Council to have forfeited their rights of citizenship, including the privilege of holding Pueblo lands and of living in the Pueblo. This judicial holding rests upon the fundamental postulate that Utset, the founding culture creator, vested all Pueblo land in the Pueblo per se.

From this is derived the corollary of Pueblo usage: no individual may claim ownership of any Pueblo land qua individual. Any plot assigned to a family head is then transmissible to successive family heads in univeral succession (see Gluckman in this volume), for which the Sia term is *diwait ukwaini* (etymology unknown). It involves a perpetual right of use vested in a family line and bilaterally inheritable, but subject to revocation if for any reason the family permanently leaves the village. Like the Barotse and many other primitive gardeners, "If you leave the village, you lose your gardens in it." The Sia council took its stand on the proposition: extrusion from the pueblo nullifies all claims to a share in the pueblo estate. Therefore, the ruling held, since the land on which the homes of the Pentecostal families stood is owned by Utset, there could be no monetary compensation for the loss of use of these plots. Likewise, the earth and stone materials of which the homes were constructed are part of the unalienable pueblo earth; ergo, no compensation for the walls and plastered floors of the houses. However, the ceiling beams had been brought down from the mountains outside the Pueblo grant and are therefore private property; likewise, the doors and windows, which had been purchased from a mail-order house. The Herreras and their associates were given the option of leaving the beams, doors, and windows for liberal compensation or of tearing them out to take away with them. As for the gardens, there could be no compensation for the land but (with an eye to possible outside reaction and sense of justice) fair compensation would be paid for such "improvements" as fencing and grading as had gone into the land through personal effort. Privilege of access to communal range land by Herrera herds and use of water from the communal ditch was again formally nullified.

George Herrera was still stubbornly defiant, but he was given three months' grace to move or dispose of his herds and properties in the pueblo. He and his brother moved out to Albuquerque, but others of the converts remained quietly in the pueblo. In 1948 officers were chosen who were committed to a policy of cleaning up the issue for good. A final hearing was held; [9] the heretics living in Sia were given one last chance to recant or accede to the pueblo's terms: some capitulated, others of the holdouts agreed to leave the pueblo.

George and Viviano Herrera, backed by their church, entered suit against the governor and the Pueblo of Sia in the United States District Court for the District of New Mexico in November 1947, but their case was nonsuited for lack of jurisdiction.

The Herrera heresy is three generations deep. The family line to which most of the Pentecostal converts from Sia belong is descended from Lorenzo Shije, who is said by Sians to have been the leader of the conclave of witches described in my earlier note on Keresan witchcraft (Hoebel 1952:587–588). He was "accidentally killed," and his alleged assistant in the society of witches in Sia "fell off a high place; he was

9. The outside legal counsel for the Pueblo at this trial was not William Brophy, as White (1962:72) reports, but Soia Mentschikoff.

killed by falling somehow." They were believed to have caused a small-pox epidemic.

The grandsons of Lorenzo—George, Viviano, and Velino Herrera—became individualistic deviants, "artists and craftsmen where women's pottery is the only craft product" (Hawley 1948:273). They married outside their own pueblo, and Viviano further showed his defiance of the pueblo by painting ceremonial scenes, for which he found a good market in Santa Fe. One Herrera went further in betraying Sia secrets by submitting a modified representation of the sacred Sia sun symbol in a public contest for a design to be chosen as the official symbol to be used on auto license plates and state highway markers by the state of New Mexico. His design won the contest. I have heard a Sian say, "Whenever we see that on the highway, it hurts us here"—pounding his heart with a closed fist.

The Herrera heresy points up the unending struggle of dissenters who would like to move as individuals against the vested guardians of the law of the collective whole. "The system," writes Hawley, "is ultra-conservative, with religion as the basis for preserving that conservation, and any change which touches the pueblo from the standpoint of participation in the ceremonies is considered to strike not only at its health and subsistence but even at its very existence" (Hawley 1948:273–274).

The system was challenged once again in 1951 by the Pentecostals in a suit directed against the neighboring pueblo of Jemez, into which one of the exiled Sias had married. This time the case was tried directly in the United States District Court on the issue of whether the disabilities imposed upon the Pentecostals in Jemez came within the scope of the Civil Rights Act. The power of the pueblo officers was upheld under the federal law; the suit was dismissed (United States 1954).

As a system of tribal law, the Keresan Pueblo type is probably unique. It is totally centralized and spectacularly concentrated on societal maintenance and unyielding commitment to a specific set of cultural and jural postulates. Pueblos are highly segmentary social structures, as Kroeber noted fifty years ago.[10] But the Pueblo type, unlike the acephalous segmentary states of Africa, does not rely upon the balanced opposition of lineages to neutralize conflict (Fortes and Evans-Pritchard 1940). Lineages and clans are important in the social structure, but they do not function in the legal process. There is no private law whatsoever and not even a vestige of feud. Nor is there a trace of monarchy, such as characterizes many highly developed systems of centralized tribal gov-

10. "The clans, the fraternities, the priesthoods, the kivas, in a measure the gaming parties, are all dividing agencies. If they coincided, the rifts in the social structure would be deep; by countering each other they cause segmentations which produce an almost marvelous complexity, but can never break the nations apart" (Kroeber 1917:183).

ernment. The comparative counterpart is the totalitarian oligarchy, whether secular or theocratic, and its use of repressive authority to maintain order and conformity of belief and action in societies based on dogmatic ideology.[11]

11. The conflict over the powers of the pueblo oligarchies within the framework of United States constitutional law will not rest. In October, 1968, dissident members of Isleta Pueblo, in the form of a Committee for Religious Freedom at Isleta, filed suit before the United States District Court at Albuquerque. Named as defendants were the entire Tribal Council, three members of the Tribal Court and two ex-governors. The complaint charged that since June, 1965, "Catholics at Isleta have been threatened with physical violence and beating if they worshipped in the religion of their choice." On January 21, 1969, the Federal Court once again ruled in favor of the pueblo officials. Justice H. V. Payne dismissed the suit, holding that the defendants had acted simply as one body of Catholics against another in an intra-congregational dispute which lies outside the jurisdiction of the court. The central issue was avoided.

ANDRÉ J. F. KÖBBEN

Law at the Village Level:
The Cottica Djuka of Surinam [1]

This paper is about law in a nonstratified tribal society, or at least about those institutions having the same functions here as law in Western society, although their form and content may be very different. After a few introductory notes about Djuka society and culture in general, first legal situations are discussed in which physical coercion or the threat thereof is exercised and second cases in which only psychological sanctions—such as ridicule, avoidance, or denial of favors—are present. For analytic purposes this distinction is deemed important by the author, even though to the Djuka themselves there is no such difference.

Every Djuka individual is the center of an intricate social network; with most members of his network he has not just one but several relationships, some of which are coordinative while others are subordinative or superordinative. This system is at the basis of an important mechanism of social control, as is shown below. Still, Djuka law with its emphasis on nonphysical sanctions has its inherent weaknesses.

Further themes of the paper are: (1) Djuka law in the context of the wider judicial system of Surinam; (2) gossip and slander as a functional equivalent of law; (3) the Djuka judicial process.

1. The field work on which this paper is based was carried out from August 1961 to July 1962 mainly in the village of Langa Uku on the Cottica River. During the same period Mr. (now Dr.) and Mrs. Thoden van Velzen worked in Dritabiki, the village of the Paramount Chief on the Tapanahony River. The Netherlands Organization for Scientific Research in Surinam and the Netherlands' Antilles made this fieldwork financially possible. I wish to thank the following persons for valuable suggestions and help: H. D. van Leeuwen, L. Pospisil, J. Th. de Smidt, H. U. E. Thoden van Velzen, W. F. Wertheim. The translation was done by Mrs. M. J. van de Vathorst-Smit.

117

The Djuka, one of the Bush-Negro tribes of Surinam, live in the interior of this vast country along the Tapanahony, Marowijne and Cottica rivers (see map). Population figures for the Djuka are not precisely known, but they probably number about 15,000. They live in villages, averaging some hundreds of inhabitants, the core of which is formed by one or more matrilineages. They practice shifting cultivation and in addition they have long derived an income from rendering transport services on the rivers. Nowadays many young Djuka leave their villages to work as migrant laborers in the capital (Paramaribo) or elsewhere. The tribe has a Paramount Chief (*Gaman*) who lives in the village of Dritabiki on the Tapanahony River, where his power and influence are preponderant (van Velzen 1966: chaps. 6–9, 12, 13). However, in the Cottica region, which is the subject of this paper, the influence of the Paramount Chief is negligible, although his name is held in the highest esteem. For all practical purposes, therefore, in this region there is no tribal political power higher than the village level.

We know more about the history of the Bush Negroes than about that of most other nonliterate peoples. (For the history of the Bush Negroes see Wolbers [1861: chap. 3]; R. A. J. van Lier [1949: chaps. 1, 2, 3, and 6]; de Groot [1963]. Two important ethnographical sources are W. F. van Lier [1940] and Thoden van Velzen [1966].) From the last quarter of the seventeenth century, large numbers of Negro slaves were brought to Surinam from West Africa to work in the sugar plantations. Their life was extremely hard and in spite of the great risks involved many of them ran away to hide in the immense forests of the interior. These runaway slaves raided the plantations to procure necessary tools and implements and thus were a menace to the colony. The administration organized numerous expeditions in an attempt to wipe them out, but these proved unsuccessful. Ultimately, a solution was sought by means of a treaty accepting the *status quo* if the Bush Negroes would cease their raids on the plantations and hand over new escapees. Such a treaty was finally concluded with the Djuka in 1760. From that time on the Bush Negroes could develop their society virtually without interference, although their relations with the whites continued to be strained. In this development they made full use of their African heritage, without, however, copying their society of origin. Even today the Bush Negroes are to a large degree a nation within a nation. They harbor a considerable measure of distrust of the outside world, an understandable attitude when we take into account their past history.

Law: The Use of Physical Sanctions

Do the Djuka have law, and if so how much? How many of their social actions are regulated by law? Naturally the answer to these ques-

The distribution of Bush Negro tribes in Surinam.

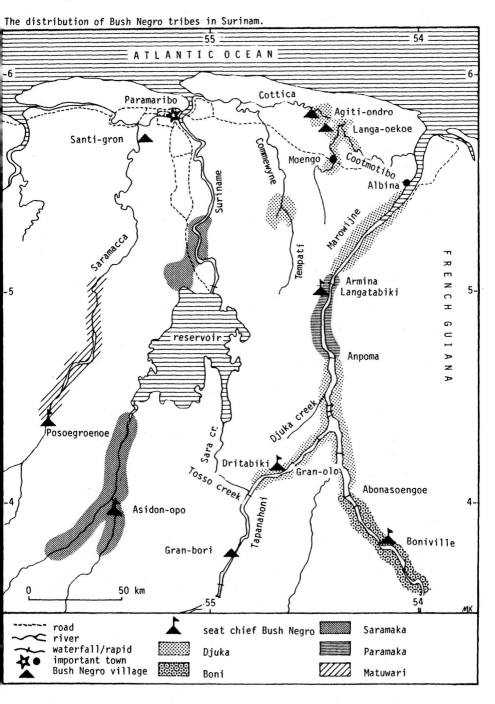

------ road	▲ seat chief Bush Negro	▨ Saramaka
～ river	⬚ Djuka	▤ Paramaka
～ waterfall/rapid		
✪● important town		▨ Matuwari
▲ Bush Negro village	⬚ Boni	

tions depends on how we define law.[2] Let us take Hoebel's well-known definition as a starting point: "A social norm is legal if its neglect or infraction is regularly met, in threat or in fact, by the application of physical force by an indivdual or group possessing the socially recognized privilege of so acting." This definition, the core of which lies in the words "physical force," is in accordance with what is usually considered law in Western society. This is both an advantage and a disadvantage, as we shall see,[3] but it is the disadvantage that strikes us first; the definition seems too "Western" to be suitable for intercultural use, especially if we want to include simple societies such as the Djuka in our discussion. By a broad interpretation of the terms of his definition, however, Hoebel makes it practicable for use in anthropology. This broad interpretation applies in particular to the words "socially recognized privilege." In a simple society, like the Eskimo, when an aggrieved individual himself takes action to redress a wrong, for instance by thrashing or killing the wrongdoer, Hoebel regards this as a legal deed provided the individual enjoys the approval or tacit support of public opinion. In situations like these public opinion, he reasons, functions as a court; the individual taking action acts as a public official *pro tempore, pro eo solo delicto*.[4] If we interpret our terms as broadly as Hoebel does, we can say that the Djuka have law. This is true in particular with respect to adultery. The aggrieved husband has the privilege-right of beating the adulterer, in which he is assisted by his lineage brothers and/or his wife's. The wife may also be beaten. Adultery is a much practiced sport among the Djuka, and thus this privilege-right is important. The punishment is subject to a number of rules and restrictions. The executors may beat the offender only with their fists, not with sticks or iron-weighted ropes; they may hit, but not stab, him in the eye; there must not be too many of them. The adulterer is not supposed to fight back but may only try to ward off the blows. He is, however, allowed to run away into the forest or to seek sanctuary in the hut of the village headman. If he comes out again, he risks another beating. For this reason the elders of his lineage get in touch with the lineage of the wronged husband. The affair is discussed, a fine is determined and paid *stante pede*. (Note that part of the punishment—i.e., the thrashing—precedes the trial!) Upon payment of the fine, the matter is finished; if the aggrieved husband beats the other man after this, he is himself committing an offense.

The Case of the Adulterous Couple. About ten o'clock at night the silence of the village is rudely disturbed by cries and sounds of wrangling. Ba

2. Cf. Kuper and Kuper (1965:3–5); Nader (1965b:4–8); Köbben (1967b:6). Substantialistic or "realistic" symptoms are found even in the work of otherwise perceptive authors (Bohannan 1965:34, 35, 40; Pospisil 1958:248, 257, but cf. 249, fn. 9). On the notion of substantialism (realism), see Alder (1964).

3. Cf. also Nader (1965b:11).

4. Hoebel (1954:27; cf. also Chapters 5 and 6).

Atonsé has caught his wife Sa Teti with a stranger.[5] That afternoon when she left her garden, she pretended she was going to the camp (where she and her husband have a hut); but in fact she went to the village to meet her lover. She knew there would be few people at home, since there was a mortuary feast in a neighboring village. She thought Ba Atonsé would also be at the feast, but he has been suspecting her for a long time, and he therefore came home to spy on her. He listens with his ear to the wall of the hut and hears two people breathing: "they were sleeping peacefully after having copulated until they'd had enough." He goes in and shines his flashlight on them, at the same time shouting loudly to wake up others, so that he will have witnesses and people to assist him. A few fellow villagers come running and try to catch the intruder; but he slips away between the huts to the river and is gone in his boat. Ba Atonsé himself does not beat his wife and tells others not to do so either. This is not forbearance on his part; on the contrary, it is meant (and interpreted) as an insult to show he has such a contempt for her that he does not consider it worth his while to beat her. But the people of her own lineage give her a good thrashing; the honor of the lineage is at stake. Finally she is rescued by two men, giving her the opportunity to escape to the village headman's hut. The two men are affines (*konlibi*), and it is their duty to intervene in cases of physical violence between members of the lineage into which they have married.

The shouting and quarreling goes on for many hours; the next day, too, the affair is the talk of the village.

The Case of the Stupid Adulterer. Ba Langabasi is in a pitiable state. Last night he was sitting in a woman's hut talking to her when the husband came in. The husband, assisted by another man, gave him a sound beating. He managed to keep the husband off by clasping the latter's arms, but this gave the helper a chance to deal him especially hard blows in the face. Finally he succeeded in escaping to the headman's hut. The cuckold was wild with rage and tried to follow him inside but was forcibly stopped by his own friends. At night, when everyone was asleep, Langabasi stole out of the village. Back in his own village, people laughed at him; the general opinion is that he was stupid to visit the woman while her husband was in the village. "You should do something like that when the husband is in town or else make sure beforehand that the woman is willing so that you don't have to waste hours talking. Now he got nothing except a beating." (Note that his action is thought stupid but not wrong.)

Carrying on with another man's wife is not sinful, only an infringement of the other's rights of ownership. (As far as the woman is concerned, she is throwing away the honor of the lineage by allowing herself to be seduced. But even this is not so much a question of sin as of a breach of contract.) The men are not ashamed of sexual adventures of this sort; on the contrary, they take pride in them and are admired for their prowess by their own kin. A man once praised his father to me in the following

5. *Ba* (literally brother) and *Sa* (literally sister) are terms for (young) man and (young) woman respectively.

words: "He always had a lot of luck with women; he got as many as eleven beatings in his life." The reactions are different, however, when a man seduces the wife of a member of his own lineage, or a classificatory mother-in-law.

The Case of the Sinful Adulterers. During a nocturnal mortuary feast Ba Napang (see Diagram 1) retired with Sa Jolina to the latter's hut. Although she is no older than he, she is a classificatory mother-in-law, being his wife's mother's brother's wife. They are caught by Ba Napang's cross-cousin (see 3 in Diagram 1), who raises the alarm but without disclosing

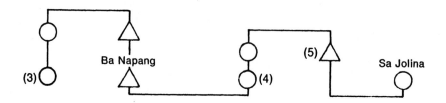

Diagram 1

the culprit's name because of her special relationship with him. Ba Napang gets away by a bold leap through the roof, which is made of leaves. He mingles with the dancers again and even joins in the search for Sa Jolina's assailant. He also helps to repair the roof. Nevertheless, his secret leaks out; at least, the rumors point more and more in his direction. He hides a few days near the river by the landing stage of the boat to Paramaribo (the capital), and when the boat calls, he climbs aboard at the last moment when it is too late to stop him. "He'll be staying in town one or two years; after that the affair is dead and he can come back." If anyone runs into him in town they will not make trouble, for in town the law is different.

Napang's wife (4) and Jolina's husband (5) both declare that they will not have anything more to do with their respective partners. Sa Jolina has left and gone to her father's village. (I do not know whether this affair ended in actual divorces.) Everyone denounces the adulterous couple.

The guilty party is not supposed to fight back, but this is a weak spot in this form of law: [6] the person acting as public official is a party at the same time. He may think that he has a right to beat the other, but his victim may be equally convinced that he does not, in which case he will fight back. In the past this situation has often led to serious trouble.

Intervillage Fights as a Result of Adultery. Da Jukun [7] tells me that "formerly" (about thirty years ago) he caught his wife with another man. He beat the man, but the latter fought back. Both men received assistance, and the ensuing fight lasted for hours. The following morning both parties went

6. See in the same sense Hoebel (1954:99).
7. *Da* (literally father) is the term for elderly man.

to fetch reinforcements, each in his own matrilineal village; as a result, there was a virtual war (*botofeti*) between the villages concerned. This sort of conflict no longer occurs.

As we saw, such cases of adultery are settled by a meeting of elders. It is in the interests of the adulterer that this should take place quickly, for until then he is outlawed. In one case a man spent eleven days in the village headman's hut and only crept out in the middle of the night to relieve himself.

The Settling of a Case of Adultery. A big mortuary feast is being held in the village of Lantiwé, and elders from the whole district have assembled there. They take this opportunity to decide all sorts of pending matters. A group of them settle the case of Ba Bembe, who seduced Sa Pobieng. Ba Bembe himself is not present, nor is the wronged husband or Sa Pobieng. They do not even know that the matter is being discussed on this particular afternoon. The elders divide the different roles; they form two parties—one representing the wronged man, the other the wrongdoer. Kinship is the criterion, but some of the elders are only distant relatives of one of the persons concerned; others are equally closely related to both of them. This is no reason, however, for them not to take one or the other side. Although there is no question of being personally involved, they act their parts with all the appropriate emotions.

The first speaker for the wronged party is Da Daose. He gives a detailed account of what happened, expressing a noble indignation: "While the lawful husband was staying with his second wife, suspecting nothing, Ba Bembe shamefully took advantage of this to seduce the first wife." The other party implores forgiveness and goes aside. This "going aside" is standard procedure; standing a few paces away from the meeting place, they confer in whispers. They return and offer to pay a bottle of liquor as a fine. But Daose says that it is too early yet to determine the fine; first he wants to know exactly what happened—whether the couple was caught before or after sexual intercourse, for the amount of the fine will depend on that. In the latter case, moreover, there is a greater chance of divorce. Another member of the tribunal proposes hearing a woman who witnessed the whole affair from the beginning to end. She arrives but does not join in the circle of men; she sits down a little aside on a stool, with her back half turned to the elders, and keeps saying that she is not a man and will not have any part of the matter. Even so, she tells her story with great eloquence. Of her own accord Ma Kawtiki [8] joins the gathering. She is the eldest woman of the lineage and has great authority. She sits in the circle of men.

Another member of the tribunal fulminates against Ba Bembe once more: "The wronged man is my brother's son, I feel shocked and insulted. We can't just settle this quietly . . . he should be made to pay a big fine; we should put an end to this sort of thing. . . . He should pay at least fifteen bottles of liquor." (But of course he relents; all this fulminating is part of the procedure.) Members of the other party clap their hands in the ceremonial way and humbly ask for a smaller fine (*begi mendi*). Agreement is reached at two bottles, which are partly consumed there and then.

8. *Ma* (literally mother) is the term for elderly woman.

In each of the cases cited above the adulterous couple was caught *in flagrante delicto*, so there was hardly need of proof. This is not always so. Sometimes there are only strong indications of guilt at first.

The Case of the Wife Suspected of Infidelity. Sa Kalima attended the mortuary feast in Pikin Santi. A few days later someone confidentially tells a classificatory brother of her husband's that he thinks she betrayed him there with another man. Ba Asindo (her husband) is informed, very discreetly. He closely questions Sa Kalima: has she committed adultery, and if not, did the man perhaps touch her or make improper proposals? She denies everything, but she cries all night and does not eat on the following day. This behavior is regarded as a strong indication of her guilt. Asindo says: "God helped me; I had just bought all sorts of things for her—soap, kerosene, cloth—but now I'll keep it all for myself. Tomorrow I'll go and help my mother clear a garden plot, not Sa Kalima." His "brothers" urge him not to leave the matter there if he does not want to become a laughing-stock in the village. "If she keeps denying, make her go through the ordeal [*akondia*]." Asindo says that he will inform his father and the village headman, so that they may start proceedings.

A few days later the ordeal takes place. Before it starts, the woman's relatives attempt to have it canceled, "The ordeal will injure her vital force [*aka*]." The request is dismissed. Both friends and enemies are watching intently: a machete is made red hot in the fire and will be passed along a tightly stretched liana. If the liana breaks, the woman is guilty; if it does not, she is innocent. The woman herself is not present; she is in a hut in the village, waiting for the verdict. She stands the ordeal successfully; the liana does not break. From now on there should be no more backbiting about her (but of course there is). A week later, Ba Asindo finds two notes among Sa Kalima's things, and he asks the ethnographer to read them aloud to him. They are most incriminating.

Asindo loudly expresses his anger and calls the ordeal a "shitty ordeal." Others, too, are upset and indignant, but this does not detract from their faith in the test's effectiveness. Apparently this particular ordeal was not much good, but nothing is said against the principle as such. During the next few days four different explanations for the ordeal's failure are spontaneously offered. Most frequently heard is that the man who carried out the ordeal was prejudiced in favor of the woman: "He is a member of her father's matri-group. They should have had it done by a neutral person, or even by someone of *his* matri-group." Others think the executor was unskillful rather than prejudiced. Still others think the woman herself brought about the failure of the ordeal through magical means—"A certain other woman escaped in this way as many as six times before the priests of the Great Deity [the Deity that deals especially with witches and sorcerers] discovered her tricks and deprived her of her powers." The last explanation was that in the ordeal the wrong question was asked: "Perhaps they asked whether the couple had had sexual intercourse and perhaps they hadn't got as far as that yet."

Asindo, with a few comrades, could have sought out the adulterer to give him a thrashing. But there is a difficulty—the man in question works in the mine at Mungo, and this place has a police station; he might go and complain to the police. Ba Asindo saves his face by saying, "It will be all the more humiliating if I don't fight for her." Next day Ba Asindo puts all her things outside the hut to indicate that he considers himself divorced (the woman herself is not at home but staying in a camp near the gardens with her mother). And he loudly proclaims, for everyone to hear, "I have no wife anymore, I'm divorced." But is this divorce permanent? Asindo complains to me that he does not like it: "The divorce is to my loss; if her family ask me forgiveness, I might take her back." That night he goes to the mortuary feast in Manjabon, where he tries himself what he condemns in his rival—to seduce a married woman. As a matter of fact, his rival (the seducer of his wife) is also present at the feast. (That meeting is less dangerous than it would seem, for there is a general truce during such feasts.) "If I were to beat him there, I would have to pay a substantial fine myself; what I can do is announce that I'll be giving him a good beating soon, and he can't say anything in return."

A good two weeks later there is a small mortuary feast in Ricanaumofo. Though there are not many elders present, it is nevertheless decided, as is customary, to settle all pending matters for the whole district, including the Asindo affair. None of the protagonists is present, nor are any of their close relatives, but still two parties are formed. Spokesman for Ba Asindo is Da Kuli, his father's mother's half-brother (the connecting link is a man,

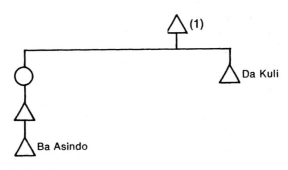

Diagram 2

No. 1 in Diagram 2), and a man is not a significant link in this matrilineal society). Da Kuli lives in a different village, has never heard of the affair, and does not even know Asindo. Nevertheless, he acts his part splendidly, gives a lively description of what has taken place (in which he sometimes mistakes names and places—he is prompted by a man from Asindo's village), and reproaches the adulterer for his conduct in a booming voice. A fine (four bottles of liquor) is determined and paid in the customary way. One bottle is consumed on the spot; the others are taken back to Asindo by people from his village as a sign that the matter has been settled. Asindo and his father are not happy with the fact that Da Kuli acted as their spokesman, for the father has an old difference with him. But they cannot ignore the verdict. A few days later Ba Asindo and Sa Kalima are reconciled. Another few days later they have a ritual ablution, together with some relatives, to cancel the evil effects of the angry words that have been spoken.

In the cases reviewed so far the use, or threat, of physical force clearly played a part—that is, they fall under the definition of law in Hoebel's sense. In addition to these, there are borderline cases, when there is no actual threat of physical force although it is present in the background.

One Man Against Many. Two young women, (1) and (2) in Diagram 3, have a quarrel. First they hurl abuse at one another and finally they come to blows. Other people interfere, and two of them—Ma Dow (the mother

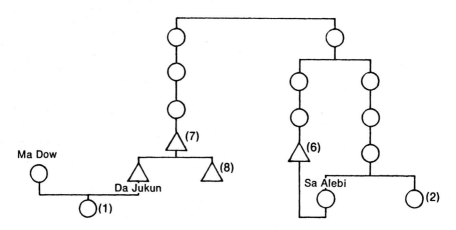

Diagram 3

of the one) and Sa Alebi (the sister of the other)—also exchange blows. Sa Alebi is the village headman's wife, and as such she should behave with dignity and under no circumstances fight in public.

The following morning the matter is discussed in a palaver (*kutu*). The headman has not slept very well; he was nervous, and very early that morning he went to fetch the headman of the neighboring village to act in his place; he is too closely concerned to act himself. Ma Dow—who is not present at first—is represented by her husband, Da Jukun. The headman's wife is present herself. After much deliberation Da Jukun is declared the guilty party, and he pays a fine of three bottles of liquor. Ma Dow and Sa Alebi are made to embrace each other in public (*basa*), which they do, though obviously halfheartedly and with their faces turned away.

Afterward I discuss the matter with Jukun. He does not consider himself (i.e., Ma Dow) in the wrong at all; on the contrary, Sa Alebi, being the headman's wife, should not have meddled in the fight. But of course one cannot publicly say that the headman is wrong. He (Jukun) can at the most tell the headman in private what he thinks of the affair, and he intends to do so. He particularly stresses the fact that he has to accept the verdict, although he is innocent, because all the others are members of the matrilineal group but he and his wife are not; he is only a son of a male member of the matrilineage (*dada meke pikin*) "and they are eager, in this place, to chase the *dada meke pikin* from the village." This seems rather farfetched to me, for his father (7 in Diagram 3) was the revered former village headman and on that account (and because of his own personality) Da Jukun has great authority in the village. However, he refers me to the case of his brother (8 in Diagram 3) who came into conflict with the other villagers a few years earlier because of a woman. In that conflict he was practically alone, with all the lineage members against him. After having been beaten a few times, he took refuge in his own matrilineal village.

Local Law and Government Law

In the past the Djuka formed a state within the state, and in many respects this situation still holds. They still settle most of their disputes without referring to the Surinam authorities. Only for the most serious matters do they go to the police of their own accord. Usually it is the headman who does this. This happens in cases of murder or homicide and rape of a young girl—offenses that are rare. In the villages near the administrative centers, Mungo and Albina, however, it has become more and more usual in the last few years for young men who have taken a beating for seducing a woman to go to the police and complain.

Two Legal Systems Collide. In the village of Ajumakonde a man and a woman are caught *in flagrante delicto*. A few of the woman's brothers want to beat her and the man, but the man fights back. In the heat of the fight he is bitten by one of his assailants. The man goes to Mungo to lodge a complaint with the police; before going into the office, he rolls about in the mud to make himself look really pitiable. The police go to Ajumakonde, where they arrest two men ("not even the one who did the biting").

This event is the talk of the whole district. People are indignant at the man's action but equally at the police. "The one who broke the rules is put in the right and the others in the wrong. The police are stupid, they should ask what was the reason for the fight. It is just like a snake; when it is lying curled up and a person passes, it won't do anything. Only if a person treads on the snake will it bite. That is what we do; we don't just strike a man; we only strike him when there is a reason."

Two legal systems collide here. I try to explain that the police do not want people to take the law into their own hands, but I have little success. Da Jukun thinks he understands: "The police don't think people ought to fight at all; whoever fights is punished. So if a man seduces your wife you should put up with it. I suppose the whites don't mind such things." [9]

9. The officials with whom the Bush Negroes have dealings are Surinamers and are all more or less colored. Yet the Bush Negroes call them whites (*bakra*), as they fulfill the same functions and behave in the same way as the whites did formerly.

We might wonder why some people go to the police in spite of the public disapproval incurred by so doing. It is too simple an explanation to say that only the "detribalized" go to the police; those concerned are not in fact detribalized to that degree. The probable explanation occurred to me when some men were talking about the case described above. One of them said, "If I don't feel I'm in the right I'll never go to the police; the Deity would kill me if I did. But if someone hits me without good reason, I will." In those cases in which a person lodges a complaint, he is probably firmly convinced that he was beaten undeservedly, while his opponent is equally convinced that the punishment was deserved. Such differences in interpretation, according to the interests of the persons concerned, are of frequent occurrence.

The Case of the Badly Wounded Seducer. (This case, which occurred in 1963, I did not witness myself. The data are derived from the official reports and a newspaper account.) Ba Foliké has seduced Ba Jada's wife. One day he is suddenly attacked by Ba Jada and a few comrades. They give him a sound beating, hitting him on his back, on his head, and in his face, until some bystanders intervene. Ba Foliké's right eye is bleeding profusely. The Hindustani shopkeeper, who lives in the village, takes him in his boat to the doctor in Mungo; Foliké's eye is so badly damaged that it has to be removed. It is not clear whether one of the attackers inflicted the injury with a stone or a piece of iron or whether it was caused by an unfortunate fall during the fight (nor does this become clear during the lawsuit that follows). In any case, Ba Foliké blames his assailants and considers them guilty of a crime. Together with his father he lodges a complaint with the police, urged on by the Hindustani shopkeeper. When questioned, Ba Jada and his helpers do not deny having attacked him; they feel they were quite justified in doing so. After tumultuous court sessions (the case is fought out all the way to the highest court) they are sentenced to one year in prison.

We see, then, how the official Surinam law [10] can thwart and disturb Djuka law. This is regrettable, since the Djukas' own law works reasonably well on this point (the handling of adultery and everything connected with it). In many cases the Surinam authorities are not aware, or not sufficiently aware, of the background, as in the case cited above. They regard punishment of an adulterer not as a legal deed but as an offense. However, even if they did recognize the legal nature of these actions, the situation would not be materially altered. The Bush Negroes are regular citizens of Surinam, to whom the law of the country fully applies. But this is obviously only a legal fiction; to mention just one example: education is compulsory in Surinam and has been for a number of generations, yet only a small minority of Djuka children go to

10. Surinam criminal law is largely in conformity with Dutch criminal law (Wijnholt 1965:2–3, but cf. 67–74).

school, and no attempt is made to enforce the statute. Nevertheless, it is difficult to part with this fiction, since it is hardly admissible for a modern government to let its judicial principles vary according to the different ethnic groups concerned. At the most, it might be admitted that the Public Prosecutor would decide not to prosecute in some cases, or, if he did, would take this background into account as extenuating circumstances.

On the other hand, there are certain cases in which Surinam law upholds Djuka law by providing it with the *ultima ratio* it does not itself possess. This is true in cases of rape. For this offense the palaver of elders nowadays imposes a compensation of fifty Surinam guilder (almost thirty dollars), to be paid to the girl's family. For the Djuka this is a large sum of money. The elders themselves have no physical means of coercion to enforce payment, but they threaten to inform the police, in which case the offender would face a stiff term of imprisonment. (The idea of imprisonment is very repellent to the Djuka.)

During a period of a little over ten years (1950–1961) there were about one hundred lawsuits involving Djuka, altogether 155 individuals from a total Djuka population of at least 15,000—enough, that is, to acquaint every member of the tribe either directly or indirectly with the phenomenon of Western justice.[11] These cases may be classified, according to their nature, as follows:

Assault, attempt to kill .... 40 cases
    Most of these cases are concerned with persons who gave others a beating for seducing a woman.

Theft, embezzlement .... 20 cases
    Most are cases of theft committed in Chinese or Hindustani shops in the administrative centers Mungo and Albina, *not* in the Djuka villages.

Illegal cutting of timber, gold smuggling .... 5 cases
    In the eyes of the Djuka these actions are not reprehensible at all.

(Attempted) rape of a girl less than 12 years old .... 5 cases

Murder, homicide .... 4 cases

Sundries .... 20 cases
    Including traffic offenses and drunkenness, in the larger centers.

Penalties

Reprimand, conditional sentence, and fine (ranging from Sf.2 to Sf.60; about $1 to $17 .... 106 cases
Prison sentence from 5 days to 9 months .... 30 cases
Prison sentence from 1 to 6 years .... 4 cases
Acquittal, discharge .... 15 cases

11. My thanks are due to Mr. H. Pos, at the time the highest jural authority in Surinam, for allowing me to look through the records in question.

Law: The Use of Psychological Sanctions

In all the cases cited above we may speak of "law" in Hoebel's sense. We should ask ourselves the question, however, whether a more inclusive definition of law would not be more appropriate for this society. We might consider Pospisil's (1958b:257) definition: "Law is conceived as rules or modes of conduct made obligatory by some sanction which is imposed and enforced for their violation by a controlling authority." Following this definition, the term "law" is also used when the sanctions are of a psychological nature, such as ostracism, ridicule, avoidance, or denial of favors (Pospisil 1958b:267). To Pospisil the effect of the sanction is more important than its form, and he reasons that psychological sanctions often exercise as strong a control as do physical sanctions. He came to this position through his study of a Papuan society consisting of small political units with an extremely simple formal structure.[12] In such a situation his criterion for law is a significant one, whereas it is less so in Western society. In the latter type of society pure psychological sanctions without the threat of physical force (for example, public reprimands) do occur, but only in a small number of cases and for minor offences.[13]

Pospisil's definition undeniably has advantages for the Djuka situation. When Djuka elders in a formal palaver try to correct an individual who has deviated from the socially accepted norms, there is much to be said for calling this "law" even if only psychological, not physical, coercion is used; these proceedings have the same functions as "law" in a Western society. It should be noted, moreover, that the Djuka handle a case the same way whether physical coercion comes into it or not; to them there is no difference. Any distinction we make here is merely a construct of our minds.

The Case of the Absent Couple. Sa Lomina, a woman from Langa Uku, is married to Ti Valisi.[14] For over three years they have been living on the Commewijne, where the husband is working on a timber concession. During this time they have not been back to the wife's village, although in the meantime her father has died and the woman herself has had a child. This is against the established norms.

Now Ti Valisi comes to the village for a visit, having left his wife behind because she is pregnant again. His arrival, in his boat with a brand-new

12. Cf. Pospisil (1958:67–68, 76–77).
13. It may be noted that in many Kapauku cases where psychological sanctions are applied, they are accompanied by the threat of physical sanctions, and it often seems to be the latter that make them effective; the reader gets the impression that (the threat of) physical force plays a far greater role in the Kapauku legal system than Pospisil suggests (cf. Pospisil 1958:223–224, 267–271, and cf. Hoebel's definition).
14. *Ti* (literally uncle) is the term for middle-aged man.

outboard motor, is a glorious one, but early the next morning there is a palaver of elders in which he is the accused party. In the customary way, two sides are formed, sitting facing each other in two semicircles. One side consists of classificatory fathers-in-law of Ti Valisi, the other of men who live in the village as affines (*konlibi*) like him (he plays no active part himself—the defendant himself never does). Ti Valisi is sharply rebuked for his conduct, and he is required to fetch his wife at once. "If she has to have her baby on the way, never mind! That can take place in any village she happens to be passing. Or hasn't Ti Valisi brought her because he thinks there are witches here who may hurt her? There is no question of that." Every possible suspect has been ritually cleansed,[15] and the village is free of all blemish. In fact, the contrary is true: "if Sa Lomina is not here during her pregnancy and confinement, it will be bad for her." Ti Valisi's representatives ask for mercy, which is finally accorded. He offers half a bottle of liquor, some bottles of soft drink, and bread.

The following day Ti Valisi goes to fetch his wife. She will have to stay in the village for at least five or six months, until she has her child, and three months after that. Strictly speaking, Ti Valisi should also stay in the village all that time, but he largely ignores this obligation; during this period he is more often absent than present. In this case there is no question of physical coercion; is there coercion of some other kind? We might think of "denial of a favor," meaning that the lineage will take the woman away from her husband if he does not obey. But no such threat is pronounced during the session, nor could it be carried out without the wife's consent. What happens is really an appeal to the man's common sense; it is more fitting and better for the woman to have her baby in the village. One is strongly reminded here of Gluckman's (1963b: Chapter VII) "reasonable man" concept.

The Case of the Polygynous Husband. (In this case the threat of "denial of favor" is more clearly expressed than in the previous case.) Ti Aki has two wives—an older one, Sa Budulu, by whom he has five children, and a younger one, who is a recent acquisition. With this second and favorite wife he has lived in town for about ten months. When he left Sa Budulu she was pregnant, and in his absence she gave birth to a child. When Ti Aki finally comes back to Sa Budulu's village, the child is already five months old. Sa Budulu refuses to receive her husband and chases him away. She does not really want a divorce, but she must do so to save her face. Ti Aki asks two elders of the lineage (one of them a woman) to plead in his favor, and at the end of the day they come to settle the case. It is a small—almost a household—affair; initially, apart from the two elders, only the parents of Sa Budulu and two of her brothers are present. However, in form as well as in function it has all the qualities of the larger palavers, and I see no reason therefore to deny it the quality of "law."[16] Sa Budulu and Ti Aki

15. For this purification rite (*dingi sweli*), see W. F. van Lier (1940:182–183) and Thoden van Velzen (1966:150–156).
16. Cf. Pospisil's statement on "legal levels" (1958b:272–278).

sit about 100 yards away from where the "court" convenes, he hidden inside their hut, she before it in a sulking position.

Budulu's brother, acting as the first prosecutor, attacks Ti Aki: "We have always been benevolent to him. When he came to live here, many years ago, I helped him with my own hands to build his hut. Now he has two wives; that is not bad in itself, not at all, but he neglects the first one, her he considers as 'light,' the other one as 'heavy.' " One of the elders continues the attack: "I have a knife in my belt, I cut myself. [This proverb means: "This man has asked me to help him, but in so doing I do harm to my own kinsmen."] He did not send anything to his wife, neither money nor presents; he behaved badly; his whole family behaves badly—take his [clan] brother X, who stole the wife of one of our [clan] brothers . . ." and so forth. The third charge comes from Sa Budulu's mother, who hurls accusations in so loud a voice that her son-in-law is perfectly able to understand them in his hut. "It is a shame! When the baby was born, the woman's brothers had to cut the firewood to keep her and the baby warm; he was not there to do it. He did not even come to bury his father-in-law. [The "father-in-law" in question was a very distant clan-brother of Sa Budulu's father.] Let him stay away with that other woman, and leave this woman alone."

But then the elders begin to plead forgiveness: "That other wife of his is perhaps the culprit; she does not know how to behave; she should have urged him to go and see her co-wife. So let us forgive him, although he did bad things." A clan-sister of Ti Aki, also married into this village, has come in the meantime and pleads for him as well. Finally everyone gives in, last of all the mother-in-law (but the opinion of Sa Budulu is not asked). A bottle of liquor is offered on behalf of Ti Aki and its contents drunk.

The following day it appears that Sa Budulu is still not satisfied, and she refuses to let Ti Aki sleep with her. But an informant says: "She will give in all right; if not, she would give shame to her family, who have already accepted him back." There is thus quite a measure of mere show in the demonstration of anger in cases like this. Nevertheless, when the husband neglects his wife too often or too long or when he does not show the appropriate submissiveness and tact on the occasion of the trial, a divorce may ensue. Since divorces are common in Djuka society (of all adults, about half have been divorced at least once) and since a woman may very well take the initiative for a divorce, this is a real possibility.

The Case of the Man who is Coerced by Ridicule. On the previous night old Da Jonga chased his wife, Ma Jaja, out of their hut because, as he asserts, she has refused sexual intercourse with him for the past seven months. Turning a woman out without a formal divorce is a reprehensible action. If the woman simply went back to the hut after this, she might fall ill.

The case is tried. Ti Djoisi, Da Jonga's son-in-law, acts as his spokesman, but he refuses to talk about the sexual aspect of the affair: "That would not be proper for me in front of all my mothers-in-law and fathers-in-law." Da Jonga will not admit that he has committed a wrong, he keeps shouting, "Seven months! Seven months!" and boasts amid general laughter of his sexual prowess. But the opinion is that he is in the wrong; he should have left the hut himself to go and sleep elsewhere, and then he should have called his wife to account in public. The meeting decides to impose a fine on him. Da Jonga refuses in forcible language and walks off, shouting that he will never, never pay. There is laughter and shouting all around. Ma Dada, who is at least eighty, pats him admonishingly on the back. My informant says: "He goes off now, but he'll be back for sure. You don't just ignore the decisions of the *kutu* [palaver]; *they force you with their mouths.*" True enough, in a little while Da Jonga returns and after much pressing he agrees to "go aside." [17] When he comes back he grudgingly admits: "It is true, I did wrong." He is fined one bottle of liquor. Da Jonga immediately flares up again: "That is far too much." Ma Dada says, "But you must pay for what you've done wrong," and amid roars of laughter she pats his buttocks. A moment later the liquor is fetched and drunk. Now Da Jonga too is laughing, and he reveals that altogether he must have paid for at least eighteen bottles of liquor in this way. Da Todi—Ma Jaja's brother—now appears on the scene; he starts railing at Da Jonga afresh. But Ti Djoisi begs him to forgive too and adds another quarter pint of liquor to the fine.

The Case of the Cursed Husband. Ti Sapatia suspects his wife, Ma Amaini, of being unfaithful. He publicly accuses her, adding, "If it isn't true, may the Great Deity I have swallowed kill me." Ma Amaini undergoes the ordeal and proves to be innocent. A dangerous situation has now arisen, for the god Ti Sapatia so rashly invoked is the most feared of all Djuka deities and knows no mercy in his punishment of such acts.[18] Ma Amaini will not tolerate the man any more, and they separate. Shortly afterward Ti Sapatia falls ill. Illness, to the Djuka, is a sign that something is wrong in human relations. He goes to Agitiondo, in which village the Great Deity has a temple.[19] The deity is consulted, and the illness proves to have been caused by the curse Sapatia has called down on himself. The priests impose a fine on him and instruct him to reconcile with Ma Amaini; they make a libatory offering to conciliate the Great Deity.

Ti Sapatia now makes a real attempt at reconciliation with Ma Amaini and her relatives. As many as three times he sends an elder to plead his case, but to no avail. "We dare not permit him to come back, for we are afraid the woman may fall ill; forgive us for being afraid," her kinsmen say. Some of them, however, who think differently privately urge the woman to take him back: "He's grown accustomed to this place, after all, and it's not good for a woman to be alone. And sexually he is pretty good." And be-

---

17. See p. 123.

18. The punishment need not strike the sinner himself. More often than not it strikes a member of his lineage, his wife, or his child.

19. Beside the one in Agitiondo, the Great Deity has a tabernacle in Dritabiki and one in a village on the Sara Creek. In Dritabiki the tribal chief (*Gaman*) acts as the high priest. A detailed description of the functions of the tabernacle and its priests, with particular emphasis on law and political control is given by Thoden van Velzen (1966:Chapters 7, 8, 9, 13). As a group, the priests of the Great Deity in Dritabiki, the political center of the tribe, are without doubt more powerful than those in Agitiondo. Nevertheless, the latter are the most powerful group on a supralocal level among the Cottica Djuka. Note that the power of these priests is based on psychological, not on physical, sanctions.

hold, the fourth time it is a man of great authority who comes to plead forgiveness; now the request is granted—"so that the elder won't be put to shame," as the stereotyped phrase goes. Soon afterward the man and the woman go together to Agitiondo to make a libatory offering to the Great Deity.

Nevertheless the relationship remains strained. The man does not really return to the village, and finally an unexpected occurrence definitely puts an end to the marriage. A boat carrying ore runs into the riverbank,[20] causing some trees to fall right on Ma Amaini's hut, which is totally destroyed. The people of the village spontaneously attribute this to machinations (black magic) on Ti Sapatia's part. Amaini meets him on the river and heaps abuse on him. After this she considers herself definitely divorced.

"I Caught You There"

A special form of law in Pospisil's sense is the one the Djuka call (literally translated): "I caught you there." When a person has been wronged by another or by a group, he will seldom attempt to get redress at once; instead, he will wait, for years if need be, until one day he happens to occupy a superior position with respect to the person(s) concerned, for example as a bride-giver or as a priest. Then he will say: "I caught you there; you planted bananas," meaning, that on that past occasion the culprit did not realize the consequences of his action. (The banana is an annual plant, but after the first year new shoots sprout out of the ground in unexpected places.)

The Case of the Angry Mother's Brother. There is a palaver, in which the relatives of Ba Nofé come to ask a girl in marriage. The two parties (Ba Nofé's relatives and the girl's) take a long time to reach an agreement. The match is opposed by a classificatory mother's mother's brother of the girl: "We will never consent, for Ba Nofé has treated me disrespectfully." He relates that some years before, at a big mortuary feast, Ba Nofé gave him foul water instead of coffee and laughed at him with his comrades when he became furious after drinking some of it. Ba Nofé's party humbly begs forgiveness, supported by "neutral" elders; they offer to pay a fine of one bottle of liquor. The old man bitterly reproaches them again: "Forget about that liquor, bring me some more of that delicious coffee." But of course he relents in the end.

The Case of the Gossiper. Da Papun's wife has gone to her village, according to rumors, to complain about her husband. Da Papun catches Ti Bento gossiping about this matter. He says nothing and waits. Less than a month later, Bento asks him to make an offering to the Great Deity on his, Bento's, behalf (Da Papun is the local priest of the Great Deity). Papun refuses at first and does not agree until Ti Bento has publicly admitted his guilt. As Da Papun said later: "In this way I put Ti Bento to shame and took vengeance."

---

20. Ships regularly pass on the Commewijne and Cottica rivers on their way to the mining town of Mungo, where they load bauxite.

The Case of the Refused Woman. Some years ago Ba Jan, a member of matri-group I seduced the wife of Ti Adadi, a member of matri-group II (see Diagram 4). The affair became known, and the elders of matri-group II told those of group I some home truths. Now, however, the roles are reversed, for Ti Dolaini (of group II) wants to marry Sa Aliéti (of group I) and a group of elders come to ask for her hand in marriage. Da Djodji, classificatory mother's brother of Sa Aliéti, rails at the delegation: "When Ba Jan had stolen your wife you took all sorts of liberties with respect to us and we had to put up with it, *but now I catch you;* I refuse to give you our woman!"

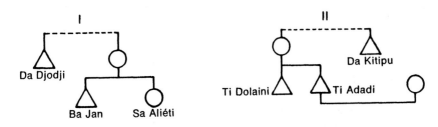

Diagram 4

(A short comment is needed here. One may argue with good reason that this case is no "law" at all, not even in Pospisil's sense. Objectively, since no wrong was committed by those of matri-group II in scolding group I, the "I-caught-you" institution cannot be seen here as an action to redress the transgression of a social norm. I give this case to point out once more the inherent weakness in Djuka law. Here, as in many other cases, the party who acts as public official or judge is himself involved in the case and is consequently not much given to objective criteria.)

Do Djodji in speaking thus meets with resistance. Da Kitipu in particular, a member of the visiting delegation, flares up and even wants to start a fight: "You ought to be glad things turned out so well for you; we didn't even beat Ba Jan that time." Da Kitipu's conduct is contrary to the rules. The negotiations are stopped, and the delegation has to leave empty-handed. Sa Aliéti declares her solidarity with her lineage and says that she is through with Ti Dolaini.

A few days later Ti Dolaini comes to see her, but she will not let him into her hut (she chases him away). "She has nothing against him, indeed she loves him, but she has to do this out of respect for her family. The situation is not as tragic as it seems, however, for she knows as well as everyone else that the matter will soon be settled.

Some days later a small palaver is devoted to the matter. An elder says, "Ti Dolaini's mother has asked me to make it up. Dolaini can't help it if Da Kitipu acted badly; he [Kitipu] has done Dolaini an ill service, apparently he doesn't care for him. So don't blame Dolaini, a thousand pardons!"

Thus this elder, by deserting his own kinsman, opens the way to reconciliation. Members of the other party note emphatically that Da Djodji had
a right to speak as he did: "We do not want him to come out of this with
a bad reputation." But finally they relent, and by way of reconciliation the
eldest man present makes an offering to the ancestors: "O great ancestors,
you heard those two men quarrel; that is all over now. Please see to it that
Da Kitipu does not fall ill and that Da Djodji doesn't fall ill."

The Case of a Man versus His Fathers-in-Law. Sa Bobi has betrayed her
husband, Ba Anaki, with another man—at least, there are strong indications
that she has. While the matter is still pending, Ba Anaki comes into the
village one day and catches two brothers, Ba Asapoti and Ba Daleki, speaking disparagingly of him and of his lineage: "What he says about Sa Bobi is
probably all lies; anyway, his whole family is no good, his grandmother was
a witch and his mother very likely has an evil heart too." Ba Anaki is
furious and gives them the rough side of his tongue. When the two brothers
attempt to go off in their boat, Ba Anaki tries to stop them by hewing at the
boat with his machete for all he is worth. Others arrive on the scene and
take the infuriated man away.

Two days later, there is a palaver about this case. From an objective
point of view Anaki was right: such gossip about another man's lineage
(*kosi mama pima*) is a serious offense. However, Anaki is put in the wrong;
he has to beg forgiveness and pay a fine of one bottle of liquor. Asapoti
and Daleki go scot free. The governing factor is that Ba Asapoti and Ba

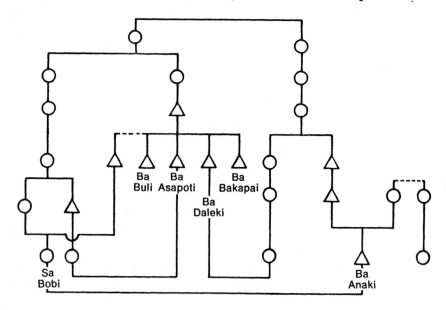

Diagram 5

Daleki are Ba Anaki's classificatory fathers-in-law (see Diagram 5), and as such they should be treated with respect by him. As "fathers-in-law" they may, on the other hand, take all sorts of liberties toward him. A person's conduct is thus judged not only on its own merits, but also according to his relationship with the other persons involved.

After the court session a few men, including Anaki, are talking about the affair. Anaki gives vent to his annoyance: "In actual fact I was right, nevertheless I have to pay, only because they are my 'fathers-in-law.' Perhaps that was thought proper in former times but we people of these times [*bakakio-sama*] don't want this any more." These words, which meet with much approval on the part of the younger men, *seem* to illustrate an important change of attitude, and we might expect this to cause a change of procedure before long. The rest of the conversation, however, indicates that we must not be too sure. Ba Anaki's father consoles him: "You'll get your bottle of liquor back soon; think of Ba Buli! They have planted bananas!" Ba Buli (a brother of Asapoti and Daleki) wants to marry a widow in the village of Pikin Santi; such a marriage is a risky undertaking, since one must be prepared for the dead husband's vengeance. If the new husband wants to have some hope of success, he will need at least the support of the woman's matrilineal kin. *And she is a (classificatory) sister of Ba Anaki's* (see Diagram 5). When Ba Buli comes to ask for her hand in marriage, Ba Anaki will make sure he is present, and then the roles will be reversed, *he* will be the one to make demands and can have his revenge. It is significant to note that Ba Anaki does draw comfort from this prospect and at once abandons his objections against the proceedings. Here too, as is so often true, the person concerned was dissatisfied with a social institution only for so long as it operated against his personal interests. There is no real urge for reform behind such expressions of discontent.

Note that the three brothers and Anaki are related in all sorts of other ways as well. They all live in the same village,[21] Langa Uku. They all have the same relationship with this matrilineage: it is the matrilineage "that begot them" (that is, their father and grandfather respectively were members of this lineage). And finally all three of them have effected an affinal bond with the same lineage through their marriages (see Diagram 5). According to the situation, one or another of these relationships will be stressed. For example, a few days after the events described above, a palaver took place in a different village, at which the case of Anaki versus his wife's seducer was treated. Bakapai, a brother of Asapoti and Daleki, happened to be present. On this occasion he counted as a fellow villager and acted (with others) as Ba Anaki's spokesman. He did make a reference to the quarrel between Ba Anaki and his brothers, but several elders took exception to this: *hic et nunc*, this did not fit into his role.

21. This is only true in part; like many Djuka, these brothers have huts in different villages, and they live in Langa Uku only part of the year (cf. Köbben 1967a:39).

The analysis of this last case explains why the "I caught you" institution can be a fairly effective means of social control. A person has not one but several relationships with most individuals of his social network, and some of these are coordinative whereas others are subordinative or superordinative. If he treats another person unfairly at a moment when that person is in a subordinate position with regard to him, the other has only to wait until the roles are reversed to strike back. The knowledge that this may happen has a preventive effect.

The Efficacy of Sanctions

Let us return for a moment to the definitions of Hoebel and of Pospisil. The latter has taken us a step further, but this definition has a drawback as well. All definitions of law contain the word *sanction;* such a sanction must be effective. Hoebel (1954:26) expresses it as follows: "The law has teeth: teeth that can bite if need be." Is the "bite" of psychological sanctions effective enough? Pospisil thinks that it is in the case of the Kapauku Papua,[22] but in Djuka society such sanctions are rather less efficacious.[23] We have already seen an example: a man should stay in his village for a few months following the birth of his child—especially if it is his first or second child—"to look after the belly"; but often he does not. If he neglects this duty, he is publicly rebuked and promises to behave better in the future, but such promises are by no means always carried out.

At a burial feast each category of relatives must contribute a particular gift (money, liquor, rice, or textiles). If someone neglects to do so and is found out, he is put to shame in a public palaver. Many people take the risk, however; it seems that their ego-image can very well stand it. Even if they are found out, they do not always pay up. They will keep putting it off, and no one can force them. In other cases, also, a public reprimand is not always effective.

The Case of the Defiant Thief. Ba Mangala has stolen and thus disgraced the name of the village. A letter is written to him at the headman's request, ordering him in forcible terms to come home, or else. But what else? The headman has no means of adding force to his authority. Mangala receives the letter and says that he will go at some time when it suits him. In fact he does not go, although people reprimand him for his attitude. Some months later the subject is raised again. The village headman gets

22. Although he points out that in some instances "the advice and solutions of the authorities are not respected" (1958:255, 260).
23. Thoden van Velzen (1966: Chapter 14) did his field work in the village where the power of the Paramount Chief (*Gaman*) of the Djuka is at his highest, yet he comes to fundamentally the same conclusion.

very worked up about it: "Ba Mangala must be deaf, he doesn't come back to the place where his navel-cord is buried. . . . When he dies, he'd better stay where he is."

If a headman is obeyed, it is because of his personal prestige. Many headmen, however, do not have sufficient prestige. Their impotence is covered to some extent by the fact that at a palaver the headman customarily speaks in a tone of command and the person addressed always promises most humbly to do what he is told. But this is no more than outward appearance, or it need be no more than that. As a result, some headmen grossly overestimate their own influence and importance. Others, however, are more realistic, such as one village head from the Cottica region who said openly in a session of the Oracle at Dritabiki (the residence of the Paramount Chief): "We, the village heads of the Cottica, are in a difficult position because we lack the *Gaman's* [Chief's] help. Take my case: I warn my villagers time and again to do as they should, but they don't follow my advice and even agitate against me. They throw me to and fro like a ball." [24] It should be added that this headman had a particularly weak personality.

Stories are told about legendary former headmen who exercised a strict authority; about Da Dandilo, for example, who was village headman of Agitiondo for over forty years and who even dared defy the Surinam government. (The archives show that the Djuka do not exaggerate in this instance; in 1923 Dandilo was deposed as "chief captain" by the government, and another man was put in his place. But since the other had no authority, the situation did not really change.) "If someone did something Dandilo didn't like, he would say go and sit on your buttocks in the dust and the other person would actually do so. Or else he would beat him with a stick or with a whip." Evidently this man's authority was great enough to permit him to use corporal punishment. In this respect he must have been an exception, even in former times, although his authority is probably partly explained by the fact that formerly government interference with the Djuka was even less than it is now.

The Efficacy of Gossip

Undoubtedly there are other instruments of political and social control in Djuka society. One of them is gossip. It is not at all unusual for a group of people to lavish praise on some elder in his presence, only to abuse him as soon as his back is turned. Every person knows that he is being closely watched and that no mistake of his will be passed over silently. That is why certain transactions, such as buying food and

24. Thoden van Velzen 1966:287 (my translation).

drink for a village feast from communal funds, are carried out as much as possible in the presence of witnesses. Gossip occurs, of course, in all societies, but it is my impression that in this society, with its absence of significant hierarchical differences and its lack of privacy, gossip plays a bigger part than in most others and that it is a more important element in social control. I would not, however, regard gossip as a form of "law." Pospisil (1958b:257–272) mentions, besides sanction, three other attributes of law: authority, *obligatio,* and intention of universal application. These same attributes are also to be found in Hoebel's definition. "Gossip" does not possess these attributes, or possesses them only in a very imperfect form. In this connection it is worth noting that for the Djuka themselves, too, gossip is something *sui generis.* It is considered improper and undesirable, even dangerous; the Great Deity or the avenging spirit (*kunu*) [25] may punish gossip by causing illness or misfortune. At a palaver it is quite usual to hear it said that a particular case is being treated in order to put an end to gossip—and equally usual is the pious exclamation of the elders that, thank god, they are not gossipers.

We have seen that too narrow a definition of law is unsatisfactory; here we see that too broad a definition is equally undesirable. If we want one concept to include everything, what we get is a concept explaining nothing.

If we categorize all eighteen Djuka cases given in this paper as law, we do so because they have to a greater or lesser extent the functions of what is called "law" in Western society. This does not mean that Djuka law and Western law are identical. Hoebel (1954:Chapter 12 and passim) has introduced an evolutionistic element in his book on law, and I follow his example. Djuka law is less perfect than Western law, and the order it creates is a precarious order. Where physical sanctions are applied, objectivity is lacking; and where objectivity is practiced, the coercive element is lacking. But in this society law *can* be imperfect because groups are small and social structure is simple. We might almost say that one element implies the other.

25. All or almost all Djuka matrilineages have one or more revenge spirits (*kunu*) —the spirits of persons sinfully murdered by the group.

Ontology of the Judicial Thought
of the Kabrè of Northern Togo

The intent of this paper is to examine how the judicial norm is defined
in relation to the religious norm in Kabrè thought. I am concerned more
specifically with grasping how, in this system of thought, the temporality
of one is reconciled with the eternity of the other; how, in the man-God
relationship, the law, divine emanation, is made by human beings and
made sacred in God; how, in this coming and going from one pole to
the other, the priests are in charge of communication in the direction
God-men, and the ancestors in the direction men-God.

In Kabrè thought, justice means to *conform* to the plan of the creating
God and to *respect* the ancestral customs.

To Conform to the Plan of the Creating God

Eso, the creating God, to whom the whole earth belongs, and who is
the father of mankind, gave order to the world by his word *Esotom;* [1] the
first man, *Esotisa,* "God's messenger," was made the trustee of God's
plan, *Esodutu,* and of all the rules meant to regulate the relationships of
individuals among themselves and to govern society.

The trustee of these rules, *sonsi,* is the priest *Coco,* descendant of the

---

1. The word *tom* is a very general term, which has very different meanings: (a)
the speech, the word of a culprit, one will say: *nyo tom siba,* your word is dead;
(b) the order, commandment; (c) the manner, way, habit; (d) the case, litigation:
tomhuye "judgment."

first man and representative of God on earth; the transgression of these rules impairs social equilibrium and the transmission of life (fertility-fecundity), for which he is accountable and responsible.[2]

If God, owing to his immensity and infinity, is impenetrable to those who have not received from him the gift of prophecy or divination, he nevertheless does not cease to act and be present among men.

Eso laki: God acts; he acts either directly or indirectly. The God who assists and forgives (*Eso sinam, Eso kpem*) is also the one who chastises (*Eso nasa i*) by brandishing lightning, by "striking" (*Eso kpala i*), by sending epidemics, droughts, sterility. When truth is impenetrable to men, they rely on God (*Eso kana we,* "that God sees them") or they solicit his judicial powers in trials by ordeal.

Eso we: God is; he is present in the holy places, *diweri* ("places of presence"), sanctuaries of the great ancestors who revealed God's might and who today are the mediators between men and the Creator.

These spirits, *Akoloma,* who bear witness to Eso's word and sacred ordinances (the term Kadé, which designates the sacred, is applied not only to the places of divine presence, but also to the rules emanating from Eso), are at the same time men's mediators with God; they are at the junction of the two worlds, human and divine, and they insure *communication* from one to the other.

To Respect Ancestral Customs

Atètèna are the ancestors—literally, those who are in the grave. They watch over men and are present among them. Death, in fact, only affects the body; the two spiritual principles of *kaliza* and *wayitu* that exist in the person are immortal, so that death does not mean cessation of life, but passage from one mode of existence to another; after the performance of the funeral ritual and the setting of his altar into the family home, the deceased takes his place henceforth in the lineage of his ancestors and, by perpetuating it, insures the transmission of life to future generations.

Lakasi (from the verb *labu,* to do) designates in a wide sense everything one does; in a more specific sense, it designates ancient customs, customary norms that one must respect; these customs emanate from the ancestors and draw their obligatory force from tradition, *sosa daa bi i wè'lè* ("in days of the ancestors, how it was").

Should one see in the *sonsi* and *lakasi* two independent sources of law: justice from above, the sovereign law of God; justice from below, the

2. The priest *Coco* is also designated by the expression *Tètutu,* the one of the earth; he is indeed the keeper of the ancestral land, and in the old days he settled matters of land boundaries.

customs of man? This interpretation would be too rational and systematic, because the *sonsi* and *lakasi* do not arise from two different levels but are essentially two poles of a single inseparable reality, the world of God and men: the *sonsi*, insofar as they regulate human society, participate in its humanity; the *lakasi*, insofar as they take root in ancestral tradition, receive their consecration from it. The priests who worship God and the mediating spirits between God and men, *Akoloma*, are precisely the guardians of the justice that is human and divine at the same time, and the transgression of which leads to retribution.

The verb *kètu* expresses on the one hand the idea of resemblance, on the other the idea of conformity to bounds of measure: *kètu* can indeed be used, either to designate resemblance, physical or moral (one will say of a child resembling his father: *biha kanè kètina ka ja*), or to indicate a person or an action that conforms to the rules and customs.

Kitèkètim means nonconformity to norms, overstepping the bounds (not to follow, *tingu*, transgress, *yu*, the rules and customs). Thus one who lies, *cètu*, to harm his fellow man, *kpèntu*, will be reproached in these terms: *bi fey dew*, this is not nice; *bi laki mbu*; this is not done; *bi kisa*, this is forbidden.[3]

The "delinquent," *kitèkètu*, is an agitator, an agent of disorder and corruption, *kiwèkim*;[4] his infraction calls for justice in its double aspect, sacred and profane: if the culprit is not eliminated (capital punishment, expulsion), he must be reinstated; one must then re-establish the disturbed divine order and rebalance the ruptured human order.

Re-establishment of divine order: it behooves the *kitèkètu* to rectify *daanu*,[5] the disturbance he caused, with a sacrifice of retribution and expiation, *nyozuu*.[6]

Rebalancing, establishing human order: this role was the obligation of the *sosa*, the great men of the village, who held a meeting under the "presidency" of the most influential man, *wiyau* (traditionally the Kabrè had no chieftainship); this judicial assembly was called upon to pronounce judgment "in the last resort," when the dispute could not be settled by the family heads concerned or by the head of the market *kiyakudu* if something arose in the market place (a brawl, a theft), or

3. Note with regard to the last expression that the notion of prohibition by the term *kisu* is only the negative counterpart of the prescriptions emanating from God and the ancestors; "that which is not done" refers to "that which is done."
4. *Kiwèkim*, from the verb *wèku*, "to trouble, to spoil, to deteriorate"; *tètu weka*, "the country is spoiled," is an expression one often hears from old people.
5. *Daanu* means "to put order into, to make good," in the material and moral senses.
6. The sacrifice *nyozu* is distinct from the sacrifice of communion and alliance, *kpayu*, that is practiced by the priests in the name of the community at certain times of the year (for example, at the time of the opening of the hunting season) and in certain exceptional circumstances (for example, the day before a fight). In the case of an expiation sacrifice, the person offering it does not eat the sacrificed animal.

by the priest *Coco* in the case of contested property or land boundaries. Today it is the tribunal of the chief, surrounded by notables acting as assistant judges, that is called upon to pronounce itself on any litigation that has not been settled privately, excluding "penal" matters. The "traditional" procedure has been maintained in these matters, but the authority of the old supreme jurisdiction has been considerably weakened by, on the one hand, the possibility of appeal to the tribunal of first instance of the district and, on the other hand, by the fact that certain chiefs are challenged by the population.

To specify the function of the village tribunal, we shall briefly examine the two main types of tension and social conflicts [7] internal to the peasant society of the Kabrè country, namely women's affairs, *halatom*, on the one hand and, on the other, matters of witchcraft, *alukendatom*. It is, in fact, in these two areas that the disputes carried to the chief's tribunal are the most numerous; [8] this results, on the one hand, from the present instability of marriage, because the couple's union is less and less a part of an alliance of families, and, on the other hand, from the important place held by beliefs in witchcraft and by the murderous doings of a certain number of individuals, eaters of "souls."

Divorce, *dama kisu* (literally "to refuse oneself to the other"), is a rupture that one seeks to avoid at all costs, and everything is done to reconcile the parties. The woman who abandoned the marital home and whose husband desires to take her back is summoned to return: *"Nya walu labi nyo kunyong sin . . . . ; kudumtu wèna se nting nya walu yoo"* ("Your husband suffered so much for you . . . ; the only thing to do is to follow your husband"). If necessary, she is returned by force. It is only after several attempts at reconciliation, and generally only when the woman has a child by a lover, that the judges will recognize the separation and will compel the lover to compensate the husband for the marriage payments that he made at the time of the engagement: *"Kiyaku nku ki wiye mo sun na bisina buye ndè me cèba cihda naa na mo toolin bicèkiyè yo, xèyim bi lide"* ("From the day that I 'paid bridewealth' for you to the day that I took off your pearls, and put the loincloth on you, give me the money for that").

7. On the economic level, the shortage of land, as a result of the very strong demographic pressure, has caused emigration of numerous farmers to virgin land in the center and in the south; although the problem of land is thus partly and temporarily solved, raising only matters of secondary importance to justice—loans of plots not returned, claims to their ancestors' fields by emigrants who come back to their native land—Kabrè colonization nevertheless raises numerous disputes in the already populated areas in which the Kabrè settle and where they claim rights to the land in the name of the improvements they have made.

8. Out of the forty-five trials we attended in 1962 and 1965, twenty concerned women's affairs and ten concerned matters of witchcraft.

The judges are called upon to weigh the reciprocal wrongs and griev-ances in order to eliminate the grounds for disagreement, with a view to arriving at a reconciliation and not to granting the divorce for the benefit of one spouse or the other. The departure of the woman, whom the husband obtained at the price of hard work and gifts, must be compen-sated for in any case. Several features of the procedure particularly illus-trate the major concern of the judges with re-establishing conjugal peace (separation leading to reunion) or, failing that, to liquidate a hopeless situation in order to set up a new one (divorce leading to remarriage):

1. The judges cannot automatically take the case; they can judge it only at the request of one of the litigants.

2. The parties are their own counsel for the defense; if they can call upon witnesses, the litigants must, in turn, formulate their arguments themselves; one notes that literate people are not allowed to rely on written notes.

3. The case can be judged only through cross-examination.

4. Debates, deliberation, and decision are public. Public debates are necessary because any trial implicates not only two individuals, but also the groups of which they are members; all the words spoken by the judges are intended to appease the spirits and must be heard by the audience; the judicial scene is a spectacle for all and gives the elders the oppor-tunity to recall precepts and customs.

The justice of men is called upon to yield to the justice of God for all evil acts that set invisible forces in motion.

The spirits *Alewa* are only visible to those who possess second sight, the *kenatina;* the latter have a particular power, *hama,* that they can use for beneficent or evil ends. We shall mention here only two types of *kenatina*—the diviner, *tiwu,* who has been able to dominate the *Alewa,* and the sorcerer, *efelu,* who is dominated by their might.

The diviner is in a position to detect the *afela* (plural of *efelu*) and to liberate the *kalizase* that they captured, the deprivation of which quickly brings about death. Called in consultation to the side of the sick person whose *kaleza* has been imprisoned, the diviner must discover the place of its imprisonment and determine the author of the evil spell, *nima hokiyu* ("the binder of ropes"); most often, it is a close relative or an ally of the victim, whose identity, although it is not revealed, is not doubted by anyone.

The assertions of the diviner put a heavy presumption of guilt on the person singled out, but his testimony can be appraised as partial or in-sufficient by the judges who will then request another diviner; but, even should the latter confirm the declarations of the first, the judges cannot condemn the supposed culprit who persists in denying the charge; it rests with God to pronounce Himself during the trial by ordeal, *kpesiyè* ("refutation").[9] If the accused overcomes the ordeal, he is declared innocent; if he is reinstated in society, his accuser is cut off from it.

9. The ordeal is also designated by the term *kasanga* ("purification"). One of the currently practiced rituals consists of plunging the right hand into a pan of blazing oil and retrieving an iron ring from it without burning oneself; it is said of the one who succeeds: *bi li sa i,* "it got him out"; of the one who does not succeed, *bi kpa i,* "it took him," or *bi doki i,* "it held him."

Struck by Speech:
The Yakan Concept of Litigation

tiyaq ku tawwaq bissāh
Here I am struck by speech
(Remark of an accused in a trial)

The Yakan legal system is manifest almost exclusively through one kind of behavior: talk. Consequently the ethnographer's record of observations of litigation is largely a linguistic record, and the legal system is a code for talking, a linguistic code. In this paper we focus initially on a small part of this talk, that representing the concept of litigation. We subsequently attempt to illustrate how a definition of this concept guides a description of the legal system and, finally, points the way toward meaningful comparisons with legal systems of other cultures.

The Yakan are Philippine Moslems inhabiting the island of Basilan located off the southern tip of Zamboanga Peninsula, a western extension of the island of Mindanao.[1] Southwest of Basilan stretches the Sulu archi-

1. Fieldwork among the Yakan in 1962, 1963–1964, and 1965–1966 was supported by a United States Public Health Service Grant under the National Institute of Mental Health and by an auxiliary research award from the Social Science Research Council. The statements in this paper are at a level of generality applicable to the Basilan Yakan as a whole and represent knowledge that any adult Yakan could be expected to have. Yakan expressions are represented by a linguistically motivated orthography, but certain canons of traditional phonemic analysis are ignored ("a," for example, represents both /a/ and /e/ where this contrast is neutralized). This practice enables dialect differences to be accounted for by special rules applicable to a uniform orthography. /q/ is a glottal catch, /e/ a mid-front vowel, /j/ a voiced, palatal affricative. The ethnographic record upon which this description is based includes the investigator's observations of court sessions, transcriptions of forty-three tape-recorded trial sessions at all jurisdictional levels, and informants' interpretations of the content of these observations and texts. In addition, by living in Yakan households during the entire field period, the investigator was continually exposed to conversations related to litigation. Special acknowledgment is due to Samuel Pajarito and Reuben Muzarin for assistance in recording and transcribing court sessions and to Hadji Umar of Giyung for many long discussions about Yakan law.

pelago, a chain of small islands extending some 200 miles to within a few miles of the northeast coast of Borneo. Some 60,000 Yakan share Basilan's 1,282 square kilometers with Christian Filipinos concentrated along the north coast and with Taw Sug and Samal Moslems living mostly in coastal villages all around the island.[2] The Yakan are close linguistic kin of the sea-faring Samal but, unlike them, practice an exclusively land-oriented economy: diversified grain, root, and tree-crop agriculture on plowed fields and swiddens, commercial copra production, and cattle raising. Supplementary economic activities include plantation labor, distribution of cigarettes smuggled from Borneo by their Moslem brothers, and banditry. These economic activities bring the Yakan into close contact with the Philippine economy, political system, and army. Having been given this much information, the anthropological reader has probably already classed the Yakan as "peasants," which is appropriate as long as the concept does not bring to mind a downtrodden, economically exploited, culturally deprived people submerged by the weight of some "great tradition."

Houses, mosques, and graveyards dot the Yakan countryside, rarely revealing any obvious patterns of spatial clustering. Each, however, represents the focus of a pattern of social alignment. Houses are occupied by nuclear families, independent units of production and consumption. The family is the unit of membership in a parish, a religious and political unit under the titular leadership of a mosque priest (*qimam*). Parishes are alliances of independent families; affiliation is by choice, not by residence or kinship ties. Parishes comprise only several dozen families, and any family has a network of social relations with kin and neighbors extending beyond the parish. Ancestors, buried in conspicuously decorated graves, define networks of cognatic kinship ties among the living. Although these networks are unsegmented by discrete, corporate groups of any kind, the Yakan talk about groupings of kin in ways that would do credit to a social anthropologist. Note, for example, the contrast between *paŋkat baqirah*, "the unrestricted, nonunilineal descent group defined by an ancestor (female) named Baira," and *qusba baqirah*, "the kindred centered around an ego named Baira." Like the legal expressions we are about to discuss, this talk about social groups must be understood to be a part of social behavior as well as a description of it.

Defining Litigation

A description of a culture derives from an ethnographer's observations of the stream of activities performed by the people he is studying. As a

2. There are also Yakan speakers on Sakol, Malanipa, and Tumalutab islands just east of Zamboanga City. These communities are beyond the scope of this paper.

first step toward producing an ethnographic statement, the investigator must segment and classify the events of this behavior stream so that he can say, for example, of two successive events that one is "different" from the other, and of two nonsuccessive events that they are repetitions of the "same" activity. If the ethnographer claims his people do X three times a week, verification of his statement requires not simply counting occurrences of X, but also assessing the criteria for distinguishing X from all the other things people do during the week and for deciding that all the different events construed as instances of X in fact represent the "same" activity. Information about what is the "same" and what is "different" can only come from the interpretations of events made by the people being studied.

Within the stream of behavior observable in Yakan society, there are some events that are difficult to characterize initially except as "a group of people talking together." There seems to be no focus of activity other than talk—no distinctive settings, apparel, or paraphernalia. We might postulate that all such events are manifestations of the same category of cultural activities, that all are repetitions of the same scene. At a very general level we could justify this decision. All these activities can be labeled *magbissāh*, 'talking to each other' in response to a query such as *magqine siyeh*, 'what are they doing?'[3] But, as the English glosses indicate, this categorization is not particularly informative, especially to an observer of the scene. To discover a more refined categorization we must attend to the way the Yakan talk about talking.

Yakan, like English, provides a large number of linguistic expressions for talking about a great variety of aspects of speech behavior. Of these, we sort out for consideration the following set of semantically related expressions, all possible responses to the query "What are they doing?" (Only the variable portion of the response is shown.[4] Some of these forms, especially *hukum*, have different, but related meanings in different contexts. Etymological information is given for later discussion):

1. *mitiŋ* (from English), 'discussion';
2. *qisun*, 'conference';
3. *mawpakkat* (from Arabic), 'negotiation';
4. *hukum* (from Arabic), 'litigation.'

The structure of inclusion and contrast relations manifest in the use of these terms to denote events is shown in Figure 1. Let A, B, C, D represent situations that can be labeled as *mitiŋ, qisun, mawpakkat,* and

---

3. Single quotes enclose English glosses. These are to be assigned the meaning given to the Yakan expressions for which they substitute.

4. In response to *magqine* (< *N*, 'active,' + *pag*, 'mutuality,' + *qine*, 'what'), 'What is the mutual activity or relationship?' the forms cited, all unanalyzable morphemes, replace *qine*, 'what': *magqine siyeh*, 'What are they doing?' *magqisun*, 'Conferring with each other.' Note also: *magqine siyah*, 'How are they related to each other?' *magpoŋtinaqih*, 'As siblings.'

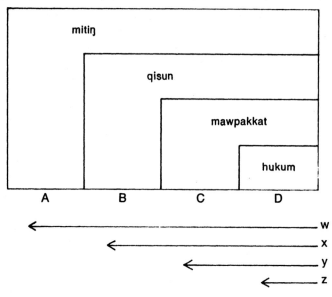

A, B, C, D: situations represented
w, x, y, z: features of meaning

Figure 1.   Semantic structure

hukum, respectively. Then it is the case that *mitiŋ* can label the set of situations {ABCD}, *qisun* the set of situations {BCD}, *mawpakkat* the set {CD}, [whereas] *hukum* can label only {D}. Thus these expressions form an ordered series, the situations labelable by a given term including all those labelable by each succeeding term. However, it is also the case that *mitiŋ* can be used to contrast situation A with each of the other situations (A not B, C, or D) as in the exchange: *magqisuŋ qenteq siyeh,* 'They seem to be conferring.' *Dumaqin, magmitiŋ hadja qiyan,* 'No, they're just discussing.' The form *hadja,* 'just, merely,' specifies that *mitiŋ* is to be construed in its minimal sense, but its use is not obligatory to convey this sense. Similarly, *qisun, mawpakkat,* and *hukum* can be used to contrast B, C, D respectively with each of the other situations. We have, then, a case of the use of the same form at different levels of contrast, a situation common in semantic representation (Frake 1961), and one that has caused some controversy over interpretation (Bright and Bright 1965:258).

In the use of the same expression at different levels of contrast, there is in Yakan a distinction between those cases, such as the present example, in which use at the less inclusive level is specifiable by a de-emphatic particle (for example, *hadja*, 'just, merely') and those in which it is specifiable by an emphatic particle (such as *teqed*, 'very, true, real').

Contrast *magmitiŋ hadja qiyan*, 'They're just discussing' (and not 'conferring,' 'negotiating,' and the like), with *magpoŋtinaqi teqed qiyan*, 'They're real siblings' (and not 'half-siblings,' 'cousins,' and so on). The use of the same term at different levels of contrast results, in the former case, from a *specification* of the basic general sense of an expression. In the latter case it results from an *extension* of the basic specific sense of an expression. Cases of specification, such as the present example, can be interpreted a manifestations of "marking," a phenomenon widespread in linguistic representation in phonology and morphology as well as in semantics (Jakobson 1957, Greenberg 1966).

Semantic marking means that given two expressions, A and B sharing some feature of meaning x but differing with respect to some feature y and in that sense contrasting, the difference is not

term A represents the meaning: $x\ y$
term B represents the meaning: $x\ \bar{y}$

but rather

term A represents the meaning: x
term B represents the meaning: $x\ y$.

The use of term B necessarily implies feature y, but the use of term A does not necessarily say anything about the presence or absence of y. Term B is marked for y. In our series each term is marked for a feature (or features) not necessarily implied by its predecessor:

mitiŋ, 'discussion': w

qisun, 'conference': $w\ x$

mawpakkat, 'negotiation': $w\ x\ y$

hukum, 'litigation': $w\ x\ y\ z$

The next task is to characterize the features of meaning represented above as w, x, y, z; w being what the set has in common and x, y, z being sucsive increments to this common meaning.

At the outset we should be clear about just what linguistic and cognitive operations of our informants we are trying to account for. It is not simply a case of determining the perceptual cues for distinguishing one object from another. If a Yakan sees some people engaged in mutual speech behavior (that categorization he can make perceptually) and wants to know what they are doing, he will in all probability ask them. In this case the object of categorization, a group of people engaged in some activity, is aware of what it is doing. This awareness is, in itself, an attribute—a necessary one—of the category. Just as in classifying a plant one might apply a test of taste or smell to determine a criterial property, in classifying these speech events one applies a test of eliciting a linguistic response from the performers of the activity. It is impossible for people engaged in 'litigation' or in 'conference' not to be aware of what they are doing and not to be able to communicate their awareness. For people engaged, say, in 'litigation' to be able to state that they are 'litigating' is a necessary condition for the activity to be 'litigation,' but it is not a sufficient condition. They might be lying or, more probably in Yakan life, they might be joking. Being funny is a prominent goal of Yakan speech behavior, and semantic incongruity is a standard way of adding humor to speech—but the effect is dependent on the hearer's ability to recognize the incongruity. What we are trying to formulate, then, are the conditions under which it is congruous, neither humorous nor deceitful, to state that one is engaged in 'litigation.' These conditions are the semantic features of the concepts in question. Our evidence for semantic features does not come from informants' statements about the linguistic representations of these concepts (though such explicit definitions of terms are often useful guides for preliminary formulations), but from informants' interpretations of the situations that the concepts represent. Our aim is not to give an elegant formulation of minimal contrastive features, but a statement that reflects the various dimensions of speech behavior revealed in the use and interpretation of these expressions.

Let us consider first the features common to the whole set, those that distinguish all events construable as *mitiŋ*, 'discussion,' from other things Yakan do. This set of events includes the events labeled by the other expressions. Then we will consider what each successive term adds to these common features. Four dimensions of speech behavior appear to be involved in contrasting 'discussion' with other activities.

1. Focus. The focus of 'discussion' is on the topic of messages. There is a subject of discussion. Excluded are speech events in which the focus is on message form: storytelling, riddling, exchanging verses, joking, prayer (which, being in Arabic, has no semantic content for the Yakan).

2. Purpose. The purpose of the gathering is to talk. Excluded are activities in which the intent to accomplish something other than talking is responsible for the gathering of participants.

3. Roles. Speaking time is distributed among the participants. Each role in the scene, whatever its other characteristics, is both a speaking and a listening role. Excluded are monologues, in which speaking time is monopolized by one person.[5]

4. Integrity. Integrity refers to the extent to which the activity is construed as an integral unit as opposed to being a part of some other activity. A 'discussion' must have sufficient integrity not to be construable as incident to or accompanying some other activity. A 'discussion' can occur within the context of another kind of event, but only as a recognizably bounded interruption, as when participants disengage from some

5. The mutuality of the behavior is represented by the prefix *pag* in the sequence *N + pag > mag*. See footnote 4.

other activity to talk something over. (This dimension will sound less fuzzy when we consider its relevance to the contrast between 'litigation' and other kinds of 'discussion.')

The expression *mitiŋ*, 'discussion,' necessarily implies only these features. Each of the succeeding expressions in the series adds some necessary implications along one or more of these dimensions (Table 1):

Table 1. *Semantic Features*

	Topic	Purpose	Role Structure	Integrity
'discussion'	subject	talk	undifferentiated	minimal
'conference'	issue	decision	undifferentiated	minimal
'negotiation'	disagreement	settlement	opposing sides	moderate
'litigation'	dispute	ruling	court	maximal

QISUN, 'CONFERENCE'

1. Focus. The subject of discussion is an *issue*, some topic that presents a problem to be decided: when to plant rice, when to go on a trip, what price to pay in a transaction.

2. Purpose. A 'conference' has an expected outcome, a *decision* about the issue. Participants meet in order to reach a decision, and, if a decision is made, the conference is concluded.

3. Roles. No added implications.

4. Integrity. No added implications.

MAWPAKKAT 'NEGOTIATION'

1. Focus. The issue in 'negotiation' is a disagreement, a topic over which participants have conflicting interests.

2. Purpose. The decision is a *settlement*, a legally binding resolution of the disagreement.

·3. Roles. Participants are divided into two protagonistic sides. Witnesses may be present.

4. Integrity. No clear added implications. Although *mawpakkat* is more likely to refer to an integral event than *qisun*, and *qisun* than *mitiŋ*, these are not necessary implications.

HUKUM, 'LITIGATION'

1. Focus. The disagreement is a *dispute*, a disagreement that arises from a charge that an *offense* has been committed. A dispute can also be handled by negotiation, but the topic of litigation is necessarily a dispute. A dispute handled by litigation is a *case*.

2. Purpose. The settlement takes the form of a legal *ruling* based on precedent and having special sanctions.

3. Roles. In addition to protagonists and optional witnesses, 'litigation' requires a *court*, a set of neutral judges who control the proceedings and attempt to effect a ruling.

4. Integrity. 'Litigation' is always an integral activity. If it is interrupted by a different kind of activity—eating, for example—there is a new instance of litigation, a different court session. "Discussion," "conference," and "negotiation," in their minimal senses, can occur as parts of "litigation," but "litigation" cannot occur as a part of these other activities.

Each expression in our series except the terminal one has a maximal and minimal sense, depending on whether the speaker intends to include or exclude the meanings marked by succeeding expressions. 'Mere discussion' (*mitiŋ hadja*), the minimal sense of *mitiŋ*, implies the features listed as common to the whole set, but the topic is simply a subject to discuss, not an issue to be decided, a disagreement to be settled, or a case to be ruled on. The purpose is to talk, but there is no expected outcome that terminates the event, no decision to be reached, no settlement to be negotiated, no ruling to be handed down. Role structure is undifferentiated and integrity minimal, although it is still greater than that implied by *magbissāh*, 'talking to each other.' A *mitiŋ* in its minimal sense more closely resembles an American "bull session" than what we would call a "meeting."

"Mere conference" applies to situations in which the issue is not a dispute, the decision not a settlement, and role structure remains undifferentiated. 'Mere negotiation' applies to situations in which, though the disagreement may be a dispute, the intended outcome is a settlement that is not a legal ruling and that is reached without the aid of judges.

The flexibility of reference afforded by this semantic structure, the ability to be ambiguous about whether a general or specific sense is intended, reflects the fact that not only are these expressions used to talk about speech behavior, but their use is also a part of the behavior they describe. A Yakan uses terms like *mawpakkat* and *hukum* not simply to give serious answers to probes for information, but also to further his own objectives in speech situations by advancing a particular—perhaps ostensibly incongruous—interpretation of an event and by representing this conceptualization linguistically in an effective way. He can, for example, call for a 'conference' without immediately committing himself to an interpretation of the divisiveness of the issue; he can call for a 'discussion' without implying that there is an issue at stake.

For these reasons, stylistic features of expressions—selections among alternative linguistic representations of a given conceptual distinction—figure importantly in their use and affect their semantic properties. In our set, *mawpakkat* is considered more learned than the other terms, all of which are ordinary, everyday words. Although the word is widely known, it occurs most often during 'litigation' when 'negotiations' are being talked about. In other contexts the notion of 'mere negotiation' is more likely to be referred to as *qisun*, using 'conference' in its general sense. It is probably a consequence of this stylistic difference that the semantic contrast between *mawpakkat* and *qisun* seems less sharply drawn than that between the other pairs of expressions. In direct questioning about the meaning of these terms, many informants have stated offhand that *mawpakkat* and *qisun* have the same meaning. No one has said that of *hukum* and any other term in the set. The same informants will still agree that if, for example, several guests at a festivity get together to decide when to leave, that this is a case of *qisun* but not of *mawpakkat*. The two expressions are not synonymous but the difference between them is somewhat harder to uncover than is the difference between the other terms. The concept of "negotiation" can also be represented by expressions referring to the distinctive aspects of the event, for example: *pagsulutan*, 'agreement, settlement'—not including legal rulings (*hukuman*); *qalegdah* (from Spanish), 'to settle a dispute by any means'; *janjiqan* (from Malay), 'negotiated contractual promise.'

Any citation of Yakan legal terms illustrates another property of these expressions—that is, the large percentage of forms that are loan words from the languages of both of the "great traditions" impinging on the Yakan: Arabic and Malay of the Malaysian-Moslem tradition, English and Spanish of the Filipino-Western tradition.[6] These loans have been acquired through contact with intermediary languages (Taw Sug and Zamboangueño), and their prevalence is not a reflection of a crushing impact of either Moslem or Western legal concepts upon Yakan law, but of the stylistic coups a speaker of Yakan scores by displaying a knowledge of foreign words. This process apparently has a long history. Many loans, such as *hukum* (from Arabic), are now completely assimilated and are not now recognized as foreign. The term *mitiŋ*, currently much more popular than alternative designations of 'discussion,' seems to be on the verge of losing its loan-word aura. English loans used in current litigation include: *wantid, holdap, kidnap, wadan* ('warrant'), *supenah, pospon, pendiŋ, qokeh* ("approval"), and *qistodok* ('strategy,' from "stroke").

Describing Litigation

Our formulation states that litigation is a kind of topic-focused mutual speech behavior, the distinctive attributes of which pertain to the content

6. The source of etymological information on Malay and Arabic loans is Wilkinson (1932). Yakan expressions are marked as Malay loans only when there are phonological grounds for distinguishing loans from inherited cognates.

and role structure of talking. An observer of Yakan litigation would have difficulty finding any other element that sets it apart from other activities. There are no distinctive settings, no courtrooms in which litigation takes place. A site for a trial should be neutral and should require no one to play a host role—a role that requires the offering of food. A typical result of these considerations is convocation on the porch of the house of one of the judges (in Yakan terms, "on" the house but not "within" it). But a wide variety of other activities takes place here as well. There are no distinctive paraphernalia associated with litigation: no law books, no gavel, no judges' bench, no witness stand. There is no provisioning of participants. They may smoke and chew betel, but the rules for soliciting and proferring smoking and chewing makings are the same as for other informal gatherings. There is no distinctive dress associated with litigation—no judges' robes—and participants do not dress up to go to court as they do to go to ceremonies. If one were to make distinction in Yakan activities between festive and nonfestive, formal and informal, litigation would clearly fall on the nonfestive, informal side. As speech-focused activity, litigation is outside the domain of ceremonies, feasts, technological tasks, and other object-focused activities. We must therefore organize a description of litigation along those dimensions of speech behavior found to be significant.

CASES

The topic of litigation is a 'case' (*pākalaq*, from Malay from Sanskrit), a 'dispute' brought to court. A 'dispute' arises when an identified party is 'charged' with an 'offense' and the accused counters the charge. To make a charge is to publicly proclaim a particular interpretation of an act. To counter a charge is to advance another interpretation. Clearly the key descriptive problem is to state the rules for interpreting an act as an offense. Equally clear is that these rules cannot be perfectly consistent in their formulation or straightforward in their application. There must be room for argument if there is to be litigation.

Offenses. 'Offenses' (*salaq*) are a subset of 'wrongs' (*duseh*)—those wrongs aganst persons that can lead to a dispute. There are also wrongs against God (*tuhan*), such as desecrating a Koran; wrongs against this-world supernaturals (*saytan*, from Arabic), such as cutting down a tree they inhabit; and wrongs against ancestors (*kapapuqan*) now in the other world (*qahilat*, from Arabic), such as selling an heirloom. But these beings need not rely on courts to seek redress.

The Yakan employ a large number of linguistic expressions for talking about different kinds of offenses, along a variety of semantic dimensions dealing with the nature and consequences of acts as well as with the social relationships between offender and victim. The saliency of dimensions with respect to one another can vary in different portions of the domain. For example, physical assault with intent to kill (*bonoq*) and sexual assault (*hilap*, from Arabic, and many other expressions) are terminologically distinguished unless the offense is also a wrong against God, as is the case if victim and offender are primary kin or primary affines. There is one term, *sumbaŋ*, to cover these grievous sins against both man and God. One might say that the contrast "sex versus killing" is neutralized when an expression is marked for "interference by God." (It might be noted that sexual relations are often designated euphemistically or facetiously by metaphors based on expressions for killing or fighting. "To make a killing" in Yakan does not refer to business success.) We will state here only a few general inferences about the nature of the concept of 'offense,' which have been drawn from Yakan talk about particular kinds of offenses.

At the most general level, for an act to be interpretable as an offense it must be a threat to a *dapuq* relationship. The term *dapuq* occurs together with a possessive attribute in response to the same query that elicits kinship terms and other relationship expressions. Unlike kinship relations, however, a person may be *dapuq* of an object as well as of another person. Being someone's or something's *dapuq* implies having an economic interest in him (it) and a responsibility for him (it). The notion includes, but is broader than, that of ownership. To be a *dapuq* of a person in no way implies that the person is one's slave. One is *dapuq* to his children, his legal wards, his spouse, and himself. To be a *dapuq* of an object does not necessarily imply that one has rights of use, possession, or sale, but only that one has a legitimate interest in its use or disposal. A water source, for example, has its *dapuq* (*dapuq boheq*)—those who use it and who would suffer economic loss if it were destroyed—but it has no owner. The *dapuq* of a mosque (*dapuq laŋgal*) is not its owner—there is such a person—but the entire congregation. The *dapuq* of an inheritance (*dapuq pusakaq*) is a potential heir. Any threat to a *dapuq* relationship can be interpreted as an economic threat, a threat whose gravity is expressible in pesos and centavos. All offenses, including murder, can be compensated for by money. The purpose of Yakan litigation is not to mete out punishment, but to award compensation for injury.

There are two ways in which an act can be an offense. First, it can challenge a person's status as a *dapuq*, usually in the form of a claim that some other person is properly the *dapuq* of a given object or person. Second, an act can damage an object or person in such a way as to reduce its economic value to its *dapuq* (including, in the case of persons, the victim himself). Since a given object or person is likely to have more than one *dapuq*, an offense generally produces several plaintiffs. A sexual assault, for example, is an offense against the victim (*dapuq badannen*, 'dapuq of one's body'), her parents (*dapuq qanakin*, 'dapuq of the child'), and if she is married, her husband (*dapuq qandahin,* 'dapuq of the wife'). *Charges.* It is up to a victim of an offense to make a charge (*tuntut*); all Yakan law is civil law. He must, furthermore, determine the identity of the offender and assume responsibility for the identification. Offenses in which victim and offender do not meet face to face or in which the victim does not survive are difficult to prosecute. Even though theft, ambush shootings, and murder are among the more common—and certainly the most complained about—offenses in Yakan life, they rarely reach the courts. It is largely sex and, to a lesser extent, fights and property disputes that keep court agenda full.

An initial charge can be made in the form of a complaint (*diklamuh,* from Spanish) to a court or even by directly confronting the accused. More often an accuser will utilize gossip channels to make his charge known to the accused. In this way he can feel out the response of his opponent before being irrevocably committed. A way out is left open through denying the truth or serious intent of the gossip. One of the dangers of Yakan life is *limorok* (literally, 'slip through'): 'inadvertently instigating a dispute by incautious gossip in the presence of someone who is likely to relay the accusation to the accused.'

There are three strategies available for countering a charge:

1. One can deny the validity of the accuser's definition of the offense in question, disputing the meaning of a concept. Does, for example, the notion of sexual offense include all acts in which a male makes unnecessary physical contact with a female not his spouse, or only those acts in which a male has sexual designs on the woman?

2. One can deny that the act in question has the properties to qualify it as an instance of an offense, disputing what really happened. For example, granted any physical contact as described above is an offense, did any such contact actually occur in the particular instance?

3. One can deny responsibility for the act because (a) someone else committed it; (b) the accused was provoked by the accuser; (c) the accused was incited by some third party (a much stronger excuse for wrongdoing among the Yakan than among ourselves); (d) the act was unintentional.

To deny a charge is at the same time to make a charge against one's accuser, for a false charge is in itself an offense: it threatens the economic interests of the accused. The set of arguments propounded by one side in a dispute to counter the charges of the other is their *daqawah* (from Arabic) or "case" in the sense of "the defense rests its case."

Disputes. Once a charge has been made and countered, a dispute exists. Disputants may simply decide to live with the dispute, they may attempt to dispose of each other, or they may seek a settlement. If they decide on the last course of action, they may either 'negotiate' or 'litigate.' In 'negotiation' two opposing parties meet to settle a disagreement by mutual agreement. The disagreement need not be a dispute (that is, the outcome of a charge). Negotiating a contract, property settlements, marriage (which involves all of the preceding) are cases to point. Negotiations are often sufficient to handle minor disputes and are necessary for major disputes difficult to place under the jurisdiction of any Yakan court. An agreement is specific to the negotiating parties and need not derive from legal precedents; the breaking of an agreement, however, is an offense and can result in a dispute taken to court. Marriages are made by negotiation but dissolved by litigation. To settle a dispute by litigation requires that it be reported to a court, at which point the dispute becomes a legal case. The party that considers itself offended against should report first, but often by the time a case reaches court, there is such a complex of charges and countercharges that any distinction between plaintiff and defendant becomes obscure.

COURTS

What distinguishes litigation from other methods of settling disputes is the presence of a court (*saraq*, from Arabic)—a set of persons, performing the role of judge, who are ostensibly neutral on the issue and whose task it is to formulate a settlement. The Yakan court has few of the tangible manifestations of its Western counterpart: professional judges holding an office, court houses, explicit and continuous schedules, and well-defined jurisdictions. On the other hand, a set of judges is not recruited ad hoc to try each case that appears. Particular sets of judges meet more than once and may try more than one case in a single session. Furthermore, there is a fundamental difference between a single case appearing again in a subsequent session of the same court—a continuation of a single trial—and a case appearing again in a different court—a retrial of the same case. One may also report to a court when the court is not in session—to file a charge, for example, or to seek asylum. The crucial problems in a description of Yakan courts are those of legal authority and of jurisdiction. How are persons recruited to the role of judge? How are cases assigned to particular courts?

Judges. To act as a judge, a person must be a parish leader with the ability and knowledge to perform the role and with sufficient political power at the jurisdictional level of the court to make his voice effective. Parish leadership is not a political office with formal rules of recruitment, but a position achieved by accumulating influence and prestige by a variety of means: religious learning, economic success, military prowess, forensic ability, acquisition of a title, pilgrimage to Mecca, election to a local office in the Philippine political system (councilor or barrio captain), or simply growing older. (The most common expression for a leader is *bahiq*, 'elder.') Typically, parish leadership is vested in a small group of close kinsmen, each specializing in one or more of these routes to power. One man may be the priest and litigator, another the entrepreneur, another the fighter. Larger political groupings are informal and unstable alliance of parishes. To exert leadership at this wider level, one must also be a leader at the parish level. One does not rise to higher positions; one merely extends the range of his influence. An exceptional position is that of titular tribal chief (*datuq*) of all the Yakan, a hereditary office now held by the Westernized son of a Christian Filipino escaped convict, who, during the latter part of the Spanish regime, fled to Basilan. There he assumed political leadership over the Yakan and achieved formal recognition of his position by both the Spaniards and the Sultan of Sulu.

Jurisdiction. The jurisdiction of a court is a function of the social distance between the judges who comprise it and the disputants before it. This distance, in turn, is a response to the need to preserve neutrality with respect to the cases brought before it. The rule for assignment of a case to a court is to maintain minimal social distance between court and protagonists consistent with preserving neutrality. This rule has the effect that the greater the social distance between protagonists and the more serious the case, the higher the jurisdiction of the court that can try the case. If both protagonists belong to the same parish, then one or more of their own parish leaders may be found who, by kinship and other dimensions of social affiliation, are equidistant from both sides. If, however, the protagonists belong to different parishes, the court must comprise representatives of both parishes. The seriousness of a case is measured by the number of active supporters recruited by each disputant. As the number of active supporters surrounding each disputant increases —that is, as each party of protagonists grows larger—the further afield one must go to find judges who are not involved on one side or another. Because of these considerations, there is a certain ad hoc nature to the formation of courts as adjustments are made to handle particular cases. Nevertheless, three basic jurisdictional levels can be distinguished: parish, community, and tribal.

The tribal court, composed of leaders appointed by the tribal chief, meets in the yard of the chief's Western-style house in the town of Lamitan. Although in theory it is a sort of supreme court for all the Yakan, handling cases local courts have failed to settle, in practice its jurisdiction and its composition is geographically limited to the side of the island where the court meets. Parish courts are generally formed ad hoc to try relatively trivial disputes—fights among young men, for example—among parish members. Occasionally a parish trial will be conducted with the absolute minimum personnel: two disputants and one judge. The bulk of litigation occurs at what might be called the community level. In most areas there are regular court sessions about once a week. Adjustments are made in these courts to handle particular cases. Any court intermediate between a regular community court and the tribal court is an ad hoc formation to handle a special case. Before reaching the tribal level, however, there is a limit beyond which jurisdiction cannot be stretched, where judges who are neutral and at the same time sufficiently close socially to act together cannot be found. Disputes at this level may be referred to the tribal court or to government courts, or a settlement by negotiation may be attempted. Frequently, however, disputants resort to violence at this point.

Other roles. Added to the basic role structure of litigation—a court and two opposing sides—there is a further differentiation of roles within each party of protagonists: (a) the principal, the one primarily involved in the original dispute, the person who, as the Yakan say was 'struck' by speech (*tawwaq bissāh*) or who 'collided' with litigation (*lumaŋgal si hukum*); (b) his guardian, the one who assumes responsibility for accepting or rejecting a ruling and complying with it. The guardian may be the principal himself, a parent or parental surrogate, or a spouse; (c) senior and peer supporters.

The Yakan speak about this role structure in the language of kinship, using an ideal model in which the principal is a child, the court his elders, the guardian his parent, and his supporters his senior and peer kin. A final role is that of witnesses, who may be called by either side or by the court.

RULINGS

The intended outcome of litigation is a ruling (*hukuman*) on a case handed down by the court. The crucial fact shaping Yakan legal rulings is that the court has no powers of coercion to force compliance with a ruling. It must resort to persuasion. What distinguishes a ruling from an agreement arrived at by negotiation consists largely of the elaborate verbal trappings that go along with a ruling and lend it a sacrosanct aura. The ideology expressed in talking about rulings during the process of proclaiming them should not be taken as an expression of the manner in which rulings are actually derived, but as part of the behavior of making a ruling in the most effective way. The basic principle for actually arriving at successful rulings seems to be the same as those for agreements, namely to give each side somewhat less than full satisfaction but something better than the worst they might expect—in other words, to effect a compromise. The basic objective of both litigation and negotiation is to eliminate a dispute, to re-establish normal social relations between the disputants. It is not to do justice whatever the cost.

A ruling may call for one or more of three acts: payment of a fine (*multah,* from Spanish; *qātaq,* from Malay from Sanskrit), listening to an admonition (*nasihat,* from Arabic; *pituwah,* from Arabic; *tōqan*) from the court, and performing a prayer (*duwaqah,* from Arabic) of reconciliation. A fine, in turn, has one or more of three components: a compensation for the offense, an amount serving to "wipe away" any sin against God associated with the offense (which the court collects), and a payment to the court, the *baytalmāl* (from Arabic 'treasury'). Fines are calculated in ten-peso units (*laksaq*) and paid in Philippine currency (₱1 = $.25). In proposing a ruling, the court must explain in detail how the amount was arrived at, relating it to traditional fines for the offense and to the particular exigencies of the case at hand. In one case involving two youths who had been in a fight, one side claimed damages for bodily injury and presented a medical bill for the amount of ₱180.25 from a Christian Filipino physician. The court suggested a fine of ₱100 to the injured party, explaining its decision as follows:

> ₱120 for paying the medical bill (principle: never give full satisfaction);
> −50 in recognition of the countercharge of collusion between the plaintiff and the physician. The court was careful to state that it did not necessarily believe the countercharge, but since there were no witnesses, account must be taken of the possibility.
> +50 for the offense against the plaintiff.
> −20 for the plaintiff's responsibility in instigating the fight.
> ‾‾‾‾‾
> ₱100

If an admonition is part of the ruling, it is given in the form of a lecture by the court to both sides at the end of the trial. It is designed to make both parties feel their share of responsibility for the dispute, to smooth ruffled feelings, and to warn of the grave consequences of repeating the offense. Admonitions are especially common in rulings over marital disputes and fights among youths.

If a prayer of reconciliation is called for, it is performed at a later time in the form of a different scene, a religious ceremony. Its performance involves expenses, instructions for the payment of which is an important aspect of the ruling. The prayer unites the former disputants in a divinely sanctioned ritual-sibling tie. A call for prayer is especially common in cases of violence.

Upon suggesting a ruling, the court argues for compliance, not only by carefully justifying the form of the decision, but also by pointing out the dire consequences of refusal to comply. God and the ancestors may mete out sickness upon the offender and his kin. Opponents may resort to violence against the offender and his kin. The offender's kin, under threat from these sanctioning agents, may withdraw support or even disown the offender. Judges threaten to wash their hands of the case and withdraw political support, and finally the case may be referred to Philippine government legal system with its expensive lawyers and pris-

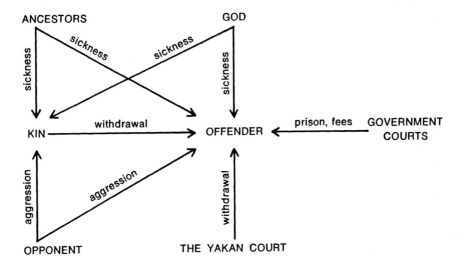

Figure 2.   Sanctions and Sanctioning Agents

ons. Figure 2 diagrams these sanctioning forces converging on an offender.

If the litigants agree to the ruling, those who are called upon to hand over money almost never pay in full on demand, this being a rule in all monetary transactions. They ask for *tanguh*, a deferment of part of the payment until a specified later date. As might be expected, failure to pay *tanguh* when due is itself a major cause of disputes.

If a court fails to formulate an acceptable ruling, the litigants may attempt to take the case to another Yakan court, seek redress in a government court, or drop attempts to settle the dispute by litigation. Another alternative is to turn the decision over to God. In a religious ceremony each disputant swears (*sapah*) on the Koran to the validity of his arguments in the case. God decides who is right and announces his decision by inflicting fatal illness (*kasapahan*) upon the person who swore a false oath or upon his kin. Swearing is a serious matter, rarely resorted to in fact. The threat of it, however, figures prominently in legal debate. One can protect himself from false charges by challenging his opponent to participate in a swearing ritual. In several recorded cases young men saved themselves from conviction on charges of sexual assault by this tactic. The fact that God may punish not only the offender but also his kin may seem capricious to Western moralists; yet it greatly increases the effectiveness of the punishment. Support of one's kin is crucial in a dispute, but they will be extremely reluctant to carry this support to the point of swearing unless they are firmly convinced of their kinsmen's innocence. Furthermore, if the disputants are in any way related to each other, as they often are, this relationship tie must be dissolved before swearing. Consanguineal kinship ties can be formally broken in a religious ceremony. The term for the ritual payments required to disown a kinsman is *tallak*, from the Arabic word for the formula spoken by a husband to divorce his wife (Yakan divorce is not that simple).

PROCEDURES AND SCHEDULES

Our formulation of the concept of litigation states that litigation is an integral activity never performed as part of another scene. It is a maximal unit of planning and scheduling. The description of the manifestations of this aspect of the concept requires a statement of the constituent structure of the scene—the sequence of parts that make up the whole—and of the scheduling of litigation with respect to other scenes in the society.

Procedures. Unlike mere negotiation or conference, litigation is conducted according to definite procedural rules. Although these rules are much looser than those of Western courts, they are, by Yakan standards, fairly strict and explicit. During proceedings judges frequently make reference to the following general rules governing the conduct of court sessions.

1. Speaking time is a free good available in unlimited quantity to any person present as long as what he says is relevant to the case.

2. A speaker has the right to finish before being interrupted.

3. Judges have the right to call on a person to speak, but one may speak without being called upon.[7]

4. Litigants should address all their arguments to the court.

5. Overt expression of anger, and especially any violence, must be avoided. Allowance should be made for the necessity, in litigation, for people to say unkind things about one another. Disputants must be allowed to accuse, judges to admonish.

6. Each party of protagonists, as well as the judges, has the right to confer in private whenever necessary.

7. A continuous period of time should be allotted to each case during a single court session.

Although there is some variation by type of case, the usual sequence of events is as follows:

1. Presentation of the case by the person to whom it is reported.

2. Taking testimony from each side and from witnesses.

3. Arguments from each side presented together (one side does not present its complete case and then defer to the other side).

4. Private conference of the judges.

5. Presentation of a ruling.

6. Further argument (optional but inevitable).

7. Private conference of each side (optional).

7. The question of someone's refusing to testify never seems to arise.

8. Expression of acceptance or refusal by each side.
9. Final decision for disposition of case.
10. Payment of fines, listening to courts admonition (if required).
11. Ritual handshaking (*salam*, from Arabic) with the judges signaling the termination of a trial session.

Steps 2 and 3 often occur simultaneously; steps 4–8 may be repeated several times.

Schedules. Fixed timing is not an attribute of litigation, as it is, say, of some calendrical religious ceremonies and agricultural activities. Court sessions are fitted into vacancies left by the schedules of other scenes. As a matter of convenience, community courts generally have regular scheduled meetings (Friday afternoon after mosque service is a favorite time), but these are easily accommodated if schedules conflict. The tribal court meets two afternoons a week. Court sessions must be scheduled between meals, with allowance made for participants to return home to eat. The five daily prayers of Islam, performed in most localities only by a few religiously inclined individuals, cause no problem. If someone wants to say a prayer, he can always go off and do so.

Comparisons

In this section we make a few summary comparisons with another Philippine legal system. The purpose is not to offer an explanation of these differences, but to demonstrate that the ethnographic approach argued for here, rather than hampering cross-cultural comparison as some critics seem to fear, provides a basis for determining which units are comparable and points up significant dimensions of comparison.

The Eastern Subanun are pagan swidden agriculturists inhabiting the interior of Zamboanga Peninsula on the island of Mindanao.[8] The Yakan and Subanun are not in direct contact, but they speak related languages and, along with other central Malaysian peoples, share many basic technological and social-organizational features. Subanun communities are much smaller and more scattered, although the basic principles of settlement pattern are the same: nuclear family household dispersed in individual fields. The difference is that the Yakan practice continual exploitation of privately owned fields and groves. Both groups have long been subject first to Moslem, then to Christian cultural influence, political authority, and economic exploitation. The Yakan accommodated where necessary and resisted where possible. They became Moslems, they participate in Philippine politics; and they market copra. At the same time they have retained a marked cultural distinctiveness and some freedom to run their own affairs and, above all, their land. The Subanun, on

8. Reference is to the Eastern Subanun of the Lipay area of Zamboanga del Norte, studied in the field in 1953–1954 and 1957–1958.

the other hand, retreated or succumbed entirely. They have remained pagan and retained temporary economic and political independence at the price of increased isolation and loss of land. Perhaps not unrelated to this difference in adaptation to external pressures is a marked difference in the behavior of the two peoples today: the Subanun drink, whereas the Yakan fight.

There is among the Subanun a set of activities that, in contrast to other Subanun activities, can be defined in much the same terms as Yakan litigation: an integral speech event concerned with settling disputes by means of a ruling formulated by neutral judges. A brief description of litigation in one Subanun community appears elsewhere (Frake 1963). Here we will restrict ourselves to a few comparisons along the dimensions of topic, outcome, role structure, and integrity.

TOPIC

Subanun legal cases arise in much the same way as Yakan ones, except that they need not be initiated by a plaintiff. A judge can try someone for an offense even if no complaint has been made. It seems ridiculous, however, to call this criminal law, since the offenses in question are generally slanderous or flirtatious remarks made by an incautious drinker, often not at all resented by the victim. Otherwise the definitions of particular kinds of offenses are similar. (A major difference is that the Yakan consider sexual relations with an affine as incestuous, whereas the Subanun practice levirate and sororate marriage and sororal polygyny.) There are great differences, however, in the kinds of offenses that occur (violence is almost unknown among the Subanun) and the types of cases that reach court. Adultery, for example, fills the agendas of Yakan courts, whereas it is rarely the overt basis of a Subanun legal case. This fact is not a comment on Subanun virtue but on the weakness of Subanun legal sanctions.

OUTCOME

The rulings of a Subanun court, like those of the Yakan, generally demand financial compensation (but fines are calculated in units of twenty centavos rather than of ten pesos) and may call for admonitions and rituals of reconciliation. But not only does the Subanun court have no legal sanctions of force to back up a decision, there is also little realistic threat of illegal force it can bring to bear. The Subanun offender may fear a certain amount of social censure—a real enough sanction, to be sure—but he need not fear a shotgun blast interrupting his evening meal, the outcome of more than one Yakan dispute. The Subanun also lack an Almighty God to mete out justice when litigation fails. For this reason, "A large share, if not the majority, of legal cases deal with offenses so minor that only the fertile imagination of a Subanun legal authority can magnify them into a serious threat to some person or to society in general" (Frake 1963:221). Yakan courts, too, cannot cope with the full range of offenses committed, but the Yakan, by absolute standards, commit much more serious crimes. A Parkinsonian cynic viewing Yakan and Subanun life and law might conclude that the severity of crime increases with the ability of a legal system to cope with it.

ROLE STRUCTURE

Subanun courts are always formed ad hoc to try a particular case. There are no court schedules or regular meeting places. The role of judge is open to any adult male with the ability to formulate successful decisions, and performance in the role is largely a route to community leadership, rather than a result of it. Unlike the Yakan, where a parish priest is generally a political leader as well, Subanun roles of legal and religious authority are quite distinct and typically filled by separate individuals. Subanun litigation less often musters bodies of kin in support of disputants, partly because there is usually less of common interest at stake and kin do not share collective responsibility under mortal and divine sanctioning agents.

INTEGRITY

The striking difference between Subanun and Yakan litigation, and one that does not derive from differences in socio-economic complexity in any obvious way, is the place of the activity in the over-all structure of cultural scenes. Subanun activities are sharply divisible into festive and nonfestive scenes, the former always involving feasting and drinking (Frake 1964b). Subanun litigation is festive behavior, performed as part of a larger scene and accompanied by eating, drinking, and merrymaking. In this respect it is the same kind of behavior as the performance of religious offerings; the two activities, in fact, often occur together as parts of the same festivity. Subanun litigation, then, is less of an integral unit of performance and scheduling than is the comparable Yakan activity. Subanun legal arguments, as they develop in the course of drinking, exhibit more obvious attention to message form. Litigants and judges employ esoteric legal language, often arranged into verse and sung to the tune of drinking songs (Frake 1964a). Thus, whereas the Yakan try relatively serious cases in scenes of informal discussion, the Subanun devote themselves to trivial disputes in scenes of formal festivities. This difference is crucial to any functional interpretations of litigation in the two societies. Participation in litigation has different meanings and different consequences in the two societies because of it.

PART II

Law and Innovation in Non-Western Societies

INTRODUCTION BY JAMES L. GIBBS, JR.

The dominant focus in legal studies of nonliterate societies has been on the search for regularities in conflict resolution. This emphasis began with Llewellyn and Hoebel's (1941) pioneering delineation of the trouble-case method and has culminated in the current concentration on the judicial process. A secondary focus is on the structural correlates of variations in conflict resolution, which has resulted in incipient taxonomies of legal systems (for example, Gulliver 1963). An outgrowth of this has been a third (and largely futile) focus, the attempt to find a universally applicable definition of law.

Studies of the legal institutions of nonliterate societies contrast with judicial studies of our own society in that they show little concern for the role of the individual. The extent of legal scholars' preoccupation with the individual in Western legal systems, sometimes referred to as "gastronomic jurisprudence," is indicated in the review of the literature in Gibbs' paper, which appears in this section, and is also touched upon by Aubert in his introduction to Part III.

The four papers in this section mark a break with the past in their common concern with the interaction between the individual and the legal process in nonliterate societies.[1]

The papers by Pospisil and Schapera focus on the legislative role of the individual legal figure, the chief-adjudicator.

1. In framing the comments on the papers included in this section, I have drawn on my own thoughts and upon the substance of the discussion of the papers that followed their presentation at the Burg Wartenstein symposium. While I wish to acknowledge my debt to my colleagues, responsibility for what appears here is my own.

169

Pospisil's paper, "Structural Change and Primitive Law: Consequences of a Papuan Legal Case," presents a lively account of a change in the Kapauku law of incest introduced by a headman who himself contracted an incestuous marriage and later enunciated a change in the law to institutionalize such unions for the wider community. This paper is both biographical and longitudinal in that it traces out the consequences over time of a legal change introduced by a particular individual and attempts to assess that individual's motives and goals. Pospisil offers two orders of explanation for the headman's actions and the ensuing results. First is a biographical or psychological explanation, and second is a structural one.

Pospisil's psychological and structural explanations are not mutually exclusive. They can be resolved by using a paradigm of the sort introduced by Abram Kardiner, an early writer of the culture-and-personality school (1939, 1945).[2] Structural pressures operate on individuals so as to produce intrapsychic tensions. Individuals are motivated to commit various actions in an attempt to reduce these societally induced tensions. Among such attempts to reduce tension may be an innovative act. Wallace (1956b) in his paper on revitalization movements has shown graphically how innovative acts may be a response to structurally induced tensions caused by acculturative pressures.

Pospisil indicates the structural pressures for endogamous marriage that existed in Kapauku society. The headman's response to such structural pressures—entering an endogamous marriage—was not innovative, inasmuch as such unions had been formed occasionally in the past. However, his act of proclaiming a change in the law *was* innovative, and this response, too, was an attempt to reduce stress. Pospisil suggests that it was idiosyncratic stress, not societally induced stress.

In attempting to decide whether the innovating Kapauku headman was relieving unique tensions or shared, societally induced ones, we should not overlook the possibility that a successful legal innovator may introduce for idiosyncratic reasons a change that is accepted by the population for structural reasons. The innovation may resolve widely shared, structurally caused tensions. The simple fact necessary to the understanding of the routinization of innovation is that different people may engage in the same action but for diverse reasons. Wallace (1961) refers to this phenomenon as "unity in diversity" and uses the concept of equivalences to explain how it comes about. Such a construct seems to explain what happened in the Kapauku case, and it is implicit in Pospisil's presentation. The headman's account to Pospisil of his actions suggests that he (the headman) would fully understand Wallace's unity-in-diversity concept. He obviously understands its pragmatic applications.

2. This approach also characterizes the work of John Whiting (Whiting *et al.* 1958) and Beatrice Whiting (1963).

Orthodox contemporary field studies in the ethnography of law involve a general study of social structure as well as a study of the legal system itself. Thus, patterned structural strains that characterize the society being studied are customarily reported. Case reports such as Pospisil's, which analyze the role of the individual innovator and his relationship to the legal system, need to consider systematically some additional factors that Pospisil's study only touches upon:

1. What is the range of variation with regard to the conformity to a particular norm *before* the change or innovation is introduced?

2. In what forms do the intrapsychic strains that result from the society's structural strains manifest themselves?

3. How widespread in the population are these patterned manifestations of tension?

4. To what degree does the innovator share these tensions, and in what form do they manifest themselves?

5. What other personal features of the innovator are significant?

One could consider such measures of *personal attributes* as: (a) intelligence, persuasiveness, empathy—assessment of these qualities is necessary to determine why the innovator succeeds or fails in getting his innovation adopted; (b) *deeper-lying personality trends,* such as manner of relating to authority, impulsiveness, degree of autonomy; (c) and *physical condition.* Clyde Kluckhohn suggested that a complete biographical study should include a physical examination, because such somatic factors as hypertension may play a significant role in behavior. The relevance of Kluckhohn's suggestion has been highlighted by the results of Wallace's (1956a) study of the Handsome Lake movement, which pinpoints the role of physiological factors in the transformation dream that is the genesis of the innovations extolled by the revitalizing prophet.

6. What are the personal features (other than societally induced tensions) that characterize the population as a whole?

Such a battery of information would enable the anthropologist to gauge the extent to which the innovator is giving expression to what is felt by many persons in his society—or rather, to truly unique desires. In short, how unique is the innovator? In addition, noting such methodological caveats forces us to examine *explicitly* the socio-psychological side of the process whereby an innovation is either accepted and routinized or rejected.

The Kapauku case study raises the question of whether the major finding of the study can be generalized. Under what conditions is legal innovation inaugurated by the commission of a deviant act? Does it occur more often in certain areas of the law, for example, where moral considerations are important, as in family law or in religious law? Is it more apt to occur in areas where institutions converge, thus making normative change more likely to be particularly disruptive? For example, a change in the Kapauku law of incest involved changes not only in kinship practices, but in economic and political ones as well. In such cases a frontal assault on substantive law is particularly devastating, and people may feel this intuitively. If so, presenting a *fait accompli* may be the only way to effect the change. As Schapera questions in his paper, does the institutionalized possibility of arbitrarily imposing new laws by fiat allow more scope for the operation of individual personality traits of the innovator?

How innovative is the innovation, and why is it accepted? Pospisil indicated that intrasib marriages had taken place before that of the innovating headman. Why did these not lead to a change in the law or at least in marriage practices? An analysis of these unions might help to validate Pospisil's analysis more fully.

Schapera's study, "Uniformity and Variation in Chief-Made Law: A Tswana Case Study," compares legislative innovations made by several chiefs of four Tswana tribes that share the same ecology and language and have closely similar social systems and even similar acculturative movements and pressures. The rigor of his analysis is enhanced by the fact that Schapera compares each chief's legislative innovations in the same three areas of substantive law—innovations concerning practices expressly forbidden by the dominant Christian denomination active in the Tswana area. By selecting practices contrary to the imposed Christian doctrine, Schapera attempts to control as variables, the presence of mission influence and the content of the innovation. Thus, Schapera uses the method of controlled comparison to demonstrate that the individual personality attributes of Tswana chiefs are a dominant causative factor in their actions as legislative innovators. The elimination of all the other major possible factors leaves the personality factor as the operative one.

Although Schapera is to be commended for his use of the method of controlled comparison, which lifts his paper beyond the intuitive humanistic approach, the paper has some possible shortcomings that should be noted.

The study presumes the identity of the four tribes on the variable of the legislative power of the chiefs. But there is some question whether in fact the chiefs were equal in this regard. From Schapera's description it seems quite clear that the chiefs varied in the extent to which they imposed new laws arbitrarily or, on the contrary, sought consent before enunciating new legislation.

The Tswana study differs from the Kapauku one in that the personal data on the legal innovations are not based on first-hand knowledge but on contemporary accounts transmitted either orally or in missionary chronicles and diaries. One can question the objectivity of both orally transmitted personal descriptions and written ones screened through missionary values. Schapera does not tell us how he assessed the comparability and validity of the biographical data that he uses.

A question raised in the commentary on the Pospisil paper also applies here. To what extent were the motives that are ascribed to the Tswana chiefs also characteristic of their subjects? Again, without this knowledge, it is not possible to understand fully the fate of an innovation.

A related problem, also raised by the Kapauku study, is suggested by the fact that some Tswana chiefs proclaimed the *same* law but for *different* reasons. This underlines the point made in the comments on Pospisil's paper: subjects may accept the new law for the reasons that motivated the innovator—or for different reasons.

The Pospisil and Schapera studies taken together suggest some methodological features that should be utilized in future research aimed at understanding the process of legal innovation and the role of the individual in it. These are:

1. A focus on the individual, requiring that certain features be measured not only in the innovating individual, but also in the population as a whole (see Inkeles and Levinson 1954). Naturally the adequacy of such measures must be carefully considered.

2. A longitudinal focus in order to demonstrate the full results of the adoption of an innovation. Such a diachronic focus should include detailed study of the means by which the innovator gains adherence to his innovation. For example, how does he mobilize support and reduce opposition? Where the innovation is successful, there is a process of routinization that undoubtedly shows cross-cultural similarities. Wallace's revitalization paradigm (1965b) cited earlier offers a model that could be adapted for use in analyzing the process of legal innovations. This step would advance us toward our ultimate aim of explaining the incidence and form of legal innovation. In addition, ethnographers of law who wish to work in this field will have to examine much more fully than they have the literature on innovation and creativity that offers additional useful methodological and conceptual insights.

3. An attempt to observe and record all sorts of legal innovations such as: (a) legislation; (b) deviate acts; (c) novel judicial decisions; and (d) other actions, such as revitalization acts or other innovations cast in a ritualistic idiom.

4. An attempt to delineate systematically the conditions (or structural covariates) that lead to such innovative legal acts.

Werbner's paper, "Constitutional Ambiguities and the British Administration of Royal Careers among the Bemba of Zambia" deals with the substance of law among the Bemba. It indicates that in the precolonial period Bemba political succession was not absolutely fixed. The outcome of succession depended partly on which of several categories of potential heirs was available. Certain other ambiguities were built into the system.

As Gluckman (1955) has indicated in his analysis of Barotse law, such institutionalized vagueness allows flexibility while giving the appearance of certainty and sameness. Thus Werbner's paper documents further the widespread existence of that feature in the legal systems of nonliterate societies.

In addition, the Bemba succession process considered the personal qualities of heirs to the extent that a candidate's power vis-à-vis other candidates was a factor affecting the final selection of royal officeholders.

During the colonial period the British administration attempted to manipulate the succession process by reducing the ambiguities in order to create a more fixed outcome. More predictability was desired for administrative reasons—for example, in order to groom an heir. The British also wanted a system that would make eligible those younger heirs who would be more amenable to receiving a Western education and, as a consequence of this education, more likely to agree with some goals of the colonial administration.

Gibb's paper, "Law and Personality: Signposts for a New Direction," differs from the others included in this section because it does not deal with the process of legal innovation, nor does it deal with the role of the individual in this process. It is broader in scope, focusing on the interrelationship between the individual and several aspects of the process of dispute settlement.

The paper begins with a review of the major literature on law and personality; however, it is devoted primarily to a report of some preliminary findings from an on-going study of law and personality among the Kpelle of Liberia. A quantitative analysis of cases suggests that the frequency of disputes is not random but patterned. It reflects not only the structural features of the social system, but also patterned personality dispositions characteristic of the population as a whole. Similarly, the Kpelle data indicate that "surface" legal features, such as the grievance that is seized upon as the basis for bringing a suit and the form of bringing a suit, also reflect personality features as well as structural ones. The psychic roots of other procedural features, such as the time lag between the commission of an offense and the presence of conditional oaths, are also noted.

In essence the Gibbs paper raises the question of the extent to which personality attributes characteristic of a society's members as a whole will help to shape both the level of the case load with which that society's legal system must cope and the contours of that case load. It also raises the question of the manner in which personality trends affect the recognized procedures for disposing of cases. The frame of reference used is much more explicitly socio-psychological than that used in any of the other three papers. It also differs from the other three in that the concern is not with individual personalities but with recurring or shared personality trends.

Like the other papers included in this section, the Kpelle study has its shortcomings. The hypotheses tested are based on inferred personality data rather than on data measured directly in individuals. The reader may wonder, rightly, whether the direct personality data collected in further field work will support the tentative findings reported in the present paper.

It should be noted that Gibbs' approach goes beyond that used by Nader in her work on the Zapotec (Nader 1964b). Like Nader's method, which it builds upon, it requires the systematic collection of information about the traditionally recognized features of litigants and cases, such as the major status attributes of litigants (sex, age, place of residence, kinship links) and the major features of the case (offense, decision, sanctions). But it then attempts to relate the generalizations one can draw from such descriptive data to another type of systematically collected data, personality variables.

Taken together, these four papers shed light on the role of personality factors in the legal process, both in the instituting of legal innovations and in the process of dispute settlement. They suggest that we should study both the relationship of particular personalities to the legal process and the connection of shared personality traits to that process. In their common concern with process all four papers reflect a general trend in social anthropology, a movement to focus on dynamics as well as structure.

Law and Personality:
Signposts for a New Direction

In Nader's review of the anthropology of law she correctly notes that in the ethnography of law "the tendency has been to treat the legal system as an institution virtually independent and isolated from the other institutions of society" (Nader 1965b:17). This is not the only oversight of the legal anthropologists. They have treated the legal system in isolation from the personalities of the members of society also. The magnitude of our blindness is indicated by the fact that even Nader (1965b:23) in formulating questions that point to new directions in the ethnography of law exhorts us to ask: "What are the manifest and latent jobs of the law and how are they related to the *social structure?*" (italics added). Bohannan (1965:41), too, in answering his own question, "What should we and our students be doing?" makes the same omission.

If we rephrase Nader's question to read: "What are the manifest and latent jobs of the law and how are they related to social structure *and to personality dispositions?*" we bring the frame of reference of psychological anthropology to the study of legal systems. This step forces us to ask other new questions, and answering them will require us to refine our old methods as well as to develop new ones. This assumption was anticipated in a paper of Spiro's in which he cautioned that *the functions of social systems should be explained more "by reference to their capacity for the gratification and frustration of personality needs* (cf. Cohen 1966)" (Spiro 1961:472).

The first part of this paper is a review of selected literature on law and personality. Next is a call for more research on law and personality. Some data from my own field research in this area conclude the paper.

Studies of Law and Personality

The considerable body of research on the relationship between law and personality is scattered in the literature of such diverse disciplines as *psychology* (general, clinical, criminal, social, and legal); *sociology* (the sociology of law, and the sociology of deviance); *anthropology* (social anthropology—especially ethno-law—and psychological anthropology); *law* itself (notably jurisprudence); and such related fields as psychiatry and social work. Obviously a complete review of this extensive literature is out of place here, but a rough mapping of the field can be sketched and some illustrative studies pointed out as landmarks.

Research relating law and personality is rarely global or holistic in scope, but usually posits a link between some particular aspect of "law" on the one hand and a specific aspect of personality on the other.[1] It then proceeds to examine this link. In broadest terms, the law-personality links that have been studied can be grouped into the following general categories that reflect fundamental dimensions of conflict. They are: (1) the psychic sources and functions of the breach of norms (including the societal incidence of the breach of certain norms); (2) the psychic sources and functions of institutionalized procedures for dealing with the breach of norms; and (3) the results of institutionalized counteraction to breach of norms.[2] Some studies representative of each of the categories are cited below.

THE BREACH OF NORMS

A series of studies of Western societies have noted that different social classes and ethnic groups show characteristic but different patterns of crime. For example, Kardiner and Ovesey's (1951) classic study of the American Negro sees drunkenness, one of the most common offenses committed by that group, as having roots in the ethnic personality.[3] Drinking in this subculture functions as an escape from the psychic pain of a societally instilled low self image.

1. My thinking in this area has benefited from the contributions of the student members of a graduate seminar on Law and Personality that I taught at the University of Minnesota in the spring of 1965. They were: Rachel Bonney, Margo Liberty, John Poggie, Katherine Salter, and Gretel Whitaker. I would also like to acknowledge the comments and criticisms of my fellow participants at the Wenner-Gren symposium on the ethnography of law in August 1966 for which an earlier version of this paper was prepared. In particular I would like to express thanks to Sally Falk Moore, the discussant for the paper.

2. It should be noted that there is no significant body of research literature on the psychic sources and functions of norms, a fourth dimension of social control.

3. I define "ethnic personality" as those recurring basic personality dimensions that are most characteristic of a culture or community. This definition is meant to parallel the term "national character" but stresses the presence of more than one representative "character." Ethnic personality is multimodal, not unimodal.

Winick, Gerver, and Blumberg (1961:129) deal with the phenomenon of judges who breach norms of their profession by issuing what are "deviant" decisions. They state that "inconsistency between social class background and judicial attainment may have resulted in some unusual decisions and opinions." Implicit in this view is the assumption that this inconsistency results in certain intrapsychic tensions that are resolved by issuing a particular type of decision. Parsons (1962:65), classifying deviant behavior among lawyers, notes that excessive formalism stems in part from the fact that "the legal profession probably has at least its share, if not more, of 'compulsive personalities.'"

Berndt's (1962) controversial study of law in the Eastern Highlands of New Guinea characterizes the ethnic personality of the Highlanders as showing admiration for and focus on power, strength, and physical force, as well as a fusion of aggression with sexuality. Some of the breaches in that culture, such as necrophilia and cannibalistic incorporation of sexual organs, are not only memorable for the reader, but patently rooted in Highland ethnic personality dispositions.

A germinal cross-cultural study by Bacon, Child, and Barry (1963) documents a similar hypothesis. The authors find a correlation between lack of strong male identity in men (and a derived defensiveness against a feminine identity) and a high incidence of theft and personal crime. Poggie (n.d.) shows that in Tepoztlán the high crime rate, which is rooted in weak male identity, is perpetuated by the role in socialization of the dominant male personality type.

Wife-beating and the wife's reporting to the authorities of the assaulting husband are both deviant acts in our society, part of a related syndrome studied by Snell and his associates (1964). They found that such behavior occurs in families where both the husband and wife have a need for role reversal; she, for punishment for her usual hostile, castrating activity directed toward her husband; he, for asserting his masculine identity, about which he has great anxiety. The beating goes unreported for years until an older son reaches adolescence and intervenes in his parents' fighting, an act that his physical size and reactivated Oedipal position makes potentially dangerous.

These and similar studies indicate that one level of explanation of the types of breach committed is a psychological one.

THE COUNTERING OF BREACH

The largest body of personality-law studies deals with the relationship between personality and institutionalized social control procedures for dealing with the breach of norms. One focus of research is the degree to which the decisions of judges in Western societies are reached by forming a personality-influenced, intuitive, over-all impression of the case and its issues. Several studies have shown that the sentencing behavior for an identical offense varies from judge to judge (Winick et al. 1961: 134–135). As early as 1923 it was suggested (Haines 1923) that personality factors are responsible for this variation, a conclusion supported by some of the autobiographical writings of judges who discuss the way in which they reach decisions (Winick et al. 1961:132–135). Thus the citation of precedents and legal reasoning rationalizes what is a more private, psychically colored process. This position is summarized well by Cowan (1962:109), who refers to law as "a system for organizing and systematizing *feeling* judgments" (italics added).

The customary behavior (rather than deviant acts noted above) of the attorney in the dispute-settling process, like that of the judge, also has some psychic roots. Winick et al. (1961:137) imply that there is some self-selection of trial lawyers in terms of their interest in the adversary system with its focus on conflict and differences. The same authors (ibid.) and lawyer-turned-sociologist Riesman (1962:37) note that attorneys have a strong component of egotism, which is satisfied in the "exhibitionism" of the courtroom (and for judges, in the fact that opinions are signed rather than anonymous [Winick et al. 1961]). It is obvious that there are also psychological bases for the self-selection of other lawmen such as policemen, jailers, and wardens (Frenkel-Brunswik 1954).[4]

There has been a good deal of recent research on jury processes in the United States, although most of it has been sociological rather than psychological. However, Winick (1961) reviews a series of psychological studies and cites those with findings directly relevant to understanding what he terms the "psychology of the jury." The studies, drawn from many fields of psychology, deal with the processes of projection, displacement, ability to make accurate judgments, recall, suggestibility, decision-making, and so on.

An anthropological study that relates personality dispositions to institutionalized reactions to breach is the study of New Guinea Eastern Highlanders mentioned earlier (Berndt 1962). The accepted forms of self-help to which the Highlanders turn to counter a breach of norms are markedly violent in flavor: warfare, suicide, sorcery, sexual assault, and cannibalism. Berndt sees this development as connected with the ethnic personality trends centering on physical force, aggression, and the fusion

---

4. Frenkel-Brunswik (1954:232, 233) notes that in a study of ethnocentrism in children she found "variations of the authoritarian personality syndrome to be related to parental occupation." In a fleeting comment she states that salesmen, policemen, firemen, and their families are more likely to be found among authoritarians and that choosing to be a policeman "may reveal identification with authority and aggression and poor adjustment to work *per se*." A rather thorough bibliographical search fails to reveal any other studies that deal with the relationship between authoritarian personality variables and legal occupations, a surprising gap in research foci.

of sex and aggression. He also indicates (p. 325) that those who render judgment in the informal courts of the Highlanders often mete out violent punishment, and that it "gives emotional satisfaction not only to the person administering the punishment but also to the complainant and the spectators." It is clear that Berndt is speaking of something other than Durkheim's (1933) concept of repression when he notes (p. 312) that: "There is some reason to believe that if the punishment is not too severe it may also be suffered with some degree of *excitement* if not *pleasure* by the victim" (italics added). A case in point is the use of forced copulation as a way of shaming guilty adulterers, an action that, the field worker notes (p. 336), expresses violence as well as providing indirect sexual stimulation to the Highlander judges, litigants, and spectators.

Hoebel (1954:316), in discussing law among the tribes of the American Northwest Coast, cites Crane's (1951:144) observation that "the big stick which is relied on in this control system [is] not physical punishment, but social attacks upon the extremely vulnerable egos of the members of the group." Further consequences of the ethnic personality's sensitivity to shaming are noted by Hoebel (idem.), who adds: "this same vulnerability leads to wanton killing and strains the legal machinery to the utmost."

Gibbs (1963a), in an analysis of the Kpelle moot as a forum for the settlement of marital disputes, states that it functions as successfully as it does because it stimulates and capitalizes on certain psychic responses in exactly the same manner as does group therapy in Western society.

In a comparative study of preferred modes of dispute settlement among the Gusii and the Nuer, LeVine (1960) observes that the Nuer prefer to settle disputes by a resort to physical force, whereas the Gusii, whose culture is similar in many ways, prefer to utilize the courts. The hypothesis offered to explain this discrepancy is that there is an underlying difference in ethnic personality and in related child-training patterns. The Gusii ethnic personality is characterized by an avoidance of the direct expression of aggression, and socialization patterns include an authoritarian concentration of power in the hands of the father. Among the Nuer the ethnic personality is one that values the direct expression of aggression, and socialization patterns involve an egalitarian locus and use of power.

More broadly cross-cultural studies also offer insights into certain features of the dispute-settlement processes. Roberts (1965:205–206) in his exploratory cross-cultural study of oaths and autonomic ordeals finds that oaths are found primarily in societies where adults show anxiety about responsibility, a personality disposition that is rooted in the stress on responsibility-training in the child-socialization procedures of those societies. Autonomic ordeals, on the other hand, are found in societies where adult anxiety centers more on obedience because of cultural stress on obedience-training in socialization practices. Beatrice Whiting (1965), in a study that draws upon the concepts of Bacon, Child, and Barry (1963) mentioned earlier, seeks psychological roots for certain types of assault and concludes that a high incidence of certain types of physical violence can be interpreted as an expression in the adult male personality of "masculine protest" as a reaction against identification with women in infancy.

If we include judicial concepts as a significant aspect of the institutionalized procedures dealing with breach, as Bohannan (1957) rightly urges us to do, we should also cite Cohen's (1964) cross-cultural study, which relates the concept of liability to initiation rites and puberty. He finds that the presence of "several" (individual) liability for a wrong correlates with the presence of a sense of identity focused on the nuclear family, whereas the presence of "joint" (shared) liability is associated with a sense of identity focused on the wider kin group.

The studies that have been reviewed, diverse as they are, remind us that psychological hypotheses provide one order of explanation for a cultural preference for one mode of institutionalized reaction to breach as opposed to another. Similarly, psychological factors may also explain the existence of certain procedural features of social-control mechanisms.

RESULTS OF INSTITUTIONALIZED COUNTERACTION

Some writers have reminded us that the result of counteraction is not always the restoration of equilibrium. The counteraction may not end the deviance of the offender but may lead to a cycle of progressive alienation that may result in the commission of progressively graver offenses (Parsons 1951). Legal anthropologists have not systematically studied this "failure" of social control. However, Whitaker (1965) uses the Parsonian paradigm in discussing the effect of being convicted upon defendants in Chiapas courts. Noting that the convicted litigant may undergo an "identity struggle," she asks, "does the acceptance of the identity, wrong-doer, alienate the defendant and push him into a position where he will commit further deviant acts?"

A Plea

The purpose in citing the research reviewed above is not to suggest that the psychological explanation is the only order of explanation we should seek in ethno-law; it should be apparent to any behavioral scientist that psychological and socio-cultural explanations are not mutually exclusive. Nor is it my purpose to imply that the studies cited are without flaws. Many of them, for example, set forth "psychological" explanations without having measured the relevant personality variables in the individual with valid psychological indices (cf. Inkeles and Levinson 1954). Others ignore alternative explanations or confuse cause and effect. In the case of the cross-cultural studies, one can raise the usual questions about the completeness and comparability of the data.

I have soft-pedaled critical comment because legal anthropologists have almost completely neglected the contribution of such studies. Unless we believe that what has been cynically referred to as "gastronomic jurisprudence" is relevant only to our own society, we must ask more often than we have the question raised in the introduction to this paper: "What are the manifest and latent law jobs of the law, and how are they related to social structure and to personality dispositions?"

Even brief contemplation of the rephrased question germinates some profitable hunches. For example, where a litigant—whether he is Kapauku, Lozi, Arusha, or whatever—has a choice of settlement modes for harmonizing his dispute, to what extent will his choice among the alternatives reflect psychic as well as social structural factors? Further, a question is raised when Hoebel's (1954) work on the correlation between features of the law and societal subsistence levels is placed alongside Bacon, Child, and Barry's (1963) demonstration that there are different personality patterns associated with the basic societal subsistence modes. It must be decided to what extent Hoebel's "trends of the law" are rooted in psychic as well as economic and social features. Suggestive in this regard is Liberty's (n.d.) hypothesis that holds for the Cheyenne: "in societies where male model personality is disintegrating, or showing radical stress or adjustment to change, the 'trend of the law' (with increase of public over private law and kin-dominated dispute settlement . . .) may halt or reverse."

A NEW TREND

There are two portents of an awakening anthropological interest in law and personality. Nader (1965b:12) singles out as indicative of a new trend the publication of two cross-cultural law papers by anthropologists (Roberts 1965, Whiting 1965) that bring the Human Relations Area Files cross-cultural approach to bear on legal material. Perhaps it is not simply fortuitous that both these new-wave papers make use of psychologically oriented hypotheses.

An even more encouraging sign on the horizon is Swartz' (1966) study of the bases of political compliance among the Bena of Tanzania. In many ways his study is a model of the sort for which the present paper is calling. Swartz questions the Bena's obedience to the orders of their local political officials "even when doing so does not provide them immediate or direct gratification" (p. 89). In particular, he is concerned with why the Bena take their disputes for settlement in adjudicatory hearings—*barazas*—of political leaders.

Swartz did measure personality variables in the individual, and from his analysis of motives concludes that among the Bena "distrust" and "dependency" are fused in a search for security. Bena seek aid and succor from their fellows in both specific and diffuse ways and yet do not trust each other to provide the expected support. Moreover, they are reluctant to express even indirect hostility because they are fearful of return counter-hostility. Even within the nuclear family the three common Bena goals of getting aid and succor, avoiding distrust, and escaping hostility are difficult to achieve because of the relative absence of community of interests.

Why, then, do the Bena turn to the courts? Swartz suggests that the *baraza* satisfies Bena dependency needs by insuring that one's kinsmen do as "they ought to do." Thus, even though they may not do so out of kin loyalty, they will do so because of the external control of the court. The courts also reduce the fear of hostility from others because they are believed to short-circuit the process of retaliation and counter-retaliation. The *baraza* gets disputants to forswear their grievances, to eschew hostile counteractions, and to re-establish harmonious relations.

Swartz' analysis indicates that the Bena's motives for agreeable, winning behavior are harnessed in the procedures of the *baraza* so that the parties are likely to tell the truth and to come to agreement on the facts and the appropriate solution. As Swartz puts it: "the disputants are motivated not only to participate in [the adjudications] but to participate in such a way as to increase the likelihood of their success." He adds: "Successful adjudication does not remove the distrust and conflict from within the community, nor does it obviate the fear of others' hostility. However, the adjudication removes these desiderata from being the individual's unaided concern and brings them out where they can be subjected to broad social pressures. When they succeed, the adjudications do not ensure complete harmony, cooperation, or freedom from fear, but they provide a *social* mechanism that ameliorates the failure of attainment of these goals on a strictly *interpersonal* basis" (pp. 104–105; italics added). In Swartz' view a key aspect of the *baraza* is the fact that the Bena feel it is "objective," allowing a solution to emerge rather than imposing one. Swartz, like the Bena, seems to feel that the *baraza* is objective, and he traces this objectivity to the way in which the hearings capitalize on and manipulate the dispositions of the most common Bena needs. In any case, Bena *barazas* are strikingly consensual in flavor and show a basic mechanism markedly parallel to what I describe as underlying the Kpelle moot (Gibbs 1963b).

Finally, it should be noted, Swartz concludes that the dispute-settling process of the *baraza* bestows legitimacy upon the political official who represents and organizes the process (p. 108).

Swartz is concerned *primarily* with the political consequences of the Bena adjudicatory process and sees the adjudicator's role more as political than as legal. Nevertheless, his study is an important contribution to the ethnography of law because he is concerned explicitly with the psychological as well as the structural factors that shape legal procedures.

Law and Personality Among the Kpelle [5]

Partly in response to my own plea, I am in the midst of a long-term study of law and personality among the Kpelle of Liberia that incorporates the basic asumptions of the present paper. Some preliminary findings follow.

THE KPELLE: AN ETHNOGRAPHIC SKETCH

The Kpelle are a Mande-speaking, patrilineal group of some 300,000 rice cultivators who live in central Liberia and the adjoining regions of

5. The field research reported here has been supported by several bodies whose support I acknowledge with gratitude. The 1957–1958 field period was carried out while I held a Ford Foundation Foreign Area Fellowship, and it was also supported by a grant from the Laboratory of Social Relations of Harvard University. Initial analysis was done while I held a pre-doctoral fellowship from the National Science Foundation; further analysis was made possible by a Faculty Summer Research Grant from the University of Minnesota. The 1965–1966 field period and subsequent analysis has been supported by the National Science Foundation. I would also like to acknowledge the assistance of the Center for International Studies of Stanford University.

The research design was drawn up in 1963–1964 while I was the holder of a post-doctoral fellowship from the Social Science Research Council for training in methods of personality assessment; the Council's support is gratefully acknowledged. During that year I learned much from the staff of the Departments of Psychiatry and Psychology at the Hennepin County General Hospital, Minneapolis, Minnesota, and from the faculty members of the Department of Psychology and the Institute of Child Development at the University of Minnesota.

Both periods of field work were facilitated by the cooperation of the Liberian Government. I would also like to thank all those individual Liberians who have contributed to the research effort. Space precludes my mentioning all of them here, but I would particularly like to thank my primary field assistants: Lewis T. Currens, John Kellemu, and John Wealar. I am grateful to Daniel Pearlman of the Peace Corps and University of Liberia Law School and his students, who helped to compile the case inventory of Kpelle disputes, and also to Cuttington College for numerous courtesies and for student clerical assistance. I also owe appreciation to the United States Peace Corps and to many individual Americans too numerous to mention here.

I extend my appreciation to my Stanford research assistants, Peter Dolan and Patrick O'Grady, who have carried out their assignments with diligence, enthusiasm, and high competence. The first version of this paper was typed in Liberia by Mrs. Bonita Estes; the present one, by Mrs. Millie Dunn and Mrs. Anne Gamble.

the Republic of Guinea. In contrast to many African societies, strong corporate patrilineages are absent among the Kpelle. The relatively minor role of descent groups is explained partially by the presence of secret societies—notably the tribal fraternity, the Poro Society, and its sister organization, the Sande Society for women. The functions of these exotic societies, strongly diagnostic of the culture area of which the Kpelle are a part, have been much discussed in the anthropological literature. Among these functions are political ones (cf. Little 1965–1966). Other political functions inhere in the secular political structure, which is centralized. Although there is no single king or paramount chief, there are a series of paramount chiefs of the same level of authority, each of whom is superordinate over district chiefs and town chiefs. The Kpelle form of political organization can be termed the polycephalous associational state.

The structure of the formal Kpelle legal system parallels that of political organization. In Liberia the highest court of a tribal authority and the highest tribal court chartered by the government is that of a paramount chief. A district chief's court is also an official court. Disputes may be settled in these official courts or in unofficial courts, such as those of town chiefs or quarter (clan-barrio) elders.

Parallel to and overlapping that legal structure is another system of courts that was added in 1964, with the introduction of the Liberian county system to the interior regions of the country (previously administered by a type of indirect rule). The newer courts are those of the justices of the peace, magistrates, county commissioners, county superintendents, and the circuit courts of appeals. In some areas paramount chiefs hold appointments as justices of the peace, thereby creating a fusion of the two court systems at the lowest levels. Thus, Kpelle litigants have a whole series of courts to which they may carry their grievances. In addition to this, disputes are settled informally by associational groupings such as church councils or cooperative work groups as well as by the secret societies.

The systematic study of Kpelle personality is the aim of a forthcoming phase of the present research. Until it is completed, it is useful to draw a highly tentative outline of some of the features of Kpelle ethnic character based, *faute de mieux*, on inferences from cultural data. The Kpelle ethnic character includes the following traits: deference to authority, dependency, lack of ability to cooperate easily with other people, detachment, autonomy, preference for indirect forms for expressing aggression, male feelings of inadequacy vis-à-vis women, practical orientation, self-concept centering on work, instrumental orientation, manipulativeness, secretiveness, and suspiciousness.

THE LEGAL DATA

This section of the paper is based on data collected during two field periods. The first field period, seventeen months in 1957–1958, provided a description of Kpelle social organization and the Kpelle legal system. The second field period, which involved a more narrow problem orientation (the relationship between law and personality) covered twelve months in 1965–1966. Specifically it contributed additional quantitative depth for the analysis of Kpelle disputes. To provide this depth, a case inventory was completed for courts in Fokwele, Panta Chiefdom (the primary research site) and Gbarnga (the chiefdom's county seat). The complete case inventory includes elemental data on 1,967 cases. In addition, a census survey of Fokwele provides data on 999 other cases in the form of self-reports.

Although the case inventory currently undergoing analysis contains an impressive number of instances, the data on the cases are disappointingly uneven because of the nature of record keeping in Kpelle courts. Most often there is no record at all, the only documentary evidence that a hearing took place being the presence at a writ of summons or subpoena. Decisions are often not recorded. Similarly, where a recorded decision indicates, for example, that damages are to be paid at a later, specified date, there is often no recorded follow-through. Except in higher courts, there is usually no indication whether a case was heard *de novo* or on appeal. Ethnic affiliation, age, sex, and home town of litigants are not recorded, although some of these attributes can often be inferred either from knowledge of the culture or from the internal evidence of the case or from both. The implication for the present research of this pattern of record-keeping is that, even with a large sample of cases with which to work, it is sometimes impossible to glean enough cases with comparable, complete data from which indices can be constructed to quantitatively test hypotheses of the sort listed below.

Fortunately, however, the large body of varyingly complete cases in the case inventory and the self-report inventory are supplemented by other cases for which there are more complete data in the form of tape-recorded case transcripts or informants' accounts. All these sources of legal data are utilized in the analysis and discussion below.

THE PRELIMINARY HYPOTHESES

The 1963 research proposal for the 1965–1966 law and personality study included the following hypotheses, which were tested in the field period.

1. The Kpelle preference for the indirect expression of aggression will be reflected in: (a) failure to fulfill a commitment as a common offense;

and (b) a tendency to sue a person for a reason other than that revealed in court.

2. A high incidence of disputes about rights over women is rooted, not only in structural factors (cf. Gibbs 1963b), but also in male feelings of inadequacy vis-à-vis women.

3. Authoritarian submission will be reflected in a tendency to acquiesce in a judge's decision in the courtroom; but, when out of authority's view, to appeal the case.

4. Ordeals and conditional oaths will be resorted to when there is an absence of proof or conflicting testimony that there is no more "rational" way of resolving. *But* conditional oaths will be resorted to when the offense is one which, analytically viewed, is an attack on self-identity as defined by the Kpelle.

5. Individuals whose personalities show a high level of hostility or blocked aggression will tend to be involved in litigation repeatedly; further, they will be more likely to appeal cases they have lost in the first hearing.

FREQUENCY OF DISPUTE TYPES IN KPELLE LAW

The analysis of the case inventory described above is still in process, but a picture of the frequency of various types of disputes can be obtained from the census survey of Fokwele conducted in 1965–1966. Household heads were asked to report the number of times they and each adult member of their household had been involved in disputes that were aired either in a court or in a moot (house palaver). They were also asked to describe very briefly each of the disputes reported. A frequency distribution for the disputes reported appears in Table 1.[6]

Some explanation of the case categories included in Table 1 and the way in which they were devised will make the subsequent analysis more meaningful. The census-survey protocols were given a content analysis, and an extensive classification of dispute types was constructed. Each of the self-reported cases was assigned to as narrow and specific a category as possible. The general, more inclusive categories that appear in Table 1 and the narrow, specific categories were derived from the actual universe of reported cases. Thus, both the detailed taxonomy and the general categories into which it is divided emerge from the data rather than being imposed upon it. As will be noted below, where categories were not clear, specific dispute types were categorized as the Kpelle categorize them, making the heuristic scheme used here both "emic" and

6. Table 1 represents self-reported cases collected, as noted, in a census survey of Fokwele. There is evidence that respondents did not report all the cases in which they had ever been involved, especially house palavers. However, there is no evidence that the under-reporting was not random or that some kinds of cases were reported more than others.

Table 1. *Frequency of Dispute Types in Kpelle Courts and Moots*

	Courts		Moots		Total		Rank Order
	n	*%*	*n*	*%*	*n*	*%*	
1. Rights over women ("women palaver")	253	53.4	168	32.1	421	42.2	1
2. Derivative rights over women	...	...	17	3.2	17	1.7	11
3. Other conjugal disputes	9	1.9	146	27.9	155	15.5	2
4. Derivative conjugal:	0	0.0	40	8.0	40	4.0	7
(a) Co-wives	(0)	(0.0)	(35)	(7.0)	(35)	(3.5)	
(b) Affines	(0)	(0.0)	(5)	(1.0)	(5)	(.5)	
5. Discord in family of orientation	1	.2	28	5.4	29	2.9	10
6. Supernatural assaults	...	...	2	.4	2	.2	12
7. Other wrongs against the person	40	8.4	16	3.1	56	5.6	5
8. Nonperformance of an obligation:	70	14.8	10	1.9	80	8.0	4
(a) Debt	(36)	(7.6)	(6)	(1.1)	(42)	(4.2)	
(b) Other "breach of contract"	(13)	(2.7)	(4)	(.8)	(17)	(1.7)	
(c) Failure to fulfill an obligation to government	(21)	(4.4)	(...)	(...)	(21)	(2.1)	
9. Using or transferring the property of others without permission	20	4.2	13	2.5	33	3.3	8
10. Other property disputes	22	4.6	8	1.5	30	3.0	9
11. Other	39	8.0	47	9.0	86	8.6	6
12. Incomplete, nonclassifiable	21	4.4	29	5.5	50	5.0	3
Totals	475	99.9°	524	100.2°	999	100.0	

° Percentages do not total 100% because of rounding to tenths.

"etic." However, the broader Kpelle categories turn out to be rather congruent with those from the common law.

The content of each of the twelve general categories of dispute types will be briefly noted.

Rights Over Women ("*woman palaver*"). The first category refers to certain types of sexual, marital, and personal wrongs, such as adultery or allegations of adultery, divorce, refusal of sexual access by the wife, and nonfulfillment of specific wifely duties. It includes cases of "improper marriage" (for example, when the alleged wrong is the improper transfer of bridewealth), and cases where a woman's guardian is sued to determine if bridewealth has been paid for her. Beating or verbal "abuse" of the husband by the wife is classed here rather than in the third category because this method fits the Kpelle way of thinking. In such a case a woman is violating her duty to be overtly submissive *to* her husband, not asserting a right to be assertive *over* him. The case will be viewed as stemming from a fault of the woman rather than from a lack in the man.

Derivative Rights Over Women. The second category refers to disputes that do not involve the operation of the marriage itself but are closely related to its formation. Generally the disputes raise issues that are not specific enough to be taken to court or that are not amenable to traditional legal sanctions. Thus, cases in this category are heard only in moots (house palavers). Such issues as the moot is expected to air include whether a person should marry, whom a particular person should marry, or how bridewealth should be raised. There are relatively few of these cases, and an argument could be made for grouping them with the first category, "rights over women."

Other Conjugal Disputes. The classification of other conjugal disputes refers to arguments that, if we used a more Western-oriented, etic approach, we would categorize as *"man* palaver," since they involve wrongs against women committed by men: the husband's refusal to consort with his wife, nonsupport by the husband, nonfulfillment of other specific husbandly duties, beating or verbal "abuse" of the wife. Because of the androcentric bias that characterizes Kpelle treatment of spouses' rights over each other, these cases are aired largely in moots.

Derivative Conjugal. The fourth category subsumes disputes that center on a marriage but do not involve a husband-wife pair but other parties to a marriage—either co-wives or a spouse and his or her affines. Thus, it includes discord between co-wives centering on accusations of jealousy or verbal "abuse" and in-law problems involving either spouse's mother.[7]

Discord in the Family of Orientation is a grouping that includes wrongs such as nonsupport by a parent and beatings or verbal "abuse" by a parent or member of the nuclear family other than a spouse or co-wife. This category is used in order to distinguish marital discord (categories 1 through 4) from other types of family discord.

Supernatural Assault. This minute rubric covers cases of accusation of sorcery or witchcraft. Because of the difficulty of proof there is no doubt that there are more allegations mentally phrased than are ever actually articulated in moots or courts.

Other Wrongs Against the Person. This category refers to various types of assault against the person that are not directly or derivatively marital: beating or verbal "abuse" by peripheral kinsmen or nonkinsmen, other physical assaults, and actual or attempted homicide.

Nonperformance of an obligation includes three subcategories. The first, *debt*, contains cases in which the offense is nonpayment of a mone-

7. Fathers-in-law do not pose a major problem to families of the next descending generation.

tary obligation. Cases in the second subcategory, *other breach of contract*, involve nonfulfillment of a specific or implied contract—for example, where a person has agreed to thatch a roof in return for a payment he has received and yet refuses to provide the service or to return the payment. Also included here are cases in which a court has ordered a payment, such as adultery damages or return of bridewealth, and the order has been ignored. By including this last type of case here we follow Kpelle thinking, which stresses the unmet obligation to the other party rather than the obligation to the court. *Failure to fulfill an obligation to government* is the last subcategory. This may consist of nonpayment of hut tax, refusal to perform public-works duty, or contempt of court for ignoring a summons or failure to appear in court as a bondsman or witness.

Using or Transfering the Property of Others Without Permission. The ninth category includes such wrongs as borrowing and not returning property and misappropriation of funds or goods (including embezzlement).

Other Property Disputes is a category that includes cases of misappropriation of land, of livestock's damaging crops, and of theft. The number of cases is smaller than one would expect from a middle-level horticultural society in Sub-Saharan Africa.

Other. There is a residual category for cases that fit nowhere else and are primarily singular, so that they cannot be combined into additional significant rubrics.

Incomplete and Nonclassifiable cases are those for which the interviewer's report of the informant's accounting of a case is too incomplete or too ambiguous for classification.

TESTING THE HYPOTHESES

Judicial Implications of Indirect Expression of Aggression. The self-reported cases from Fokwele and a review of the larger case inventory indicate that the judicial results of the indirect expression of aggression were more wide-ranging than predicted in the original first hypothesis. It suggested that the Kpelle dislike of expressing aggression directly, as in physical assault, will be reflected in: failure to fulfill a commitment as a common offense and a tendency to sue a person for a reason other than that given in court.

At first glance the incidence of nonperformance of an obligation tallied in Table 1 seems small. But the rank order of frequency is fourth, and it is the most frequent single category of breach apart from woman palaver and other conjugal disputes.[8] This finding confirms the first con-

8. The rank remains fourth even when the subcategory "failure to fulfill an obligation to government" is excluded.

dition of the hypothesis. A review of some actual cases reveals the underlying causal relationships.

The Case of the Delinquent Marketwoman. In a typical case heard before
a justice of the peace, the defendant, Kɔtu,[9] was a woman who had borrowed
six dollars [10] from the male plaintiff, Zo Gbelai, in order to engage in petty
trade. After four months she had failed to make a report of the earnings,
as she had promised, or to return any of the capital. Her backer sued in
order to recover his investment and a portion of her profits.

A lender always makes a loan in the presence of witnesses, inasmuch
as Kpelle society is basically nonliterate, making the use of promissory
notes cumbersome. Thus the borrower is almost certain to lose his case
if the dispute is taken to court because the lender's witnesses confirm
the existence of the obligation. He then has to repay the loan as well as
the courts costs.

Why does a litigant allow himself to be placed in a position so disadvantageous from the point of view of the economics involved? The hypothesis suggests that it is because of the somewhat ulterior (and largely
unconscious) motivation of the defendant. David Aberle (personal communication) has suggested an alternative explanation: that in a culture
making the transition from a subsistence economy to a cash economy
individuals commonly perform acts that seem highly uneconomic simply
because they are undergoing a type of monetary socialization.

Aberle's suggestion is plausible, and it and the present hypothesis are
not mutually exclusive. However, a look at further Kpelle cases heightens
the feeling that another factor beside economic motives or monetary
inexperience is involved. This idea is suggested initially by the fact that
often very small sums of money are at stake.

The Case of the Indebted Fisheater. Dennis Flumo sued Yakpawolo before a justice of the peace. The words of the complaint on the writ speak
for themselves: "That defendant Yakpawolo of Gbarnga is justly indebted
to him in the sum of $0.36 for two tins of fish, notwithstanding plaintiff
has made repeated demands for payment, defendant has failed so to do.
Plaintiff prays for redress."

In one case a father sued a son for failure to provide services in return for expenses the father had incurred on the son's behalf. In Kpelle
society, as in our own, to sue a kinsman is unusual. There such a case
would normally be heard in a moot, if at all.

9. Pseudonyms are used in all the cases presented here to preserve the anonymity
of the litigants, although all cases are a matter of public record.
10. American currency is used in Liberia as legal tender, although there are some
specially minted Liberian coins. Thus monetary figures used in the cases are actual
dollar figures.

Finally, it should be pointed out that the failure to fulfill an obligation takes forms other than reneging on a debt, notably failure to perform a service. For example, a typical case involved a man who agreed to make some doors for $16.00, accepted $15.40 in payment, and failed to construct the doors or to return the payment.

The cases cited above supply some of the connotations implicit in the rubric "failure to fulfill an obligation"—connotations that gave rise to the hypothesis. In the case of the father who sued his son, it is clear that something other than the actual tangible obligation must have been involved. Similarly, in the Case of the Indebted Fisheater, the loser had to pay not only the debt of 36 cents, but also court costs of at least $8.50. I suggest that the defendant did not renege on paying the 36 cents for lack of money or for lack of skill in the handling of money. For whatever reason, he wished to cause the shopkeeper some difficulty, even though it would hurt him in his own pocketbook. Then, too, the shopkeeper must have had more than his 36 cents in mind when he went to the trouble of instituting suit. On one level, many cases of this sort represent Kpelle instrumentality, the attempt to get more from the other person than he gets from you. If someone will let a friend forfeit on repaying an obligation without pressing him, that is the debtor's good fortune, and a Kpelle does not expect to meet an obligation until he is asked to do so or even until he is pressed by the person to whom he is obligated. On another level, we see the failure to honor a commitment as serving to express aggression indirectly, as is most apparent in those cases in which a person fails to meet an obligation even after being pressed repeatedly. Finally, the two needs are not mutually exclusive. The high incidence of reneging may simultaneously gratify both needs widespread in the Kpelle population: the need to manipulate others to one's own end and the need to channel aggression obliquely.

The hypothesis suggests that suing a person for a reason other than the one stated in the complaint and allegations is another manner in which Kpelle express aggression indirectly.

The Case of the Defaulting Workman. In the case of Flumo Zao (plaintiff) versus Sua Kweli (defendant), heard before a district chief, this dimension emerges baldly in the words of the writ of summons: "That you, Sua Kweli, have failed to repair Pl. Flumo Zao's house and you have his wife." In this instance both the overt *and* more covert grievance are listed. However, more characteristic is the following case to which the hypothesis applies, where the covert grievance does not emerge.

The Case of the Vengeful Shopkeeper. Tokolong Dolo (plaintiff) sued Wua Lopu (defendant) before a justice of the peace in an "action of debt for the sum of fifty cents being value for a tin of carbide which [you] have failed absolutely to pay for." However, the case was more complicated than these words of the plaintiff's formal complaint indicated.

My inquiries into the background of the case indicated that Wua had bought the fifty-cents can of carbide from Tokolong Dolo's small shop on credit. Wua is the *koti* for the quarter in which he and Tokolong live. The *koti* is the tribal authority responsible for seeing that the members of the quarter carry out their primary obligations to the central government—paying taxes and reporting periodically for the public labor in lieu of taxes which the Kpelle often refer to as "government work."

Wua in his capacity as *koti* had exempted Tokolong from public works duty because he operates a shop for which he pays a license fee to the government. Tokolong's father, Nang Ba, was also exempted because of his extreme old age. Because of these exemptions the *koti* had granted him and his father, Tokolong did not press Wua Lɔpu for payment of the fifty cents.

One day a small detachment of soldiers came to town, and it was Wua's quarter's turn to lodge and feed them. Everyone in the quarter, except Tokolong's father, had gone to his farm. Wua told the soldiers that the old man was obligated to feed them because he and his son were exempted from other public-works duty. But the old man had no food and the soldiers beat him.

When Tokolong came home from the farm, the old man told him what had happened. Tokolong said, "I won't sue Wua for letting them beat you. But he has owed me fifty cents for a long time, and I haven't bothered him about it. So I will sue him for the fifty cents."

In the court hearing Tokolong never even mentioned that beating of his father. Wua admitted that correctness of the debt charge, and agreed to pay the fifty cents, court costs, and expenses.

This case is a very clear-cut example of use of a cover grievance in bringing suit. Suing for other than the stated reason is reflected in a concomitant descriptive attribute characteristic of the configuration of Kpelle dispute settlement—frequent long delays between the time of the alleged wrong and the time of filing suit. Such a delay is often a cue to the fact that a long-smoldering grievance has been revived to serve as the means for countering a more recent act committed by the offending party. Normally the cue can be verified only for those cases for which the researcher has more than the court records as a source of information and can obtain a more complete account of events.

The syndrome of failure to state the actual reason for bringing suit is often also reflected in cases thrown out of court for "suing without sufficient reason."

Other manifestations of the indirect expression of aggression that appear in the configuration of dispute settlements are: (a) failure to honor a promise to a litigant to appear as a witness on his behalf; (b) a plaintiff's suing and subsequently failing to appear in court for the trial; (c) verbal aggression (called "abuse" by the Kpelle) and supernatural aggression; (d) adulterous actions directed at the wives of another man.

These manifestations were not predicted by the original hypothesis but emerged from analysis of case incidences summarized in Table 1.

Examination of some additional cases sheds light on the subhypothesis that actions directed at another man's wife can be a vehicle for the expression of aggression or hostility. Adultery and divorce cases, lumped by the Kpelle as "woman palaver," most often reveal a flavor of desire for the woman combined with hostility directed against the husband.

The Case of the Amorous Herbalist. Mulruba (plaintiff) sued Surong Tei (defendant). Mulruba's wife, Nowai, had a headache for a week, and she asked him to take her to the clinic for treatment. He demurred, saying that he would make medicine for her himself. He then left, saying that he had to go to his farm but that he would see about the medicine when he returned.

Surong Tei was a friend of Mulruba's and, according to local gossip, the lover of Mulruba's wife. Surong Tei saw Nowai looking unwell and asked what the trouble was. She told him, and he suggested that she accompany him to the bush, where he would show her a leaf for preparing medicine for her headache.

While they were gone, Mulruba returned and people told him that his wife had gone into the bush with his friend. When the couple returned, Mulruba asked Surong Tei why he had taken Nowai into the bush without his permission. He added that this action confirmed the tale that Surong Tei and Nowai were lovers and that, accordingly, he would sue Surong Tei.

Mulruba sued for damages in a complaint holding "that you the above defendant have administered medicine on [sic] the plaintiff's wife without telling him, which was very illegal." Surong Tei was found guilty and fined twenty-five dollars. The case was treated by the justice of the peace as a criminal matter, the fine being paid to the government.

In analyzing the case, it is important to know that the Kpelle feel that normally a man and woman who are not husband and wife should not go to the bush together, even if they are brother and sister. If they do, the assumption is that they have engaged in sexual intercourse. This explains Mulruba's reasoning and consequent action. In addition, Surong Tei assumed a role that is expressly allocated to the husband—that of providing medicine for an ill wife. Thus his actions were doubly demeaning of Mulruba.

I have argued elsewhere (Gibbs 1963b) that the status of Kpelle men is highly dependent on the economic contribution of their wives, especially in polygynous households. Thus, when one man acts to seduce another man's wife, he is attacking not only that man's self-identity as a sexually and conjugally adequate person, but also his means to high status and therefore his psychic security. In short, Kpelle men use actions toward women not only as a means of asserting power over women, but also as a way of communicating their negative feelings and power needs toward their fellow males.

Examination of the frequency distribution of dispute types and of some individual disputes indicates that the first preliminary hypothesis can be extended. It can be rephrased as follows: Among the Kpelle the need to discharge aggression or hostility is reflected judicially in a relatively high incidence of the following type of offenses: (a) failure to fulfill a commitment; (b) tendency to sue for a manifest stated grievance rather than the covert one that actually troubles the plaintiff; (c) woman palaver, much of which begins with adulterous actions directed at the wife of another man. Aggression may also be discharged through offenses with a relatively low frequency, such as verbal aggression and supernatural assault.

In Llewellyn and Hoebel's (1941) terms, the preference for the indirect expression of aggression provides the Kpelle legal system with much of its "law work"—in particular with a substantial percentage of its disputes. To be sure, structural as well as psychological factors are at work. Thus the question can be raised concerning the structural factors producing the recurring strains that are resolved by this patterned discharge of aggression in courts and moots. I have done this for woman palaver in a previous paper (Gibbs 1963b).

This type of hypothesis is similar to the one advanced by LeVine (1960). As noted in the review of the literature above, he explained the difference in the over-all incidence of litigation among the Nuer and the Gusii in terms of a differential preference for the direct expression of aggression.

The present study indicates that the judicial implications of modes of discharging aggression are more sweeping than the LeVine study suggests. More results from different styles of expressing aggression than merely a preference for litigation as opposed to other types of dispute settlement. These styles even affect the types of wrongs that most commonly occur and, as we shall see, the procedural steps used to adjust those wrongs.

PSYCHOLOGICAL ROOTS OF WOMAN PALAVER

The Kpelle themselves say, "The only palaver we have in this land is woman palaver." Table 1 indicates that this assertion is not much of an exaggeration. As noted in the discussion of the first hypothesis, the adulterous acts Kpelle men direct at other men's wives suggest a need for power over women, for power over other men, and for directing hostility against other men. The second hypothesis holds that this need for power is partly an expression of male feelings of inadequacy vis-à-vis women.

Actions such as those of Surong Tei, the defendant in the case cited above, often result ultimately in divorce and the woman's remarriage to the lover. Analytically, this pattern of alienation of affections followed by remarriage can be viewed as wife-stealing. If so, then theft—broadly conceived—becomes one of the most common offenses among the Kpelle. This fits Bacon, Child, and Barry's (1963) suggestion that theft by males is sometimes a defense against a feminine identity. In support of this interpretation, it should be recalled that we have already observed that Kpelle men do owe much of their status to women; thus they have a not-too-latent envy of women as powerful figures and, correspondingly, some uncertainty about their identity as males. Thus hypothesis two builds upon my own earlier analysis of Kpelle marital instability and the thinking of the Whiting-Human Relations Area Files school to suggest that there are psychological as well as structural roots for the incidence of disputes over women among the Kpelle.

The Case of the Sensitive Husband. George Keller, a Kpelle evangelist, sued Tia, a Bassa tribesman, for "abusing" his wife. The case was heard before a justice of the peace. Tia lived with a fellow tribesman who, like himself, was a sawyer. Keller's wife, Nyeei Puu, used to visit the wife of Tia's landlord, who was her friend. She would often see Tia there and jokingly started to call him "Big Head" because of his physical appearance. He, appraising her appearance, in turn began to call her "Big Behind."

One day, when Nyeei Puu was on the way to the bush with another man, she passed Tia washing his clothes in the creek. She greeted him: "Good morning, Big Head." He returned her salute in the usual fashion, saying, "Good morning, Big Behind." However, because Nyeei Puu was with someone else, she became worried that her companion would misunderstand their joking and report her to her husband as being too familiar with another man. She therefore acted insulted, claiming Tia had greeted her by saying, "Good morning, Big Ass." She reported her version of the incident to her husband when he came home that night.

The next morning Keller went to Tia's house to ask if his wife's account was true. However, Tia and his landlord had already gone into the bush to saw. Therefore Keller went immediately to the justice of the peace and filed suit against. Tia.

When the case was heard, it came out that Nyeei Puu and Tia had established a kind of joking relationship and that they always used the same nicknames in addressing each other. Moreover, the man who had accompanied Nyeei Puu on the morning in question testified that he had heard Tia address Nyeei Puu by the inoffensive term, "Big Behind."

The court stated that Keller should have checked with Tia before bringing suit. It found in Tia's favor and ordered Keller to pay court costs and incidental expenses. Tia wanted to file a countersuit for defamation of character, but the court dissuaded him.

Nyeei Puu's discomfort and consequent shame at the creek indicates that she was fully aware of the explosive potential of male-female interaction in Kpelleland. She also anticipated her husband's concern with face, which led to his precipitous suit. He shows to a higher degree what is common to many Kpelle men—nagging uncertainty about his ability to uphold his masculine authority and prestige.

Further evidence of male feelings of inadequacy vis-à-vis women emerges in a sequence analysis of what occurs in Kpelle divorce cases.

The Case of the Sojourning Wife. In this case, heard before a paramount chief, Nyema (the plaintiff) sued her mother, Gopuu, requesting that the old lady return the bridewealth that had been paid for her because she no longer wished to live with her husband. This was therefore a suit for divorce and the "real" defendant was Nyema's husband, Kwi Kwili.

When Nyema was asked why her mother—who for purposes of the suit acted as her guardian in place in her deceased father—should return her bridewealth, she replied in the manner customary for Kpelle wives seeking divorce: "I do not want my husband's home anymore." To substantiate her charge, she recounted the history of her marriage as first wife to Kwi Kwili, a classificatory father's sister's son. Kwi Kwili, in turn, gave his chronicle of their marriage. A crucial element in the dissension between them was the fact that after their marriage Kwi Kwili inherited some additional wives from his deceased father who, at the time of his death, was living in Guinea. There was jealousy between Nyema and the new wives. Quite some time after that, Nyema's father had died in another chiefdom and she went to the funeral and stayed, remaining away from her husband for a year and a half. She came back to institute suit for divorce.

Nyema made her allegations against Kwi Kwili in the following order:

1. A child of hers had died because of her husband's mother's witchcraft.

2. Her husband had not supported her because he failed to clear a rice farm for her.

3. He had disrespected her by not going to offer condolences whenever any of her relatives died.

4. He had not shown appreciation for special wifely acts: (a) treating his illnesses, (b) helping him to acquire money to offer the chief in lieu of having to perform public-works duty, (c) showing more concern and consideration than her co-wives.

5. Her husband "overlooked" her, did not treat her with kindness or gratitude.

The key allegations seemed to be the witchcraft charge and the nonsupport charge, because each was repeated. But when questioned by her husband at the beginning of his testimony, Nyema indicated that she was not leaving him because of the child's death but because of the nonsupport.

Kwi Kwili made the following allegations of his own:

1. Nyema was guilty of promiscuous behavior, notably the taking of frequent lovers.

2. She objected to his inheriting additional wives.

3. When he did accept his inheritance of plural wives, Nyema, as the headwife, treated the co-wives badly, causing dissension in his household.

4. By staying away so long, she had deserted him.

Finally, Kwi Kwili countered his wife's primary allegation by referring to two of his own. He stated that the reason why he had not cleared a farm for her was that she was living elsewhere and forming liaisons with another man or men.

At the beginning of the case the chief established that Nyema wanted to leave Kwi Kwili "because of his ways." He then questioned her.

Chief: All right! Nyema, it reaches you. What did this person [the husband] do to you?

Nyema: The thing he did to me . . . when a person is in a home her child should live. And when a person is in a home, someone should work for her.

Thus a veiled accusation of a child's death by alleged witchcraft opened her allegations, which continued for many minutes. She catalogued the additional complaints noted above. Finally the chief, a bit exasperated and weary, turned to her and spoke:

Chief: The thing that you are saying, say it to the point. What are you saying? Say it to the point.

Nyema: This person they gave me to—when I have a child, his mother eats it. [She has restated—more baldly—the witchcraft accusation with which she opened her allegations.]

Chief: Who is that who eats human beings?

Nyema: This person's [indicates her husband, Kwi Kwili] mother. This is one of his mothers sitting here. When they are doing like that to you in a home, can you stay there?

Chief (to spectator): Man, you who are sitting like that, if you lift up your head, that piece of stick will hit your head. What did you come to look for?

Man: No. [Meaning: I didn't come to look for anything special.] I just came to sit and listen to the case for a while.

Chief: You are sitting in a bad place. You will strike your head and hurt it. [Turning to Nyema] Are you through?

Nyema: There [In all I have said] is why I say: I don't want him. [It is] Because I took him from death and he overlooks me. He is just behaving like that to me.

Even though Nyema ranked nonsupport as her major allegation, it was clear that the child's death was also a great concern to her. It is equally clear that the chief was not anxious to probe into the matter and found a subtle way to avoid it by distracting Nyema, who was prone to ramble in testifying. We cannot be certain of whether or not the chief's gambit was conscious or unconscious. The effect was the same in either case.

The paramount chief granted the divorce, holding Nyema at fault, and he ordered Nyema and her mother to return Kwi Kwili's bridewealth and to pay damages. This is the usual pattern in Kpelle divorce actions. The person who brings suit for divorce is felt to be at fault, and the plaintiff in divorce cases is almost always a woman.[11]

11. The guilty party pays damages fixed by statute at $100, and if it is the wife, as it most often is, the refunded bridewealth her guardian repays on her behalf is fixed by statute at a minimum of $40. The man retains filiation of the children re-

Although fault seems presumed in a Kpelle divorce case, it must be proven. It is in the pattern of proof that we find some psychological ramifications. In the case of the sojourning wife the only allegation of Nyema's investigated by the chief was that of nonsupport. In finding her at fault he accepted Kwi Kwili's counterallegation that he had not farmed with her because she had deserted him. The chief did not delve into Nyema's plea that she waited in vain at her deceased father's house, expecting Kwi Kwili to send for her. In effect the chief said that inasmuch as Nyema's primary reason for holding her husband at fault had been vitiated, she herself was at fault and the divorce would be granted on the grounds that she no longer wanted to live with her husband. There was no attempt to see whether she could substantiate any of her other reasons for holding her husband at fault—even the fairly serious charge of witchcraft. Even in delving into the nonsupport charge, the chief questioned Nyema in such a way that it was all but impossible for her to win her point. At a point early in Kwi Kwili's testimony, when the chief interrupts him to question Nyema, the transcript reads:

> *Chief* (to Nyema): *Nee* Nyema, during the *whole time* you were in this man's hand, didn't he make any rice farm for you? [Emphasis added]
>
> *Nyema:* When we were at Zowa, his mother and I used to make rice farms. He used to go to Firestone [Plantation] and we made swamp [rice] farms. But he used to just up and go across the river. . . . Then I told his mother that "I will be with you here, making farms for you."
>
> *Chief* (to Nyema): *Mama*, did you say this person has not made *any* farms for you? [Emphasis added]
>
> *Nyema:* I said that he used to make farms for me. But since we crossed the river, he has not made farms for me nor built a house for me.
>
> *Chief:* And since you two came here?
>
> *Nyema:* It was just recently that they told him that if he didn't come back across the river, his women will no longer be his. This is why he came here.
>
> *Chief:* Since he came here, has he made any farm for you?
>
> *Nyema:* I told you that I was at our home.
>
> *Chief:* Go and sit down. That is just what they said about you.

By rephrasing Nyema's question to make it seem that she was holding that Kwi Kwili had *never* made a rice farm for her, it made it easy for Kwi Kwili to disprove her allegation simply by showing that he had farmed with her at some point in their marriage. Moreover, the chief led Nyema to the point of repeating that she had lived at her father's home for a long period of time, thereby setting the stage for Kwi Kwili's subsequent allegations of promiscuity and desertion. Thus the chief used his investigatory initiative to act somewhat as a prosecutor.

---

gardless of whether he is held at fault. If the man is held at fault, he forfeits bridewealth and has to pay damages. No bridewealth is deducted for children born to the woman, regardless of where fault is assigned.

The incomplete investigation of the wife's allegations can be explained in two ways. The first is a judicial explanation. A Kpelle woman sues for divorce because she no longer wishes to stay with her husband. The chief hearing the case has only to determine that this is indeed so and to find a single basis for allocating fault. Having done so, he need proceed no further. Thus, as I have indicated elsewhere (Gibbs 1962), Kpelle divorce cases take on something of the cut-and-dried flavor of Monday morning drunkenness cases in American municipal courts. Finally, having assigned blame, the Kpelle judge determines the bridewealth to be returned.

However, there is a second, psychological, interpretation, based on the fact that the incompleteness of investigation operates to the woman's disadvantage. The chief, seeking out a single ground for allocating fault, usually airs the one most likely to show the woman at fault, not the one or two that have contributed most to the bad feelings between the litigants. This selective manner of focusing on allegations is a way in which Kpelle chiefs not only handle divorce cases with dispatch, but also express male control and dominance. Although chiefs can see fault on both sides in the divorce cases they hear, Kpelle conventions with regard to the handling of divorce cases require a unilateral ascription of blame. Thus, regardless of his actions toward his wife, the husband is almost always declared the winner and to his wife is ascribed the fault. The divorce court is one arena in which a Kpelle man—either litigant or spectator—can find counterbalance for feelings of inadequacy vis-à-vis women.

The judicial and psychological explanations are not mutually exclusive but complementary. The incidence of woman palaver—including divorce —is rooted in both structural and psychic factors, as was noted earlier. The treatment of divorce cases is patterned by the hardened nature of the estrangement, which demands severance of the union. But logically the biased investigation of allegations and assignment of blame could equally well go against the husband. However, if such were the case, additional psychic tensions would be created for Kpelle men. On the other hand, the androcentric bias in the investigation of allegations and assignment of fault serves to alleviate Kpelle men's feelings of inadequacy vis-à-vis women. Thus we see the law functioning, not only to settle disputes, but also to gratify the personality needs of litigants.

Qualitative case analysis suggests confirmation of the second preliminary hypothesis in its original form: A high incidence of disputes about rights over women is rooted not only in structural factors, but also in male feelings of inadequacy vis-à-vis women.

JUDICIAL IMPLICATIONS OF AUTHORITARIAN SUBMISSION

The Kpelle tendency to submit to authority figures and their stress on autonomy in interpersonal relations sometimes combine to produce a type of passive resistance to the decisions of judicial figures. Some of this resistance is predicted by the third preliminary hypothesis. This syndrome emerges very clearly in the Case of the Contemptuous Debtor, in which a justice of the peace sued the defendant, an acculturated Kpelle named James Reeves, for contempt of court in a debt case. The words of the summons were: "that you were sued in the above court and writ of summons issued; you failed to appear; two (2) consecutive letters were sent to you as friend but you never care to appear."

The Case of the Acquiescent Farmer. A more complicated case, also heard before a justice of the peace, involved Labla Kweli as plaintiff and Kiamu Pee and Goma Tokpa as co-defendants. All three litigants lived in the same quarter of their town. Kiamu Pee was entrusted with a steer owned by a Malinke from a nearby town. Goma Tokpa was also entrusted with a steer, in this case one owned by the paramount chief. The two steers went to the farm of Labla Kweli and ate much of the knee-high rice crop. Labla reported as much to the two caretakers, each of whom replied that he was not the owner of the beast and that Labla would have to sue the owners. The cattle went to the farm a second time and consumed the balance of the crop; Labla then sued both caretakers. Both owners of the cattle, the Malinke and the paramount chief, also appeared in court, although they were not named as co-defendants in the summons.

Although not named as a co-defendant, once in court the Malinke was held responsible for the acts of his steer and was ordered to pay $150—the value of the rice crop—and incidental fees."

In the pleadings Labla asked $150 from Goma Tokpa and the paramount chief. The paramount chief who appeared with Goma Tokpa admitted that the second beast was his and that it had destroyed the rice crop. He stated that he (the paramount chief), Goma Tokpa, and Labla were all related, implying that Labla could not sue him and Goma Tokpa because he would —in effect—be suing himself. Labla and the court accepted this argument.

The paramount chief then paid the court costs and gave Labla $20, saying that because the steer was Labla's, too, he should drop the matter. Labla agreed, saying that inasmuch as he was a co-owner of the beast, he would accept only $10 from the paramount chief.

The paramount chief stressed a kinship link that, under other circumstances, might be ignored. Because of Labla's submissiveness, the Malinke, as an alien in the chiefdom, bore more than an equitable share of the damages.

In this case Labla's deference to the paramount chief was open and apparent. However, informants reported that one reason the suit was filed in the first place—even though the paramount chief was a shadow defendant—was that the people of the town in which the three litigants lived were angry with the paramount chief. In fact, they filed a formal complaint against him with the county superintendent about the same time. Thus, as in some previous cases, we also see in this case the indirect expression of a grievance, suing for both overt and covert reasons. However, Labla's timorousness robbed the community of a complete victory in their covert goal.

Examination of the census survey figures of frequency of types of disputes and selected individual cases suggests a modification of the third preliminary hypothesis, to read: Authoritarian submission and stress on individual autonomy combine to produce a type of passive resistance to some aspects of the judicial process. This takes the form of litigants ignoring summonses and subpoenas and/or ignoring court decisions in which they have concurred before the court.

FUNCTIONS OF CONDITIONAL OATHS

The fourth of the original hypotheses suggests that the use of conditional oaths is found not just where there is an absence of other means of proof, but also where the issues in the case take on marked psychological salience.

This is found most commonly in cases of woman palaver in which a man's wife is leaving him. Before returning the brideprice and thus severing the union, the man who is being divorced will ask the court to have the woman swear a conditional oath that she has revealed all the names of any lovers she has had. The primary reason for this action is that the husband wishes to avail himself of the right to collect adultery damages from each of these men—a right that he will lose as soon as the divorce is effected. However, it seems probable that a second reason is that the husband can "get back" at those men who have attacked him by consorting with his wife.

The association of the use of conditional oaths and psychological salience emerges most dramatically in a type of case that is relatively rare in Kpelle courts—when the wrong is what can best be termed supernatural assault.

The Case of the Menacing Blacksmith. Yakpawolo Gbanga and Sumo live in the same quarter of their town, where Sumo is the quarter blacksmith. Yakpawolo is crippled by a disease which caused both of his lower legs to swell so greatly that he cannot walk. One day when Yakpawolo was in Sumo's blacksmith's shed, Sumo told him that the reason he was crippled was that he (Sumo) had once obtained a sheep and made a sacrifice using Yakpawolo's name.

Yakpawolo sued Sumo before the district chief, demanding that Sumo indicate why he had sorcerized him. At first Sumo denied having made the statement, but there were several witnesses to the incident who testified otherwise. The court found Sumo guilty and ordered him to bring a sheep to sacrifice to clear the bad feelings. In handing down his decision, the chief explained: "then the spirits of the old people [the] ancestors would leave them, . . . otherwise they would continually be in trouble." Since Sumo did not have a sheep, he brought a white dog instead, white being the color Kpelle associate with having "good heart" toward others. Yakpawolo refused to accept the suggestion of the sacrifice, saying that what he desired was to know why Sumo had directed a sacrifice against him. The district chief suggested that they should kill and eat the dog and that Sumo should drink the dog's blood and swear on it that he had not made a sacrifice against Yakpawolo.

Yakpawolo still refused to accept the court's decision and appealed the case to the paramount chief's court, where it was heard the following day. The paramount chief also found Sumo guilty and offered him two alternatives. One was that first suggested by the district chief, that Sumo swear his innocence on the blood of the dog; the other, that he swear it on *kafu*.[12] This time Yakpawolo accepted the court's decision, and Sumo swore his innocence on *kafu*.

This case illustrates both functions of the use of conditional oaths. First, for the tension of grievances to be dissipated at all, it was necessary for the court to use the conditional oath to find out whether or not the alleged act of sorcery had taken place. By swearing the oath, Sumo said in effect that he had been lying when he told Yakpawolo that he had performed sorcery against him. It was then necessary for the effects of the admitted wrong, malicious lying, to be reduced. This second result was also achieved by the use of the conditional oath. It served the second function of allaying anxieties aroused in Yakpawolo by Sumo's boast. Sumo's swearing on *kafu* assured Yakpawolo that the blacksmith's feelings against him were not so hostile that they had led him to perform sorcery, although the false boast was itself an antagonistic act, albeit of lesser magnitude.

In effect Yakpawolo asked the court to require Sumo to issue a supernaturally buttressed denial of sorcery, a form of redress that was rooted in his own psychic needs, his desire to institute the process of repression (or even denial) of what he had heard that painful day in the blacksmith's shed. Because Sumo's denial was cast in the potentially boomeranging form of a conditional oath, Yakpawolo found it all the more believable and all the more soothing. However, this interpretation must not be overextended. Yakpawolo was not ruled completely by his anxieties, for he admitted that he had appealed the case partly because he hoped that the paramount chief would require Sumo to pay him $100 to use for medical treatment!

Qualitative case analysis suggests a slight revision of the fourth pre-

12. *Kafu* is a colorless liquid kept in a stoppered whiskey or wine bottle and is believed to have supernatural potency. In taking it a witness swears that, "if I bear false witness . . . then the *sale* [medicine] should kill me." It is believed that a person who breaks such an oath will be "caught" by the *kafu*. His stomach will swell and he will die, or some other illness will eventually strike.

liminary hypothesis. It can be stated as follows: Ordeals or conditional oaths will be resorted to when there is an absence of proof or conflicting testimony that there is no more "rational" way of resolving. But conditional oaths will be resorted to also when the offense is one that is psychologically very disturbing to the wronged party's psychic equilibrium. Usually this wrong will be one that is, in Kpelle terms, an assault on the wronged party's self-identity. However, the incomplete nature of Kpelle court records makes it impossible to test the revised hypothesis quantitatively.

PERSONALITY DISPOSITIONS AND INCIDENCE OF LEGAL INVOLVEMENT

The data suggest modification of the fifth original hypothesis, which states that people with a high degree of blocked aggression show a greater frequency of involvement with the law. It is more accurate to predict that persons with a high frequency of involvement in litigation may be deviant psychologically. Of course, some instances of frequent appearance in court can be explained by structural factors. Thus, shopkeepers in Kpelleland—whether they be Kpelle, Malinke, Lebanese, or Americo-Liberian—are more likely to be involved in suits for debt than other people. Other instances of frequent appearance in court yield to a more psychological explanation.

The Case of the Bellicose Suitor. This pattern is illustrated by the case of Dolo Gbia (plaintiff) versus Kiakula (defendant). Dolo Gbia had Kiakula working on his farm, and he noticed that Kiakula had a sexual interest in his wife, Nyeme. Dolo Gbia then offered the woman to Kiakula as his consort, and Kiakula thus became his client.[13] After six months the woman and Kiakula terminated their relationship by mutual agreement. Kiakula then directed his attention to Dolo Gbia's and Nyeme's daughter. The daughter spurned his advances, saying that she could not have an affair with her mother's former lover because she now thought of him "as a father." This angered Kiakula, who assaulted the girl. He was sued by Dolo Gbia before a justice of the peace, found guilty, fined, and ordered not to return to his home town for three months but to work on the farm of the justice of the peace instead. However, Kiakula violated this injunction, and before the three months were up he returned to his home town and assaulted the girl

13. This is a type of union which I referred to as "male concubinage" (Gibbs 1965). A man who does not have the means of obtaining a marriage payment will go to a wealthy man and ask to be given one of the wealthy man's wives as a consort. The woman remains the legal wife of the *tɔ ńuu* (patron) but the *lɔɔ pɔlɔong* (client) cohabits with her in a house provided by the patron-husband. Although the patron gives up sexual access to his wife, he retains the right to collect any adultery damages that may be incurred by her actions, and children born to her and the client legally belong to the patron. The client and the woman work on the farm of the patron, and they may also work a farm of their own. In a formal sense the client gains little more than sexual access to the woman.

again, threatening to beat her to death. This time he was arrested and tried at the county seat, where he was jailed for a month.

The court clerk who was my informant with reference to this case observed that Kiakula, a man with a withered arm, was "always in trouble." It is probable that the withered arm affected Kiakula's sense of adequacy and consequently led him to assert himself in ways that brought him into conflict with the law. The nature of Kiakula's offense and the repetition of it both lend support for this type of hypothesis.

Until the next phases of the research are completed, it is not possible to test quantitatively the correlation between high involvement in litigation and psychological deviance predicted by the preliminary hypothesis because of the absence of "hard" personality data. However, qualitative examination of some cases and substantial personal knowledge of many individuals in the culture yield subjective support for the fifth preliminary hypothesis.

The preliminary hypothesis, which was phrased in too narrow terms, can be modified to read as follows: With a few statable exceptions (such as merchants, chiefs), persons with a high frequency of involvement in litigation or who are frequent appellants are likely to be psychologically deviant.

This type of psychologically oriented hypothesis does not preclude a complementary sociological (or structural) one. Frequent involvement in litigation may be reflective of a person's status attributes, such as occupation (trader) or rank, wealth, and responsibility (chief).

THE REVISED HYPOTHESES

The preliminary hypotheses can now be stated in less tentative form, as dictated by the preceding analysis. Among the Kpelle:

1. The need to discharge aggression or hostility is reflected judicially in a relatively high incidence of the following types of offenses: (a) failure to fulfill a commitment; (b) tendency to sue for a manifest stated grievance rather than the covert one that actually troubles the plaintiff; (c) woman palaver, much of which begins with adulterous actions directed at the wife of another man.

2. A high incidence of disputes about rights over women is rooted not only in structural factors, but also in male feelings of inadequacy vis-à-vis women.

3. Authoritarian submission plus stress on individual autonomy combine to produce a type of passive resistance to some aspects of the judicial process. This takes the form of litigants' ignoring summonses and subpoenas and/or ignoring court decisions in which they have concurred before the court.

4. Ordeals or conditional oaths will be resorted to when there is an absence of proof or conflicting testimony for which there is no more "rational" resolution. But conditional oaths will be resorted to also when the offense is one which psychologically is very disturbing of the wronged party's psychic equilibrium. Usually this wrong will be one that is, in Kpelle terms, an assault on the wronged party's self-identity.

5. With a few statable exceptions (such as merchants, chiefs), persons: with a high frequency of involvement in litigation or who are frequent appellants are likely to be psychologically deviant.

AN ANALYTICAL NOTE: INDIVIDUAL DIFFERENCES AND GROUP TRENDS

The careful reader will observe that all these hypotheses can be phrased and investigated from either of two viewpoints: one is that of individuals' differences; the other, that of group trends. For example, as phrased, the fifth hypothesis suggests that when Litigant A appeals his lost case and Litigant B does not, we may explain this in terms of differences in their two personalities; that A has more blocked aggression, which he discharges through being litigious. On the other hand, we may derive figures both for the level of blocked aggression and the incidence of appeals from lower courts characteristic of the group as a whole. If both are high, we can say that the high incidence of appeals may reflect a personality trait that is characteristic of the *group*. To be sure, one would not wish to overlook other factors that contribute to the frequency of appeals, such as what our society calls "judicial error" or simple uncertainty as to what the law (in the sense of rule) is. Obviously these various independent variables must be weighed differently when explaining the separate appeal frequencies of particular offenses. Thus, in cases involving "new" laws, a high incidence of appeals is likely to reflect uncertainty about the law and judicial error; in cases involving "old" laws, it is more likely to reflect a widespread psychodynamic factor.

This distinction between the "individual" and "group" approach is seen in beautiful simplicity with regard to the second hypothesis, which explains the incidence of disputes in rights over women. The approach espoused here is not so much concerned about why particular Kpelle men get involved in adultery or divorce cases or both as it is with why 44 per cent of all self-reported litigation in the town in which I have done most of my field work involves rights over women or marital problems. The concern is with the impact such "group" incidences has on both the procedures and the substance of the law.

The present study is oriented to the "group" point of view for several reasons. First, the aim is to examine and explain the regularities of Kpelle law. Second, most of the presently available personality assessment techniques lend themselves more readily to discerning recurring traits than to validly isolating differences (particularly when used in nonliterate societies). Third, the concern is not with explaining the particular behavior of particular individuals in particular litigation situations, for neither our assessment techniques nor our predictive models are yet sufficiently sophisticated to do this.

A review of the literature scattered across several behavioral science disciplines reveals numerous studies that relate personality variables to particular aspects of law and social control. However, these studies have had little impact on the mainstream of work in the ethnography of law of nonliterate and peasant societies. Research in this area has concentrated primarily on dispute settlement, particularly the judicial process. Even when anthroplogists (who form the majority of scholars working in the subdiscipline) analyze the relationship between personality and law, they have explored the relationship between personality and a single aspect of law rather than attempting to relate it to the profile of major descriptive attributes characteristic of a single legal system.

The writer's on-going study of law and personality among the Kpelle is broader in scope than preceding studies in that it traces connections between personality variables and several dominant features of the judicial system.

Structural Change and Primitive Law: Consequences of a Papuan Legal Case

One of the unfortunate effects of sociology upon some social anthropology has been the banishment of the consideration of the individual's role in the social and cultural history of the various tribal societies. This divorce of the individual from his society has given rise to the well-known cultural descriptions and social analyses in which a native innovator has no place, in which the "group as a whole acts, decides, and changes," being equipped by various writers not only with a structure and existence that is termed "superorganic" or "supraindividual," but also with such amazing faculties as "group mind" and "group will." Human society somehow has been promoted to an organism in its own right. It is not surprising, therefore, that an account (Pospisil 1958b) of a Papuan innovator who initiated changes in social structure became controversial and drew the following categoric refutation: "the operations of his primitive legislator had no effect whatsoever on the social structure" (Leach, 1959: 1096). I intend in this article to carry the controversy a bit further.

Fortunately, many contemporary social anthropologists, who have somehow escaped the sociological influence referred to above, do allow for the importance of the individual in shaping tribal cultures. Hoebel made his position on the native innovator quite clear when he wrote: "In the primitive world volitional inventiveness is truly a rare occurrence. Conscious tinkering with the social structure or with gadgetary improvement is not the order of the day. Most primitive inventions are nonvolitional" (1949:470). By this statement he allowed for a possibility of cultural change owing to an individual's volitional effort. Since many societies have been studied for a relatively brief period of time (one or two consecutive years), and since many of the investigators have been heavily influenced by the early sociological dogma that divorces the individual actors from the "social processes," it follows that there are very few accounts of volitional innovations, especially in the area of law. This article is intended to contribute to the growing literature on this topic and to present the history and analysis of an innovation made by a Papuan headman and to relate its subsequent fate and effects upon the Kapauku Papuan society during the nine years that followed my original investigation in 1954.

During my first research among the unacculturated Kapauku Papuans of West New Guinea, conducted in the non-"pacified" Kaumu valley in 1954 and 1955, I recorded a dramatic modification of the laws of incest and a series of subsequent changes in the social structure of a Papuan community. The modification of the incest laws was initiated by Awiitigaaj, the headman of the village of Botukebo. I had the opportunity to record the pertinent history and motivations of this man and to observe the attitude of his tribesmen toward the innovation. In my article "Social Change and Primitive Law," which appeared in *American Anthropologist* in October 1958, I interpreted the modifications of the laws of incest, and the subsequent changes in the social structure of the village, as an example of a rare volitional invention made by an influential individual in a tribal society. I also proposed a hypothesis for the social acceptance of this unprecedented innovation and made several predictions about changes that would follow. In a letter to the editor Professor Leach criticized my interpretation and claimed that what I had actually observed was a normal, unexciting, and necessary process of fission, such as is present in any segmentary society. According to his letter, the headman "had no effect whatsoever" on this development (1959:1096). In a subsequent rejoinder I defended my original position, and in 1959 I returned to the Kapauku to verify my predictions. The results of this endeavor formed the content of my paper presented at the Annual Meeting of the American Anthropological Association in Philadelphia in 1961. I went to New Guinea for the third time in 1962 to restudy the Kapauku and to test my theories of political change and those specific predictions made in my paper of 1961. The results of my investigations made in 1959 and 1962, and my interpretations of the structural changes that occurred in the social relations of the people of the village of Botukebo, are re-examined in this article.

A Brief Sketch of the Kapauku Culture and Society

The Kapauku, who inhabit the Wissel Lakes region of the Central Highlands, subsist by shifting and by complex cultivation. The latter technique employs rotation of crops, construction of beds and drainage ditches, composting, and the use of green-vegetable fertilizer. In addition to the sweet potato, which is the main crop and occupies 90 per cent of the gardens, the Kapauku plant taro, sugar cane, bottle gourd, squash, bananas, and several varieties of greens. Their cultigens are augmented by pork from domesticated pigs and by hunting, fishing, and gathering. The main characteristics of the social structure are patrilineal descent, patrilocal residence, Iroquoi type of kinship terminology, and—ideally speaking—patriarchal polygynous family. On the average, 150 individuals, living in about fifteen households, form a village. Inhabitants of one or several neighboring villages constitute a localized lineage that, if large enough, may be subdivided into sublineages. The Kapauku localized lineages belong to nonterritorial, traditional, exogamous patrisibs whose membership, living in the localized lineages, is scattered over the whole Wissel Lakes area. Members of two, three, or more localized lineages of different sibs unite themselves for defense and offense into relatively permanent political confederacies, which may comprise as many as 600 individuals, living in from four to seven villages. War and diplomatic relations prevail beyond this unit. Within the group, law and order are administered by wealthy headmen. Every lineage and sublineage has its headman, and the most influential of these is elevated to the confederacy leadership.

Botukebo, the village of the headman Awiitigaaj, belongs to the Ijaaj-Pigome Confederacy, which is composed of four lineages whose members belong to three different sibs; two lineages are subgroups of the Ijaaj sib, the third is a segment of the Pigome sib, and the fourth belongs to the Dou sib. Because almost all the Kapauku sibs are subdivided into named nonlocalized subsibs, the two Ijaaj lineages of the confederacy belong to the Buna-Ijaaj, the Dou lineage to the Dou-Pugaikoto, and the Pigome lineage to the Pigome-Umaagopa subsibs (see Figure 1). The historical core of the confederacy is formed by the intermarrying Ijaaj-Gepouja and the Pigome-Obaaj lineages. The old Kapauku tell about the creation of the political confederacy by a treaty concluded by the ancestors of these two lineages approximately a hundred years ago. The present membership of the two "founding" lineages resides in five of the seven confederacy villages—the Ijaaj-Gepouja people live in Botukebo, Aigii, Jagawaugii, and Kojogeepa and in one half of the Obajbegaa village; the less-numerous Pigome-Obaaj Kapauku inhabit only the other half of the Obajbegaa community. As time went on, to this core of the two lineages were added the Ijaaj-Notiito and the Dou-Pugaikoto lineages, whose members make their homes in the villages of Notiito and Bunauwobado, respectively. They still remain rather peripheral members of the political union, participating only in some of the wars of the confederacy.

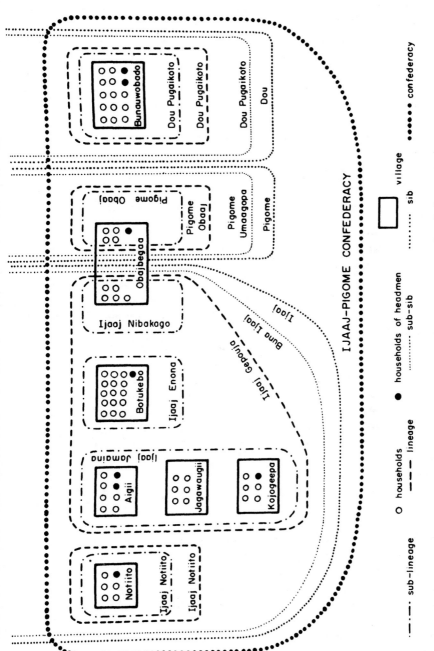

Figure 1: Societal Structure of the Ijaaj-Pigome Confederacy

Because the Ijaaj-Gepouja people grew too numerous, they divided their localized patrilineal group into three sublineages: the Ijaaj-Jamaina, which occupies the villages of Aigii, Jagawaugii, and Kojogeepa; the Ijaaj-Enona, whose members live in the single village of Botukebo; and the smallest, Ijaaj-Nibakago, restricted to half the village of Obajbegaa.

These subgroups as well as the Ijaaj-Pigome Confederacy as a whole have their own informal leaders, whom the Kapauku call *tonowi*. All these headmen possess the four Kapauku attributes of leadership: wealth, generosity, eloquence, and health. There is a rule that the headman of a more inclusive group must be the leader of the group's most numerous constituent segment. Thus political statuses are cumulative. The *tonowi* of a political confederacy, for example, retains his position as *tonowi* of the confederacy's strongest lineage, *tonowi* of the latter's most numerous sublineage, and head of the largest household of that sublineage. His body of constituents, his scope of power, and the content of law he administers differ in every instance, according to which type of status he activates on a given occasion. His main functions are to settle disputes within his constituency and to represent his group as a leader vis-à-vis the outsiders. In the latter function he maintains what we may call diplomatic relations and decides matters of war and peace.

Following these Kapauku rules of political leadership, the power within the Ijaaj-Pigome Confederacy was delegated to Ijaaj Ekajewaijokaipouga, the wealthiest man of the Ijaaj-Jamaina sublineage. In this group he was until 1958 the head of the most numerous household, located in the village of Aigii. Since this sublineage is the most numerous subgroup of the Ijaaj-Gepouja lineage, he, rather than Awiitigaaj, the headman of the smaller Ijaaj-Enona sublineage, was headman of the lineage. Because the Ijaaj-Gepouja lineage is the largest constituent of the whole confederacy, Ekajewaijokaipouga functioned as the head of this inclusive political unit.

History of the Change of the Incest Regulations

The story of the structural change in the Botukebo village, which ultimately affected the whole Ijaaj-Pigome Confederacy, started about 1935. At that time Awiitigaaj—the wealthy, courageous, and shrewd headman of Botukebo—fell in love with his beautiful third paternal parallel cousin, who unfortunately belonged to his own sib. Kapauku law is very explicit about the matter of incest. It categorically states: *keneka bukii daa*, which means, "to marry one's sibmate is tabooed." Nevertheless, Awiitigaaj did not hesitate to break the taboo and to elope with the girl. The infuriated relatives of the couple pursued the lovers, and the girl's father, Ugataga, who was a co-headman of the Ijaaj-Jamaina sublineage and lived in the neighboring village of Kojogeepa, ruled that both his daughter and her seducer must be punished according to the Kapauku customary law by being shot to death. His decision was upheld by the head of the Ijaa-Pigome Confederacy. This dangerous situation was accepted as a challenge by the fugitive Awiitigaaj, who was well versed in native law, politics, and intrigue. Although he was the first man in the Kamu Valley to conclude such an incestuous marriage, he knew that in the neighboring Pona Valley some individuals, who belonged to the Adii sib, had broken the incest taboo in a similar way and had managed to survive. He hid in the bush, assuming that the girl's father would soon realize the futility of pursuit and in time, after his temper cooled off, might be willing to forego the punishment and accept a handsome brideprice. After all, Awiitigaaj reasoned, Ugataga was a clever businessman and politician; he would see the personal disadvantage of killing his daughter and forfeiting a handsome brideprice; he would end up with no daughter and no money—a very hard prospect to be contemplated by even a very moral Kapauku. It was much more likely that Ugataga would show great anger in public and make exhausting expeditions into the forest until he tired out the patrilineal relatives and bored the other tribesmen. If he eventually gave up the search and accepted the inevitable, he would preserve the public's high opinion of his morality, the life of his beloved daughter, and the prospect of an unusually large brideprice. Thus, reasoned Awiitigaaj, any sensible Kapauku headman of the status of Ugataga would act. The acceptance of the brideprice would make the marriage formally valid and would legally absolve him. The only problem seemed to be to play the socio-political game properly and avoid detection by his patrilineal kin, who were combing the forests. To accomplish this, Awiitigaaj cleverly utilized the behavior patterns that require maternal relatives, especially mother's brothers, to protect a fugitive from Kapauku justice; these relatives supplied him with food and with information about the plans and movements of the searching parties of his paternal kin.

The patrilineal relatives of the two fugitives diligently combed the forests, ostensibly trying to catch the incestuous couple. Actually, however, they played the required role of moralists, thus reaping admiration and respect from the residents of the surrounding, but not involved, communities. In the evenings in front of a large audience of their neighbors they talked about their dilemma—having to do justice and, by this very act, killing their close relatives. As time passed, the pursuers tired of the game, and so did their audience. Actually the noninvolved witnesses of the man hunt played the most important part in this affair: they were the ultimate umpires, who were expected to decide when enough effort had been expanded in hunting the fugitives and when the requirements of morality and justice had been satisfied. Indeed, they constituted what Durkheimean enthusiasts would call the group mind, or public opinion. The guilty couple's maternal relatives on one side and the couple's patrilineal relatives on the other were scrutinizing the mood of this noninvolved audience. Both groups of adversaries waited for the moment when the bystanders would get tired of the futile game and suggest a settlement. Finally this day came, and headmen of two of the noninvolved confederacy lineages began publicly to demand an end of the hunt and a peaceful settlement. Although Ugataga desired this resolution most, he knew better than to show eagerness. Like Caesar refusing the laurels of emperorship, he continued to reject the idea of peaceful conclusion of the affair. "Morality and not the money of the prospective brideprice," as he put it, "is the important issue." Thus his prestige as a man of high morality grew with every rejection of the overtures. However, even in this game there is a limit between the image of a very moral individual and a stubborn fool. Ugataga knew this limit, and constantly reverting to temper tantrums—manifested by the Kapauku mad dance directed against the fugitives—he properly and finally began to give in. Thus, I have been informed, his brilliant performance as an indignant and vengeful father slowly changed to that of an ostensibly subdued man, "crushed by public opinion" and by the futility of his attempts to administer justice. Finally, at the suggestion of Awiitigaaj's maternal relatives, who acted as go-betweens, he very reluctantly gave in to "the public pressure" and asked Awiitigaaj's paternal relatives for a brideprice.

Legally speaking, this act implicitly recognized the incestuous marriage. For his financial demand he was able to enlist the support of his own sublineage as well as that of the head of the Ijaaj-Pigome Confederacy. Awiitigaaj seemed to have won the case. However, being a sly individual, he had an additional scheme in mind. Through intermediaries he let it be known to his patrikin that, contrary to the general opinion, he was actually poor and insolvent, which meant that the burden of payment of the brideprice would fall fully upon the purses of his brothers, paternal uncles, and patri-parallel cousins. As he hoped and expected, this ploy resulted in the inevitable: his paternal relatives refused to pay the price and continued to insist on the death penalty for the couple. The infuriated girl's father and his sublineage lost control of their emotions and attacked Awiitigaaj's relatives with sticks. By this act of violence, which inflicted bleeding wounds upon several of the seducer's kin, Awiitigaaj and his relatives were absolved, in conformance with well-established Kapauku customary law, from payment of the brideprice. A Kapauku may legally either accept payment of damages (in this case brideprice) or avail himself of the pleasure of corporally punishing the offending party; but he may not do both.

Release from their financial obligation induced the beaten relatives of Awiitigaaj to accept the settlement and recognize the incestuous union.

The happiest man, of course, was Awiitigaaj, whose scheming genius had accomplished the seemingly impossible. Not only did he manage to go unpunished and keep his incestuous bride as his wife, but he was also absolved from the usually onerous payment of the brideprice, for which his patrilineal relatives had to pay with bleeding scalps, a couple of fractured noses, and bruised bodies. Whereas they were beaten and the girl's father suffered the loss of the brideprice, Awiitigaaj gained the woman, was absolved from payment for her, and successfully broke an established taboo. This clever manipulation of individuals and groups of relatives, and utilization of the knowledge of the Kapauku law, brought him deserved (in Kapauku eyes) prestige and recognition and enhanced his political influence and fame.

So much having been accomplished, one matter still remained to be corrected. As a sublineage headman and a well-to-do Kapauku business-man, Awiitigaaj could ill afford to be regarded as a violator of law. Therefore, to clothe his action with an air of legality, he promulgated a new law, which stated that it was permissible to marry within the same sib, lineage, and even sublineage as long as the couple were at least second cousins. This new boundary of incest that he laid down was easily understandable. Another Kapauku law of incest specifies the prohibition of marriage between any first cousins, even if they do not belong to the same sib. Thus Awiitigaaj, while breaking one law of incest, upheld another one and applied it to paternal kin, formerly covered by the sib exogamy rule. When asked in the presence of other Kapauku about his motives for changing the laws of incest, he gave this explanation: "To marry a *keneka* [a sibmate of the same generation] is good as long as she is a second paternal parallel cousin. In the old days the people did not think of the possibility, but now it is permissible. Adii people [members of a Kapauku sib who live south of the Kamu Valley] have started this change [incest violation], and so I thought we were the same as they and I introduced the new custom. I married my cousin only after I became *tonowi*, so that either other people were afraid to object or they agreed with me. To marry *keneka* is not bad, indeed it is nice; in this way one becomes rich."

On hearing this justification of his action, given in the presence of other people, it was immediately obvious to me that I was listening to a political speech rather than to an honest explanation of Awiitigaaj's motives. Later, when we were alone, I received the following confidential statement: "Why did I marry my relative? Well, I will tell you but don't tell the others. I liked her; she was beautiful." As to his new incest regulation, he had the following comment, accompanied with a sly smile and a friendly punch under my ribs: "Please don't tell the others. They wouldn't like me and I would lose influence. As far as I am concerned, it would be all right if first cousins were to marry. To marry your own sister is probably bad, but I am not convinced even of that. I think whoever likes any girl should be able to marry her. I set up the new taboo in order to break down the old restrictions. The people [Kapauku] are like that. One has to tell them lies."

Sociological Consequences

The successful breaking of the incest taboo by a headman of a large sublineage established a precedent that, in the course of time, brought about far-reaching change in the law and social structure of the entire Ijaaj-Pigome Confederacy. Following his own precedent, Awiitigaaj later married three second paternal parallel cousins from his own sublineage and village. As time went on, more and more young men followed the example of the innovator, until in 1954 seven of fifty-two Botukebo married couples were living in "incestuous" unions. One more man married "incestuously" before my departure in 1955; four incestuously married women of the Enona sublineage of the Ijaaj sib died prior to 1955; four Ijaaj-Enona women married men of the related Ijaaj-Jamaina sublineage (two) and Ijaaj-Notiito lineage (two) and resided outside the village of Botukebo; one woman married an Ijaaj man of the Bibigi village and therefore resided beyond the boundaries of the Ijaaj-Pigome Confederacy; and one Enona sublineage man with his incestuously married wife moved to the village of Magidimi. There were therefore actually eighteen incestuous unions concluded within the Ijaaj-Enona sublineage between 1935 and 1955. Furthermore, within this period one additional incestuous marriage occurred between a man and a woman who belonged to the related Ijaaj-Jamaina sublineage, bringing the total of the incestuous unions to nineteen. If we assume that my timing of the marriages prior to my first research in 1954 (based on genealogical evidence and age computation) is correct and that, consequently, 295 marriages were contracted in the Ijaaj-Gepouja lineage during that twenty-year period, the nineteen incestuous unions represent 6.44 per cent of the total.

In 1954, on the basis of a test I administered to all adults of the Botukebo village (Ijaaj-Enona sublineage), I found that 57.5 per cent of the Botukebo people accepted, 37.5 per cent rejected, and 5 per cent were indifferent to the newly promulgated law of marriage that violated the old incest taboos. The acceptance and rejection of the new regulation, of course, varied in intensity, motivation, and content from individual to individual. The innovator of the new law, Awiitigaaj, privately defended almost complete freedom of choice of a spouse. Ijaaj Imopaj, who married his third paternal parallel cousin, offered this comment: "All people should be permitted to marry as they wish. However, it is bad to marry one's first paternal parallel cousin. I would beat my younger brother if he tried to commit such an outrage." A Botukebo man whose sister married her third paternal parallel cousin accepted that marriage but raised strong objections to any union closer than that of the fourth degree of collaterality. Another co-villager objected to any marriage within the same sib: "It is bad. I would never marry my sib-sister. I would beat my son or younger brother if he should try to marry his sibmate." There was also one old man in the village who proclaimed that he would shoot his son with an arrow if he were to marry a girl from his own sib. Although there was quite a variety of opinion among these men of Botukebo (Ijaaj-Enona sublineage), all of them admitted the possibility that a close relative of theirs might commit such a violation of the established prohibition of intrasib marriage. As a contrast, Enaago of the Dou sib (who comes from a lineage that belongs to another political confederacy), who had recently married a brotherless Botukebo girl and had gone to live in her parents' house, was unable even to conceive that his close paternal relative could commit such a crime. In his mind there was no alternative, not even an illegal one, to the old incest taboo. Typically, his reaction to my question about the propriety of the sexual behavior of the Botukebo Ijaaj people was highly emotional and reflected what might be called incest horror: "Bad, bad, a sib-sister is never a spouse. They are all bad. Their vital substance will deteriorate, and they all will die of their crimes."

However, in spite of the opposition, acceptance of the new legislation of Awiitigaaj spread from his sublineage to the rest of the Ijaaj-Gepouja lineage, and also to the politically allied but genealogically unrelated Ijaaj-Notiito lineage of the confederacy. Finally, both lineages accepted, with some modifications, the new incest regulations. Consequently the law of incest in the Ijaaj-Pigome Confederacy became complicated and, to a casual observer, bewildering. In the Ijaaj-Enona sublineage marriages between second paternal parallel cousins became permissible, but in the rest of the related Ijaaj sublineages and in the Ijaaj-Notiito lineage only a marriage between third paternal parallel cousins, and preferably between those who came from different sublineages, was regarded as legal. These rules stood in sharp contrast to the laws of the Pigome and Dou lineages. Pigome intrasib marriages remained prohibited and were punished by severe beating with a stick. The Dou proved to be the most conservative and resistant to the innovation: in accordance with the old tradition, its authorities continued to insist on the death penalty for offenders against the intrasib marriage taboo.

Perplexed by the complexity of incest regulation in the Ijaaj-Pigome political confederacy, the reader might well wonder how the legal discrepancies among its various subgroups could be reconciled under a unified headship. Ekajewaijokaipouga, the confederacy headman in 1950–1958, had publicly rejected the old rule of sib exogamy, and his immediate successor, Jokagaibo, was even "incestuously married." These men had to rule over lineages whose authorities punished violations of the incest taboo by beating or execution. The solution to this problem is found in the organizational principles of the Kapauku societal structure (patterned segmentation of the society into constituent subgroups) and the rules of jurisdiction. One of the basic rules of the Kapauku legal procedure is that an individual is tried by the headman of the group to which he and his co-litigant belong. Since in the confederacy there is only one lineage of either the Pigome or Dou sibs, a couple could commit incest only if both were members of the same lineage in one of these sibs. Consequently, the lineage headman of the Pigome or Dou people, rather than the confederacy leader, always adjudicates such violations. Because by a rule of the Kapauku jurisdiction there is no appeal from a verdict, the decision rendered by either of the two lineage headmen is final and never subject to revision at a higher structural level of the society. The same principle of jurisdiction applies within the Ijaaj-Gepouja and Ijaaj-Notiito lineages. Since second paternal parallel cousins have to belong to one sublineage of the three that compose the Ijaaj-Gepouja lineage, the law of incest in these three subgroups can have different content: although the Ijaaj-Enona sublineage permits second cousins to marry, the other two sublineages permit no closer marriage than that of third cousins. The latter regulation is also true of the Ijaaj-Notiito lineage. In none of these groups is incest violation carried to the confederacy headman for adjudication.

With the increase of intrasib marriages appeared an additional phenomenon; by 1955, of eighteen marriages in which at least one party was a member of the Ijaaj-Enona sublineage of Botukebo, nine (50 per cent) of the unions were concluded between partners not only from the same sib, but also from the same village. Awiitigaaj, with his political genius and his need to establish his incestuous innovation on a more convincing moral basis, seized upon this new trend toward village endogamy. For reasons of prestige, as well as to refute the incessant criticisms and accusations of immorality and criminality hurled at him by his domestic opponents and his external enemies, he decided to render his new incest law more appealing by making it more formal and complex. By drawing a line (AIL, in Figure 2) through the community, he divided the village of Botukebo into two halves, to which he assigned the names *weejato* and *auwejato*. The line was so cleverly drawn that in each half of the village resided adult members of the Enona sublineage who were as far related as first cousins. Awiitigaaj spoke in favor of marrying across this line into the other "incipient moiety." Moreover, he even managed to induce one of the villagers, whose place of residence did not agree with his scheme, to move his house across the newly established incest boundary.

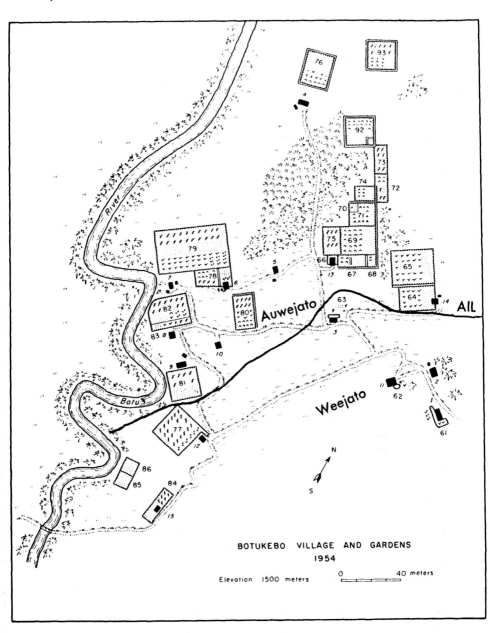

BOTUKEBO VILLAGE AND GARDENS
1954

Elevation 1500 meters

0 _____ 40 meters

Figure 2: AIL is Awiitigaaj's Incest Line

In his legislative enthusiasm he did not stop at this point but advocated a new and revolutionary compact settlement pattern. He proposed to change the Botukebo village from a loose and completely irregular cluster of houses into a lineal village, in which the houses would stand in a single line, divided in the middle by a wider gap, representing the incest boundary line. One of the new moieties was supposed to occupy the southern, the other the northern half of the settlement. By a linear village, he thought, the moiety structure would be even more accentuated. His argumentation and public speeches never failed to attract a favorably inclined audience. Because I knew Awiitigaaj's persuasiveness and influence, as well as his wealth and the network of extended loans that tied him to many important village debtors, I wrote in 1958: "We may expect that in the near future Botukebo village will be linear, with a main street in front of the houses" (1958b:835). In the same article I made three other predictions. First, I viewed the abrogation of the sib exogamy rule as a serious blow to the cohesiveness of the Ijaaj-Pigome Confederacy. Since I knew that the marital ties uniting the four lineages into a political confederacy represented the mainstay of this alliance, I expected that with more marriages occurring within the sibs (represented here by their lineages) the important affinal bond would be weakened and the esprit de corps of the political union would vanish. A fragmentation of the confederacy appeared to me to be a possibility. Unfortunately, with the Dutch pacification of the Kamu Valley in 1956, it was not possible to test this hypothesis. Because of the variety of political and economic factors brought into existence by the acculturation process, the original system of confederacies had fully disintegrated by 1962, when I undertook my third field study of the Kapauku people.

Second, I predicted that the decrease in the number of interconfederacy marriages (which would slowly abrogate the affinal relationships that provided one of the main channels for regional understanding and for peaceful settlement of interconfederational disputes) would eventually lead to a perceptible increase in local hostilities and open wars. Again, the pacification of the area prevented a test of this hypothesis.

Third, with village endogamy I visualized a trend to an elevation of the status of women. Under a lineage or even village endogamy, the married women would no longer be strangers marrying into another locality, where they would have to depend entirely on their husbands' affection and justice. An intravillage marriage provides women with relative independence, immediate support from their consanguineal relatives in disputes with their husbands, and ultimately with a greater influence over their spouses. We may even speculate further that such lessening of emphasis on the male line favors a change from patrilineality to a bilateral social organization. As in the two previous instances, pacification interfered with this process, enhanced the security and prestige of women, and made them less dependent upon the whims of their consanguinal or affinal kin.

Fortunately, my explanation of the nature of the sociostructural change in the Ijaaj-Pigome Confederacy and my predictions of the changes in the village plan and residence pattern, could be tested in spite of the advance of Western civilization. In the rest of this paper I shall concentrate on these problems and shall confront my original analysis and Leach's criticisms of it with the changes recorded during my two subsequent research periods in New Guinea.

Nature of Awiitigaaj's Innovation

In his letter to the editor of *American Anthropologist*, Professor Leach expressed appreciation of my data on the social change in Botukebo, but he was very critical of my interpretation of the change. He states: "Pospisil's primitive legislator . . . did not change the law but only its application." Moreover, he rejected my claim that the headman Awiitigaaj made a volitional innovation in promulgating a new law of exogamy and in creating moieties in his village. He maintained, "all that has really happened here is that one major segment of the society, which was formerly exogamous, has split up to form two segments, each of which is now exogamous." And subsequently he states: "The existence of a fission process of this kind is a necessary mechanism in any segmentary structure; its operation signifies the continuity of structure and not its breakdown" (1959:1097).

In my rejoinder of 1960 I defended my original interpretation. As to the first criticism, I pointed out that Awiitigaaj had indeed changed the native law and not merely its application. The traditional law states literally: *keneka bukii daa,* which means "to marry a *keneka* [sibmate of the same generation as Ego] is forbidden [tabooed]." Since Awiitigaaj promulgated a law by which a *keneka* became eligible as spouse (if she or he was at least a second cousin of Ego, or a more distantly related sibmate) he broke the law of sib exogamy and substituted a new one for it. What actually happened, therefore, was a change of law and not merely of its application.

Leach's second criticism of my analysis arises from what appears to be superficial reading. First, to make his interpretation of the changes consistent with the data, he promoted the Ijaaj-Pigome political confederacy to a "maximal lineage" (1959:1096), in spite of the fact that I devoted an entire chapter (Pospisil 1958b:64–94) to the Kapauku confederacy, in which I show that it is not a consanguineal group, but a purely political union of several lineages that belong to different mutually unrelated and nonlocalized sibs. Furthermore, he equates sib with a lineage that seems, in his interpretation of the Kapauku culture, to be a localized segment of the confederacy. After thus having engineered the data of the Kapauku society, he proceeds to correct the findings and claims that what actually happened was simply that "one of the major exogamous lineages had grown too large for convenience and fission in this major segment took place" (1959:1096). Of course I must agree with Leach on the point that every segmentary society employs the fission process as a necessary mechanism of change. Indeed, the Kapauku have such a mechanism; fission occurs there along political, economic, and residential lines. A group that separates from its parental societal segment usually settles a new area and becomes a member of a different political confederacy. Nevertheless, it retains the old sib exogamy. Thus fission in Kapauku society has nothing to do with the regulation of marriages and the rules of exogamy.

Figure 1 demonstrates this point quite well. On it can be seen that the only localized consanguineal groups of the Kapauku are the lineages and sublineages. The subsibs and sibs, on the contrary, represent nonlocalized, traditional social units, whose members live in lineages that are scattered throughout the vast Kapauku territory. As stated above, the rules of incest pertain primarily to the nonlocalized and traditional sibs and not to their segments, the localized patrilineal corporate groups—which are, of course, logically also exogamous. Consequently, if a localized sublineage or lineage divides into two segments because of population pressure, such a split has nothing to do with the incest regulations themselves. This is true because the most inclusive exogamous unit is not the parental sublineage or lineage but the nonlocalized sib to which the two newly split societal segments belong. A process of fission that is due to population pressure results logically in the creation of a new localized sublineage rather than of a new exogamous sib. On the basis of this argument, Leach's interpretation of structural changes in the Botukebo village is definitely incorrect, lacks any factual support, is based on superficial reading of my work, and is contradicted by a mass of ethnographic, demographic, and case material.

Social Acceptance of the Change in Incest Law

Having dealt with the nature of the change initiated by Awiitigaaj, we can now inquire into the reasons for the social acceptance of this innovation. At the outset of the discussion we may dispose of Leach's interpretation of the reasons for the split of the Ijaaj-Enona sublineage. He claimed that because one of the major exogamous lineages had grown too large for convenience, fission in this major segment took place (1959: 1096). That this interpretation does not stand the test of empirical evidence is obvious from the following facts: the Ijaaj-Jamaina sublineage of the same confederacy is much larger than the one in question and has not undergone fission because of size. Nor did the large villages of Jotapuga, Ugapuga, and Mauwa in adjacent confederacies, split, although each of them was more than three times as large as Botukebo. It is obvious that population pressure had nothing to do with the division of the village of the Ijaaj-Enona sublineage into incipient moieties.

In several tribes in New Guinea abolition of the rules of exogamy and incest followed a marked decline in the population (Bureau for Native Affairs 1957:15, 21). A sharp decrease of population was without question the reason for changes of incest regulations in those tribes, but this explanation is not applicable to our case, since the Ijaaj-Enona sublineage and the more inclusive Ijaaj-Gepouja lineage have increased remarkably, rather than diminished, during the last 120 years.

Lowie (1920:157–162) and Murdock (1949:137) regarded particular techniques of food production, types of residence, and rules of inheritance responsible for changes in forms of social organization. Although this explanation is unquestionably correct for many tribal societies, it does not apply to the situation in Botukebo. If the remembered history of social change of this village is borne in mind and if the culture patterns of the members of the Ijaaj-Enona sublineage are compared with those of the rest of the inhabitants of the Kamu Valley or with those of the peoples of surrounding Kapauku regions, it is unquestionably clear that none of the factors mentioned can be considered responsible for the willingness of the Ijaaj-Enona people to accept Awiitigaaj's new legislation. In all these regions division of labor, techniques of food production, type of residence, and rules of inheritance are the same as in Botukebo; yet, according to several old informants of mine, there has been no change comparable to the one I recorded in Botukebo. One possible exception is provided by a few members of the Adii sib, who lived in the Pona Valley, south of the Kamu. However, far from being legalized behavior, the incestuous intrasib unions of these tribesmen remained violations of the prevailing law. No headman comparable to Awiitigaaj elevated these exceptions to the status of legal rules. Finally, the recorded sequence of events in Botukebo shows that the incest violation and the subsequent changes in the law, as well as the development of "incipient moieties," preceded rather than followed the alterations in residence patterns.

In my original article (1958b) I considered that social acceptance of the modified incest taboos had a political basis. Members of the Ijaaj and Pigome lineages were latecomers into the Kamu Valley. Approximately 120 years ago, after a natural drainage of the valley had occurred and its floor became suitable for cultivation, ancestors of the two lineages migrated from the adjacent Mapia ad Paniai regions. They settled in the southeastern part of the Kamu Valley and claimed the vacant, flat, and only recently dried fertile land and slowly desiccating swamps. Their newly acquired territory was surrounded by political confederacies, whose members looked with envy and hostility upon the usurpers of the land, who were regarded as thieves of the territory. Inevitably, battles ensued and the Ijaaj-Pigome Confederacy became intermittently involved in wars with their numerous neighbors. Marriage, as a consequence, presented a serious problem. Because the Ijaaj people far outnumbered their Pigome and Dou lineage allies, in order to comply with the rules of sib exogamy they had to marry the women of their hostile neighbors. In times of war such unions did not prove felicitous. The wives from the neighboring political units were of questionable loyalty. Many of them betrayed the war plans of their husbands to the enemy or even deserted them, and their desertions became further causes of war. Of eleven wars in the Kamu Valley during the twenty years preceding 1954, five were fought because of the desertion of wives from hostile confederacies, whose members then refused to refund the brideprice. Even when an Ijaaj girl was married to a traditional enemy, matters were not rosy for the newcomers. The brothers, fathers, and paternal parallel cousins of those girls were never sure of receiving the full amount of the stipulated brideprice. Often their hostile in-laws managed, under the threat of violence, to obtain a substantial reduction from the sum originally agreed upon.

Although war and political negotiations prevail on the interconfederational level, law and order are enforced within a confederacy. Consequently, an intraconfederacy and intrasib marriage virtually eliminates the possibility of causing war and eventual economic losses. In such marriages no killing and violence results from a divorce, because a full return of the brideprice is legally guaranteed. Similarly, it is very difficult to cheat on the amount of brideprice in an intraconfederational marriage. The headmen who administer the law are vitally interested in keeping order within this political unit and would regard such an action as a dangerous crime. Because of the political problems, which make an interconfederacy marriage for an Ijaaj man most insecure, and because not enough women were available in the allied Pigome and Dou lineages for the Ijaaj men, sib endogamy appears to be the logical answer to this particular political situation. This contention is further supported by the fact that the Pigome and Dou people, who found enough wives in the much more numerous Ijaaj lineages, firmly maintain the traditional rules of exogamy and were utterly disinterested in the legislative products of Awiitigaaj's jural genius.

This political interpretation of the acceptance of the modified laws of incest received additional convincing confirmation during my research in 1959. Since my first fieldwork in 1954–1955, the Kamu Valley has been brought under administrative control by the Dutch government, and the whole region has been pacified. If my interpretation in the article of 1958 was correct, this pacification and enforcement of law and order across the old boundaries of political confederacies must have removed the cause for social acceptance of Awiitigaaj's innovations. Although the moiety system could meanwhile have been formalized in terms of residence, there should have been some signs of weakening observable within the new system. However, if an increase of population were the cause of the abolition of sib exogamy (although this proposition sounds absurd and is contradicted by my structural analysis of the Kapauku society, as presented above), the pacification of the area, introduction of modern medical care, and the resulting acceleration of the population increase not only should have upheld the moiety system and the concomitant legal changes made by Awiitigaaj, but should even have intensified them. Indeed, my prediction of the changes not only in the residence of the people of the Ijaaj-Enona sublineage, but also in the village plan of Botukebo materialized in 1959, as postulated on the basis of a questionnaire submitted in 1955. My statement of 1958 that in the near future Botukebo village would be lineal, with a main street in front of the houses, became literally true, as is apparent from Figure 3. A survey and a systematic inquiry into the attitude toward Awiitigaaj's innovation revealed that in 1959 as many as 55.32 per cent of the adult and adolescent males of the Ijaaj-Enona sublineage opposed the innovation and regarded it as unjustified and even immoral. An additional 2.12 per cent would offer no opinion about the innovation; 10.64 per cent of the population gave Awiitigaaj's changes only a qualified support ("I myself would not marry a *keneka*, but would not punish others if they did"), and only 31.92 per cent of the males fully supported Awiitigaaj's legislation at that time. This represents quite a loss of support, compared to the year 1955, when 57.5 per cent of the Botukebo men fully and wholeheartedly supported the new regulations of incest and the resulting changes in the social structure. In 1959 even Awiitigaaj, who was still publicly defending his legislative actions, in private seemed uncertain about the justification of his legal actions, probably because he already had ten wives and at his advanced age had lost interest in collecting additional specimens of female beauty. By 1959 his legislation indeed appeared to be unjustified and unnecessary because under the Dutch rule an Ijaaj man could safely marry a girl outside his own sib and confederacy. In spite of the decrease of popular support for laws allowing intrasib marriages, in 1955–1959 four of a total of fifty-nine marriages of the Ijaaj-Gepouja lineage members were concluded between partners belonging to the same (Ijaaj) sib. Thus the percentage of "incestuous" intrasib marriages had actually slightly increased, to 6.8 per cent of the total. This statistic does not affect my interpretation of the change, however, because three of these intrasib

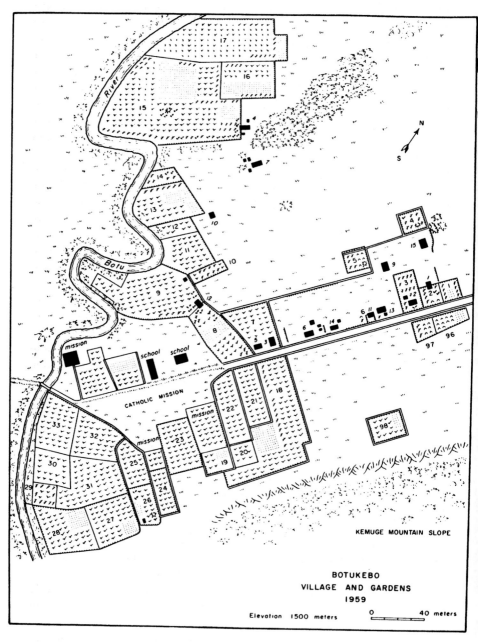

Figure 3

marriages were concluded *prior* to the pacification of the Kamu Valley area in 1956.

In the paper read at the American Anthropological Association meeting of 1961, I predicted, on the basis of these as well as other findings, that if the pacification of the Kamu Valley continued, sib exogamy would again be emphasized in the Ijaaj-Pigome Confederacy, the village plan would revert to an irregular pattern, and the moiety system created by Awiitigaaj would be abolished. The abolition of the formal aspects of Awiitigaaj's innovation would logically disintegrate as an immediate reaction to the failing popularity of his new law. The law itself, however, would persist longer, because the leaders—a minority of influential men such as Awiitigaaj, Ekajewaijokaipouga (the former Confederacy headman), and Jokagaibo (the Confederacy's headman since 1958)—had become committed to it and could not tolerate that their marriages, or those of their close kin, be pronounced illegal or even criminal. The vested interest of the several leaders would thus keep the intrasib marriages permissible as long as these leaders kept their status, in spite of the adverse opinion of their followers.

The changes postulated in 1961 had indeed materialized by the time of my third research, in 1962. Because of the impact of the pacification of the valley, and the stubborn support of the abolition of the taboo on intrasib marriages by the leaders and their immediate close kin and friends, the opinions of the natives concerning the support or rejection of Awiitigaaj's innovation became sharply defined. The category of individuals with no opinion and that of people who gave only qualified support to the legal change in 1959 (together comprising 12.76 per cent of the adolescent and adult males of Botukebo) had disappeared by 1962. The former qualified or unqualified support of the abolition of the intrasib incest taboo diminished from 42.55 per cent (in 1959) to 34.14 per cent by 1962, all of which was unqualified. Consequently, a full 65.86 per cent of adolescent and adult males of the Ijaaj-Enona sublineage wholeheartedly rejected abolition of the incest taboo and advocated its reinstatement. Against the powerful clique of the headmen, the supporters of the intrasib marriage taboo still proved ineffective. Thus it happened, paradoxically enough, that in spite of the loss of popularity, there were three more intrasib marriages concluded in the Ijaaj-Enona sublineage between 1959 and 1962. Indeed, Ekajewaijokaipouga, who had formerly only advocated intrasib marriage but had not practiced it, in this period selected a sibmate as his sixth wife.

In contrast to the persistence of the official recognition of intrasib marriages as legal, the formalistic accessories of Awiitigaaj's legislation disintegrated very fast indeed. Since these were not regarded as crucial and their abolition would not affect adversely the intrasib marriages, Awiitigaaj did not insist on a compulsory perpetuation of the moiety

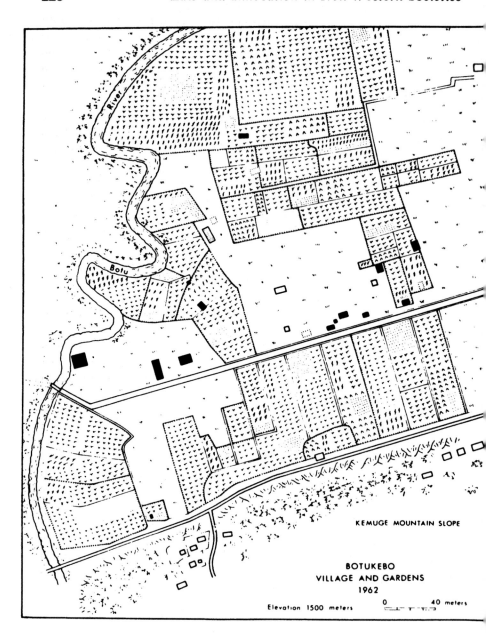

Figure 4

system and his lineal village residential pattern. As can be observed from Figure 4, in 1962 his compact lineal pattern disintegrated, and the community reverted to the old irregular traditional Kapauku settlement. The moiety segmentation of the village was not only disregarded but even openly rejected by the majority of the Botukebo residents; indeed, most of the younger people had virtually forgotten it.

This, of course, may not be the end of the story. The acculturation situation, created by the arrival of the Indonesian administrators and Western missionaries, may provide new support for the abolition of sib exogamy. The Catholic missionaries may succeed in destroying the idea that intrasib marriages are incestuous by proclaiming the taboo an outmoded and sinful pagan superstition; the Indonesian government officers, in turn, through their pacification activity will certainly abrogate the death penalty for intrasib marriages—indeed they may, in turn, punish the executioners as murderers. Enforcement of the native prohibition of intrasib marriages will consequently become not only a religious sin, but also a legal delict. Thus, sib exogamy may ultimately disappear from the Kapauku culture. When that time comes, it will not occur as a consequence of Awiitigaaj's legalistic change, but because of the advance of the Western civilization.

No matter what the ultimate outcome, the data collected over a period of nine years testify to the importance of the individual's role in legal change and structural transformation of a tribal society. Therefore, in spite of Leach's criticism and of the possible displeasure of some orthodox social anthropologists, I feel justified in reiterating the conclusion of my article of 1958: "a volitional invention among primitives may not be as exceptional as has been often assumed" (1958b:837). Furthermore, the collected material documents the importance of analysis of law for understanding basic changes in the social structure of tribal societies. In this respect the importance of the role of the techniques of food production, of technology in general, and of rules of residence may have been overstated in the anthropological literature. Indeed, precise and systematic exposition of native law (so often lacking in anthropological analyses) may bring the study of the various types of social structure into a new perspective and supply answers that are sought in vain in those aspects of human culture traditionally explored by the anthropologist.

Uniformity and Variation
in Chief-Made Law:
A Tswana Case Study

Historical Introduction

In a monograph published in 1943 I showed that Tswana chiefs in what was then the Bechuanaland Protectorate could formerly add to or otherwise change the laws of their people by means of decree and judicial decision. That power they continued to exercise after Bechuanaland came under British rule in 1885, and in some chiefdoms or "tribes" (the English term locally used) they have in recent times made many new laws.[1] The present paper deals with one of the comparative problems arising in this connection: how and why chiefs in four related tribes, all exposed to the same Christian missionary influence, legislated about certain social reforms sought by that mission. I choose related tribes because of their common origin and culture, and missionary objectives because these were identical in all four. In both respects basic uniformity is thus established; my hypothesis briefly is that tribal variations in the legislation were due ultimately to the different personal characters of the chiefs involved. I suggest also that an experiment in comparison such as is here made reveals more about the process of legal development than does a historical study of law-making in a single community.

The four tribes concerned—Kwena, Ngwaketse, Ngwato, and Tawana —occupy neighboring territories.[2] The Ngwaketse and Ngwato are offshoots of the Kwena, from whom they broke away separately about

1. Schapera (1943) deals with Kgatla, Malete, Rolong, and Tlokwa, in addition to the four tribes discussed in the present paper.
2. Their populations are (1964): Kwena, 73,000; Ngwaketse, 71,000; Ngwato, 201,000; Tawana, 42,000. For background information about them and other Tswana, see Sillery (1952; mainly historical) and Schapera (1953; mainly ethnographical, with comprehensive bibliography).

A.D. 1760–1780; the Tawana are a later offshoot from the Ngwato (circa 1800). The chiefs of the first three claim agnatic descent from a remote common ancestor, and the founder and eponym of the Tawana was a brother of the Ngwato chief Kgama I. There has been much intermarriage among the royal families of all four. Their chiefs have sometimes also collaborated politically, notably in dealings with the British administration.

For many years all four tribes were served by one missionary body alone. The London Missionary Society started work in 1817 among Tswana farther south.[3] In 1845 David Livingstone settled as its agent among the Kwena, and African evangelists settled among the Ngwaketse in 1848 and the Ngwato about 1857. After Livingstone's departure to explore central Africa (1851), Hermannsburg Lutheran missionaries worked for a time among the Kwena (1857–1864) and Ngwato (1859–1862). The LMS then reoccupied the field, stationing European missionaries among the Ngwato (1862), Kwena (1866), and Ngwaketse (1871). In 1878 the society also sent African evangelists to the Tawana, and in 1893 it sent a resident European missionary (who left in 1898 and was not permanently replaced until 1926).

Until fairly recently the LMS was the only Christian mission in each tribe. Instances are even known, especially among Ngwato and Ngwaketse, of chiefs deliberately excluding any others. Except among the Ngwato, that policy was not maintained; the Church of England, for example, gained access to the Kwena in 1912, and the Seventh Day Adventists went among the Ngwaketse in 1922. In 1931 the LMS also handed over its station among the Kwena to the United Free Church of Scotland. But in all four tribes the vast majority of Christians still belong to the LMS church (Congregational). The same LMS missionary, moreover, often worked successively in at least two of them, so that his personal influence was not necessarily confined to only one. Such a man was usually also, in the early days, the chief's secretary and adviser when he had to deal with other Europeans; missionary influence might thus extend beyond the sphere of religion alone.[4]

For many years, too, the chiefs themselves have been Christians, though sometimes only superficially or temporarily. The earliest convert of all—in fact, the first of his tribe—was Sechele I (Kwena), baptized by Livingstone in 1848; Khama (Ngwato) was baptized by the Lutherans in

3. The main published sources on the Society's history are, R. Lovett, *The History of the London Missionary Society, 1795–1895* (1899), and N. Goodall, *A History of the London Missionary Society, 1895–1945* (1954). For many of the details given below I am indebted chiefly to missionaries' letters and annual reports preserved in the LMS archives (London). For the Lutherans, see G. Haccius, *Hannoversche Missionsgeschichte*, Bd. 2 (Hermannsburg 1910).

4. For the general history and effects of missionary activity in Bechuanaland, see Schapera (1958:1–9).

1860, during the reign of his heathen father, and when the Lutherans left, he joined the LMS; Moremi II (Tawana) became a church member in 1881, and so did Bathoen I (Ngwaketse) in 1894, after having been an "enquirer" for several years. Though Moremi renounced Christianity soon afterward, Khama and Bathoen remained in the church until they died. Sechele was suspended from "fellowship" for adultery within a few months of his baptism, but he persistently sought during the rest of his long life to be readmitted. The successors of these four chiefs were almost all brought up as Christians and often received part of their education at mission schools abroad. But some, especially among the Kwena, later abandoned or were severed from membership of the LMS. Only among Kwena and Tawana, incidentally, did the chiefs in whose reign Christianity was introduced adopt the new faith; neither Khama's father (Sekgoma I) nor Bathoen's (Gaseitsiwe) became converts, though the latter did learn to read.

A chief's personal acceptance of Christianity did not mean that he then compelled the whole of his tribe to follow suit. Indeed, he could not have done so had he wished, for the LMS normally insisted on a lengthy period of instruction in dogma and literacy before admitting any person to church membership. But both Khama and Bathoen held public prayers daily in the tribal council place before starting official business, and Sechele habitually conducted Sunday services when his missionary was absent. By 1890, observance of the Sabbath had itself become part of tribal law everywhere; for example, people were liable to punishment if they worked in their fields on that day, traveled by ox-wagon, or hunted. In addition, chiefs in all tribes helped the missionaries to build churches and schools, supplying free labor when needed and sometimes imposing a levy of cattle or money to meet other costs. Such levies for church-building were made, for example, by Sechele, Khama, and Bathoen, as well as by later chiefs.

Usually the chiefs also exhorted, but did not compel, parents to send children to school. Initially the teachers were employed and paid by the LMS, which derived some of the money from school fees. To overcome the hardship this measure caused poorer people, and to make free education possible, Bathoen I in 1903 imposed upon every Ngwaketse taxpayer a special annual rate of two shillings. Sebele I in 1909 did the same for the Kwena. But Khama, although "personally anxious" for his people "to advance in education," rejected the idea of a similar tax when it was suggested to him by a visiting expert in 1905; the reason he gave was that "he did not believe the tribe as such would endorse such a proposition." [5]

5. E. B. Sargant, quoted in Schapera (1943:16); see the same work, p. 30, for the educational levies imposed by Bathoen and Sebele (the date given there for Sebele's is wrong). By "taxpayer" I mean a man paying the annual "hut tax" due to the Protectorate administration from 1899.

Imposition of Church Laws

The chiefs not only enforced Sunday observance and made heathens as well as Christians help build and pay for churches and schools. Sometimes they also commanded their people to abandon certain traditional practices condemned by the mission. The LMS made abstention from those practices a condition of church membership and disciplined offenders. But it had no such powers of jurisdiction over heathen tribesmen, who still greatly outnumber professing Christians everywhere.[6] Insofar as the mission code (*melao yaphuthego*, "laws of the church") also became part of tribal law, to be universally observed, it was the chiefs who were directly responsible.

To simplify comparison, I confine the rest of this discussion to three important Tswana usages explicitly forbidden by the church: polygamy, "circumcision" (*bogwera* and *bojale*), and payment of *bogadi* (bridewealth).[7] The first was banned by the LMS from the beginning; circumcision was also condemned fairly early (before 1830), and *bogadi* was forbidden in 1875.[8] Government legislation (1917) prohibited the subjection of youths to circumcision rites without their parents' consent but did not otherwise reinforce the church laws (except that when taxation was introduced in 1899, polygamists were required to pay more than other men). Nor were those laws common to all mission churches: it was reported in 1916 of the Anglican missionary then among the Kwena (Fr. Deacon) that he both "commended *bogwera*, and insisted on *bogadi* as a preliminary to marriage in church" (Willoughby 1916).

In 1943, my last year of systematic field work among the Tswana, the extent to which the church laws were also part of tribal law was as fol-

---

6. Schapera (1958:4). By "still" and similar expressions, I mean the period during which my field work in Bechuanaland was done (1929–1943).

7. The "circumcision" rites were—in some tribes still are—those immediately preceding the creation of a new age set, at intervals of about five to seven years. All boys of suitable age are then initiated together and so, very soon afterward, are the girls. The boys' ceremony is named *bogwera*, the girls' *bojale*. Only the former includes actual circumcision, but in government legislation and missionary literature both are grouped together as "circumcision rites," which term I retain here simply for convenience. For a general account of the rites, see Schapera (1938:105–108). It should be noted that all Tswana tribes still continue to create age sets periodically, even where "circumcision" has been abolished. *Bogadi* (bridewealth) normally consists of cattle, which are theoretically due to the wife's parents before she goes to live at her husband's home; see Schapera (1938:138–147). The LMS and various other Christian missions stigmatized the payment as "wife purchase."

8. In October of that year the Bechuanaland District Committee of the LMS formally resolved: "That bogari [sic] being an evil, we endeavour to discourage it by the following means: (a) by refusing to marry, unless a promise is given that there is no bogari; (b) by circulating a printed statement that the missionaries are entirely against it; (c) Church members who countenance bogari, either in giving or receiving it, to be regarded as under Church discipline."

lows: in all four tribes circumcision was forbidden; the Ngwato and Twana had also abolished *bogadi,* the Ngwaketse insisted on its payment even by Christians, and the Kwena had no legislation about it; finally, the Ngwaketse, but no other tribe, prohibited polygamy (except under certain conditions and to relatively young men only).

Not all the laws in force had been imposed by the first Christian chief in each tribe. Since this fact bears directly upon my thesis, I must now survey briefly the history of the relevant legislation. Where possible, I give the date when a law was decreed; a phrase such as "by 1880" means that its existence was first mentioned in that year, though it may have been (and probably was) imposed somewhat earlier.

Among the Kwena, Sechele I (ruled 1831–1892) made no laws at all about any of the three practices. Sebele I (1892–1911) abolished circumcision (1901). Sechele II (1911–1918), on becoming chief, reaffirmed the ban, but in 1916 he restored the boys' ceremony (*bogwera*), though not the girls' (*bojale*). Sebele II (1918–1931) retained the *bogwera.* It was abolished again in 1937 by Kgari (1931–1962), who said at the same time that people taking part in ceremonies outside the tribal area also would be liable to punishment.

Among the Ngwaketse, Bathoen I (1899–1910) abolished circumcision (1901). Seepapitso (1910–1916) reaffirmed the ban in 1911, decreed (also 1911) that all men except Christians must give *bogadi* for their wives, and (1915) prohibited the practice of polygamy, without special permission from himself, by any member of the two junior age sets (created respectively in 1901 and 1909). After his death there followed a period of regency (1916–1928), during which some of his laws on these and other matters were widely disregarded. Bathoen II (1928–   ) enforced the ban on circumcision more strictly (1929), decreed (1930) that Christians as well as heathens must give *bogadi,* and extended (1931, 1935) the law against polygamy to men of the four junior age sets (created in and after 1909) and all future ones.

Among the Ngwato, Khama (1872–1873, 1875–1923) abolished circumcision (1877) and *bogadi* (by 1880). Some sources say he also prohibited polygamy, but according to his own evidence he merely tried to discourage the practice.[9] Neither of his successors (Sekgoma II and Tshekedi) made laws that are relevant here.

Among the Tawana, finally, Moremi II (1876–1890) also abolished circumcision and *bogadi,* though he restored the former in 1886. It was retained by his successor Sekgoma (1891–1906) but was abolished again in 1910 by Mathiba (1906–1933). There has since been no relevant legislation in this tribe.

As the survey shows, the first Christian chiefs abolished circumcision

9. See below, p. 238.

in three tribes. Sechele I, however, retained it among the Kwena, though he would not let his own children go through the rites. Only two of those chiefs (Khama and Moremi) also abolished *bogadi*, and none abolished polygamy. Circumcision was first abolished among the Kwena by Sebele I (who was not a church member, though he had received a Christian education); it was restored fifteen years later by his successor and then abolished again twenty-one years afterward by yet another chief. The same ban was repealed among the Tawana within five years by the chief who had first imposed it and was reimposed twenty-four years later by the next chief but one. Among the Ngwaketse, lastly, the laws about polygamy and *bogadi* made by Seepapitso (the second Christian chief) were both extended more widely by his son Bathoen II. In this tribe, it must also be noted, the law about *bogadi* is diametrically opposed to that of the church.

Motives for Legislation

The survey indicates also that the chief's legislation was not dictated solely by acceptance of Christianity. Not one of the first chiefs to be converted abolished all three of the practices condemned by the mission, and Sechele I in fact abolished none of them, though he ruled for more than forty years after being baptized. A non-Christian chief (Sebele I) abolished circumcision among the Kwena, and a Christian chief (Seepapitso) enforced payment of *bogadi* among the Ngwaketse.

Perhaps the only instance in which conversion was immediately effective, and even then only partially, occurred among the Tawana. Moremi II was baptized in 1881 during a visit from the missionary stationed among the Ngwato (Rev. J. D. Hepburn); as Tawana headmen informed me in 1940, he then prohibited circumcision and *bogadi* "because he had become a Christian." There is indirect confirmation for this statement. When Moremi restored circumcision in 1886, he told Hepburn, again visiting him, "that he had abandoned himself wholly to heathenism, and forsaken God as his helper, although he still read his Bible" (Hepburn 1895:280).

The reasons given for such laws as other chiefs imposed show that here LMS doctrine was only sometimes the prime inspiration. Nor, it might be noted in this context, do chiefs ever seem to have been directly influenced in their legislation by the views of their Christian subjects. Kwena informants said, indeed, that Sebele I refused a request from some evangelists for the abolition of *bogadi;* and it is on record in official correspondence that both Sechele II and Sebele II allowed circumcision rites to be held despite protests from the local LMS congregation.

The original prohibitions of circumcision were certainly due at least partly to pressure from the LMS. "The first missionaries," Livingstone wrote in 1857, "set their faces against the boguera [*sic*], on account of its connection with heathenism, and the fact that the youths learned much evil, and became disobedient to their parents." He himself regarded it as probably "only a sanitary and political measure." He nevertheless thought it "better" for "young missionaries" to follow the lead of their predecessors, because of the "evil" that might result "from breaking down the authority on which the whole system of our influence appears to rest" (Livingstone 1857:148–149).

However, according to what people say nowadays, the main argument used by the chiefs who first abolished circumcision was that it "hindered the advancement of education"; it was essentially a form of training for Tswana youths, and now that better schools had been provided by the LMS, where children could be taught "in an enlightened way," *bogwera* was no longer needed. Sebele I, for example, "stopped circumcision and told the Kwena that school education of boys and girls must now take the place of the ceremonies"; but, another source adds, he said also that "these customs did not please the Government." [10] Khama further held that "some of the rites and teachings were morally pernicious, and some uselessly cruel." Bathoen I similarly said *bogwera* was "bad morally as well as from a disciplinary point of view, and tends to undermine the chief's authority," though Ngwaketse also attributed his abolition of the practice to the influence exercised upon him by Khama, with whom he had become very friendly (Willoughby 1924:76; Schapera 1940:145). All three chiefs, it may be added, had themselves been circumcised, Sebele in spite of his father's opposition.

The prohibition of circumcision was nowhere popular. To both parents and children the rites were above all the hallowed method of initiation into the social status of adult. In every tribe the heathen element, and sometimes even church members, accordingly persisted in wanting them continued. But they could not be held locally unless sponsored by the chief. If he withstood agitation to restore them, the malcontents had either to organize ceremonies of their own outside the tribal area or to attend those of neighboring tribes that still had them (for example, Malete and Tlokwa). Among the Ngwato, where Khama abolished circumcision in 1877, he had to suppress strong demands for its revival in 1883 and 1890. Among the Ngwaketse it was abolished in 1901, and both Bathoen I and Seepapitso subsequently often fined people for going elsewhere to organize or take part in circumcision ceremonies. But in June 1940 Bathoen II still found it necessary to declare that he would punish

10. See Schapera (1940:60) for information from Sebele's contemporaries; B. P. archives, Mafeking Registry J. 2667.

any man taking a son to the ceremonies about to be held among the Malete.[11]

Elsewhere chiefs readily gave way to public pressure or personal inclination. Among the Tawana, as was shown, Moremi II simultaneously renounced Christianity and restored circumcision. Sekgoma at first supported the church but later withdrew for "political" and other reasons, "posed as the head of the heathen section," and gave it *bogwera* (Jennings 1904). The main "political" reason was a dispute about whether Sekgoma was the rightful chief or merely regent for his half-brother Moremi's son Mathiba. The administration decided in favor of Mathiba, who was duly installed (1906). Within a few years many of the more "conservative" tribesmen had moved away to join Sekgoma in exile. This may partly explain why Mathiba apparently met with little opposition when he again abolished circumcision (1910); but except for the fact that he was a church member, and also greatly under Khama's influence, I cannot account for his action.

Among the Kwena, Sechele II repealed his father's ban partly because of "persistent requests" from two large subject communities of Tswana stock and partly because his heir (Sebele II), then working in Johannesburg, refused to come home "until he was given *bogwera.*" Sechele himself also favored the ceremonies. Having fallen out with the LMS, he had admitted the Church of England (of which a foreign concubine he had recently taken was "a zealous member"), and it is said that his restoration of circumcision was done with the approval of the local Anglican missionary (Willoughby 1916). The renewal of the prohibition in 1937 arose from another request by the same two subject communities for permission to hold local ceremonies. The matter was discussed at several tribal meetings, where opinion was so sharply divided between heathens and Christians that Chief Kgari could not or would not make a final decision. Tired of waiting, the applicants hired land on a neighboring European farm and went ahead. Kgari punished them for acting without his permission. Pressed by his district commissioner, to decide one way or the other, he also announced that the ceremonies would now be illegal again.[12]

Although LMS influence contributed to the abolition of circumcision rites, it nowhere resulted in legislation against polygamy. Livingstone had noted during his early travels that fear of having to give up their "superfluous" wives was, for many men, perhaps the greatest obstacle to acceptance of Christianity (Livingstone 1841–1852, Schapera, ed., 1961). Sechele I, before being baptized, divorced four of his five wives; Khama,

11. See Schapera (1943:59–60) for sources and more detail.
12. District Commissioner (Molepolole), annual reports, 1936, 1937; see Schapera (1943:59–60).

while still heir to the chiefship, resolutely and successfully resisted his father's command to take a second wife; Bathoen I was also a monogamist. Yet none of them made polygamy illegal.

Nor was Seepapitso's law derived from the church code. It was due directly to the frequent tendency of young men on taking a second wife to neglect the first and her children and to the many complaints of desertion consequently brought to court. But this particular problem was not confined to the Ngwaketse. Presumably therefore Seepapitso, in thus seeking to protect the first wife, was prompted by personal views of a kind not shared by other chiefs. However, the prohibition was not absolute, since if the wife was childless, her husband could (and still can) usually get permission from the chief to marry another as well.

Khama was the only other chief openly opposed to polygamy. In 1904, for example, he stated to a Government Commission: "I have spoken to some of the younger men in the tribe who have taken several wives and told them they have a church in their village and a Missionary amongst them, and that they should not take more than one wife, but my words seem to be unwelcome to the people." [13] This implies that his opposition was founded on Christian doctrine. It implies also that he nevertheless did not feel able to prohibit polygamy—though fear of offending his subjects had not prevented him from prohibiting both beer-drinking and circumcision. Since polygamy, always practiced by only a minority of men, was already becoming less common everywhere with the spread of Christianity and similar influences, he (and other chiefs) may possibly have thought prohibition not worth the trouble of enforcing. However, that is mere speculation and certainly does not apply in regard to Seepapitso. I should mention also that Moremi II, after renouncing Christianity, himself became a polygamist, as did both Sebele I and Sebele II (Kwena); and several other chiefs—for example, Sekgoma (Tawana), Sechele II (Kwena), and Sekgoma II (Ngwato) —were notorious for their matrimonial irregularities. They were therefore unlikely to impose upon their people what they themselves did not practice.

Some sources say Khama's abolition of *bogadi* (by 1880) was likewise due to his desire that "people should enter Christianity and marry in church." It followed so soon after the church ban (1875) that the explanation seems plausible. But reliable Ngwato informants, including Khama's son Tshekedi, discounted LMS influence. They said he objected to *bogadi* mainly "because it bound a woman to her husband's family"; in particular, the latter could claim any children she bore, even if she married again after becoming a widow, "and this was the cause of much trouble." He dealt with the problem by deciding in court cases that if

13. Source quoted in Schapera (1943:41).

a woman married a second time, any resulting children belonged to her new husband, whether or not the first had given *bogadi*. In practice, too, his "abolition" meant merely that a wife's parents could not sue in court for payment of *bogadi;* no cases are known, I was assured, of people having been punished for giving it. Nor did he apply the ban to his many subjects of alien stock (Kalaka, Sarwa, and the like), whose systems of "marriage payments" differed from that of the Tswana proper.

In those tribes (Kwena and Ngwaketse) where the practice still prevails, payment of *bogadi* has allegedly become less common among heathens as well as among Christians. That was why Seepapitso began to enforce it among the Ngwaketse. Addressing a public assembly in March 1912, he asked, "Why have you abandoned the custom that is yours, I mean the custom according to which you used to marry?" He went on to say, "If you marry according to our usages, you ought to give *bogadi*, so that it may be known the marriage is proper"; and he explicitly likened *bogadi* in this respect to the wedding ring of "the white people." [14] But although he subsequently prosecuted and fined several men who had not yet given *bogadi* for their wives, he repeatedly had to keep urging the people to do so. Bathoen II has been equally persistent, yet as recently as 1939 he had to announce once more that there was a tribal law requiring the payment of *bogadi*. Data I collected in 1940 showed that, of 141 married men, 85 (60 per cent) had not (yet) given *bogadi* for their wives. Among the Kwena, where payment of *bogadi* is not similarly reinforced by decree, the corresponding number in a group of 88 men was 72 (82 per cent). Presumably, therefore, the Ngwaketse law has had some effect. But the high proportion of defaulters suggests that the chiefs have not been particularly successful in stopping the decay of the *bogadi* practice. Nor, I may add in this context, is there any marked desire among either Ngwato or Tawana to revert to it.

The Chief's Legislative Powers

What I have said about resistance to some of the laws raises a question crucial to my argument: is a chief free to legislate as he wishes, even if his people object? He has to inform the public assembly of any new law, since that is the only method by which he can make it known. In principle, the Tswana say, the assembly should also discuss and agree to the law before it can come into force. As Khama stated in 1905, when he refused to impose an eduaction tax, "under tribal government it was necessary that the people themselves should endorse any suggestion emanating from the Chief." [15]

14. See Schapera (1947:51) (minutes of Ngwaketse tribal assemblies).
15. See above, p. 232, and footnote 5.

A good example of legislation by consent was Seepapitso's action against polygamy. On deciding to restrict the practice, he told the assembly that "he was worried by women because their husbands had left them." After "full discussion," his proposal was adopted. "Chief Seepapitso gave us a chance to refuse or accept. We said at the time it was a good law." And when his son Bathoen II renewed it in 1931, "It was we ourselves who told the chief of this law. Those who ruled after Seepapitso did not apply the law and did not pursue it fully. When Seepapitso's son became chief, we pointed out his father's laws and asked him to revive them." [16] Similarly, Moremi's decision to restore circumcision was discussed at a specially summoned assembly, where the Tawana "with one voice" resolved "to go back all the way" and "take up" the rites again (Hepburn 1895:262).

But some of the laws here discussed were certainly imposed without formal aproval, and even despite much opposition. Khama himself noted about his laws against circumcision and "secular work on the Sabbath" that "He carried out these reforms solely in virtue of his powers as Chief, against the wishes of the majority of his people, but believing them to be for their advantage"; and when Bathoen I abolished circumcision among the Ngwaketse, "this decision was arrived at in a very small meeting, the tribe in general did not agree, the Chief forced matters through his power." [17] Similarly, Seepapitso, when speaking about *bogadi* in 1912, added to the remarks quoted above: "This is still merely a warning, but if you do not take heed you will have a new law made for you concerning marriage." In April 1914 he likewise announced: "I have continually said you must give *bogadi*, but you just do nothing about it; now I say, let *bogadi* be paid before I summon anyone" (Schapera 1947:51, 77). It seems very unlikely from this that he had given the tribe the option of deciding whether or not it wanted his "new law."

The chief's right to act so arbitrarily is, however, a recognized feature of tribal rule. *Lentswe lakgosi kemolao,* says the proverb—"The chief's word is law." At a meeting of the (Protectorate) Native Advisory Council in 1930 Bathoen II stated, during a debate about early castration of cattle, "We know Chiefs who have been educated by white men in some cases tell their people to do what is impossible. When we tell our people to castrate early, they reply that we are troubling them." Thereupon one of the other members (not a chief) commented: "The

16. The quoted statements were made by speakers at a tribal meeting in March 1936, when the Assistant Resident Commissioner held an inquiry into reports "that the chief had imposed a levy on all men with more than one wife." Bathoen had in fact fined several men for taking second wives without his permission and had also dissolved the marriages. (Mafeking Registry J. 236.)

17. See Sargant, as quoted in Schapera (1943:17) for Khama; see also *Minutes, Native Advisory Council,* 12th session (1931), p. 41 for statement about Bathoen's law by Ratlhaodi Bome.

father must see to all that the child requires. The tribes are children and the Chiefs should enforce early castration—it is a good thing even if we do not like it. The Chiefs should compel it. It would not be compulsion, it would be help." Another said, "It is the duty of the Chiefs to order the people to castrate in due time"; and yet another added, "If a man is blind and someone wants to lead him to a safe place, he cannot refuse. Unless the Chief enforces the law, nothing can help." [18]

People thus look to the chief for guidance, and expect him to initiate and enforce what he thinks will help them. His own behavior, moreover, tends to set a fashion; as the proverb says, *Kgosi eatlhotsa malata reagogoba*—"When the chief limps, his subjects crawl." In 1848, for example, Sechele I told Livingstone, "the immemorial custom of the people in this country has been to imitate their chief. If he is fond of oxen all the men live at the cattle posts, if fond of hunting all rear dogs and hunt with him." In 1878 it was reported of the Ngwato that "a great proportion attend the mission services, probably more induced to do so by the example of the Chief than by any wish to learn," and Hepburn was told by a Tawana tribesman in 1886, "We were learning nicely. Then Moremi left the Church, and we all followed" (Schapera 1960: 299; Patterson 1879:238; Hepburn 1895:272).

The Personal Factor

We have seen above that certain practices forbidden by the LMS to church members were also forbidden by chiefs to all tribesmen, heathen as well as Christians. The tribal prohibitions were not uniform everywhere, the chiefs imposing them were not always church members, and one Christian chief (Seepapitso) made compulsory a practice condemned by the church. The reasons given for the enactment of the laws show too that, although LMS teaching was sometimes directly responsible, the prime determinant might also be something else. We have seen further that among the Tswana a chief was relatively free to legislate as he wished. His laws sometimes met with general assent but were sometimes imposed without regard for public opinion. If determined to have his way, he might rigorously enforce a law (whether his own or a predecessor's); if not, he might disregard its violation, or he might even repeal it.

The two constant factors in the situation just summarized were the LMS code and the powers of the chief. Both were essentially the same in the four tribes considered. In all tribes except the Tawana the LMS also began work (1845–1857) and established permanent mission stations (1862–1871) in roughly the same decades. But as the chiefs obviously did not behave alike everywhere in regard to the church code, some

18. See *Minutes, Native Advisory Council,* 10th session (1930), pp. 13–17.

additional factor must be sought to account for the variations. That factor, I suggest, was the chiefs' personalities; it was, in other words, mainly because chiefs differed from one another in character and outlook that they differed also in their legislative response to the missionary stimulus.

To substantiate this conclusion fully would require more biographical evidence than space will permit me to give here. But even a few brief comments may suffice to show how greatly the chiefs whose legislation is here discussed varied in personal characteristics.[19]

Of those chiefs, Khama was by far the most famous internationally. Aged about thirty-five when he began to rule, he was an ardent Christian, whose renunciation of "heathenism" had led to long and bitter conflict with his father. Upright, honest, courteous, and a fanatical opponent of intoxicating liquor, he was the missionary ideal of a model convert. But his views were "narrow and stern," and in later life he became increasingly autocratic and intolerant, with the result that some of his closest relatives seceded from him or were driven away. Even his critics, however, give him credit for sincerely wanting to "elevate" his people, and during his long reign he made many beneficial changes in tribal life.[20]

Both Bathoen I and Seepapitso were also "progressive" men, under whose guidance the Ngwaketse advanced economically and socially. Seepapitso, in particular, had been relatively well educated, and he used his knowledge of the outside world to try to make his people more "civilized." Although he died at the age of only thirty-two, after reigning six years, he was a prolific law-giver, with many constructive measures to his credit. The regents who followed him in rapid succession were well-meaning but sickly men; their poor health is said to have been one reason for the slackness of their rule. Bathoen II, the present chief, was twenty years old when installed. He too received a fairly good education. A practicing Christian and lifelong teetotaler, he has ruled firmly and well and is now one of the most influential and highly respected chiefs in all Bechuanaland.[21]

Of the Kwena chiefs, Sechele I belonged to the generation when European influence first became established, and (unlike Khama's father, his contemporary) he eagerly embraced many of the white man's ways. But he was nearly forty years old when converted, and he could never bring himself to abandon some of the heathen rites (such as rainmaking) it was his duty as chief to perform. His missionaries described him as vain, vacillating, and hypocritical. His own people remember him with affection and gratitude; they speak of his rule as severe but just, and

19. The comments are based partly on tribal traditions and partly on the writings of Europeans who knew the chiefs well. The former are summarized in Schapera (1940); some of the latter are cited below.

20. Several biographies of Khama have been published. The most useful account for the present purpose is Willoughby (1924).

21. See Schapera (1942:1–26); for Seepapitso, see Schapera (1947).

they honor him as the man who made their tribe great. Of Sebele I, in contrast, few Kwena have anything good to say. The government officer who has most to do with him described him in 1908 as "underhand, irascible, utterly selfish, addicted to drink, always ready to sacrifice the interests and welfare of his people to his own, and therefore often acting by himself and keeping them in the dark." Sechele II and Sebele II were also bad chiefs. Their drunken habits, neglect of tribal affairs, and personal misconduct in other ways gave rise to several petitions against them by influential headmen. Sebele proved so thoroughly hopeless that the Administration finally deposed and exiled him. His younger brother and successor, Kgari, much better educated and a good churchman, became a relatively able and sympathetic ruler, under whom the tribe recovered social order and stability.[22]

Among the Tawana, only Sekgoma has the reputation of having been a "real" chief. Although his occasional severity made some of the headmen his enemies, he kept the tribe under firm control and decreed several good laws. Moremi II and Mathiba were both kindly and easygoing, and therefore more popular; but Moremi was a weak ruler, and Mathiba was so incompetent that two years before his death special "councillors" were chosen to help him manage tribal affairs.[23]

Enough has been said, I think, to indicate the wide range of variation in the character and ability of the chiefs. I do not claim that the laws a chief made were always and inevitably determined by such personal traits alone—that, for example, church laws were imposed tribally by "strong" and "progressive" chiefs only, ignored by "amiable nonentities," and repealed by "reactionaries." My contention is merely that in a political system like that of the Tswana, where "the chief's word is law," his special characteristics as an individual may have much to do with the nature of his legislation. That was one of the conclusions reached in my 1943 monograph. What I have tried to demonstrate now is that the importance of the personal factor becomes especially apparent when we observe how variously chiefs in different tribes responded to what was essentially the same kind of stimulus and how, even when they made the same laws, their motives were often different.

The value of such intertribal comparison may be illustrated by a final example. The Ngwaketse chief Seepapitso (1910–1916) and his cross-cousin the Kwena chief Sechele II (1911–1918) ruled at about the same time and for roughly equal periods. We have already noted that their fathers both abolished circumcision and that Seepapitso retained the ban

22. E. W. Smith's biography of the missionary Roger Price (1957) contains much useful information about Sechele I (and Khama). See also A. Sillery (1954; popular biography); Mafeking Registry J. 766 and other files (Sebele I, and so on); M. O. M. Seboni (1956; vernacular biography).

23. See Mafeking Registry J. 1023 (Moremi and Sekgoma); District Commissioner (Maun), annual reports, 1930–1933 (Mathiba).

whereas Sechele repealed it. Sechele's other legislation forbade the drinking of *kgadi* (a very intoxicating honey beer) and the sale, without permit, of cattle to traders. Seepapitso enforced the same prohibitions among the Ngwaketse (where they had originally been imposed by Bathoen I). He himself also forbade polygamy to younger men, the unauthorized sale of grain to traders, residence at fields or cattle posts, dancing and beer-drinking at night, and cruelty to domestic animals; he made *bogadi* payments compulsory; he decreed that wives and daughters should receive cattle from a dead man's estate, that in divorce cases an offending spouse (whether husband or wife) must pay five head of cattle to the other, and that certain kinds of contract (such as loan or gift of fields) must be made in his presence; he framed regulations controlling the use of public roads and the tribal dam, the activities of magicians, and the prices to be charged for transporting traders' goods; and he increased the standard rates of penalty for stock theft and defamation of character. Almost all the problems and practices he dealt with here existed also among the Kwena, but Sechele did nothing about them. It can only be concluded that Sechele's conception of his duties as chief differed markedly from Seepapitso's. It may be added in this connection that when Sechele was installed as chief, at the age of about forty, his uncles in the usual speeches of congratulation referred openly to his "wild ways and *kgadi* drinking," his "bad advisers and bad companions," and his "life unbecoming of a chief's son"—evidence enough that they did not look forward to his rule.[24]

In view of what has just been said, and of the preceding discussion as a whole, I would urge that in the study of legal history it is not enough to list successive changes in the law and to account for them by referring merely to prevailing social conditions or pressures. We need surely to investigate also how far the characters and motives of the lawmakers themselves contributed to the changes. I would suggest, too, that the roles of personal influence should not be overlooked in studies of social change generally. The Tswana are, of course, by no means the only African people whose tribal institutions Europeans have sought to reform. Comparison with what has happened elsewhere may possibly show that chiefs, where they ruled, were not always important agents of change. But I think it equally possible that not enough attention has been paid on the whole to how much they, as individuals, have done in deciding whether or not to make missionary and similar norms binding on all their subjects.

24. See report on installation of Sechele II, 2 February 1911 (by J. Ellenberger; Gaberones District records SP 15).

RICHARD P. WERBNER

Constitutional Ambiguities and the British Administration of Royal Careers Among the Bemba of Zambia [1]

Disputes over succession to chiefship, when tried before an administrative tribunal, involve more than the choice of a successor. Like the claimants, the administrator who tries the dispute may reason from a mixture of premises, administrative and tribal, and hold that only a decision shown to be in accord with earlier precedents is just. Each decision is not isolated but is linked to past decisions and regarded as setting up a line of future decisions. The claimants' manipulation of the precedents can be seen as depending on the "flexibility" (Gluckman 1955:293–294, 311) of their legal concepts: their rights and qualifications for succession have multiple, competing, and shifting references (Stone 1947:696–735). They make use, implicitly or explicitly, of concepts (such as "eligible senior" and "ineligible" or "excluded senior") which, if polar, are indefinite in their limits and must be defined with reference to current standards of political authority. Claimants argue over which are the past breaches of norms of succession, and their arguments pivot on assumptions about the rightful relations among various tribal positions and between chiefs

1. This essay embodies part of a course of lectures on Central Africa given at the University of Manchester. In 1964–1965 the University of Manchester generously gave me a Hayter Travel Grant, which enabled me to consult files in the National Archives of Zambia and to revise this essay. I am grateful to my students and my colleagues at Manchester, particularly Professor Max Gluckman, for much constructive criticism. I wish to thank also Dr. A. L. Epstein, who read an earlier draft of this essay and allowed me to consult some of the unpublished notes he made on tribal administration during five months of research in 1953–1954. This rural research was preparatory to his research on the Copperbelt. To the late Professor Paul Radin I am most indebted for the many discussions I had with him about the way authority may be "leased" to the holder of a ritual office.

245

and other officials in the hierarchy of colonial government. The manner in which the disputes are resolved tests the validity of these assumptions and may change them.

Under British rule the traditional constitution and modes of succession among the Bemba of Zambia were modified in legal disputes. At stake in the disputes were the political interests of tribal rulers and their superiors in the colonial administration. Whether the goal was efficiency and progress or defense of established authority, both the tribal rulers and the nonhereditary colonial officials had legitimate political aims. Administrative expediency alone did not lend either rule legitimacy. Both types of administrator manipulated tribal rights and historical claims. Both ruled with traditional justifications. The efforts of specific tribal rulers to extend or entrench their rule came into conflict with the efforts of colonial officials to establish and to administer a bureaucracy. But neither the hereditary rulers nor the other servants of government seem to have opposed each other consistently. There have been convenient, if transitory, alliances between particular Bemba rulers and other officials of government. Theirs has been a mutual accommodation, each making some use of Bemba constitutional traditions.

Discrepancies in statements of Bemba law lead Gluckman (1963a:99) to suggest that:

1) the succession through brothers, full and classificatory, born of a group of sisters, in order of genealogical seniority, to a number of chieftainships of ascending status up to the kingship;
2) the succession to the titles of chieftainesses through full sisters and then to uterine granddaughters; and
3) the titles CANDAMUKULU and MUKUKAMFUMU carry the right to bear the king.

Gluckman (1963a:103–104) goes on to discuss the working out of the conflict in the history of the present royal lineage:

> Within the first three generations there was no dispute about who was the rightful heir to the kingship, though there were irregularities in the succession to, and struggles for, the big chieftainships. When it became time for an heir to be taken from the fourth generation (D), there was a dispute between the senior men in two branches, and Government had to settle this matter.

Underlying Gluckman's discussion are stable rules: roughly the same rules are inferred to apply throughout the reigns of the present house, and a conflict, intrinsic in the rules, is linked to recurrent processes in the Bemba kingdom, both before and during British administration. The extent and nature of instability in the rules needs to be analyzed before the development of disputes can be understood.

From the start it is essential to recognize where the genealogical appearance of the royal lineage, in isolation, is misleading. Seemingly evident on the genealogy is a regularity of succession to kingship, and not to the other royal offices, according to a single set of rules (Gluckman 1963a:97). Also apparent on the genealogy is a coincidence between lineage segmentation and the sharing of the territorial "seats of power"; that is, when the lineage proliferates, in three generations there appears to be an increasing spread of offices among more distant relatives. The coincidence appears to be a process of politics intrinsic in the systematic development of the descent group. But the genealogy makes plain that the set of senior uterine siblings has not met in each generation the demographic requirements for the major royal posts—one fertile sister and three brothers. Because of demographic chance alone, there has been opportunity for the spread of titles to junior parallel cousins. Who regulated succession and how has been crucial here. But the genealogy does not show the key struggles over the counterposed offices of electors and king-makers or the pivotal realignments in territorial posts. It does not show how marriages within the *lupwa*, the "bilateral kinship group" affect the relationships within the royal descent group (see Werbner 1967:39–42). It does not give any hint of how a new organization of administration radically altered the interrelations between the offices of the royals and those of their extraclan kinsmen, the nobles. Disputes over succession among the Bemba have been directly related to changes in the distribution of political power and authority under British administration. An evaluation of the use of genealogical precedents or an assessment of regularities in succession must comprehend these changes.

To some extent the Bemba "authorities," recognized and sustained by the British officials, have been "purposefully adapted" to the requirements of the British South Africa Company's conquest, to those of the Company's administration, and after 1924 to those of the Northern Rhodesian Government under the Colonial Office. Prior to British rule, none of the Bemba kings [2] had advanced directly to the kingship from one of the other major chieftainships that were held by princes of the ruling house. There had been no definite territorial rota or series of promotions from the great royal chieftainships to the kingship: a prince, not the titled ruler of a big territory, was elected king. Under the Colonial Office's administration, a career of territorial advancement came to be the only way for a prince to succeed to the kingship. The career system that evolved was a compromise between an electoral competition among

2. One king, Sampa (B6 in the genealogical chart), is recalled to have controlled a major post for a brief time while he was a prince. The Bemba did not regard him as having been promoted from the post of NKULA to the kingship. Before he acceded to all the prerogatives of the NKULASHIP, he is said to have been driven away from the post by the reigning king, Citapankwa. (See Brelsford 1944b:37, 43-44.)

rightful contenders and a regularized order of uniform promotion from one territorial post to another. Under Northern Rhodesian administration there arose among Bemba a new distribution of noble and royal power, a new paramountcy for the kingship, and new hierarchies of office. Other royal houses, excluded from the kingship and the greatest posts, continued to hold lesser territories and to claim the greatest ones. But within the ruling house opposed dynasties developed, based on control of major divisions of the country. And in order to accommodate the claims of these opposed dynasties within a federation no longer expanding, Bemba have had to gloss legally incongruous instances in their past to reconcile these with the congruous instances; and they have had to gloss the congruous instances to distinguish relevant precedent from the irrelevant and the unconstitutional.

In many respects the legal activities of British civil administrators have weakened the application, but there is a sense in which Maitland's comments on the Saxon title do apply to the Bemba title. Maitland (1961: 301) wrote: "Hereditary and elective elements were mixed up in the title: we can define neither the one nor the other." If a set of genealogical precedents—or what Maitland might have regarded as the "hereditary elements"—had been decisive in succession among the Bemba, there would have been a single heir with overriding rights to a title. But in contrast to the monarchy in a nation or unitary state, the kingship among the Bemba has been the kingship in a federation of dominions. Constitutionally this has meant a political election to kingship: the holders of offices counterposed to the kingship make the king. Thus the realities of struggles for dominance among the kingdom's rulers—the realities of age and sterility, of demographic chance, of unequal ambition, of major upheavals in the kingdom—these realities have opened the kingship to caretakers, to "young men in a hurry," or to heirs of secondary recourse and, in turn, continually have redefined the precedents for succession.

In the choice of a successor Bemba have held to hierarchies of unlike and unequal rights which, ideally, precluded a logical "conflict of rules": in a given legal order one set of qualifications prevailed, and rights of succession constituted an order of precedence. This fact should not be mistaken, however, as evidence for legal certainty of succession among the Bemba. For where a candidate must be elected, legal contention and uncertainty over succession is prior to a set of rules—indeed, it is the stuff out of which the rules are derived. Because the particular reference of antecedent norms was uncertain, an order of precedence and legal grounds for struggles over succession could co-exist without contradiction among Bemba, even prior to British rule. Accession was conditional on a candidate's own or his mother's personal competence and on his election by other officeholders. When was political office first to be transferred from one generation to another? Should adelphic succession rightfully take place because of the minority or incompetence of an otherwise legitimate heir? When do the rights of a female title lapse? Among the Bemba there could be no a priori and logical agreement or disagreement over these issues, from one generation to the next. There could only be uncertainty of reference and political ambiguity.

At each accession the uncertainty was resolved, but only temporarily and not in all senses; there emerged a prevailing coalition of supporters and thus a dominant alignment of political power and authority within the ruling strata. The uncertainty was not resolved in all senses because the electors and kingmakers did not allow the phases of succession to be completed when a prince acceded to power as king. The holders of office counterposed to the kingship always granted to a particular ruler a conditional legitimacy; and they allowed him to be promoted to kingship, in its divine and ritually validated senses, only gradually. The making of a king did not mean a successive or general promotion of other princes. Some princes succeeded to great royal chieftainships and became ineligible for kingship. Some princes became excluded royals; strategically, they became "odd men out." In the Bemba federation it was conditional, specific, and not general promotion that produced categories of excluded royals and also legitimate heirs ready to seize the throne out of turn—"young men in a hurry." Advancement to a post or exclusion from it was not ordered by a uniform progression within a descent group. If a set of legal rules for succession of monarchs has told anything of past and potential political struggles, it has told this: no king is safe by rule from the dangers of "odd men out" and of "young men in a hurry."

Under British rule the political processes came to be radically distinguished from the earlier processes of ritualized election. Under British rule an heir could be chosen and could accede as a legitimate administrator, and yet he could lack a dominant alignment from within the ruling strata of Bemba, or at least lack the public and ritualized demonstration of such electoral support. Each coalition or alignment came to be influenced by the political involvement of European priests, company officials, and, eventually, civil administrators under the Colonial Office. They affected the political support of an heir, and then they sanctioned the accession. Precedents took on a new legal and political value: there was a change from one unstable legal system to another.

These struggles over succession must not be regarded as grossly cyclical. They do not arise out of repetitive conflicts within a single set of rules for succession. There is a basic flaw in any effort to abstract a single set of rules for the succession of Bemba kings in the precolonial or slave-trading phase of the nineteenth century and for the succession of kings in the imperial phase of the twentieth century. That effort puts beyond analysis the cumulative changes within a single period. It allows for no more than an acknowledgment, and not an assessment, of the radical changes that distinguish the earlier period from the later. A set of genealogical precedents does not stand in an immutable and ideal isolation. People give it meaning in relation to other sets of precedents, and they amend it as a new rule emerges. There is, therefore, an element of conjecture in any attempt to reconstruct from ossified history what the Bemba regard as the legal and the ritual norms of their kingdom prior to 1896.

Ossification and Contingency in an Unstable Legal Order

Disputes over succession need to be set in relief. This effort requires interrelating the early precedents, those for the preconquest kingdom, and inferring the norms of succession that Bemba had to modify, as their polity evolved within Northern Rhodesia—that is, "as-if" speculation is necessary. For purposes of exposition, precedents are to be taken as if interconnected at a period in time, and a later change is to be focused by reference to an ideal abstraction of these earlier precedents. This mode of exposition is particularly appropriate for Bemba legal history. It takes account of a special legal definition and certainty given to the Bemba past.

Neither we nor Bemba confront the long-past events of an unrecorded legal memory when we turn to the royal genealogy. After the Northern Rhodesian Administration took charge, it took pains to try to define certain events of the Bemba royal house. The official royal genealogy was compiled by E. H. B. Goodall, a Native Commissioner of Luwingu, in 1911–1912, and this served as the bedrock of later legal disputes such as those in the Willis Enquiry of 1924 and those in the Hudson Enquiry, the government adjudication of 1946. This eleven-foot-long genealogy has also been the basis of the royal genealogies that Richards (1940: 102) and Brelsford (1944a:44) and, after them, Gluckman (1963a:108–109) have presented. The point at which one version of preconquest royal history was legally ossified was the point at which a new system of succession began to develop, in the reign of Makumba Cimfwembe (B7). Along with legal ossification came a change in elective kingship, which led to the political compromises that may be called rotational succession.

Within a fixed type of positional succession, the following rule is implied by the precedents for the period before the British South Africa Company took charge. All the great royal offices—the major royal and appointing posts, the kingship, as well as a female title—would revert to the senior uterine siblings; and an adjacent generation would be the caretaker and "elector" generation between alternate generations. All the major *and* royal territorial offices in the kingdom would rightfully be

Abbreviated genealogy of the present Bemba royal house show-ing matrilineal descent.

NOTE: Some descendants in the sixth generation are omitted and no descendants in the (E) seventh gen-eration are shown. Male titles in capitals; female titles in capitals, underscored. * indicates dubiousness of ritual accession; dotted line . . . . indicates uncer-tainty of specific kinship relation. Genealogy revised from Gluckman 1963 (b.). Sources: Goodall 1911–12; Brelsford 1944a; Epstein 1953–54; Richards 1940.

controlled by the group of uterine siblings born of the senior Queen-Mother (CANDAMUKULU [3]) or, in the next and caretaker generation, born of her daughter, the Princess-Mother (MUKUKAMFUMU). Neither these precedents nor the later realties of succession show a repetitive cycle, proceeding from a small family monopoly of all territorial power to major branches sharing power and then back to a small family monopoly. (Contrast Gluckman 1963a:14, 104.)

Diagram 1

Paradigm of Precedents for Alternate Generation Succession

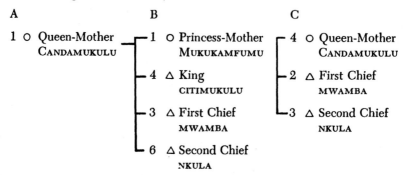

To accord with new political realities, precedents—such as those for the status of titles—have in some respects been extinguished; and this will continue to concern us *and* Bemba. Until roughly the time when Brelsford wrote *A Guide for District Officers*, the Queen-Mother (CANDAMUKULU) had been superior in position to the Princess-Mother (MUKUKAMFUMU). Brelsford's facts do not contradict those of Richards on this point. Brelsford (1944a:12), however, argues against his own evidence and contributes to the extinguishment of precedents:

> One name is as good as the other. . . . We hear of the big house (*ng'anda ikalamba*) and the little house (*ng'anda inono*). The house of Chandamukulu is the big house at the moment because she is the senior daughter of a senior *namfumu* [mother of the chiefs]. . . . Chandamukulu and Mukukamfumu are but names and the relative seniority of their mothers decides which is senior at any particular time.

That Bemba have concepts of positional succession is concealed in Brelsford's special pleading for an order of rotation according to genealogical seniority. To succeed to one of the titles, CANDAMUKULU, has been to succeed to the position of "mother of the earliest CITIMUKULU." Brelsford himself reports, "The name Candamukulu is said to be the oldest name and traditionally the name of the mother of the earliest CITMUKULU, but Mukukamfumu does not make its appearance until the beginning

3. Titles are shown in small capitals; female titles begin with a full capital.

of the present lineage" (Brelsford 1944a:12). At the beginning of the present lineage its rebel founder, Cileshye, took the superior and most ancient title from the house he dispossessed and gave this title of CANDA to his sister (A 1), thus securing rights of succession for the next generation. CANDA (A 1) became, by positional succession, a mother to her real mother, Mukukamfumu.[4] Only this view is compatible with the rule Bemba persistently hold that a granddaughter succeeds to her grandmother's position. Thus Bemba have regarded as Queen-Mother not the MUKUKAMFUMU but, to quote an informant of Richards, "the great CANDAMUKULU the mother of the CITIMUKULU, whom they used to call 'the Sun of Lubemba'" (Richards 1936:20). The royal genealogy shows, in the precedent of A 1, that the CANDAMUKULU has the prior right to bear the divine king (the CITIMUKULU) and also the other royal rulers who have major powers of appointment (MWAMBA and NKULA) and the Princess-Mother (MUKUKAMFUMU).

Within a fixed type of positional succession, the early precedents [5] in the official genealogy point to a legal dominance for the senior uterine line. Yet, as has been indicated, this does not imply the legal definiteness of a "legitimatist" type of succession; no royal could reign as divine king by right of primogeniture or genealogical seniority alone. A royal's right to reign depended on his being ritually elected.

If this view is right—that is, if Bemba have had legal precedents for an order of preference in succession to royal titles and also an electoral procedure—why, it may well be asked, has there been so much confusion over succession? Here, among the many forms of confusion, several forms need to be distinguished: (1) a writer's imprecise or perhaps tendentious exposition; (2) a logical inconsistency in the ideological "principles" of the people studied (Gluckman 1963a:99); (3) the ambiguous and variable policy of a conquering company which becomes an administration; and (4) the people's ambiguity (the flexibility of their concepts) that admits of change, allows of adaptability in their social relations, and may become a means of resistance to superordinate authority.

4. Two titles, CANDA WE IYAYA and CANDA MUKULU, seem to have been distinguished here. In Bemba myths, Mukukamfumu's daughter is regarded as having taken the position of her "grandmother," CANDA WE IYAYA, and then she (A1) or her successor (C4) became CANDAMUKULU WE CIBUNDU (Epstein 1954b). According to the myths, the title CANDA WE IYAYA has reverted to royals of the old house of CIMBOLA. But now their possession of the title of CANDA WE IYAYA has come to be symbolic of their exclusion from the throne: only a woman past the age of childbearing can now take the title (Brelsford 1944a:12).

5. B2 has seen the precedent for the right of the Princess-Mother to bear the Queen-Mother and, secondarily, the appointing chiefs. Precedents for the relative standing of the appointing chiefs were MWAMBA I (A3), the first, and NKULA I (B6 or C3), the second among these chiefs. Bemba cast some uncertainty over B6's title. The relative standing holds true also if C3 is considered.

Much of the seeming inconsistency in the statements of Bemba law does not stem from Bemba contradiction. Rules for succession to female titles and to male titles appear to be discrepant or conflicting partly because necessary distinctions are not made in the writing of one of the government's main authorities on Bemba, Mr. Brelsford. In his *Guide to District Officers* imprecision is crucially evident in Brelsford's reference to the Princess-Mother and the Queen-Mother as "sisters, mothers." [6] Bemba speak of these offices as *namfumu*, "mothers of chiefs." Brelsford explains that he has spoken of CANDAMUKULU and MUKUKAMFUMU as "sisters because these mothers, the holders of either title, may become the sisters of a Paramount and because succession appears to him to be initially sororal: "For the succession to each name is separate and is from sister to sister, or, if there are no sisters, to the granddaughter" (Brelsford 1944a:11).

Diagram 2

King-Bearing Titles of Females
(Based on Brelsford 1944a:44)

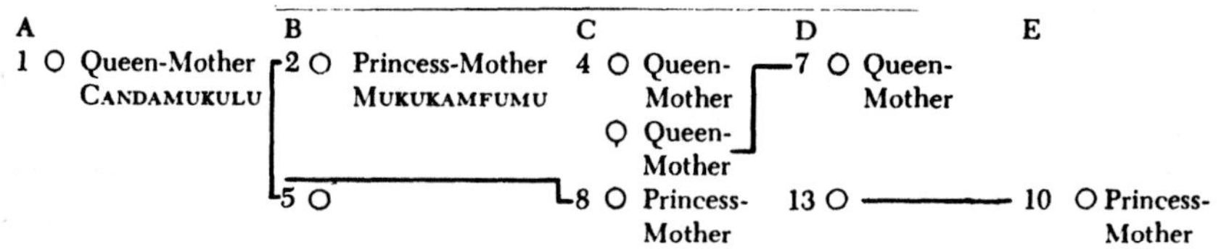

A	B	C	D	E
1 ○ Queen-Mother CANDAMUKULU	┌2 ○ Princess-Mother │ MUKUKAMFUMU	4 ○ Queen- Mother ○ Queen- Mother	┌7 ○ Queen- │ Mother	
	└5 ○	└8 ○ Princess- Mother	13 ○ ——————— 10 ○ Princess- Mother	

Brelsford does not make clear on what evidence he bases his opinion that succession is sororal. Richards (1960:224) remarks that in general "a woman [is succeeded] theoretically by her sister, but actually by her uterine granddaughter." According to Epstein's unpublished evidence, Bemba prefer a granddaughter to succeed her grandmother to the titles of MUKUKAMFUMU and CANDAMUKULU. The only instance of a sister (C5) apparently succeeding her sister (C4) as titleholder occurs as a last resort—in the absence of any granddaughter and also any suitable daughters, D4 being barren. Epstein was told by a Councillor in 1954: "In the case of these two titles the holder is succeeded by her grandchild, but a daughter can succeed if there is no available grandchild . . . and

6. Brelsford appears himself to have been uneasy and at pains to justify his usage of "sister": "I use the word sister frequently as a matter of convenience but the word mother represents the ultimate test. A man takes his seniority from his mother. . . . Succession is traced from *namfumu* [mother of the chief] to *namfumu* and the order of precedence is the order of the mother. The sons of a senior *namfumu* are senior to those of a junior *namfumu* although the sons of the latter may be older in years" (Brelsford 1944a:2).

normally it would be the first-born who would succeed" (Epstein n.d.). Brelsford's imprecise use of "sister" need no longer confuse analysis. The notion of a fixed type of positional succession may be applied in order to understand rank and status relations among titleholders. The paradigm for the two female offices is that of "mother and daughter." It can be seen that where the two offices of Princess—Mother and Queen-Mother were forced into the same generation—like biological "sisters," —Bemba readjusted this so that in the next generation the distinct office-holders were of adjacent generations. (C4 and C8 were succeeded by D7 and E10 of adjacent generations.)

A Bemba was astonished and perplexed at the height of a succession dispute when Gluckman questioned him about the MUKUKAMFUMU. But the perplexed Bemba was more precise than Brelsford who wrote that "one name is as good as the other" (Brelsford 1944a:12) and appeared to imply that "the titles of CANDAMUKULU and MUKUKAMFUMU are equal in status" [7] (Gluckman 1963a:96). These titles, as Brelsford himself revealed, were and still are unlike and unequal in a variety of ways, both legal and ritual. The perplexed Bemba did make this clear in the first half of his reply to Gluckman's question, "Has MUKUKAMFUMU IV (E10) the right to bear kings?" "No, she hasn't," he replied [and she has not or had not at that moment], "but she doesn't know it," the Bemba concluded, in astonishment (Gluckman 1963a:103).

Why should she not know it? There are at least two basic reasons, which also clear up Brelsford's confusion. These are: (a) The MUKUKAM-FUMU had a residual right to bear kings and not a primary right, like that of the CANDAMUKULU. That is, if the holder of the title of CANDAMUKULU fails to bear a prince in time for him to succeed as an adult king, then the next in line to the throne is a son of the Princess-Mother, MUKUKAM-FUMU. The MUKUKAMFUMU cannot know in advance that she has no right to bear a king; her son conceivably could become a king, if there should be no son of CANDAMUKULU. (b) The second reason has grown out of the first in a historical sense, though not necessarily in a logical one. The MUKUKAMFUMU might know that, according to the earlier precedent, she had only a residual right, but she would also know that times had changed; that a new order was in the making; and that there was considerable doubt that the old precedent would be observed—particularly since it no longer accorded with the present distribution of royal property or political office, and since the more recent precedent of Nakasafya (B5) could be used to extinguish the precedent of CANDAMUKULU I (A1).

7. By "equals in status" Brelsford seems to have meant, in the context of his report, those who are neither superiors nor inferiors in an order of official advancement. He meant "peers," having priorities. He meant that in the case of holders of comparable, graded offices—such as professors, for example—their capacities relative to other such officeholders may legally be exercised according to an order of precedence so that a senior's exercise of capacity may block a junior's.

The MUKUKAMFUMU and the perplexed Bemba knew even more than this. They knew what Brelsford reports in his *Guide for District Officers:* that from 1924, when MWAMBA IV (D1) acceded as Paramount Chief, a struggle over the status of MUKUKAMFUMU had been waged by NKULA IV (D12) and his successor (D14). In 1943 the reigning king, formerly MWAMBA IV (D1), won a strategic victory for the unity of the whole royal house and for the continued superiority of CANDAMUKULU. NKULA (both D12 and D14) had attempted (a) to gain for the MUKUKAMFUMU (and thus for the royals of her womb) legal and ritual independence of the king's capital, (b) to bring the MUKUKAMFUMU's ancestral relics to his territory, and (c) to obtain for her staves of office and a salary equivalent to the CANDAMUKULU's salary. Previously, the MUKUKAMFUMU had had neither staves nor salary. In Brelsford's account (1944a:15) "The NKULA house had lost the fight in one respect and hung on to rights in another way. The attempt to gain complete control of the MUKUKAMFUMU in their own district had failed. But by surrendering at the last moment they had prevented a still more junior branch of the clan from taking their important posts."

In 1946 some of the uncertainty over the king-bearing rights of the MUKUKAMFUMU should have been eased, though not ended, by the succession of NKULA V (D14) to kingship. I consider that the succession of this last Colonial Paramount, the son of a MUKUKAMFUMU, legally confirmed a promotional pattern of alternation between houses (see Diagram 3, Paradigm of Rotational Succession). Lord Hailey (1950:141)

Diagram 3

Paradigm of Rotational Succession
(Arrows show order of promotion)

Line of Queen-Mother	Line of Princess-Mother
(CANDAMUKULU)	MUKUKAMFUMU
King	King
↑	↑
First Chief (MWAMBA)	Second Chief (NKULA)
↑	↑
Third Chief (NKOLEMFUMU)	Fourth Chief (CIKWANDA)

wrote to the Colonial Office, "The position of Paramount has alternated between the two senior families." The holder of the most important post in MUKUKAMFUMU's house, like his immediate predecessors from the alternative house of CANDAMUKULU, advanced to kingship through a series of promotions from other territorial posts and was also, like his parallel cousins and predecessors, of the senior set of full brothers in his house. *For the moment,* the succession of MUKUKAMFUMU's senior son gave the Princess-Mother a status in her house (that of B5) akin, though not equal, to the status of the CANDAMUKULU in hers. But (I stress that my view of Bemba succession is of an unstable legal order) in its evolutionary processes *doubt* can and must continue to exist. A new legal standing for, in Brelsford's terms, "a third sister" or third king-bearing title could affect the standing of the others. And the continued inequality in the statuses of MUKUKAMFUMU and CANDAMUKULU could also be manipulated to serve the changing interests of princes, and others.

I have suggested that the perplexed Bemba was more precise than Mr. Brelsford, in Brelsford's apparently loose designation of the CANDAMUKULU and the MUKUKAMFUMU as equal in status. In remarking on Brelsford's imprecision I intend in no way to slight his work. Indeed, I stress that to understand the realities of recent Bemba political struggles it is necessary to be clear about the nature of Brelsford's imprecision and his role in these struggles. Brelsford acts on behalf of political interests crucially different from those of the other learned authorities on the Bemba, such as Richards. Subsequently I shall analyze Brelsford's role further to demonstrate the administrative use of Bemba traditions by officials of the Northern Rhodesian Government.

Bureaucratic and Bemba Decision-Making in a Magistrate's Hearing

Who was to make the king and for what purposes? What were and ought to be the relations between the legalities of seniority and the realities of power as seen by British civil administrators and by different Bemba rulers? Was there to be a regular promotion from one office to another, as would suit some of the British administrators, or was each accession to kingship to depend on the power struggles of the moment? These questions were at the core of the dispute of MWAMBA (D1) and NKULA (D12) over succession in 1924. It is important to evaluate this dispute because the grievances expressed in it rankled and were carried forward into quarrels over various offices—including those of the priest councillors—until, and even after, the accession in 1946 of the last of the Administration's Paramounts, NKULA IV (D14). Fortunately the Magistrate's hearing, the Willis Enquiry of 1924, is now a public document, which may be cited here to show the nature of the reasoning and decision-making in the dispute.

At the hearing the Commissioner, Mr. Willis, regarded himself as reluctantly acting in his role as a magistrate: he was to treat the case within the government's canons of legal justice when he heard the evidence and when he sought to make a legalistic decision. Willis wrote in the letter accompanying his report to his Superior, the secretary for Native Affairs (District Commissioner 1924b):

I considered it advisable to postpone interfering in the matter until the rival parties had been given every opportunity to arrive at a friendly settlement amongst themselves. I urged upon both sides that this would be the better course. I pointed out to them (1) that the Government had no particular anxiety for an immediate appointment, (2) that the Government did not favor one more than another, (3) that we only wished them to nominate a Chief who would be acceptable to the whole tribe. By October 1 I had however realised that there was little likelihood of an agreement ever been [sic] reached and that the parties would prefer to state their respective cases.

Willis was, according to his own account of himself, an aloof and imparitial outsider; a just decision had to be and was taken free of specific bias in favor of one contender and irrespective of political expediency. Willis (1924:1) believed simply that "The opinion I have given in favor of MWAMBA has been arrived at entirely on the evidence in connection with a claim of right." In the justification of his action he concealed, from himself and others, the judicial problems presented by his combining the two roles of magistrate and district commissioner—judge and administrative bureaucrat. The combination of his roles required that he decide not exclusively in terms of Bemba claims of right; he had to bring his decision publicly in line with past administrative decisions about other offices while, at the same time, he determined upon the policy most likely, in his view, to make succession or future administrative relations regular and unhampered by disputes. His judging would have had to take into account administrative premises and interests, even if, when arriving at a decision, he had more successfully distinguished and not confused his roles.

To take the District Commissioner's opinion about his part as an analytic conception would be a gross mistake. The District Commissioner was an insider in various analytic senses. He was not an outsider in the grossest sense of one at once unrelated and "excluded both as a participant and as a subject from the gossip and backbiting of the community" (Frankenberg 1957:156). There is clear and full evidence that in this and other succession disputes among Bemba, the district commissioner and even more senior officials participated in the backbiting and politicking of the succession disputes. Various officials took different sides, marshaling arguments and defamatory tales counter to those of their opponents. These officials were career administrators superior to the hereditary rulers and thus within a common hierarchy of administration; together with their changing Bemba allies they participated as parties having special or local interests to defend in the disputes.

In 1924 the District Commissioner as magistrate did not shed his executive experience and administrative competence when he assessed the evidence and made a recommendation. Toward the end of his letter to his superior he did warn about the undesirable Bemba who might have to be promoted if his, the District Commissioner's, recommendations were not considered right. Moreover, because Willis appreciated succession in career terms—that an appointment of a royal to one post was seen by other royals as affecting their chances of advancement—Willis argued that for administrative purposes it was not enough merely to make an immediate decision in favor of MWAMBA for the post of Paramount Chief. Willis (1924:4) recommended "that in the event of His Excellency upholding MWAMBA's claim today then the latter's nearest relatives must in course of time fill all the important posts." This would eliminate the prospect that the undesirable royal would hold an important post and, in Willis' words "There will be no future difficulty . . . ," for sons of CANDAMUKULU would then succeed to the kingship in order of seniority through a fixed rota of offices.

A line of future decisions had to be set up about other offices as well as the Paramount Chiefship if all the District Commissioner's recommendations were accepted and not merely his immediate choice of a Paramount Chief. Willis advocated a policy that would have clearly graded the major royal posts, defined the relations between the posts in different administrative districts, and unified the control of these posts in the hands of full brothers. His immediate choice was accepted; his policy was not carried out. Just as Bemba rulers represented different territorial interests, so too some of the British administrators spoke for the special interests and claims of different districts. The District Commissioner of Abercorn, writing at Willis' request, stated his objections to the recommendations of his colleague at Kasama (District Commissioner 1924a):

> I understand that once a man accepted the appointment of MWAMBA it was beneath his dignity to accept the appointment of CHITIMUKULU as the positions were almost equal. On the other hand there is record that when a man was appointed NKULA it was a step towards being made CHITIMUKULU. The Wemba House has certainly been divided for some time and if MWAMBA is appointed now as Paramount Chief over the whole country I think there will be disappointment amongst the people of the Luwemba [CITIMUKULU's] and Ichinga [NKULA's] sections as it is obvious these sections favor NKULA while MWAMBA is supported by the Ituna [MWAMBA's] and Miti [NKOLEMFUMU's areas].
>
> It might possibly be wise on the part of the Government to accept the position and have two Chiefs of equal authority, MWAMBA as the Chief of the Ituna and Miti and NKULA (as CHITIMUKULU) in charge of the Luwemba and Ichinga. Personally, I would prefer to divide the Authority than give one man the absolute control of the whole Wemba country.

Within the ranks of government and elsewhere there continued to be criticism of Willis' decision; in 1935, Goodall, then Provincial Commissioner of the Central Province and one of the most learned among the government's authorities on the Bemba, wrote to a colleague: "I thought and said at the time that Willis was making a mistake in favoring the nomination of the then MWAMBA. I still have little doubt that if we had not been in the country, he, the present CHITIMUKULU, would not have secured the stool, it would have gone to NKULA" (Provincial Commissioner 1935).

Willis seems to have disregarded considerations of the past and present realities of power among the royals themselves: their political strengths and allegiances were irrelevant to justice. And in his letter to his superior he went even further. His case against NKULA raised what is in effect a civil administrator's critique of the methods of conquerors who were his predecessors. For Willis' reasoning was that such political considerations ought not to have weighed even under the early rule of the British South Africa Company. Mr. Young of the British South Africa Company, with the agreement of Ponde (C10) and CITIMUKULU V (B7), had allowed CIKWANDA (C6) to appoint Bwalya as NKULA (D12). Willis saw no legal basis for this action; it was wrong for an order of seniority to be overridden, and it was wrong for the strongest royals to exercise elective and appointive powers in their own interests. "I very much doubt whether this [succession of NKULA] was in order or in accordance with native custom but Mr. Young may have had some other reason for approving it" (Willis 1924:3). Willis (1924:3) found that "It is very clear throughout that these posts are always given to the eldest of the line."

Willis held that there was "native custom" that fixed "the right man," and struggles over office were native in succession only insofar as such struggles were beyond the realm of right and within the realm of might and conquest. For this reason he judged the most telling argument against NKULA to be NKULA's own admission of MWAMBA's seniority: "They [NKULA's] faction openly admit that was [sic] it not for the quarrel [a struggle over the offices of NKULA and MWAMBA, and the resulting division of the country between the houses of MUKUKAMFUMU and CANDAMUKULU] MWAMBA is the proper person to become CHITIMUKULU" (Willis 1924:3). Willis further contended that "NKULA's claim is purely a hostile one, his party asks the Government to do another wrong in order to undo a previous (alleged) wrong."

When NKULA recounted at the hearing his version of how new political divisions came about between royals, dividing them into distinct houses, he was careful to avoid directly blaming the officials of the British South Africa Company for illegitimate appointments (such as Kanyanta's to the MWAMBASHIP). But the implication of blame for such illegitimate appointment was unavoidable. This fact further lent a hostile direction to NKULA's case before the District Commissioner. In a closed letter to his superior, the District Commissioner was willing to voice doubts whether Mr. Young, an earlier Native Commissioner, had appointed NKULA "in

accordance with native custom." But in public, at the Enquiry, the District
Commissioner so addressed the contenders as to leave no doubt that
whatever might be the grievances between the houses over a past appointment, right rested with a past appointment "approved by the
officials at the time." And this point was a key element in the District
Commissioner's decision against NKULA IV—the public upholding of past
administrative action as just.

In a sense the District Commissioner was right when he branded
NKULA's claim as a "purely hostile one"; NKULA did have to play a part
more hostile than MWAMBA's in the Enquiry, and it was NKULA's followers
who threatened to leave their homes in Lubemba, in defiance of the
administration, if their claims were not upheld. NKULA had to begin by
attacking legal arguments that might have applied had circumstances not
changed. To NKULA fell much of the task of first establishing that there
were significantly new political relations—that where there had been an
old division of power between counterposed great rulers of a single house,
MWAMBA and CITIMUKULU, there were now opposed dynasties, the houses
of MUKUKAMFUMU and CANDAMUKULU, each having its own territories.
Then NKULA had the further task of stretching some Bemba concepts of
succession to cover these new relations and, at the same time, opposing
new arguments that identified the MWAMBASHIP with other, unlike, posts
(and thus extinguished the ineligibility of a MWAMBA to become king).

The Reasoning of the Bemba Claimants

MWAMBA was the first to testify at the Enquiry. He traced his matrilineal descent from the eldest sister of CITIMUKULU Cileshye, then recounted a history of rebellion and succession to the CITIMUKULUSHIP, the
MWAMBASHIP, and the NKULASHIP. MWAMBA declared, "I make this claim
because I am now the elder. NKULA, the other claimant, is my younger
brother." He continued his case with his opinion of who the electors were
and what the electoral procedure was by right: "The biggest Chief; that
is the eldest person present speaks first. In this case it would be me.
The eldest present by birth has the right to say that he will be Chief.
He would not do this if the deceased had a brother living who was
elder. If the word of the eldest was not accepted, then it always ended in
fighting" (Willis 1924:5). In conclusion, MWAMBA rejected the claims of
either the perpetual "Son of CITIMUKULU," the MAKASA, or a priest-
councillor, such as the CIMBA or any other, such as CANDA WE YAYA, to
be the one to appoint or nominate the CITIMUKULU.

NKULA then questioned MWAMBA very briefly:

Q. When Mubanga Cipoya [MWAMBA III C2] died, were there any bigger
people than yourself? A. Yes, there were two CHIKWANDA, and Ponde.

Q. At that time who appointed you to be Chief MWAMBA? A. I was appointed by Chimfwembe Makumba [CITIMUKULU V B7]. Chief Nkula here states that is not true. MWAMBA continues: What I meant was that my mother CANDAMUKULU appointed me, and I understood that she did so with the approval of Chimfwembe Makumba. . . . Mr. MacKinnon [of the British South Africa Company] told me that CHITIMUKULU had approved my succeeding. [Willis 1924:7]

NKULA here sought to establish that Kanyanta's appointment as MWAMBA was, for Bemba, illegitimate: CANDAMUKULU had appointed Kanyanta to be MWAMBA without the approval of CITIMUKULU or any other great royal ruler. NKULA claimed that Kanyanta's wrong and unapproved succession had brought about a division of the country, leaving Luwemba, CITIMUKULU's area, and Ichinga, NKULA's area, for the house of MUKUKAMFUMU. The importance of this for NKULA's case is reflected in the fact that several pages of his testimony are given over to an account of the MWAMBA succession and the way his uncle Ponde (C10) was cheated of the MWAMBASHIP. NKULA testified that Kanyanta's wrongful succession had led to his own rightful succession to the NKULASHIP. CIKWANDA had then resigned the NKULASHIP in his favor because CIKWANDA was very angry that Kanyanta had become MWAMBA: "that MWAMBA had now more power than he had as NKULA, and that it was wrong for him [Nanyanta] to be MWAMBA, because he [Kanyanta] was only his nephew" (Willis 1924:8). NKULA tried to prove that Kanyanta's politics were opposed to the wishes of all the royals then greater than Kanyanta; CIKWANDA, Ponde, and CITIMUKULU all condemned Kanyanta when he sought, unsuccessfully, to have Native Commissioner Young oust NKULA from office. NKULA then hypothesized about Kanyanta's rights, in order to suggest that as NKULA Kanyanta would have had a claim to the Paramount Chiefship and he would not then have usurped Ponde's place as MWAMBA "If MWAMBA (Kanyanta) had not succeeded in the way he did but had Ponde become MWAMBA, then this trouble would not have happened. I say that MWAMBA's claim to be CHITIMUKULU today would be right, if that had not happened . . . Kanyanta would have become NKULA on CHIKWANDA becoming CHITIMUKULU, and on CHIKWANDA's death Kanyanta would have become Paramount Chief" (Willis 1924:9).

In these hypothetical statements about rights and an order of succession NKULU did not admit seniority alone to be a sufficient criterion for succession: "It is not quite true what MWAMBA said that it is always the elder who succeeds, it could happen that a younger man such as NKOLEMFUMU [D3] or CIKWANDA [D12] could succeed" (Willis 1924:10). NKULA cited precedents [such as Citapankwa as CITIMUKULU (B4) and Kanyanta himself as MWAMBA], but these precedents were of rebellion and, from his own view, usurpation of office—instances where the senior was not strong enough to hold office against a junior. At this point NKULA implicitly contradicted the premise of rightful promotion from one major territorial post to another. Such a contradiction endangered his case because it struck at a basic premise that he, along with his opponent and the magistrate, had followed in the dispute.

Another argument could have been and later was used to meet claims based on seniority. NKULA IV's younger brother, NKULA V (D14), in the succession disputes of 1944–1946, made use of the flexibility in the concepts of seniority. One of his arguments was in effect that his opponents' claims based on a senior title should be placed on the side of excluded or bypassed senior and not unaltered senior. According to Brelsford (1944a:4): "The post of Paramount went three times in succession to sons of junior, second sisters [Makumba B7, CIKWANDA C6, and Ponde C10—sons of A4 and B5], and NKULA [D14] of the present day always asserts that this altered the rule, and he states his intention to follow this up with his own claim when CHITIMUKULU Kanyanta [D1] dies." I note that Mr. Brelsford, in 1944, misprophesied when he continued his remarks in his *Guide to District Officers:* "But, as I shall show, it is a futile claim and is not supported by traditional rules." NKULA V's reasoning was: CANDAMUKULU *was* senior, but now the rights of her title have lapsed and have been limited by the succession of a son of Kanyanta Bwalya, A4, and sons of Nakasafya, B5, both women being "second sisters" and not the holders of the title CANDAMUKULU. There were other houses of seniors excluded from succession, like the house of Ngoshye, which still had many kin and supporters. Are their pretensions to the throne to be admitted, based on limited titles like that old title of CANDAMUKULU? Bemba have no statute of limitations on a title, and royals of the house of Ngoshye did continue to claim at least the chieftaincy of NKULA and, perhaps also, the kingship throughout the reigns of NKULA IV and NKULA V.

In 1924 NKULA IV did not manipulate the indefiniteness in the extension of seniority for the title of CANDAMUKULU. When he tried to counter the notion that a senior takes precedence in succession, NKULA IV was not able to keep to a purely legalistic argument: he had to appeal to precedents where the realities of greater political strength had swung the succession to a junior man. Elective and political realities were essential to his case. Legalistically and in terms of his manipulation of other Bemba rights of succession, NKULA had a dual argument at the simplest. On the one hand, NKULA sought to disqualify Kanyanta as the holder of an office that could never be the steppingstone to the CITIMUKULUSHIP; and, on the other hand, NKULA sought to establish that if there were a steppingstone to kingship it should be the NKULASHIP according to precedent. NKULA buttressed his case with the claim that CITIMUKULU V (B7) had recognized his right to succeed: "CHITIMUKULU's last words to me when outside his house . . . were 'You NKULA have two uncles, and

when both are dead you will succeed as CHITIMUKULU'" (Willis 1924:8).
NKULA also countered MWAMBA's version of the electoral procedure and
gave his own version: "this is the business of the Washiluwemba, after
they have consulted with MAKASA . . . when they want to appoint a new
Chief, MAKASA has to gather the people together, and state the man he
has chosen, but if the people do not agree, MAKASA cannot press the nomination. He will then choose someone else" (Willis 1924:9).

Kanyanta questioned NKULA on two points—the lack of a precedent for
the succession of a MWAMBA to kingship and the dubious legitimacy of
his own accession to the M.,AMBASHIP. He phrased his question to pose
an identity of norms between unlike posts, his own and an ancient post in
the same area. In reply to MWAMBA's question NKULA denied that a CITI-
MUKULU of an earlier house, one before Cileshye's had come from Ituna,
the area of MWAMBA, and NKULA added, "It [an alleged succession from
the area] is not the same thing, I spoke of no MWAMBA succeeding"
(Willis 1924:13). On this point MWAMBA extended the reference of a
precedent and obliterated a distinction in order to include his unprecedented claim within an accepted order of succession. NKULA and his
supporting witnesses maintained, in effect, that MWAMBA did not come
under a general category of rulers from the Ituna area; the MWAMBASHIP
was legally distinct from any previous post that, though in the same area,
was of another royal house, differently titled, and of a different political
rank vis-à-vis the kingship. The ineligibility of the holder of the MWAMBA-
SHIP was established by the specific precedents of the previous three
MWAMBAS of their house. NKULA and some of his supporting witnesses
did acknowledge that past MWAMBAS were offered the CITIMUKULUSHIP;
but the refusal of these MWAMBAS to take the CITIMUKULUSHIP was binding for the present MWAMBA also. Here it was NKULA and his supporters
who had to struggle against the shifting reference of precedents and thus
against a further development of the laws of succession. The m.,istrate,
in his concluding remarks, disallowed that the earlier MWAMBAS' refusal
to become king was the binding aspect of the precedent: he considered
sufficient for the present MWAMBA's case that past MWAMBAS were offered
the post of CITIMUKULU.

Kanyanta's second major defense was the legitimacy of his appointment
to the MWAMBASHIP. Kanyanta pointed his questioning to reach to an old
field of political competition between titled holders of a major royal post
and their untitled royal rivals. These were princes not controlled within
an established order of subordination yet great in following and in power.

Briefly, his predecessor as MWAMBA (the third) had sought to turn a
powerful and independent rival, the prince Ponde, into an underling with
a claim to, if not a powerful prospect of, advancement from the underling's post of NKOLEMFUMU to the superior office of MWAMBA on the
MWAMBA's death. Instead, Ponde extended his conquests over the Lungu,

refused to abandon his base of power among these foreigners to the north of MWAMBA, and refused to accept one type of legitimacy at the price of subordination in a small post. Ponde further secured the base from which he could seize the MWAMBASHIP in an accession war against any other contender: Ponde did not yield up his claims to the MWAMBASHIP.

In the dispute of 1924 Kanyanta seized on the significance for authority of Ponde's rejection of subordination. Kanyanta argued that any heritage of illegitimacy in the present situation must be traced to his opponent's own uncle, Ponde, and to Ponde's politics, which were opposed to the control of the ruling MWAMBA. NKULA's own mother's brother, Ponde, and not Kanyanta, had rejected legitimacy and an orderly progression from the lesser office of NKOLEMFUMU to the office of MWAMBA. At the end of his questioning of NKULA, MWAMBA used the notion of legitimate promotion to confront his opponent with a question that NKULA failed to answer. MWAMBA asked, "If Ponde had agreed to go and succeed NKOLEMFUMU, I could not have been sent for?" and NKULA replied, "I do not like to answer this, because I may answer wrongly" (Willis 1924:13). Since Ponde, NKULA's own uncle, had refused to accept this subordinate office from MWAMBA III, Kanyanta reasoned, it was his own fault that Ponde never advanced to become MWAMBA. Kanyanta's question was telling, and NKULA was unable to put in legal terms this earlier struggle between MWAMBA and Ponde.

On this dispute of 1924, which took place before her field research, Richards (1940:101–102) writes:

> Bwalya [NKULA O12] claimed that he was [the] own maternal nephew of the dead chief, Ponde [C10], and Kanyanta [MWAMBA D1] that he came of an older line and that it had now become established that the MWAMBAS always succeeded the CITIMUKULUS. The Government supported the latter claimant, but there seems to have been very little to choose between the legal rights of the two rivals, and the rather complex machinery of tribal deliberation on such matters [a reference to the council of the *bakabilo*] was not called into motion.

I quote Richards' statement because it has itself become a part of the practical as well as theoretical discussions over succession: government officials considered it in deciding later disputes, and Gluckman built on it in his theories of Bemba succession. But nowhere in the magistrate's evidence of the succession dispute of 1924 did Kanyanta claim "that it had now become established that the MWAMBAS always succeeded the CITIMUKULUS." Nor was NKULA's argument simply that he was the own nephew of the late king. Richards' account is right insofar as it hints that NKULA did not deny Kanyanta's seniority in all senses; NKULA unsuccessfully used other Bemba qualifications for succession to legitimize himself and to disqualify MWAMBA.

Both contenders had to adapt Bemba legal categories to fit new political circumstances. Of this Richards gives no hint. She suggests that their claims were of equal validity: "there seems to have been little to choose between the legal rights of the two rivals." Yet, however little it was, it was enough to allow for a meeting of bureaucratic and Bemba reasoning in the dispute. For, along with the British magistrate, the Bemba parties in the dispute of 1924 did come to argue from a premise that, prior to that time princes had rejected—that a prince ought to accept the position of underling in order to advance to the kingship. Because they agreed in the main on the notion of promotion to the Paramount Chiefship from another major post, they could not dispute their claims to the Paramount Chiefship without disputing their rights to the holding of other offices and also the rightful relations between the offices. NKULA, whose arguments wavered about promotion and seniority, lost his case.

Conquest and Political Compromise

Where and why under Northern Rhodesian administration precedents came to be extinguished may be clarified if I here give a brief account of the first appointments made by the British South Africa Company. Irregular succession to kingship and to other offices was legalized by these appointments. They settled disputes involving members of the second, third, and fourth generations in the royal lineage and ended the restriction of office within a single uterine line. Because royals were prevented from excluding or eliminating their collaterals, royals of three generations, each from a different uterine line, came to hold offices at once, and the basis for a rotational system between houses was laid.

The Company's intervention began with Makumba Cimfwembe (B7). He was an "odd man out" at first. His mother was an untitled and young sister of a CANDAMUKULU. In the minority of a son of a CANDAMUKULU— or a MUKUKAMFUMU also, perhaps—he might have had a contingent title to the throne. He was a junior prince, an heir of secondary recourse, depending on circumstances. None of his uterine siblings could or did legally hold any major political office along with him. Nor could any own sister's son of his. Major political office had remained with those of the senior womb, of which he was not a member. His accession to kingship pivotally affected the transfer of political office to another generation of the senior uterine line: the other offices had already passed to his nephews. Such an "odd man out," unsupported by any powerful brothers, was an ideal puppet king for an "outside power." In reality, Makumba Cimfwembe became at once a puppet king and, in a sense, a usurper. For it was not the major chieftains then ruling among the Bemba, the MWAMBA and the MAKASA (The Perpetual "Son" of CITIMUKULU) who appointed this king.[8] To quote Makumba Cimfwembe's contemporary and one of the earliest British authorities on the Bemba, George Pirie (1905–1906:142), "Makumba Chifwimbi, the present [1906] KITIMU-KULU, was assisted to the chieftainship by the British South Africa officials in 1896." Makumba Cimfwembe was weak, ineffectual, senile, and regarded by many as near death on his accession, though in fact he reigned for fifteen years. If it had not been for the continued protection of the British South Africa Company, this CITIMUKULU's frail life might more quickly have been taken in the care of a priest-burier.

To recognize Makumba Cimfwembe's as the most legitimate claims, the administration—or armed company, as it then was—had to recognize them in isolation. It could not, and it did not, consider whether the Bemba had constitutional provisions for the political election of a divine king by the Bemba themselves. The conquerors reserved for themselves the power and the authority to be the political electors. Since an understanding of the foreign politics of this accession is crucial to my analysis, I quote at length from Pirie's account of the conquest of North Eastern Zambia by the British South Africa Company and its campaign to end the slave trade and the influence of Arab slave traders. Pirie records the death, late in 1895, of CITIMUKULU Sampa (B6) and the gradual surrounding of the Bemba with the Company's fortified stations and protected tribal allies. Pirie (1905–1906:143) continues:

> While this was being done, the MWAMBA had sent and taken possession of Maruli village (the burial place of the kings) and driven off the WINI MARULI or priest (SHIMWALULE, the External Priest-Burier) and all the inhabitants.[9] This, I infer, was after MWAMBA's victory over CIKWANDA. Assistance was asked by these people from the official in charge of the new station (Mirongo), and was readily granted. The Awemba were driven off, and the village was given back to the former inhabitants. The MWAMBA was determined to avenge this, and, taking a great quantity of arms and ammunition, set out for Maruli. They reached the Chambezi river, but halted there

8. Makumba Cimfwembe did initially become a contender with the support of the army of another junior royal (C6), who reigned in the south as CIKWANDA. But before a ritual election had taken place, MWAMBA III (C2) defeated CIKWANDA's forces (Brelsford 1944a:8).

9. MWAMBA may have had customary grounds for his action against the SHIM-WALULE: the precedent may have been that a SHIMWALULE buried only one great royal ruler. Brelsford records that "Cimbwi was the SHIMWALULE, but a typical intrigue had been in progress and before the funeral [of B6, who had died at the same time as NKULA [C3] MWAMBA Chisenga told Cimbwi that his nephew Nsufya Metueme was to become SHIMWALULE. Cimbwi fled to the government station [which was then at Mirongo with "Bobo" Young in charge] and laid a complaint" (Brelsford 1942:211). Brelsford continues that Young intervened, deposed the External Priest's nephew, reinstated the External Priest, and later, on other grounds, once more intervened and replaced the External Priest with his nephew again. "Bobo" Young's version is in Young 1953:65–71.

and never attempted to cros. . . . Meanwhile, Makumbu Chifwimbi, who was next in succession to KITIMUKULU, and who had been hiding at a village near Maruli came forth and, laying his claims to the kingship before the Administration, asked their assistance against the MWAMBA, who were conspiring against him. His claims were recognized, and he was declared KITIMUKULU 18th, under the protection of the Administration, a generous subsidy from whom he now enjoys.

Presented with a "capital opportunity," the company officials "on the spot"—Young, McKinnon, and others—took legalistic grounds for extending their influence; and they were not concerned to appreciate the customary nature of political struggles at a ruler's death. This appreciation came later. In 1911, after the administration was established, Hubert Sheane, a former official, did record a customary practice of fighting over a late king's estate in slaves and ivory, a practice that, this former official said, "gave no right to succession" (Sheane and Gouldsbury 1911:20). Though the Willis Enquiry of 1924, too, disregarded the role of an electoral council, this inquiry significantly reflects the replacement of British South Africa Company expediency by the legalistic policy of a later civil administration. Eventually, in the 1940's—when the civil administration had become more rationalized and centralized—district officers were publicly guided by W. V. Brelsford with facts on the political and ritual relations between territorial rulers and priests. And these facts suggest a further dimension of the company's early actions.

When the company fought to become sovereign and to delegate powers to its officials, Bemba and others, it had to wield influence over the rituals and shrines of kingship. There was in reality no separation between the Bemba rulers' participation in the ritual and in the election of a king; one affected the other and was a part of it. According to Brelsford, the MWAMBA had the right and the duty "to give the signal that it was burial time" (Brelsford 1944b:28) and the MAKASA to go "over to the capital as soon as the body of the chief starts its journey to the burial grove at Mwalule and [to stay] in command of the capital until the new paramount is appointed. He [MAKASA] has to make the culminating remark acknowledging that the proposed CHITIMUKULU is his 'father' and therefore the right man to succeed" (Brelsford 1944b:31).

For Bemba rulers the perpetuity of their federal association was symbolized, and in a sense regulated, through their interdependent roles in the rituals of burial and accession. The company radically altered this in the irregular accession of Makumba Cimfwembe. It demonstrated a new overriding sovereignty. This subordination of all territorial rulers to a new authority was demonstrated as the company protected and sustained those who became its delegates, its king-elect and its External Priest Burier, SHIMWALULE. It was helped to effect this change by the French missionary, Msgr. Dupont of the White Fathers. For Msgr. Dupont counselled MAKASA "not to interfere in the struggles over a succession which was being regulated by the English authority and to benefit from the occasion by himself making an act of submission" (Dupont 1937:127; see also Kittler 1957:275–285; Rea 1964:6). MWAMBA III (C2) also sent his petition for peace through Msgr. Dupont and turned to the missionary to secure his domains.

The later stages of the company's intervention struck further at the political authority of powerful princes. The accession of Makumba Cimfwembe was the first stage of intervention. The second stage was the sharing of the great royal and appointing posts among distant and openly hostile relatives. Toward the end of 1898 MWAMBA III (C2) died. His own younger brother, NKULA I (or II, C3) had died in 1895. The rulers' deaths, close on one another, left no royal in the senior uterine line holding a major office. This was an opportunity for powerful junior royals, the brothers CIKWANDA (C6) and Ponde (C10), to fight for the major offices while their younger rivals in the senior line were without the support of any reigning great prince or king. Ponde, who seems to have commanded the strongest forces, did try to capture the MWAMBASHIP, but failed. The late MWAMBA's own sister's sons, young men apparently under thirty,[10] did not drive Ponde off; "Bobo" Young and his company did. Ponde had, in Young's words, "got impatient and thought he had Might so must be Right" (Young 1953:68 475–476). The defeat of Ponde, another contemporary wrote, "was the last of the Awemba trouble" (Pirie 1905–1906:303).

In 1900–1901 the new administration divided the major posts between the different families of opposed relatives: the young Kanyanta (D1) of the senior uterine line was appointed to the post of MWAMBA, and CIKWANDA (C6) of the junior line was recognized as NKULA. It was only when the British South Africa Company took charge that uterine princes lost a monopoly over the greatest among the royal territorial posts—the CITIMUKULUSHIP and the MWAMBASHIP and the NKULASHIP. This monopoly was first broken by the intervention of the company officials at the accession of Makumba Cimfwembe; and it was the company's officials who prevented a set of royal and powerful full brothers from monopolizing the electoral posts, the MWAMBASHIP and the NKULASHIP. The legal wars of the new administration grew out of the company's wars of conquest. And here the Bemba had to make constitutional compromises and had to extinguish legal precedents.

10. D2 was born about 1876, according to a guess made in 1910 and recorded in the Mpika District Notebook KSD 4/1:205; to guess from their deaths in the 1940's, D1 and his siblings were probably under thirty in 1898. D1 might have made other claims for himself. He is reported to have been born in the early 1860's and to have spoken "of those memorable days when as a young boy he sat quietly and watched his great uncle negotiate with the explorer [Livingstone]" (Thomas 1959:478).

The Legitimation of Administrative Change

It has been suggested that learned authorities on the Bemba, Brelsford and Richards, disagreed because each authority worked mainly in one or other half of the country, under different "branches" of the royal house, and thus each authority correctly reported only the claims of a single faction (Gluckman 1963a:14, 98–101). However, Richards' field work seems to have been too extensive to have been bound by such local or factional bias.[11] The suggestion of local bias neglects the more significant contrast between Brelsford and Richards. In 1940, and before District Officer Brelsford wrote his accounts of the Bemba, Richards observed that there were "Government officials who naturally prefer a fixed system of succession to the discussion of rival candidates' rights that seems to have been the older procedure" (Richards 1940:101).

In this period of indirect rule, Richards recommended extending the council to include "representative elders attached to the territorial chiefs in the full council of the CITIMUKULU's *bakabilo*." She argued that the time for "the appointment of a body of younger men, probably better educated, but without that tribal tradition of service" would come subsequently (Richards 1935:22, 23). Eventually, in her article of 1940, she argued against continuing "to deny to the commoner the experience of administration he will require to have in the future" (Richards 1940:120). In his *Guide to District Officers*, Brelsford, as he himself frankly declares from the outset, points to tendencies in Bemba history that may be made to serve the interests of efficient indirect rule, "tendencies that might simplify and stabilise the succession to the Paramountcy" (1944a:2). Brelsford's *Guide* is no merely academic exercise in theory: Brelsford does indulge in influential and prophetic "theorizing," as he terms it (Brelsford 1944a:17). But it is "theorizing" that events, in part, disallow.

Various though its guises may be,[12] there is basically one central issue over which Brelsford challenges Richards. It is an issue of vital interest to an administering officer such as Brelsford and of objective concern to an anthropologist such as Richards. As a responsible yet lower-echelon officer of the administration, Brelsford views as a danger Bemba tendencies toward local consolidation of power and sectional independence. This attitude is sharply evident in the following remarks (Brelsford 1944a:23) as well as throughout his *Guide*.

> The desire to give the branch of MUKUKAMFUMU one or more of the higher posts . . . was the reason openly given in 1934 when Bwalya NKULA IV D12

11. Richards details her "visits to different villages from one end of the country to another" (Richards 1939:11).
12. See especially Brelsford 1944a:11, where he begins his argument with Richards on the "sequence of Chiefly names," and the following pages, where he misreads his own evidence on the king-bearing titles.

died [and when D14 and not D5 succeeded, as the Willis inquiry had recommended]. Such a reason emphasizes the dichotomy of families, and Dr. Richards' statement that certain chieftainships are being stabilised in certain branches of this family may be true in a limited way such as this. But it is a dangerous argument for the present junior branches to press because if carried to logical conclusions it would freeze such chieftainships as the NKULA and SHIMUMBI in their own lines and tend to imply that they could not leave them to pass on to the MWAMBA.

Brelsford, and not Richards, is concerned with a universal "direct and straight-forward" (Brelsford 1944a:26) rota of office that locally entrenches no "branch of the royal family" and also does not continually throw up a "series of old, conservative chiefs" (Brelsford 1944a:19). It is in the interest of indirect rule, from the viewpoint of a lower-echelon officer, to bring forward young men. They can be educated; they may become more efficient and less resistant to carrying out progressive government policy; they have no entrenchment in a local following and may primarily represent the administration to their people.

For the administration, the manipulation of constitutional traditions was essential to progress.[13] During the early 1940's, and particularly during the interregnum after the death of Paramount Chief Kanyanta (D1), the government carried out its policy of amalgamating and rationalizing Bemba territorial units. As in succession to office, the government required, to quote Brelsford (1944a:1): ". . . both opportunity and precedent for exercising influence." It required a review of what had been sanctified by tradition. One expert definition seemed to fix certain territorial claims. In 1944 Brelsford (1944b:2) wrote: "Dr. Richards fully develops the spiritual association of land and spirits but there is a more practical aspect that has recently been emphasised and may become more important in the future."

Brelsford appealed to history for proof that the proposed policy of amalgamation was closer to tradition than any other method and thus not newly subversive of Bemba "spiritual associations." He cited, aptly, parts of past struggles and he commented, "The point that has not been emphasised is that history seems to show that the association was only permanent when it was backed by political control of the land" (Brelsford 1944b:4).

Brelsford did argue, in the main, that administrative changes had to be made for the sake of efficiency and economic progress: "There is little doubt that in the future the rigid preservation of chiefs' boundaries is going to become an increasing hindrance to many administrative changes. These boundaries cut across agricultural schemes, demarcation of Game

13. For published evidence on Brelsford's and others' participation in the disputes involving SHIMWALULE, CITIMUKULU, NKULA, and NKWETO, see Brelsford 1942:212–219 and 1944b:15, 46–47. In another essay I discuss king-making under British Colonial administration and the role of the priestly keepers of the symbols of mystical authority, the *bakabilo*.

Reserves and plans for closer settlement, already, and in my opinion too much stress is laid upon the theory of the sanctity and the spiritual attachment of chiefs to their areas" (Brelsford 1944b:7).

This administrator did not justify reform on purely technical grounds. He argued further that tradition, in any event, had always bent to those with ultimate political control of the land. The very names of Bemba geographical units, Brelsford wrote (1944b:9):

> show how one chiefly area has been divided between several chiefs and thus give an indication of how they might be amalgamated on traditional lines. And, from the view of administration, the few incidents quoted above show that the system of chiefly land tenure was in the past extremely flexible. Areas could be split up or divided and given new names: so that if we insist too much, in our political developments, on the sacredness and rigidity of chiefs' areas we are emphasising a textbook theory, not a traditional practice.

"A textbook theory, not a traditional practice;" this contrast—which does not name any textbook—has a political force. It legitimizes the revision of policy from one period of indirect rule to another phase of local government under an alien administration; and it liberates that administration from being so hidebound. It must now be officially recognized that Bemba have always been tradition manipulators—or the administration itself may become hindered and hidebound by its own creation. When ossified, custom or history becomes a fetter upon the actions of rulers as well as ruled.

Bemba have been contentious, at points, as to what have been their precedents and which aspects of past events have been precedents for the present. Along with the British officials, Bemba have been contradictious; their *rules* have not been logically contradictory. Historically, a new legal basis for struggles over succession to hereditary office, for pretenders to assert opposed claims, developed under British administration; and this basis was consistent with the absence of a logical contradiction in the rules of matrilineal succession. The evidence from the Bemba of Zambia suggests that one set of rules no longer specified the next heir to the throne—first, because precedents were amended from one reign to the next; second, because there was major constitutional change in the allegiance of subjects to rulers and to the state and also in the allegiance of rulers to each other; and third, because there emerged a new sovereignty to override what was a federal polity of dominions.

Under colonial administration, Bemba extended their legal categories of succession and appointment and included concepts of rightful promotion from major office to the kingship. The use of Bemba constitutional traditions for bureaucratic purposes admitted of compromise between hereditary rulers and their alien superiors in the civil services, for tribal administration was not to be rationalized in terms of a simple hierarchy of authority and a uniform mode of advancement to superior office.

PART III

Case Studies of
Law in Western Societies

INTRODUCTION BY VILHELM AUBERT

There is a danger in attempting to spell out the differences between ethnography (social anthropology) and sociology—the danger of perpetuating unnecessary cleavages and of furnishing a systematic rationale for what are merely historically conditioned divergences. If this is true of the two disciplines, ethnography and sociology, it is also true of the two branches of these social sciences that deal specifically with law. However, the differences in approach, in the choice of topics, in methods, in concepts, and in theories are sufficiently marked to make it unrealistic to pretend that the two fields are really one. They ought to become one. Until such time it is useful to pay some attention to differences in the traditions and circumstances that have influenced the development of the two disciplines.

The methods and concepts of ethnography have been shaped to a large extent by the concern with preliterate, tribal, or "folk" societies. From these foreign cultures the ethnographer has recently brought his tools back to his home society and applied them there with considerable success. A similar process has been initiated in the sociological study of law, but it will not necessarily run parallel to the general transference of ethnographic methods from tribal to modern societies. In order to elucidate this point, it is useful to look at the functions of a social-science approach to law in different societies.

In a modern society law is an old academic discipline that has produced a great deal of empirical knowledge about the operation of the national legal system. Doctrinal law does not have description, or the formulation of social regularities, as its main task. Such knowledge has nevertheless been produced by legal scholars and has also been derived from the systematizing efforts of legislators and judges. Thus, in a modern society the position of observer and recorder of the legal system is already occupied when the social scientist enters the field. He cannot simply go ahead and report "facts" in the legal area. Such an effort would often merely duplicate work that has already been done, and usually by someone more qualified to understand what he observed.

The previous presence of a well-developed field of scholarship is probably a major reason why it has taken so long for a sociology of law to develop, and why it is still making such halting progress. In order for the sociological approach to be accepted as legitimate in this area, an intensive philosophical debate on "the nature of law" has to be conducted. For some time it seemed as if the sociology of law would never emerge as an empirical science out of the essentially philosophical and programmatic "legal realism." Quite apart from the more fundamental doubts about the accessibility of law to an empirical approach, the presence of the formidable analytic tools of the lawyers may have scared off many social scientists. It is less rewarding to apply new tools to a field crowded with knowledgeable professionals than to be the first on virgin territory.

The early ethnographers of law were the first to acquire any knowledge whatever about the legal institutions of primitive societies, often the first to discover that they had legal institutions at all. There was no competition with lawyers and not much need to legitimate the empirical approach. For doctrinal law is a parochial science in the sense that it is of little concern to the traditional lawyer how other legal systems are treated, as long as his own system is approached with the proper respect. Lawyers who were serving in colonial areas had reason to be grateful to the field ethnographer for collecting information on legal customs in tribal societies. Far from constituting a threat to lawyers, the ethnographer aided them in their legal work.

One aspect of the sociology of modern law that seemed threatening, at least initially, was that it directed attention to the legal personnel. Sociology of law became to a large extent the study of legislators, judges, administrators, and practicing lawyers. The servants of the law were treated with no more, and sometimes with less, respect than other people subjected to scrutiny by the social sciences. Although the term "breakfast jurisprudence" was never very fitting, it seemed aptly to symbolize the "debunking" aspect of some early attempts in the sociology of law.

Insofar as social science is used to study the habits—the beliefs and customs—of the ordinary man, cooperation with more traditional types of professionals and rulers is relatively unproblematical. When social research directs the attention to the rulers themselves and to the normative structure—the values and institutions of the home society—the relationship becomes more uneasy. There are several reasons why the attention of the sociologists of law has been directed precisely toward these aspects of their own society. Sociologists of law have, for example, been much concerned with the behavior of judges, simply because the legal tradition itself has tended to define law in terms of court decisions. If you want to study law, study the judiciary. And if you want to study it sociologically, study those aspects that the lawyers themselves have ignored—for example, how judges are influenced by extralegal social factors.

If the sociologist of law directed his attention to the beliefs and customs of ordinary people, as much early ethnography of law did, he would find himself competing with all kinds of social scientists. If he were studying the customs of marriage, sex, and family life, he would, for example, become indistinguishable from a family sociologist. Insofar as there has been an attempt to delimit a field for legal sociology in a modern society, it has seemed reasonable in terms of a fruitful division of labor to stay away from such studies. In early ethnography of law this division of labor could not be practiced.

Lately there has been an attempt to define the "distinctly legal" institutions of preliterate societies. This has been undertaken in several ways. One method is to analyze "trouble cases," to look for the types of disputes that in a modern society are handled by the legal machinery, and to discover how they are handled in a preliterate society. More generally this approach leads to a search for mechanisms of conflict resolution in preliterate as well as in modern societies, unbound by any a priori definition of "law." Another approach in the study of preliterate legal institutions is to use Western legal concepts for the purpose of revealing the covert meaning of conflict-solving behavior.

In recent years there has been a certain convergence between the ethnography of law and the sociology of law, and there has been a certain amount of mutual influence. As mentioned, the modern approach to trouble cases and conflict resolution within the ethnography of law has been influenced by modern law and sociology of law. Conversely, the sociological approach to the study of the legal institutions of the home society has been influenced by the approach of the ethnographers to primitive institutions.

Doctrinal legal research has had the practical purpose of providing decision-makers with the tools needed to reach decisions on an immensely varied assortment of problems, usually with limited time and resources at their disposal. This explains the pervasive normativism of traditional legal research, a normativism that has had important implications for the direction of research. For one thing, it makes the question of rates relatively unimportant, as long as one or a few good precedents can be analyzed. Since the precedents are primarily to be found in supreme-court decisions, these decisions constitute the universe from which empirical materials are drawn, while the actual practices of the lower courts and of administrative agencies with semi-judicial functions are left un-mapped. Insofar as judges' opinions have been scrutinized, the normative purpose of the research has made it uninteresting to follow up on the influence from factors outside the recognized sources of positive law.

What differentiates the sociology of law from doctrinal law is the removal of the former from the task of preparing for decision-making. Once this pressure is removed, it becomes possible to investigate rates, to count, to tabulate, and to correlate. Once the emphasis is put not only upon what happens in court, but also upon how often it happens, the attention is drawn to the lower courts and to agencies that fall outside the judiciary but that perform parallel tasks in the administration of justice and in the settlement of disputes. The response of the citizen to the law becomes an interesting empirical problem, and no mere matter of speculation for lawyers, who include references to the sense of justice or to public opinion in their technique of arguing. When the behavior of judges, of civil servants, and of ordinary citizens is to be explained, it appears arbitrary to limit the attention to influences that are normatively respectable. The operation of interests, passions, and prejudices becomes a legitimate concern for legal research.

Empirical studies of this kind, with their emphasis upon stochastic processes, can be oriented toward aims that are more or less removed from the concerns of the legal profession. As representing two ideal types we may speak about a lawyer's sociology of law and a sociologist's sociology of law. The study of the decisions of the lower courts may well come to influence the decision-making process itself, directly or indirectly, through legislative or administrative interference with the functioning of the judiciary. A charting of the tendencies in the decision-making process cannot very well go unnoticed by judges who will pass on similar issues in the future, whether the charts and tables establish precedents or not.

From the sociologist's point of view the field of law offers many opportunities for studying phenomena that occur in, as well as outside of, legal institutions. The pervasive problems of conflict and conflict resolution are central in legal studies, as they are also in the study of racial tensions, industrial relations, and international affairs. In legal doctrine many of the problems of conflict resolution are already dealt with, explicitly or tacitly. The sociologist who comes to the law comes to a set table. Some of the disadvantages of this circumstance have been mentioned above, but there are also advantages. In the available body of legal rules, with their preambles and commentaries, and in the law records the sociologists can find a vast body of materials where conflicts and modes of conflict resolution are already classified and analyzed. Though the classification and analysis are not carried out on the basis of sociological principles, they may nevertheless aid the sociologist a great deal in achieving mastery of the data.

The lawyer may become attracted to the sociology of law primarily because the social sciences offer methods and techniques of data collection and statistical analysis. He needs these new tools in order to prepare legislation or to formulate doctrinal points of view in areas where new legal rules are developing and where the supreme court has not formulated clear precedents. The basic scheme of reasoning and arguing may, however, remain relatively unmodified by the encounter with sociology. The sociologist, for his part, is also often attracted by some technical advantage inherent in studying legal materials. But the sociologist may have other reasons for studying legal institutions, of which two will be singled out for mention in this context.

Sociology is concerned with the study of values—of the preferences and evaluations that underlie basic structural arrangements in a society. Presumably many of these values are embodied in the law, in substantive rules as well as in the guiding procedural principles. In this respect there is little or no difference betwen the tasks of the ethnography of law and those of the sociology of law. Whether the scene of research is a moot in a tribal society or a court session in an industrialized society, the principles and values according to which the dispute is handled and the final decision are made may be equally suggestive of pervasive structural features of the society under scrutiny. From this point of view the study of law is a diagnostic tool, applied to a part of society that may be particularly sensitive to values.

The second major reason for sociological concern with law is of a different order. It is sometimes striking how much the vocabuldarly of sociology resembles the language of law. The emphasis upon rights and expectations, upon predictability and sanctions within sociology directs the attention to the sophisticated analyses of these concepts within the tradition of legal scholarship. Hohfield's (1923) conceptual scheme was rooted in this tradition, but it would not seem too odd as part of a general sociological analysis of social interaction. It seems likely that in the future, when the need for maintaining independence and originality has lessened, social theorists will come to use these kinds of legal analyses as a resource in the development and refinement of sociological conceptual schemes.

The last point illustrates an interesting duality in the relationship between law and sociology. Lawyers are the subjects of sociologists, but they are simultaneously collaborators—even teachers and mentors. Legal thinking and methods of decision-making are an interesting subject matter for sociological analysis. In this respect the sociology of law could be construed as a branch of the sociology of knowledge, dealing with the social circumstances under which certain modes of thought are applied to solve problems. Insofar, however, as sociology is using legal analyses to improve upon its own analytical tools, the relationship shifts from one of observer-subject to one of partnership. Although this duality is particularly marked in the relations between law and sociology, it is probably a much more general phenomenon, derived from the social role of the sociologist. The legal scholar has a similarly dual role in relation to his subjects. He observes and describes the judge and the legislator, but he also gives advice to them, and he is always in some sense bound by them.

There is a difference between the use of law as a diagnostic device for revealing value assumptions or principles of social interaction and the study of legal institutions in their own right. It is to the latter kind of work that the term sociology of law can most confidently be applied, although the division of the social sciences into such specialties is always a mixed blessing. The sociology of law in this more narrow sense has three or four foci: the legislative process, judicial decisions, the legal profession, and the administrative process. Whether, or to what extent, problems of administration and bureaucracy ought to be dealt with in a context of legal sociology may be doubtful. As two of the papers in this section suggest, however, the exclusion of administrative problems from the sociology of law might lead to erroneous conceptions of the way in which legal rules and the decision-making machinery actually function in a modern society.

Of the following papers, Kay's deals specifically with the rule-making process. It does so in a way that should illustrate to the sociologist that the functional approach can be made operationally testable. A set of rules is enacted and put into practice. The consequences of the decisions rendered are observed, and it is described how those responsible for the application of the rules react and propose changes in the rules. New rules are enacted. Usually when a sociologist makes statements about the functions of a certain social item, these are based upon speculations or upon a limited knowledge of the antecedents, correlates, or consequences of the item in question. Very rarely is he able to show the feedback from consequences to causes, the way institutions produce effects that either become the causes of perpetuation of the institution or which cause changes.

Among the various possible definitions of the term "function" here is one that permits the social analyst to remain empirical throughout the analysis. The future fate of the social item under scrutiny provides the test of functional hypotheses. Kay's paper ought to show that legislation offers particularly good opportunities for carrying out a certain kind of functional analysis. True, the example selected is unusually simple and clear-cut. But this is in accordance with the methodological stratagem of trying out propositions in laboratories that offer simplified conditions.

Legislators provide the social sciences with many such laboratory situations.

There is the danger of an exaggerated emphasis upon a narrow range of rational reasons and motives inherent in a functional approach that takes the reasoning of rule-makers and law-enforcement personnel at face value. On this point Sykes' paper has a message. Although essentially concerned with the enforcement of the law, rather than with law-making, it bears on the latter as well, since the operation of the decision-making machinery is regulated by law and is discussed in terms of general legal ideals. Sykes further deals with an institution that, in its present state, produces undesirable consequences—delay in court. Why the failure to develop remedies that could do away with such consequences? The answer is sought, not within a narrow range of rational motives for opposing change and preserving the status quo, but rather in a variety of social factors—unplanned, and to some extent unrecognized—that combine to perpetuate the perceived malaise of congestion. While the lawyer Kay explains a piece of social change in terms that are derived from, and readily understood by, the subjects of her inquiry, the sociologist Sykes explains resistance to change in terms that may well be alien to his subjects. While the former deals with manifest functions, the latter deals largely with latent functions. This contrast is not simply because of differences in professional orientation, but because of the very different nature of the two phenomena explained in the two papers.

That the explicit or implicit functionalist approach is common to all three papers in this section is certainly not accidental. Anyone who deals with institutions of law is met with the claims of the legal personnel, legislators as well as judges, that they act purposefully and rationally. Of course most individuals tend to make such claims in a variety of situations. But legal personnel claim that they act purposefully and rationally on behalf of society as such, not merely as individuals or as representatives of subsystems. This claim, inherent in the legal process, makes it well-nigh inevitable that a sociological approach to these problems will represent some brand of functionalism.

The three papers share a certain concern about the functioning of the courts in a modern society. Sykes discusses why it is difficult for the courts to reform themselves so as to become more efficient. So does Aubert in the emphasis put upon the "flight" from the courts to other conflict-solving devices. Kay's paper deals with one of those administrative agencies that is taking over judicial tasks and discusses specifically the division of labor between the judiciary and administrative agencies.

Although the papers converge on these points, their divergencies are probably equally apparent to the reader. If they jointly illustrate anything, it is that the sociology of law is far from being a unified field with a commonly accepted approach. Further they may raise doubts about whether it is at all advisable to look forward to a consolidation of such dispersed efforts into a discipline. The sociology of law has relatively little internal consistency, beyond that which is common to an empirical social-science approach. In a modern society law is a phenomenon with ramifications too wide to become the subject matter of a neatly delimited scientific discipline.

As for the future relationship between law and the social sciences, the three papers seem to suggest the need for a more sustained concern with the problems of conflict solution in modern society. Sykes' and Aubert's papers suggest that there are serious limitations to the conflict-solving capacities of the courts. Kay makes the further point that some conflicts may be insoluble, and that the problem is not one of dispensing with them but of living with them. In the task of solving conflicts—and particularly conflicts of values—the developments in science and technology have not led to any breakthrough. Conflicts that prove resistant to other devices of conflict solution end up in courts or quasi-judicial agencies, where they are handled in a way that often appears to be unscientific and has overtones of magic.

Thurman Arnold (1935) made the point that the courts, and the theories surrounding the courts, function as a repository of social ideals that can neither be reconciled nor discarded. For the elucidation of such normative tensions in the social systems of modern societies, a study of the functioning of the courts and of the many quasi-judicial agencies seems to be a commendable approach.

If it is true that the courts and the quasi-judicial agencies in a modern society provide favorable opportunities for the investigation of values and tensions between values, this must also be true with respect to legislation. For the sociologist, the distinction made by legal philosophers between law in books and law in action has struck a responsive chord. In consequence, perhaps, there has been a neglect of the obvious: that some of the enactments are seriously intended and widely abided by. Whenever that is so, society itself has produced an important piece of self-description. The distinction between normative law and actual social regularities is an important one, but it may become blurred when ideals and practice correspond fairly well to each other.

To the social scientist concerned about the social functions of knowledge, of forecasting and rational planning, the legislative process and its aftermath provide unique opportunities to gain new insight. The basic problems concerning the interplay between science and morals, the ought and the is, appear in the legislative process in a way that may render them researchable. On the one hand one may observe how the available knowledge about social mechanisms at times is manipulated by the legislators to achieve ends that have no connection with the implications of the available knowledge, as these appear to an outside spectator. The decision-maker reduces knowledge to tools of argumentation. On the other hand it may sometimes be observed how legislators through their efforts render predictable important areas of social action not by mere insight and knowledge, but by edict. Quite apart from specific findings, a closer scrutiny of the legislative process on the part of sociologists would lead to a disturbing rethinking of the social function of the social sciences.

The conflict-solving agencies and legislation having been dealt with, there remains the important subject matter of the legal profession. A rationale for studying the legal profession and its subculture is suggested in Aubert's paper. In the study of law as a profession the lines of distinction between sociology of law and other types of sociology are necessarily blurred. Many of the problems of the modern professions—recruitment, status, specialization, ethics—are general and can best be approached on a comparative basis. In order to make interesting statements about lawyers, they must be compared to someone else, most profitably probably to some other professionals. The recruitment problem leads back to the general problems of the universities, for example. Far from being a disadvantage, this need to join forces with other kinds of social scientists makes it easier to set the legal institutions in a broader social perspective. If there is any sense in searching for the distinctly legal elements in rule-making, in conflict resolution, and in the work of professional lawyers, the task has to be approached by a comparative method.

Law as a Way of Resolving Conflicts: The Case of a Small Industrialized Society

Law has manifold functions in a modern society. Although the problems of law and those of conflict resolution often merge in preliterate legal institutions, this overlap is only partial in modern legal institutions. The growth of legislation in industrialized societies suggests that law is used as an instrument to further many interests other than peace-keeping and conflict resolution. Not infrequently legislation creates or intensifies social conflicts, a consequence that may even have been anticipated by the legislator and accepted as a necessary social cost in the efforts to further an action program. Nevertheless, conflict resolution has remained an important concern of legal institutions. Whatever the purpose of new legislation, the instruments and the language employed have been shaped through a development in which peace-keeping and conflict resolution have always loomed large.

The purpose of this paper is to discuss some trends in the development of institutionalized methods of conflict resolution in a small industrialized society (Norway). As a basis for this discussion a scheme of interpretation will be presented consisting in a typology of interpersonal conflicts and a corresponding typology of conflict-resolving devices. Two types of conflicts and two types of conflict resolution are contrasted. It is not claimed, however, that in their pure form these types correspond to actual instances of conflict resolution. Normally the elements of one of the two models are intermingled with some elements of the other. The polar types serve merely as reference points for the analysis of the social functions of empirically observable methods of conflict resolution.

Conflicts of Interest (Competition) and Negotiation

A conflict of interest derives from a situation of scarcity. Ego and Alter want the same thing, but there is not enough of it to satisfy both. Such a basis of conflicts is very common in interpersonal relationships. In most selling and buying there is some conflict of interests; the customer would like to acquire the commodity at a low price, and the seller would like to obtain a better price.

Even if a source of conflict is present in commercial dealings—marketing and selling—the conflicting interests are not wholly incompatible. It is true only to some extent that the gains of one party must become the losses of the other. There usually exists an area where the interests are overlapping—that is, where both parties have an interest in the completion of the transaction. The relationship between Ego and Alter is characterized by partly incompatible and partly overlapping interests.

In relations between Ego and Alter where interests are partly incompatible and partly overlapping, *negotiation* presents itself as a normal procedure to resolve the conflict. Since each party has something he may gain from the adversary, the actions of one are calculated to extract concessions from the other. Ego will attempt to motivate Alter to increase his contribution or to reduce his demands by a promise to offer Alter some reciprocal concession. Ego and Alter search for a solution through a compromise. A fundamental motive underlying such negotiations and determining the strategies chosen by the parties is the wish to minimize the risk of a maximal loss (the minimax principle—see Luce and Raiffa 1957:118), leading to the sacrifice of the chance to obtain the maximal gains in order to achieve security against inviting the worst (loss).

In negotiations concerning a sale, a loan, or some other business transaction, Ego and Alter are apt to behave more or less in accordance with the minimax principle. Since very often the least desirable alternative is that no transaction will take place, both parties are motivated to make concessions and yield in relation to their initial preferences. They may be willing to concede some point even though concession may bring them to feel that the terms of exchange are becoming unfair—that is, contrary to the demands of justice. By refraining from the insistence upon moral rights, they have smoothed the way for a negotiable settlement.

When a conflict is being solved through negotiations between the parties, it is not necessary to arrive at any agreement regarding the factual origin and development of the conflict or regarding the norms that are applicable. Consequently, a great freedom of movement is bestowed on the negotiators. Strictly speaking, the parties need not reach agreement on anything beyond settlement of a point where the demands of both sides meet—that is, where they would rather accept the solution offered them than face a broken relationship and no agreement at all. The advantage of negotiated solutions is that they need not leave any marks on the normative order of society. Since the solution does not become a precedent for later solutions to similar conflicts, the adversaries need not fear the general consequences of the settlement. However, from another point of view this is a weakness of such a settlement because a kind of predictability is often needed that would result if the solution could be interpreted as the application of a norm generalizable to other similar cases.

So far we have dealt with conflicts where the interests are partly overlapping and partly contradictory. There are, however, also situations where the incompatibility of the interests is total with regard to a specific set of values. What is a gain for one side must necessarily appear as a loss to the other side. When gains and losses are evened out in this fashion, the relationship has been described as a zero-sum game (Luce and Raiffa 1957:71–72). The competition as such does not generate value; it merely serves to distribute existing values on the basis of an either-or choice, where a benefit on one side reappears as a cost on the other side. Such conflicts are not so readily solved by means of negotiations between the contestants.

In economic transactions a relationship may be transformed from a non-zero-sum game to a zero-sum game if disastrous events intervene in the relationship of exchange. This transformation may occur if the commodity representing Ego's contribution disappears after the contract is signed but before Alter has received the commodity.

It seems that negotiations are a less than adequate means of solving conflicts where the interests are contradictory to the extent that gains and losses must cancel each other—where, in other words, we are faced with a zero-sum game. In such situations the parties may bring the case to the courts and demand a legal settlement. The courts will then solve the conflict in accordance with principles very different from those governing commercial negotiations.

A conflict of interests does not presuppose a disagreement between Ego and Alter over values or factual matters. On the contrary, competition rests upon consensus in the evaluation of a scarce good. Jealousy springs precisely from an unfortunate consensus over the value of a woman. Nor would rivalry over positions of leadership arise if the contestants had not tended to evaluate incumbency of the position in rather similar terms. This agreement tends to draw Ego and Alter together; the conflict thus emphasizes their communality of value premises.

Conflicts of Values and Dissensions

A conflict of values means that Ego and Alter have different attitudes to a value. They are in disagreement over the valuation of some benefit or burden. The disagreements over factual matters concerning what has actually happened or the explanation of facts are quite as important as this normative dissension. Dissension over values or facts does not necessarily imply that Ego and Alter clash with each other in a conflict. Rather, the disagreement may tend to keep them away from each other and may reduce the probability of a clash if for other reasons they are not brought in touch with each other. This fact notwithstanding, dissension often leads to conflict behavior.

Conflicts about values or about the truth of facts are different from conflicts of interest and are not in general amenable to the same types of resolution. Conflicts over values and facts are more public. A solution implies a stand on what has actually happened or on what norms ought to be applied to conflicts of this kind. This has implications for the solution of other, similar disagreements. Actors other than those directly engaged have a stake in the outcome because a certain definition of the truth of a factual matter or of a point of value can come to mean something for them also. For these reasons and others such dissension over facts or values is not so readily amenable to negotiation between the conflicting parties. The antagonists have no private rights in values or in the truth of the matter at issue. Compromise does not present itself as the obvious solution, as it so often does in commercial negotiation.

Disagreements over facts or values may be settled in many different ways. A third party usually participates in the solution in one form or another. Feuds between politicians are solved directly or indirectly by the electorate, or occasionally by appeal to the court of history operating through the judgment of posterity. In principle at least debates between scientists are solved by reference to objective methods that may be applied by other persons as well as by the protagonists themselves. Conflicts over guilt and responsibility in private matters may be solved by delegating the decision to a court of law.

Verdicts and Litigation

When a case is dealt with in court, the conflict between the parties has been formulated as a controversy over facts and/or norms applicable to the case. In criminal proceedings the court decides whether the defendant has committed the crime he is accused of, and in civilian litigation it must decide whether a contract of specified content has actually been entered into or whether a certain amount of injury has been caused. The court is further invited to decide what norms have validity and what inferences are to be drawn from the norms when the specific suit at hand is subsumed under them. Irrespective of the source of the conflict between the parties, it must be formulated in court as a disagreement over norms and/or over factual matters.

The verdict of the court has an either/or character; the decision is based upon a single, definite conception of what has actually taken place and upon a single interpretation of the legal norms. When a conflict of interest passes from the stage of negotiation to that of litigation, one of the parties must be prepared to suffer a total loss. He runs the risk that the judge will make no allowance for his demands and will decide wholly in favor of his adversary. In addition, the loser may have to pay the legal costs. This raises the question of why all civilian suits are not settled out of court after negotiations.

One reason is that there may be considerable uncertainty about who is more likely to win the case, and both adversaries overestimate their chances of victory in the legal battle. Aggression and unwillingness to meet the antagonist in negotiations may also play their part. Some feel that concession in the course of negotiations is a symptom of moral weakness and that a defeat at the hands of the judge is preferable. If Ego represents interests that he shares with others—like his family, colleagues, or partners—he may prefer to run the risk of an adverse verdict rather than accept some voluntary sacrifice, since he might be rebuked by his relatives or colleagues for having sold out. If the government, an insurance company, or a bank is party to a conflict, its desire to achieve certainty with respect to future claims may gain overriding importance and reduce the significance of a possible loss in the present suit.

There are, in other words, many reasons why adversaries choose to accept the increased risk implicit in litigation, provided that the prospects of a compromise solution are dim. However, the fear of an either/or solution if the conflict is brought before a judge is, no doubt, one of the most important reasons people attempt to settle their controversies out of court. In the course of such settlements no one needs to take a definite stand on what is right and what is wrong or on who is responsible, nor is it necessary to find the one proper interpretation of the relevant legal rules. This flexibility gives the negotiations a somewhat less moralistic flavor, a more matter-of-fact character, than that associated with litigation.

The Legal Model of Conflict Resolution

The either/or aspect of legal thinking is linked to a whole cluster of elements in the decision-making process. A subculture has developed within the legal profession through a very long tradition. The patterning of elements in the decision-making process constitutes a subculture in the sense that changes in one element tend to induce changes also in other elements. Studies have shown that modifications on some points in the legal process, without corresponding alterations throughout the whole pattern, cause serious problems and produce dysfunctional consequences.[1] Some of the most important characteristics of the legal model for handling human affairs will be briefly enumerated.

One aspect of legal decisions that is closely linked to their either/or character is the marked orientation toward the past. The major legal task is to establish guilt or some other operative fact, from which legal consequences follow. They do not "follow," however, in the sense that the established facts are assumed to furnish a reliable basis for making predictions. The occurrence of a crime may actually lead to a certain type of penalty, but the vast amount of undetected, hidden criminality shows that such a prediction would run a great risk of being falsified. Legal rules that establish a relationship between a crime and a penalty must, obviously, have a different basis; they establish that it would be normatively right to apply a certain sanction, not that the process is going to happen.

From the preceding it follows that law is primarily not concerned with causal processes, nor with phenomena that have a dimension in time. "Causality" as a legal concept is something rather different from the causality, correlation, or invariance of the natural or social scientist. In the final analysis the concept of "causality" in law turns out to hinge upon a normative criterion. If an act shall be taken to have caused some damage, for which the actor is to answer in terms of criminal or civil liability, this depends upon the reasonableness of expecting the actor to foresee and forestall the damage.

The absence, or the distortion, of scientific causal explanations in law is related to the modest place of utilitarian considerations in the judicial process. The judge is far from free to select the proper means to reach preferred goals. Insofar as legislators indulge in utilitarian thinking, and they often do, they must get their advice not from law but from the causal sciences. When the judge argues in terms of means selected to produce desired ends, he is not held responsible for erroneous predictions, as he would be if he were wrong about legal rules or about the past facts of the case. The task of the judge is above all to interpret the existing legal rules and to subsume established facts under them. The legal decision follows from this process of subsumption, although not as neatly as it has sometimes been claimed in traditional jurisprudence. The judge seeks to establish a balance between that which is general

1. See, for example, Thomas Mathiesen and Vilhelm Aubert (1964).

and that which is unique in the case. He has a double task. On the one hand he is assumed to reaffirm a normative invariance in the relationship between operative facts and legal sanctions. The courts are producers of predictability, real or illusory, insofar as they, for example, leave the impression that anyone who has committed the crime of drunken driving is put in prison. But the furtherance of predictability, including deterrence, is only one of the functions of the judge. He is also assumed to mete out justice in the individual case, paying due respect to the variability of human problems and conflicts.

If the judge wants conformity to the standards of concrete justice, he must be on his guard not to make the future behavior of the judiciary too easily predictable. Otherwise he would either tie the hands of other judges so as to make it difficult to pay enough attention to individual justice, or he would increase the likelihood of falsified predictions. Falsifiable propositions are admired in the causal sciences, but in law falsification is taken to imply normative errors. For this reason, among others, the opinions of judges are normally written in a somewhat individualizing style, which tends to make each decision unique, if only on some minor point. However modest the feature that makes the case unique, it may serve a future judge as a peg on which he can hang his reservations against treating the case as a binding precedent if he finds the verdict unacceptable.

With these elements that put law in a certain contrast to the natural and the social sciences goes a lack of specialization upon any particular aspect of the physical or social world. The lawyer is in this respect a generalist. His specialization lies in his method, not in his subject matter. Insofar as he is an expert on certain categories of facts, these are the products of his colleagues in the legislative and judicial branch of government. The lawyer is an expert upon what other lawyers have done and do. In this sense the lawyers are unique in the academic world. As professionals they perceive society as filtered through the rules and decisions produced collectively by the legal profession over the centuries.

This "professional self-analysis" has also put its mark upon the lawyer's conception of equality. The structure of legal thinking is oriented toward comparisons between actions and sanctions, rather than around utility and effectiveness. Equal cases ought to be treated equally at the hands of the law. Thus, the social significance of the ideal of equality before the law depends directly upon the relative scope and significance of those sanctions and resources over which the judiciary and the legal profession have command. In a society where the major bulk of resources and opportunities, of rewards and frustrations, is distributed by non-legal institutions, equality before the law is a less important ideal than it is in a society where the judiciary disposes of a larger share of the resources.

The judiciary in Norway and elsewhere is a passive agency; it waits for cases to be brought in, and it functions in many respects as a service institution rather than as an executor of plans or a dispenser of power. Again, this circumstance is probably related to the relative absence of causal and utilitarian thinking in law. Passivity is also an important asset of the judge as an impartial umpire in disputes, protecting him against suspicions and commitments to specific factions or programs. Passivity and a modest emphasis upon utility seem to be prices the judiciary has to pay in order to retain confidence and respect. But here lies a basic dilemma: the courts run the risk of paying so high a price for retaining an unblemished image that their decisions are rendered largely irrelevant to the concerns of a rapidly developing industrial society.

Let me summarize the argument so far. A distinction was drawn between conflicts of interest and conflicts of values and facts (disagreements). It was pointed out that conflicts of the former type often are particularly well suited for settlements after bilateral negotiations, whereas conflict of the second type usually presupposes the intervention of a third party for its settlement. Among the third parties who intervene in conflicts is found the judge. Although most litigation has one of its sources in a conflict of interest, it can be handled by a court and by the application of legal methods only when the conflict has been reinterpreted as a disagreement over norms or facts or both. This follows from the structure of legal thinking and of the legal model of decision-making and conflict resolution. Some important elements in this model have been specified above. With a background of these general concepts, some hypotheses may be advanced concerning the trends of development in the conflict-solving machinery of the Norwegian society.

Some Trends in the Development of Conflict Resolution in Norway

As a concomitant of the social process of modernization (industrialization, urbanization, secularization, and so forth) there has taken place a change in the relative preponderance of types of conflict resolution. The courts, as well as the specific techniques of the judge, have come to play a diminishing part in conflict resolution relative to other modes of settling disputes. More generally, the legal model of thinking about interpersonal relations and problems has lost ground to other models of social reality, typified by economics, psychology, and other scientific disciplines.

It would probably be misleading to claim that law in Norway today is less important than it was one hundred years ago. The vast growth of legislation contradicts such a sweeping generalization. The process of "delegalization" is specifically related to the techniques of conflict resolution. Even within this area it must be observed that a quantitative reduction in the relative scope of court decisions and of legal personnel does not automatically imply a reduction in importance. Another qualification should be added. While court proceedings may have been supplanted by other modes of conflict resolution, there has been a growth of quasijudicial procedures within private organizations. Thus, for example, professional associations have developed tribunals for the settlement of disputes between colleagues as well as between the professionals and their clients.

The general hypothesis will be specified by reference to the following trends in the Norwegian legal system during the last one hundred years: (a) a numerical stagnation in the case load of the regular courts; (b) a feeble expansion of the personnel of the judiciary and increasing use of the "judge apprentice";[2] (c) growth of institutionalized mechanisms of conflict resolution outside of the judiciary and reliance, to a greater or lesser extent, upon methods that deviate from the court model; (d) a relative decline of the legal profession in numbers, political eminence, and perceived usefulness in public and private administration; (e) a relative diminution of the sanctions and resources at the command of the courts; (f) internal changes in legal thinking and decision-making, characterized by an influence from social science on the one hand and from bargaining procedures on the other.

These trends have not been completely synchronized. Some of the changes have preceded others, and in some respects there have been ups and downs. The cumulative effect becomes apparent only if a very long time perspective is applied. Thus, it may be claimed that the first half of the last century in Norway was characterized by a rapid growth in the application of legal methods and personnel. Some aspects of the "delegalization" of society have only become apparent in the period after World War II. In a brief survey it is not possible to do justice to the complexities of the historical process.

In 1814, when the old united state of Denmark-Norway was dissolved and the new Norwegian state was joined with Sweden in a looser union, there were approximately 100 functioning judges; 150 years later this figure had doubled, whereas the population had quadrupled.[3] If the judge is regarded as an expert who has a service to contribute—namely to solve conflicts in a peaceful way—it is remarkable that there should have been so little growth in the personnel of the courts. It should be

2. The judge apprenticeship usually lasts for a year or two and offers young jurists a unique opportunity to familiarize themselves with a wide spectrum of practical legal problems. The judge apprentice (*dommerfullmektig*) does not receive instructions from the judge in specific suits but handles the case independently. In practice his decision-making authority is indistinguishable from that of the judge.

3. These and the following figures are taken from Vilhelm Aubert (1967).

noted that great changes have taken place in the allocation of tasks among the judiciary and various other public agencies, relieving the courts of many administrative duties. The efficiency of the courts has been increased, not least as a consequence of the contraction of settlement patterns and the improvements in communications. To this must be added that the "judge apprentice" has come to take over a substantial part of the total case load. If the number of "judge apprentices" were added to the judges, the total figure would have more than tripled during the last 150 years.

In spite of the qualifications that have to be considered when the modest growth of the judiciary is interpreted, it is apparent from the figures on the case load that the activities of the courts have expanded rather less than the growth of the population alone might explain. This is very much at variance with the trend in other areas, where the growth of the supply of the service of experts has been very great—for example, in medicine, engineering, architecture, the teaching profession, and various branches of economic advice. Such a trend was also true of attorneys in private practice until relatively recently.

One might thus be left with the curious impression that the demand for a service that consists in the dispensation of justice and peaceful settlement of disputes has remained stable or has even decreased throughout a period of vast social changes and great economic progress, while the demand for most other kinds of services has multiplied at a very rapid rate. The only parallel exception to the general trend is the numerical lack of growth in the ministry. But although there exist good grounds for assuming that the real demands for the services of the clergy have diminished, there is no reason to assume that the demands for justice or for peaceful settlements of conflicts have been diminishing—rather the opposite.

The problem has probably not been phrased adequately. It is only part of the story to describe the courts as the contributors of a social service. They are at the same time the wielders of coercive power—a power which is channelized into a structure of decisions characterized by either/or choices. Although the courts on many occasions present themselves as the protectors of the common man, they appear on other occasions as menacing distributors of punishment and other threatening sanctions, ultimately backed by naked force. Thus it is dubious whether the ordinary citizen should wish for more or fewer judges if he wants to maximize his welfare. It is not at all clear whether a welfare state is one characterized by a large judiciary or by a small one.

This ambivalence is not only due to the fearful consequences of some trials; it also has to do with the fact that conflict resolution as such is not an unequivocal service to an individual. It is a service to society or to the dyad that has run into an unmanageable situation. But there are two sides to a case, and the nature of the legal decision is such as to make the gains of one party a loss to the other side. Legal decisions cannot provide for any increase in welfare that is not bought at the cost of reduced welfare somewhere else. Although medical, technical, and educational innovations may lead to continuous expansions in some aspect of human welfare, the most refined legal techniques do not hold out any certain promise of increased utility to any particular individual. The service provided by the application of first-rate legal methods on the part of the judge is of a much less tangible kind, and the recipient is society as such.

Although it seems rather obvious that a modern society is as much in need of sophisticated methods of conflict resolution as the preindustrial societies are, if not more, the need is difficult to locate. It presents a very serious measurement problem to evaluate the functions of a legal system with an expansive judiciary as compared to the functions of a more modest judiciary. It may also be difficult to evaluate the operation of courts with more or less well-qualified personnel, since no measurable output is to be expected and no increased welfare of the clientele can be expected as a consequence of more highly qualified personnel. This may be one of the reasons it is possible to run the Norwegian judiciary with such a heavy reliance upon the institution of the "judge apprentice."

The permanently appointed judges in Norway come to the bench after a long period of service in some other branch of the legal profession, mostly from the departments of state. Their average age today is above sixty. The judge has at his side an assistant who normally comes fresh from his final law examination without any practical experience. After a few months he will very often take over a substantial part of the case load of the court, not merely being restricted to the most trivial and simplest types of cases. In the courts of first instance, outside the four major cities where judge apprentices are not used, these young and inexperienced lawyers share the task of adjudicating rather equally with the permanent judge, although there are great variations from one jurisdiction to the next.

When the post of judge apprentice was introduced in 1845, the intention was that he should serve as an apprentice and as an aid to the judge, not as his equal. However, the growth of the population and of the case load created pressure to delegate more independent authority to him. The system has functioned well in the sense that no serious criticism has been raised against the institution, in spite of the fact that within the Norwegian governmental system it is exceptional to entrust young people with that much authority. Although there may be grounds for assuming that the apprentices are about as well qualified as the older judges, it is surprising that no serious demands for reform have been raised simply on the bais of appearances. This fact is probably related to a lack of faith in the likelihood of multiplying the beneficial effects of the judiciary through improvements in the formal qualifications of the personnel.

There exist alternatives to the explanation given for the numerical stability of court personnel. The hypothesis that the actual occurrence of conflicts in society has remained relatively stable and that there has been no expansion in the demand for legal decision-making seems highly unlikely. The process of industrialization and urbanization must have vastly increased the probability of conflicts among the citizens and, not least, between the citizens and the state. The growth of the private legal profession as well as the emergence of new methods of conflict resolution seem to refute this explanation. It is, however, conceivable that some of the most intractable human conflicts—disputes that defy settlement through negotiations—have diminished in significance. This speculation might apply to certain types of religious and sexual deviance, which used to be punished but which are now exempt from legal sanctions. It might also apply to property disputes between farmers in an agrarian society, disputes that today have a much less personal flavor.

A more likely explanation, however, relates to the increase in legislation and of legal personnel outside the judiciary. It is difficult to find an adequate quantitative measure of the amount of legislation. If we use as criterion the number of printed pages of statutory law produced each year, Norwegian legislation has increased by a factor in the neighborhood of five during the last 100 years. If we use the number of statutes as the criterion, the growth has been somewhat more modest, because a great deal of new legislation consists of revisions of and amendments to old statutes. According to these two criteria of legislative activity, the growth was much more pronounced up to the time of World War I than it has been since. The picture might have been a different one if it had been possible to include also that production of legal rules that takes place on the basis of delegation from the legislature. It is a characteristic of modern Norwegian statutes, especially within the large area of administrative law, that they leave a great deal of the rule-making to the administration itself. In any event, it seems clear that a modern society has a more developed system of formal rules specifying the rights and obligations of the citizens than does a preindustrial society.

The expansion of trained legal personnel has been very great during the last 150 years, although it seems that the growth is coming to a halt now. In 1815 there were altogether 329 academically trained lawyers in Norway, of whom the majority were judges or other local decision-makers who shared many characteristics with judges. According to the census of 1960, there were 5,603 trained lawyers. The largest subcategories of lawyers, which together made up nearly two-thirds of the profession, were the advocates, the civil servants of the central administration, and administrative personnel in private enterprise.

One aspect of the changes in the scope of legislation and in the size and composition of the legal profession is a shift of emphasis from conflict resolution to the prevention of conflict or, at least, of litigation. The growth of statutory and delegated law may have clarified many legal issues, previously open to doubt and contradictory interpretations. The increasing formalization of rules has made the outcome of litigation more predictable, thus encouraging conformity to rules and avoidance of conflicts, as well as facilitating settlements out of court.

The development of a large public bureaucracy staffed with lawyers has presumably had a similar effect, although it is also clear that bureaucratic growth and the expansion of government intervention has given rise to a large number of new conflicts. These conflicts are not, however, in all respects similar to the older conflicts arising out of the criminal law or to the disputes over property and private contracts. The strong injection of legal expertise into business management may also have had the effect of preparing the actions of the enterprise in order to conform better to the laws or of taking precautions in contractual arrangements in order to prevent the rise of future disputes.

Although it seems plausible to deduce that the function of law and of the legal profession has undergone a change from conflict resolution to conflict prevention, it must be admitted that the distinction between resolution and prevention is far from clear. The decision whether an advocate or a legally trained business executive is preventing or solving a conflict through negotiations with a customer, competitor, or government agency may often be no more than a matter of words. However we interpret the effects of a growing system of rules, served by a growing legal profession, it remains indubitable that for the most part conflict resolution has been removed from the judiciary. In some instances it may be fitting to describe the change in terms of legal influences that prevent dispute from arising in the first place. In other cases it may be more appropriate to talk about alternatives to conflict resolution in the courts.

The feeble growth of the judicial activities of the courts is clearly demonstrated by the figures on the case load of the Norwegian courts over the last century. Around 1870 there were approximately 4,000 sentences in criminal cases (felonies and misdemeanors). In 1965 there were 9,720. The amount of court activity in criminal cases has increased by a factor corresponding roughly to the population increase during the last 100 years. The situation is much the same with respect to civilian suits. In the years around 1870 the Norwegian courts handled somewhere between 3,000 and 4,000 cases, with considerable variations from year to year. In 1965 they delivered verdicts in somewhat more than 8,000 civilian cases.

During the last century the majority of civilian disputes has always been settled outside the regular court system, namely by the "reconciliation boards." These boards, through which most civilian disputes have to pass, function in part as summary small claims courts, in part as vehicles of mediation. The relative numerical importance of the reconciliation boards has been decreasing during the last 100 years. In 1870 the reconciliation boards handled approximately 100,000 cases, as against 40,000 in 1965. In 1902 the activities of the reconciliation boards reached an all-time high, with 157,000 cases. During the years of the World War II and the first years that followed, the figures were down to around 10,000. However these variations in the use of the reconciliation boards are to be explained, it is clear that the stagnation of the activities of the courts in civilian suits cannot be explained by reference to a growth in the use of the reconciliation boards, since they also have been declining with respect to the scope of decision-making.

An inspection of recent statistics for civilian suits suggests that the lower courts deal frequently with conflicts where there probably has been little disagreement. Possibly as many as one-fourth of all the cases have been instigated because the parties, or one of them, had to obtain a legal basis for further action, his claim being undisputed by the adversary. This is the case with divorce, when the parties have agreed upon the dissolution of marriage but still need an official stamp upon their agreement. The underlying conflict of interest is often "solved" prior to the lawsuit.

According to Norwegian law, reconciliation may take place also subsequent to the initiation of a lawsuit, and the judge is authorized to attempt mediation in court. Of all the suits that were terminated before the lower courts in 1962, 33 per cent ended with reconciliation, no sentence being delivered. The various types of lawsuits differ a great deal with respect to the frequency of reconciliation: 63 per cent of the suits concerning owner-tenant relations end in reconciliation; 38 per cent of damage suits and 33 per cent of suits involving real estate end by reconciliation; 21 per cent of marriage cases, 13 per cent of paternity suits, and only 2 per cent of suits to obtain a declaration of legal incompetency are settled by an agreement between the parties.

One would expect to find the conflicts that lend themselves to resolution through traditional legal methods by an examination of the case load of the courts of appeal and especially that of the supreme court. The composition of the case load of the latter deviates substantially from that of the lower courts. Suits concerning marriage, tenancy, and bills of exchange together make up 46 per cent of the case load of the lower courts, as against only 8 per cent of the supreme-court cases. Damage suits are about equally represented on all levels of the judiciary. Cases that are particularly likely to be appealed to the top are those concerning expropriation, which make up 21 per cent of the supreme-court cases, as against a few per cent of the lower-court cases. Cases concerning other decisions of public authorities comprise 6 per cent of the supreme-court cases, as against 0.5 per cent of the lower-court cases, and cases concerning farm succession constitute 4 per cent of the supreme-court cases, as against 1 per cent of lower-court cases.

The most striking aspect of this examination is the extent to which the supreme court is concerned with settling disputes between the public authorities and the citizens. This circumstance may have to do with the belief that only the supreme court is in a position to set aside decisions made by other public authorities. It may also be owing to an inability of the civil service to engage in bargaining on behalf of the government, thus debarring a settlement out of court. Sometimes—for example, in certain expropriation cases—the appeal to the top is related to the magnitude of the issue at stake.

Two points have been made concerning the settlement of civilian suits: that the majority of them are settled outside a regular court and that the methods even in court deviate from the ideal of legal thinking as outlined in our model. The statistics suggest that the courts may have represented a more attractive, or inevitable, alternative for conflict resolution 100 years ago than they do today. The situation is rather parallel with respect to criminal cases. The development of the case load of the trial courts has been shown above. If we look at the contemporary situation, it is clear that the procedural rules in practice function so as to limit the interference of the courts to a small proportion of even those cases where some legal action is taken. In those cases where a trial is initiated, the manner of treatment frequently deviates from the legal model.

A legal clause may tacitly assume that bargaining can lead to more favorable results than a sentence by a criminal court. Thus, in the case of embezzlement or of assault and battery, criminal proceedings cannot normally be initiated by the public prosecution unless an indictment has been sought by the victim. Especially in cases of embezzlement it is very common for the victim to reach an agreement with the offender over the settlement of his debt. In 1965 38 per cent of all Norwegian cases of embezzlement that had been investigated by the police were withdrawn from prosecution at the behest of the victim. The plea for an indictment was withdrawn in 37 per cent of the investigated cases involving assault and battery, in 32 per cent of libel cases, and in 28 per cent of fraud cases. In these instances a bargain is probably struck between the offender and the victim. In other instances the bargain primarily involves the prosecution and the offender.

In 1965, 83 per cent of all delinquencies (including misdemeanors) were disposed of on the basis of an option of a fine in lieu of prosecution. This option, called "forelegg," amounts to a bargain between the offender and the police. Strictly speaking, the offender need not plead guilty in order to be dealt with in this informal, discreet, and quick way. It suffices that he declares himself willing to accept a writ issued by the police and imposing a fine. Thus, the basis of the penalty and the termination of the conflict between the offender and his society assume a form strongly reminiscent of a private contract. However, it is hardly legitimate for the offender and the police to haggle about the price of the crime. The element of bargaining creeps into the transaction in a different shape.

Since the alternative to "forelegg" is a trial by the courts, the police as well as the defendant have reasons to prefer the "forelegg." It offers the defendant a chance to avoid publicity, to stay out of the court, and to protect his self-image against the taint of real criminality, and it is all finished quickly and at no extra costs. For the police it saves time, man power, and money to deal with most offenses in this way. Since the defendant is free to choose a trial, whatever the circumstances of the case, the offenders may collectively exert a rather strong pressure upon the police to keep fines down. If the police raise the fines above a certain critical point, the defendants may be more prone to take their chances on trial, in order to be acquitted or at least to obtain a reduction of the fine.

Of those criminal cases that reach the trial stage, two thirds are dealt with according to a summary procedure presided over by a single professional judge. This is also a relatively quick way of disposing of cases, and one that normally avoids publicity. The condition for the application of this procedure is that the defendant has pleaded "unreservedly guilty." In these cases, as in those mentioned above, the prosecution and the offender have to agree in order for the case to be settled. Thus, much of the conflict resolution, in the sense of settling a disagreement, must have taken place prior to the operation of the legal device.

In criminal cases the disagreements over facts or rules come to the surface in that one-third of the trials before the lower courts that take place according to a more elaborate procedure with two lay judges in addition to the professional judge. Only 11 per cent of the defendants plead guilty without any reservations, while 9 per cent plead partly guilty, according to a study of all criminal cases that occurred before six selected courts near Oslo in the period 1950–1960. However, the disagreements over guilt are most heavily concentrated in the cases concerning misdemeanors, where the defendant might have opted for a fine in lieu of prosecution if he had felt unable to protest his innocence. Of those charged with larceny, as many as 22 per cent pleaded unreservedly guilty, whereas 24 per cent admitted partial guilt.

The disagreements that are brought out and finally settled in courts concern, above all, the meting out of penalities. In recent years the methods of settling this question have become more detached from the traditional legal model of applying rules to an established guilt of a certain magnitude. Psychiatric and psychological considerations may intervene, and so may predictions concerning the probable effects of the punishments. This loosening up of trial methods has introduced new opportunities for a kind of tacit bargaining. Suspended sentences have become frequent, usually granted on the condition that the defendant fulfill certain demands, such as paying damages to the victim, abstaining from the use of alcohol, getting a job, or maintaining contact with some kind of welfare agency. The judge may let his sentence be influenced by the credibility of the promises made by the defendant and by the arguments advanced in this respect by the counsel for the defense.

Although those conflicts that originate in criminal offenses have traditionally been considered fit for treatment in a traditional legal form without much legitimate scope for negotiations, today an element of bargaining also plays a large part in this area. Most of the bargaining takes place outside the courtroom or prior to a trial. However, the humanitarian and psychological trend in modern penology opens a certain tacit element of bargaining also at the trial stage. At the same time, a utilitarian thinking, based upon scientific models, has become more widely used. There remain areas of application for the relatively undiluted legal model, however, and the fact that some cases are handled in this way gives a symbolic reassurance out of all proportion to the frequency of the occurrence of such trials. Jerome Frank's notion of the courts and the criminal trial as symbols, arising out of the needs for a certainty beyond the vagaries of human weaknesses, has its application also today (Frank 1949).

Modern criminal trials also bring out another aspect of the trend in social development, one that has been termed "delegalization." The judicial techniques for arriving at just decisions have been improved upon during the last century. In addition, the ability to foresee the consequences of the verdict has developed, and the opportunity of the judge to choose sanctions in the light of such insight has also been expanded. Nevertheless, there is some reason to believe that criminal trials function haphazardly in terms of justice as well as in terms of social utility. The crimes that result in relatively severe penalties represent a very one-sided sample of wrongdoing. The sampling is ill suited to bring into focus the kinds of activities against which a modern society has to protect itself. And although the efforts of the judge to adapt the penalty to the situation of the criminal have resulted in a more humanitarian penal law, no real system of treatment and rehabilitation has emerged.

One major reason for this state of affairs is that the courts have at their disposal only an infinitesimal part of the total resources and sanctions of a modern society. The judge may decide that a year in prison will do no irreparable harm to a convict, but he cannot see to it that the man gets a job when he is discharged. The judge may find that a short stay in prison is an adequate penalty for drunken driving, but it is not in his hands to secure the livelihood of the convict if he looses his driver's license and perhaps his job. In the area of civilian litigation, the results one's trade union obtains in the recurrent negotiations with the employers' organization or with the government are more important than what happens in most private disputes with contractual partners.

It is safe to assert that there has been a vast growth during the last century of those resources that are at the command of the government or of the large-scale organizations that dominate a modern society. The distribution of these resources—of advantages and disadvantages, of benefits and costs—take place through mechanisms located outside the legal machinery for conflict resolution. Much of this distribution is done through private or public administrative decisions, with relatively little publicity and formality. A good deal takes place through bargaining between the interest organizations, often with the government as an arbiter or mediator. The direct influence of the courts in these matters is negligible. However, this does not exclude the possibility that a relatively small number of court decisions may have considerable indirect influence through their impact upon the methods and principles employed by the new conflict-resolving devices that have sprung up and that often borrow some characteristics from the courts and from the pure legal model.

The emergence of the new conflict-resolving devices shows that an increasing number of recognized and important conflicts are steered willfully and by legislation outside the courts. Thus, conflicts arising out of taxation or the social pension schemes are, with few exceptions, handled by administrative bodies, with greater or lesser resemblance to court procedures. The number of social-pension cases alone corresponds roughly to the yearly number of criminal trials. In such areas as insurance and building, and in many other relationships between firms, conflicts are settled through arbitration on a private basis. The child-welfare agencies handle the largest amount of juvenile delinquency as well as other conflicts between parents and children.

It is difficult to develop one single explanation for the extrajudicial growth of the modern machinery for conflict resolution. In some conflicts the need for experts on something other than law has been apparent. Insight into causal relationships in a specific area is deemed a necessary requirement of those who make the decisions, and it is difficult to combine this type of expertise with the legal model as practiced by the courts. Nonlegal expertise is important on the wage arbitration boards, in the role of management-labor mediators, on the price council, and also on the boards of private arbitration between insurance companies or between contractors and house buyers. In other institutions—as for example in the boards for tax appeals—the opportunity to reach compromise solutions seems to be an important function of the deviations from the legal model.

One of the extrajudicial institutions that expanded greatly during the latter half of the last century and during the first decades of this was the private legal profession of advocates. In 1814 there were about as many advocates as there were judges in Norway. The advocates were government-appointed until 1848, at which time the law was made a free profession as the consequence of a general move to abolish protectionism and privilege. In 1960 there were 1,500 lawyers in practice as advocates. Thus, while the judiciary had only doubled during 150 years, the private legal profession had expanded by a factor of 15. The advocates have probably taken over from the courts a large share of the task of preventing conflicts through advice and of solving conflicts through negotiations. It should be emphasized, however, that many lawyers spend a great deal of time on work that is only marginally related to the tasks of conflict prevention and resolution.

There may also exist a relationship between the expansion of the legal profession and the relative decline of the activities of the reconciliation boards. The latter seem to have served as the poor man's lawyers in a society rather modestly equipped with experts, especially in the country.

The expansion of the private legal profession did not continue after 1930. In recent years the profession has lost more practicing lawyers than it has gained through new recruitment, and the age composition suggests that this trend will continue. The number of students does not at the present time hold out any promise that the trend is likely to be quickly reversed. The situation raises the question of whether the welfare state will develop new professional roles as capable of defending the individual's rights and settling his conflicts as the advocate is when full use is made of his techniques and skills. To the extent that new institutions develop as substitutes for the legal advisor or counsel, the personnel will base their professional services upon a theoretical foundation that is at variance with the legal models, be they economists, accountants, psychologists, or social workers.

Between 1814 and 1960 the total number of Norwegians with legal training had increased by a factor of 17. Although there have been ups and downs, as a result of poor synchronization of supply and demand, the number of lawyers has been rising until the present day. It should be noted, however, that the great increase has taken place within the categories that perform functions only distantly related to the application of the legal model of conflict resolution. This has occurred in the civil service, where lawyers have taken on all kinds of administrative tasks, as they have also in business management and to some extent even in private practice.

Law served for a long time as a general education for participation in managerial, administrative, and political tasks. In the latter half of the nineteenth century as many lawyers were trained as there were students in all other academic fields taken together. In terms of student numbers the University of Oslo was very much a school of jurisprudence, as the University of Copenhagen 100 years earlier had been a school of divinity. In politics and in the civil service the lawyers were completely dominant. Since more than 90 per cent of all positions in the civil service above the clerical level were filled by lawyers, it is clear that lawyers must have acted as experts in a great number of fields outside their own. Thus the numerical hegemony of the legal profession was bought at the cost of a dispersion of tasks and rather divergent orientations to the handling of human affairs.[4] Nevertheless, the legal model of thinking must have put its stamp upon many activities that are today in the hands of other experts.

In this century the relative share of law students in the total Norwegian student body has been greatly diminished. They have been outnumbered by engineers, by students of science and of the humanities, and often also by medical students. In terms of high-school grades, the grades that can be compared across academic fields, the lawyers' averages have fallen below those of the other student groups in scholastic achievement. During the last two or three years the grade level has declined

---

4. Rather than emphasizing the "delegalization" in recent years, one might emphasize the "artificiality" of the previous growth of the legal profession. It may seem that the legal profession expanded during the last century not so much because of a demand for legal services as because of a more general and diffuse demand for individuals with an academic background. In England this demand has been satisfied by the training of classical scholars; in Norway, and many other countries, by the training of lawyers. If we consider an academic career as a kind of economic enterprise, demanding an investment and yielding a profit on the investment, it may be pointed out that it is cheap to train lawyers—much cheaper than to train engineers, natural scientists, medical doctors, or even philologists. In Norway during the last century, three or four professors sufficed to train all the lawyers, and they needed no equipment and no laboratories—only a few books. It is, of course, also a crucial fact that law existed as a well-developed field of scholarship while the other academic fields, except theology, were in an immature and budding state. The generality of the training of lawyers is also very important in a society in the process of industrialization, where specialization is poorly developed and where it is difficult to foresee and satisfy demands for highly specialized expertise. Further, the fact that the government was a going concern as an economic enterprise favored the legal profession relative to those professions that are more dependent upon private demand. I think that a more thorough investigation of the economic premises of the growth of the professions would reveal further evidence for the thesis that law offers very special economic opportunities in a society that is moving from a preindustrial to an industrialized stage. This supposition might also explain why so many students in the underdeveloped world choose law rather than the more "productive" specialties of medicine, engineering, agricultural science, and the like.

even further, and there is considerable apprehension that the present shortage of recruits to the legal profession is aggravated by the low quality of new candidates of law. Whether this acute setback is temporary or the consequence of a long-term trend is uncertain. Against the background of the general analysis of the changing position of the legal profession, there may be some reason to believe that the present crisis is nothing but a particularly sharp symptom of a social development that has rendered the function of law more equivocal than it once was.

During the first decades after 1814 every fourth member of parliament was a judge. Later on, the advocate took over the political role of the judge, concomitant with a shift in debating style in the direction of open acceptance of the legitimacy of representing interests and not only wisdom. Between 1814 and 1884 every fifth member of parliament was a trained lawyer. After the introduction of a parliamentary government in 1884 no more than 10 per cent of the members of parliament were lawyers, and today there are only 7 per cent. Until the beginning of this century half the members of the cabinet were lawyers. In recent years one-fourth or one-fifth of the cabinet members have been lawyers. A comparison of advocates in 1932 and in 1950 suggests that lawyers have withdrawn also from other types of political activities. This may well be related to the labor take-over of government, which left the relatively conservative lawyers with fewer opportunities to achieve political positions.

One conclusion that may be drawn from the preceding analysis is that the pure legal model plays a modest part in actual instances of conflict resolution in Norway today. This conclusion is based upon a tentative answer to the question: how frequently is the model, or a relatively close approximation to it, actually applied? However, there may well exist a contrast between the usefulness of the legal model in concrete conflict resolution and its function as a last-resort eventuality, which the other methods of conflict resolution have to take into account.

The possible dysfunctions of the legal model have been outlined above with particular emphasis on the exclusion of compromise and bargaining, as well as on the relative absence of causal scientific thinking oriented toward utility. In the various functional alternatives to the courts, one can see that either it is more convenient to bargain and reach negotiated settlements or easier to apply utilitarian schemes of scientific thinking or both. There may also be other reasons, related to the relative expenditures of time and money, that favor the alternatives to judicial methods. These are not necessarily intrinsic to the legal model. It is not warranted to draw the conclusion that it is impossible to improve upon the functioning of the courts and to enable them to recapture more of the conflict resolution in a modern society if this is thought desirable.

The pure legal model has an important bearing upon the function of legislation. Although most types of modern legislation in Norway are put into practice without much interference from the courts, the statutes are always formulated with the eventuality in mind that they should form an adequate basis for the solution of conflicts before a court of law. Although the legislators may assume that negotiated settlements of disagreements are normal, or that conflicts will be handled by other conflict-resolving agencies, statutes are formulated to fit into a legal model of conflict resolution.

It is not certain whether the changes that have taken place during the period of industrialization are to be interpreted as symptoms that the legal model quite generally plays a more modest role today than it once did. What seems established is that other models of conflict resolution have become more popular than the trial in court and that other types of experts have multiplied in numbers and importance, in part at the expense of the legal profession. To some extent, however, this circumstance should probably be interpreted as a symptom that the legal profession has succeeded in making itself dispensable. The systems of social organization and communication have expanded enormously from preindustrial days to the present time, making it possible to service large areas of social activities through relatively few full-dress legal decisions, the consequences of which flow out through well-oiled channels in many directions. It is possible today to run the control system with a high degree of economy in terms of actual application of the legal model. The court is a social institution that may be indispensable but that also has a number of dysfunctional consequences when its methods actually are used. It is an institution that is exposed to a certain risk of having its authority undermined if it follows an expansive policy.

The Offer of a Free Home:

A Case Study in the

Family Law of the Poor

Anthropologists interested in the study of tribal law have thus far tended to concentrate on the "trouble case" decided by a court, moot, or other judicial group. They have used the "trouble case" both as a field-work tool for the collection of data and as an analytical instrument for probing the relationship between a people's law ways and their generalized culture (Malinowski 1926; Llewellyn and Hoebel 1941; Hoebel 1960–1961; Gluckman 1955, 1965b; Bohannan 1957; Nader 1964b, 1965b). As the chief model for such studies, the Western judge may not provide an image that is flexible enough to fit the tribal pattern. The judge in Western political systems is commonly a figure in a three-part governmental structure: the judicial, the executive, and the legislative. That observation is important to this paper because Western judges typically are not charged with policy-making functions. In deciding specific cases, judges of course "make law" and occasionally even initiate sweeping new policies (Cardozo 1921; Llewellyn 1960); but they are not given responsibility for governing in this fashion. In some tribal societies, however, and particularly at the village level, the political head of the society is also one of its judges. (Gluckman 1955:1–34; Bohannan 1957; Nader 1964:266–267.) In the analysis of the law ways of such a society, the Western administrative agency may be more useful than the Western court as a model for anthropologists.

It is the purpose of this paper to describe the promulgation of a rule by an administrative agency, the evaluation of the workings of that rule through cases heard and settled within the agency, and the ultimate withdrawal of the rule partly as a result of the experience developed through the hearing process. The same point could have been made using any rule issued by an agency and then tested through case appeals. The particular illustration chosen for treatment here, however, has broader significance: the rule to be described was finally withdrawn, partly because the agency believed itself to be an inappropriate forum for the resolution of the problem it had raised. Ultimately the question is posed whether any conflict-resolving agency in the society, including the courts, could have satisfactorily accommodated the conflicting values found to exist in these particular cases. This question, too, may be relevant to anthropologists, for it suggests, first, that the choice among available remedy agents made by persons with grievances may depend in part on how broadly a particular remedy agent conceives its own functions and powers, and, second, that certain conflicts cannot be entirely resolved within the existing social system. It goes without saying that these indissoluble problems will probably be different for different societies and that much could perhaps be learned about a given society by asking which conflicts it has been unable to resolve.

The administrative agency discussed in this paper is the California State Department of Social Welfare, which, among its other duties, is charged with supervising the Federal Social Security programs in California. The particular program under discussion is one of the categorical aid programs administered under the Social Security Act and called Aid to Families with Dependent Children (AFDC); the nature of the rule that was progmulgated by the Department as part of the AFDC program will become apparent from the material that follows.

Background: Structure of the AFDC Program and the Fair Hearing Appeals

The Federal Social Security Act of 1935 authorized an appropriation of $24,750,000 to be used for payments to the states equal to one-third of the sums expended by them for Aid to Dependent Children in Their Own Homes. (Carstens 1936:248.) The program can be traced to the White House Conference of 1909 called by President Theodore Roosevelt, at which Rabbi Emil G. Hirsch suggested that public moneys be made available to mothers of dependent children so that the children could be supported at home rather than in institutions. Although the idea did not gain immediate acceptance on the federal level, the individual states took it up. In 1911 Illinois enacted the first mothers' aid law; by the end of 1913 twenty states had passed similar laws, and by 1936 only two states lacked such provisions. The statutes were in general broadly phrased; but it is reported that in practice the aid was extended mainly to widows and their children (Carstens 1936:246–247).

The federal act followed the now familiar technique of the grants-in-aid. The federal government provided part of the funding to states that met the approval of the Social Security Board, the federal administering agency. State plans could not be approved for matching funds unless certain conditions were met, including the provision that the state must "provide for granting to any individual, whose claim with respect to aid to a dependent child is denied, an opportunity for a fair hearing before such State agency" (Social Security Act, Tit. IV § 401 [a]).

In California, the AFDC program is administered through the County Departments of Public Welfare under the supervision of the State Department of Social Welfare. Applicants seeking to establish their eligibility to receive aid under the program must first apply to the county departments. If the county either declares the applicant ineligible to receive aid or discontinues aid previously granted because of a discovered fact establishing that eligibility is no longer being maintained, the applicant may ask for a "fair hearing" before the state agency. According to Dr. Jacobus tenBroek, then Chairman of the State Social Welfare Board, in testimony before a Senate investigating committee, the procedure for obtaining a hearing is quite simple: "All they [the recipients] have to do to appeal is to make this [their dissatisfaction with the county decision] known to the county or to the State department and this can be done very informally and is generally done very informally. Once we have a knowledge, then a hearing officer is assigned to set up a hearing and conduct the case." (Hearing of Senate Fact Finding Committee on Labor and Welfare, Sacramento, Jan. 18–19, 1962, p. 52.) Testifying before a Senate Committee, the Department's Chief Legal Officer, Mr. Michaels, said of the hearing procedure: "The classic case is a letter we once received on a little piece of paper four inches by six inches which said, 'Dear Sir, I have been did wrong and I want to be did right.' We considered this and as far as I know always will consider this as a request for a hearing." (Executive Session of Senate Fact Finding Committee on Labor and Welfare, Sacramento, Dec. 10, 1962, p. 42.)

Despite the ease of the procedures for obtaining a fair hearing, however, some doubt has been expressed that recipients actually make wide use of their right of appeal. Thus, in reporting the results of interviews with a sample of ninety-six recipients of AFDC-U (the new program that provides aid to intact families with dependent children in which the father is unemployed, rather than absent from the home, the requirement for aid under the AFDC program), Briar (1966:55) discovered that 60 per cent of the families said they were not informed of their right to a fair hearing. Briar concludes that the informants were probably given the information by the social worker, but "this information probably is not particularly meaningful and useful to a person who sees himself as a suppliant, and therefore it may be ignored or soon forgotten." Much the same point is made by J. M. Wedemeyer, the former Director of the California Department of Social Welfare, who reported in 1966 that "the prosecution of an appeal demands a degree of security, awareness, tenacity, and ability which few dependent people have. The same factors which compel the dependent person to avoid controversy in settling grievances make him avoid this avenue. He may create more immediate problems than he would face by accepting the intitial decision" (Wedemeyer and Moore 1966:18).

During the period discussed here, the procedure was as follows: if an applicant from Los Angeles County, for example, had been found ineligible for aid by the county welfare worker, she could notify either the county or the state department in Sacramento that she objected to the ruling. One of several state hearing officers (called referees) would then be assigned to the case and a date would be set for a hearing at Los Angeles.

Referees are social workers, not lawyers. In Dr. tenBroek's view, the experience of the Department has been that lawyers "were at their best when they were handling problems that are of the type that lawyers frequently handle, questions involving the distinction between real and personal property, but when they came to the types of questions that involve social work, issues which are also embedded in the laws and which need to be decided in these cases, for example, the suitability of a home, there they are weaker" (Hearings of Senate Fact Finding Committee on Labor and Welfare, Sacramento, California, Jan. 18–19, 1962, p. 48). Since "the important issues in our field and the more numerous issues in our field are social-welfare type issues, "the department chose to use social workers as hearing officers under the direction of a Chief Hearing Officer who is a lawyer (tenBroek 1956:248–253; and Hearing before Senate Fact Finding Committee, Jan. 18–19, 1962, p. 48).

At the appointed time the applicant, representatives of the county department, and any witnesses that either desired to call appear before the referee. The applicant is entitled to representation by counsel of his choice, but such representation is extremely rare. An effort is made to be informal. The governing statute provides in part that "The hearing shall be conducted in an impartial and informal manner in order to encourage free and open discussion by participants" (Welfare and Institutions Code §10955, 1965). The applicant is encouraged to tell her own story in her own way, without the hindrance of technical rules of evidence applicable in courtroom proceedings. The aim of the proceeding is to establish the true facts bearing on eligibility. The hearings are recorded.

After the hearing, the referee prepares a proposed decision. A conclusion is reached, together with its supporting facts and reasons, on the issue of eligibility for aid. The proposed decision must be approved by the chief referee of the State Department of Social Welfare, who is a lawyer. After his approval, the proposed decision went, at the time of the cases here discussed, to the State Social Welfare Board for final action.[1] The Board consists of seven members, who are chosen by the governor with the advice and consent of the state senate. They serve at the pleasure of the governor and are chosen "for their interest and leadership in social welfare activities without regard to political or religious affiliation or profession or occupation" (Welfare and Institutions Code §10700, 1965).

The Board's method of deciding the Fair Hearing Appeals Cases, as they were called, has been described in detail elsewhere (tenBroek 1956). Briefly, the procedure was for the Board to divide the cases among its members for study. The proposed decisions were available at each meeting and could be acquired by board members, the department staff, the parties to the cases—including the county representatives—and other persons present at the meeting who had a legitimate interest in the work of the board. At the board's monthly meeting the cases were read out by number and a motion was made to adopt the proposed decision of the hearing officer. Unless a board member objected to the decision in a certain case and asked to have it considered separately, the cases were approved en masse. From time to time the director or a board member might call the board's attention to a specific case that could be precedent-setting if approved. The board's decisions were based on its own prior actions; its staff recommendations; its own notions of what the policy and fair administration of the program required in the individual case; and its understanding of California law embodied in statutes, court decisions, and the state constitution. If the Board upheld the county's decision to deny or discontinue aid, the applicant could appeal its decision to the courts.

At the time of these cases, the board was the only body empowered by statute to make the rules and regulations that implemented the state statutes in the administration of the welfare programs. The function of the appeals cases in helping the board make policy was clearly understood by the Chairman, Dr. tenBroek. He commented (tenBroek 1956: 254) that "The appeals serve the board as an active and continuous test of policy . . . They indicate whether a given regulation is working well and as contemplated when adopted. They quickly bring to light the inequities of policies in operation, their harsh, undue, and unanticipated results."

---

1. The cases are now sent to the Director for final decision. (Welfare and Institutions Code §10959, 1965.) Judicial review of the director's Welfare and Institutions Code decision is available to recipients and to the Counties (W. & I. §10962, 1965). (Government documents and Codes of the State of California are not referenced in the Bibliography.)

The Offer of a Free Home: Promulgation of an Administrative Rule

Public moneys are granted only to families who can establish their need for such support. Proof of eligibility involves many elements, including the federal requirement that the state must "take into consideration any other income and resources of any child claiming aid to dependent children" (Stats 849, 1956:42 USC 602(a) (7)). The impetus for the "offer of a free home" rule came from the ambiguity of the phrase "any other . . . resources" in the federal act.

Section 11264 of the California Welfare and Institutions Code provides that

> No child maintained in an institution for whom a bona fide offer of a proper home has been made is eligible for further aid; but no institution shall be required to surrender a child to any person of a religious faith different from that of the child or the parents of the child. [Added 1937.]

No appellate cases interpreting this section have been found. Its intent, however, appears to be similar to that of the earlier mother's aid laws: wherever possible, children should be kept in family homes rather than in institutions. There is a significant difference: the mother's aid laws, as we have seen, provided public funds to support the child in the mother's home. Thus, a child was not denied public support by his removal from an institution to a private home. Section 11264, however, appears to contemplate that the "proper home" will also be a "free home" —that is, the public obligation to provide aid for the child will terminate if it can be established that a private home is available where the child will be cared for and supported by private means.[2] Section 11264 required the department to take account of an offer of a proper home as a resource affecting eligibility for continued aid only when the child was

---

2. Another section of the California law supported this view. Section 1580, no longer in existence, provided that

> A county may transport needy children to proper homes without the State, when such homes are offered, and the State shall pay one-half of the total expense necessarily incurred in effecting such transportation. [Added 1937; repealed 1957.]

In the cases to which Section 1580 applied, it is clear that the acceptance of the offer of a proper home would remove the child from California's relief rolls. The Social Welfare Board, however, seems to have denied requests for transportation funds unless it was assured that the family would be taken care of in the other state. The Attorney General of California in his Opinion #NS 4085 (Feb. 11, 1942) advised the department that if a responsible agency in the other state authorized the indigent person's return in such a way that "it may logically be concluded that the agency recognizes a responsibility to care for, and that it will provide a proper home for, the children upon arrival," then California could properly provide one-half of the transportation cost. Thus the board's interpretation of the section was substantially upheld by the Attorney General's office.

institutionalized. The rule that was ultimately adopted by the department as Regulation C–316, however, was not limited to children living in institutions, but was extended to all children receiving public support, even to those living at home with their mothers or fathers.

It should be made very clear what was involved in the offer of a home. If, for example, a child was living in its mother's home and AFDC funds were being paid to the mother for the child's support; and if the father living with his second wife, offered a free home to the child; the AFDC case worker was required to determine whether the father's offer was a financial resource available for the child's support that must be considered in establishing the child's continued eligibility for public support. If the worker decided that the father's home was proper from the point of view of the child's financial and emotional security, she might conclude that the child was not in need of public support for the reason that the father was able and willing to assume his private support obligation for the child. Once this conclusion was reached, the child was no longer eligible for aid in the mother's home. The caseworker's decision was not, of course, a legal requirement that the child go to the father's home. The welfare agency lacked authority to force a change of custody in such cases; and, indeed, the referees took great comfort in this point. Neverthelesss, in practice, if the mother could not afford to keep the child without public support, the agency's decision to terminate aid forced the child to change homes. This reality appears to have haunted the case workers from the beginning.

It is not clear exactly when the State Department staff first expanded the requirement of considering an offer of a home as a resource for institutionalized children to include all children receiving public support. The departmental records on this subject begin with a letter dated May 3, 1941, from the AFDC (then ANC) supervisor to a county welfare official from Santa Clara County. The county had before it the following case: two illegitimate children, aged 11 and 13, were living with relatives who had been appointed the children's legal guardians. The natural father had been located and, although he had never before contributed to the support of his children nor had they ever lived with him, he now professed himself willing to take them into his home and support them. What should the county do? The supervisor, foreshadowing later departmental policy, replied in part that "while it is true that an offer of support must be considered in determining eligibility, it should also be ascertained whether or not it is to the best interests of the children to be placed in the home offering such support." Santa Clara was advised that the children should continue to receive aid while the father's home was being investigated.

It is significant that the close relationship between child support and child custody that embodied the conflicting values underlying these cases made its appearance in the first case raising the issue of the offer of a free home. The legal standard for deciding custody matters, binding on courts in cases involving two parents, is "the best interests of the child." In effect Santa Clara County was being asked to decide whether these two children would be better cared for in the home of their legal guardian or of their natural father. To be sure, even if the county decided to terminate public support, the guardians would still retain their legal authority, but their legal rights to the child's physical custody might become practically unexercisable.

The next mention of the offer of a free home appears in an office memorandum from the ANC supervisor to the department head and staff, dated January 8, 1943. The memo called attention to a fair-hearing appeal case scheduled for hearing by the board later in January. The case involved the denial of aid by Los Angeles County to two illegitimate children who were living with their mother. The mother's husband, who lived in Mississippi, offered to support his wife, his own child, and the two illegitimate children provided they returned to him in Mississippi. The mother refused to return. The county thereupon ruled that she had refused to take advantage of an offer of private support available to her and the children and denied her application for public support.

Calling attention to the fact that "the major question raised is presented for the first time, therefore the decision will be important as a precedent for future guidance," the supervisor pointed out that Section 11264 (then §1524) was limited to children living in institutions. She continued, "Section 1503 outlines the purpose of the ANC law to keep children in their own home wherever possible, and Section 1526 provides that a mother, who is living separate and apart from her husband, may establish residence for her children. The appeal therefore raises the question as to whether the denial by Los Angeles County is a proper one." The Board ruled that the offer by the father, since it was conditioned on the mother's return to his home, would not suffice to render the child ineligible for aid (*C.*, January 1943).[3]

Questions from the counties continued to be handled informally for the next several years. Letters from the supervisor to Los Angeles County in 1944, San Luis Obispo County in 1945, and Imperial County in 1946 reiterated her understanding of the basic policy: the offer of a home would be considered as an available resource that should be explored by the county, but aid should not be terminated unless the free home was found to be "suitable" for the children.

---

3. The cases discussed in the text are confidential (Welfare and Institutions Code §108–50), and are available only in the offices of the State Department of Social Welfare in Sacramento. Citations to fair-hearing appeals will therefore give only the applicant's initial and the date on which the appeal was heard before the Social Welfare Board.

In 1949 a new supervisor was appointed for the ANC bureau. In reply to a question regarding the offer of a free home from Butte County, he reviewed the files and cases that had accumulated since 1941. His summary of the department's working policy was sent to the area offices in Los Angeles and San Francisco, as well as to the Butte County inquirer. The memo covered the following points: if the child was living "in a foster home, institution . . . or with a relative other than a parent" and the offer was made by a parent, it would be considered a potential resource that should be explored. "If the offered home was entirely suitable in every way, the child would be ineligible on the basis of need." If, however, the home was not suitable, the offer would not be considered an available resource. If the child was living with a parent who had legal custody and the other parent made the offer, the county need not consider the offer unless the parent having custody was willing to let the child go. If the child was living with a nonparent and another nonparent offered to take him, the department would consider the child's desires in the matter.

Inquiries from the counties continued to appear, and it became apparent that the question could no longer be handled informally by the staff. In 1951 a declaration of working policy in the form of a handbook section, Manual Section C-390, was presented to the State Social Welfare Board together with a supporting memo from the ANC staff. C-390 provided that

> If a child receives an offer of a home from a relative, other person, or agency, the county shall assist in evaluating such offer and in determining whether the child would benefit thereby.
>
> The county shall make its services available to the family for such purposes as investigating the suitability of the home and interpreting the legal, social, and emotional implications of the offer. Usually the county can request qualified agencies to investigate the suitability of distantly located homes.
>
> If a child has adequate emotional and physical security in his present home, moving him might have a serious effect on him. If it is decided that it would be best for the child's growth and adjustment that he be moved, the suitability of the home offered should be evaluated to determine whether it can provide the necessary physical and emotional security, or educational, financial, and social benefits.
>
> When the family has reached a decision and a suitable plan has been made, the county may be able to provide other related services, such as preparation of the child for the move, preparation of the new family for the child, or, if the home is rejected, interpretation of the decision to the person who made the offer. [Welfare and Instructional Code § 1524, 1560]

Following a meeting with the board in May 1951, a memo was circulated to the field representatives of the Department describing the policy arrived at in the discussion:

There was complete agreement on the basic principle that "economic ability" of the person offering a free home is not the determining factor in arriving at a decision that the offer is a resource. The Board did not encourage the staff to draft specific rules and regulations as it was pointed up again and again in the discussion that cases would have to be handled on their own merits. . . .

It was recognized by the Board that under our rules the county should not make the decision as to where the child should live or in whose custody the child should be placed. These are questions for the parents or courts. The county responsibility is to determine whether or not the child is eligible for ANC on the basis of an available resource which would meet the need if the resource were used.

Despite this directive from the department staff, the counties continued to have difficulty in applying the policy thus developed. By 1952 the ANC supervisor had recognized that the pattern of the cases had altered. In a memo to the board dated June 6, 1952, he stated in part that after the passage of a new law that broadened the coverage of the ANC program by abolishing a three-year waiting period necessary to establish eligibility, the cases increasingly involved offers of a free home made by parents. Before the passage of AB 40, the new law, the offers had come mainly from relatives or friends. With the new cases, the department faced the problem of deciding whether the child was to live with the mother or the father. In August 1952 the supervisor advised the director of the Salinas County Department of Public Welfare that "as yet neither the Department staff nor the Board has arrived at a final and firm interpretation of this manual provision (Section C-390). The Board has expressed a desire that questions involving this provision should reach the Board by the appeal process, and further attention should be given to the problem before instructing the staff to prepare a revised policy statement on the offer of a free home."

In May 1953 the staff again made a presentation to the State Social Welfare Board, asking for a clarification of policy on the offer of a free home. In September of that year a memorandum was circulated that stated four basic principles the Department wished to follow:

    I. Where one or both parents are available to participate in planning for the child and the child is not a ward (of the juvenile court), the child cannot be deemed to be needy if the parent makes a bona fide offer to take the child in his own home and to provide reasonably adequate support and care in keeping with his circumstances.

    II. Where one or both parents are available to participate in planning for the child and the child is not a ward (of the juvenile court), and the child is not living with either parent, the child cannot be deemed to be needy if a person other than a parent makes a bona fide offer which will assure the child of reasonably adequate support and care, and

(1) the offer is acceptable to a parent who has a legal right to custody, or

(2) the offer is acceptable to a parent who does not have a right to legal custody and the parent who has a right to legal custody is not available.

III. Where neither parent is available to participate in planning for the child and the child is not a ward (of the juvenile court), the child cannot be deemed to be needy if there is an offer of a home by a person other than a parent if the home is determined to be a proper one in accordance with the provisions of Manual Section C-390.

IV. Where an adult or an emancipated minor parent with a child is offered a home for himself and the child, the child shall be considered needy if the parent does not voluntarily accept the offer.

So matters remained through 1955 and 1956. Then, in 1957, the board acted formally to promulgate its first regulation on the subject. Regulation C-316 was issued effective July 1, 1957. It read

OFFER OF A FREE HOME: Decision as to the eligibility of a child who is offered a free home by a relative, other person, or agency, is to be made on the basis of the legal, social, emotional, and financial security for the child in the home offered as compared to his present home.

The accompanying handbook material, which interpreted the regulation to the county case workers and which is suggestive rather than mandatory for the county personnel, amplified upon the point as follows:

C-316   OFFER OF A FREE HOME

Sometimes an offer of a free home is made by a parent, relative, other person, or agency for a child receiving ANC. When this happens the worker is responsible for deciding if the offer is resource to be considered in determining if the child is needy.

In general, if the child is living with a parent, and the offer is made by a person other than a parent, the offer would not be considered a resource. If, in such a case, the parent with whom the child is living requests the agency to evaluate the offer, the worker should make the agency's services available for this purpose.

In other instances where such an offer is received the worker should consider the following in determining if the offer is a resource:

1. Was the offer made in good faith, i.e., is the person making the offer actually interested in giving the child a home and the necessary care; or, for example, was the offer made by a parent only for the purpose of evading his responsibility for support regardless of the child's location?

2. Can the offered home provide the necessary physical and emotional security, financial and social benefits; are there any aspects of the offer, the home, or the new family situation which would be detrimental to the child's welfare?

3. Would it be detrimental to the child's welfare to remove him from his present home? Such factors as relationships and emotional ties with the present family, health problems, length of time he has been in the present home, number of times the child has been moved in the past, his adjustment to neighborhood and school, are taken into consideration.

The study necessary to these determinations is primarily the responsibility of the worker. Assistance and consultation should be obtained as indicated by the individual situation from school authorities, psychologists, physicians, psychiatrists, etc. Where the offered home is distantly located, a qualified social agency in the locality should be requested to make the study of that home.

On completion of the study the worker makes an analysis of the total situation and decides if the offered home is a resource to be considered in determining if the child is needy. It is considered a resource only if the offer was a bona fide one, if the home can provide the child with the necessary physical and emotional security and financial and social benefits, and if it would not be detrimental to the child's welfare to move him from his present home.

The above decision is made only for the purpose of determining eligibility to ANC. The decision as to whether the offer is to be accepted belongs to the parent or relative with whom the child is living or who has custody, or the court if the child is a court ward. If the responsible person rejects an offer which the study has shown to be an acceptable resource, the worker should explain why the child is ineligible to ANC. In this event, as well as where the study indicates that the offer is not an acceptable resource, the worker should explain the reason for the decision to the person making the offer.

If the responsible person or agency decides to accept the offer, the worker offers the services of the agency in preparing the child for the move, and preparing the new family for the child.

Thus was created Regulation C-316 and its accompanying interpretive material. From July 1, 1957, when it became effective, to November 1, 1962, when it was withdrawn, the regulation accounted for a total of twenty-three fair-hearing appeals cases that were decided by the State Social Welfare Board. In addition, sixteen appeals cases had been decided by the Board under C-390, making a total of thirty-nine cases that had to do with the interpretation and enforcement of the Board's policy in this matter. To these cases we now turn.

Offer of a Free Home: The Fair Hearing Appeals Cases

A sampling of the cases will provide an illustration of their range.

Case 1. A husband and wife had been divorced without obtaining a custody order from the court. The two children of the marriage, together with another child whose paternity the husband denied, lived with the mother. After the divorce she had established a "stable relationship" with another man and had had four children by him. The father, meanwhile, had remarried and was earning approximately $500 per month. He and his second wife offered a free home to the oldest child, a girl aged 10. The mother, now living alone with the seven children, wished to keep the girl at home. Although a careful evaluation of the father's home indicated that it was a "good one in terms of love, understanding and emotional and financial security," the board decided to continue the AFDC grant to support the girl in her mother's home. The decision was based on the girl's attachment to her mother, her express desire not to be separated from her brother and sister, and because "we cannot consider that the home offered is a suitable substitute for her present home or that the care reportedly available to her in the home of her father and stepmother . . . might adequately replace the emotional security that a mother can give her own children and which is essential to their well-being" (E., September 1957).

Case 2. Although their mother had their legal custody, the children were living in the home of their paternal grandmother in California and were being suppported by AFDC funds. Their parents were divorced; the father was serving a prison sentence for having forged AFDC checks, and the mother had remarried and was living in Texas. The case arose because Los Angeles County had discontinued the aid payments to the grandmother when the mother offered to take the children into her home in Texas. The mother and stepfather and their two children were living in a federal housing project. Their home was investigated for Los Angeles by the State Department of Public Welfare of Texas, which reported that "the relationships within the home seemed to be good. Mr. and Mrs. B. seem to provide a stable and secure home for their children who appear to be well-cared for and well-adjusted. [The two B children] speak of their sisters in California and would like them to live with them." The second husband had not met his wife's children, but he was willing to support them. He had a minor police record for gaming and petty theft. The paternal grandmother did not wish to let the children go; she testified that the mother had not communicated with the children for five years. The grandmother was fifty-seven years old and worked as a cleaning woman in office buildings. The board denied the grandmother's appeal, affirming the county's decision to terminate aid to her. The decision read in part that

> We must take note of the fact that the children are deprived of their mother's care. They are deprived of a meaningful relationship with a seemingly understanding stepfather who might provide the paternal care which they have lacked for so long. In addition, the children are separated from their siblings.
> From all indications, the children are offered a home which is acceptable and in which they will be wanted and loved. Whatever the reasons for their mother's past seeming indifference, whether attributed in some measure to aspects related to finances or to limitations related to youth, the advantages of having the children with their mother, who also has legal custody of them, far outweigh other considerations related to appellant. (E., November 1962.)

Case 3. The mother and father, who were both married to other spouses, had been living together for four years and had produced two children. The couple had separated, and the mother applied for AFDC support for the children. Los Angeles County denied her application on the ground that "appellant has been offered full support for her family if she would reconcile with her common-law husband. However, she has chosen a father-less home in order to get public assistance, rather than a united family without dependence." The mother testified that the father had never fully supported her; that he drank to excess and that he was violent and abusive to her daughter when he drank, although "when he became sober and calmed down, he expected everybody to forget all about his behavior when he was drinking." The Social Welfare Board held that the aid should be granted (V., July 1961), despite the County's insistence that the mother be forced to reconcile with the father of her children (in whose home, it might be pointed out, it was a crime for her to live, since their adulterous cohabitation constituted a "double misdemeanor" for which both could have been fined $1,000 or imprisoned in the county jail for one year, or both (see California Penal Code § 269b).

Case 4. The mother, a woman of forty-seven, maintained a home for her nine children. She had three children by Mr. A, three by Mr. B, two by Mr. C, and one—the subject of this application—by Mr. D, a married man. The facts indicate that "during the fifteen years the County has known the appellant and her family, the County has been led to the conclusion that the appellant has rejected each of her children from the time of conception with the result that six of them have juvenile records and three of the older children also have adult records and are presently in San Quentin." The child here involved had lived with her father and his wife since she was nine years old, and they intended to file legal proceedings to obtain her custody. Meanwhile she was with the mother, and the father had offered a free home. The county had removed the child from the AFDC allowance to the mother, and she appealed. The board upheld the county. Pointing out that "efforts . . . made during the 15 year dependency history of this family by many community agencies to provide services calculated to strengthen the family . . . do not appear to have been productive," the board concluded that "necessary physical and emotional security, financial and social benefits for [the child] would be met more adequately in her father's home than in the home of the appellant" (J., June 1961).

Case 5. This illustrates the use of the offer of a free home as a device for expressing family hostility. In this case the child had lived with his maternal grandmother since he was three months old, when she had removed him from the prison hospital ward where he had been born. His mother was released from prison when he was about two years old; she lived with him and her mother until the boy was three. At that time the mother married and left to establish a home with her husband. The child was supported by AFDC in his mother's home for two months following her marriage; but the grandmother, unhappy because he was in his mother's home, offered to provide a free home for the boy. An evaluation determined that the grandmother's offer was a resource available for the child's support; AFDC to keep him in his mother's home was terminated, and he returned to the home of his grandmother. Some years later, when the grandmother was fifty-eight, in poor health, and partially blind, she became unable to support the boy and applied for AFDC to maintain him in her home. His mother, upon being informed of the application, offered to provide a free home for her son. Investigation of the two homes disclosed that the grandmother lived in a small, two-room apartment, while the mother lived with her husband and their two children in a small house. The board found that the long-term advantages offered to the child by his mother and her husband, when coupled with the mother's preferential legal right to custody, indicated that the boy's best interests would be served by placement with the mother even though he would probably suffer a "temporary emotional trauma" at leaving his grandmother. Aid provided for his support in the grandmother's home was therefore discontinued (*T.*, March 1958).

The thirty-nine cases suggest some of the strains in the California welfare system. Of the thirty-nine cases, twenty-three arose from Los Angeles County, six more from its neighbor county, San Diego, and only six were from the San Francisco Bay Area. The impact on Los Angeles County of California's population explosion is reflected in these cases, and the cases illustrate the county's attitude that many of the AFDC mothers had left other states for the purpose of getting relief in California. In many of the cases the worker appeared convinced that the mother, having left her husband in Oklahoma, Louisiana, or Mississippi, was motivated by California's high welfare standards to come to California in order to qualify for relief. In one case the county workers seemed to believe that the size of California's monthly payment had motivated the family break-up: the mother, they claimed "forsook her spouse for a monetary advantage, looking to the high ANC standards in California." (*S.*, September, 1961). In twenty-seven of the thirty-nine cases, the person offering the free home resided outside of California; in only twelve of the cases did the offer come from persons living within the state. Thus, the cases lend support to the suspicion that the regulations concerning the offer of a free home, with their emphasis on the child's financial security, could be used to send the child (and sometimes the mother) back to the state he or she had left.

One of the pervasive problems of Regulation C-316 was the question of establishing the good faith of the person offering the free home. In most of these cases the absent father had been located by the district attorney and reminded of his duty to support his children. All too often the offer to take the child into the home was a compromise with the alternative of paying the mother for the support of the child. As one staff member expressed it, "We will no doubt get more 'offers' as absent fathers are located and support demanded. Somehow, they always feel it would be cheaper to give the support at their home—or they're mad at momma and will punish her by offering to take the children away." The appeals cases lend support to this view: in thirty-two cases the child was living with the mother, and in all cases (not all the same cases) the offer of a free home was made by the father.

In outcome, the appeals cases were heavily in favor of the appellant. In twenty-eight cases the State Social Welfare Board reversed the county to order that the aid payments be granted, if they had been denied, or continued, if they had been suspended. In only eleven cases were the county's refusal to grant or termination of the grant upheld. The board was consistent, however, in looking at all the cases from the point of view of the AFDC program. Although the staff had at one point suggested that if the child were living with a person having legal custody, the offer of a free home would not be considered without the consent of the person having custody, the cases do not treat the question of legal custody as decisive. At the same time, however, the point is not ignored. Thus, in several cases the mother had legal custody and the children were receiving AFDC in her home. In these cases the board tended to refuse to permit the withdrawal of funds to be used as a lever to force the mother to give up custody to the father (*E.*, November 1962; *J.*, November 1962; *W.*, September 1960; *S.*, April 1954). This decision was made in one case even in the face of an indication that the mother's home might be considered unfit (*D.*, May 1961). If, however, the father held legal custody and the children were being supported by AFDC in the mother's home, the decisions were in conflict. In some cases the grant was continued because the father had not "actually exercised" his right to legal custody (*M.*, June 1962); because his home was not immediately available for the child (*A.*, January 1962); or, in one case, apparently because the worker thought the child was better off in the mother's home (*R.*, August 1960). In other cases, including one where the mother had deserted the family prior to reclaiming the children (*J.*, November 1962), the father's right to custody was enforced by terminating the aid (for example, *F.*, May 1957; *S.*, October 1955).

Other unique problems were presented by fathers who agreed to provide a free home for their children only if the mother would consent to return as well, and by grandparents who agreed to provide for their grandchildren if the minor mother-daughter would return to the family home. Without exception the board properly refused to permit the withdrawal of AFDC funds to be used to force marital reconciliations. Nor was the erring daughter required to return home, at least if she was within a year or so of attaining full majority and it was not entirely clear that her parents' offer was bona fide (*T.*, December 1956; *M.*, December 1956; *McC.*, March 1954).

Withdrawal of Regulation C-316

Attention has previously been directed in this paper to Dr. tenBroek's emphasis on the function of the appeals cases as a test of the policy and regulations formulated by the Social Welfare Board. The point is illustrated by these cases involving the offer of a free home. The primary impetus that led to the ultimate withdrawal of Regulation C-316 came from an appeal case heard before the Board in April 1961. The facts in the *D* case were as follows:

> The mother and father were divorced in April 1952 in Missouri. Custody of the three children was given to the mother; the father was ordered to pay $20 per month per child as support. Following the divorce, the mother came with the children to live in Santa Clara County. Although the father made the monthly payments provided in the divorce decree for the support of the children, the mother applied for ANC in October 1952 to supplement this meager allowance. In 1955 she moved with the children to San Diego County to live with her parents and again applied for ANC. The father was notified of the application and asked if he was able to increase the payments. He had remarried and was living in Missouri with his second wife and their child. Both were schoolteachers. They lived in a small home with one bedroom (he planned to enclose a large porch for additional sleeping space), which they were purchasing. The father's annual salary was approximately $4,000 per year. When notified of his first wife's application for ANC, he replied that he was unable to increase the monthly support payments to the children but that he and his wife would be glad to take the three children into their home. The district attorney, upon being notified of the father's offer, declined to seek legal action to increase the father's support payments.
>
> The County Welfare Department elected to consider the father's offer of a free home as a resource available for the children's support, and aid was terminated as of August 31, 1960.
>
> The mother appealed, and the case was set for hearing in San Diego County on January 24, 1961. At the hearing it was disclosed that San Diego County had initiated proceedings through the juvenile court to test the fitness of the mother's home. The probation report alleged that the children had been observed at least once in the street without adult supervision at 1 A.M.; that they were habitually allowed to roam the streets in a filthy condition, begging the neighbors for food; that on two occasions adult males had remained overnight in the home; that the children were taken away and kept away from their home for a week by the mother following an argument with her mother about a man; that the public health nurse at the school was concerned about the children because of their dirty clothing and their apparent lack of proper food; and that the children were nervous and inclined to petty theft, fighting, and other attention-getting devices at school. All allegations contained in this report were denied by the mother and her witnesses, who were present at the ANC hearing. At the time of the ANC hearing the case was pending before the juvenile court.

The State Department referee filed a proposed decision on March 17, 1961, affirming the county in deciding that the father's offer of a home was a resource available to the children. The draft opinion stressed the father's stable remarriage, the intellectual advantages his home would provide for the children, and his strong desire to have the children in his home. When the case came before the Board for hearing on April 20, 1961, the director of the state department, Mr. Wedemeyer, asked that the case be put over so that another draft opinion could be prepared. He stated before the Board that the current situation pending the appeal was that aid had been terminated, the juvenile court was involved on the question of placement, and

in the meantime because of the cessation of aid we have left the children in effect in an undesirable home situation without even the basic needs for support for several months, thus I think miscarrying the basic ideas that have been advanced around the program and for which I have felt we should stand, that is . . . not penalizing the children by leaving them in a situation where they were in want unless other alternatives have been developed which would assure that their needs were being taken care of. . . . Now, in view of these facts, I think we should take this back and deal with the question of where these children are and their need and whether or not . . . the denial of the grant is a proper way to enforce the proper placement of the children. It certainly does not appear to be one that is serving that purpose at the present time. The question of who has custody of the children should be a court decision in my opinion. [Minutes, April 20, 1961, pp. 124–125]

Following the board meeting, Wedemeyer sent a memorandum to the Chief Referee, dated April 25, 1961, in which he made the point that the *D* case illustrated a new trend in the offer-of-a-home cases in that it furnished detailed evidence of the living conditions in the home provided for the children as well as evidence of the children's eligibility for aid. The director suggested that the department had a dual responsibility in such cases:

first of all financial help to the persons having the responsibility for the care of the children, and second, the protective service to see that the situation is constructive for the children. The latter is carried out wherever possible [within the Department] by counseling, guidance, and help to the parent or custodian of the children. When this is not adequate it is carried out by working with and referring to those agencies or sources [outside the Department] who have responsibility for determining matters of custody and developing the base on which alternative plans can be carried out. *Until such steps are taken, the children must be provided for to the extent that they lack the essentials for adequate maintenance.* We need to observe here the principle that denial of aid cannot be used in the absence of an adequate alternative, which can be achieved either through the cooperation and voluntary effort of the caretaker or through the intervention of the proper enforcement agency. [Italics added]

The rewritten decision was submitted on May 4, 1961, and approved by the board on May 25, 1961. The reasoning, which conforms to the director's views expressed to the Board and in his memo to the legal staff, stated in part that

The evidence presented in this matter indicates the children may well be benefitted socially and emotionally and may enjoy increased financial security if they were living in the home of their father. However, the legal aspects of the situation are such that the offer of a free home cannot be considered a resource in determining eligibility for Aid despite the apparent benefits arising from the other factors.

At the time of the hearing, the appellant had the legal custody of three minor children. The question of custody is exclusively for the courts to decide and so is the question of the fitness of the home provided by the mother. Since the question of custody is outside the jurisdiction of this Board, a finding of ineligibility based upon the present circumstances would not be proper in this case. It is necessary that Aid be rendered in order to assure the maintenance of the children, for the appellant has the legal custody and the children are living with her. The granting of such aid is necessary in the absence of a voluntary acceptance by the mother of the offer of a home so that the children's physical needs may be met while they are in her home. Any contrary finding, no matter how desirable, would by indirection be the probable cause of a change of duly authorized legal custody as denial of Aid in this case would necessarily operate as a lever to force this mother to relinquish the custody of these children to their father and thus interfere with judicially-determined custody. The solution to the problem of the unfitness of the mother's home as shown by the evidence presented is being sought by the county through the juvenile court.

Thus, dissatisfaction with the Department's policy in the offer-of-a-home cases had already been expressed by the director and concurred in by the board when a report prepared for a senate committee by a law professor (Sweet 1961:75–78) on the role of the Board in the ANC program criticized, almost in passing, the Board's policy in these cases. Sweet found that the Board's actual decisions in the offer-of-a-home cases had "by and large, shown good sense." But he stressed the inappropriateness of allowing the board's decision on aid to thwart, in practice if not in theory, the court decision on custody of the child; and he pointed out that the board's action in extending the concept of an offer of a free home as a resource from institutionalized children, as provided in Section 1524, to all children receiving public support was wholly gratuitous. He indicated that federal officials did not concur in the board's interpretation of the federal requirement of considering all resources available to the child as including the offer of a free home. He suggested that a feasible solution would be to grant aid based on physical possession of the child, but to condition such aid on the custodian's obtaining a court decree granting her custody within a specified period of time.

In a response to the Sweet report prepared by the Department staff, the point was conceded that the offer of a home regulation "represented an extension of W & I Code 1524 and was also promulgated to be consistent with the basic rule in ANC that all income and resources for the support of the child shall be determined and related to the total needs to establish that a child is needy." And in a memo to the ANC staff, dated July 20, 1962, the point is made that the Department's present position was based on Director Wedemeyer's decision in the *D* case of 1961:

> The Director actually initiated the revision of this policy in April 1961 on the basis of the *D*. appeal. In his memo of April 25, 1961, he set forth the principles which he later confirmed in response to the Sweet report. His position that the Department's two basic responsibilities in these cases are payment of financial aid and protection of the child rules out the offer of a free home as a resource to an otherwise eligible child. This in effect requires that Regulation C-316 be repealed. The offer of a Free Home in essence would become a factor to be taken into consideration in providing services for the protection of children.

On November 1, 1962, by recommendation of the Department staff, Regulation C-316 was changed to read as follows:

> OFFER OF A FREE HOME. Except as provided in Welfare and Institutions Code 1524, aid shall not be denied or discontinued for an otherwise eligible child who is offered a free home.

Section 1524, now renumbered 11264, is the section covering children who live in institutions for whom an offer of a proper home is made. Appeals cases involving Regulation C-316 after 1962 appear only rarely. For all practical purposes, the books are closed on the Offer of a Free Home in California. Practical experience with the actual cases presented by the appeals process had convinced the board that its broad interpretation of the federal requirement of considering all resources was unwise in this situation. Therefore the board, acting in its role as legislator and informed by its experience as a judge, changed the law.

Conclusion

Public welfare exists today in the center of controversy and conflicting interests. One such conflict is long-standing; its adversaries are found chiefly among the more conservative tax-payer groups, on the one hand, and, on the other hand, the social workers who are the professionals of the welfare system. Thus, at a hearing in California before the Senate Fact Finding Committee on Labor and Welfare in 1960, District Attorney Nedjedly of Contra Costa County charged that the welfare caseload exhibited "on the one hand moral decline evidenced by the casual acceptance of illegitimacy and the abrogation of marriage or any marital or family responsibility and upon the other side the collapse of the character of the individual who finds it simpler to qualify for welfare than to seek assistance first from himself" (63–64). Other witnesses expressed the similar view that AFDC mothers regularly produced illegitimate children in order to increase the size of their monthly checks and that, in any event, the money was as likely to be spent by a mother to buy the boyfriend's gin as to provide the baby's milk. Nor are such views confined to senate hearings. For a time in California it appeared likely that local judges had found an effective means of terminating illegitimacy: AFDC mothers charged with welfare fraud, or even with being in a place where narcotics were unlawfully smoked with knowledge that the activity was occurring, were to be placed on probation instead of being jailed only if they consented to "voluntary" sterilization. Happily for the administration of justice in California, this practice was brought to an abrupt end when a superior court held that such orders were beyond the power of municipal judges (*In re Hernandez,* Superior Court, Santa Barbara, 1966).

The professional social workers tend to counter such charges with the argument that the AFDC program's chief problem is that it mistakenly provides only money to the recipients rather than money plus services. Miss Angell, testifying at the 1960 Senate hearing on behalf of the California Social Workers' Organization, urged that if more trained social workers could be made available to work with the AFDC families, more damaged individuals could be helped to reclaim themselves and get off the relief rolls.

A broader controversy, just beginning to be noticed by lawyers sensitive to infringements of individual liberty and to the right of privacy, concerns the vulnerability of poor persons to the regulations of the system, and to pressure from social workers. Thus, Professor Reich (1964–1965:1245–1246): "the poor are all too easily regulated. They are an irresistible temptation to moralists, who want not only to assist but to 'improve' by imposing virtue. They are subject to social workers' urges to prescribe 'what is best.' It is significant that 76 per cent of Briar's informants thought that when the welfare social worker suggested that a recipient see a psychiatrist, the recipient should be expected to go and 66 per cent thought the recipient must go in order to continue receiving aid (Briar 1966:56–57).

Dr. Bernard Diamond (1966:37–41), a psychiatrist, has concluded that deeper emotions than mere concern over the proper use of public funds produce these sweeping attacks on welfare recipients. Speculating that "society simultaneously loves and hates its poor, its dependent, and its disabled," he suggests that this ambivalence gives rise to a typically neurotic solution in the shape of welfare policy which

provides aid and nurture, but only to the degree that it ensures that they [the recipients] remain nonpersons. Nonpersons must not be allowed to suffer to the point where they might be tempted to reverse the social order. At the same time, they must be constantly reminded, through the infliction of punitive sanctions and discriminatory exclusions, that they are nonpersons.

This alleged unconscious aim of the welfare system has been recently attacked by two staff members of the Columbia University School of Social Work. In two articles, Cloward and Piven have announced a strategy they hope would create a political crisis "that could lead to legislation for a guaranteed annual income and thus an end to poverty" (1966:510). The strategy, proposed in 1966, was "a massive drive to recruit the poor *onto* the welfare rolls" with the result of causing "bueraucratic disruption in welfare agencies and fiscal disruption in local and state governments," which in turn would "generate severe political strains, and deepen existing divisions among elements in the big-city Democratic coalition: the remaining white middle class, the white working class ethnic groups and the growing minority poor." If this strategy were followed, the authors predict, "to avoid a further weakening of that historic coalition, a national Democratic administration would be constrained to advance a federal solution to poverty that would override local welfare failures, local class and racial conflicts and local revenue dilemmas" (1966:510). In a second article in 1967 the authors report substantial progress toward organization of the poor but reiterate that the movement's most potent strategy lies in continuous recruitment of eligible persons to the welfare rolls. Only then, they suggest, will the "nonpersons" described by Dr. Diamond be able to command enough numerical strength to create a crisis and thus force major reforms in the system at the national level.

Regulation C-316 and its attendant fair-hearing appeals cases must be seen within this context. The power to determine the fitness of a child's home obviously must be exercised with great restraint. As the decisions made clear, the welfare laws and regulations did not require the case workers to assess the fitness of the home as a condition for eligibility. The assumption of this power must have greatly threatened the recipients. Other agencies in the community, notably the juvenile court and its probation department, are charged with the responsibility of providing protective services for children. If the probation department has reason to believe that a home is unfit for child-rearing, it may bring an action to have the child declared a "dependant of the juvenile court" (Welfare and Institutions Code §600). Strict standards of proof are required under the statutes to establish the unfitness of a home; even if the court takes jurisdiction, the child may be returned to the home under supervision of the probation case worker. Referrals from the AFDC caseworker to the probation department are by no means rare; although precise figures showing how many AFDC children are referred to probation departments or other protective service agencies as "neglected" children are apparently not available, a two-months sample of neglect referrals from all sources in the Minneapolis-St. Paul area showed that, although only 3 per cent of families in the general population were on public assistance, 42 per cent of the families against whom neglect petitions had been filed were relief recipients (Boehm 1964:459). A California study estimated that during the twelve months ending June 30, 1964, a "substantial" number of the 21,264 children who were referred to probation departments from all sources as possible dependent and neglected children were located in the AFDC case load (National Study Service 1965:8-12).

When the welfare worker was instructed by Regulation C-316 and its accompanying handbook material to evaluate the home offered the child in comparison to his present home, the worker was in effect directed to make a determination similar to that required of the probation staff, but without its attendant safeguards. Director Wedemeyer's decision to limit the function of the welfare worker to seeing that the children were protected in the sense of being provided with the necessities of life, pending the investigation of the home by the probation department or other protective service agency, must be seen as a recognition of the differing functions of other local welfare and probation departments.

Thus the conflict posed by Regulation C-316's implicit requirement that the welfare case worker balance the adequacy of a child's present home against his need for public support was finally resolved by a complete separation of task and authority; the agency providing public support was forbidden to evaluate the child's home, and the agency charged with investigating the fitness of the home had no public funds to disburse. The conflict between what is best for the child and what is most economical for the taxpayer no longer arises within a single agency.

The point is not merely that the conflict could not be resolved in a fair and equitable manner, given the setting in which it arose. Possibly no other agency could have resolved the conflict posed in those terms. The narrower point of this paper is to call attention to the process by which the law-giver set himself a problem to solve, promulgated a solution in the form of a rule, discovered that the rule was not adequate in the light of case-developed experience, withdrew the rule, and abandoned the problem as one proper for him to solve. The recognition of this process, I suggest, may provide an additional tool to supplement the "trouble case" for discovering law and legal institutions in tribal settings.

Cases, Courts, and Congestion

In attempting to understand the relationship between law and social structure, it is obviously necessary to go beyond the legal rules and to examine the law in operation. The rules constitute a blueprint for behavior, not behavior itself, and they can give only a rough indication of what individuals in a society will do in fact.

A crucial element in the transformation of rules from legal imperatives to social reality is to be found in the social organizations or social subsystems that create and enforce the law. Even in supposedly simple cultures these subsystems may be complex structures; and in modern industrial societies they have become intricate enterprises that play a major part in shaping legal norms in ways that far transcend their culturally assigned role. Legislative bodies, the police, the courts—all leave their mark in terms of both manifest and latent consequences.

One important aspect of this transforming function involves the capability of the legal system in relationship to the demands that are placed upon it. The courts are particularly significant in this respect, for the number of disputes they can handle and the speed with which they do so have a heavy influence on the paths that the members of a society will come to choose for securing just or equitable solutions for the conflicts inevitably arising in the course of social interaction.

Now many subsystems suffer at times from the problem of congestion or overload due to the vagaries of input. The cost of occasional delay or congestion, however, is held to be outweighed by the cost that would be entailed by creating and maintaining a subsystem designed for the rare peak performance. But in the case of the courts in the United States,

327

the problem of overload appears to be chronic. In part this circumstance can be attributed to a steadily rising volume of demand placed on the courts, stemming from a growth of population that has approximately doubled in half a century; and it appears that few courts have been provided with the resources to keep pace with this vastly expanded number of legal disputes. It is also necessary, however, to examine the cultural setting of the courts and their internal social structure in order to understand the way in which American society attempts to grapple with its quantity of legal conflicts.

In most of the literature on the administration of justice in the United States, delay in court is treated as an unmitigated evil. The congestion of our courts, we are told, is a critical social and professional problem, a basic threat to legal rights, and a major weakness of our judicial system.[1] Although much of the current discussion of court congestion sounds a note of contemporary alarm, delay in court has long been seen as a serious defect dogging our legal system. Over the years society has attempted to cure delay with a great variety of remedies, yet despite the imagination and effort devoted to getting rid of this *malaise* of the law, it appears that we are not much better off than we were fifty years ago, when Roscoe Pound delivered his address on "The Causes of Popular Dissatisfaction with the Administration of Justice" at the annual meeting of the American Bar Association.

Delay in court seems to belong, then, to a more general class of social problems—that is, where many people are concerned, much is said and attempted, and little progress is made. The difficulties cannot be attributed to the sources of social malfunctioning so often singled out for attention, such as early patterns of socialization or supposedly immutable components of personality structure. Why does the problem persist?

In part, of course, much of the difficulty lies in the complexities and costs attending any form of planned social change involving more than minor social tinkering. Even more important, however, is the fact that delay in court (like many social problems) often stubbornly resists solution because society fails to come to grips with the socially acceptable goals and values that are enmeshed in the social reality defined as troublesome or undesirable and that society seeks to eradicate. Part of the difficulty in getting rid of court congestion appears to be because it is not simply an accidental defect of the law, but is rooted in some of the legal system's most cherished characteristics.

In any event, the argument here is that there are serious barriers to the solution of the social problem of delay in court that transcend the

---

1. Concern with the problem is well summarized in *Lagging Justice, The Annals of the American Academy of Political and Social Science*, March 1960. For one of the few attempts to analyze the possible positive functions of delay in court, see Maurice Rosenberg (1965).

specific details of particular reforms. It is these more general points of resistance, involving the social structure of the court and its place in society, with which this paper is concerned.

Delay in Court

The definition of delay in court poses hard issues, as many writers have indicated.[2] Where we should begin counting delay and where we should end remain more than a little arbitrary, although the date when a case is "at issue" and the date when trial begins are commonly accepted as the start and finish for the measurement of delay.[3] Much more troublesome, however, is that the word "delay" suggests some extra or unnecessary time beyond a normal or reasonable amount, but what is normal or reasonable is far from clear. An interval of more than six months is sometimes taken as being beyond the "normal" limits of a case, but this gross categorization seems to be designed more for ease in preparing judicial reports than as a reflection of an agreed-upon standard. The problem is that there is no socially defined crisis point, no fixed, definite level of delay at which corrective action *must* be taken, in the manner of quality controls in many other areas.[4] In fact, it appears likely that many courts do not possess systems for handling information that allow them to determine promptly and easily the precise status of cases in their backlog. With vague—or at best arbitrary—definitions of what constitutes an unreasonable length of time for bringing a case to trial, with inadequate data, and with a lack of clear-cut consequences, many courts find themselves drifting deeper and deeper into difficulties, rather than being driven toward a solution.

This administrative flaccidity of the courts finds a counterpart in the society at large. The mobilization of public support for an attack on a social problem often requires the evocation of a crisis mood, a sense of urgency, and a sharp awareness of the consequences of failure to take ameliorative steps. The crisis may be real or imaginary, but it is the

2. See Zeisel, Kalven, and Bucholz (1959: Chapter 4).

3. As Milton Green (1960:9) has pointed out, "Considerable difficulty is encountered in ascribing a precise meaning to the term 'at issue.' It usually refers to the status of a case when final pleadings on both sides have been filed and preliminary motions have been disposed of. In some jurisdictions, however, the term is used in a different sense. For instance, in New Jersey a case is considered 'at issue' when the first answering pleading is filed, whereas in New York a case is not considered 'at issue' until the pleadings have been completed, all preliminary motions made and determined, and a certificate filed by the attorneys indicating that the case is ready for trial."

4. One exception to this attitude is to be found in those states where criminal cases are required to be brought to trial within a designated period of time after the filing of an indictment. It is significant that the "necessity" for a speedy trial created by such rules can have a dramatic effect on the problem of delay in criminal matters.

perception of crisis that is important and that galvanizes the public into a demand for solutions and the provision of necessary resources. In the matter of delay in court, however, the public is apt to have an even less clear idea of what is normal or abnormal than has the legal system itself. Instead of creating an atmosphere of emergency, an increase in the time necessary to bring a case to trial is likely to generate an ill-focused irritation.

Of course there are some individuals—and their attorneys—with cases awaiting trial who are quite certain that *their* cases have long since passed any possible limit of reasonable delay. Against these, however, there must be set those individuals who have filed cases simply as a means of harassment, without any intention of ever reaching the trial stage, or who are merely using the court as an arena in which to stage a settlement. And if those individuals who are now suffering from delay in court do provide some sort of "constituency for reform" in the administration of justice, their appetite for such efforts is likely to be dulled with the passage of time once their case has been disposed of.

In general, litigation in court is outside the experience of most people in our society, or it is a once-in-a-lifetime event. For delay in court, then, as for a variety of other social problems, it is difficult to find a strong and continuing interest based on personal involvement that can serve as a powerful lever of social change. In addition, there is the problem that those who have been involved in the slow course of justice are likely to be a heterogeneous social category rather than an organized social group—a crude sample of the population, united only by the fact that they have been exposed to the law's lagging movement. It is not a promising basis for a program of legal change.[5]

The Structure of the Judiciary

Even though the concept of delay in court is a muddy one, and though sustained, organized public support for alleviation of the problem is a difficult matter, it might be supposed that a powerful movement to ameliorate the problem could be found in the judiciary itself. Public declarations of concern over the issue are certainly not lacking among lawyers and judges, as has been suggested earlier, and it is true that sections of bar associations at both the national and local levels have dedicated themselves to the issue.[6] Nonetheless, I very much doubt that

5. Newspapers on occasion may mount an attack on delay in court. Such efforts, however, are all too often little more than a superficial political maneuver, aimed at embarrassing the party in power, rather than a serious attempt to build and sustain an informed public concern.
6. See, for example, American Bar Association (1961).

there are many who would claim that a full-scale attack on the problem had yet been undertaken, and there are probably few who would have the hubris to disagree with the statement that "Progress toward bringing about any improvement in the machinery for the administration of justice is all too often impeded by lethargy and inertia, if not by downright opposition" (American Bar Association 1961: xiii). To understand the nature of this inertia and opposition, we must turn to the social structure of the court.

In his analysis of the different types of legitimate social order, Max Weber (1947: chapter III) distinguished the informally organized group centered on the person of the charismatic leader, the patrimonial feudal system based on tradition, and the bureaucracy with its rational and explicit rules. It is too often forgotten, however, that these are pure, or heuristic, types and that even in a modern industrial society such as our own, with its dominant stress on bureaucratic structure, many organizations contain important traditional or charismatic elements. It is in this light that we must examine the court, for despite its outward appearance of a bureaucracy, the court possesses many of the aspects of a loosely organized feudal order, with an emphasis on fiefs, patronage, and personal loyalties.

The judge—the lord of this quasi-feudal system—is distinctive for the extent to which he is autonomous within his realm; there are few social roles invested with such power in American society that are yet subject to so little control. For example, a few years ago in Colorado the judges of the Supreme Court ruled that no bar association or court could institute disciplinary proceedings against any judge for any reason. There was no one to deny them. The movement for political reform that swept Europe in the early part of the nineteenth century and found expression in the United States as Jacksonian democracy had as one of its aims, of course, the popular control of the judiciary. And from that time to the present, our legal system has struggled with questions of judicial selection, the removal of incompetent judges, and so on, with rather indifferent success.[7] All this, however, has left untouched the more mundane and yet perhaps more serious issue—the control and supervision on the judge in the day-to-day operation of the court.

In the analysis of the judicial function, great stress is laid on the elements of unhurried deliberation, freedom from external constraints, and the dignity attaching to the judge's position. Rebecca West speaks of the majesty of English judges in their courts, "weighty with earned honors,"

7. See, for example, Joel B. Grossman (1965). The United States Judicial Conference is now considering two proposed laws to deal with the problem of incompetent federal judges, since the only constitutional provision for the removal of a federal judge consists of the cumbersome process of impeachment by the House and conviction by the Senate.

and the prestige in the United States of such a strong and independent occupational role unquestionably places the judge near the top of the occupational hierarchy.[8] We cannot ignore the fact, however, that judges generally do not exist simply as isolated figures of magisterial splendor. Typically, there are a *number* of judges who are members of a court and who somehow must be bound together in a complex administrative system. Thus, for example, in the Denver District Court in Colorado there are fourteen judges whose activities must be coordinated; and in larger courts, such as the Supreme Court of New York County and Bronx County, there may be forty or more (Zeisel et al. 1959:26).

Unfortunately there are acute difficulties posed by the supervision and control of such individuals who by tradition, training, and experience find the usual bureaucratic orientation alien. As one writer has said, "It is realized that judges are not ordinary employees and that the problem, if the judiciary is to retain its dignity and independence, is not simply one of time-clock efficiency" (Zeisel et al. 1959:14). Such a delicacy may or may not be justified. The important point, however, is that the efficiency of the court and the problem of delay is likely to be subordinated to the autonomy of the judge. The social problem thus created is not held to be desirable, but its elimination would require disturbing deeply held traditions of the legal system.

Perhaps it seems somewhat unfair to characterize the judges of our superior courts as prima donnas, for despite examples of arrogance and willful behavior, we can assume in general that they are men of high purpose and serious intent. Nonetheless, the connotations of the phrase convey some of the problems of the court in binding the judges together by explicit lines of authority, standardized procedures, closely geared time schedules, objective measurement of performance, and subservience to a general plan, all of which are basic to modern bureaucratic organization. As Weber has indicated (1947:337), "For the needs of mass administration today, bureaucratic administration is completely indispensable. The choice is between bureaucracy and dilettantism." For many of our courts, with budgets of one million dollars or more per year, scores or hundreds of employees, and a growing number of cases to be handled, the need to avoid dilettantism is clear, but the ability to allocate and control judicial manpower in a rational fashion is uncertain. It is imperative, therefore, in introducing modern administrative methods into the court, to distinguish between problems involving personnel policies, bookkeeping, and paper flow and those such as the assignment of judges and the proper length of hearings. The former are relatively easy to solve, but the latter involve the touchy issues of spheres of influence, competing professional careers, and the personal status of those we have called the

8. See Wilson and Kolb, 1949, pp. 464–474.

lords of a quasi-feudal system; and here both judges and lawyers interested in legal reform begin to move with caution.

The appointment of an administrative officer for the court can ameliorate these problems, but it is no guarantee of a cure. If, on the one hand, the administrative officer is a lawyer, serving as chief clerk of the court, he may find himself without the prestige or personal standing necessary to deal with the men he is trying to direct and supervise. He may, indeed, hold his position as a political appointment of the judges sitting *en banc*, and they may deeply resent any serious attempts on his part to mold them into an effective judicial unit. If, on the other hand, the administrative officer of the court is an administrative judge or a presiding judge, selected for this position by his peers, he may be somewhat better off in dealing with his colleagues in some matters, but his efforts to develop efficient procedures are just as likely to be sabotaged or disregarded as an undue bid to stand *primus inter pares*.

It seems possible, then, that the arguments for "modern administration" in the court are often seriously incomplete and do not really get to the heart of the matter. It is all too easy to mistake the trappings of rational organization—the routines of "housekeeping," salary schedules, and so on—for the more fundamental factor of rationally organized effort devoted to a central purpose. As matters stand today, courts are apt to become that sociological monstrosity, the headless organization, with the men who have the potential power for control and leadership refusing to exercise it and holding a dog-in-the-manger philosophy, refusing to let anyone else do it either.

The forces hindering the building of a coherent court structure are strengthened by the fact that thirty-six states still select judges in the political scramble of an election rather than by appointment—which has not proven to be an effective means for popular control of the judiciary. And in this situation the judge is all too likely to feel that he has a grant of power that stands free from any possible administrative machinery. In fact, his supposed colleagues may be viewed as actual or potential political rivals, to be avoided or hindered rather than cooperated with; and the judge follows his individual course in his courtroom, his barony, surrounded by his retainers in the form of the bailiffs and clerks he has personally chosen.

Legal Procedures

The lack of a coherent court structure becomes apparent in the matter of creating a trial calendar that assigns cases for trial at a specific time and place. Ideally, there should always be one case before one judge in an orderly sequence. No judge should be left inadvertently idle for lack of a case to be heard, and no case should go untried for lack of an available judge. In fact, however, this ideal of full utilization of the court is seldom reached.

A portion of the court's failure to use its resources with maximum effectiveness can be traced to the inevitable mishaps that attend the close scheduling of human events, such as illness, emergencies, and so on. In addition, however, it appears that the trial calendar frequently exhibits "holes" or unused time, owing to two factors that are linked to the organization of the court and its mode of operation. First, the length of trial time required for cases placed on the calendar is often overestimated by the court, and thus the early conclusion of cases going to trial leaves a large amount of unemployed judicial manpower. Second, many cases scheduled for trial suddenly reach a settlement shortly before their trial date falls due. If no other cases can be substituted—and frequently the announcement of a settlement comes so close to the scheduled trial date that no substitute can be found—the court again is left with vacant time.[9]

Now it might be argued that these factors are beyond the control of the court and should be classified with those other "inevitable mishaps" that make the plans of mice and men so often go astray. Courts, however, like many other social subsystems with the potential of rational planning, are not necessarily the creatures of chance. It is at least theoretically possible to predict the length of trial time with greater accuracy, just as it is possible to predict with greater accuracy which cases will reach a settlement prior to trial. Furthermore, the court can overschedule its trial calendar on the expectation that a certain number of cases will reach a settlement, thus reducing the amount of time left idle for want of a case. And, in fact, this procedure is followed; but courts seldom push overscheduling very far for fear of falling into the error of having more cases than judges.

The creation of a court calendar is, of course, a gamble; and a balance must be struck between being too daring and too cautious. The temptation, however, is to err on the side of caution and to schedule too little work rather than too much, since a judge without a case is far less public, far less likely to arouse criticism and indignation, than attorneys who have been promised a trial of their case that they do not get. Given the social structure of the court, there is little pressure to be brought against

9. If a case has definitely been scheduled for trial, settlement may become more likely because the uncertainties of trial loom larger in the minds of attorneys and a settlement becomes preferable. It is also possible that full, detailed work on a case on the part of attorneys may be delayed until it seems certain that a case will go to trial. As this process comes into play, a basis of a mutually acceptable settlement is more likely to emerge, and a trial becomes unnecessary. Robert Merton has analyzed the phenomenon of the self-fulfilling prophecy in which the prediction of an event makes its occurrence more likely (Merton 1949:Chapter VII). We seem to be dealing here with the phenomenon of the self-defeating prophecy.

the judge who is guided by an excessive concern with the safe and comfortable administrative course. And the autonomy of the judge locked in the sanctuary of his courtroom often makes it difficult or impossible to assemble the information necessary for the better prediction of trial time and settlements so essential for the reduction of court congestion.[10]

In many forms of anthropological and sociological analysis, we are apt to overlook the ordinary details of the speed with which a social process takes place. The details of timing, however, may be no less significant than the goals, values, norms, and so on, that are often the focus of our attention. In the case of the legal process, the temporal dimension is particularly important, since the orderly, regular disposition of cases lies at the heart of the work of the court.

In the United States, as indicated in this paper, delay in court has been a persistent problem; and a rapidly increasing demand for the services of the courts, stemming in large measure from an increasing population, has often been held to be the major cause. The demand for services, however, is only one side of the coin, and it must be analyzed in light of the human resources assigned to the courts as part of the legal system and their willingness to organize their efforts in a rational fashion.

The courts may perform an integrative function for a culture, as a number of writers have argued, by providing a "fair," "impartial," referee institution transcending factional disputes.[11] But the very elements that make such a function possible—such as a stress of the independence of the judiciary and the dominance of traditional forms beyond the influence of individuals in conflict—may so impede the performance of the courts that disputes flow into new channels of adjudication.

The problem of delay in court, then, is a serious issue that may have profound consequences for the administration of justice. From the point of view of sociological theory, however, the problem can serve as an illuminating example of a more general dilemma that is frequently encountered as we examine the relationship between law and social structure. Western societies have generally placed great emphasis on the idea that government should be a matter of laws rather than men. The exercise of authority is not to be based on individual caprice, but is to flow from agreed-upon rules and accepted procedures. No set of rules, however, is so complete, so detailed, that the rules do not require interpretation and human judgment in their application. And Western societies have thus been confronted with the problem of creating not only just and equitable laws, but also just and equitable administrators of law.

The solution in part has been to free the administrators of law from many of the social pressures that might undermine their position as im-

10. See Sykes, 1967, pp. 377–386.
11. Compare Parsons (1954:Chapter XVIII).

partial dispensers of justice in the settlement of disputes. Judges, as we have pointed out, are made relatively autonomous; in addition, lawyers are given a large share of self-determination through the operation of professional guilds, courtrooms are protected with the demands for dignity and decorum, and so on. Society, in effect, attempts to seal off portions of the legal system from the passions and the special interests that so influence the ordinary course of men's affairs.

The dilemma, as we are now discovering to an ever greater extent, arises from the fact that subsystems within such spheres of freedom are likely to develop their own dynamic, their own institutional goals, which may subvert the function that provides the rationale for their autonomy. Society, then, finds itself caught up in an almost insolvable paradox: to build a government of laws rather than men, it must make the administrators of law at least partially autonomous; yet this autonomy may mean that the administrators of law are no longer fully responsive to the demand for justice. It is only in light of this larger problem that we can begin to understand the meaning of the assertion that justice delayed is justice denied.

PART IV

Comparative Studies

INTRODUCTION BY SALLY FALK MOORE

Identifying a common link among the three papers that follow, the conference group gathered them under the rubric, "Comparative Studies." Nader's own interest in designing a research project that would obtain comparable legal data from several concurrent field studies is evident in her work on the Berkeley Comparative Village Law Project. It is probably this interest in the problem of comparability that led the group to emphasize the comparative aspect of the essays that follow. For reasons that will be made plain, it is my view that, despite their form, the papers have more in common as discussions of the place and nature of concepts in law, than as essays on (or in) comparison. However, two of the papers do talk directly about descriptive problems in cross-cultural legal comparison, and the third compares the varied uses of a single law-related concept within one society and hence might be characterized as an intracultural comparison. It will be evident to any reader not only that comparison has a very different place in each of the papers, but that deeply imbedded into the two that discuss methods of comparison, there are differences of opinion about what is being compared and to what end.

It does not seem sensible to attempt here another brief review of the past applications of what is called the comparative method in anthropology, since these have been recently summarized by Eggan (1965: 357–372). The comparative studies Eggan cites are very diverse in subject matter, and in technique, and they vary enormously in scale. They range from the comparison of whole societies, of contrasting social types, of systems, of sequences of development, to small-scale studies of selected variables within limited types, studies of particular institutions, regions or periods of time. Eggan diplomatically makes no critical evaluation of the validity or worth of the results of the works he mentions. In very general terms he calls for more sophisticated research design and testing. He concludes rather blandly that "the comparative method is still a useful procedure in cultural anthropology despite the considerable variation in the conceptions held by different anthropologists as to its nature . . . the comparative method is not a "method" in the broad sense, but a technique for establishing similarities and differences" (Eggan 1965: 366).

Comparison can be said to be simply a technique, but it would be closer to the facts to say that it is very complicatedly a technique. The basic, double-ended dilemma is, *what to compare in order to find out what*. Theoretically, in the social sciences much research proceeds by setting problems in the form of hypotheses. These often concern the causal significance of the association of phenomena or of similarities and differences among phenomena. A class of data is selected to test (or illustrate) the propositions, but in fact what is usually tested (or illustrated) is the association or the degree of similarity. Another comparative procedure is to construct certain ideal types or models, producing them logically on the basis of explicit principles. Then social evidence is examined and analyzed in order to note and explain conformities and divergences from the typology. The objective is to test the adequacy of the principles as explanatory or descriptive devices. What is really tested is the degree to which the model and social realities are congruent.

Where the attempt is to prove, rather than to illustrate, much attention is given to obtaining a suitable number and sampling of instances; when possible, the results are quantified. Comparison may be more or less extensive, more or less rigorous in its attention to precision about comparability, more or less illustrative. A scholar has the methodological option of trying to prove his contentions by checking through all available data and adding up their results, or he may choose instead to illustrate his propositions by selecting what seem to him a few persuasive instances and leave it to others to try to refine or disprove them. Both methods have been used creatively by anthropology, and both have been used in studies that are worthless. Method alone does not guarantee significant results.

Such comparisons as have been made in the published material on anthropology and law have been illustrative. Probably the best-known are Hoebel's comparison of the legal systems of a handful of societies of varied degrees of political centralization and complexity, and Gluckman's comparison of his model of tribal society and its legal concomitants with the data from the Barotse and other pre-industrial peoples (Hoebel, 1954; Gluckman, 1955, 1965b). The question is where to move next in comparative work in anthropology and law.

Many of the current apparently technical discussions about legal comparisons are really about what ought to be compared—the what, not just the how. The merits of comparison itself are generally agreed on, and no one could object to a call for more thoroughness, more exactness, greater extensiveness. Where anthropologists differ—and they differ radically—is on the issues: what are *significant* problems, and what is *relevant* to them.

On the whole, the greatest disagreements and difficulties concerning comparisons do not lie at the comparative stage of study. It is the other stages that have the biggest hazards, the formulation of the problem and the choice of the criteria of relevance on the basis of which data are selected and classified for study. There are no mechanical techniques for deciding what questions to ask and what kind of information is necessary to answer them. The fact that today there are phenomenally improved methods of recording, storing, and retrieving information greatly increases the number, scale, and refinement of possible comparisons. However, it does not in any way answer the fundamental questions of what information to gather and what problems to resolve. In this area it is often each man for himself.

The anthropologist with an interest in law must face these basic questions, all the while taking care not to drown in the great oceans of existing information. Most of what is known about law is a huge mess from the standpoint of systematic sociological research. Legal data have been recorded for centuries for myriad purposes, but only relatively recently and to a very limited extent for the purpose of sociological analysis. The question of what can be used of this glut of stuff, and to what ends, raises to emergency proportions the issue of defining problems and determining relevance. The anthropologist is a late-comer into this morass. Because of the nature of anthropology, he may exercise the option of turning his back on the law libraries, but he cannot by doing so avoid the issues involved. They confront him in his field work as urgently as they would in the analysis of the existing sea of legal literature.

In investigating legal phenomena, on what basis is the anthropologist to decide what he is looking for and what to look at? Is he comparing legal concepts or behavior? Are these different from each other, or are they facets of the same entity? Is he comparing whole legal systems? Cases? Rules? Systems of rules dealing with particular substantive matters, land, inheritance, family, property transfer, and the like? Procedures? Is he interested in dispute settlement exclusively or in systems of social control in general? There is no end to the possible topics. Each person in the field defines somewhat differently what he is looking at and looking for. There is serious question whether there should be, or even whether there can be, consensus in the discipline about such matters.

Another basic problem in the law field is to what extent the anthropologist should look to the body of established knowledge when he plans a field of study or other investigation, and to what extent he should (and can) maintain a calculated looseness of approach in order to remain open to new observations. Law is a field of social activity that has been under close, self-conscious scrutiny as far back as there are written records. Anthropology has built its own theoretical frameworks and its own literature for looking at social materials. Unless the anthropologist conceives his research in terms of some such body of established knowledge and ultimately in terms of comparative work, there is not only the risk that the information each field worker collects will have no comparability to that found by any other, but also the opposite risk that the discipline will never advance but, endlessly naive, will forever retread the same paths, repetitively discovering the same phenomena. Other dangers attend the formulation of questions too tightly framed in terms of established knowledge. Traditional standardization of the form of inquiry may produce comparability of the data gathered, without such equivalence being a real quality of the phenomena observed. The possibility of having new insights may be inhibited by too narrow a definition of the field of observation, or by too strict an adherence to established ways of looking at the data. The dilemma of legal studies in anthropology is not in these respects different from that of any other research. Comparative studies emphasize all the problems inherent in single studies.

Anthropology advances through an integration of planned, rationally designed research and fortuitous discovery and insight. Since the instrument of this technique is the anthropologist himself, it is important that as much as possible of his reasoning be accessible to those who are interested in evaluating his results. One of the merits of the kind of discussion that took place at the Wenner-Gren Conference, and that is evident in published debate, is that it tends to produce a considerable degree of explicitness about basic assumptions, the general mental models of how things work and why, that underlie a scholar's choice in formulating questions and identifying evidence as relevant. It is for this reason that the discussion of concepts and comparisons that follow are not simply a discussion of techniques. Bohannan and Gluckman's papers ask, "What is a valid unit of comparison?" but, in a deeper sense, the answers show differences in point of view about the question, "What is the subject of study?" Gluckman's paper was presented at the Conference, Bohannan's was written afterward. Since Bohannan's is in a large measure an attack on Gluckman's mode of analysis and comparison, it is only fair to indicate that Gluckman's paper is a response to previous criticisms, not to this particular paper.

A great deal of discussion between Gluckman and Bohannan takes place in the form of an argument about what is a suitable language in which to describe another people's legal system. Bohannan argues that the vocabulary of English jurisprudence is a vocabulary developed for talking about English law and is unsuitable for the description of the folk systems of other peoples. His case is that to describe another people's system, one must spell out at length the implications of native terms and categories in order to approximate as closely as possible the indigenous system being examined, and then one must use these native terms rather than substitute English equivalents. Then, and only then, can one begin to think about making comparisons. This part of his argument starts as an argument against an ethnocentric Anglo-American legal vocabulary. Then he faces the difficulties inherent in trying to use indigenous vocabularies when making comparisons. In his paper Bohannan proposes that this problem may be dealt with in the future by means of a "new logical and independent language," and he suggests that Fortran or some other computer language may be the most suitable medium into which to translate folk concepts for comparative purposes. His argument is fundamentally that English legal terms are so inextricably bound up with the content of English law that they cannot be used effectively to describe another system. The number of redefinitions and qualifiers that must be used to make a term of English law fit an alien legal category is such that, in his view, it is less distorting and less confusing to use certain key indigenous terms and try to describe their referents. This last, since he is writing in English, he does in English words, but with an effort to avoid technical legal terms as far as he can.

Gluckman agrees that the first task of the ethnographer is to describe what Bohannan has called the folk system. He also agrees that vernacular African terms sometimes have no English equivalents, and that in such cases indigenous terms must continue to be used after they have been explained in English. However, where it is practical to use English terms without having to add too many qualifiers—where, in short, there is a satisfactory English equivalent or approximation—he not only sees no objection to using English (or whatever is the language of the investigator), but also thinks it far preferable to do so. He argues that only if the same term is used to cover the notions of diverse legal systems is it possible to discuss where the notions in each system differ, as well as the common elements across the systems. What Gluckman does, further, is to argue that after the notions of an African legal system have been described, they can be compared profitably with those of English law at various stages of its development. Similarly, he also draws on the terms and ideas of Roman law and other legal systems where they seem appropriate.

Presented in this way, there seems a limited area of disagreement between the two. After giving and explaining native terms, Gluckman is prepared to shift to terms of English law more readily than Bohannan, and he has a strong interest in particular comparisons of African with English legal notions that Bohannan does not share. Bohannan explains in English and then continues to use more indigenous terms and makes a studied effort to avoid terms of English law when he can. Both are acutely aware of the difficulties of translation and definition in the task of describing an alien legal system, and both realize that those difficulties are multiplied when the level of analysis and comparison is reached.

Certainly, the English forensic vocabulary does contain many words that may be considered loaded with connotations of English law, though even of these, few have meant the same thing over long periods of time, and many have different legal connotations in different jurisdictions. However, it is useful to recognize that there is also a legal vocabulary of what I can only describe as neutral terms, and there are many combinations of these terms that can be conveniently used by anthropologists in making ethnographic descriptions.

This may not be the place for an extended list, but a few examples may be suggestive. It is a convention of Anglo-American opinion writing for the judge to describe the facts before him initially in such neutral terms. Then he gives the facts their legal significance by recasting into more precise legal language the situation he has just described. An example: Two men discuss a possible *transaction*. One of them may afterward claim that they reached an *understanding* about the potential terms of the transaction, and that they *concurred* on those terms. The Anglo-American legal question would be whether in the circumstances this alleged *understanding* and *concurrence* constitute a *contract* or not. In some ethnographic descriptions there would be reason to avoid using "contract," but the words *binding agreement* would serve in such cases without much culture-bound loading, while the words "understanding" and "concurrence" would serve very neatly to describe reaching an *accord*, or giving *mutual assent* that may not necessarily be legally binding. One of the merits of using such words in ethnographic description is that they force the ethnographer to ask himself what agreements are binding and when and how and between whom they become binding in a particular society.

The word "transfer" is another very good example of a neutral term, since it tells only that something moves from one person to another or from one place to another. It remains for the ethnographer to describe what is being transferred, how permanently, whether for a fixed period of time or not, whether irrevocably or revocably, whether the transfer gives rights to the transferee, at what point these rights are transferred, whether the transfer creates firm or contingent reciprocal obligations, and so forth. Another useful word is "interest," because it is applicable to almost any kind of right. *Transactions, agreements, obligations, transfers,* and *interests* cover a great deal of the legal universe, and they do so with convenient neutrality. There are many other "neutral" words that are equally useful. Whether their use can capture the full flavor of indigenous categories would be partly a matter of skill in filling in the particular specifications for the system under study, and this aspect relates to the subtleties involved in particular folk notions. The use of well-chosen adjectives and appropriate combinations of nouns can adapt these terms to special ethnographic needs without the awkwardness and confusion caused by using an overabundance of indigenous terms and avoiding the perils of Anglo-centrism. Blank-check words have another virtue. Their very emptiness requires the ethnographer to fill in the potential legal connotations of acts that he is in the habit of looking at in other senses. They oblige him to think about the possible legal consequences of mundane behavior.

Hohfeld (1923) proposed another, highly specialized "neutral" vocabulary for describing *all* legal relationships in terms of the various elements encapsulated in the notions of right and duty. Despite having been brought up, as Hoebel was, in the Hohfeldian religion by Karl Llewellyn, I would reject Hohfeld's terminology for ethnographic description for the following reasons. First, it is hopelessly clumsy. Second, it cuts up all legal relations into dyads, which is sometimes a very artifical and distorting procedure. Third, it cuts up legal relations into analytically distinguishable, but not always pragmatically distinct, qualities, until sight is lost of the relationship as a whole. Lawyers, who usually seem to have no need to write gracefully and who are only occasionally concerned with trying to communicate the flavor of a relationship, nevertheless avoid Hohfeld's system because it is so awkward. In my opinion legal anthropologists should read Hohfeld and then, cheerfully, should do without him.

The dispute between Bohannan and Gluckman about what is a suitable language for legal description is really only the surface of a much more profound difference of emphasis and interest. Bohannan has described the difference in this way: "The comparatists, from Tylor to Gluckman, want to compare substantive material; I want, rather, to compare viewpoints or theories of substantive material." Gluckman's statement on the difference in their approach is: "it may well be that we are interested in divergent problems. Bohannan may be aiming to compare folk conceptions in themselves. . . . I am interested . . . in specifing the folk conceptions of a particular people as clearly as I can and then trying to explain why they are as they are, and how they differ from the folk conceptions of others, in terms of economic and social backgrounds."

Implicit in these statements is the basic difference in point of view between Gluckman and Bohannan—a difference only indirectly confronted in the discussion of the language of description and the language of analysis. Gluckman sees the concepts and principles of law as *part* of legal systems, whereas Bohannan is most interested in studying the concepts *themselves,* because he considers them a reflection of the whole organization of the legal system.

To Gluckman, these concepts and principles are manipulable tools within legal systems, part of their equipment, not reflections of their organization. He looks to social and economic backgrounds for broader underlying explanations and describes himself as interested in "the relation of legal ideas to the general social system of a tribe" (1965b:xiv).

Bohannan is passionately interested in perception, in the way a culture sets up and classifies reality into categories. In his text *Social Anthropology*, while describing Whorf's theory with approval, Bohannan says, "The proper subject for study—indeed the only possible subject for study— is . . . perception" (1963:46). This is his view of culture in general. In another place in the same book he says, "culture and social action become organized into sensible chunks or schemes that form sensible connected wholes of one sort or another. . . . It is precisely this system of categories, as it is preserved in the language and recurrent social behavior, that the ethnographer must report" (1963:9–10). He goes on, "Thus, a language is not merely part of the culture, but is also a reflection of the total culture. It is a reflection, more importantly perhaps of the *organization* of that total culture" (1963:42).

When Bohannan objects to the use of terms other than carefully defined indigenous ones and stresses the theme of the distortions in translations, it is because he sees the categories embodied in indigenous legal language as a key to the organization of indigenous thought. In fact, he emphasizes that "every culture has certain key words in its language" around which the major part of the ethnographer's knowledge of the culture may be communicated (1963:11–12). However vigorously Bohannan argues for a systematic methodology of comparison once these key words are described, he does not provide a way in which the key words themselves can be systematically selected. As far as I can tell, they have to be chosen rather subjectively (1963:12). A careful control of techniques of handling data does not get around the problem of how the data are chosen in the first place. This is a problem of which Bohannan is certainly aware, and he discusses it in his paper. The total pattern of thought condensed into key words if what Bohannan is after as an ideal ethnographic aim. This is what he means when he says, "I want to compare viewpoints or theories of substantive material."

Gluckman has an entirely different ultimate aim in mind when he approaches legal materials. The large pattern he is inquiring into is the interrelationship between the legal system and its social and economic setting. The assumption underlying his work is that these are often related phenomena, and that they are related in complex and various ways. They are not at every point interdependent, but frequently they can nevertheless be shown to be significantly connected. To demonstrate such relationships, comparison is not only illuminating but even essential. Gluckman uses comparative examples to show the ethnographic foundation of his ideas, and he supports his arguments about the relationship of phenomena by offering examples. His technique is one of presenting illustrated hypotheses.

Bohannan is as critical of Gluckman's mode of comparison as he is of Gluckman's mode of description. Some of it he suspects to be too much based on a priori categories and concepts. Some of it he finds simply an argument supported by selected favorable illustrative instances. In his paper Bohannan is in effect saying "You have not proved them," to Gluckman's hypotheses and ideas in general.

Whatever the ultimate validity of Gluckman's hypotheses may be, it seems evident that the systematic mode of comparison that Bohannan proposes for the future is not a solution to the kind of problem Gluckman has set himself. The controlled comparison of concepts proposed by Bohannan may well prove to be a very fruitful line of investigation. However, it can never be an answer to the problems in which Gluckman is interested. The pursuit of such a study as a key to legal systems is not congruent with Gluckman's conception of the place that ideas, categories, legal principles, and the like have in legal systems.

In Gluckman's analysis law involves, among other things, a hierarchy of principles: some of these low in the hierarchy are very precise and explicit rules, whereas those high in the hierarchy are very vague and general; and in between there are medium-level principles that are more encompassing than a rule for any single set of facts, but less grand and abstract than the highest level principles (Gluckman, 1955: 291–326). Anywhere above the lowest level of law (and morality), principles conflict, overlap, have fuzzy edges. Many have a generally definable import; some are multireferential; for others the referents are not altogether precise. The imprecision and multireferential quality increases the higher up the hierarchy of princples one goes. Gluckman's view, which is in accord with the view of many jurists, is that these very vaguenesses of a multiplicity of logically independent principles and the conflicts between some principles are an inherent part of legal systems—part of the living law in terms of which people conduct themselves and in terms of which disputes are settled. The vagueness of and conflicts between principles, the multiplicity of principles, the combination of precise and imprecise principles, give the law the quality of flexibility that enables it to work and makes it applicable to the unbelievable variety of contingencies involved in human affairs. Clearly, if this complex analytical scheme about legal principles is one's point of departure, a legal system is only partly to be understood in terms of its categories. Gluckman wrote in summary of *The Judicial Process Among the Barotse of Northern Rhodesia* (1955; see also 2nd Ed., 1967):

> I found a multiplicity of meanings and possibilities of application to the facts
> of social life inherent in all the key terms of Barotse law. . . . I was able to

accept that this multiplicity of meanings—what the philosophers call "open texture"—of terms was an inherent attribute of legal concepts, . . . I tried to work out how the judges manipulated the uncertainty of words. [1965b:22]

Despite the fact that Bohannan casts his argument in terms of methodology, I think the basic disagreement between Bohannan and Gluckman is one over the *significance* of legal categories. They both agree that such categories should be accurately and fully reported. They have some difference about what is the most suitable language to do the job, and Bohannan is critical of Gluckman's style of comparison and of what he perceives as Gluckman's preoccupation with parallels in the history of English law. Gluckman, in fact, was aiming in his books at a "developmental morphology of law, relating law to techno-economic development" (unpublished lecture). He uses his data on Barotse law to illustrate how they fit into this morphology of development. When he cites other ethnographic data, it is to argue that Barotse law is typical of what he calls "tribal law." He did not attempt a systematic march through the totality of the ethnographic literature. It was never his intention to attempt anything of the sort.

But these issues follow from the much deeper difference in approach and interest of the two men concerning what the categories *mean*. Bohannan is apparently convinced that the categories themselves can reveal the "system." Gluckman's analysis of how legal principles work would seem to make him necessarily less optimistic about such an outcome.

My own paper is an illustration of the complexities attendant upon any investigation of basic concepts. In looking at descent and legal position among the Lango, I have chosen a vast umbrella concept and have tried to show how many levels of organization and how many kinds of legal rules are framed in terms of it. Driberg's ethnography of the Lango, on which the paper is based, is an old-fashioned, conventional one, not written with any of these problems in mind. Nor do the Lango seem particularly unusual in the fact of their variegated application of descent principles. Though the paper is not to any extent a cross-cultural comparison, the implications of the argument go far beyond the Lango, since the general question raised concerns the manner in which concepts are used in legal affairs. Following one thread, the paper examines the variety of law-related situations in Lango life that invoke descent principles. Following another, it inspects some of the techniques by which legal rules and principles are manipulated. The two are, of course, intertwined.

The legal aspects of Lango descent are approached from the point of view of the practical situations in Lango life, in which descent figures as an element. I do not see how one could reliably delineate a "Lango concept of descent" without this information. In a field-work situation it would perhaps be possible also to elicit statements from informants about what descent is considered to be in the abstract, but this would scarcely be exhaustive. The very specificity that makes case studies more revealing than informant's statements about legal rules makes information about the kind of situation in which descent is invoked more telling than some abstract definition of it. But this is not to say that either terse statements of rules or the abstract definitions of principles are of no importance. They are part of the way people think and talk about social life in general, which is quite distinct from (though related to) the way they deal with it in concrete instances. Law involves both. But it is no small matter to try to work out the relationship between the principles and the supposed "applications" of them, the concepts involved in law and the uses of them.

It may be, in fact, that the role of certain concepts and principles is less one of defining rights and duties than of defining the general ideological framework in terms of which rights and duties are expressed. Partly it is a question of different levels of specificity. Gluckman has discussed the hierarchy of legal principles to which Barotse judges have reference. Gulliver discusses hierarchies of rules in this volume. Hierarchies of rules are regularly mentioned by judges in British and American courts when several principles apply to a case and some are considered to have a moral or political superiority over others. My paper uses the descent concept to show that certain very general ideas can *reappear at many levels* and in many guises in the hierarchy of legal rules. I suggest that these metamorphoses are separable both for indigenous pragmatic purposes and for the anthropologist's analytic purposes.

Innumerable specific legal rules among the Lango have reference to descent, but, as I have tried to show, descent is not in itself either directly a source of these rules nor in any other way exclusively determinative of them. For example, though the Lango are patrilineal, descent is legally established by the payment of bridewealth cattle, not by filiation. Thus a man's offspring may be members of the descent group of his mother's brother if his mother's brother supplied the marriage cattle with which he obtained his wife. The analysis of the connections among the legal rules, the descent ideology, and the varied courses of action available to people acting in terms of the rules raises questions about the nature of legal rules in general and the legal significance of descent in particular. If the same ideological reference point—descent—is used by the Lango in a whole series of entirely different social contexts and is varied and highly manipulable in those contexts, how is cross-cultural comparison of such an idea to be undertaken? Surely not without detailed attention to the context.

Divergences from what anthropologists sometimes think of as the "descent ideal" are frequently considered by them to be exceptions to, or inadequate approximations of, the ideal. Some even think they have found a new organizational type where or when they find that divergences are commonplace. My argument is that this is not a matter of ideal-real dichotomies, nor of norms and violations. On the contrary, such "exceptions" are part of the system. They are legitimate alternatives to other arrangements and there is legal provision for them.

What becomes evident is that among the Lango descent is used as an explicit justifying framework for arrangements that actually are frequently as much based on other exigencies and criteria. When these criteria are lacking, the supposed consequences of relationship do not follow. This means that the idea of descent—that is, the set of interrelated principles of which it is composed—exists concurrently with a more lowly assortment of legal rules, legal legitimators, and qualifying conditions that are the legally and pragmatically effective aspects of the general notion.

The most basic ideas of unilineal descent are very simple and found around the world, yet the jural consequences that are justified in terms of these basic models are very variable. Thus, I conclude that such fundamental ideas in a social system account for only a very limited aspect of its shape. How much lower down the ladder of folk ideas and explanations must one descend before arriving at those that are special to the system (or type of system) being examined? When one gets to these special concepts, what does one know? Are the concepts reflections of the social system, conditioners of perception, or manipulable ideological constructs? Are they perhaps all three? These are some of the questions with which Bohannan, Gluckman, and I are concerned.

Concepts in the
Comparative Study of Tribal Law

Despite the great importance of earlier studies of what may in the widest terms be called social control, or law and order, in tribal societies,[1] the big recent theoretical advance in this field was marked by the publication of Llewellyn and Hoebel's *The Cheyenne Way* (1941). This book was preceded by Hoebel's own *The Political Organization and Law-Ways of the Comanche Indians* (1940) and Richardson's *Law and Status Among the Kiowa Indians* (1940) and has been succeeded by other studies of American Indian law. Nevertheless, *The Cheyenne Way* is still a model in the total field of research, for it set new perspectives in the study of all tribal law. I here use "law" in the widest possible common-sense way. Since its appearance, attempts at specialized studies of law in other tribal zones, both ethnographic and theoretical, have appeared.[2] In 1954 Hoebel published his theoretical analysis of problems and "evolution" in *The Law of Primitive Man*. Recently a special issue of the *American Anthropologist* reported the results of a small seminar to discuss "The Ethnography of Law."[3] My aim in this paper is to attempt to clarify certain of the controversies that have accumulated during the course of these studies.

1. Barton (1919, 1949); Malinowski (1926); Kroeber (1928); Hogbin (1934); Schapera (1938); Evans-Pritchard (1940, 1951); Fortes (1945, 1949); Nadel, (1947). I cannot refer to all, and there are recent bibliographies by Nader in *The Ethnography of Law* (1965a) and by Nader, Koch, and Cox in *Current Anthropology* (1966).
2. Pospisil (1958); Berndt (1962). For books on Africa see below.
3. Vol. 67, part 6, no. 2 (December, 1965), edited by L. Nader.

This is not the first time I have written on this theme; [4] but though I necessarily repeat here some of my earlier arguments, recent restatements of controversial points enable me both to develop and to refine the presentation of the approach to these problems that, among anthropologists, is I think best represented by Epstein (1953, 1954), Hoebel, Pospisil, Schapera (all cited above), and myself. I judge that we are the anthropologists who have deliberately applied the theories and work of Western jurisprudents to the analysis of tribal law. This procedure has been queried by some other anthropologists on the grounds that it leads to certain fundamental errors and distortions. I shall argue that this charge has never been validated in detail by its critics, and I shall try to establish that it remains a most illuminating approach to the problems of tribal law. I do not, of course, assert that there are not other illuminating approaches.

Since Epstein's work on the processes of law in African Urban Courts established by the former Government of Northern Rhodesia appeared in the series of mainly anthropological Rhodes-Livingstone Papers, it apparently escaped not only the appreciation it deserved, but also the ill-based criticism meted out to my own work. Nor do I know of any substantial criticism of Hoebel's, Pospisil's, and Schapera's work. Hence I shall appear to be defending mainly myself, but I am sure that the others will be pleased to associate themselves with me in the dock. I must note at once that my reply to one line of criticism of my approach does not mean that I do not acknowledge the weight and validity of many of the criticisms that have been made of my studies of Barotse and, more generally, of tribal law. I note that lawyers have not found our use of Western words and even concepts misleading, nor have many other anthropologists.

My first main study of tribal law was my book, *The Judicial Process among the Barotse of Northern Rhodesia* (1955). It appeared at about the same time as Epstein's *Juridical Techniques and the Judicial Process* (1954), Anderson's *Islamic Law in Africa* (1954), and Howell's *A Manual of Nuer Law* (1954). In 1957 there appeared Bohannan's book on *Justice and Judgment among The Tiv of Nigeria*. This set of books on African law produced a number of review articles (some commenting only on my book) in journals dealing with anthropology, with law, and with Africa, and in one book edited by Janowitz on *Community Political Systems* (Ayoub 1961).

4. Gluckman (1962, 1965c); see also 2nd edition of my 1955 *The Judicial Process among the Barotse of Northern Rhodesia* (1967:Chapter IX, "A Reappraisal, [1966]"), where I give a fuller account of points discussed in the present essay. This, however, gives my views more briefly, after further consideration and clarification, and takes account of points made by my colleagues at the seminar on which the present book is based. I am most grateful to them, and additionally to Sally Moore, who has written to me comments on my paper.

The main controversy established by some of these writers was seen to be between Bohannan and me. The sharpness of separation of our points of view is perhaps demonstrated by the publication of summaries of each of our books and one essay comparing them (Ayoub 1961), as well as of an essay, "Sociological Jurisprudence Revisited, A Review (More or less) of Max Gluckman" (March 1956), in Schubert's *Judicial Behavior: A Reader in Theory and Research* (1964). March's revisitation to sociological jurisprudence via a critique of my book on the Barotse judicial process takes the view that my attempt to look at Barotse law in comparison with Anglo-American law is—if I may put it more harshly than perhaps he does—meaningless and misleading; he raises the same points (among others) against me, therefore, as other critics. The criticism has been repeated by Nader in her editorial introduction to *The Ethnography of Law* (1965a), though she does not say that she endorses the criticism. Indeed, she generously acknowledges elsewhere for another of my books "the stimulus value of Western jurisprudential ideas" (Nader 1965b:25). Nevertheless, she has in my opinion helped here to give currency to a completely false myth about what I have done and has put in sharper opposition than in fact exists the difference between Bohannan's approach and mine.

In social science, controversy and judgment accumulate all too easily around misconceptions. For example, anthropologists have criticized Maine's generalization in the last sentence of Chapter V of *Ancient Law* (1861) that "If then we employ Status, agreeably with the usage of the best writers [to designate powers and privileges anciently residing in the Family], and avoid applying the term to such conditions as are the immediate or remote result of agreement, we may say that the movement of progressive societies has hitherto been a movement *from Status to Contract.*" (By "Family," in this quotation, Maine meant a Roman "familia," or what we would call an extended family or lineage.) But those who have criticized Maine have concentrated on the end of the sentence, starting from "the movement . . . ," and have not taken into account his definitions of status and contract or the limitations he set upon these terms. Thus they have failed to see the high degree of validity in the generalization, and have lost the opportunity to develop its implications (see Gluckman 1965b:Chapter VI). And once one anthropologist had stated this misunderstanding of Maine, it was repeated by others from that initial misconception. Therefore it appears to me important to clarify the extent of agreement in, as well as the issues that divide, different approaches to the analysis of exotic legal systems.

This is how Nader (1965a:11) summarizes the controversy:

Bohannan's contribution to methodology of description lies in his formulation of the folk versus the analytical system—while not "new," an argument that strikes at the very core of the translation and meaning problem in anthropology. He raises for inspection statements made by Hoebel (1954:46) and more recently by Gluckman (1962) that encourage anthropologists to discuss tribal law using the principal concepts of Western jurisprudence. Gluckman states, "The very refinement of English jurisprudence makes it a better instrument for analysis . . . than are the languages of tribal law" (1962:14). Bohannan (1957), on the contrary, contends that to describe and analyze the system of justice and judgment of one culture through the interpretation of a system indigenous to a second society can only lead to confusion and distortion. He implicitly charges Gluckman with having converted the Western legal folk system into an analytical system and with having forced the Lozi folk concepts into a Western model. He presents a variety of instances illustrating for example how the Tiv concept of "correction" when translated to "sanction" may misconstrue what final action does actually involve for the Tiv. Ayoub (1961), Gluckman (1962) and Hoebel (1961) discuss the problems inherent in Bohannan's approach, Nadel (1956) and Ayoub (1961) discuss the perplexing questions inherent in Gluckman's assumptions, as does the whole body of literature in ethnoscience. See in this volume the paper by Metzger and Black. The answer probably lies solely neither with Gluckman nor Bohannan, for how an ethnographer goes about laying bare or describing his society is intimately related to what use he believes can be made of such a description. This brings us to the question of comparison. Bohannan's intention is to discover and portray the Tiv view of justice and judgment. He shirks the problems that such a relativistic approach implies for comparison, but then he was not interested in comparison at the time. Gluckman's work has been characterized as analogous to that of a linguist who attempts comparison by jamming Barotse grammar into Roman Dutch categories.

Nader then discusses more seriously some of my proposals on how to set about comparison. Unfortunately Nader does not state who has characterized my work "as analogous to that of a linguist who attempts comparison by jamming Barotse grammar into Roman Dutch categories." [5] This is a vague and imprecise—and an unvalidated—indictment, which would be thrown out in any court of law as not specific enough to enable the defendant to answer. I do make some explicit comparisons of Barotse law with some Roman-Dutch and Roman, as well as with English, legal institutions and rules, but these are explicit attempts made in order both

5. Nader may have noted a statement in Vansina (1965:117) about a Congolese tribe: "Kuba law is thus very different from any European legal system, and to try to define it in terms of European legal concepts is like trying to fit a Bantu grammar into a Latin model of grammatical categories, something that was actually done until descriptive linguistics taught us better." The analogy is not developed, and it is worth noting that the Kupers in their editorial "Introduction" to the book in which Vansina's essay appears, comment: "In fact, Vansina is able to describe the Kuba system in terms of the concepts of Western jurisprudence" (1965b:5). Vansina's footnote reference is to Bohannan's book, not to mine.

to illuminate by contrast and to try to generalize. I shall return below to some of these comparisons.

What I did have to do, writing in English, was to use words like "evidence," "agreement," "right," "duty," "obligation," "law," "tort," and "delict," "injury," "wrongdoing," and so forth; but I attempted on each occasion clearly to specify the Barotse word that corresponds and to set out with examples its connotations and limitations. For of course once we write in English, we have at some point to translate, and this involves using English (or Roman-Dutch) categories. Even Roman-Dutch words, Latin or Dutch, are commonly translated into English save where the Latin is part of our legal vocabulary. But the alternative for an ethnographer, even at the first descriptive level and before analysis, is to remain in the vernacular; and he can then never escape from that vernacular to get into analysis. For at some point in an English work vernacular categories—whether Roman-Dutch, Tiv or Barotse—have to be expounded in a series of English words, whether commonplace words or social-anthropological technical terms or jurisprudential technical terms. In my opinion, indeed, it is the use of the simplest English words, such as connecting prepositions and conjunctions, that is potentially most dangerous.

Hence I do not consider that even Bohannan is able to escape the difculties of translation, and at many crucial points he uses English terms. But I do of course agree with him that the first task of an ethnographer,[6] or of any recorder of a system of ideas or practices, is to describe as fully and subtly as he can, taking account of all the problems of translation, what Bohannan has called the "folk system." One of the effects of this accumulating, falsely based controversy between Bohannan and myself has been to suggest that I do not agree with Bohannan on this point. On the contrary, whenever I have argued that to stop at the folk system stultifies further analysis, which I consider to depend on comparison, I have at the same time stated how much I admire—and at times envy—the skill, subtlety, and comprehensiveness with which Bohannan reports on Tiv "folk-concepts." (I have added, however, that fortunately he does not abide by his precept and that he continually does compare in words drawn from outside the folk system.)

Despite these statements of mine, the development of the controversy in other hands has made my opposition to Bohannan appear to condemn altogether his procedure; and I am therefore taking this opportunity not only to defend the procedure of comparison through Western jurisprudential words and concepts, but also to try to dissipate this other confusion and to make clear where Bohannan and I are in agreement.

6. I made clear in my preface to the first edition of *The Judicial Process Among the Barotse* that "my first duty was to describe Lozi legal institutions clearly" (1955:xix).

The long citation from Nader above, itself emphasizes that Bohannan and I formulated our problems at different levels. She writes (I recapitulate and supply emphasis): "Bohannan's contribution to methodology of *description* lies in his formulation of the folk versus the analytical system." She then cites my statement that "The very refinement of English jurisprudence makes it a better instrument for *analysis* . . . than are the languages of tribal law." When she goes on to write that Bohannan "contends that to *describe and analyse* the system of justice and judgment of one culture through the interpretation of a system indigenous to a second society can only lead to confusion and distortion," two steps —description and analysis—are brought together in a way that Bohannan (1957) did not combine them in his study of Tiv justice and judgment, in contrast to what I tried to do in my own work. There I essayed a comparison of different folk systems.

Bohannan and I are agreed, in fact, that the first duty of an ethnographer is to record clearly the facts in the society he is studying. We are further agreed, as became apparent at the seminar which led to this present book, that we have then to devise terms to bring together for comparison parallel, similar, and different, conceptions and procedures in various "folk systems," and then to devise terms for yet more abstract analytical generalizations. This raises the question of what it is one is attempting to compare, and here it may well be that we are interested in divergent problems.[7] Bohannan may be aiming to compare folk conceptions in themselves; we shall know when the new edition of *Justice and Judgment among the Tiv,* with a promised additional comparative chapter, is published. I am interested, like most social anthropologists, in specifying the folk conceptions of a particular people as clearly as I can and then trying to explain why they are as they are, and how they differ from the folk conceptions of others, in terms of economic and social backgrounds (Moore 1966).

In practice it is almost impossible to write in English about a foreign system of law without using English words that may appear to import English "folk conceptions" (I think "conceptions" is here more accurate than "concepts"). For example, to explain the Tiv conception of a *bumenor,* Bohannan (1957:33–34, 84, 86) in the end translates it as "unreasonable man" and specifically compares it with my discussion of the importance in the Barotse judicial process of "reasonable man," an alleged importation by me of a Western conception that has been criticized by several authors (see below). Here Bohannan is using, in reverse, the same English term—which is not necessarily using the English legal conception—in order to argue that Tiv courts, established by the British, do not explicitly use the idea of the reasonable or unreasonable man in their judgments; and hence he maintains that we are not justified in using

---

7. See Moore's (1966) discussion of Hoebel's and my comparisons.

it for analysis of their court proceedings (see Epstein 1959 and Gluckman 1966 for a discussion of these proceedings in relation to this problem).

The same difficulty attends one of the most important sections of Bohannan's book. He insists (1957:passim) that Tiv categorize in terms of "debt" and not in terms of "contract" or "tort." But he does not discuss whether the Tiv use their words for "agree" and "injure" to talk about cases in "debt" (except possibly by implication in a statement by Bohannan that they have contract and tort in the way that M. Jourdain spoke prose). I suggest here that what the Tiv do (as English law did until the seventeenth to eighteenth centuries) is to class together as "debts" the actions arising both from agreements and from injuries. I recently noted in the Authorized Version of the New Testament that the Lord's Prayer in two of the Gospels has "Forgive us our debts [trespasses], as we forgive those who are indebted to us [have trespassed against us]." Elsewhere in the Gospels "debt" is used where we would now use sin, transgression, and even guilt (cf. German *schuld*). Thus debt was, and is, a very complex English folk conception.

Again, he does not discuss Tiv conceptions of ownership. But he says: "The simplest sort of debt *jir* [disputes] called by Tiv involve livestock: disputes over ownership of livestock and disputes over damage caused by livestock." He illustrates this with a *jir* in which WanIgarwa calls Gbilin about the ownership of some goats. "WanIgarwa told the *jir* [court —*jir* is a multivocal word] that three or four years ago she was going to Asawa market in Obudutown to sell her two goats" (Bohannan 1957: 102 f.). Very complex problems of translation, in terms of legal problems, are involved not only in the use of "ownership" from English here, but also in the possessive in "her goats, as well as in 'damages.'"

I myself struck this problem among the Barotse. First in an article published in 1959 and then in my *Ideas in Barotse Jurisprudence* (1956b: Chapter V) I reported in detail on how the Barotse used the word *mung'a*, and its abstract form *bung'a*, both in cases in court and in everyday life. I described how the words are used to refer to persons with quite different kinds of claims on the same piece of land or chattel. Thus the king, and a village headman to whom the king grants rights to administer land and distribute it to his villagers, and these villagers, are all called *mung'a*. In some circumstances a husband is called *mung'a* of his wife, in others his wife is called *mung'a* of the husband; or the wife's father or brother or mother's brother may be called her *mung'a* as against the husband in yet other circumstances. Litigants address a judge often as *mung'a*, and sometimes a judge may address a litigant as *mung'a* when reprimanding him. An adult may address a child as *mung'a* when he is reproving it. These last two uses are to be understood as indicating that the judge toward the litigant and the adult toward the reproved child are showing that they are discharging an obligation to the other in administering a rebuke to him. I begin here in order to stress the extent to which Barotse emphasize the element of obligation contained in masterful relations. The same theme runs through their relations to one another in connection with land. The king is *mung'a* of land in which he has rights and privileges; but in addition he owes all his subjects the duty to provide arable and building land for them and to allow them free access to common pastures, fishing sites, and the woodland's wild products. And through these obligations of the king, which constitute both claims and privileges for subjects, these subjects in turn owe him duties. Barotse society is dominantly structured in permanent status relations; and the element of *bung'a* (the abstract form of *mung'a*) is ascribed to anyone who has a masterful relationship of responsibility and demands on services over another in some situation. This masterfulness may or may not arise out of property. Barotse jurisprudence sees every situation that arises out of status relationships as containing an essentially similar element, which it calls *bung'a*. They distinguish relatively few forms of *bung'a*, for the rights and duties involved in any particular form are defined by the status relationship involved in a dispute, and the main clarification of Barotse law lies in the multiplying of names for status and for different kinds of property. Suits in court may raise questions about rights, but the courts tend always to lay stress on obligation (Bohannan makes the same point about the Tiv, who "use both the institution of self-help and the jir (court) to enforce their rights. This is not, however, the way they put it. Their emphasis is on means of making others carry out their obligations" (1957:131).)

This situation is to be understood in the total social context of Barotse society, constituted as it is by prescribed status relations. As a result, therefore, when a court hears a case in which there is dispute about claims over and the duties toward property or person, the court can deal with the situation according to who is the *mung'a* in that particular situation in relation to a certain contestant. If a man, king or commoner, is judged to be *mung'a* of a piece of land, the judges are not asserting that he has any exclusive power over the land, nor are they denying that other persons have enforceable claims on the land. The successful contestant is only *mung'a* in relation to another contestant. (I suggested that this may explain also the background of the mediaeval seisin.)

I cannot pursue here this summarized analysis, which is set out more fully in my earlier works (1959, 1965b), without going into the role of goods within Barotse social relationships, and in other similar societies, as well as in our own. I have cited, I hope, enough to show that when discussing Barotse *bung'a*, I expounded its varied contexts fully and explored its ramifying significance in cultural belief and social relationship. I could perhaps have left it as *bung'a* and *mung'a* without ever making them equivalent to ownership and owner. But I do not feel that I could have brought out the implications of the Barotse concept without this translation: as it is, to make their significance clear, I have had to use other English phrases, such as "masterful relationship." But I consider that use of "owner" for *mung'a,* with the full explanation of the Barotse use and contexts of the word, does not at all result in a jamming of the Barotse concept into English categories. On the contrary, I consider that when writing in English, the use of the English equivalent term, general and multiferential in its common-sense meaning, brings out implications in the English meaning of "owner" as well as perhaps a significant core of similarity in the Barotse meaning of *mung'a.* The alternative in the extreme is to make communication impossible; we should be writing about "owner" or "proprietor" in English, *eigenaar* in Dutch, *Eigentümer* in German, *proprietario* in Italian, *proprietaire* in French, *dominus* in Latin, *mung'a* in Barotse, *umnini* in Zulu. This procedure would obscure differences and similarities, not keep distinctions clear. There is much in common in the conception of some different languages, which may be hidden by different word forms. There are differences obscured by common word forms. I shall return with other concepts to the important point that use of a term from one language for the conceptions of another society alone makes it possible to emphasize difference as well as similarity. Here, in conclusion, I note that I moved from *mung'a* to "owner" because I analyzed in English. Biebuyck (1963:4 f.), as a Belgian, discusses the equivalent Nyanga *mine* in terms of French law, *domaine,* after referring to my early treatment of *mung'a.* I do not find that when I read his analysis I am kept from the Nyanga by the French words that are all clearly referred to Nyanga facts.

There are, of course, conceptions in some folk systems that cannot be rendered directly into an English or other equivalent. I have been striving since 1943 [8] to persuade my colleagues how inappropriate it is to use the Roman and Roman-Dutch law concept of "usufruct" to describe certain levels of African tribal landholding; and in his *The Nature of African Customary Law* (1956) Elias, a leading Nigerian lawyer, also argued thus. So has Mr. Justice Ollennu of Ghana (1962:10). Bentsi-Enchill (1964:232–233), a Ghanian barrister, argues that there is a type of landright in Ghana to which the expression "usufructuary interest" might be confined; this "would have the merit of bringing us into closer, though not complete, harmony with the use of the term 'usufruct' in Roman law." The *Concise Oxford Dictionary* defines usufruct as the "right of enjoying the use and advantages of another's property short of destruction or waste of its substance." And it did not note that the Roman right was for life only. African rights, far stronger than usufruct, were also inheritable or otherwise transmissible. Here, if I may say so, was a case in which I

8. *Essays on Lozi Land and Royal Property* (1943); *The Ideas in Barotse Jurisprudence* (1965b:Chapter III).

took the lead in trying to prevent the jamming of African concepts into an inappropriate Roman-Dutch category. After carefully surveying the rights and obligations involved in African tribal landholding, I argued that to call them usufruct would muddle any attempt to compare African land tenure with land tenure in ancient Rome or elsewhere where true usufructus occurred. I also argued that feudal terms were unsuitable. Therefore, I proposed a set of neologisms. The king granted land for village headmen to distribute to dependents, who might make further grants to their dependents in turn. The rights and duties between adjacent holders in the series were similar at all levels of the hierarchy: hence all were called *mung'a* (owner). Therefore, I proposed a terminology by which the king granted primary estates of holding to the holders of secondary estates, and they to holders of tertiary estates, and so forth. I chose "estate" because of its wide, general, and multireferential meaning in English, because it was etymologically connected with status, and because Radcliffe-Brown had given authority for using it in his own writings—as had Maitland and Cheshire in discussing similar general proprietorial rights in English history. Sheddick (1954), writing on the Basuto, adopted my hierarchy but pointed out that rights in the hierarchy varied from administration at higher levels to use at the bottom level. In this light, I proposed that we distinguish between estates of administration and estates of production, the latter covering the actual cultivating, grazing, fishing, and the like. A holder of a higher estate of administration also often holds subordinate estates of administration, down to an estate of production within his own higher estate. I argued that this neologistic set of terms had the merit of bringing out the close connection of landholding with the social organization, which I felt gave it advantages over the neologisms proposed by the Dutch adat lawyers, by Goodenough (1951, 1956), and by Holleman (1952). The seminar of the International African Institute on African law held in Addis Ababa in January 1966, which was attended by lawyers and anthropologists, agreed to a formulation of the type I have advanced (Allott, Epstein, and Gluckman 1969), for a similar style of formulation was independently advanced there by Allott (1969), a lawyer.

There are a number of conceptions in any one system that it is thus difficult to transpose into even general concepts in other systems. In these circumstances, careful description remains the first step; and then I consider it helpful to readers, and essential for comparative analysis, to give some kind of clear terminology, speaking for itself as much as possible, in the language of analysis.

Sometimes an explicit comparative excursus may highlight problems in different types of systems, and perhaps lead to generalization. Thus, I made a comparison betwen the Roman universal succession and certain forms of African succession (Gluckman 1965b:123); but in doing so there was no jamming into categories. First I cited a series of Barotse cases, and I went on to consider other anthropologists' analyses. To make what I did clear, I must cite myself at length:

This case . . . [and others] shows that the Barotse at once identify, and distinguish between, a social position like headmanship and its present incumbent. They speak of the present incumbent as if he were the position, and often as if he were the past holder. But they also say, "There is the title and there is also its holder" . . . , and "The title is greater than the holder." . . . Hence they see clearly what is factually true, that the title persists through a series of incumbents. It is the persistence of titles that is the enduring part of Barotse social structure. This continuity is made possible by a mechanism which is found in many societies and is known best in the Roman form of succession to a *universitas juris*. Maine, whose views still prevail among students of Roman law [Jolowicz, 1939:128, cited in support], held that the chief form of universal succession was the replacement of a dead person by a live one. He wrote: "A *universitas juris* is a collection of rights and duties united by the single circumstance of their having belonged at one time to some one person. It is, as it were, the legal clothing of some given individual. . . . A universal succession is a succession to a *universitas juris*. It occurs when one man is invested with the legal clothing of another, becoming at the same moment subject to all his liabilities and entitled to all his rights." When a man died the most important demand was for an heir on whom could be bestowed the universal succession: *haereditas est successio in universum jus quod defunctus habuit* (an inheritance is a succession to the entire legal position of a deceased man) (1861:191 f.).

The mechanism of universal succession is found in many African societies, who describe it as "taking the name" or "the spirit," or "eating the name" (in Barotse, *kuyola libizo* or *kuca libizo*). Richards (1933, and 1960) called it "positional succession" and "positional inheritance" for the Bemba and Professor Mitchell (1956) accepted this term in his analysis of the Yao village. And many other anthropologists have drawn attention to similar types of succession in different societies, and have applied various terms to them; in essence they are all the universal succession of early Roman law.

Dr. Richards' use of the adjective in *positional* succession draws attention to an important limitation of universal succession in most African societies. The heir of a dead man succeeds to his *universitas juris* in a particular position, and not to his individual legal clothing, as in Maine's phrasing. Clearly even Maine erred in his choice of words, for he hmself pointed out (p. 144) that "the Patria Potestas did not extend to the Jus Publicum"—so that a man dying in public office did not pass to his private heir the rights and duties of his official position [an example from the Barotse cited by me for this distinction].

I then cited from Holleman (1949, 1952) on the Shona how several such positions, which I called "estates," might be united in one person and dispersed among different other persons on the former's death. I cited also how among the Zulu each rich man's estate develops into several estates, each centered on an important wife. I noted that in some systems, therefore, conflict arises in practice between the principle of community of estate, with its unified control, and the preferential claims of different houses within the groups involved, and that authorities on these tribes have discussed how the disputes arising from such conflicts are adjusted at law. I used the comparative discussion to emphasize how in several African tribes cited, and in others not cited, universal succession is to a position or *persona* rather than to an individual, in a variety of ways, and that certain positions, mostly based on land, become permanently linked together, irrespective of who occupies them. In some tribes the headman of a new village is linked to the headman of the village from which he leads out his following as, say, brother, son, sister's son, brother-in-law, son-in-law. Thereafter the two incumbents of these headmanships will always regard each other as related in this specific way, whatever their actual genealogical tie as individuals. They are in what Cunnison (1959; also Mitchell 1956; Watson 1958; Richards 1960) called "perpetual kinship." The incumbents observe norms of behavior that fit with their perpetual kinship. One of the linkages between villages, and between a chief and his headmen, is a series of "perpetual kinship" ties of this sort. These ties form a permanent structure of relations.

I then proceeded to follow a comparison of Maine's (1861:200). He compared the results of the Roman universal succession with the endurance of the English corporation sole, "an indivdual, being a member of a series of individuals, who is invested by a fiction with the qualities of a Corporation," as the King, or the Parson of a Parish. "The capacity or office is here considered apart from the particular person who from time to time may occupy it, and, this capacity being perpetual, the series of individuals who fill it are clothed with the leading attribute of Corporations—Perpetuity. Now in the older theory of Roman Law the individual bore to the family [that is, the extended family or lineage] precisely the same relation which in the rationale of English jurisprudence a Corporation sole bears to a Corporation aggregate."

I argued that these concepts were "almost cast to fit the structure of Barotse society." On Maine's view, each Barotse village is a corporation aggregate, with its rights and duties vested in a headman, who holds a specific title, a corporation sole. The village is in set and permanent relations with the king, also a corporation sole, and with other villages and headmen. But the nation as a whole is a corporation aggregate, organized in an elaborate structure of subsidiary corporations aggregate and corporations sole.

My argument then was pursued with a detailed analysis of national buildings, the placing of seats of officials, the significance of the king's right and left sides, and so on, in an attempt to arrive at an understanding of the relation between the Barotse approach to holding of land and holding of chattels.

This is the manner in which I used the technical conceptions of Roman and Western law. Even if "universal succession" is inappropriately brought in as a comparison with what Richards called "positional inheritance," a term adopted by other anthropologists, it does not confuse the issues arising from the Barotse data, nor (since this is a common Central African institution, reported by others) is it likely that my preliminary awareness of what universal succession, corporation sole, and corporation aggregate are in European legal systems distorted my perception and reporting of what went on around me when I was in Barotseland. "Succession" is, of course, a word in general use, as well as technical legal use, in English, as is "corporation" and both words ("corporation" frequently in the form of "corporate groups") figure constantly in analyses of tribal legal system. But I shall turn shortly to the use of this type of word in the analysis of tribal systems of law. (Bohannan himself uses "succession" and "inheritance," though as usual he defines their Tiv connotation clearly.)

Let me make clear that I am not claiming that my analysis is always clear. Ayoub (1961), Nadel (1956), and Krige (1956), as well as others, have criticized me for failing (in my book on the Barotse judicial process) always to use the terms I stipulate to have certain meanings consistently, and also because it is not always clear to them when I use a term to report Barotse ideas and when for comparative analysis. These are undoubted weaknesses. But in general I have always described Barotse concepts as clearly and fully as possible before using English equivalents (as demonstrated above), and they are not distorted by translation into English. I have perhaps not always attained for the Barotse the precision and detail shown on Tiv ideas by Bohannan's skill and subtlety, which —I repeat—I greatly admire, but I have certainly *as a first step* reported as well as I could, through case material, Barotse ideas and procedures before proceeding to further (and usually by implication at least, comparative) analysis.

For I maintain that it is impossible to describe, let alone analyze, without at least implicit comparison. Because I realized this, in my book on *The Judicial Process Among the Barotse* (1955) I made clear from the outset where the roots of my implicit comparison might lie. In the second paragraph of the *Preface* I therefore stated that my own studies in law "were in Roman-Dutch and Roman Law; and English lawyers will find that my implicit comparative background for Lozi law is South African law." The extent of explicit comparison or use of Roman-Dutch conceptions was limited to my citing of a few Roman maxims and legal doctrines. Thus the Barotse maxim that "if you are invited to a meal and a fish-bone sticks in your throat, you cannot sue your host," clearly invited me to cite, in parenthesis, *volenti non fit injuria* (Gluckman 1955: 206, 325). But the whole of my analysis was concerned to show that even if principles of law of this kind are similar in different systems, at least from Roman times into the modern age, they are what I called "permeated" by quite different economic and social conditions—and this is what lends flexibility to legal systems. This being so, it is nevertheless important to state where there are similar principles. Hence, in appropriate discussions on when the Barotse considered a valid "contract" to have been set up, I cited *ex nuda pacta non oritur actio*. I noted explicitly the presence or absence of Barotse equivalents of *vinculum juris*, fair price, *laesio enormis*, and *negotiorum gestio*. These were not built into the argument so as to obscure Barotse data. Again, when I cited Barotse decisions on cases where both parties had committed breaches of law or morals, I stated that they agreed with the Romans that *in pari delicto potior est conditio defendentis*. Explicitly, therefore, I made reference to Roman and Roman-Dutch principles; and an English lawyer might have made different comparisons of this kind, or seen comparisons or differences I did not. How far I was implicitly influenced by Roman-Dutch law I do not know: I think relatively little, but I had to make my credentials, and my possible biases, clear to readers. Then I let facts about the Barotse speak for themselves.

Nevertheless, clearly if "the whole body of literature in ethnoscience" is puzzled by my assumptions, as Nader alleges, I may have failed sufficiently to clarify the structuring of my argument. I thought that wherever I discussed any important word used in Barotse trials, I had examined its connotations carefully before translating it by an English word. I refer here, for example, to my discussion, with parallel citations from Schapera's study of Tswana law (see Gluckman 1965b:Chapter IV), of the multivocal Barotse words *mulao* and *mukwa* before I used for them our equally multivocal "law" and "custom," respectively. Other Barotse concepts, particularly those involved in evidence, are carefully discussed in the context of trial or series of trials. These discussions should bring out that I was fully aware, like "the whole body of ethnoscience," of the difficulties and dangers involved in any kind of translating of a word from one language into another language, of comparing ideas or customs in one culture with those in another, and of equating an official in one society with an official in another. I was aware, too, that each word used in jurisprudence also carries technical connotations. I was aware of this, but I stressed (1955:xx) that I would not become "involved in complex discussions of the meanings of [English] terms, nor considered whether my definitions for this particular analysis will cover the fact of law in other systems. I . . . tried to use terms with due regards for their instituted use in comparative jurisprudence; but in general analysis I . . . found it best to use the most common terms (law, right, duty, etc.) with the connotations given in the Concise Oxford Dictionary." I used also such general terms as agency, principal, tort (pp. xix–xx), delict, contract.

I tried as best I could, in the light of my research, while writing in English to expound the structure of Barotse courts, the roles of judges and other officials, the course of trials, the background of social relations and institutions in which the trials were set, legal concepts and legal maxims, the logic of judges' reasoning, and the like. At every point I made clear from my case material how the Barotse conceive of, and operate with, such ideas as *bupaki* = evidence—whether direct, circumstantial, or hearsay; and proof, also *bupaki*, or *niti* = truth.

I have already stated that I judge that I did not do so as comprehensively or as subtly as Bohannan analyzed many Tiv ideas. On other ideas, I was, I believe, clearer. But I set about my task in the same way as he did. The difference is that, as he admits (Bohannan 1965), at the time he wrote his book, he did not take the further step and make any comparison. I made the further step to essay a comparison, as Epstein did. We compared the Barotse judicial process and the Barotse use of principles and concepts of their law with, for example, Cardozo's analysis of the Anglo-American judicial process. I believe I showed similarities as well as differences in the cases I cited; of course, I may have missed other similarities and other differences in these cases; and perhaps cases I did not cite—or did not hear!—may exhibit yet others. My use of C. K. Allen's discussion of custom, particularly, and precedent, equity, natural law, statute, public policy, laws of nature, good morals, as sources of judicial law in Anglo-American law also, I believe, is validated by the evidence I produce and illuminates my Barotse data in similitude and difference. Again, when I took up the problem of certainty and uncertainty of law in the light of what Western jurists have written on this theme, I did so with my Barotse data given in detail; and this light illuminated the Barotse data. I argued that rules of law remain "certain" through the vicissitudes of judicial decision coping with many varied situations and with social change, because judges are able to specify and redefine the multivocal concepts of legal and moral rules.

Hoebel's (1965:53) discussion of "Fundamental Cultural Postulates and Judicial Law Making in Pakistan" similarly shows that it is now held that the opinion of mufti, or religious interpreter of the law, "is binding only so long as it 'correctly' relates Quranic precepts to the social environment of the day." This is in Nader's *Ethnography of Law* (1965a), which also includes an article by Kay on how Californian courts are redefining the family and kinship system in considering the rights of illegitimate children. It may be that more could be made of my data. But I reject sweeping statements that this kind of comparison distorts the Barotse facts, unless the critic gives an example of such a distortion—or at least cites data from another tribal society, to show that there is potential distortion; or unless he shows specifically that my analysis could be improved throughout because in making these particular comparisons, I went wrong, or that the analysis could be improved in some particulars, or that the comparison has inevitably led to a neglect of important problems. A complex argument merits an examination in its totality and its parts. It has to be examined in the light of the data it presents; how it handles those data explicitly and where, in detail, any implicit assumptions lead to distortion or sterility; and how far its argument advances or retards our understanding.

I have, in considering my colleagues' work on law (Gluckman 1962; 1965b:251 f.; 1965c:209, 230–232; 1965a), extended to them the courtesy, as far as I was able, of careful citation and re-analysis; and I am entitled to the same privilege, even if it not be a demand-right. There is a habit in sociological, anthropological, and jurisprudential controversy of seizing on one sentence like a straw, blowing it up to a straw man, and enjoying a Guy Fawkes bonfire. The result is only ashes.

In this light I do not feel that my use of words in common as well as in technical use in English was misleading. In a study of government one may use the word "legislature" to cover British Parliament, American Congress, German Bundestag and Reichstag, French Chambre des Députés, Japanese Diet, all for purposes of general discussion in order to draw attention to similarity while insisting on differences. Some word is necessary for purposes of general discussion. In discussing several systems of law, therefore, one may speak of ownership, contract, property, succession, marriage, betrothal, judge, decision, all to draw attention to a core of similitude while defining differences. It must be a very blinkered mind that, when an anthropologist speaks of contract in an African tribe, immediately thinks of the English or French or Roman-Dutch or Roman contract. "Contract" has a general meaning of enforceable agreement; and one can use it—and must use it—to discuss the different conditions, forms, incidents, and remedies for breach of contract in various social and economic conditions (Gluckman 1965b:Chapter VI).

I used English words because I was writing in English, and I have always felt that it is unfair to readers to ask them to carry in their heads a large number of vernacular terms. Bohannan uses many Tiv terms. And when he does translate, he sometimes avoids obvious English parallels; for example, "Anongo *calls* Iyorkyaha" avoids "summons," with its many implications of complicated processes, though the "call" is apparently authoritative to come before a court, since there is presumably a penalty if the defendant fails to attend; "calls" appears to me to be too weak, and hence misleading. Ayoub (1961:248) considers that Bohannan's method makes for greater conceptual clarity than does my use of English terms. But in fact Bohannan, since he writes in English, can avoid the use of only a certain number of English jurisprudential terms, such as tort, contract, sanction, court, judges. He nevertheless makes

considerable use of English words that have many technical jurisprudential connotations, such as right, duty, obligation, and, in the end, crime.
He avoids "contract" and "tort" because Tiv categorize actions akin to
these as "debt." But "debt" itself is a very complex conception: and I have
argued in the final chapter of *The Ideas in Barotse Jurisprudence* that
we can only understand what this Tiv category of "debt" means if we
examine also this particular type of categorizing as it occurred in early
English law and in a variety of other tribal and early legal systems (Gluckman 1965b:Chapter VII). I cite this example to show here, first, that
however determined one is to present a folk system in its purity, one
cannot escape from the use of one's own language. Second, and more
importantly, it emphasizes that, for deeper understanding, the presentation solely, allegedly, of the ideas of a folk system, restricts one's analysis
severely. In sociological jurisprudence, comparison puts problems in
more illuminating perspective. If Bohannan insists that Tiv do not distinguish tort and contract but see them as debt only, neither did Roman
law until postclassical times (Jolowicz 1939:285–286, 531–535), while
only in the seventeenth to eighteenth centuries did the distinction begin
to become clear in England (Winfield 1931:20 f.). We may well ask why
these several societies had similar categorizations.

Insistence on uniqueness constantly obscures problems. The following
example illustrates this point clearly. When the Tiv conduct an autopsy
on a man to see if he has practiced witchcraft, guilt is shown by the presence near the heart of colored sacs—presumably collections of arterial
and venous blood—called *tsav;* hence Tiv speak of innocence as "empty-
chested." Bohannan (1957:199) says that "empty-chested" in Tiv means
two things: "a man of no talent and consequence, if he is alive and
healthy. Applied to a dead man, it means a person who died for some
reason other than his own evil propensity [his witchcraft bringing his
doom through the operation of good ritual]. It resembles our own word
'innocent' in that it has connotations of good, but in other usages the de-
rogatory connotations of lack of experience are dominant."

There is, of course, nothing unique in this Tiv idea that to be innocent
is to be guiltless, and therefore in some way to be guileless, naive, simple,
and foolish, as any dictionary shows. The existence in such widely separated societies of this feeling that the guilty are somehow clever and that
the weak and poor are somehow innocent, while the innocent are also
somehow foolish, poses a general problem. The same identification is
found in Hebrew, Arabic, Latin, and in at least some Bantu languages.
There are also differences. Tiv "empty-chestedness" involves beliefs about
the responsibility of persons for their kin's misfortunes and successes
quite different from our own, and comparison of these differences leads
us into fundamental problems of social relations and dogma (see Gluckman in press).

Again, Bohannan has a brilliant and subtle discussion of Tiv concepts of truth (1957:47–51). To oversimplify, this discussion focuses on two words, *mimi* (more or less our truth) and *yough* (to maintain the even flow of social relationships), as against *yie*, which covers lies, broken promises, and disturbing the even flow of relationships. The weakness comes in the explicit statement that here the Tiv differ fundamentally from the Western judicial systems' view of "truth" as "verifiable 'facts' of what took place." We have only to think of our difference between "white lies" and "black lies" to see that there are similarities; and the fact that one should not tell "white lies" in court against the verifiable facts shifts the focus of comparison to the role of Tiv courts in maintaining permanent social relationships as against the role of our courts. This comparison draws attention to the possible existence of equivalent valuations in other institutions among ourselves, such as the manner in which lawyers, marriage guidance counselors, and similar "adjusters" of disturbed relations work and urge clients to speak the truth. Bohannan's example of a woman who had to be compelled by an oath to give evidence that she had seen her co-wife becoming involved in an adulterous relation could be paralleled, too: in personal relations, the subpoena and the oath excluding perjury may similarly excuse a person for not lying to maintain smooth social relationships.

There are, of course, specific concepts in particular systems that are unique. For these, the vernacular term has to be used, or some descriptive phrase has to be coined. Thus, after the Barotse liberated their homeland from Basuto conquerors, their king allowed returning Lozi to *liulula* —reclaim or liberate—their ancestral lands. In 1927 his successor barred these claims and made it an offense to bring one. The offense is called *muliu:* and I either speak of *muliu* or of the offense of making an ancestral claim (Gluckman 1955:54, 56 f., 287–288). But putting cattle out to be herded, though it has somewhat different incidents from agistment in Anglo-Saxon law, can be called agistment. The Tiv ideas involved in *tsav* (Bohannan 1957:passim) are so complex that it may be wiser to use *tsav;* "witchcraft substance" is misleading, but "mystical heart-blood" might do.

I feel therefore that everyone will agree with Bohannan that the first task in reporting a legal system is clearly to describe its "folk-concepts." I consider that, after careful and perhaps lengthy description and discussion, very many of these concepts can, without distortion, be given English equivalents, at least out of courtesy to one's readers. But some such step is essential at the next stage, when one essays comparative work. The problem must be tackled at several levels: first, delineation of the tribal conception; second, its comparison with other conceptions of similar type; third, determination of some general word, perhaps with a qualifying adjective, to arrive at a word for comparative analysis. In some cases it may be better to use neologisms, which Ayoub (1961) favors though he does not suggest any. But his discussion of the problems involved is clear and stimulating. Goodenough, Sheddick, Holleman, the Dutch adat lawyers, and I have done so for land tenure. I did so in making a distinction between "tribute" and "things of kingship" among the Barotse, in *The Ideas in Barotse Jurisprudence* (1965b:Chapter V).

Failing the use of neologisms, a research worker writing in his own language is, in my opinion, entitled to try to specialize by stipulation the riches in the vocabulary of that language; and it seems to me that the refinements of English, and in general European, jurisprudence provide us with a more suitable vocabulary than do the languages of tribal law. It might be helpful to use heavy black type or block letters or other printing devices to mark when a word like "law" or "reasonable" is used for general analytic comparison as against reporting.

The Reasonable Man

Several critics have objected to my analysis of Barotse cases in terms of "the reasonable man," and then to my making "the reasonable man a central emphasis" of Barotse law. These criticisms vary in kind. Anderson, in a review (1955), says when I argue that here there is a parallel with Western law, "Surely it amounts, in fact to no more than a regard for what an ordinary man, or an average headman, father, son, or husband would normally do in given circumstances—and, as such, represents a canon of judgment which is basic to human thinking, however inarticulate it may be?" If the canon is "basic to human thinking," it surely merits analysis; and there is a wealth of litigation, both among ourselves and the Barotse, contained in Anderson's "it amounts, in fact, to no more than a regard."

I here repeat that I believe my cases demonstrate that something like this idea is fundamental in Barotse reasoning, both of judges and of litigants. I have elsewhere recorded, in published broadcasts (1963b), how this vision of the reasonable man in Barotse law suddenly burst on me during the hearing of a case I called the Case of the Violent Councillor (1955:83–90). This insight illuminated all my other cases. The whole concept had been overlooked in the records in tribal law known to me. I examined the role of the reasonable man in cross-examination and judicial reasoning. Epstein also showed that other tribes in the region argued similarly, in his *Juridicial Techniques and the Judicial Process* (1954). Following on my work, Howell (who acknowledges reading my work before publication) reported the conception among the Nuer (1954) and Meggitt found it among the Walbiri of Australia (1962). Bohannan described clearly how the Tiv have this conception (1957:33–34), but he stated that it is not employed by judges in courts. Here Epstein (1959) and I (1965a) agree with him that it may not be used explicitly, but that an analysis of Bohannan's cases shows that these cannot be understood unless one sees that the conception is constantly, if implicitly, in the "judges'" minds. Gulliver has similarly stated, in a study of the Arusha of Tanganyika (1963:300), that he did not find it "empirically or analytically valid to adopt Gluckman's hypothesis of 'the reasonable man.'" Insofar as this concept "corresponds closely with the concept of 'the *role* of a particular *status*' [in Gluckman's words] Arusha, like other people, have some idea of it which they more or less explicitly put into words, and which can be readily inferred from their behavior, at relevant times." Gulliver proceeds to state that disputes are argued, "not altogether as a conscious technique . . . by reference to reasonable expectations." Yet reanalysis of his longest case, the only one of which anything like a full record is given, shows that at every point protagonists argue as reasonable men about what reasonable incumbents of social positions should do in the light of demands on their resources (Gluckman 1965a).

This implicit use of the conception of a reasonable man by Tiv in court judgments has ben conceded by Bohannan (see Gluckman 1965a), but he considers that since the conception is not explicitly formulated, it is not a Tiv "folk-concept." But clearly, then, some such analytic concept should be used to make sense of Tiv judgments. More generally, Bohannan states that Tiv elders and judges do not give a public explanation of the logic by which they have come to a conclusion and state their verdict. Gulliver says the Arusha also do not publicly expound the logic of their arguments; and he suggests that explicit analysis by judges of cases may occur only where there are courts with power to summons, hear, and cross-examine parties and witnesses. This suggested association that clear and explicit argument emerges only in courts needs careful checking.

As far as the use of the conception of "the reasonable man" is concerned, I consider that two things have to be kept clear. First, I insist that primarily I report a Barotse conception that is akin to what we call "a reasonable man"—their phrase is *mutu yangana*. Epstein has reported the same conception from other Zambian tribes. This being so, it is impossible to analyze the way judges cross-examine and give decisions in these courts without dealing with "the reasonable man" and what Epstein calls "reasonable expectations." Allott (1956), a lawyer specializing in African law, lends his support to the utility of the conception, in a review of my study of Barotse judicial reasoning:

> The court, by setting custom as its standard, makes what is otherwise normal, normative; that which is done, ought to be done. But custom *alone* [Gluckman's italics] will not always yield a rule of decision, and in such cases another standard is required. This standard is that of the reasonable man: what would an ordinary, prudent or reasonable man have done in the cir-

cumstances of the case? The conduct of the reasonable man, since he steps into the shoes of the defendant, must vary according to the circumstances posited. In societies without written law the two standards, the customary and the reasonable, often overlap; for, as that percipient Gold Coast judge, Sir W. Brandford Griffith C. J. remarked: "Native custom generally consists of the performance of the reasonable in the special circumstances of the case" (Yerenchi v. Akuffo (1905) Renner's Reports, 362,367).

Allott then discusses my use of the concept in explicating how Lozi judges use reasonable standards to incorporate prevailing ideas of morality and justice changing standards, and the like, but he does not approve of the extent to which I argue that the judges may be seen as "interpreting" ideas in the law. He also draws attention to what he considers to be my too "flexible" use of "reasonable behaviour."

None of those who have criticized my use of the conception of the reasonable man on general grounds have attempted to re-analyze the cases I reported without using the conception or some similar conception. It is easy for March (1956:733) to say, in the abstract, that I include so much under the single rubric of the reasonable man that it becomes virtually meaningless, and that the confusing use of this concept, with its extensive connotations in Western law, is "simply rhetoric related to [an] unfortunate attempt to strengthen [a] claim of similarity between Lozi and Western law." But I would like a demonstration that the cases can be better analyzed otherwise. March, in fact, goes on to extract from my book itself three forms in which social norms enter into judicial reasoning. But I still insist that the social conception that pulls these together is an assemblage of norms, with reasonably defined leeways, into a total view of "the reasonable man" and "the reasonable incumbent of a specific social position."

Having established that "the reasonable man" is a Barotse concept, perhaps I would have been wiser to use the Barotse term when reporting and to confine my use of the English phrase or to invent a neologism or use a printing device for analytical purpose. I did not do so because I wished to suggest that the central position of the conception in the Barotse judicial process encouraged me to believe that a more meticulous examination of how, in Britain, litigants or accused in a large number of cases presented their evidence and of how this evidence was cross-examined by counsel and adjudicated on by judges and juries would reveal that a series of reasonable men of somewhat different types exist in British social life and therefore in British courts. That is, I suggested that research in Western courts of trial in these terms would reveal what are the shared and the divergent norms that various types of persons attach to different roles. Some of the lawyers who reviewed my book (Stumpf 1955–1956, Kilgour 1955, and Schiller 1957) have seen value in this suggestion. But, above all, I used the established phrase to state my hypothesis that "the reasonable man" appears to dominate the Barotse judicial process, and possibly the judicial process in similar societies, because most disputes involve persons in related status positions, so that courts are dominantly concerned with the roles of such positions and with much of a litigant's total social personality. In a more differentiated society, contractual relations and injuries by one stranger on another are what primarily come to courts. Hence what "the reasonable man" would have done in certain circumstances appears to be only a judicial device to assess reasonable duty, care, support, and so on, in specialized branches of law. But law becomes divided into specialized branches only as the society of which it is a part becomes more differentiated. My whole argument is that this specialization had developed very little in Barotseland. That is, my hypothesis is that in the relatively undifferentiated law of Barotseland "the reasonable man" emerges as a more clearly and concretely defined social cluster of rights and duties around a specific status than he does in the developed law of Britain, where he is in a sense a judicial fiction—but possibly not a fiction for juries. And "reasonable" is everywhere a means primarily of measuring duties in relation to the wealth of the parties and other specific conditions in a particular case brought under a general rule.

Moore (1966:621) makes this important difference clear when she writes that "One of the difficulties with the concept of reasonableness has been its judicial use (in both Barotse and Western systems) for two entirely different kinds of cases: those in which reasonableness is simply a condensed term for well-known standard role expectations, and those in which reasonableness is a way of dealing with situations in which the norms are unclear." She proceeds to discuss the controversy. I would add that the application of even clear norms to particular sets of facts is unclear, as is the setting of role expectations in the economies of individuals. But the distinction is important; and cases of the two types occur with different frequencies in Barotse and in Western law.

If this is seen, it is, I believe, quite clear when I am reporting Barotse use of the conception of "the reasonable man" and when I use the concept for objective analysis. March did not see that I used the device to emphasize divergence as well as similarity between Barotse and Western law. I also saw (1955:129) "the reasonable man" as representing the forensic aspect of roles, and hence as a means to link analysis of the judicial process to this central concept in sociology and anthropology (compare Epstein's "reasonable expectations"). As I show in Chapter V of *The Ideas in Barotse Jurisprudence* (1965b), where modern Western law is specialized in defining types of rights and duties, Barotse law is developed in definitions of social positions and types of property. The concept of reasonableness in modern Western law, therefore, applies to rights and duties; in Barotse law it applies to social positions in relation to property.

I would add a further merit of the word "reasonable." African law, like English and Roman and Roman-Dutch law, insists that men have "reason." Indeed, in Africa, as with us, it is reason that is regarded as distinguishing man from the animals; this appears in cases in which judges compare wrongdoers with animals, lacking reason and respect (Epstein 1954:32; Gluckman 1955:148 f., 206 f., 240, 259). If reason is the essence of law in human society, we need the concept of reasonableness.

Analytic Models

Having considered concepts, let me turn to models. An essay by Bohannan, "The Differing Realms of Law" (1965), emphasizes for me that too little thought has been given to the problem of how far the application of Western jurisprudential analytic models distorts other systems of law. Let us look at Bohannan's relation of what he calls "custom" to what he calls "legal," to see if there is a fundamental logical difference between his procedure and my procedure (following Western jurists) whereby I call "custom" a source of what I call "law" and hence of what I call "forensic" (formerly legal) rulings. Bohannan states (pp. 34 f.) that:

A norm is a rule, more or less overt, which expresses "ought" aspects of relationships between human beings. Custom is a body of such norms that is actually followed in practice much of the time. . . . A legal institution is one by means of which the people of a society settle disputes that arise between one another and counteract any gross and flagrant abuses of the rules . . . , of at least some of the other institutions of society. Every on-going society has legal institutions in this sense, as well as a wide variety of nonlegal institutions.

. . . Seen in this light, a fairly simple distinction can be made between law and custom. Customs are norms or rules (more or less strict, and with greater or less support of moral, ethical or even physical coercion) about the ways in which people must behave if social institutions are to perform their tasks and society is to endure. All institutions (including legal institutions) develop customs. Some customs, in some societies, are *re*institutionalized. When this happens, therefore, law may be regarded [the first time he stipulates how he will personally use one of these multivocal words] as a custom that has been restated in order to make it amenable to the activities of the legal institutions. In this sense, it is one of the most characteristic attributes of legal institutions that some of these "laws" are about the legal institutions themselves, although most are about the other institutions of society—the familial, economic, political, ritual, or whatever.

We might rephrase this: the customs of all institutions of society are liable to be involved in a dispute, which may be settled by a legal institution. In such circumstances, the legal institution restates [certain?] customs in the institution involved, that is, it reinstitutionalizes these. These customs can be called "law." Customs are therefore the source of law in legal institutions. We are then back with the standard jurisprudential approach, but with a difference.

The difference is that Bohannan sees the re-institutionalization into legal institutions of custom as occurring out of "familial, economic, political and ritual, or whatever" institutions (domains of life, Fortes calls them), and out of the legal institutions (or domain), into the legal institutions. He does not discriminate between types of custom. The Western jurisprudential approach, which I have followed to analyze the Barotse judicial process, not only discriminates between the domains of social relations, but also discriminates between the types of rules and regularities that are restated as "law" or as "legal" or as "forensic rulings" in the judicial process. I have described these, for the Barotse, as statutes, precedents, moral exemplifications, public policy, good morals, equity, natural law (called by the Barotse, laws of God), laws of nature (also called by the Barotse laws of God), and reasonableness. Bohannan might say that these are in fact Barotse ideas on public policy, ideas about good morals, ideas about the laws of nature, and hence that they can all be called "customs" in his definition of the word. To do so would in my opinion obscure the complicated balancing of these different types of rule—practice, principle, and the like—that is involved in a judicial process or a process of settlement, mediation, negotiation, and so forth. I therefore believe that the standard jurisprudential approach to this process is, *for certain problems*, more refined and fruitful than Bohannan's. His approach may be useful if we shift our interest to examine problems involved in the maintenance of norms within specific domains of social relationships, though I consider that even then we would have to bring in the jurisprudential discriminations for refined analysis. But my major point is that there is no difference between using the language of Western social anthropology and using the language of Western jurisprudence in tackling these sorts of problems. Theoretically, both are equally distorting, even while they may be illuminating. It is mere prejudice for social anthropologists to consider that the schemes that jurisprudents have used successfully for the analysis of Western law cannot be applied to clarify the law of another "folk-system." It is particularly prejudice if in fact their own systems of analysis can be reduced to exactly the same logical procedures.

I would suggest that if we examine Hoebel's analysis of Eskimo law (1954:Chapter 5) we will find that there, too, it is profitable to use the approach from the different sources of law to classify Eskimo "jural postulates." Some of these postulates embody laws of nature (as that a hunter who harpoons a seal with a harpoon to which a bladder is attached can claim the quarry, because it is slowed down). Others (the punishment of recidivist homicides and persistent breakers of taboos) involve public policy. And so forth.

Epstein and I also took certain analyses of the Western judicial process (particularly Cardozo's) as a model from which to approach the study of the African judicial process. Nader (1965a:22) therefore adorns me with the mantle of greater men when she says that "Gluckman's conceptual model [is] . . . much too general for comparative usefulness." Using this model, Epstein and I were able to illuminate the processes of trial we studied. Thus, surveying Barotse cases, where gaps in the law had to be filled, I was able (1955:28 f.) to show that in their reasoning the Barotse judges used Cardozo's methods of the logic of analogy, the development of tradition, the development of custom, and the development of social principles. This model made sense of Barotse judges' reasoning. Some very intelligent men have been working on legal systems for a long time, and it is unwise not to use the products of their labors —not all of which were phlogiston theories. I do not say that judicial procedures could not have been classified in another and also fruitful way; but no one as yet has shown that this can be done. Those anthropologists who have not used Western methods do not appear to me to have produced any kind of theory on this point. On the contrary, I consider that some of them have gone seriously astray in this and other fields. For example, Bohannan (1957), Krige (1939), and Krige and Krige (1943), by insisting on the great difference between Tiv and Lovedu, respectively, as against Western, judicial processes, have made statements contradicted by their own material. I give one example only: Bohannan insists that Tiv "mbatarev (elders) suggest a settlement, and the litigants must concur if the case is to be thoroughly successful" (Bohannan 1957:61, discussed in Gluckman 1965c:185). But his own cases show that Tiv judges in courts established by the British laid down decisions that litigants had to accept. I dare say English judges consider their judgments to be "thoroughly successful" if a convicted criminal acknowledges his felony and a defeated civil suitor that right was on the other side.

I do not say that an anthropologist who has not studied jurisprudence cannot study tribal law; such a statement would be nonsense. But jurisprudence, insofar as it is scientific, is a social science; and hence I consider that its concepts are propositions that must be taken into account for profitable analysis of certain problems in social anthropology. Use of the terms can be dangerous; but there is no adventure of ideas without risk.

Descent and Legal Position

Descent systems are part ideas and part social realities. While culturally defined modes of tracing relationship and classifying kin clearly belong to the realm of ideas and ideologies, they serve as rationales of real social arrangements. Legal consequences are often said to flow from descent. Hoebel lists descent among the basic jural postulates of a number of peoples (1954:Ifuugao, 104; Trobriand, 191; Ashanti, 253). Fortes puts descent in the jural and political domain (1959:207). Bohannan notes that in almost all societies some legal rights are linked with actual or putative descent (1963:59).

Although the jural importance of descent is frequently acknowledged in this general way, its legal significance can be estimated only by asking first what is meant by descent, and then by seeing exactly what rights and duties are in fact derived from descent in a particular society. That is what this paper proposes to do. The first two sections—this one and the next—define the problem to be dealt with as one of the relationship between concepts and rules, arguing that on one level descent is an ideology, not in itself a set of legal rules; and that certain studies that take as their point of departure the notion that ideological descent by itself has legal consequences are failing to make important distinctions between ways of thinking about social organization and the operative realities. The third, fourth, and fifth sections examine the ethnography of the Lango as a detailed illustration of the complex relation between the jural rule level and the conceptual level. The last section summarizes the general significance of the data examined.

I rely on Driberg's description of the Lango as they were fifty-odd

374

years ago, supplemented by some additional data recorded later by Hayley (Driberg, 1923; Hayley, 1947). I came upon the Lango more or less fortuitously. I had read Driberg's book in the course of collecting comparative material on collective liability in Africa, and it struck me as a concise and uncomplicated illustration of the points I wanted to make in this paper.

What emerges from the analysis of the Lango is the fact that descent, although relevant to many rights and duties, is in the instances examined neither exclusively nor absolutely determinative of them. Descent is seen, not as a principle that has clearly definable, invariable legal consequences, but rather as one of the more significant of a number of considerations pertinent to rights and obligations. Descent sometimes figures more prominently in the conceptualization of rights and obligations than in their operation. These facts—that rights and duties arise from the concatenation of a number of circumstances; that descent is not in and of itself an absolute definer of obligation, but rather a contributory definer of it—bear on the whole question of rules of law and what they are made of.

The present examination of the jural consequences of descent in one cultural milieu is not undertaken to reiterate the already long-established fact that descent systems do not operate as neatly as elementary charts of uterine and agnatic links. That would be a useless and repetitive exercise. This paper will undertake to explore, on the one hand, the concepts, models, and rationales in terms of which Lango rules are framed, and, on the other hand, the operational level of the rules, and the relationship between them.

All jural rules may be analyzed in terms of general principles, categories, and concepts that are not themselves narrow enough to be described as rules. Hoebel, Bohannan, and Gluckman, each in a very different way are seeking this body of material when they respectively pursue the jural postulates, the folk systems, and the hierarchies of principles (Hoebel 1954; Bohannan 1963:13; Gluckman 1965b:295). Legal systems classify types of relationships and types of acts. Any particular case fits within wider concepts and categories. From one view, legal systems are amenable to study purely as systems of classification.

A great deal is known about descent. Descent is an idea woven through many binding relationships and transactions. With descent as a well-marked point of departure, it is possible to have a look at the intricate relationship between the rule level of legal matters and the concept level in terms of which the rules are framed. The rule level has received diminishing attention in some anthropological quarters for both practical and historical reasons.

It was once the fashion to include in ethnographies a section on laws and to give lists of rules worded like the Ten Commandments. These simply stated rules had been extracted from informants, perhaps even suggested to them, and not observed in operation. Only the crudest of hypothetical cases usually were put to informants for their comment. Driberg's book on the Lango is in some respects a museum piece of this method, but happily his ethnographic material is fuller than his law lists. A tremendous reaction against these sterile citings of rules has produced instead an emphasis on case reports. The preoccupation with cases has had a salutary effect. A case is something that really happened, not some abstract precept told the anthropologist, and it presents conflict and crisis situations in condensed form, ready-made for analysis.

But as soon as analysis is undertaken, one is returned to the problem of the nature of legal concepts, rules, and settlements. Bohannan (1965: 39) has said that in stateless societies trouble cases are settled by compromises rather than by the kind of decisions rendered in unicentric power systems. This, he feels, "leads to very much less precise statements of norms as law than does the decision-based unicentric solution." The procedural difference between compromise and decision may well affect the way norms are stated, but there are also many other reasons why many legal norms are imprecise in both types of systems. One of these is the fact that there frequently are many contingencies that affect legal relations, and these make the problem of formulating norms quite complex, as every statutory draftsman is well aware. I think there is a good reason why norm statements appear least precise in the structurally least differentiated societies—a reason that has nothing to do with particular dispute-resolving procedures. It is this: the more multiplex the social relations, the more contingencies there are that may affect any particular act or transaction. This multiplicity not only makes it difficult to state norms precisely, but sometimes it may even make it impossible, since the assortment of contingencies can vary so much from one case to another. The Lango material illustrates this quite clearly.

The riches of the case method of research should not make one forget that the most important place where legal rules and ideas operate is outside the courts (and other dispute-settlement institutions), not in them. However, in the context of ordinary social life, just as in court cases, legal rules do not usually appear as discrete, simple directives or prohibitions in terms of which people behave. Instead, they appear in clusters, framed in concepts, hedged about with special circumstances, with variations and conditions, with exceptions and accommodations of contradictory principles. Not one rule but a whole complex of rules and legal ideas apply to any social relationship, and some of the rules are alternatives.

Unsatisfactory studies of the rule aspect of law have generally been the result of the naïveté with which rules are sometimes conceived and treated, simply and one at a time. Instead of assuming that legal rules are simple and definite and certain, and can legitimately be considered one by one, it is more profitable to start with very different assumptions. One must postulate a *complex of rules* for any situation and also assume that there is in many legal relations a measure of indefiniteness and uncertainty, and that these qualities are essential to the operation of legal systems.

In introducing Cory's book, which attempted to codify Sukuma law, Mr. J. P. Moffett, Local Courts Advisor to the Government of Tanganyika, said, "One of the principles of the Rule of Law, fundamental to the British way of life and an indispensable part of any system of British administration, is that the law should be certain" (Cory 1953:xi). This kind of statement may be found in many judicial opinions on both sides of the Atlantic. Certainty is one of the themes of the Anglo-American legal creed. But a major task of the legal scholar is to apply himself to the study of those very aspects of the law that do not comfortably fit such a conception.

Gluckman has illuminated important facets of this problem in his study of Barotse judicial process. He has shown the indefiniteness of the highest legal principles and the way these are used as a tool by Barotse judges (1965b:295 ff.). On the lowest level, in application to the facts of a particular case, he shows how legal rules appear very precise. The apparent precision comes from the facts of the case and the necessity of decision. In a particular dispute, by definition, there is a specification of all the conditions that surround the dispute. Any attempt to generalize about rules at a level lower than the "highest principles" and higher than the facts of a single case shows that indefiniteness at this intermediate level derives not only from the vagueness of legal principles, but also from their very multiplicity. Indefiniteness at this level also flows from the endless variation of factual possibilities.

Any attempt to state normative rules at an intermediate level (that is, without narrowing the statement down solely to the facts of a particular case) requires that one try to specify a whole range of possibly relevant conditions, contingencies, and alternatives, which are always part of the complex of rules, concepts, principles, and facts that bear on legal relationships. Ordinary people acting in ordinary social situations usually take the whole complex into account. They act in terms of it. One of the purposes of this paper in tracing the theme of descent through Lango law is to show in what varied ways descent figures in such rule complexes. Three aspects are of particular concern here: the justifying, legitimizing, and symbolic frameworks in terms of which rules are conceived and expressed; the rigidity, flexibility or manipulatability of rules; and the contingencies that affect obligations.

A Minimal Definition of Descent

In a paper published in 1964, L. L. Langness makes an analysis of a New Guinea society in which he touches on the connection between descent and law. He deals with descent in terms that I think confuse some of the very issues he sought to clarify. He contrasts the ideological definition of local units as patrilineal descent groups with their actual genealogical composition, describing this as a contrast between *jural rules and statistical norms* (1964:163). Underlying his analysis is the not-unusual conception of law as a set of rules that are obeyed or disobeyed with statistically measurable frequency. He conceives of patrilineal descent as such a "jural rule."

Langness' "detailed quantitative description" of a New Guinea people is offered in order that "whatever discrepancy exists between the sociological facts and the cultural ideology can be made apparent" (1964: 164). He sees the problem of analysis as twofold. First he mentions Barnes's discussion (1962:5–9) of whether it is profitable to use models developed for African segmentary systems in examining New Guinea societies, and second he asks "whether one is discussing, in the New Guinea case, jural rules or statistical norms." And he adds, "It seems, in fact, that the comparisons made are often between jural rules (ideologies) of the lineal segmentary societies of Africa, and presumed (but not actual) statistical norms of New Guinea" (1964:163). The key to his conception of the problem lies in his speaking of jural rules as identical with ideologies.

Langness describes one of four subgroups of a tribe. The Nupasafa group is localized, corporate, exogamous, and a "patrilineal descent group . . . *by ideology* (dogma)" (1964:165). The Nupasafa group considers itself to have been founded by an ancestor named Gooyi. It consists of a total population of 232 persons. Langness carefully distinguishes the local Nupasafa group with which he is concerned from a much larger nonlocalized category, the Nupasafa "clan," which would include all those persons who on the basis of descent might call themselves Nupasafans. Confining himself to the local group, he indicates that nearly all male residents claim to be members of the subgroups founded by Gooyi's five sons, though they cannot all show a genealogical connection. Thus they are all ideologically members of Nupasafa, which is conceived as a descent group. When Langness gets down to genealogies, he explains that there are thirty-five adult male agnates, fifteen nonagnates living in Nupasafa. Sifting these down by eliminating adolescent, aged, or ineffectual individuals, he judges that the active core consists of thirty males. These constitute the fully participating nucleus of the Nupasafa group, and of these ten are nonagnates. The grounds on which these nonagnates were resident varied. Some were the children of people who had settled there as refuges from war defeats, some were subject to sorcery in their own communities, two had Nupasafa wives and still claimed land in their own communities, and one had a father who had once been temporarily resident in the community, which was considered sufficient reason to allow him to attach himself to the community.

All nonagnates considered themselves full members of the local Nupasafa group. All were addressed by kinship terms. The two married to Nupa women did not, of course, claim common descent, but the others evidently did. When pressed, they would admit that they were not actually descended from the Nupasafa ancestor, but it was clear from the shallow memory of genealogies exhibited that this point would soon be forgotten and that they would be totally assimilated in a generation or two. Immigrants assimilating in this manner observed all the Nupasafa rules of exogamy and would have found it unthinkable to marry a Nupa girl. Langness argues from these data that "the sheer fact of residence in a Bena Bena group can and does determine kinship" (1964:172).

Langness argues that "To say that Nupasafa group is patrilineal in terms of its 'core' may be descriptively adequate, but the implication that Nupasafa group is truly a 'patrilineal descent group' with the connotations that are usually associated with the term, and which might easily result from such a description, is a very serious over-simplification" (1964:167). He returns repeatedly to what he considers to be the African model. "It may well be that the number of agnates living elsewhere than in their natal group may be significantly larger for a New Guinea group than an African one, or that genealogical depth is greater or remembered more precisely in an African group, but this does not necessarily mean an absence or weakness of the dogma of patrilineal descent. What it does mean is that the dogma of patrilineal descent operates weakly as only one principle among several, rather than as the sole principle implied in the African materials" (1964:171).

Apart from passing introductory allusions to African segmentary models, Langness never makes absolutely clear what he conceives the African situation to be. In fact, many of the points Langness has made about the Nupasafa can be illustrated easily from the African materials. A serious difficulty would seem to arise, not from differences between African and New Guinea ethnographic data—and there certainly are important differences as well as parallels—but from the conception of descent that Langness has chosen to use. He takes the position that there is a jural-ideological model in which true genealogical descent, and descent alone, gives a person legal rights in a patrilineal descent group. I think this is the way he conceives the African systems. Since the Nupasafa do not fit this model, Langness ends by classifying them as *quasi-unilineal.* He says, "the fundamental problem is the discrepancy between ideology and statistical norms."

I would argue that descent ideology and jural rules are distinct concepts and cannot be used interchangeably, as Langness has done. In my view descent ideology in its most basic form is an *ideology of identities*, a model of relationships in the sense of *homologies*, not of behavior. As such, it is an idea that can be used in many different ways, and it is enormously adaptable and manipulatable. It may be used literally to define the membership of social categories or units. It may be used symbolically to represent identities of interest or category that, in fact, are not genealogical descent relationships at all. It would appear that it is used for both purposes by the Nupasafa. But Langness considers only the literal use as fitting the "descent ideology." He treats the metaphorical use of descent (to assimilate nonagnates into the group) as a statistical deviation from the "jural rule," from the "ideology," as he uses those words.

I. M. Lewis' recent paper approached descent in a entirely different manner. His was a much more flexible conception of descent, though it, too, was very much tied to the idea of descent as a principle of social organization. He inquired into the question of "how unilineal descent varies in different unilineal descent systems, and how such variations can be assessed, or measured" adding parenthetically, "(if indeed this is possible)" (1965:87). He begins by asking the question, "are some societies more or less 'strongly' patrilineal or matrilineal than others; and, if so, in what respects: and, further, by what criteria can such differences be objectively established?" (1965:87).

Lewis touches briefly on a wide range of applications of patrilineal descent principles in segmentary lineage systems. He starts off with "national" genealogies that embrace the whole society or culture, then he moves down a level to maximum corporate groupings. He struggles with the problem of the "functional significance of descent" in politico-jural and religious contexts and tries to make tests of consistency and exclusiveness of application. He presents a whole smorgasbord of variations in uses of patrilineal descent, essentially to demonstrate the hopelessness of trying to make a total quantitative evaluation of the over-all significance of descent in any particular society, let alone in comparisons between societies. He touches on matrilineal societies to the same effect.

Throughout his paper Lewis speaks of descent as an "organizing principle"; this is the aspect that interests him. For example, he argues that "The fundamental test of the functional importance of unilineal descent in a particular society must surely be the extent to which it is empirically the organizational basis for social activities in the widest sense" (1965: 94). Lewis is well aware of the idiomatic use of descent to represent relationships founded on other bases, but his preoccupation is with organization, rather than with ideology. The problem he set himself was an impossible one, and he carried the test of "strength" of unilineality bravely through a maze of facts and asides, to a very sensible conclusion: that is, that it cannot be measured.

If descent ideology is approached as an ideology of identities that can be adapted for use as an organizing principle, rather than as an organizing principle in the first place, it is not difficult to cope with the varieties and irregularities observed by Lewis and Langness. The basic element of the ideology of descent is a way of thinking about the procession of the generations. It postulates certain identities between ancestors and descendants and consequently also categorizes contemporaries. In no way does this minimal model itself dictate what specific social consequences this series of identifications shall have. Descent is essentially an infinitely expandable system of identities. As it has to do with sequences of generations, it often gets involved with facts and myths about sex and procreation, with rules of incest and exogamy, and with the distribution and handing on of property and status. Social units may describe their boundaries in terms of it.

The regulation of these matters involves jural rules. However the rules are not inherent in the system of identities itself. The jural rules may or may not be built partly or wholly in terms of the descent ideology or rationalized by it. Even if descent is invoked, the model itself is nonspecific in these matters, and *quite a variety of jural possibilities can be built on the same minimal descent base.*

One way to sift out the connections between descent and law in a particular society is to examine the rights and obligations of individuals, two legal questions being asked throughout. First, is descent by itself the effective source of the rights involved, or is descent operative only when combined with other factors? Second, is descent (with or without other elements) the only source of the rights involved, or may the same rights be acquired by alternative means not involving descent at all?

These questions are not answerable unless one distinguishes among the ideological, the jural, and the statistical or behavioral levels of analysis. Thus far I have spoken of the ideology of descent in its minimal and fundamental form, isolating identities as the lowest common denominator of descent ideologies. Built on this basic set of identities are elaborations special to particular cultures. For example, a conception of society at large and of its component parts may mix basic descent principles with others to arrive at a constitutional theory of society. This is a *way of thinking* about social organization that may be more or less metaphorical. It is only on the jural level that one finds those practical binding rules that actually regulate the "on the ground" operations of a particular society. These rules may be stated in terms of the descent ideology, but they vary greatly from society to society, whereas the minimal forms of descent ideology (the identities between ancestors and descendants) by definition are very much the same in many cultures. On the statistical level one investigates the incidence of action under the various alternative jural rules, not simply violations nor the extent to which a population fits or does not fit preconceived notions of what constitutes a "descent group." The basic descent ideology, the constitutional theory, the jural rules, and the statistical frequences should be kept conceptually distinct whenever this is possible.

The Lango: Descent and Constitutional Theories

Insofar as a society has a conception of what constitutes a formally legitimate political subunit and what is the proper relationship among such subunits, it has a constitutional theory. A constitutional theory "explains" the vagaries of the political reality by describing in very general terms the model system within which political events supposedly take place. Some cultures seem prone to conceptualize their political relations in terms of a single dimension—segmentary lineage systems, for example. Others, like the Lango, do not rationalize the whole in such unitary terms, but simply operate with a varied set of interlocking constitutional categories and principles.

The fact that a constitutional theory is couched in terms of one repetitive idea does not mean that the whole polity is really operationally organized on the basis of only one principle. It suggests rather that there are political reasons for emphasizing unity and minimizing diversity by means of the *model*. For example, for some purposes the Inca conceived of their empire as everywhere subdivided into units of 100 taxpayers, these being included in larger units of 1,000 taxpayers, which in turn were grouped into units of 5,000 taxpayers, and so on. Each larger unit was contained in a still larger one, until the whole empire was encompassed. This categorization produced an apparent organizational homogeneity from top to bottom, from emperor to merest villager. In fact, the decimal conception concealed real diversity. It provided a simple set of terms in which an empire of many disparate and relatively autonomous local units could be conceived as a single integrated whole.

Apparent formal unity is achieved in some other constitutional theories by representing the relationships among the large-scale constituent parts as if they were homologues of relationships within entities of the smallest scale. Hilda Kuper (1961:40) indicates that the Swazi kingdom is for some purposes represented in sayings and customs, as if the whole Swazi nation were a magnified model of a single homestead with the king at its head. (This is not to say that other constitutional conceptions were not available to the Swazi and invoked when convenient.) Segmentary lineage systems are another instance of this use of the internal organization of a small unit to depict the relationship among larger ones, since relationships *between* lineages are represented as relationships between ancestral individuals *inside* lineages.

This use of the internal organization of small units as a descriptive model for the depiction of the entities of large scale produces a repetitive pattern in which each level of formal organization seems built out of the same elements as every other one. By this means differences of kind seem reduced to mere differences of scale.

Why did the Lango not develop some such unitary over-all conception? Was there anything about the decentralized Lango system that would have precluded the development of a fixed model of the relationship among villages? They had patrilineal clans which segmented. Why did they not develop a segmentary lineage system? One can only guess at the answers.

M. G. Smith (n.d.) has argued that a segmentary system of the Nuer type cannot develop where lineage groups are structurally differentiated from one another by such matters as differential marriage rules. The Lango system has another differentiating characteristic that would seem to be inconsistent with a segmentary lineage rationale: unstable military alliances among villages. No descent rationale of alliance is possible where alliance is unstable.

The Lango were organized into named exogamous patriclans. Genealogical connections were recognized among some, but not others, and there was no over-all "national" genealogy or other total descent framework into which they were fitted. Some clans were subdvisions of others, having segmented and broken off. These named subdivisions could intermarry (Driberg 1923:191).

The economic basis of Lango life was a system of shifting agriculture combined with cattle-keeping. The Lango lived in villages that were chronically at war. Each village tended to have a numerically dominant clan. Driberg (1923:71) gives figures on one such village in which sixty-seven men belonged to one clan, and the remaining twenty-six belonged to seven different clans. Villages were led by the head of the dominant clan and had local fighting alliances with other villages under the leadership of one of the village heads. Numbers of these village groups would join forces from time to time under a common temporary leader. Such alliances were constantly changing (Driberg 1923:206–208; Hayley 1947: 56–58).

Village composition was not altogether stable. The Lango rule of residence appears to have been one of considerable flexibility. Usually the eldest son continued to reside in the village of his father, but other sons did not always remain (Driberg 1923:71). There were many reasons why a man might take his family and move from one village to another, or why several families might start a new village. An individual or group might leave because of internal disputes, or because when the village moved to a new site the place selected did not meet with everyone's approval, or because there was illness in the family, or on the advice of a diviner (Driberg 1923:71). There seems to have been no binding obligation of any kind on the Lango to remain with a particular village if he thought he would be better off elsewhere.

Villages moved every three or four years. Consequently, land was frequently redistributed, and adjustments could be made easily as the composition of the village altered. Each man had his own plot (Driberg 1923:71). There was no land shortage, and individual "ownership" was temporary and more or less equivalent to the period of cultivation. Evidently a village that moved retained rights in the land it had abandoned for a year or two after moving, but thereafter lost all rights to its earlier site and fields. Agricultural land, then, though it was the basic means of production, was not really an inheritable asset of a descent group or a village; it could be temporarily inherited (Driberg 1923:175). But clearly such rights were no more durable than the occupancy of the site by the village itself. Clearly, also, land distribution would have been no impediment to additions of persons to the village. The social composition of the village could change without affecting existing land rights in any way.

Four named geographical territories were distinguished by the Lango. These were the largest categories that ever acted as a unit. Driberg (1923:191 footnote) tried to discover a genealogical rationale for these divisions but was unable to find any. Nearly all the clans were represented in all the regions. Three of the territories regularly functioned as ceremonial units, the local clans coming together at one place for the age-set initiations. These took place in a four-year cycle, and there were four age sets, linked alternately. A nine-year gap was observed between cycles. The period of the initiation ceremonies was a time of intratribal truce, culminating in a raid against another tribe. Groups of normally hostile Lango villages cooperated peacefully in the age-set ceremonies and the raid.

The age sets had a major ritual function in the annual rain-making ceremonies. These also took place at one traditional site in each of three of the geographical sections mentioned earlier. The fourth region appears to have been less cohesive and organized. There the ceremony was performed clan by clan (Driberg 1923:248–263; Hayley 1947:63–80).

Clans were bound together locally into what were called *etogo*—sets of clans whose initiated males met periodically to partake of a ritually killed animal. Women and children also attended these ceremonies, but sat apart. The *etogo* group controlled the spirits of the dead, and in this capacity it performed essential services for the living. Clan dead were dangerous only to their descendants. Hence, when the occupants of the spirit world became troublesome and brought a man illness or misfortune, he turned to the members of his *etogo* group for help. Since other clans were immune from the acts of his clan spirits, they could take measures to scare away the ghost without fear of reprisal. The *etogo* also performed ceremonies at ordinary funerals and played the major role in the great burial rites for the tribal dead held every two or three years (Hayley 1947: 17–21, 63–71).

A man belonged to the *etogo* group of his father. However, if he moved away from his own *etogo*, he could attend the ceremonies of the local *etogo* in the place to which he moved, although not as an initiated member. His son, however, could later be initiated as a full member. At initiation into the *etogo*, each boy was sponsored by a ceremonial father of the linked age set. The sponsor belonged to a clan other than that of the boy, yet the boy was not allowed to marry his adopted father's daughter. The same adopted father sponsored him at the age-set initiation ceremonies (Hayley 1947:63–71).

In sum, the localized segment of a clan, one basic unit of social cleavage, was connected with other clans through the regional organization, the age-set structure, the *etogo* groups, and the kinship networks established by exogamous marriage. The ceremonial system tied the whole bundle together in periodic ritual observances. Certain of the constituent elements of Lango society are evident from this summary. However, it omits two very significant facts of life for the Lango: the village and the military alliance of villages. There is no evidence on the question whether the smallest groups of allied villages were also the members of the *etogo* groups, but Hayley (1947:57) feels that such a presumption fits with the logic of the system.

The constitutional theory of Lango society could be described as founded on patriclans and age sets (which existed both in localized subunits and in dispersed form), these in turn functioning in the context of villages, village military alliances, *etogo* groups (united for minor ritual), and regions (united for major ritual). Every male belonged to every one of these units. His place in the polity depended upon how he fitted into or manipulated his membership in these constitutional categories. I consider the constitutional categories themselves as much a part of the Lango legal system as the narrower rules under which individuals acted within them.

Although the *types* of categories and connections were fixed in the Lango system, both the composition of social units and their particular relations with each other could shift within the system. Village alliances were variable. Patriclans could split or fuse. Not only the relationships among groups, but also, as will be shown, the relationships of individuals to groups was not absolutely fixed, despite the importance of the descent element threaded through the system.

It remains to be seen whether the place of descent in constitutional theories is a useful criterion for distinguishing organizational forms. It also remains to be seen whether particular sorts of constitutional forms can be consistently correlated with economic, social, and historical circumstances as Sahlins (1961:322–345; 1965:104–107) has sought to show. It may turn out, instead, that some constitutional theories are a formal dress that may clothe quite varied types of social arrangements. These questions lie beyond the scope of this paper. For present purposes it suffices to suggest the usefulness of employing the concept of constitutional theory in order to place notions of legitimate over-all organizational form in the comparative law framework where they belong.

Clans, Cattle, and Contingency: Variations on the Descent Formula

THE LEGITIMATION OF MEMBERSHIP IN THE DESCENT GROUP

Technically defined, each Lango patriclan was composed of persons whose mothers were married with cattle belonging to the clan, plus other individuals—such as war captives—who were adopted into the clan. Where there was no cattle payment, children belonged to the mother's clan. However, the initially "illegitimate" children of a woman who later married into the clan became full clan members through the marriage payment. Payment also made it possible for kinsmen who were not clan members to father children who were. A mother's brother could provide his sister's son with marriage cattle, whereupon the children of the sister's son would belong to the patriclan of the mother's brother.

There is nothing unusual about these facts. But from a legal point of view, this classic case is instructive. What it shows is that it is not patrilineal descent principles by themselves that have legal consequences in Lango society. The addition of new members to the patriline, while *conceived* in terms of genealogical descent, is only *legally effective* through cattle payments. A woman's lineage had full primary rights to her reproductive powers and to her offspring unless these were transferred to another lineage through the marriage payment. The formal device by which the transfer of rights in offspring is made from one patrilineage to another serves in the ordinary case to legitimize patrilineal descent. But the same device by which descent is legitimated serves also as a means of deviating from genealogical descent when it is convenient to do so. Thus the very legal formalities that make descent principles binding are the means by which the descent rule is made manipulatable.[1] Because the ordinary Lango case is one in which cattle payment and descent go together, these elements are noticeably separated only in the exceptional cases. But from the legal point of view, it is useful to treat them as analytically separable elements in all cases. The purpose that is served in distinguishing descent from its formal legitimations is obvious as soon as comparative studies are made. A look at the New Guinea societies in which not marriage payment but long residence and the allocation of land are the legal legitimators of descent makes it clear, not only that descent systems frequently have built into them legal legitimators quite separate from genealogy, but also that these legitimating procedures may be quite different in different societies. (See Meggitt 1965 for a beautifully clear description of the operation of a New Guinea system.) It makes one wonder, in fact, whether all unilineal societies do not have some such formal means of adjusting genealogy to convenience. The extent to which this is done in any particular society is a statistical question, which may be some index of social change or type. However, the very existence of the legal device shows something of the complexity of operational descent "rules." They are founded on a multiciplicity of circumstances of which genealogy is only one.

LEGAL ADJUSTMENTS IN THE DEFINITION OF THE DESCENT GROUP TO ACCOMMODATE DEMOGRAPHIC CHANGE

A Lango clan could split by dividing its cattle. If the seceding group also adopted a new name and new food taboos, it could thereafter intermarry with the remainder of the clan with which it had once been united. In such cases separation and social autonomy (and its validating symbols) were more important than common descent interpreted in strict accordance with genealogy. New clans also could be formed through the coalescence of branches of two old ones, and the fused clan could then intermarry with either of the original clans (Driberg 1923:191). Hayley confirms this report by Driberg, giving a number of additional details. He evidently witnessed a case of incipient segmentation in which a clan had grown to proportions such that half of it did not feel itself closely related to the rest. They were awaiting a case of incest to formally declare the two divisions distinct clans (Hayley 1947:41).

In the previous section we saw that descent ties that did not follow the lines of genealogical patrilineality could be created through cattle transfers at marriage. Here we see that genealogical descent ties already

1. This point adds a dimension to the Leach-Fortes debate on the relative importance of kinship, descent, and affinity as "crucial" links between corporate unilineal descent groups. The manipulatability of descent-group composition, as well as local constitutional theories, may bear on the relative emphasis given to one element or another in particular structures (Fortes 1959:193–309; Leach 1961:114–123).

acknowledged and existing in a clan could be *unmade* by splitting cattle holdings and by formal declarations. Physical separation could be effected without formalities. However, social separation sufficient to permit marriage could be managed only on the occasion of a precipitating case and through public statements and formal symbolic acts. Here again, as in the matter of indivdual membership, descent grouping is seen as an arrangement that could be modified by procedures involving manipulation of the symbols of legitimation.

CONTINGENCIES RELATING TO THE ASSEMBLING OF BRIDEWEALTH
AND THE DISTRIBUTION OF AN INHERITANCE

Family composition, prosperity, and degree of internal harmony, are all factors that bear on what are often thought of as descent-determined rights and obligations. The priorities for the provision of a Lango boy's marriage payment were as follows. The obligation (moral? legal?) lay primarily on his father. If he had no father or if his father were poor, he could appeal to other agnatic relatives. If they could not help him or were dead, he might then turn to his mother's brother for help (Driberg 1923:155). Usually, in point of fact, the animals received for a man's sister were the actual source of his marriage cattle, but as male and female children cannot be counted on to arrive in pairs, the other means existed.

Lango exogamy had a characteristic that seems logically consistent with the marriage-payment arrangements. The rule was that a man could not marry anyone in his father's *or* his mother's clans. This would seem to fit with the position of the Lango as a potential quasi-member of his mother's patrilineage, should it honor his contingent claims to marriage cattle from maternal kin.

The rules of inheritance were also consistent with this close tie to maternal relations. A man's eldest son was normally his heir. But if the eldest son were a ne'er-do-well, another son could be chosen. In the absence of sons, or suitably responsible sons, the inheritance might pass to the deceased's brother's son or, if he were ineligible, to the deceased's sister's son (Driberg 1923:174). The wives of the deceased could choose among the various possible heirs the one with whom each decided to live. The general order of eligibility for inheritance was the same as the order of claims or appeals for aid.

The heir was selected at a ceremony held from four to sixteen months after a death (Driberg 1923:168). Livestock were the principal inheritable property and were distributed by the clan after the selection of the heir. Customarily goats were inherited as they had been distributed in the decedent's lifetime among the houses of his wives, and cattle were inherited in accordance with the distribution of milk among the various wives. The heir got what livestock were left, and he held them subject to certain rights of his siblings. He was under obligation to help provide his unmarried brothers and sister's sons with marriage cattle. His uterine brothers (whether or not they were physiologically sons of the same father) and the sons of a uterine sister had claims on him prior to those of any sons of other wives of his father (Driberg 1923:174).

On an ideological plane, the cattle of agnates among the Lango may be regarded as symbolic of the real, genealogically traced patrilineal descent group. But then, with only the slightest legerdemain, the symbol itself could be used jurally to create or break membership. This is the kind of legal fiction Sir Henry Maine was talking about. It is possible to argue that all this does is to extend the mantle of descent over a few instances that would not otherwise be included or to allow for other un-usual circumstances. One can stress the contrast between the ordinary route to membership and the less usual ones and make much of the usual rule fitting the patrilineal paradigm, treating the others as deviations from rules postulated as "ideal." However, I think such a procedure is distorting; it overstresses the ideology and undervalues jural rules. The same reservations apply to the acquisition of cattle; what may be statis-tically exceptional among individuals—the young man without sisters or helpful agnates, the war captive, the orphan, the irreconcilable dispute between brothers, the shrunken or overgrown clan—may be part of the ordinary experience of every village. Certainly the rule of exogamy that barred members of mother's patriline as well as father's was part of the ordinary experience of every individual, and the contingent claims for assistance and inheritance that lay against the mother's patriline was a part of general knowledge, as were cattle dealings outside the agnatic circle. These must all be taken into account as aspects of Lango descent.

It seems to me to be a serious mistake ever to consider a complex of jural rules, such as the rules that govern membership and rights in Lango patriclans, without considering as *built in* to the basic rule those devices and extensions by which it is adapted to the vagaries of reality. The ideological model is one thing; the jural rules are another. When one gets down to the legally binding rules, patrilineality among the Lango had its own local twists, its own accretions to the bare-bones model, its own local forms of manipulatability.

DESCENT GROUP CORES AND CLUSTERS OF CONTINGENT CLAIMS

Neither the Lango definition of bridewealth obligations nor the de-termination of inheritance distributions is governed solely by a fixed gradation of closeness of agnatic relationship. Individual character, emo-tional preferences, accidents of family composition, wealth, and com-peting claims, all affect who pays what and who gets what. The priorities are as much determined by the contingencies as by a descent formula. Clearly not all rights in cattle were strictly agnatic rights, either for brideprice financing or for inheritance. Nor can one look upon the clan cattle from a jural point of view as "owned" in common by the descent group—though Hayley (1947:46) speaks of them in this way. Ideologically the cattle wealth of agnates may have been identified with the descent group. But in jural fact there were simply many separate networks of claims, each nucleated around the holdings of individuals. This situation is in some respects the obverse of Gulliver's concept of "stock associates," which he developed in connection with his analysis of the Jie and the Turkana. Gulliver (1955:196) defines "stock associates" as the circle including all people with whom a man maintains "well-recognized reciprocal rights to claim gifts of domestic animals in certain socially defined circumstances." What is being described here for the Lango are circles of *stock claimants.*

Each individual's stock holdings were at the center of a set of concentric circles of *contingent claimants.* The more peripheral the claimant, the weaker was the claim. Certain agnates, at least theoretically, were supposed to be closer to the center. One could perhaps postulate theoretical reciprocity over the long term among agnatically related descent lines, but this is quite different from the expectation of actual reciprocity between particular individuals in their lifetime.

If the whole of a localized Lango descent group were depicted as concentric circles of contingent claimants, one would probably find that certain people had only a few peripheral claims and that others were close to the center of many claim circles. That is, there would be persons who had high-priority claims on a number of cattle holders, and persons who had only weak peripheral claims where they had any. There would, of course, be mixtures also—individuals who had some high-priority claims and some peripheral ones as well. The fortuitous composition of families would have much to do with these variations.

Such inequalities of position were not mapped out individually in the Lango field work, but they follow from the descriptions of the system. This finding has significant theoretical implications, since it adds an inside perspective to the conventional picture of agnatic descent groups in which everyone is seen from the outside as jurally equivalent to everyone else. Perceived instead from the inside, in terms of concentric contingent claims, a picture emerges of internal differentiation in the descent group, not only of property, but also of rights. One sees the descent group as having a *core*—a core of persons who have many overlapping claims of high priority against one another. On the edges of these dense clusters of overlapping claims are persons more peripherally attached. Very likely aliens (nonmembers of the locally dominant descent group) also fitted into the periphery of some claim circles, as did nonresident affinal kin.

This cattle-claim model could be elaborated for other types of rights, and one would, I think, find similarly variable concentrations of other overlapping and multiplex ties. (See Pospisil 1963 on variations of individual wealth among the Kapauku.)

Presumably, with the vagaries of birth and mortality and the ups and downs of stock breeding, to say nothing of disputes among brothers and variations of individual character, the lineage core thus identified would not be stable over long periods of time. Shifts in the relevant contingencies would alter the alignments of priorities, and so on. Surely this Lango contingent cattle-claim complex is a common enough aspect of corporate unilineal groups to merit analysis as a legal type. In it, descent operates as a guideline for priorities of contingent claims rather than as a clear determinant of ascribed, invariant, and enforceable rights.

LAW AS A RULE-COMPLEX PERTAINING TO A FIELD OF ACTION

The whole matter of stock rights among the Lango is further complicated because it was possible to acquire cattle in various ways that did not depend on inheritance or claims on the generosity of kin. It was a common practice to place cows with friends for long periods of time, and this custom also served as a means of obtaining cattle, for if the cow calved more than once during the period of care, one of the calves was given to the friend in payment (Driberg 1923:92–93). Cattle borrowing was also very common. A man might borrow cattle, giving as security the promise of betrothal of his daughter or even of an unborn daughter (Driberg 1923:155).

Cattle also could be bought with grain (Driberg 1923:92–93). This not only has implications of opportunities for the buyer, but also reflects on the whole notion of communal ownership by the clan of the seller. Hayley (1947:46) notes: "he would always inform at least his brother should he intend to kill or sell an animal." Inform? Under what circumstances, one wonders, could the brother object, and could he implement his objection beyond making his wishes known? One senses in the whole description a distinct conflict between agnatic claims and individual autonomy, with shadowy areas where it was not clear which was paramount. When observed, then, the Lango had within their legal system at least two competing sets of rules—those relating to contingent kinship liens and those pertaining to the discretionary rights of the individual in property in his possession. Any picture of the descent-connected kinship rights in cattle is incomplete unless the countervailing individual discretionary rights are also considered. The Lango possessor of beasts held them under a great variety of conditions. The extent of his discretionary power over their disposition, however, depended not only on the manner in which he acquired possession—whether by agistment, as a brideprice payment, by inheritance, and so on—but also upon his family situation, the urgency of the claims upon his animals, whether by wives or marriageable sons or by other persons.

When the possessor of cattle does something with them that alters existing legal relations he is acting in a legal field of choice. Multiple ends and means confront him, and he picks his way, usually in a manner that can be rationalized by some legal principle. At the risk of exciting the ire of colleagues who see red whenever universality is mentioned, I would venture to say, not only that all legal systems have such areas of discretionary action, but also that it is over the very stuff of these fields of action that a great many disputes arise. Writers on economic anthropology are aware of the importance of the weighing of alternatives. Legal anthropology could profitably give more attention to these problems. Lawyers are all very acutely aware of choice as an aspect of law because much of their professional life is spent, not simply in settling disputes —which seem to have become the focus of legal anthropology—but in giving advice, advice about legally legitimate choices open to a client who wishes to achieve certain ends. The legal choices available to the Lango possessor of cattle did not involve his consulting Dibble, Dibble, and Dabble; he had to make his decisions himself. But the fundamental element of choice is similar.

One way of looking at legal systems is to identify and analyze the legal rule complexes that surround particular fields of action. Seen this way, the law is not a simple normative standard one does or does not conform to. It is much more complicated than that.

Village Membership: Descent Group Membership

EXPULSION: THE LOSS OF LEGAL CLAIMS ON THE DESCENT GROUP WITHOUT THE LOSS OF NOMINAL MEMBERSHIP

Perhaps an even more telling aspect of the jural implications of Lango descent emerges when one examines the occasions and causes for which a Lango could be abandoned or expelled from the community by his patriclan, from which he normally would expect to receive help and protection. The most extreme example of obligation is perhaps that of collective liability for homicide, yet on close scrutiny one discovers that such liability is not precisely collective, that it is not absolute, and that a man's agnatic relatives may decide not to back him in certain cases.

Driberg first describes the rules in terms of conventional collective liability terms. He tells us that when a man of one patriclan killed a member of another, the interclan dealings that followed were all directed toward the repair of the damaged patrilineage as a corporate unit, the replacement of the lost individual. The Lango equation was the familiar one: men are produced by women who are obtained by cattle. As indicated earlier, membership in the patriclan itself was calculated in these terms rather than in terms of descent itself.

The rules governing compensation followed logically. When a member of one patriclan killed a member of another, and the killer was known, cattle had to be paid in compensation by the kin group of the murderer to the kin of the decedent if blood vengeance were to be averted. The killer tactfully went into hiding until a settlement was concluded between the clans, when he could again emerge safely (Driberg 1923:210).

The injured kin group had lost a member. It was compensated in the currency that could replace the dead individual through the birth of new ones—that is, in cattle, which could be used to obtain a bride for a man in the decedent's kin group and hence to increase its numbers. The Nuer were more direct in this matter than the Lango, using the payment to buy a wife to marry to the name of the deceased. But the essential basis of the Lango practice was clearly the same, for if the Lango murderer had a marriageable sister or daughter, the deceased's brother could accept her instead of the cattle as full requital (Driberg 1923:211). The seven head of cattle that were the standard number paid were more or less equivalent to the brideprice, which Driberg cites as ranging anywhere from four to ten head (1923:157).

Liability for payment was not inevitably collective. It rested initially on the murderer himself. His relatives took all the cattle from his herd if he had the necessary seven animals, or they took his sister instead. But, if he had neither, Driberg notes that the obligation to pay was shifted to his agnatic relatives (1923:211). Primary responsibility thus rested on the actor, contingent but ultimate responsibility on his kin group. Viewed from the outside, the fundamental obligation was from one patriclan to another, and the debt was paid in cattle, the core of the clan patrimony.

But from the inside of the patriclan, the obligation rested on the individual who had committed the homicide. Where possible, all the animals came from his herd. Only if he did not have them and had no available sister did his close kinsmen help him out. Even then there was a question; his kinsmen had a choice. They could help, or they could deliver him to his enemies. In this respect the position of the kinsmen is quite different from that of the killer. He has a binding and inescapable obligation to his enemies. Among his principal assets are his claims for aid from kinsmen. But these are contingent claims, which the kinsmen may or may not honor. They are under no absolute and unambiguous obligation to him. He can exhaust his claims on them.

Driberg tells us that "whether the offender pay the full compensation for his offence himself, or whether he is assisted by his relatives, both the family and clan are poorer by the loss of so many livestock, and consequently, the crime of an individual weakens the whole clan. The offender is accordingly in temporary disgrace for weakening the clan, and if the offence is serious, is publicly reprimanded by the clan headman, not (be it noted) for his offence, but for its communal consequences: and a hardened offender who squanders his patrimony or constantly requires assistance from the clan is driven away or eventually given up to the vengeance of an injured claimant" (1923:208–209).

Insofar as it exists, the collective liability then is not an automatic consequence of membership in a descent category, but rather it follows on being a member *in good standing* of a patriclan in a particular localized group. The descent model (with the jural elaborations indicated earlier) defined the membership, but not the conditions for remaining a member with full privileges in a localized segment of the clan group. Hayley (1947:58) tells us that "Unsociable individuals were driven away," driven out of the village. Expulsion seems to have been a recourse available for a wide range of reasons, from shirking one's share of the communal agricultural work to mere quarrelsomeness. It could also be resorted to for unwarranted exposure of the village to the vengeance of another village (Driberg 1923:208; Hayley 1947:59).

Membership in the community or expulsion from it were not the only possibilities. One could be a community member and yet be tenuously attached. As indicated earlier, rights of members were characterized by shifting concentrations, overlappings, and priorities. Certain persons had many strong claims, others had few weak ones. The material on expulsion suggests that individual behavior as well as agnatic position was important in these matters. A "slightly attached" community member might seek his fortune elsewhere, given any provocation to do so. Whether he moved voluntarily or was expelled, his clan membership would remain fixed for purposes of exogamy but would not carry with it the rights in a particular community previously associated with it.

VILLAGES AND VILLAGE ALLIANCES: THE STRUCTURAL BASIS
OF LEGAL ENFORCEMENT

One of the interesting features of Driberg's account is that in part of his book he presents the blood feud and compensation obligations purely in terms of clan liabilities, yet when he gets down to procedure, he makes it clear that not only the clan but also the village as a whole was a liability unit.

The elders of each village, together with the local clan head and sometimes with the leader of the group of allied villages, settled all disputes between local people. Within their villages their decisions are described as binding and respected. A complainant from one village could even recover against an inhabitant of another village by bringing his case before the elders of the defendant's village; this course was effective, provided the two villages were friendly and within the same alliance district. However, notes Driberg, (1923:208–209):

> should he sue at a hostile village, or at one under another *rwot* (leader of a group of allied villages), his prospects would not be so bright, as, though the elders might find in his favor, they would be unable to enforce their decision if the defendant were unwilling to come to terms, and the defendant would certainly be supported by the younger warriors anxious for a fight. Hence, though custom has evolved an elastic scale of fines and compensations for various offenses, recourse had often to be made to violence to obtain satisfaction, and in case of murder or even adultery it was easier to make war on the village rather than to await the result of a lawsuit which would probably be unfavorable or inoperative. . . .
>
> This has resulted in the principle of the communal responsibility on the one hand of the family . . . and of the village on the other. A weak village in which lives a defendant sued by a member of a strong fighting village would insist on the defendant's punishment to save themselves from invasion, and to save the defendant, his relations and clansmen, if he is poor and has not committed an offence which is incompoundable, will help him to find the necessary amount of the fine or compensation.

Villages evidently fought as units and were raided as units; presumably attached elements were as involved as dominant clan members. Here edges of any purely clan definition of the blood feud become blurred. The fighting was carried on between villages, not simply between patriclans. Clearly much depended upon the strength mustered by each side of any intervillage dispute, leading to what Gulliver has called essentially political processes of dispute settlement (Gulliver 1963:297 ff.).

Conclusion

Descent ideas appear in Lango rule complexes in many varied forms. The Lango evidence shows, on the one hand, that there were simple techniques by means of which the definition of descent and patriclan could be adjusted to fit variable social circumstances (cattle transfers, patriclan fission and fusion). It shows, on the other hand, that there were conditions under which not the definition of descent, but its social concomitants were adjusted or changed (contingencies, withdrawals or expulsions from a village). The law can have it both ways. In some instances the covering concept for a rule has an adjustable definition. Yet in others the concept is not tampered with, but the rules under its cover are adjusted or countervened.

In reviewing the Lango material, it is extremely difficult to isolate any significant rights or obligations, with the possible exception of some ritual ones, that may be said to flow absolutely from descent and from descent alone. Even the rule of exogamy, excluding as it does the mother's patri-line as well as the father's, goes beyond descent for the definition of its scope. Lango jural rights and obligations connected with descent commonly involve other elements to make them operative, or they may be derived from alternative sources. These are the circumstances that give perspective on the difference between ideology and the jural rules. Ideology sometimes has descent and its elaborations as the be-all and end-all. The jural realities are always far more complex.

A way to approach the problem without overweighting descent is to say that many Lango jural rights depend on *social identity,* and that descent is an element in that identity. This formulation puts descent in its place as a contributory definer of the legal position of individuals and stresses that it is generally far from the sole determinant.

Gluckman (1965b:14) has spoken of rights and obligations associated with social positions. I use "social identity" to mean all those descriptive aspects of an individual's social positions that attach to his person, as well as some other elements that refer to his character. Social identity is a composite. As a concept it lends itself to the discussion of component parts. Some aspects of identity are permanent—one's sex, for example. Some may be changed, such as residence. An individual's reputation is part of his identity, and it may have a crucial bearing on his rights in the social community in which he lives. Yet reputation is not comfortably encompassed in the concept of social position.

Another way of stating the matter is to say that in a society where significant jural rights are tangled in multiplex ties, there are likely to be multiple sources of jural right. Descent, for example, may be an effective source of rights only in combination with co-residence, frequent social contact, a history of mutual support, and so on. A great many elements in an individual's social identity may have to fit to make operative rights that seem ideologically to stem from descent alone. In a single-interest-tie situation jural rights emanate more often from single sources. In Western law a man may sue another as the holder of a negotiable instrument; it is not relevant to his rights as holder where he lives, whom he sees often, what he does for a living, or whether he is faithful to his wife.

A problem of jural analysis is imbedded in this multiplicity. A training in Western legal systems pushes one in the direction of trying to specify the sources of right. But it may not always be possible to do so in the precise terms one is accustomed to expect. The Lango rights derived from co-residence in the same village serve as a good example of the problem. Co-residence in a village carries with it rights to land, agricultural assistance, cooperation in herding and care of cattle, and support in inter-village dispute. Since most co-villagers belonged to the same clan, clan membership and village membership usually ran concurrently. But of course, villagers who were nonagnates could enjoy the same benefits of communal life.

There are two ways, at least, to read this state of affairs. One can argue that the rights went with co-residence and had nothing to do with descent, since nonagnates enjoyed them. Instead, one can argue that attached nonagnates were treated for village purposes as quasi-members of the dominant clan. Which was the indigenous rationale? If I read him correctly, Driberg implies that it was the first—that village residence was treated as the key principle. The situation could have been rationalized in terms of descent ideology, and it evidently was not. Thus another related and jurally significant piece of Lango social identity was membership in a village. What does one do with Nupasafa, where membership in a village *was* rationalized in terms of the descent ideology? Is the jural situation substantially different as a result?

What about rights to cattle? A Lango man's best bet was his father's obligation to provide him with a wife. Beyond that, about all one can say is that descent gave a man a position as a legitimate *claimant* to the assets and assistance of his close agnates for particular purposes, the most ordinary and urgent of which was the financing of his first marriage. But there is a difference between contingent claims and absolute rights. There could easily be claimants with higher priorities. A father's brother might have a son of his own of marriageable age. A young man was in real trouble if he had to go so far as to depend on the generosity of his mother's brother or his sister's husband (Driberg 1923:67–68). These might simply refuse to help.

The right to claim assistance from agnates in the assembling of the brideprice is clearly related to descent. But a weighing of competing claims is involved that is not settled by descent principles at all. Once a man's father failed him, his rights were not clear-cut. The distribution of the brideprice is clear enough, but the assembling of it is very muddy. Even for the much better reported Nuer, Howell writes (1954: 97): "There are no set rules governing the actual assembling of bride-wealth cattle, and in any case the circumstances are too varied to warrant generalization on the subject."

The raw fact of descent identity itself gave him the right to claim help but by itself would not assure him of receiving help. Many things must have weighed in the balance, including the ties other than descent ties that he or his father had to agnatic kin and the history of their relationships. The fact that agnates could refuse to supply bloodwealth, or other indemnity, to redeem someone they thought contemptible is indication enough that more weighed in the balance than descent alone. Rights to the assistance of agnates seems to have been conditional and contingent.

In some respects the situation may be analogous to the obtaining of credit in Western society. Credit is not obtained as a matter of absolute right; it depends upon the likelihood of ultimate repayment. It also depends on the lender's having available capital that he does not intend to expend in some other manner. The whole business career of the borrower may be reviewed and may have relevance to his success or failure in obtaining the loan. Particular aspects of an individual's social identity may make it more or less likely that he will receive credit. As I see the position of the Lango seeking the help of his agnates, common descent gives him the position of a legitimate claimant, who may be more or less favored, depending on the surrounding circumstance.

One could generalize about the Lango that membership in a localized patrilineal clan provided the ordinary way in which an individual acquired rights in a village and the usual means by which he could gather cattle when they were needed. Nevertheless, the jural rules amply provided for other entirely legitimate possibilities. One out of every four males living in the village Driberg gave figures for had availed himself of some of these alternatives.

Descent identity, normally acquired by birth, was permanent. Yet while descent identity could not itself be lost, the rights and claims ordinarily associated with a particular group of agnatic kin could be lost. These rights could be rendered worthless or nugatory through the misfortune or decease of the agnates or the existence of prior claims. They could be lost if one did not get along with one's agnatic kin. Substitute arrangements could usually be made and legitimized by regular procedures. The permanence of descent identity was thus not matched by any invariable permanence or certainty of what appear to be descent-engendered rights. One could move to another village if one's chances seemed better there.

How, then, are the statistical facts to be interpreted? If an ethnographic description of a village indicates that the community is prevalently composed of agnatic kin, though there are present a substantial number of resident nonagnates, what is to be made of the classification? What Langness has done in his New Guinea case is to say that the ideological-jural rules require patrilineality and patrilocality, hence nonresident agnates must be explained away as deviations from the rule. He opposes the "ideal" (jural) and the "real" (statistical). Levi-Strauss' dichotomizing into mechanical and statistical models is adequate for some purposes, but not for this one. As Scheffler (1965:301) has noted, "although people may discuss their economic, political and other relations by means of kinship norms or rules we should be careful not to imply that in so doing they are attempting to attain or maintain an ideal state of affairs, not even that seemingly implied by the norms or rules themselves."

A rule may be stated in very rigid and mandatory terms yet have built into it numerous means of adjustment. The techniques by which this may be done include at least the following; there may well be others.

1. Fictional or formal extension of the rule. Fictions and formal devices can exist by which the rule can be nominally adhered to while being actually circumvented. The Lango adoptions of war captives or the rule that children of a marriage are assimilated to the lineage that provided the marriage-cattle are extensions of this type.

2. A loose application or discretionary interpretation of the rule. The existence of exceptions can be ignored and tacitly denied by behaving as if they do not exist—as if the rule, in fact, encompasses them. The rule can be applied metaphorically. This would appear to be the Nupasafa situation in which nonagnates behave as agnates do and are assimilated as quickly as their origins can be forgotten. This intentional ignoring of the facts may be done in general or only in specific contexts. However, the decision when the rule shall be applied may be in the discretion of a person or persons who may make adjustments according to their own lights. An example is the Lango agnates' option to support or surrender an accused kinsman.

3. Other rules may exist that may be resorted to instead. This characterizes the Lango residence and cattle resource arrangements.

Any of these three ways of rationalizing can be used to justify the same set of facts. They may all be used simultaneously, in fact. I think they must be regarded as different techniques for accommodating reality and as an essential part of the basic system of jural rules, not simply as deviations or exceptions from an ideal. I do not know what significance, if any, the use of one rather than another of these techniques might have, but it is a question that might be worth further inquiry. Formal extension or loose interpretation does more lip service to the exclusiveness of a patrilineal-patrilocal descent group ideology than would the open acknowledgment of legitimate alternative arrangement. But if the alternative rules are regarded as second best and there is a strong preference for maintaining membership in a patrilineal-patrilocal descent group, is there any less value given to the patrilineal ideology in the last instance than in the first two? The question, in a sense, concerns the meaning of the situation in which there are preferential rules in one case and prescriptive rules in another, yet the same statistical distributions occur in each. I am suggesting that the distinction that Needham has made between prescriptive and preferential marriage rules might usefully be investigated with reference to other rules. There seems a great variation from society to society in the *apparent* mandatoriness of particular rules.

There may even be variations within a single society of the perception of the degree of mandatoriness or of the relevant contingencies.

Social identity, the multiple source of right, and surrounding political circumstances, are all contingent factors in the Lango system that affect the enforcement or application of rules. However, the fact that rules are multiple and highly conditional in operation makes them not less but more significant as subjects of study. Legal reasoning of the sort that is common in Western courts, and that has been described by Gluckman for the Barotse, has its analogues in the justifying rationales of social systems quite outside of juridical institutions such as courts. Social arrangements, like court decisions, are usually conceived in terms of justifying principles, not simply as expedient or practical matters. Descent is often used as such a principle. Systems of legal principles, concepts, or "beliefs" (rather like systems of religious belief) provide descriptions and explanations of the nature of the social universe, and at the same time provide means for manipulating that very social universe, so that those who want to can try to make it bend to their advantage.

Descent ideologies and their elaborations are in part symbolic or metaphorical representations of social connections, in part categorical definers that affect social relations. There seems to be a two-way interaction between social structure and ideas about social structure. Any analytic framework that deals with the matter as a one way flow at this stage of knowledge has serious limitations. The dichotomizing of descent analysis into the ideal/jural and the real/statistical implies that social arrangements are simply imperfect approximations of ideal models which follow from supposed jural rules. But in fact, jural rules, though they may be stated in terms of ideology, invariably provide one way or another for the complexities, irregularities, and manipulations of real social life. By distinguishing the jural aspects of descent from the ideological and statistical, one places oneself in a better position to inquire into the relationship between justifying ideologies and social arrangements.

Ethnography and Comparison
in Legal Anthropology

Legal anthropology is, as I have remarked elsewhere, a small field in which the general quality of the work is extraordinarily high. For that reason it serves well as a microcosm in which to examine some of the problems that plague the more inclusive subject of social anthropology.

One of the recurrent problems in social anthropology is the relationship of ethnography to what is usually called comparison. Differences of opinion about the nature of data and its organization into ethnography and its reorganization into "comparative studies" have been at the heart of much disparateness within the discipline. Within legal anthropology these differences have assumed inordinate proportions.

Given the present state of the art, I find that there are four main areas on which some light can be thrown. I want to take them up in order of increasing importance: the use of native terms in reporting ethnography; the idea of the "folk system" and the way in which unavoidable warping of native ideas can be kept track of; some of the kinds of intellectual gymnastics that have been called comparison; and the difference between the theory and culture of ethnography and the theory and culture of comparison.

In the material that Gluckman added to the second edition (1967) of his *The Judicial Process among the Barotse* (originally published in 1955), he quotes a sentence from Mary Douglas' review of his book (Douglas 1956:369) which seems to touch the kernel of the problem: "C'est précisement dans cette interposition de formes de pensées étrangères que reside l'acte d'interprétation." Roughly rendered, this reads, "It is in the juxtaposition of previously unconnected ideas that the act of interpretation is to be found."

With this idea in mind, the present article will be seen to deal with four contexts in which novel juxtapositions can be made, and the kind of interpretations that can justifiably be derived from each: the new juxtaposition that comes when an ethnographer struggles to present his ideas in English to his colleagues; the new juxtapositions that arise between the models of the ethnographer and the models of his subject people; the new juxtaposition of ethnographic models with one another when they come from different cultures; and the new juxtaposition of new ethnographic models with those already accepted as theory in the subject.

Native Terms

I have been told on a number of occasions that my Tiv ethnography makes extensive use of native terms in reporting. I always agree that this is true. Gluckman (1955:380–381) takes this position: "I consider that very many of these concepts can, without distortion after careful and perhaps lengthy description and discussion, be given English equivalents, at least out of courtesy to one's readers."

Thus, the overeasy statement would seem to be that an author either uses native terms and makes it tough on the reader but easy on himself, or else he uses no native terms and makes it tough on himself but easy on the reader. This seems to me to be an erroneous way—at least an oversimple way—of looking at the problem. No one doubts that it is difficult to read an ethnographic report that is studded with foreign words. No one questions the fact that one's material should be made as easy to read as possible.

The alternative to using native words is to put a gloss on English words. That means to expand or reduce the meaning such words carry in their own culture so that they can carry an accurate meaning from the subject culture.

It is my firm opinion that the power of the word is always greater than the power of the gloss. If the ethnographer is not concerned with some (unfortunately he cannot be concerned with all) of the delicate nuances of his culture, then he may write without either native terms or glosses, "using words as the dictionaries define them"—but I brand him the lesser ethnographer. It boils down to this question: is it more difficult for a reader to keep in mind a set of native terms or a set of glosses on English words—usages of ordinary English words that will apply in no other context than the immediate one? I agree with William Empson (1951) that to introduce such a gloss is either to make a word mean so much that it becomes too blunt or to create what he calls a "negative pregnancy" to the meaning of the word—to accept only one chunk out of its ordinary day-to-day meaning. Either procedure, but particularly the latter, is to insert a trap for the reader that no amount of skillful writing or careful reading can keep him from falling into, because he subconsciously reinserts the entire range of meaning.

The result is that good ethnography is hard to read, whichever method one opts for. It is my opinion that every ethnographer owes it to himself, the people he studies, and his colleagues not to blunt the edge of his material. He must, of course, translate as much as possible; he must gauge the point at which difficulty of reading becomes impossibility of reading. But there is an analogous point at which the gloss method leads to even greater difficulty, because it simulates understanding through the use of a familiar word. Such simulation leads—almost inevitably, I think —to an assumption of comparability of everything called by the same word—and this is a difficulty that is almost impossible to correct. The most blatant examples come in the old-fashioned treatment of kinship terminology: translation of kinship terms is notoriously difficult, and we all know what a mess one can get into if he translates as "father" the words from Crow or Omaha systems that include the English "father" and then work in translation. Hocart (1937) understood this and, as far as I know, was the first really to grasp the nature of the problem that today is being attacked by componential analysis and the beginnings of a kind of ordered ethnography that its practitioners call by the unfortunate term "ethnoscience."

Hoebel, Ayoub, and some others have, when reviewing Gluckman's book and my own *Justice and Judgment among the Tiv*, claimed that Gluckman's approach leads to greater theoretical understanding. I am convinced that they have fallen into his language trap, and that in fact greater understanding has been sharply curtailed the very while our capacity to talk in demi-semantic categories gives the illusion of getting somewhere.

I see no virtue in everybody's agreeing on this matter. Differences of purpose and of personality seem to me best left to stand and speak for themselves.

While we are on the matter of language, another question can be taken care of: is the "native language" a reasonable alternative to the language of jurisprudence? Here is, indeed, another red herring. Hoebel's (1960–1961:431) statement is the earliest one I know. Although he tells me he would not stand by the statement today, I nevertheless want to review it, because the precise point was made in Gluckman's 1967 addenda. Hoebel stated that "The Tiv folk system idealizes the Tiv legal process, and it is just as erroneous to slip into an acceptance of Tiv thinking about their system as representing the real thing as it would be uncritically to carry over inappropriate Austinian conceptions to the distortion of

Tiv ideas and behavior." Gluckman (1955:382) puts it in this way: "It seems to me that the refinements of English, and in general, European, jurisprudence provide us with a more suitable vocabulary despite its connotations, than do the languages of tribal law."

Both these statements miss the point. English jurisprudence has developed a vocabulary for talking about English law (and to a lesser extent talking about comparative law and conflicts). Tiv have not developed jurisprudence. Therefore, even to get these two matters onto a comparative level, the ethnographer must do for the Tiv what they have not done for themselves—find a "theory" of Tiv legal action, for what Gluckman aptly calls forensic action. Then the job of comparison can begin. Gluckman is no doubt right that a larger proportion of what we shall below call the culture of comparison will be derived from English jurisprudence than from Tiv (or any other) ethnography. But the two "languages" per se—English jurisprudence and the native language—are not equivalent entities. In short, when you juxtapose one with the other, you are not merely changing language—you are changing media.

Hoebel's statement above has an additional difficulty in the phrase "representing the real thing." One cannot represent the real thing any way except by a grossly ethnocentric viewpoint or else by some kind of technique, such as the folk system or ethnoscience, to get at something less ethnocentric. I will have more to say below about the difficulty involved in "the real thing."

One's knowledge of ethnography and the institutions of other societies must comfortably inform the writing of any ethnographic tract the very while they are not made part of it. That is to say, if I report an institution from the Tiv that is totally similar to another institution that is described by someone else, I must neither omit to report it nor merely say that it is "like the Romans." I must describe it in Tiv terms, so that other scholars can make up their minds whether it is like the Romans. If the ideas that an ethnographer has discovered or has had to invent to explain the situation in another culture are helpful and actually do work, then any ethnographer must use them, or improve on them, and he is at fault if he does not. This is utterly different from the comparative method. It is merely utilizing the full culture of one's own profession (which Gluckman confuses with comparison). In short, Gluckman has treated what I have talked about as the folk system as if it were merely a first step toward some problem that he is interested in. In fact, it seems to me that it would never lead to the problem he is interested in, and he has therefore branded it as "unique" and as "cultural solopsism." That does not mean that it is "not comparative" so much as that he has an egocentric concept of comparison.

Folk Systems

The idea of the "folk system" formalized in my book on Tiv law has been by and large generously received. However, even at the time of its publication, Hoebel (1961) noted that it was not new; today it can be seen as a coarser and larger-scale tool, but not greatly different from what has since that time come to be called ethnoscience. The considerable thought that has gone into the epistemology of ethnography, usually under the rubric of componential analysis or ethnoscience, leads me to think a new statement about the folk system worth while.

Every cultural tradition is, in Nietzsche's phrase, "ein aus sich rollendes Rad"—a wheel rolling out of itself. No matter the origin of its cultural traits, or how internally inconsistent it may be, a cultural tradition has a character that becomes "more so" as it develops. These characteristics must be understood anthropologically in terms of the concepts and processes in which they are played out and given substance.

Without doubt, the next ten years will see the development of computer simulation programs that will allow us to isolate the vectors operating in dynamic socio-cultural systems well enough to allow us to generate the morphological stages and "types" within any given cultural tradition. In order to hasten the day, however—and I have no doubt that that day will be the one that history will remember as "scientific anthropology day"—we must be very careful in examining how we know what we know.

Gluckman (1965b:255 and other places) has taken my plea for an understanding of Tiv ethnography in Tiv terms to be quite another point: that the various cultural traditions are "unique" and have no similarities whatever, that every folk system must be different from every other folk system in all its details. It seems to me that I did not say anything so absurd. However, since a number of anthropologists have confused the admonition for analysis of a system in its own terms with a plea for uniqueness, it is worth mentioning. Simply put, the proportion of the ideas or artifacts within a cultural tradition that at one level or another are also found in other cultures is quite a different matter from whether or not we interpret whatever is there in orderly accordance with some kind of overt conception of what it means to the actors in the situation. I learned this, while a graduate student, from a lecture, given by Professor Isaac Schapera, taking anthropologists to task for not reporting the familiar. His particular target on that occasion was the lack of information in the standard ethnographies about Christianity in many African communities otherwise well reported. He went on to outline that in every sphere of life ethnographers were disposed to give closer attention to exotic items. He ended with a moral about the degree to which this process undermined the ethnographic record.

Taking his idea to heart, I think that it is necessary both to report the familiar fully (and "familiar" can, in the culture of the anthropologist, mean anything extensively dealt with in the literature, not necessarily merely something in his own ethnic background) and, specifically, to see how it is utilized and conceptualized in the subject culture.

In short, whether or not an item is "unique" is the least interesting aspect of it, except in diffusion studies. The way in which it fits into the larger conceptual system of the people who use it is what is important. It seems to me that when one gets comparative at too early a stage, this particular job is given short shrift—always to the crippling of the ethnography.

There are much more important things to say about folk systems than to argue about whether their components are unique. In the light of Ayoub's review article of Gluckman's book and mine (Ayoub 1961), I want to restate some of these points about the nature of the folk system—and this takes us back to the subject of "the real thing" mentioned above.

Ayoub points out that the description of a folk system must be in the ideolect of the analyst, and that the key elements of that ideolect may or may not be taken over into the language in which he is writing. This is, of course, one facet of the primary difficulty of almost all ethnographic reporting—that it must be done in a foreign language and hence is subject to vast distortion by the reader as well as by the writer. As a result, Ayoub is quite right in saying that we can never report *the* folk system. In one sense, obviously, there is no such thing—there are only the observable and discussable "facts" of communication and purposive action among the people. However, if the anthropologist can get the ideas so straight that he can discuss them in detail with informants in their own language, and if it is indeed the ethnographer instead of the informant who has made the major adjustment for purposes of communication, then I think he has something that can reasonably be called a folk system.

I was overeager in *Justice and Judgment* to say that a folk system is what the people think and say. I will again state my revision: a folk system is what an ethnographer thinks and says that allows him to interact successfully with the people he is studying. Goodenough (1956:212) has shown with humbling clarity that it is possible to interact perfectly well but to have different readings or models of the situation. Indeed, I have myself (Bohannan 1964) talked about the "working misunderstanding." The ethnographer ends up with a model in terms of which he can interact with the people—and, because of the nature of communication, he cannot go beyond that (although still another ethnographer may go further by virtue of his being able to see both systems).

Thus, today the question of whether or not the folk system as reported is *the* folk system strikes me as the same kind of question as whether some particular performance of a symphony is *the* symphony. Obviously, whether we like it or not, different ethnographers will come back with differing interpretations of a culture. However, those interpretations are not necessarily, and usually not actually, at odds—they merely allow us a better opportunity to discover the possibilities of a complex score. We simply must get used to the fact that every ethnography is an interpretation of only part of a culture. No amount of "scientific" fol-de-rol can avoid this fact. The scientism may give an appearance of comparable data, but (as in ethnoscience) it does so at the expense of vastly reducing the dimensions of the part of the culture that is reported. Yet there is enough overlap for us to recognize the culture in question.

There is a further difficulty: what is "out there" changes rapidly, particularly in those societies that anthropologists have been studying for the last fifty years. The problem, when two ethnographers studying the same society are separated by as little as a decade, becomes not merely "What is the real thing?" but "What is the *same* thing?"

Ayoub has inserted a third system, the concrete system. The concrete system seems to be what is "really" out there. I did not originally utilize any such idea because it seemed to me obvious that what is out there is unknowable except in terms of somebody or other's perception of it. There can be a large number of perceptions of it, but the ones I am interested in are those that can be systematized as folk systems, in the communication sense mentioned above, and as analytical systems. One perfects a folk system by arguing with informants; one perfects an analytical system by arguing with anthropologists. To go back to the text from Mary Douglas, the new milieux in which one tries out one's interpretations are once and for all different, even though the subject matter is much the same.

There is, of course, no possibility of ever arriving at a "fact" that is uncolored by that ethnographic instrument, the perceiver of the fact. The concrete system necessarily remains a mystery. All we can do is to learn more about our sensory means of perception, and mechanical and other extrinsic extensions of them, and our own cultural prison. Communication to a degree is possible, and it is the wish of most parties in most situations to refine that degree.

Therefore the "concrete" system is the "reality," and we need say no more about it—indeed, we cannot say any more about it. The folk system is the ethnographer's action-oriented reading of the concrete, which is sufficiently "collective" as to allow him to interact successfully with the other people who utilize this system of symbols and culture traits. The analytical system is a scientific (whatever we may mean by that) reading of the folk system or of many folk systems.

Ayoub claims that the difficulty is compounded, because for analytical purposes there is a necessary melding of the folk system with the concrete. What he surely means is that there is a stage of his work when any ethnographer knows more about a culture than he understands about it. Certainly he sees actions and things that he interprets tentatively before he tests the folk interpretation. But that should not be confused with "reality"—it is merely a stage in learning.

Some Chimeras of Comparison

If the core of ethnography is the creation of theory around ideas that are "discoverable" in a folk system, what is the core of comparative anthropology? To put the question another way, if the core of ethnography is the juxtaposition of a set of native ideas with a set of ideas in what we shall call below the "culture of ethnography," what is the new juxtaposition to be achieved in comparative anthropology and what are its methods and its dangers?

As long ago as 1896, Franz Boas in an essay in the pages of *Science* pointed out some of the chimeras that lay waste the fields of anthropology in the name of comparative method. His primary target was the questionable doctrine of the psychic unity of mankind. He argued convincingly that such a doctrine, more or less based on the systematic misunderstanding of Bastian (and, a latter-day investigator might add, of Jung), harbors a lurking hypothesis that the same phenomena everywhere develop in the same manner, represent the same thing, and have the same meaning. As Boas noted (1896:903) "even the most cursory review shows that the same phenomena may develop in a multitude of ways." The question for the comparative method is "when are two things the same thing?"

Boas (1896:904) went on to deplore

> the fact that so many fundamental features of culture are universal, or at least occur in many isolated places, interpreted by the assumption that the same features must always have developed from the same causes, leads to the conclusion that there is one grand system according to which mankind has developed everywhere; that all the occurring variations are no more than minor details in this grand, uniform evolution. It is clear that this theory has for its logical basis the assumption that the same phenomena are always due to the same causes.

The original grand theory of evolution was (temporarily) eclipsed, but the psychic need of some social scientists for a single grand theory that would explain everything was not. Some anthropologists have a penchant for rejecting any proposition that they can find an exception to, whether that exception leads to a valid refutation of a position or proposition or not. This is what Potter (1951) has called the "But not in the south" technique of one-upsmanship. Indeed, one reason social science has garnered its reputation for never getting anywhere can be laid to some of its most vocal practitioners who demand that theory be universal and reject all theory that is not. I have never understood how they can think their own theories can pass muster better than others.

The "psychic unity of mankind" as an idea did not die—it merely took refuge in the creed of liberalism. And as such it covertly informs much of Professor Gluckman's work. In his first Lozi law book (1955:271) Gluckman states that "it is unfortunately still necessary to demonstrate that Africans . . . use of processes of inductive and deductive reasoning which are in essence similar to those of the West, even if the premises be different." He wants, in short, not merely to study a culture and social structure, but also to prove that Africans are as good as anybody else. The point is later made even more explicit: "I am delighted in every way that his report bears witness to some similarities of social life everywhere, and to the basic similarities of all human beings in very varied conditions." Of course one must recognize that Gluckman knew his book would be read by some whites in southern Africa who might want to refute that position, and one sees his difficulty in writing with two audiences in mind. Yet he has not negotiated this passage very well, and the febrile doctrine of psychic unity stands in a way of a thoroughgoing analysis of what is to be found in his notes and cases. What *is* in question is a difficulty that Durkheim long since warned us against—the danger of a psychological *deus ex machina* in social and cultural analysis.

Boas (1896:907) claimed, and I agree, that the only way to clear up such difficulties is to have the history and ethnography of single cultures completely understood, each in its environment, with its psychic component, its history and other dimensions. "Thus by comparing histories of growth [ethnographies of structure and culture] natural laws may be found. This method is much safer than the comparative method, as it is usually practiced, because instead of a hypothesis on the mode of development, actual history forms the basis of our deductions." The words "history" and "development" meant something different to Boas in 1896 from what they do to most anthropologists in the 1960's. But if we insert "ethnography" and "integration" instead, his meaning is precisely the one I wish to convey.

I have not quoted Boas merely as an ancestral totem—indeed, he is not my totem. But on this point he spoke clearly and aptly—and a long time ago. Obviously his precepts have not yet been fully recognized or digested by the profession.

Another, and almost exactly opposite, mistake is one that is marked by Nader when—casually, so perhaps she does not deserve the brunt —she suggests that mine is a "relativist" approach. "Relativism" has created almost as much misunderstanding in the anthropological profession as has "prelogical" or the "psychic unity of mankind." Nader (1965b:11) writes: "[Bohannan] shirks the problems that such a relativist approach implies for comparison, but then he was not interested in comparison at the time."

"Relativism" seems a shorthand term for a doctrine that holds that there is no absolute. In that sense, surely every social scientist must be a relativist. But relativism also sometimes means to some people "anything goes." Only if we mean by it that no analysis can be made of any culture without some set of premises or other, and that such premises are themselves necessarily culture-bound to some degree, can we see the "relative" problem. The "correct" set of premises is that which informs the action as well as the analysis. Seen so, relativism is not merely the opposite of "absolutism" but is itself relative. Denying psychic unity or denying the omni-appropriateness of one set of assumptions (English jurisprudence, in the case at hand) does not mean that one is, for that reason, a relativist. "Relativism" is valid only if it means that every society, and hence every ethnography, must be understood on its own terms (which may or may not be unique—the point is irrelevant), and only if the theory is forged from the force of creative processes dealing with those terms.

Another "mythical beast" that sometimes masquerades under the name of "comparison" is backward translation. As we have already noted, translation from the language and culture of the subject people into the technical language and culture of anthropology is the task of every ethnographer. The danger is that, instead of starting with the culture in question, we as ethnographers begin with our own anthropological language or even our mother tongues and find equivalents in the language of the people we study. It appears to me that this is what lies behind the difficulty that has led to so much misunderstanding of Gluckman's position. In the new material to the second edition of *The Judicial Process*, he notes (2nd ed., 1967:376) that a "myth" has grown up about his methods, and he takes as his scapegoat a statement by Nader about his using the categories of Roman-Dutch law. I think he adequately defends himself here; however, in the course of the defense, he has missed what it was that led to the myth. It appears to me that instead of starting with Lozi ideas and seeking to translate them for his colleagues, he begins wih his own rather considerable sophistication in jurisprudence and translates as much as possible of it into Lozi. The original flag quote of my book, from Sir Henry Maine, was selected to warn against such a danger. Gluckman does surprisingly well at the translation—but in doing so he misses some of the Lozi point. I am not impugning Gluckman's cases or his documentation, which we all know to be the very best. I am, rather, saying that he fails to give us Lozi interpretation because his own interpretation enters too early. Here is one of the more obvious examples of Gluckman's backward translation (1955:316):

> The key concept here, equivalent to *law* in which it is embraced, is trial by due process of law (*tatubo kamulao*). The process is based on hearing evidence (*bupaki*) which established proof (also *bupaki*) on the facts (*litaba* = also things). Evidence itself is reduced by concepts of relevance (*bupaki bobuswanela*, appropriate or right evidence; *bupaki bobukena*, evidence which enters); of cogency (*bupaki bobutiile*, strong evidence); of credibility (*bupaki bobusepehala*); and of corroboration (*bupaki bobuyemela*). These types of evidence are tested as direct, circumstantial, or hearsay. The concepts of evidence have a marked flexibility, as contrasted with those of substantive law. First, they are multiple in their referents: they cover evidence given in courts about actions committed, the judge's knowledge of the social and physical world (judicial presumptions: *linto zelwaziba*, things we know), and the judge's inferences from the evidence (*lisupo*, indications, probabilities).

This sort of thing goes on. It reminds me of a witticism Margaret Mead made some years ago at a cybernetics conference, when someone in a flush of enthusiasm claimed that Kant could be translated into Eskimo. Mead's laconic reply was, "Of course, but can you make an Eskimo understand it?"

It is obvious, from the passage given above and from a number of others that might be selected, that Gluckman is translating fundamentally Western ideas into Lozi instead of translating fundamentally Lozi ideas into English. Please note that I did *not* say that the Lozi and the English do not have fundamentally similar ideas, but only that by this method of exposition there is no possible way for a reader to discover whether they have or not.

Indeed, as Gluckman goes on, the combination of the unstated bias of a belief in the psychic unity of mankind and such backward translation (1955:3–57) very nearly becomes an overt bias: "On the whole, it is true to say that the Lozi judicial process corresponds with, more than it differs from, the judicial process in Western society." Of course it does, or Gluckman could not have defined it as judicial. That is not the significant aspect. A final example: "The judges' manipulation of these concepts is *implicit* in their assessment of the evidence of the parties against the standard of 'the reasonable and upright man'" (Gluckman 1955:318). I have italicized *implicit* to make my point. Implicit in what? In Lozi social action, perhaps—in spite of Gluckman's protestations we cannot tell. This is the same kind of reasoning that led Murdock to say that the nuclear family is universal when only its components are universal.

Another bugbear of the comparativist is a tendency not to distinguish between cross-cultural and interdisciplinary. Gluckman deals with the interdisciplinary problems of communication between law and anthropology under his rubric of "comparison." In *The Judicial Process*, Chapter VII is called "Some Comparative Implications of the Lozi Judicial Process." There is almost nothing in that chapter that is cross-cultural, which is what most anthropologists since Tylor have meant by "comparative." Rather, the chapter is an examination of some jurisprudential writers and the way that some of their problems can be illuminated by Gluckman's readings of his Lozi cases. In *The Ideas of Barotse Jurisprudence* (1965b) Gluckman has added some cross-cultural material, still under his rubric "comparative." In one of the best parts of the book—that dealing with political power and treason—over half the passage deals not with the Lozi at all, but with medieval Europe. But when he does add the cross-cultural material, it is almost totally without his even trying to retain control of it. Here is his own statement (1965b:204):

> Wrongs in Barotse society arise out of aggressive actions by outsiders, or out of failure to fulfill obligations of familial life between persons in specific status relationships. I shall argue that general ideas of wrong are again best understood in terms of reaction to those wrongs arising in status relations. To demonstrate my argument I begin not from the Barotse, and their governmental system with its courts, but from societies where redress was secured by self-help and where vengeance for the killing of a man was enjoined on his kinsmen.

From that statement he goes into a direct discussion of Maitland's article on the history of malice aforethought, and on to the Nuer; he gives an Ibo reference, and then back briefly to the Barotse, with sidelights on the Zulu, Kalinga, Ifugao, Marc Bloch's Middle Ages, Wales, the Yurok, England; back to Maitland's early England, to the Australian aborigines, the Cheyenne; and other subjects that it would be tedious to list and to read.

The point that Gluckman wants to make is that theory is where you find it and that most of it has been thought of already. I agree, but the point I want to make is that if wide-ranging materials are utilized in this way, a theory of comparative method becomes necessary, as well as (in this particular case) a theory of jurisprudence. Comparison must be done in a controlled way, with great awareness and sensitivity to the original meaning, and with a set of methods that allow us to utilize what we are doing toward some specific ends beyond merely buttressing a position.

As many another social anthropologist might, I have come up with a genealogy of the various methods that have been used for comparative purposes.

There are two fundamental types of comparison, which I have called "casual" and "controlled" comparison. Casual comparison is inserted by a writer in order to aid his reader in adjusting the ethnography at hand to the vicissitudes either of the reader's own culture or some other cul-

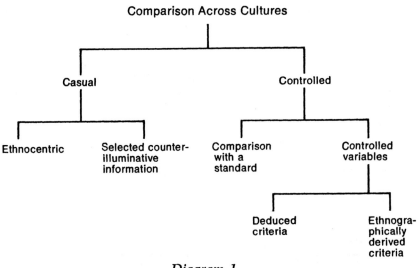

Diagram 1

ture he already knows. There are two modes of casual comparison. One I have called "ethnocentric" if the comparative examples are taken only from the culture of the writer and reader. The other I have called "selected counter-illuminative information," because it is chosen out of a very wide range of possible ethnography specifically because it illuminates the case in hand. This latter is the type of comparison Gluckman has done in the section of his book mentioned just above.

"Controlled" comparison is more complex, and for purposes of the present exposition I have oversimplified it into two sorts. The simplest form is comparison with a standard extrinsic to the particular culture in hand. The source of this standard is of considerable moment insofar as the better it is chosen, the further one can go before bogging down. However, bogging down is, I think, the inevitable end. Ultimately one can say only that something is or is not like something else—that helps, but it is limited.

The "standard" method of comparison is similar to the "application" of "general theory." It is possible to take an idea, like the overlapping spheres in Pospisil's book (1958b:257–271) or Nadel's (1947:504), or the set of boxes in the final chapters of my own *Justice and Judgment* (1957: 150), and utilize that idea as a general theory of law. That is to say, the "facts" of any system can be squeezed into any such classification with greater or lesser force required. That is, however, precisely the same mistake as forcing the data into the boxes of English jurisprudence. All these are way stations on the road to better understanding of legal anthropology; we can forge on from them only by new ethnography or new syntheses. The irony is that we never arrive at our goal—or, if we do arrive, it is at the wrong goal or else it proves to be trite. That is the fate of all science—Kingdom Come is a mirage, but the world of here and now must nevertheless be organized to deal with mirages.

The other method of controlled comparison is the method of controlled variables. These variables may either be derived from a "mass-theory," such as the *Outline of Cultural Materials* trait list, or they may be carefully selected and refined in the variation of the method Boas expounded (1896:905) and that Eggan later called "controlled comparison" (Eggan 1954). The criteria for comparison either may be deduced or may be ethnographically derived. Again, to overstate for purposes of exposition, "deduced" criteria are a prioristic. The mode of "ethnographic derivation," on the contrary, is one that is similar to the linguist's mode of determining phonemes in any language: if there is a difference in meaning in two sounds, there are two phonemes and hence a legitimate distinction. The ethnographically derived criteria are all the legitimate distinctions that are made in the culture of the sample—they will not all be ethnographically relevant in all situations, although these distinctions may sometimes be instructive by their very ethnographic absence. Therefore, the "bank" of distinctions is constantly enriched by ethnography and must be simplified and arranged and theorized about by students of cross-cultural comparison. This category of "ethnographically derived criteria" resembles what might be called, in presently fashionable lingo, "comparative ethnoscience." It is the sort of thing that Goodenough is doing with residence patterns, and the sort of thing that Lévi-Strauss began (but did not finish) in *Les structures élémentaires de la parenté* (too early he turned one brilliantly delineated model into his standard —that of kinship based on a model of economic reciprocity—never getting to the other modes of economic distribution—redistribution and market —that also obviously function in the kinship sphere).

My objection to Gluckman's "comparative" is that he swings uneasily between what I have called the "single standard" and what I have called "selected counter-illuminative information." With the first he lays himself open to the possible charge of imprinting an a priori set of categories and concepts; with the second he lays himself open to the charge of selecting only the positive cases. Both may be unjust—but we cannot be sure.

The Culture of Ethnography and the Culture of Comparison

We have now brought ourselves squarely up against the main epistemological problems in anthropology. First of all, how can we secure the

advantages of juxtaposing ideas and analyses from the corpus of ethnographic works with the materials of our own subject cultures without
implying that these ideas are *in* the subject culture? Put another way,
if we consider the ethnographic record as a subculture, how do we utilize
that subculture in our comprehension of the culture we are reporting
and analyzing? The second problem is no less difficult: what is the process by which we can derive from ethnography the variables that are to
be used for controlled culture of comparison, utilizing the very material
that is the substance of the culture of ethnography?

The key to the first problem, it seems to me, lies in exercising the
greatest care in making our own assumptions overt and, perhaps most
important of all, in not confusing the bizarre and unstructured totality
of ethnography with some kind of logical construct. The organization
of an ethnography, on the one hand, focuses on a people—and that includes the special ethnographies that focus on particular problems of a
specific people. The organization of a comparative study, on the other
hand, focuses on the logical interconnectedness of propositions. The fact
that the cultural items may be the same must not be allowed to mislead
us. What I am in fact saying, obviously, is that Gluckman is not comparative at all—he is merely calling on an admirably wide arc of the
culture of ethnography.

It seems to me that the key to the second problem—how to create a
controlled culture of comparison—lies all around us; it is included in a
statement by Gluckman (1965b:183) that he meant as a criticism: "If
[Bohannan] were correct [about a folk system being raised to the level
of an analytical system] we would have to be 'cultural solipsists,' unable
to compare or to generalize widely—unless we were to develop a whole
new independent language without national home."[1] Gluckman, both
here and in his 1967 "Reappraisal," thrusts this idea away as if one could
not possibly have meant *that.* However, I did mean that, and it cannot
be said better. In fact, the name of the "whole new independent language
without national home" will probably be Fortran or some other computer language.

The question, obviously, is how we go about developing "an independent language without national home." I have suggested above that
the data to be worked with in constructing a comparative system are

1. This investigation creates for me a direct confrontation with some of the statements that Max Gluckman has made in the last decade or so. I have not heretofore
answered any of his statements. I do so now without polemic—and I do not read what
he has said as polemic. We are using each other's statements as aids to express our
own points of view the more clearly, for we do have some differences of opinion that
I, at least, think of some importance to social anthropology. Arguments identical with
this one are going on in economic anthropology, with a different cast of characters,
and in psychological anthropology with a constantly shifting cast of characters. Obviously all this has something to do with communication among scholars who have
basically different philosophical foundations. It is a healthy sign in a healthy discipline.

the folk models that were found to be necessary to explain and describe specific cultures. The comparatists, from Tylor to Gluckman, want to compare substantive material; I want, rather, to compare viewpoints or theories of substantive material. So, obviously, did Boas (1896:908): "The comparative method, notwithstanding all that has been said and written in its praise, has been remarkably barren of definite results, and I believe it will not become fruitful until we renounce the vain endeavor to construct a uniform systematic history of the evolution of culture, and until we begin to make our comparisons on the broader and sounder basis which I ventured to outline." That is, on the basis of full and understood ethnographic accounts, each sufficiently theorized.[2]

In the creation of this "independent language without national home," there are certain things we cannot do. Whether it be a computer language or a "people language," we cannot assume that it will be without bias or known culture. I have already pointed out here that many cultures of completely different types share a good many ideas without that making them similar in origin, or use, or psychic proclivity. Obviously we cannot become biasless—rather, we must investigate our biases and institute controls for them. Obviously human beings cannot compare (or do anything else) without culture; rather, we must control the logic of the culture of comparison.

What, then, is the origin of the propositions in this new logical and independent language—this culture of comparison? We go to the ethnographies. In the best of all possible worlds, we include all of them (though some will, of course, prove useless). We must work somewhat in the linguist's mode of determining the basic phonemic system (by the comparison of controlled pairs), and then by a process that ultimately allows us to find axioms that enable us to deduce the specific folk systems (today this is called "generating" the system in a simulation project), and then by a process that allows us to compare the axioms of one society with those of another, and to investigate the ways in which they bunch, as vectors, and hence are culturally correlated.

These are the neologisms that Gluckman (1955:381) is waiting for. It will take about ten years, it seems to me. We must learn to put up with the theoretical "weightlessness" that comes from escaping from our own gravity. As a matter of fact, when he is not aware of it, Gluckman does a lot of this sort of thing. Certainly his books will be some of the major sources of the propositions for the new language. It is in his admonitory

2. Although Boas is saying all the right things, he did not himself in his ethnography of the Kwakiutl do all the right things. His ethnography is full of detail, but there is very little ethnographic theory to inform it, which is one of the reasons that it takes so much effort to use it today. Boas' Kwakiutl material can be used—but only if one puts almost as much effort into it as Boas himself did. Had he been more willing to create a theory of the Kwakiutl, this would not be so, and Boas instead of Malinowski would be the father of modern field studies.

passages that he narrows down and hides from his right hand many of the interesting and imaginative things that his left hand is doing.

To elucidate the immediate task, I shall revert to a diagram that I first published in the Letter pages of *Science* in 1959. Box A contains the mother culture of the social scientist. Box B contains the models or structures with which the scientists and the other people of his culture deal with in their own lives and their environment—the common-sense "the-

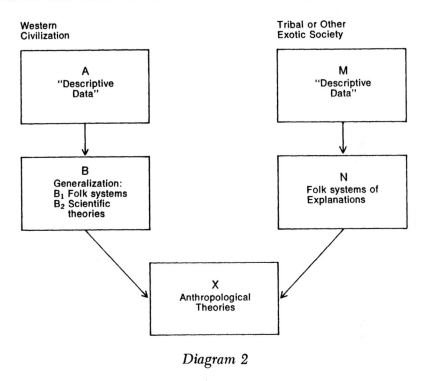

Diagram 2

ories," the myths, the scientific theories, and all the rest. Box M contains the culture of some other society (or of some other subgroup, for one cannot sensibly draw lines between cultures, except in terms of specific problems). Box N is the folk system of explanation that the anthropologist has learned and arrived at in order to explain the arrangement of the data in Box M. The "theories" or generalizations or models in Box N are sometimes also supplied, in writing or other "scholarly" modes of communication, by persons whose mother culture is M. There are, obviously, many boxes M and N—one might say $M_1 \ldots M_n$. And obviously Box A is a type of Box M; Box B is a type of Box N.

Now the new language that we are creating must take its *comparata* from all the Boxes N and including Box B. This new language, called X in the diagram, is a logical structure of interrelated propositions about the working of society and culture. We can learn a lot about it from any culture, and we can test some of the propositions in Box X against some of the models in the various Boxes N—using, of course, overt and stated criteria (hence open to criticism) of suitability for the selection of those we use.

It is in the theoretical structure in Box X that we are all ultimately interested as social scientists. We must be able to call on all the scientific theories of all the other disciplines (Box B) as well as on the folk explanations (all the other Boxes N) of other peoples of the world. May I repeat: in the immediate case in hand, that of comparative legal anthropology, I have no doubt that more of our theory can be drawn from Box B than from any other box included in the N series of boxes. But I also have no doubt that to confuse Box B with Box X is a logical error leading to a dead end.

This proposition is programmatic, I am the first to recognize. But given a decade or two, it will be well launched in the "real world"—whatever that may be.

Bibliography

Items with an asterisk are those that are quoted from a secondary source and cannot be checked; where more than one publisher has been given for some reference, the American edition has generally been used.

ALDER, F.
1964   "Social realism" and "social nominalism." *In* A dictionary of the social sciences, J. Gould and W. L. Kolb, eds. New York, The Free Press.

ALLEN, C. K.
1958   Law in the making. Oxford, Clarendon Press, 6th edition.

ALLOTT, A. N.
1956   Review of Gluckman's The judicial process among the Barotse of Northern Rhodesia. Law Quarterly Review 72:144–147.

1969   Legal Personality in African law: a comparative study with special reference to Ghana. *In* Ideas and procedures in African customary law, M. Gluckman, ed. London, Oxford University Press for the International African Institute.

ALLOTT, A. N., A. L. EPSTEIN, AND M. GLUCKMAN
1969   Introduction. *In* Ideas and procedures in African customary law, M. Gluckman, ed. London, Oxford University Press for the International African Institute.

AMERICAN BAR ASSOCIATION
1961   The improvement of the administration of justice, a handbook prepared by the section of judicial administration, 4th edition.

ANDERSON, J. N. D.
1954   Islamic law in Africa. London, Her Majesty's Stationery Office.

1955   Review of Gluckman's The judicial process among the Barotse of Northern Rhodesia. Modern Law Review 18:643–644.

419

420   *Bibliography*

ARNOLD, THURMAN
  1935   The symbols of government. New Haven, Connecticut, Yale University Press.
AUBERT, VILHELM
  1963   Researches in the sociology of law. The American Behavioral Scientist 7 (4):16–20.
  1967   Rettssosiologi (translation: Sociology of law). Oslo, Universitetsforlaget.
  n.d.   Some notes after the Burg Wartenstein conference on the ethnography of law. Memo to L. Nader (in 1966).
AYOUB, V.
  1961   Review of Gluckman's The judicial process in two African societies. *In* Community political systems, Volume I, International yearbook of political behavior research, M. Janowitz, ed. New York Free Press, pp. 237–250.
BACON, MARGARET K., I. L. CHILD, AND HERBERT BARRY III
  1963   A cross-cultural study of correlates of crime. Journal of Abnormal and Social Psychology 66:291–300.
BANDELIER, A.
  1890   Final report. Papers of the Archaeological Institute of America, Volume 3. Cambridge, Massachusetts: J. Wilson & Son.
BARNES, J. A.
  1962   African models in the New Guinea highlands. Man 62:5–9.
BARNHART, C. L., ed.
  1948   The American College Dictionary. New York, Random House.
BARNOUW, V.
  1963   Culture and personality. Homewood, Illinois, Dorsey Press.
BARTH, F.
  1966   Models of social organization. No. 23, Occasional Papers of the Royal Anthropological Institute.
BARTON, R. F.
  1919   Ifugao law. University of California publications in American Archaeology and Ethnology, 15:1–186.
  1949   The Kalingas. Posthumously published, E. A. Hoebel, editor. Chicago, University of Chicago Press.
BEATTIE, J.
  1957   Informal judicial activity in Bunyoro. Journal of African Administration 9:4:188–195.
BENEDICT, RUTH
  1934   Patterns of culture. Boston, Houghton Mifflin.
BENNETT, J. W.
  1946   The interpretation of Pueblo culture: a question of values. Southwestern Journal of Anthropology 2(4):361–374.
BENTSI-ENCHILL, K.
  1964   Ghana land law. London, Sweet and Maxwell.
BERNDT, RONALD M.
  1962   Excess and restraint: social control among a New Guinea mountain people. Chicago, University of Chicago Press.

BIEBUYCK, D., ed.
1963   African agrarian systems. London, Oxford University Press for the International African Institute.

BOAS, FRANZ
1896   The limitations of the comparative method in anthropology. Science, N.S. 4(103):901–908.

BOEHM, BERNICE
1964   The community and the social agency define neglect. Child Welfare 43:453–464.

BOHANNAN, PAUL
1957   Justice and judgment among the Tiv of Nigeria. London, Oxford University Press.
1959   Anthropological theories, Science, v. 129, no. 3345, Feb. 6, 1959, pp. 292–294.
1963   Social anthropology. New York, Holt, Rinehart and Winston.
1964   Africa and Africans. New York, Natural History Press.
1965   The differing realms of the law. American Anthropologist 67(6): 2:33–42.

BRELSFORD, W. V.
1942   Shimwalule: study of a Bemba chief and priest. African Studies 1:207–223.
1944a   The succession of Bemba Chiefs—a guide for District Officers. Lusaka, Government Printer, 2nd edition 1948.
1944b   Aspects of Bemba chieftainship. Rhodes-Livingstone Institute Communications 2:2–57.

BRIAR, S.
1966   Welfare from below: recipients' views of the public welfare system. *In* The law of the poor, J. tenBroek, ed. San Francisco, Chandler Publishing Co., pp. 46–61.

BRIGHT, J. O., AND W. BRIGHT
1965   Semantic structures in Northwestern California and the Sapir-Whorf hypothesis. American Anthropologist 67(5):2:249–258.

BUREAU FOR NATIVE AFFAIRS (HOLLANDIA, NEW GUINEA)
1957   Anthropological research in Netherlands New Guinea since 1950. A paper presented to the Ninth Pacific Science Congress, Bangkok.

CARDOZO, B.
1921   The nature of the judicial process. New Haven, Connecticut, Yale University Press.

CARSTENS, C. C.
1936   Social Security through aid for dependent children in their own homes. Law and Contemporary Problems 3:246–252

CLOWARD, R. A. AND F. F. PIVEN
1966   The weight of the poor: a strategy to end poverty. The Nation 202(May 2):510–517.
1967   The weapon of poverty: birth of a movement. The Nation, 204 (May 8):582–588.

COHEN, F.
1942   Handbook of Federal Indian law with reference tables and index.
        Washington, U.S. Government Printing Office.
COHEN, YEHUDI A.
1964   The transition from childhood to adolescence: cross-cultural
        studies of initiation ceremonies, legal systems and incest taboos.
        Chicago, Aldine Publishing Company.
1966   On alternative views of the individual in culture and personality
        studies. American Anthropologist 68(2):1:355–361.
COHN, B. S.
1959   Some notes on law and change in North India. Economic De-
        velopment and Cultural Change 8:79–93.
COLSON, E.
1962   The Plateau Tonga of Northern Rhodesia. Manchester, Man-
        chester University Press.
CORY, HANS
1953   Sukuma law and custom. London, Oxford University Press.
COWAN, THOMAS A.
1962   What law can do for social science. In Law and sociology: ex-
        ploratory essays, W. M. Evan, ed. New York, Free Press, pp.
        91–123.
°CRANE, W. C.
1951   Kwakiutl, Haida and Tsimshian: a study in social control. Un-
        published ms., University of Utah Library, cited in Hoebel
        (1954:316).
CUNNISON, I. G.
1959   The Luapula peoples of Northern Rhodesia: custom and history
        in tribal politics. Manchester, Manchester University Press for
        the Rhodes-Livingstone Institute.
CURTIS, C. P.
1954   It's your law. Cambridge, Massachusetts, Harvard University
        Press.
DE GROOT, S. W.
1963   Van isolatie naar integratie: de Surinaamse Marrons en hun
        afstammelingen. Verhandelingen Kon. Instituut Taal-Land-en
        Volkenkunde 41.
DIAMOND, BERNARD
1966   The children of Leviathan: psychoanalytic speculations concern-
        ing welfare law and punitive sanctions. In The law of the poor,
        J. tenBroek, ed. San Francisco, Chandler Publishing Co., pp.
        33–45.
°DISTRICT COMMISSIONER (ABERCORN)
1924a   Letter to District Commissioner Kasama; copy in Mporokoso Dis-
        trict Notebook KSV 1/1, National Archives of Zambia; dated
        November 14, 1924.
°DISTRICT COMMISSIONER (KASAMA)
1924b   Letter to Secretary for Native Affairs; copy in KSV 1/1 National
        Archives of Zambia; dated December 18, 1924.

DOUGLAS, MARY
1956   L'homme primitif et la loi. Zaïre, X: 367–374.
DOZIER, E. P.
1961   Rio Grande Pueblos. *In* Perspectives in American Indian culture change, H. Spicer, ed. Chicago, University of Chicago Press, pp. 94–186.
DRIBERG, J. H.
1923   The Lango. London, T. Fisher Unwin.
°DUPONT, J.
1937   Diary for 26th May 1896. *In* Eveque, Roi des Brigands, by H. Pineau. Paris, Librarie Missionaire.
DURKHEIM, EMILE
1933   On the division of labor in society. New York, Macmillan, 2nd ed., 1960.
EGGAN, FRED
1954   Social anthropology and the method of controlled comparison. American Anthropologist 56(5):743–763.
1965   Some reflections on comparative method in anthropology. *In* Context and meaning in cultural anthropology, M. E. Spiro, ed. New York, Free Press, pp. 357–372.
ELIAS, T. O.
1956   The nature of African customary law. Manchester, Manchester University Press.
ELLIS, F. H.
1951   Patterns of aggression and the war cult in Southwestern Pueblos. Southwestern Journal of Anthropology 7(2):177–201.
EMPSON, WILLIAM
1951   The structure of complex words. London, Chatto and Windus.
EPSTEIN, A. L.
1953   The administration of justice and the urban African. London, Her Majesty's Stationery Office.
1954   Juridicial techniques and the judicial process. Rhodes-Livingstone Papers No. 23.
1959   Review of Bohannan's Justice and judgment among the Tiv. Man 59(33):33.
n.d.   °*Unpublished* notes on the Bemba; author's copy.
EVANS-PRITCHARD, E. E.
1940   The Nuer. Oxford, Clarendon Press.
1950   Kinship and the local community among Nuer. *In* African systems of kinship and marriage, A. R. Radcliffe-Brown and Daryll Forde, eds. London, Oxford University Press, pp. 360–391.
1951   Kinship and marriage among the Nuer. Oxford, Clarendon Press.
FENTON, W. N.
1957   Factionalism at Taos Pueblo, New Mexico. Bureau of American Ethnology Bulletin 164:297–344.
FORTES, M., AND E. E. EVANS-PRITCHARD, eds.
1940   African political systems. Oxford, Oxford University Press for the International African Institute.

FORTES, M.
1945   The dynamics of clanship among the Tallensi. London, Oxford
        University Press for the International African Institute.
1949   The web of kinship among the Tallensi. London, Oxford Uni-
        versity Press for the International African Institute.
1959   Descent, filiation and affinity. Man 59(309):193–197.

FOSTER, GEORGE M.
1967   Tzintzuntzan: Mexican peasants in a changing world. Boston,
        Little, Brown.

FRAKE, C. O.
1961   The diagnosis of disease among the Subanun of Mindanao.
        American Anthropologist 63(1):113–132.
1963   Litigation in Lipay: a study of Subanun law. Bangkok,
        The proceedings of the Ninth Pacific Science Congress, Vol-
        ume 3.
1964a   How to ask for a drink in Subanun. American Anthropologist
        66(6):2:127–132.
1964b   A structural description of Subanun "religious behavior." *In* Ex-
        plorations in cultural anthropology: essays in honor of George
        Peter Murdock, W. G. Goodenough, ed. New York, McGraw-Hill,
        pp. 111–130.

FRANK, JEROME
1949   Courts on Trial. Princeton, N.J., Princeton University Press.

FRANKENBERG, R. J.
1957   Village on the border. London, Cohen and West.

FRENCH, D. H.
1948   Factionalism in Isleta Pueblo. New York, Monographs of the
        American Ethnological Society, No. 13.

FRENKEL-BRUNKSWIK, E.
1954   Further explorations by a contributor to the Authoritarian Per-
        sonality. *In* Studies in the scope and method of the authoritarian
        personality, R. Christie and M. Jahoda, eds. New York, Free
        Press, pp. 226–275.

FULLER, LON
(n.d.) Some unexplored social dimensions of the law. Presented as a
        contribution to a symposium on Law and the Social Sciences
        held on Sept. 23, 1967, in connection with the Sesquicentennial
        celebration of the Harvard Law School.
(n.d.) The forms and limits of adjudication. Mimeo. ms.

GIBBS, JAMES L., JR.
1962   Poro values and courtroom procedures in a Kpelle chiefdom.
        Southwestern Journal of Anthropology 18:341–350.
1963a   Marital instability among the Kpelle: towards a theory of epainog-
        amy. American Anthropologist 65(3):1:552–573.
1963b   The Kpelle moot: a therapeutic model for the informal settlement
        of disputes. Africa 33:1–11.
1965   The Kpelle of Liberia. *In* Peoples of Africa, J. L. Gibbs, Jr., ed.
        New York, Holt, Rinehart and Winston, pp. 197–240.

GLUCKMAN, MAX

1943 Essays on Lozi land and royal property. Rhodes-Livingstone Paper 10.

1955 The judicial process among the Barotse of Northern Rhodesia. Manchester, Manchester University Press for the Rhodes-Livingstone Institute, 2nd edition, 1967.

1959 The technical vocabulary of Barotse jurisprudence. American Anthropologist 61(5):743–759.

1961 Ethnographic data in British social anthropology. The Sociological Review, N.S. 9(1):5–17.

1962 African jurisprudence. The Advancement of Science 18:75:439–454.

1963a Order and rebellion in tribal Africa. London, Cohen and West.

1963b The reasonable man in Barotse law. *In* Order and rebellion in tribal Africa, M. Gluckman, ed. London, Cohen and West, pp. 178–207.

1965a Reasonableness and responsibility in the law of segmentary societies. *In* African law: adaptation and development, H. Kuper and L. Kuper, eds. Berkeley, University of California Press, pp. 120–146.

1965b The ideas in Barotse jurisprudence. New Haven, Connecticut, Yale University Press.

1965c Politics, law and ritual in tribal society. Chicago, Aldine Publishing Company.

(in press) Moral crises: magical and secular solutions. *In* A comparative study of African legal systems, J. Poirier, ed.

GOODALL, N.

1954 A History of the London Missionary Society 1895–1945, London.

GOODENOUGH, N.

1951 Property, kin and community in Truk. Yale University Publications in Anthropology No. 46, in press.

1956 Componential analysis and the study of meaning. Language, 32:(1):195–216.

GREEN, M. D.

1960 The situation in 1959. *In* Lagging justice: the annals of the American Academy of Political and Social Science, G. R. Winters, special ed. Philadelphia. March, pp. 7–28.

GREENBERG, J. H.

1966 Language universals. *In* Current Trends in Linguistics, Volume 3, T. A. Seboek, ed. The Hague, Mouton, pp. 61–112.

GROSSMAN, JOEL B.

1965 Lawyers and judges: the ABA and the politics of judicial selection. New York, John Wiley.

GULLIVER, P. H.

1955 The family herds. International library of sociology and social reconstruction. London, Routledge and Kegan Paul.

1963 Social control in an African society. Boston, Boston University Press.

GUMPERZ, JOHN, AND DELL HYMES
(in   Directions in sociolinguistics. New York, Holt, Rinehart and
press) Winston.

HACCIUS, G.
1910   *Hannoversche Missionsgeschichte,* Bd. 2, Hermannsburg.

HAHM, PYONG CHOON
(in   Religion and law in Korea. Kroeber Anthropological Society
press) Papers No. 41.

HAILEY, LORD WILLIAM M.
1950   Native Administration in the British African Territories, Part II.
       London, Her Majesty's Stationery Office.

HAINES, CHARLES G.
1923   General observations on the effect of personal, political and
       economic influences in the decisions of judges. Illinois Law Re-
       view 17(1):96–116.

HAMILTON, WALTON H.
1932   Encyclopedia of Social Sciences, Volume 8, p. 450.

HAWLEY, FLORENCE
1948   The Keresan Holy Rollers. Social Forces 26:272–280.

HAYLEY, T. T.
1947   The anatomy of Lango religion and groups. Cambridge, Cam-
       bridge University Press.

HEPBURN, J. D.
1895   Twenty years in Khama's country. London, Hodder and Stough-
       ton.

HERRERA, G.
(n.d.) This is how it start to become so bad at Zia Pueblo amon(g)
       the Gov., counciler and the people against the Christian people
       of Zia [sic]. Typescript in possession of Hoebel.

HOCART, A. M.
1937   Kinship systems. Anthropos 32:545–551.

HOEBEL, E. ADAMSON
1940   The political organization and law-ways of the Comanche In-
       dians. American Anthropological Asssociation Memoir No. 54.
1942   Fundamental legal concepts as applied to the study of primitive
       law. Yale Law Journal 51(6)951–966.
1949   Man in the primitive world. New York, McGraw-Hill.
1952   Keresan witchcraft. American Anthropologist 54(4):586–589.
1954   The law of primitive man. Cambridge, Massachusetts, Harvard
       University Press.
1960   The authority systems of the Pueblos of the southwestern United
       States. Vienna, Akten des 34. Internationalen Amerikanisten
       Congresses, pp. 555–563.
1960– Three studies in African law. Stanford Law Review 13:418–
1961   442.
1965   Fundamental cultural postulates and judicial law making in
       Pakistan. American Anthropologist 67(6):2:43–56.

HOEBEL, E. A., AND M. GLUCKMAN
1961– Comment: The role of the king in the Barotse judicial process.
1962   Stanford Law Review 14:110–119.

HOGBIN, H. I.
1934   Law and order in Polynesia. London, Christophers; New York, Harcourt, Brace.

HOHFELD, W. N.
1923   Fundamental legal conceptions as applied in judicial reasoning and other legal esays. New Haven, Connecticut, Yale University Press.

HOIJER, HARRY
1953   The relation of language to culture. *In* Anthropology today, A. L. Kroeber, ed. Chicago, The University of Chicago Press, pp. 554–573.

HOLLEMAN, J. F.
1949   The pattern of Hera kinship. Rhodes-Livingstone Paper No. 17.
1952   Shona customary law. London, Oxford University Press for the Rhodes-Livingstone Institute and the Beit Trust.

HOWELL, P. P.
1954   A manual of Nuer law. London, Oxford University Press for the International African Institute.

INKELES, ALEX, AND DANIEL J. LEVINSON
1954   National character: the study of modal personality and socio-cultural systems. *In* The handbook of social psychology, Volume II, G. Lindzey, ed. Cambridge, Massachusetts, Addison-Wesley, pp. 977–1020.

JAKOBSON, R.
1957   Shifters, verbal categories and the Russian verb. Cambridge, Massachusetts, Harvard University, Russian Language Project.

JAMIESON, JUSTICE
1957   U.S. v. La Plant. Cr. nos. 8650, 8651, Vol. 156, Federal supplement, (U.S. District Court, District of Montana, Oct. 9, 1957), pp. 660–665.

JENNINGS, A. C.
1904   Report to London Missionary Society. London Missionary Society Archives.

JOLOWICZ, H. F.
1939   Historical introduction to the study of Roman law. Cambridge, Cambridge University Press. Revised edition.

KARDINER, ABRAM
1939   The individual and his society. New York, Columbia University Press.
1945   The psychological frontiers of society. New York, Columbia University Press.

KARDINER, ABRAM, AND L. OVESEY
1951   The mark of oppression: explorations in the personality of the American Negro. New York, Norton.

KAY, H. H.
1965   The family and kinship system of illegitimate children in California law. American Anthropologist 67(6):2:57–81.

KILGOUR, D. G.
1955   Review of Gluckman's The judicial process among the Barotse of Northern Rhodesia. Canadian Bar Review 33(4):622–625.

KITTLER, G. D.
1957   The white fathers. New York, Harper.

KÖBBEN, ANDRÉ J. F.
1967a Unity and disunity: Cottica Djuka society as a kinship system. Bijdragen tot de Taal-Land-en Volkenkunde 123:1.
1967b Why exceptions: the logic of crosscultural comparisons. Current Anthropology 8(1 and 2):3–34.

KRIGE, J. D.
1939   Some aspects of Lovhedu judicial arrangements. Bantu Studies 13(2):113–127.
1956   Review of Gluckman's The judicial process among the Barotse of Northern Rhodesia. Man 56(98).

KRIGE, E. J., AND J. D. KRIGE
1943   The realm of a rain-queen: a study of the pattern of Lovedu society. London, Oxford University Press for the International African Institute.

KROEBER, A. L.
1917   Zuni kin and clan. American Museum of Natural History. Anthropological Papers, Volume 18, Part II.
1928   Law of the Yurok Indians. Atti del Congresso Internazionale degli Americanisti, Rome, Sept. 1961. Rome, Riccardo Garroni, pp. 511–516. International Congress of Americanists, 22nd session, Vol. II.
1957   Style and civilizations. Ithaca, New York, Cornell University Press.

KUPER, HILDA
1961   An African aristocracy. London, Oxford University Press.

KUPER, H., AND L. KUPER, EDS.
1965a African law: adaptation and development. Berkeley, University of California Press.
1965b Introduction. In African law: adaptation and development. Berkeley, University of California Press, pp. 3–24.

LANGE, C. H.
1958   The Keresan component of Southwestern Pueblo culture. Southwestern Journal of Anthropology 14(1):34–50.
1959   Cochiti: a New Mexico pueblo, past and present. Austin, University of Texas Press.

LANGNESS, L. L.
1964   Some problems in the conceptualization of highlands social structures. Special Issue, J. B. Watson, ed. American Anthropologist 66(4):2:162–182.

LEACH, E. R.
1959   Social change and primitive law. American Anthropologist 61:6: 1096–1097, letter to the editor.
1961   Rethinking anthropology. London, The Athlone Press, University of London.

LEVINE, ROBERT A.
1960   The internalization of political values in stateless societies. Human Organization 19:51–58.

LEWIS, I. M.
1965   Problems in the comparative study of unilineal descent. *In* The relevance of models for social anthropology, A.S.A. Monographs No. 1, M. Banton, ed. London, Tavistock Publications, pp. 87–112.

°LIBERTY, MARGOT
(n.d.)   Law and personality in acculturation: the Cheyenne Indians. Paper presented in a seminar on law and personality at the University of Minnesota, spring 1965; mimeo, ms.

LITTLE, KENNETH
1965–   The political functions of the Poro. Africa 35:349–365; 36:62–
1966   72.

°LIVINGSTONE, D.
1857   Missionary travels and researches in South Africa. London.

LLEWELLYN, KARL
1960   The common law tradition: deciding appeals. Boston, Little, Brown.

LLEWELLYN, KARL, AND E. ADAMSON HOEBEL
1941   The Cheyenne way. Norman, University of Oklahoma Press.

LOVETT, R.
1899   The History of the London Missionary Society, 1795–1895, London

LOWIE, ROBERT H.
1920   Primitive society. New York, Horace Liveright.
1927   Anthropology and law. *In* The social sciences, W. F. Ogburn and A. Goldenweiser, eds., Boston, Houghton Mifflin, pp. 50–57.

LUBMAN, STANLEY
1967   Mao and mediation: politics and dispute resolution in Communist China. California Law Review 55(5):1284–1359.

LUCE, R. DUNCAN, AND HOWARD RAIFFA
1957   Games and decisions. New York, John Wiley.

MAINE, SIR H.
1861   Ancient Law. London, Murray; Boston, Beacon Press, 1963.

MAITLAND, F. W.
1961   Domesday book and beyond. London, Fontana Library.

MALINOWSKI, B.
1926   Crime and custom in savage society. London, Kegan Paul, Trench and Trubner.

430   *Bibliography*

MARCH, J. G.
1956   Sociological jurisprudence revisited, a review (more or less) of
        Max Gluckman. Stanford Law Review 8:499–534, with a reply
        by Gluckman and response by March, pp. 767–773.

MATHIESEN, THOMAS, AND VILHELM AUBERT
1964   Crime and illness. *In* Transactions of the Fifth World Congress
        of Sociology, Volume 4, pp. 393–403.

MEGGITT, M. J.
1962   Desert people: a study of the Walbiri Aborigines of Central Aus-
        tralia. Sydney, Angus and Robertson.
1965   The lineage system of the Mae-Enga of New Guinea. Edinburgh,
        Oliver and Boyd.

MERTON, R. K.
1949   Social theory and social structure. New York, Free Press; revised
        edition 1957.

MIDDLETON, J.
1960   Lugbara religion. London, Oxford University Press for the Inter-
        national African Institute.

MILLER, M. L.
1898   A preliminary study of the Pueblo of Taos, New Mexico. Dis-
        sertation, University of Chicago pamphlet.

MITCHELL, J. C.
1956   The Yao village: a study on the social structure of a Nyasaland
        tribe. Manchester, Manchester University Press for the Rhodes-
        Livingstone Institute.

MOORE, S. F.
1966   Review of Gluckman's The ideas of Barotse jurisprudence. South-
        ern California Law Review 39(4):615–624.

MURDOCK, G. P.
1949   Social structure. New York, Macmillan.

NADEL, S. F.
1947   The Nuba. London, Oxford University Press for the International
        African Institute.
1956   Reason and unreason in African law. African 26(2):160–173.

NADER, LAURA
1964a   Talea and Juqila: a comparison of Zapotec social organization.
        Berkeley, University of California publications in American ar-
        chaeology and ethnology 48:3:195–296.
1964b   An analysis of Zapotec law cases. Ethnology 3(4):404–419.
1965a   The ethnography of law. American Anthropologist, special issue,
        L. Nader, ed. 67:6:2.
1965b   The anthropological study of law. American Anthropologist 67
        (6):2:3–32.
1966   To make the balance. Film.

NADER, LAURA, KLAUS F. KOCH, AND BRUCE COX
1966   The ethnography of law: a bibliographic survey. Current Anthro-
        pology 7(3):267–294.

NATIONAL STUDY SERVICE
1965   Planning for the protection and care of neglected children in California: report of a study by National Study Service for the Joint Study Committee on Children's Services, representing the California State Social Welfare Board.

NORTH, C. C., AND P. K. HATT
1949   Jobs and occupations: a popular evaluation. *In* Sociological analysis, L. Wilson and W. L. Kolb, eds. New York, Harcourt, Brace, pp. 464–474.

OLLENNU, N. A.
1962   Principles of customary land law in Ghana. London, Sweet and Maxwell.

PARSONS, E. C.
1933   Some Aztec and Pueblo parallels. American Anthropologist 35 (4):611–631.
1939   Pueblo Indian religion. Chicago, University of Chicago; two volumes.

PARSONS, TALCOTT
1951   The social system. New York, Free Press.
1954   Essays in sociological theory. New York, Free Press.
1962   The law and social control. *In* Law and sociology: exploratory essays, W. M. Evan, ed. New York, Free Press, pp. 56–72.

PATTERSON, R. R.
1879   British Parliamentary Bluebook C.2220. London.

PETERS, E. L.
1967   Some structural aspects of the feud among the camel-herding Bedouin of Cyrenaica. Africa 37(3):261–282.

PIRIE, G.
1905– North-Eastern Rhodesia, its people and products. Journal of the
1906   African society XVII:130–147; XIX:300–310; XX:432–436.

°POGGIE, JOHN J., JR.
(n.d.) The intergenerational perpetuation of crime in Tepoztlan. Paper presented in a seminar in law and personality at the University of Minnesota, spring 1965; ms.

POSPISIL, LEOPOLD
1958a Social change and primitive law: consequences of a Papuan legal case. American Anthropologist 60(5):832–837.
1958b Kapauku Papuans and their law. Yale University Publications in Anthropology, No. 54.
1960   Papual social structure: rejoinder to Leach. American Anthropologist 62(4):690–691; letter to the editor.
1963   Kapauku Papuan economy. Yale University Publications in Anthropology, No. 67.

POTTER, STEPHEN
1951   Some notes on lifemanship. New York, Holt, Rinehart and Winston.

POUND, ROSCOE

1906   The causes of popular dissatisfaction with the administration of justice. American Bar Association rep., Part I, 29:395–417.

1907   Sociological jurisprudence: stage one. Green Bag 19:607–615.

1959   An introduction to the philosophy of law. New Haven Connecticut, Yale University Press; revised edition; first edition, 1954.

POUWER, JAN

1964   A social system in the Star Mountains. American Anthropologist 66(4):2:133–182.

*PROVINCIAL COMMISSIONER, CENTRAL PROVINCE

1935   Letter to Jalland in Sec. Nat/416, National Archives of Zambia. Dated March 5, 1935.

*PUEBLO AGENCY, ALBUQUERQUE, NEW MEXICO: ARCHIVES UNPUBLISHED MSS.

1877   Letter, B. M. Thomas, Indian Agent, to Governor of Isleta. Pueblo Tissues, 1877–1878, Isleta, p. 23.

1879   * Letter, B. M. Thomas, Indian Agent, to Santiago Quintano, Governor of Cochiti, Dec. 23, 1879. Pueblo Tissues, 1879–1880. Cochiti, p. 101.

1882   * Letter, B. M. Thomas, Indian Agent, to Pedro Jose Esquival, Governor of San Felipe, Sept. 14, 1881. Pueblo Tissues, April 1881–Nov. 1881, p. 302.

1889a   * Letter, W. P. McClure, Indian Agent, to Commissioner of Indian Affairs, Dec. 4, 1889. Pueblo Tissues, August–May 1890, p. 113.

1889b   * Letter, W. P. McClure, Indian Agent, to Commissioner of Indian Affairs, Sept. 2, 1889. Pueblo Tissues, August 1889–May 1890, p. 46.

1897   * Annual report by C. E. Norstran, Acting Indian Agent. Pueblo Tissues, May 1897–Dec. 1897, p. 320.

1909   * Letter, Jesus Baca to Supt. C. J. Crandall, Feb. 8, 1909. File 0–1 Northern Pueblos, envelope 314.

1922   * Letter, Field Matron Mary Dennis to L. Crain, Supt., Jan. 17, 1922. File 061.1, San Felipe, Drawer 7–8.

1923   * Letter, Juan Pedro Melchor to Supt. Marble, March 7, 1923; Letter, Governor Alcario Montoya, Lt. Gov. Louis Ortiz, Indian Judge John Dixon and Principale Cyrus Dixon to Supt. Marble, March 15, 1923. File 076. "Forms of government," Drawer 8–6.

1927   * Letter, C. H. Burke, Commissioner of Indian Affairs, to Delegates from Santo Domingo, Cochiti, Sandia, Isleta. June 15, 1921. June 1927, file 8–7, Southern Pueblos 066.

1931   * Memorandum In Re: The whipping of Andrea Fragua of Jemez Pueblo. Walter C. Cochrane, Special Attorney for the Pueblo of Indians. March 31, 1933. File 153.1. Presbyterian Mission, Jemez, 6–1. Absence of religious freedom at Jemez.

1933   * Statement made by J——. B——. C. of —— to Wm. Cochrane, Special Attorney for Indians, and Supt. Towers on May 15, 1933. File 006, Drawer 7–6. Note: full names are given in the documents.

RATTRAY, R. S.
  1929 Ashanti law and constitution. Oxford, Clarendon Press.

REA, W. F.
  1964 The Bemba's white chief. Historical Association of Rhodesia and Nyasaland Local Series 13:1–19. Central Africa Historical Association.

REICH, C. A.
  1964– Individual rights and social welfare: the emerging legal issues,
  1965 Yale Law Journal 74(2):1245–1257.

RICHARDS, A. I.
  1934 Mother-right in Central Bantu. *In* Essays presented to C. G. Seligman, E. E. Evans-Pritchard, R. Firth, B. Malinowski and I. Schapera, ed. London, Kegan Paul, Trench and Trubner, pp. 267–279.

  1935 Tribal government in transition. Journal of the African Society 34:3–26 (supplement).

  1936 The story of Bwembya of the Bemba tribe. *In* Ten Africans, M. Perham, ed. London, Faber and Faber, pp. 17–40.

  1939 Land, labor and diet in Northern Rhodesia: an economic study of the Bemba tribe. London, Oxford University Press.

  1940 The political system of the Bemba tribe—North-Eastern Rhodesia. *In* African political systems, M. Fortes and E. E. Evans-Pritchard, eds. London, Oxford University Press, pp. 83–120.

  1960 Social mechanisms for the transfer of political rights in some African tribes. Journal of the Royal Anthropological Institute 90(2):175–190.

RICHARDSON, J.
  1940 Law and status among the Kiowa Indians. American Ethnological Society Monograph No. 1.

RIESMAN, DAVID
  1962 Law and sociology: recruitment, training and colleagueship. *In* Law and sociology: exploratory essays, W. M. Evan, ed. New York, Free Press, pp. 12–55.

ROBERTS, JOHN M.
  1965 Oaths, autonomic ordeals, and power. American Anthropologist 67(6):2:186–212.

ROSENBERG, MAURICE
  1965 Court congestion: status, causes, and proposed remedies. *In* The courts, the public, and the law explosion, H. W. Jones, ed. Englewood Cliffs, New Jersey, Prentice-Hall, pp. 29–59.

SAHLINS, MARSHALL
  1961 The segmentary lineage: an organization for predatory expansion. American Anthropologist 63(2):322–345.

  1965 On the ideology and composition of descent groups. Man 65:104–107.

SAPIR, EDWARD
  1933 Language. *In* Selected writings of Edward Sapir, pp. 7–32. Berkeley, University of California Press, 1949.

SCHAPERA, ISAAC

1938   A handbook of Tswana law and custom. London, Oxford University Press for the International African Institute; 2nd edition with an additional chapter, 1955.

1940   Ditirafalo tsa merafe ya BaTswana. Alice, Lovedale Press.

1942   A short history of the Bangwaketse. African Studies 1:1–26.

1943   Tribal legislation among the Tswana. London School of Economics, Monographs in Social Anthropology No. 9.

1947   The political annals of a Tswana tribe. University of Cape Town, School of African Studies, Communications, n.s. No. 18.

1953   The Tswana. London, International African Institute.

1957   The sources of law in Tswana tribal courts. Journal of African Law, 1:150–162.

1958   Christianity and the Tswana. Journal of the Royal Anthropological Institute 88:1–9.

1960   Livingstone's private journals, 1851–1853, I. Schapera, ed. Berkeley, University of California Press.

1961   Livingstone's missionary correspondence, 1841–1852, I. Schapera, ed. Berkeley, University of California Press.

SCHEFFLER, HAROLD W.

1965   Choiseul Island social structure. Berkeley, University of California Press.

SCHILLER, A. A.

1957   Review of Gluckman's The judicial process among the Barotse of Northern Rhodesia. Rhodes-Livingstone Journal 21:75–79.

SCHUBERT, G., ed.

1964   Judicial behavior: a reader in theory and research. Chicago, Rand McNally.

SEBONI, M. O. M.

1956   Kgosi Sebele II. Pretoria.

SHEANE, H., AND C. GOULDSBURY

1911   The great plateau of Northern Rhodesia. London, Edwin Arnold.

SHEDDICK, V. G.

1954   Land tenure in Basutoland. London, Her Majesty's Stationery Office.

SILLERY, A.

1952   The Bechuanaland Protectorate. Capetown, New York, Oxford University Press, 1952.

1954   Sechele. George Ronald, Towcester.

SMITH, E. W.

1957   Great Lion of Bechuanaland. London

SMITH, M. G.

(n.d.) Unpublished ms., written 1967, in possession of S. F. Moore.

SMITH, W., AND J. R. ROBERTS

1954   Zuni law: a field of values. Reports of the Rimrock Project Value Series No. 4. Papers of the Peabody Museum of American Archaeology and Ethnology, Harvard University, 43(1).

SNELL, J. E., R. J. ROSENWALD, AND A. ROBEY
 1964 The wifebeater's wife: a study of family interaction. Archives of General Psychiatry 11(2):107–112.

SPIRO, MELFORD
 1961 An overview and suggested reorientation. *In* Psychological anthropology, F. Hsu, ed. Homewood, Illinois, Dorsey Press, pp. 459–492.

STONE, J.
 1947 Fallacies of the logical form in English law. *In* Interpretations of modern legal philosophies, P. L. Sayre, ed. New York, Oxford University Press, pp. 696–735.

STUMPF, S. K.
 1955– Review of Gluckman's The judicial process among the Barotse of
 1956 Northern Rhodesia. Harvard Law Review 69(4):780–787.

SWARTZ, MARC J.
 1966 Bases for political compliance in Bena villages. *In* Political anthropology, M. J. Swartz, V. W. Turner, and A. Tuden, eds. Chicago, Aldine Publishing Company, pp. 89–108.

SWARTZ, MARC J., A. TUDEN, AND V. W. TURNER, eds.
 1966 Political anthropology. Chicago, Aldine Publishing Company.

SWEET, J.
 1961 The role of the state Social Welfare Board in the administration of the ANC Program in California. Senate of the State of California. Sacramento, State Printing Office.

SYKES, GRESHAM M.
 1967 Court congestion and crash programs. Denver Law Review 44 (3):337–386.

TENBROEK, J.
 1956 Operations partially subject to the APA: public welfare administration. California Law Review 44:242–261.

THOMAS, J. E.
 1959 Kanyanta and his times. Northern Rhodesia Journal 4:477–480.

THOMPSON, LAURA M.
 1961 Toward a science of mankind. New York, McGraw-Hill.

TURNER, V. W.
 1957 Schism and continuity in an African Society. Manchester, Manchester University Press.

UNITED STATES SUPREME (DISTRICT) COURT
 1913 United States v. Sandoval. United States Reports, Vol. 231:28.
 1954 Toledo et al. v. Pueblo de Jemez et al. CIV–A No. 2410. U.S. District Court, District of New Mexico. Federal Supplement, Vol. 119, No. 3, pp. 429–432, March 8.

VAN LIER, R. A. J.
 1949 Samenleving in een grensgebied. 's-Gravenhage, Martinus Nijhoff.

VAN LIER, W. F.
 1940 Aateekeningen over het geestelijk leven en de samenleving der Djoeka's (aucaner Boschnegers) in Suriname. Bijdragen Taal-Lan-en Volkenkunde 99.2.

VANSINA, J.
  1965 A traditional legal system: the Kuba. *In* African law: adaptation and development, H. Kuper and L. Kuper, eds. Berkeley, University of California Press, pp. 97–120.

VAN VELSEN, J.
  1964 The politics of kinship. Manchester, Manchester University Press.
  1967 The extended-case method and situational analysis. *In* The craft of social anthropology, A. L. Epstein, ed. London, Tavistock, Social Science Series.

VAN VELZEN, H. U. E. THODEN
  1966 Politieke beheersing in de Djuka maatschappij. Afrika Studiecentrum, Leiden.

VOEGLIN, C. F.
  1949 Linguistics without meaning and culture without words. Word 5:36–42.

WALLACE, ANTHONY F. C.
  1956a Mazeqay resynthesis: a bio-cultural theory of religious inspiration. Transactions of the New York Academy of Sciences No. 18, pp. 626–638.
  1956b Revitalization movements. American Anthropology 58:264–281.
  1961 Culture and personality. New York, Random House.

WATSON, WILLIAM
  1958 Tribal cohesion in a money economy: a study of the Mambwe people of Northern Rhodesia. Manchester, Manchester University Press for the Rhodes-Livingstone Institute.

WEBER, MAX
  1947 The theory of social and economic organization. New York, Oxford University Press.

WEDEMEYER, J. M., AND L. MOORE
  1966 The American welfare system. *In* The law of the poor, J. tenBroek, ed. San Francisco, Chandler Publishing, pp. 2–32.

WERBNER, R. P.
  1967 Federal administration, rank and civil strife among Bemba royals and nobles. Africa 37(1):22–49.
  (n.d.) *Fighting with constitutional traditions among the Bemba under British rule.

*WHITAKER, GRETEL H.
  (n.d.) Law and personality: an outline of perspectives and an analysis of their relationship in Chiapas. Paper presented in a seminar on law and personality at University of Minnesota, spring 1965; mimeo. ms.

WHITE, L. A.
  1932 The Pueblo of San Felipe. Menasha, Wisconsin, Memoirs of the American Anthropological Association, No. 38.
  1942 The Pueblo of Santa Ana, New Mexico. Menasha, Wisconsin, Memoirs of the American Anthropological Association, No. 60.
  1962 The Pueblo of Sia, New Mexico. Washington, D.C., Bureau of American Ethnology, Bulletin 184.

WHITING, BEATRICE B.

1963   Six cultures: studies in child rearing. New York, John Wiley.

1965   Sex identity conflict and physical violence: a comparative study. American Anthropologist 67(8):2:123–140.

WHITING, JOHN W. M., R. KLUCKHOHN AND A. ANTHONY

1958   The functions of male initiation ceremonies at puberty. *In* Readings in social psychology, E. Maccoby, T. Newcomb, and E. Hartley, eds. New York, Holt, Rinehart and Winston, pp. 359–370.

WHITMAN, W.

1947   The Pueblo Indians of San Idefonso. Columbia University Contributions to Anthropology No. 34.

WIJNHOLT, M. R.

1965   Strafrecht in Suriname. Deventer, AE. E. Kluwer.

WILKINSON, R. J.

1932   A Malay-English dictionary (romanized). Mytilene, Greece, Salavopoulos and Kinderlis.

*WILLIS, H. G.

1924   Willis enquiry of October–November 1924, copy in KSV 1/1 National Archives of Zambia.

WILLOUGHBY, W. C.

1916   Annual report. London Missionary Society Archives.

1924   Khama: a Bantu reformer. International Review of Missions, Vol. 13.

WINFIELD, P. H.

1931   The province of the law of tort. Cambridge, Cambridge University Press.

WINICK, CHARLES

1961   The pyschology of juries. *In* Legal and criminal psychology, H. Toch, ed. New York, Holt, Rinehart and Winston, pp. 96–120.

WINICK, CHARLES, I. GERVER, AND A. BLUMBERG

1961   The psychology of judges. *In* Legal and criminal psychology, H. Toch, ed. New York, Holt, Rinehart and Winston. pp. 121–145.

WITTFOGEL, K. A., AND E. S. GOLDFRANK

1943   Some aspects of Pueblo mythology and society. Journal of American Folklore 56(219):17–30.

WITTFOGEL, K. A.

1957   Oriental despotism: a comparative study of total power. New Haven, Connecticut, Yale University Press.

WOLBERS, J.

1861   Senheidenis van Suriname. Amsterdam.

YNGVESSON, BARBARA

(n.d.)   Berkeley-Albany and Oakland-Piedmont small claims courts: a comparison of role of judge and social function of the courts. Unpublished ms. in the possession of L. Nader.

YOUNG, B.

1953   "Bobo" Young relates his exploits. Northern Rhodesia Journal 2(2):65–71.

°YOUNG, R.
   (n.d.)   Awemba History as I have heard it. District Notebook Kasama,
            KDH 1/1 National Archives of Zambia, ms.
ZEISEL, H., H. KALVEN, JR., AND B. BUCHOLZ
   1959   Delay in the court. Boston, Little, Brown.

Supplementary Bibliography

BENDA-BECKMANN, K.
   1983   The Broken Stairway to Consensus: Village Justice and State Courts
          in Minangkabau. Dordrecht: Foris.
BISHARAT, G.
   1989   Palestinian Lawyers and Israeli Rule: Law and Disorder in the West
          Bank. Austin, TX: University of Texas Press.
CAPLAN, P., ed.
   1995   Understanding Disputes: The Politics of Argument. Oxford: Berg
          Press.
CHANOCK, M.
   1985   Law, Custom, and Social Order: The Colonial Experience in Malawi
          and Zambia. Cambridge: Cambridge University Press.
COLLIER, J.
   1973   Law and Social Change in Zinacantan. Stanford: Stanford University
          Press.
COMAROFF, J., AND ROBERTS, S.
   1981   Rules and Processes: The Cultural Logic of Dispute in an African
          Context. Chicago: University of Chicago Press.
CONLEY, J., AND O'BARR, W.
   1990   Rules Versus Relationships: The Ethnography of Legal Discourse.
          Chicago: University of Chicago Press.
EPSTEIN, A.L.
   1974   Contention and Dispute: Aspects of Law and Social Control in Mel-
          anesia. Canberra: Australian National University Press.
FRENCH, R.
   1995   The Golden Yoke: The Legal Cosmology of Buddhist Tibet. Ithaca:
          Cornell University Press.
GREENHOUSE, C.
   1986   Praying for Justice: Faith, Order, and Community in an American
          Town. Ithaca: Cornell University Press.
GULLIVER, P.
   1971   Neighbors and Networks. Berkeley: University of California Press.
HAYDEN, R.
   1990   Social Courts in Theory and Practice. Philadelphia: University of
          Pennsylvania Press.
KOCH, K.
   1974   War and Peace in Jalemo. Cambridge: Harvard University Press.
LAZARUS-BLACK, M.
   1994   Legitimate Acts and Illegal Encounters: Law and Society in Antigua
          and Barbuda. Washington, D.C.: Smithsonian Institution Press.

LAZARUS-BLACK, M., AND HIRSCH, S., ed.
1994   Contested States; Law, Hegemony and Resistance. New York: Routledge.

MERRY, S.
1990   Getting Justice and Getting Even; Legal Consciousness among Working-class Americans. Chicago: University of Chicago Press.

MOORE, S.
1986   Social Facts and Fabrications: "Customary" Law on Kilimanjaro, 1880–1980. New York: Cambridge University Press.

NADER, L.
1990   Harmony Ideology: Justice and Control in a Zapotec Mountain Village. Stanford: Stanford University Press.

NADER, L. AND TODD. H.
1978   The Disputing Process: Law in Ten Societies. New York: Columbia University Press.

O'BARR, W.
1982   Linguistic Evidence: Language, Power, and Strategy in the Courtroom. New York: Academic Press.

PARNELL, P.
1989   Escalating Disputes: Social Participation and Change in The Oaxacan Highlands. Tucson: University of Arizona Press.

ROSE, L.
1992   The Politics of Harmony: Land Dispute Strategies in Swaziland. Cambridge: Cambridge University Press.

ROSEN, L.
1984   Bargaining for Reality. Chicago: University of Chicago Press.

SPRADLEY, J.
1970   You Owe Yourself a Drunk: An Ethnography of Urban Nomads. Boston: Little Brown and Company.

STARR, J.
1992   Law as Metaphor: From Islamic Courts to the Palace of Justice. Albany: State University of New York Press.

STARR, J., AND COLLIER, J., ed.
1989   History and Power in the Study of Law: New Directions in Legal Anthropology. Cornell: Ithaca University Press.

WITTY, C.
1980   Mediation and Society: Conflict Management in Lebanon. New York: Academic Press.

YNGVESSON, B.
1993   Virtuous Citizens, Disruptive Subjects: Order and Complaint in a New England Court. New York: Routledge.

Contributors

VILHELM AUBERT (1922–1988) held a law degree and a Ph.D. in sociology from the University of Oslo. He was a professor in the sociology of law at the University of Oslo. He was a Fellow at the Center for Advanced Study in the Behavioral Sciences at Stanford from 1956 to 1957. Dr. Aubert has published *Om straffesn sosiale funksjon* (*On the Social Function of Punishment*), *The Hidden Society*, *Elements of Sociology*, and *Rettssosiologi* (*Sociology of Law*). He was editor of the *Reader in Sociology of Law* (Penguin), and is considered a figure of international importance in the sociology of law.

PAUL BOHANNAN has degrees from the University of Arizona and Oxford and has taught at Oxford, Princeton, Northwestern, and University of California, Santa Barbara. During 1963–1964 he was a fellow at the Center for Advanced Studies in the Behavioral Sciences. He has done research among the Tiv of Nigeria, the Wanga of Kenya, and modern American studies. He has written *Justice and Judgment among the Tiv*, *Tiv Economy*, *Africa and Africans*, and *Social Anthropology*. He is editor of the American Museum Sourcebooks in Anthropology, and has books forthcoming on sex and morality, on divorce in cross-cultural perspective, and on Tiv religion. Bohannan retired from University of Southern California in 1989. In 1995 he published *How Culture Works*.

CHARLES O. FRAKE received his Ph.D. from Yale University. He taught at Harvard University and at Stanford University before taking his present position in the department of anthropology at the State University of New York at Buffalo. During 1967–1968 he was a Fellow at the Center for Advanced Study in the Behavioral Sciences and he participated in the Social Science Research Council's *Conference on Pidginization* held in Jamaica in 1968. He has done extensive field research with both the Yakan and the Subanun of the Philippines, and his special interests are in language and culture and cultural ecology, as well as in anthropology and law. Among his important contributions are "The Diagnosis of Disease

440

among the Subanun of Mindanao" and "Litigation in Lipay: a Study of Subanun Law." In 1980 he authored *Language and Cultural Description* and more recently has researched medieval seafaring in Western Europe.

JAMES L. GIBBS, JR., is professor of anthropology at Stanford University. In 1961 he received the Ph.D. in social anthropology from Harvard University. From 1959 to 1966 he taught at the University of Minnesota. He has also taught as a visiting professor at Cornell University. Dr. Gibbs is the editor of and a contributor to *Peoples of Africa* (New York, Holt, Rinehart and Winston, 1965), and has published several articles that have appeared in anthropological journals and symposia. His field work, some results of which are reported here and as well in film, has been among the Kpelle of Liberia. Since 1996 he is emeritus from Stanford.

MAX GLUCKMAN (1911–1975) held a D.Phil. in social anthropology from the University of Oxford, which he attended as a Rhodes Scholar after studying both social anthropology and law at the University of the Witwatersrand. He was director of the Rhodes-Livingstone Institute of Social Studies in British Central Africa, and a lecturer at Oxford; he was professor of social anthropology at the University of Manchester until his death. During 1967 he was a Fellow at the Center for Advanced Study at Stanford. He directed work in India and in Britain, notably in the field of industrial sociology and did field research in Zululand, South Africa, and Barotseland, and Zambia. In 1963 the Yale Law School invited him to deliver the Storrs Lectures in Jurisprudence; these lectures were published as *The Ideas in Barotse Jurisprudence* (1965). Among his other books are *Economy of the Central Barotse Plain* (1940), *Essays on Lozi Land and Royal Property* (1943), *Administrative Organization of the Barotse Native Authorities* (1943), *Malinowski's Sociological Theories* (1948), *Custom and Conflict in Africa* (1954), and *Politics, Law and Ritual in Tribal Society* (1965). He contributed essays to symposia and journals, some of which have been published in *Order and Rebellion in Tribal Africa* (1963). In 1974 *African Traditional Law in Historical Perspective* was published.

P. H. GULLIVER is emeritus professor at York University in Canada; he has taught at the School of Oriental and African Studies, University of London. Previously he was research sociologist to the Government of Tanganyika, and research associate and associate professor of anthropology, African Studies Program, Boston University. He has undertaken several research projects in various parts of East and Central Africa since 1948. He is author of *Survey of the Turkana* (1951), *The Family Herds* (1955), *Labor Migration in a Rural Economy* (1955), *Land Tenure and Social Change among the Nyakyusa* (1958), *Social Control in an African Society* (1963) and *Disputes and Negotiations: a Cross-Cultural Perspective* (1979).

E. ADAMSON HOEBEL (1907–1993) held the Ph.D. in anthropology from Columbia University and was Regents Professor of Anthropology at the University of Minnesota. He had been a senior specialist at the East-West Center and a Fellow at the Center for Advanced Study in the Behavioral Sciences. Dr. Hoebel published extensively in anthropological and law journals. His major publications include *The Political Organization and Law-ways of the Comanche Indians*, *The Law of Primitive Man*, *The Cheyenne Way* (with K. N. Llewellyn), *The Comanches* (with Ernest Wallace), and *Anthropology*. With A. A. Schiller, he also translated from the Dutch and edited Haar's *Adat Law in Indonesia*.

HERMA HILL KAY earned her J.D. degree at the University of Chicago Law School. She has been a member of the law faculty at the University of California at Berkeley since 1960; she was law clerk to Mr. Chief Justice Traynor of the California Supreme Court, a Fellow at the Center for Advanced Study in the Behavioral Sciences, and executive director of a research project studying law and mental retardation. She is the author of many articles in legal periodicals and contributed a paper to the *American Anthropologist's* special issue on the ethnography of law. Her book *Divorce Reform at the Crossroads* appeared in 1990. Currently she is Dean at Boalt Hall School of Law.

ANDRÉ J. F. KÖBBEN is emeritus and holds a Ph.D. in the social sciences from the University of Amsterdam, where he has been professor of cultural anthropology and sociology of non-Western societies since 1955. He has done field work on the Ivory Coast and in Surinam. He is author of *Le planteur noir* and *Van primitiven tot medeburgers* as well as of numerous articles. His special interests are methodology of the social sciences, social control, and social change. *Interests, Partiality, and the Scholar* was published in 1987.

SALLY F. MOORE received an Ll.B from the Columbia University School of Law in 1945, practiced law briefly in New York, and then served on the legal staff of the prosecution at the Nuremberg Trials. The trials prompted her interest in anthropology. She returned to Columbia and obtained her doctorate in anthropology in 1957; her dissertation (published as *Power and Property in Inca Peru*) won her the Ansley Prize. Dr. Moore was a member of the faculty of the University of Southern .California, and UCLA, and is currently emeritus at Harvard University (1996). In 1967–1968 she held a Post-Doctoral Scholarship at the African Studies Center at the University of California, Los Angeles, and she completed field work in East Africa resulting in her book *Facts and Fabrications: Customary Law on Kilimanjaro, 1880–1980* (1986).

LAURA NADER holds the Ph.D. in anthropology from Radcliffe College. She is professor of anthropology at the University of California, Berkeley, where she has been teaching since 1960. In 1963–1964 she was a Fellow at the Center for Advanced Study in the Behavioral Sciences, and 1979–80 at the Wilson Center at the Smithsonian Institution in Washington, D.C. she was a founding member and Trustee of the Law and Society Association. She has done field work among the Zapotec of Mexico, Shia Moslem villagers in Lebanon, and worked extensively in the United States on the meaning of the Alternative Dispute Resolution Movement. Dr. Nader was both editor and contributor to *The Ethnography of Law*. The author of *Talea and Juquila: A Comparison of Zapotec Social Organization* led to the production of a film, *To Make the Balance*, on Zapotec court procedure, and later a PBS film, *Little Injustices*. Nader has taught at Yale, Harvard, and Stanford law schools. Her most recent book is *Harmony Ideology* (1990).

LEOPOLD POSPISIL is professor of anthropology emeritus at Yale University. He holds a Ph.D. in anthropology from Yale (1956), and a J.U.C. (law degree) from Prague, Czechoslovakia. He also studied philosophy at the Palacky University in Olomouc, Czechoslovakia and at the Masaryk's University in Ludwigsburg, Germany, and sociology at Willamette University, Oregon. His major fields of interest are political structure and anthropology of law and social structure. He has conducted field research among the Hopi Indians (1952), Kapauku Papuans of New Guinea (1954–55), Nunamiut Eskimo of Alaska (1957), and Tirolean mountain farmers (1962–63, 1964, 1965, 1966, 1967). His books: *Kapauku Papuans and Their Law, Kapauku Papuan Economy,* and *The Kapauku Papuans of West New Guinea* were followed by the *Anthropology of Law* (1971).

ISAAC SCHAPERA, D.SC., FBA, is professor of anthropology emeritus at the London School of Economics (University of London) where he taught from 1950–1969, and author of *A Handbook of Tswana Law and Custom* and *Tribal Legislation among the Tswana.* He was a pioneer in comparative perspectives on politics and leadership as illustrated by his 1970 book *Tribal Innovators: Tswana Chiefs and Social Change, 1795–1940.*

GRESHAM SYKES holds a Ph.D. in sociology from Northwestern University. He has taught at Princeton, Northwestern, and Dartmouth, where he was chairman of the department of sociology and anthropology. He has served on governmental committees and has been editor of the *American Sociological Review, Journal of Criminal Law, Criminology, and Police Science,* and the *American Sociologist.* He is the author of *Crime and Society* and *The Society of Captives.* In 1990 he retired as Professor of Sociology at University of Virginia.

RAYMOND VERDIER defended his thesis in Law in 1960 on the sociology of legal land revenue in Black Africa, which won for him the Principal Prize of the College of Law of Paris. Since 1960 he has pursued his research on African juridical systems at the National Center for Scientific Research at Paris, and in 1967 he was named Chief of the Laboratory of Legal Anthropology of the Law Faculty of Paris. In that same year he founded a Center of Study and Research on North Togo. In 1968 he was named master of conferences at the University of Louvain. He published a Dictionary of Legal Anthropology of Black Africa. More recently (1981) he published *La Vengeance,* a book on vengeance and oath taking.

RICHARD P. WERBNER holds a B.A. in anthropology from Brandeis University, and a Ph.D. (1968) from the University of Manchester. He has been a Fulbright Scholar at the University of Manchester and the University College of Rhodesia and Nyasaland and is currently at the University of Manchester. In addition to articles on the Bemba of Zambia and a longer study of the Kalanga of Southern Rhodesia and Botswana, he has published *Land Reform in the Making: Tradition, Public Policy and Ideology in Botswana* (1982) and *Ritual Passage, Sacred Journey: The Form, Process, and Organization of Religious Movement* (1984).

Name Index

Subject Index